THE
POLITICAL
VOCATION

THE
POLITICAL
VOCATION

EDITED BY
PAUL TILLETT

BASIC BOOKS, INC.

PUBLISHERS

NEW YORK / LONDON

© 1965 by Paul Tillett
Library of Congress Catalog Card Number: 65–10733
Manufactured in the United States of America
DESIGNED BY VINCENT TORRE

PREFACE

THIS BOOK grew naturally out of my association with the Eagleton Institute of Politics at Rutgers, The State University. The institute's special concern is educating young women and men for participation in the practical political life of the state and nation. For this purpose, it has, among other things, maintained since 1956 a graduate program in practical politics for students who wish to prepare for public life, but do not want the confinements or the security of civil service.

Though the book owes much in its conception to Eagleton and its program, the idea for it actually took shape while I was on leave at the University of California, Riverside, in the spring term of 1963. There, through the courtesy of Prof. Arthur W. Turner, chairman of the Department of Political Science, I received the assistance of Audley Douglas Boyes in canvassing the literature and selecting materials. The breadth of the volume owes much to his resourcefulness, insight, and industry.

Since my return to the Eagleton Institute, I have had the invaluable assistance of Miss Barbara Bilinski and Mrs. Glorianne Robbi in preparing the material for the press.

PAUL TILLETT

Wood Lawn
New Brunswick, New Jersey
July 1965

CONTENTS

PREFACE   V

INTRODUCTION: *Paul Tillett*   I

PART ONE / The Political Vocation

I   POLITICS AS A VOCATION: *Max Weber*   15
2   THE PURSUIT OF VIRTUE: *Aristotle*   62
3   THE CONSCIENCE OF A STATESMAN:
     Henry Taylor   69
4   THE PROBLEM OF MEANS: *Jacques Maritain*   72
5   THE CHRISTIAN IN POLITICS: *Reinhold Niebuhr*   80
6   ETHICAL PROBLEMS OF POLITICIANS:
     Paul H. Douglas   85
7   PROFESSIONAL ETHICS: *Émile Durkheim*   97

PART TWO / Standards of Public Conduct

8   HONEST GRAFT AND DISHONEST GRAFT:
     William L. Riordan   103
9   PUBLIC OFFICIALS OWE A POSITIVE DUTY TO
     THE COMMUNITY: *Franklin D. Roosevelt*   106
10   ROTATION—A LEADING REPUBLICAN PRINCIPLE:
     Andrew Jackson   108
11   I TOOK A CHANCE: *Welburn S. Mayock*   110
12   ONE DISHONEST OFFICIAL IS ONE TOO MANY:
     Adlai E. Stevenson   130
13   A SENATOR'S SWIMMING POOL BECOMES A
     CAMPAIGN ISSUE: *H. H. Wilson*   134

14 A SENATORIAL DISCUSSION:
        Everett M. Dirksen et al.   140
15 CONGRESSMEN WHO CHEAT   147
16 THE INIQUITY OF PRINCIPAL MEN:
        Henry St. John Bolingbroke   155
17 THE GARDEN IN THE MOUNTAINS:
        Ignatius Donnelly   158

                    PART THREE / Political Motives

18 POLITICS: *H. L. Mencken*   163
19 GLORY AND POWER: *Saint Augustine*   169
20 EGO AND COMMONWEAL: *Jacob Burckhardt*   172
21 THE POLITICAL ACT AS AN ACT OF WILL:
        Norton E. Long   178
22 MY EARLY LIFE: *James A. Farley*   183
23 WHY DID YOU RUN FOR CONGRESS?
        Jerry Voorhis   193
24 EVERY POLITICIAN IS SUBJECT TO A GREAT
        FEAR: *John T. Salter*   201
25 A *Cause Célèbre*: *George W. Pepper*   203
26 I NEVER MET AN HONEST POLITICIAN:
        M. R. Werner   205
27 MY CONNECTION WITH MRS. REYNOLDS:
        Alexander Hamilton   207

                    PART FOUR / Civic Courage

28 CIVIC COURAGE: *William James*   215
29 EXCERPT FROM *Antigone*: *Sophocles*   218
30 THE POLICY OF "DON'T CARE":
        Abraham Lincoln   221
31 MORAL COURAGE: *Mark Twain*   224
32 POLITICAL TRICKERY: *Joyce Cary*   226
33 THE DAY WE PASSED THE OATH BILL:
        Richard L. Neuberger   228
34 THE BIG DILEMMA: CONSCIENCE OR VOTES:
        William L. Benton   234
35 LIABILITIES: *Stimson Bullitt*   241

PART FIVE / The Way Things Are

36 IN PRAISE OF THE LEGISLATIVE WAY:
      T. V. Smith   255
37 WHAT MAKES A STATESMAN? *Boies Penrose*   258
38 TALKING POLITICAL: *Thomas L. Hughes*   260
39 CONFLICTS OF INTEREST: *Jesse M. Unruh*   262
40 MEN ARE SUCH FOOLS: *Christine Keeler*   266
41 PERSONAL REFLECTIONS ON BOSSES AND
      MACHINES: *Edward J. Flynn*   269
42 HOW MUCH FORTUNE CAN DO IN HUMAN
      AFFAIRS: *Niccolò Machiavelli*   276

PART SIX / Political Life

43 A RECENT TYPICAL DAY: *Clem Miller*   281
44 POLITICS CREEPS UP ON US: *Marjorie M. Beach*   285
45 THE CRUCIAL PERIOD IN MY PUBLIC LIFE:
      Robert M. La Follette   291
46 POLITICS AND THE SAME OLD STUFF:
      Maury Maverick   307
47 MARRIAGE AND POLITICS: *Finley Peter Dunne*   315
48 COMMUTING CONGRESSMEN: *The New York
      Times*   319

PART SEVEN / Social Science Assays the Politicians

49 THE PRECINCT WORKER: *Sonya Forthal*   325
50 THE JOB OF THE POLITICAL EXECUTIVE:
      Marver H. Bernstein   342
51 THE AMBIVALENT SOCIAL STATUS OF THE
      AMERICAN POLITICIAN: *William C. Mitchell*   352
52 POLITICALS AND APOLITICALS:
      Bernard C. Hennessy   364
53 THE POLITICAL SOCIALIZATION OF AMERICAN
      STATE LEGISLATORS: *Heinz Eulau, William
      Buchanan, Leroy Ferguson, and John C. Wahlke*   379
54 HOOSIER REPUBLICANS IN CHICAGO:
      David R. Derge   395

55 THE BUREAUCRAT AND THE ENTHUSIAST:
    John P. Roche and Stephen Sachs   402
56 LEADERSHIP AND PSYCHOSOMATIC ANALYSIS:
    Alex Gottfried   416

            PART EIGHT / Some Practical Proposals

57 SUMMARY RECOMMENDATIONS: *President's
    Commission on Campaign Costs*   431
58 SUGGESTED REGULATIONS: *The Association of the
    Bar of the City of New York*   437
59 SPECIAL MESSAGE ON CONFLICTS OF INTEREST:
    John F. Kennedy   443
60 PROMOTION OF PUBLIC CONFIDENCE IN THE
    INTEGRITY OF CONGRESS AND EXECUTIVE
    BRANCH: *Clifford P. Case*   454
61 REPORT OF THE SPECIAL COMMITTEE ON ETHICS,
    NEW YORK STATE LEGISLATURE   457
62 LEGISLATORS VOTE OWN ETHICS CODE:
    The New York Times   461

            PART NINE / The Citizen as Politician

63 THE PRACTICAL REFORMER: *Theodore Roosevelt*   467
64 THE CITIZEN AS A MEMBER OF A POLITICAL
    PARTY: *Elihu Root*   477
65 THE DISSENTER'S ROLE IN A TOTALITARIAN
    AGE: *Norman Thomas*   480
    INDEX   487

INTRODUCTION

Paul Tillett

I HAVE eschewed labeling politics a profession, even though it is the full-time occupation of many participants and the full-time preoccupation of many more. Politics does not possess the marks of an established profession —common, specific education and an agreed ethics imposed by and enforced by the profession on its members. And in these ways it has been slow in developing.

Who is called? We are talking about a small group in a process that, as Renzo Sereno has commented, "invites everyone; everyone either deliberately or unwittingly, with personal participation or by being absent, takes part in politics."[1] But, special though the group may be, it does not have a highly developed corporate sense, except perhaps in the United States Senate, and its special mode is competition of the members *inter se.* In this sense, politics resembles, as Sereno has also suggested, an organized professional sport—baseball or bullfighting, depending on the culture. Like such national pastimes, it involves nearly everyone:

A torero and his peers are the stars; then there is the *quadrilla;* then the friends, well-wishers and parasites, and finally the crowd that fills the arena. But the elite are those who fight and those close to them in many—and strange—ways, such as the manager, the press agent, and the unknown boy who tries his mettle with some wild bull in some remote *estancia.*[2]

So it is with politics. We are concerned with the players, their identifiable retinues, organizers, and managers; those who support the lives of individual players in immediate ways; and those in training, some of whom

[1] *The Rulers* (New York: Frederick A. Praeger & Co., 1962), p. 102.
[2] *Ibid.,* pp. 102–103.

have not heard the call or given a sign that they will respond. A beginning definition of those in the United States who follow politics as a calling should include the president and vice-president and their aides; all members of both houses of Congress; all presidential appointees (judges, businessmen, and experts brought in briefly for specific duties may be excluded *ad hoc*); the congressional staffers; the advisors from journalism and the academy; governors and members of state legislatures; state officeholders outside of the merit system; the elected officials of counties and municipalities, especially in urban areas—the mayors, sheriffs, judges, and city managers; the members and staffs of state and national party committees; and those who do not hold public office, but who play roles in determining nominations, appointments, and other significant actions.

Optimistic estimates put at no more than 25 per cent the proportion of the adult population which engages in any form of political activity other than voting. Only about two and a half million Americans deserve the label "political activists"—those who participate in a "fairly steady way in politics." This number appears small; however, it is roughly equivalent to the number of individuals employed by the federal establishment, and these activists participate on an entirely voluntary basis, for the most part without pay. Moreover, civil service restrictions, military rules, and corporate insistence on the "nonpolitical" operate to place "serious occupational disabilities" in the way of political action for two out of seven Americans.

Contrary to the stereotype, these activists are not unlettered malcontents or ne'er-do-wells. About 40 per cent are urban males in professional, managerial, official, technical, and proprietary occupations—pursuits in which only 6 per cent of the adult population as a whole appear. About one-sixth hold college degrees, compared to one-fortieth of the total adult population. Even in bygone days, high educational attainment was associated with political leadership. "Proper Philadelphia's interesting and gifted politician," Boies Penrose, boss of Pennsylvania from 1904 to 1927, "came of a long line of highly cultivated" people and graduated from Harvard *magna cum laude*.[3]

Among officeholders, formal education is even more characteristic. In the New York State Legislature which assembled in January, 1961, 42 of 58 senators and 92 of the 149 assemblymen were lawyers, which indicates in most instances the equivalent of a college education and some professional training beyond college. Investigation of the characteristics of members of state legislatures in four widely separated and diverse states showed that only 2 per cent had not attended high school, whereas 81 per cent had attended college, and almost one-half had received graduate or professional education. If, with so many formally educated politicians, we

[3] E. Digby Baltzell, *Philadelphia Gentlemen* (Glencoe, Ill.: The Free Press, 1958), p. 140.

still have complaints about politics and politicians, the thought suggests itself that either the education was of the wrong sort or that education itself cannot cure the ills of a political system.[4]

How, why, and under what conditions do individuals determine to become involved in politics to the point of choosing the political calling? Most autobiographical accounts and most biographies contribute little. This volume is offered more as a demonstration of our lack of knowledge than as the solid basis for generalization. Although most accounts by the individuals involved or those writing full-fledged lives attribute the entrance into the political life to chance, these materials suggest that the individuals concerned really do not know. A guess is that political behavior is associative, like other behavior; if so, we should look for the formation of a predisposition to political life in family background or the experiences of early life.

The very size of the United States makes it a place in which contradictory currents can run at full strength without opposition. Those who bemoan a given condition are likely to exist side by side and unknown to those who have brought the condition about as the side effects of actions taken for other purposes. For example, reformers—men and women of good will—continue to complain about the low rate of voting in the United States in the face of artificial barriers which disenfranchise more than 10 per cent of the population of voting age—disenfranchisements based on such adventitious characteristics as race, length of residence, travel, and lapsed registrations. Those worried about civic apathy expend considerable time in encouraging voting by those who would be turned away from the polls if they followed instructions and attempted to perform their civic duty.[5]

A somewhat similar situation besets the scholar who studies the recruitment of politicians in the United States. It is one of the national myths that no mother raises her boy to be a politician. It seems to be an article of faith among those who exhort the young, especially college graduates, to become active in politics that "politician" is a dirty word. In 1947, for example, the late Arthur T. Vanderbilt—the leader of a good-government group in his own state of New Jersey, the founder of what is now called the National Center for Education in Politics, and himself a politician of no mean proportions—reported the results of a national poll which asked: "Would you be willing to have your son enter politics?" According to Vanderbilt, 67 per cent of the people responded that they would not. To a

[4] That there may, indeed, be too many lawyers in public life or in Congress has been suggested by Andrew Hacker, "Are There Too Many Lawyers in Congress?," *The New York Times Magazine,* January 5, 1964, p. 14.

[5] Contrast, in this respect, the realistic "Report" of the President's Commission on Registration and Voting Participation, November 1963, with the dissenting statement on literacy tests by Brendan Byrne, executive director of the American Heritage Foundation.

second question, "Do you believe one can go into politics and remain honest?," 50 per cent responded "No." [6] These facts, observed Justice Vanderbilt, were "cause for grave concern." The results of that poll make curious reading when compared to a rating of jobs and occupations prepared by the National Opinion Research Center, also in 1947. An effort was made to determine basic attitudes toward occupations. In this ranking, six of the first ten jobs involved government employment, and five of these jobs were political, that is, elective or appointive. The first job—that of United States Supreme Court justice—received a score of 96 per cent, whereas the lowest of the political jobs in the first ten—United States representative in Congress—received a score of 89 per cent.[7]

Even in 1947, parents seemed to recognize that the importance of politics makes it impossible to agree with Swift's theory of the Brobdingnagians that, "whoever could make two ears of corn or two blades of grass to grow upon a spot of ground where only one grew before, would deserve better of mankind, and do more essential service to his country than the whole race of politicians put together." [8]

The refusal of the best people—or the sons of the average man—to enter politics was a legitimate concern a generation ago. It does not seem one today. Certainly, the best people are out in force; Harrimans, Lodges, Saltonstalls, Rockefellers, Dilworths, Clarks, Scrantons are overrepresented. And the *nouveau riche*—Kennedys, Goldwaters, and Johnsons— are, too. There is hardly a respectable university in the country that does not have a program, an institute, a research bureau, internships, or an undergraduate course dedicated to preparing students for political action.[9] In its proper contemporary perspective, public life offers the greatest challenge to talent and creativity, because now the business of America is politics.[10]

Once in politics, what steps does the politician take in his ascent to power? Is there a career pattern for aspiring politicians? It is part of the political folklore that one begins at the ward level and works one's way to the top, though it is not apparent that presidential candidates, with the exception of Harry Truman, have done this in the past generation. What does each step contribute? Does it open a new world of contacts, of access to people, money, and power? Does it make a difference whether he is

[6] "Better Minds for Better Politics," *The New York Times Magazine,* March 9, 1947, p. 10.

[7] *Opinion News* (September 1, 1947), 4.

[8] Jonathan Swift, *Gulliver's Travels,* ed. William A. Eddy (New York: Oxford University Press, 1933), p. 158.

[9] With few exceptions (the Eagleton Institute is one), these educational institutions focus their attention on the executive branch of government. One of the best known—Princeton's Woodrow Wilson School of Public and International Affairs—has what amounts to a passion for the federal executive.

[10] John Conway, "Politics as a Profession in the United States," *Daedalus,* XCII, No. 4 (Fall 1963), 840.

rich or poor? Must he have an alternate career, and, if so, will it dominate politics or become subordinate to politics? What kinds of people were important in his career? Questions of this kind cannot be answered with precision. This volume strongly suggests the need for further research.

Is there a political personality? Do politicians differ from other people? Is the typical politician as gregarious as George Washington, as smooth as Harry Truman, as profound as Eisenhower?

Whatever the personality, it can hardly be doubted that there are few natural politicians, if the testimony of both the politicians and the behavioral scientists can be respected. Few people could wish to make themselves so pliant. But it may be that something is wrong in the vision. The disease of timorousness, of sycophancy, of insecurity appears to be especially strong in the legislature. Certainly it is not unusual there. In the executive, among those who are successful, it may be that politicians differ from ordinary people in much the same way that artists differ — their fantasy lives provide material for their professional lives. Politicians act out their fantasies; an artist might paint or write them. *The Secret Life of Walter Mitty* becomes in a politician the public life of Theodore Roosevelt.

In examining the milieu, the imperatives, and the conditions of political life, we will not undertake to discuss what so often occupies those looking at the practicing politician, that is, his style and method of gaining office. Nor, except in a very general way, will we consider his performance in office. Rather, the authors selected for inclusion in this volume direct their attention to aspects of political life which do not depend so heavily on time and place. In the first section, dealing with the important ethical questions confronting politicians, our authors go far beyond the trivial question, Can a politician be an honest man? On that simple point, perhaps Harry Truman has said all that need be said: "If you can't stand the heat, get out of the kitchen." Politicians must answer ethically for serious failures of courage, energy, and detachment.[11] And Frank Kent, that minor-league Mencken, concluded a book notable for harsh things said about politicians—"dumb," purveyors of "hokum," "hypocrites and cowards"—with the observation that politicos respect their word; politics, he thought, was "purer" than business, and politicians lived by better standards in "a humbug world" than practically anybody else except newspapermen.[12]

These studies, whether they approach political life coldly and instrumentally or altruistically, find that politicians are required to respond

[11] Harry W. Jones, "Political Behavior and the Problem of Sanctions," in Harold D. Lasswell and Harlan Cleveland, eds., *The Ethic of Power*, "The Interplay of Religion, Philosophy, and Politics" (New York: Harper & Bros., 1962), pp. 195–196.

[12] Frank Kent, *Political Behavior* (New York: William Morrow & Co., 1928), pp. 322–331 *et passim*.

to more taxing demands on their moral fiber than dollar honesty. From the perspective of the politicians, which the public does not often perceive, certain really troublesome questions do not seem to differ greatly from those before a salesman, a professor, or even a clergyman. As Stimson Bullitt has commented, the real dilemmas come with such questions as the following:

What should be the rule for evasive answers, or the one for unspoken lies? How far should a candidate be held accountable for defamatory rumors which his supporters start? What should be his attitude toward a low calibre running mate for whose selection he has had no responsibility except the remote one of membership in the same party? May he protect himself by displaying disapproval of the other man, or does duty to his party constrain him to pretend respect? [13]

An undeniable source of pressure on the politician is his own constituency. One wonders whether latter-day practice has not gone overboard in requiring attentiveness on the part of the politician, and especially a member of a legislative body, to the demands, needs, and wishes of his constituents.[14] There was a time when it was thought impertinent for the people to suggest an interest in the disposition of public business. In 1714, a member of Parliament is said to have replied to some of his constituents who asked him to vote against the budget as follows:

Gentlemen: I have received your letter about the excise, and I am surprised at your insolence at writing to me at all.

You know, and I know, that I bought this constituency. You know, and I know, that I am now determined to sell it, and you know what you think I don't know that you are now looking out for another buyer, and I know, what you certainly don't know, that I have now found another constituency to buy.

About what you said about the excise: may God's curse light upon you all, and may it make your homes as open and as free to the excise officers as your wives and daughters have always been to me while I have represented your rascally constituency.[15]

In our time, pressure for service to constituents seems a source of spiritual corruption, and a United States senator finds it necessary to say in his description of an ethical code for members of the "greatest deliberative body in the world" that a good senator should "strive constantly to interpret the interests of [his] constituents in the perspective of total national interest." [16]

[13] *To Be a Politician* (Garden City, N.Y.: Doubleday & Co., Inc., 1959), p. 68.
[14] See Charles L. Clapp, *The Congressman*, "His Work as He Sees It" (Washington: The Brookings Institution, 1963).
[15] Peter G. Richards, *Honorable Members*, "A Study of the British Backbencher" (London: Faber & Faber, 1959), p. 157.
[16] William Benton, "A Decalogue for Members of Congress," *The New York Times Magazine*, August 12, 1951, p. 7.

The conditions under which politicians live and work and have their being, their relationships to their constituencies and the various publics within their constituencies, are important in this book primarily to emphasize the gulf that seems to exist between the behavior of politicians as they perceive themselves and the way they are (by implication) enjoined to behave. According to democratic theory, the politician is the primary instrument of public political education. He exhorts, informs, and persuades. In theory, he does this best by appealing coolly to reason; he eschews racial and religious prejudice, avoids personalities, does not attempt to stir the emotions, and does not stoop to crass appeals to self-interest. He is a discussion leader in a rational dialogue about the appropriate ends of government and the means to be adopted by the community to achieve those ends. Though his is only one voice among many, it is a voice that stands out for its sanity and coolness.

Political commentators suspected of cynicism deduce from their observations rules for success in politics which prescribe behavior at considerable variance to the expectations of the democrat. They make party regularity and organizational support the great desiderata and counsel the aspiring politician to avoid unnecessary antagonisms and controversial issues, not to overestimate the voters' intelligence, to forgo the pleasure of showing up one's opponent, never high-hat the voters, not to appear ridiculous, and profess no fixed principles. It is well to have money, put on a good show, and get ample publicity. That was the advice given by a newspaperman in the late 1920's on the basis of his impressions. A generation of research in political science of a hard, quantitative, scientific variety has not altered the formula in any important respect. One may deduce from the latest works of American political scientists a set of rules like the following: run scared; appeal to the ethnic and group loyalties of the electorate; appeal to the self-interest of voters; slant your campaign so as to activate your party workers; avoid issues and, if one must discuss them, attempt to do so in terms of the self-interest of the voters.[17]

This is thought to be the prescription for winning, and winning, we are told, is all-important. The nice guys—the Stimson Bullitts—finish last. In the new dismal science of politics, the activities of the politician are reduced to the calculation of a course running between threatening forces or currents of opinion. Transgression of the primitive code is thought likely to stimulate the electorate to fury against him. The politician, who is, despite prejudice to the contrary, likely to be one of the better-informed members of his community, is thus put in the position where everyone expects him to behave "political" and finds himself reduced to thinking, talking, and acting "political." The irony of the situation was delineated a generation ago by Karl Mannheim:

[17] See, for example, Warren Miller *et al.*, *The American Voter* (New York: John Wiley & Sons, Inc., 1960).

The complete disappearance of the utopian element . . . would mean that . . . human development would take on a totally new character. . . . We would be faced then with the greatest paradox imaginable, namely, that man, who has achieved the highest degree of rational mastery of existence, left without any ideals, becomes a mere creature of impulses. Thus . . . just at the highest stage of awareness, when history is ceasing to be blind fate, and is becoming more and more man's own creation, with the relinquishment of utopias, man would lose his will to shape history and therewith his ability to understand it.[18]

Are ideas about the correct form of government, theories of representation, the basis of obligation to the state or society, and the nature and source of legitimate authority important in the political process? What are the sources of political ideas, and how can the efficacy of ideas be judged?

It is possible that American politics is endemically hostile to ideas, although in the Constitutional era and for some time thereafter politically active men had no rivals from the academy in contributing to political thought.[19] It is trite to observe that American politics is a politics of compromise. Some see great virtue in this fact of our political system. Sen. Clifford Case, for example, has lauded the impetus to compromise given by our political system as making possible "a degree of domestic order and peace which is little short of a miracle in a democracy comprising a territory as large, a multiplicity of conflicting interests as great, and a population with racial, religious, and cultural backgrounds as diverse as ours." But those who demand or suggest more principled political parties, he suggested, are those "who imagine they can find in political or social strife a personal answer to the riddle of existence; happily most Americans don't feel impelled to follow that will-o'-the-wisp." In his view, ideological politics is not "an essential stimulus to creative thinking." The failure to adopt an ideology is not a sign of complacency but "plain common sense. Cerebration so feeble it cannot function without such stimulation is a dispensable luxury." [20]

Abraham Lincoln, in his address to the Young Men's Republican Union at Cooper Institute in February, 1860, included in this volume, took a sterner line. His speech exemplifies the political mind working in a relentless search for the reconciliation of moral truth and necessity, the approximation of the real to the ideal, the working out in politics of the ethical imperative. An evil can be tolerated, if it must, he seems to say, so long as it stays in its place. More than that, he is strikingly modern in recognizing in the clash of values the essence of politics.

[18] *Ideology and Utopia* (New York: Harcourt, Brace & Co., 1936).

[19] Daniel J. Boorstin, in *The Genius of America* (Chicago: University of Chicago Press, 1953), p. 97, argues that lack of theory is our characteristic and strength and in the course of his argument questions the standing of the *Federalist* as a treatise on political theory.

[20] "The Future of the Republican Party," remarks to a National Press Club luncheon, December 16, 1960.

Some minds—one is tempted to call them shallow—profess to find little of intellectual interest in politics. They may quote from Lear:

> Poor rogues
> Talk of court news;
> And we'll talk with them too,
> Who loses, and who wins:
> Who's in, who's out.

Such observers impute to those who follow politics a superficiality their own attitude betrays. They cannot understand or will not acknowledge that, in the day-to-day pursuit of their calling, politicians confront in actuality the perennial problems of political philosophy. Scorn for the practical concerns of politics and politicians has an ancient and honorable lineage. Plato was perhaps the first to separate political philosophy from politics and to denigrate the latter. He succeeded so well that today politics is the only art in which practitioners are rated lower than critics.

Politics is an operation, Graham Wallas said, "rather of art than of science, of long experience and trained faculty rather than of conscious method." [21] But is it a high art? Are the critics not correct, in the end? Politics, one replies, is the last best hope of democracy, political parties one institution of modern life capable of confronting men in their collectivity without destroying their individuality or atomizing them, the political process the only activity with the capacity to be concerned with the whole man. Not that every question is political or ought to be or that parties must or should subsume all other associations, primary or voluntary, or absorb all civic energies. It is simply that in a crowded, secular, specialized, technological world, politics is an integrative force or institution. It is one process that might in theory provide man and mankind with physical security; the opportunity to share in decisions that affect him and his work; some control over the use of his tax money; a system of education; and a framework of culture. Politics might contain the tidal wave of ugliness rushing out of urban centers, assure transport at reasonable speed and cost, and provide the basis for the construction of a community. What the family, the church, the school, the theater, the army, the corporation, and the guild have done for other times in other places must be done now by politics if it is to be done at all.

There will probably always be a gap between the sensibilities of the most advanced, the cultural leaders, and those who attend the running of the visible machinery of governing, even in a day of national cultural centers and of government support of the arts. As Emerson observed: "The history of the State sketches in coarse outline the progress of thought, and follows at a distance the delicacy of culture and aspiration." [22] And

---

21 *Human Nature in Politics* (New York: Alfred A. Knopf, Inc., 1921), p. 170.
22 Ralph Waldo Emerson, "Politics," *Essays* (2nd series; Boston: Houghton, Mifflin & Co., 1893), p. 193.

only recently Richard Nixon confirmed this statement by observing "I never saw a play I didn't like."

Out and out anti-intellectualism is not the force in American politics it once was. Politicians seem willing, if not eager, to utilize intelligence; the greater present danger is that the savants will succumb so readily and become involved so deeply that all trace of independent criticism will disappear. It is important to remember that, when McCarthy and the Yahoos were doing a war dance around the academy, a number of leading intellectuals were shaping the ice balls, poisoning the arrows, and calling the shots of the anticommunist crusade.

One may grant the centrality of politics and still demand a justification for paying attention to the practicing politicians, more-or-less awkward figures at best, masters of humbug and buncombe, shallow and uncouth or earnest and ineffectual. Individual politicians occupy a place of exaggerated significance in the American scheme, for they provide in their own persons the major links between the branches of government —especially between legislative and executive, but also between state and federal, and local and federal. Personalities must do the work of a party system which, to say the least, is not completely formed and overcome the constitutional obstacles to an articulated scheme of government.

In fact, a good many Americans argue that the curative for the ills of politics is "good men." Advocates of this remedy often seem to have as their model of the ideal political community a sleepy little town with one active party, a few bought-off dissidents, one lawyer, one doctor, one undertaker, one contractor, and "no politics." The leading citizens take turns serving on the town committee, and the local professionals perform such public business as needs doing. All very cozy, all very honest, all very nonpolitical. And all very far away and long ago.

In this political idyl, it is rational to rely on the search for good men, though in practice the "goodness" of leading citizens is never questioned in our town. But the search for the good man behind men in competitive contemporary politics is chimerical. When we ask the politician, we are apt to receive a sanguine answer. By and large, the politicos are above average.

There are no good men whose appearance will transform politics. It is not that they are nonexistent or rare, but that the system either throws them off or treats them as sports and confines them to special areas. This is the true meaning of the Senate "Club"—the difference between the "in's" and the "out's."

If this view is correct, the party system, the people, and, in a deeper sense, the society hold more responsibility for the ills of politics than do the politicians.[23] For too long we have been conservative, complacent, and

[23] See H. H. Wilson, *Congress,* "Corruption and Compromise" (New York: Rinehart & Company, Inc., 1951).

corrupt. Political questions are judged by the voters in a cynically political way—"What's in it for me?" Judgments at this level are rationalized by a hopelessly romantic interpretation of the meaning of democracy—one that substitutes actual consent for the tacit consent of the governed or consent given through representative institutions whenever governmental action immediately affects the individual. Governmental units rarely find themselves possessing power to plan and act without running a gauntlet of political and judicial interference. As a result, politics frequently has more to do with the location of a right-of-way than with engineering. These basic attitudes go a long way toward determining that our politicians will be ineffectual except when they are getting pork for the district, the county, the town, or resisting change imposed from the outside.

Of course, politicians know these things better than most, and they adopt the protective coloration afforded by the opinions about them. Their eagerness to do so makes them suspect,[24] and they are not without a portion of responsibility. Politicians are important to the system, but it is easy to overestimate their capacity to achieve reform. They are competitors for place and power, not the architects of the polity. They will more likely respond to than suggest far-reaching changes in their environment. For them, many more conditions are given than for the Prince, and it may be that much more must be forgiven them because it is so difficult to get things done.

[24] See Walter Goodman, *All Honorable Men* (Boston: Little, Brown and Company, 1963), and Karl E. Meyer, *The New America* (New York: Basic Books, Inc., 1961).

PART ONE

The Political Vocation

1

POLITICS AS A VOCATION

Max Weber

"Politics as a Vocation" was originally given as a lecture at Munich University in 1918, at the request of a group of German students.

Its author, Max Weber (1864–1920), a German sociologist, has had a powerful influence on American social scientists since World War II. Intrigued by questions of method in social science and looking for the deeper meaning of events, typically, in this lecture he announced to the audience that he would disappoint those who came for guidance on what to do in politics, for this question had "nothing to do with the general question of what politics as a vocation means and what it can mean."

*From an admirer of Bismarck's authoritarianism he turned in later years to a supporter of popular government. The change was not so great as might appear. Once, Weber told General Erich Ludendorff what he meant by democracy:**

In a democracy the people choose a leader in whom they trust. Then the chosen leader says, "Now shut up and obey me." People and party are then no longer free to interfere in his business.

Weber visited the United States once briefly in 1904, yet what he saw influenced him a great deal. Perhaps his vantage point as a foreigner enabled him to see American politics more clearly, to separate the system from its epiphenomena more readily than Americans themselves. For example, he comments in this lecture: "Naturally power actually rests in the

From *Max Weber: Essays in Sociology,* edited and translated by H.H. Gerth and C. Wright Mills. Copyright 1946 by Oxford University Press, Inc.; reprinted by permission.

   * H.H. Gerth and C. Wright Mills, ed., *Max Weber: Essays in Sociology* (New York: Oxford University Press, 1946), p. 42.

hands of those who, within the organization, handle the work continuously." *An embarrassing number of American voters continue to resist the insight.*

Weber was also subject to error or the victim of misinformation about the politics of the United States. Certainly President Wilson did not have 300,000 patronage jobs at his disposal, and it is doubtful that any president of the United States ever did.

*

THIS . . . WILL NECESSARILY DISAPPOINT you in a number of ways. You will naturally expect me to take a position on actual problems of the day. But that will be the case only in a purely formal way and toward the end, when I shall raise certain questions concerning the significance of political action in the whole way of life. [Today], all questions that refer to what policy and what content one should give one's political activity must be eliminated. For such questions have nothing to do with the general question of what politics as a vocation means and what it can mean. Now to our subject matter.

What do we understand by politics? The concept is extremely broad and comprises any kind of *independent* leadership in action. One speaks of the currency policy of the banks, of the discounting policy of the Reichsbank, of the strike policy of a trade union; one may speak of the educational policy of a municipality or a township, of the policy of the president of a voluntary association, and, finally, even of the policy of a prudent wife who seeks to guide her husband. Tonight, our reflections are, of course, not based on such a broad concept. We wish to understand by politics only the leadership, or the influencing of the leadership, of a *political* association, hence today, of a *state*.

But what is a "political" association from the sociological point of view? What is a "state"? Sociologically, the state cannot be defined in terms of its ends. There is scarcely any task that some political association has not taken in hand, and there is no task that one could say has always been exclusive and peculiar to those associations which are designated as political ones—today the state, or historically, those associations which have been the predecessors of the modern state. Ultimately, one can define the modern state sociologically only in terms of the specific *means* peculiar to it, as to every political association, namely, the use of physical force.

"Every state is founded on force," said Trotsky at Brest-Litovsk.* That is indeed right. If no social institutions existed which knew the use of violence, then the concept of "state" would be eliminated, and a condition

---

*At Brest-Litovsk, March 3, 1918, the Bolsheviks signed a peace treaty with the Germans ending Russian participation in World War I, on terms disastrous to the Soviet Union.

would emerge that could be designated as "anarchy," in the specific sense of this word. Of course, force is certainly not the normal or the only means of the state—nobody says that—but force is a means specific to the state. Today, the relation between the state and violence is an especially intimate one. In the past, the most varied institutions—beginning with the sib—have known the use of physical force as quite normal. Today, however, we have to say that a state is a human community that (successfully) claims the *monopoly of the legitimate use of physical force* within a given territory. Note that "territory" is one of the characteristics of the state. Specifically, at the present time, the right to use physical force is ascribed to other institutions or to individuals only to the extent to which the state permits it. The state is considered the sole source of the "right" to use violence. Hence, "politics" for us means striving to share power or striving to influence the distribution of power, either among states or among groups within a state.

This corresponds essentially to ordinary usage. When a question is said to be a "political" question, when a cabinet minister or an official is said to be a "political" official, or when a decision is said to be "politically" determined, what is always meant is that interests in the distribution, maintenance, or transfer of power are decisive for answering the questions and determining the decision or the official's sphere of activity. He who is active in politics strives for power either as a means in serving other aims, ideal or egoistic, or as "power for power's sake," that is, in order to enjoy the prestige-feeling that power gives.

Like the political institutions historically preceding it, the state is a relation of men dominating men, a relation supported by means of legitimate (i.e., considered to be legitimate) violence. If the state is to exist, the dominated must obey the authority claimed by the powers that be. When and why do men obey? Upon what inner justifications and upon what external means does this domination rest?

To begin with, in principle, there are three inner justifications, hence basic *legitimations* of domination.

First, the authority of the "eternal yesterday," i.e., of the mores sanctified through the unimaginably ancient recognition and habitual orientation to conform. This is "traditional" domination exercised by the patriarch and the patrimonial prince of yore.

There is the authority of the extraordinary and personal "gift of grace" (charisma), the absolutely personal devotion and personal confidence in revelation, heroism, or other qualities of individual leadership. This is "charismatic" domination, as exercised by the prophet or—in the field of politics—by the elected war lord, the plebiscitarian ruler, the great demagogue, or the political party leader.

Finally, there is domination by virtue of "legality," by virtue of the belief in the validity of legal statute and functional "competence" based on rationally created *rules.* In this case, obedience is expected in discharging statutory obligations. This is domination as exercised by the modern "servant of the state" and by all those bearers of power who in this respect resemble him.

It is understood that, in reality, obedience is determined by highly robust motives of fear and hope—fear of the vengeance of magical powers or of the power-holder, hope for reward in this world or in the beyond—and besides all this, by interests of the most varied sort. Of this we shall speak presently. However, in asking for the "legitimations" of this obedience, one meets with these three "pure" types: "traditional," "charismatic," and "legal."

These conceptions of legitimacy and their inner justifications are of very great significance for the structure of domination. To be sure, the pure types are rarely found in reality; but, today, we cannot deal with the highly complex variants, transitions, and combinations of these pure types, which problems belong to "political science." Here, we are interested above all in the second of these types: domination by virtue of the devotion of those who obey the purely personal charisma of the leader. For this is the root of the idea of a *calling* in its highest expression.

Devotion to the charisma of the prophet, or the leader in war, or to the great demagogue in the *ecclesia* or in parliament, means that the leader is personally recognized as the innerly "called" leader of men. Men do not obey him by virtue of tradition or statute, but because they believe in him. If he is more than a narrow and vain upstart of the moment, the leader lives for his cause and strives for his work. The devotion of his disciples, his followers, his personal party friends is oriented to his person and to its qualities.

Charismatic leadership has emerged in all places and in all historical epochs. Most importantly in the past, it has emerged in the two figures of the magician and the prophet on the one hand, and in the elected war lord, the gang leader and *condottierre* on the other hand. *Political* leadership in the form of the free "demagogue" who grew from the soil of the city state is of greater concern to us; like the city state, the demagogue is peculiar to the Occident and especially to Mediterranean culture. Furthermore, political leadership in the form of the parliamentary "party leader" has grown on the soil of the constitutional state, which is also indigenous only to the Occident.

These politicians by virtue of a "calling," in the most genuine sense of the word, are of course nowhere the only decisive figures in the cross-currents of the political struggle for power. The sort of auxiliary means that are at their disposal is also highly decisive. How do the politically dominant powers manage to maintain their domination? The question pertains to any kind of domination, hence also to political domination in all its forms, traditional as well as legal and charismatic.

Organized domination, which calls for continuous administration, requires that human conduct be conditioned to obedience toward those masters who claim to be the bearers of legitimate power. On the other hand, by virtue of this obedience, organized domination requires the control of those material goods which in a given case are necessary for the use of physical violence. Thus, organized domination requires control of the personal executive staff and the material implements of administration.

The administrative staff, which externally represents the organization of political domination, is, of course, like any other organization, bound by obedience to the power-holder and not alone by the concept of legitimacy, of which we have just spoken. There are two other means, both of which appeal to personal interests: material reward and social honor. The fiefs of vassals, the prebends [stipends] of patrimonial officials, the salaries of modern civil servants, the honor of knights, the privileges of estates, and the honor of the civil servant comprise their respective wages. The fear of losing them is the final and decisive basis for solidarity between the executive staff and the power-holder. There is honor and booty for the followers in war; for the demagogue's following, there are "spoils"—that is, exploitation of the dominated through the monopolization of office—and there are politically determined profits and premiums of vanity. All of these rewards are also derived from the domination exercised by a charismatic leader.

To maintain a dominion by force, certain material goods are required, just as with an economic organization. All states may be classified according to whether they rest on the principle that the staff of men themselves *own* the administrative means, or whether the staff is "separated" from these means of administration. This distinction holds in the same sense in which today we say that the salaried employee and the proletarian in the capitalistic enterprise are "separated" from the material means of production. The power-holder must be able to count on the obedience of the staff members, officials, or whoever else they may be. The administrative means may consist of money, building, war material, vehicles, horses, or whatnot. The question is whether or not the power-holder himself directs and organizes the administration while delegating executive power to personal servants, hired officials, or personal favorites and confidants, who are nonowners, i.e., who do not use the material means of administration in their own right but are directed by the lord. The distinction runs through all administrative organizations of the past.

These political associations in which the material means of administration are autonomously controlled, wholly or partly, by the dependent administrative staff may be called associations organized in "estates." The vassal in the feudal association, for instance, paid out of his own pocket for the administration and judicature of the district enfeoffed to him. He supplied his own equipment and provisions for war, and his subvassals did likewise. Of course, this had consequences for the lord's position of power, which only rested on a relation of personal faith and on the fact that the legitimacy of his possession of the fief and the social honor of the vassal were derived from the overlord.

However, everywhere, reaching back to the earliest political formations, we also find the lord himself directing the administration. He seeks to take the administration into his own hands by having men personally dependent on him: slaves, household officials, attendants, personal favorites, and prebendaries enfeoffed in kind or in money from his magazines. He seeks to defray the expenses from his own pocket, from the revenues of his patrimonium; and he seeks to create an army which is dependent on him, personally, because it is equipped and provisioned out of his granaries, magazines, and armories. In the association of estates, the lord rules with the aid of an autonomous "aristocracy" and hence shares his domination with it; the lord who personally administers is supported either by members of his household or by plebeians. These are property-less strata having no social honor of their own; materially, they are completely chained to him and are not backed up by any competing power of their own. All forms of patriarchal and patrimonial domination, sultanist despotism, and bureaucratic states belong to this latter type. The bureaucratic state order is especially important; in its most rational development, it is precisely characteristic of the modern state.

Everywhere the development of the modern state is initiated through the action of the prince. He paves the way for the expropriation of the autonomous and "private" bearers of executive power who stand beside him, of those who in their own right possess the means of administration, warfare, and financial organization, as well as politically usable goods of all sorts. The whole process is a complete parallel to the development of the capitalist enterprise through gradual expropriation of the independent producers. In the end, the modern state controls the total means of political organization, which actually come together under a single head. No single official personally owns the money he pays out, or the buildings, stores, tools, and war machines he controls. In the contemporary "state"—and this is essential for the concept of state—the "separation" of the administrative staff, of the administrative officials, and of the workers from the material means of administrative organization is completed. Here, the most modern development begins, and we see with our own eyes the attempt to inaugurate the expropriation of this expropriator of the political means, and therewith of political power.

The revolution [of Germany, 1918] has accomplished, at least insofar as leaders have taken the place of the statutory authorities, this much: the leaders, through usurpation or election, have attained control over the political staff and the apparatus of material goods; and they deduce their legitimacy—no matter with what right—from the will of the governed. Whether the leaders, on the basis of this at least apparent success, can rightfully entertain the hope of also carrying through the expropriation within the capitalist enterprises, is a different question. The direction of capitalist enterprises, despite far-reaching analogies, follows quite different laws than those of political administration.

Today, we do not take a stand on this question. I state only the purely *conceptual* aspect for our consideration: the modern state is a compulsory association which organizes domination. It has been successful in seeking to monopolize the legitimate use of physical force as a means of domination within a territory. To this end, the state has combined the material means of organization in the hands of its leaders, and it has expropriated all autonomous functionaries of estates who formerly controlled these means in their own right. The state has taken their positions and now stands in the top place.

During this process of political expropriation, which has occurred with varying success in all countries on earth, "professional politicians" in another sense have emerged. They arose first in the service of a prince. They have been men who, unlike the charismatic leader, have not wished to be lords themselves, but who have entered the *service* of political lords. In the struggle of expropriation, they placed themselves at the princes' disposal, and by managing the princes' politics they earned, on the one hand, a living and, on the other hand, an ideal content of life. Again, it is *only* in the Occident that we find this kind of professional politician in the service of powers other than the princes. In the past, they have been the most important power instrument of the prince and his instrument of political expropriation.

Before discussing "professional politicians" in detail, let us clarify in all its aspects the state of affairs their existence presents. Politics, just as economic pursuits, may be a man's avocation or his vocation. One may engage in politics and, hence, seek to influence the distribution of power within and between political structures, as an "occasional" politician. We are all "occasional" politicians when we cast our ballot or consummate such a similar expression of intention as applauding or protesting in a "political" meeting or delivering a "political" speech. The whole relation of many people to politics is restricted to this. Politics as an avocation is, today, practiced by all those party agents and heads of voluntary political associations who, as a rule, are politically active only in case of need and for whom politics is, neither materially nor ideally, "their life" in the first place. The same holds for those members of state counsels and similar deliberative bodies that function only when summoned. It also holds for rather broad strata of our members of parliament who are politically active only during sessions. In the past, such strata were found especially among the estates. Proprietors of military implements in their own right, or proprietors of goods important for the administration, or proprietors of personal prerogatives may be called estates. A large portion of them were far from giving their lives wholly, or merely preferentially, or more than occasionally, to the service of politics. Rather, they exploited their prerogatives in the interest of gaining rent or even profits; and they became active in the service of political associations only when the overload of their status-equals especially demanded it. It was not different in the case of some of the auxiliary forces which the prince drew into the struggle for the creation of a political organization to be exclusively at his disposal. This was the nature of the *Räte von Haus aus* [councilors] and, still further back, of a considerable part of the councilors assembling in the "Curia" and other deliberating bodies of the princes. But these merely occasional auxiliary forces engaging in politics on the side were naturally not sufficient for the prince. Of necessity, the prince sought to create a staff of helpers dedicated wholly and exclusively to serving him, hence making this their major vocation. The structure of the emerging dynastic political organization, and not only this but the whole articulation of the culture, depended to a considerable degree on the question of where the prince recruited agents.

A staff was also necessary for those political associations whose members constituted themselves politically as (so-called) "free" communes under the complete abolition or the far-going restriction of princely power.

They were "free" not in the sense of freedom from domination by force, but in the sense that princely power, legitimized by tradition (mostly religiously sanctified) as the exclusive source of all authority, was absent. These communities have their historical home in the Occident. Their nucleus was the city as a body politic, the form in which the city first emerged in the Mediterranean culture area. In all these cases, what did the politicians who made politics their major vocation look like?

There are two ways of making politics one's vocation: either one lives "for" politics, or one lives "off" politics. By no means is this contrast an exclusive one. The rule is, rather, that man does both, at least in thought, and certainly he also does both in practice. He who lives "for" politics makes politics his life, in an internal sense. Either he enjoys the naked possession of the power he exerts, or he nourishes his inner balance and self-feeling by the consciousness that his life has *meaning* in the service of a "cause." In this internal sense, every sincere man who lives for a cause also lives off this cause. The distinction hence refers to a much more substantial aspect of the matter, namely, to the economic. He who strives to make politics a permanent *source of income* lives "off" politics as a vocation, whereas he who does not do this lives "for" politics. Under the dominance of the private property order, some—if you wish—very trivial preconditions must exist in order for a person to be able to live "for" politics in this economic sense. Under normal conditions, the politician must be economically independent of the income politics can bring him. This means, quite simply, that the politician must be wealthy or must have a personal position in life which yields a sufficient income.

This is the case, at least in normal circumstances. The war lord's following is just as little concerned about the conditions of a normal economy as is the street crowd following of the revolutionary hero. Both live off booty, plunder, confiscations, contributions, and the imposition of worthless and compulsory means of tender, which in essence amounts to the same thing. But necessarily, these are extraordinary phenomena. In everyday economic life, only some wealth serves the purpose of making a man economically independent. Yet this alone does not suffice. The professional politician must also be economically "dispensable," that is, his income must not depend upon the fact that he constantly and personally places his ability and thinking entirely, or at least by far predominantly, in the service of economic acquisition. In the most unconditional way, the *rentier* is dispensable in this sense. Hence, he is a man who receives completely unearned income. He may be the territorial lord of the past, or the large landowner and aristocrat of the present who receives ground rent. In Antiquity and the Middle Ages, they who received slave or serf rents, or in modern times rents from shares or bonds or similar sources—these are *rentiers*.

Neither the worker nor—and this has to be noted well—the entrepreneur, especially the modern, large-scale entrepreneur, is economically dispensable in this sense. For it is precisely the entrepreneur who is tied to his enterprise and is therefore *not* dispensable. This holds for the entrepreneur in industry far more than for the entrepreneur in agriculture, considering the seasonal character of agriculture. In the main, it is very difficult for the entrepreneur to be represented in his enterprise by someone else, even temporarily. He is as little dispensable as is the medical doctor, and the more eminent and busy he is the less dispensable he is. For purely organizational reasons, it is easier for the lawyer to be dispensable; and, therefore, the lawyer has played an incomparably greater, and often even a dominant, role as a professional politician. We shall not continue in this classification; rather, let us clarify some of its ramifications.

The leadership of a state or of a party by men who (in the economic sense of the word) live exclusively for politics and not off politics means necessarily a "plutocratic" recruitment of the leading political strata. To be sure, this does not mean that such plutocratic leadership signifies at the same time that the politically dominant strata will not also seek to live "off" politics, and hence that the dominant stratum will not usually exploit its political domination in its own economic interest. All that is unquestionable, of course. There has never been such a stratum that has not somehow lived "off" politics. Only this is meant: that the professional politician need not seek remuneration directly for his political work, whereas every politician without means must absolutely claim this. On the other hand, we do not mean to say that the propertyless politician will pursue private economic advantages through politics, exclusively, or even predominantly. Nor do we mean that he will not think, in the first place, of "the subject matter." Nothing would be more incorrect. According to all experience, a care for the economic "security" of his existence is consciously or unconsciously a cardinal point in the whole life orientation of the wealthy man. A quite reckless and unreserved political idealism is found if not exclusively at least predominantly among those strata who, by virtue of their propertylessness, stand entirely outside of the strata who are interested in maintaining the economic order of a given society. This holds especially for extraordinary, and hence revolutionary, epochs. A nonplutocratic recruitment of interested politicians, of leadership and following, is geared to the self-understood precondition that regular and reliable income will accrue to those who manage politics.

Either, politics can be conducted "honorifically"—and then, as one usually says, by "independent," that is, by wealthy, men, and especially by *rentiers*; or, political leadership is made accessible to propertyless men who must then be rewarded. The professional politician who lives "off" politics may be a pure prebendary or a salaried official. Then the politician receives either income from fees and perquisites for specific services—tips and bribes are only an irregular and formally illegal variant of this category of income—or a fixed income in kind, a money salary, or both. He may assume the character of an "entrepreneur," like the *condottiere* or the holder of a farmed-out or purchased office, or like the American boss who considers his costs a capital investment which he brings to fruition through exploitation of his influence. Again, he may receive a fixed wage, like a journalist, a party secretary, a modern cabinet minister, or a political official. Feudal fiefs, land grants, and prebends of all sorts have been typical, in the past. With the development of the money economy, perquisites and prebends especially are the typical rewards for the following of princes, victorious conquerors, or successful party chiefs. For loyal services today, party leaders give offices of all sorts—in parties, newspapers, cooperative societies, health insurance, municipalities, as well as in the state. *All* party struggles are struggles for the patronage of office, as well as struggles for objective goals.

In Germany, all struggles between the proponents of local and of central government are focused on the question of which powers shall control the patronage of office, whether they are of Berlin, Munich, Karlsruhe, or Dresden. Setbacks in participating in offices are felt more severely by parties than is action against their objective goals. In France, a turnover of prefects because of party politics has always been considered a greater transformation and has always caused a greater uproar, than a modification in the government's program—the latter almost having the significance of mere verbiage. Some parties, especially those in America since the disappearance of the old conflicts concerning the interpretation of the constitution, have become pure patronage parties handing out jobs and changing their material program according to the chances of grabbing votes.

In Spain, up to recent years, the two great parties, in a conventionally fixed manner, took turns in office by means of "elections," fabricated from above, in order to provide their followers with offices. In the Spanish colonial territories, in the so-called "elections," as well as in the so-called "revolutions," what was at stake was always the state bread-basket from which the victors wished to be fed.

In Switzerland, the parties peacefully divided the offices among themselves proportionately, and some of our "revolutionary" constitutional drafts, for instance, the first draft of the Badenian constitution, sought to extend this system to ministerial positions. Thus, the state and state offices were considered as pure institutions for the provision of spoilsmen.

Above all, the Catholic Center party was enthusiastically for this draft. In Baden, the party, as part of the party platform, made the distribution of offices proportional to [number of confessors and regularity of] confessions and hence without regard to achievement. This tendency becomes stronger for all parties when the number of offices increases as a result of general bureaucratization and when the demand for offices increases because they represent specifically secure livelihoods. For their followings, the parties become more and more a means to the end of being provided for in this manner.

The development of modern officialdom into a highly qualified, professional labor force, specialized in expertness through long years of prepatory training, stands opposed to all these arrangements. Modern bureaucracy, in the interest of integrity, has developed a high sense of status honor; without this sense, the danger of an awful corruption and a vulgar Philistinism threatens fatally. And without such integrity, even the purely technical functions of the state apparatus would be endangered. The significance of the state apparatus for the economy has been steadily rising, especially with increasing socialization, and its significance will be further augmented.

In the United States, amateur administration through booty politicians, in accordance with the outcome of presidential elections, resulted in the exchange of hundreds of thousands of officials, even down to the mail carrier. The administration knew nothing of the professional civil-servant-for-life, but this amateur administration has long since been punctured by the Civil Service Reform. Purely technical, irrefrageable needs of the administration have determined this development.

In Europe, expert officialdom, based on the division of labor, has emerged in a gradual development of half a thousand years. The Italian cities and seigniories were the beginning among the monarchies, as were the states of the Norman conquerors. But the decisive step was taken in connection with the administration of the finances of the prince. With the administrative reforms of Emperor Max [Maximilian I (1459–1519), Roman emperor, German King] it can be seen how hard it was for the officials to depose successfully of the prince in this field, even under the pressure of extreme emergency and of Turkish rule. The sphere of finance could afford least of all a ruler's dilettantism—a ruler who, at that time, was still above all a knight. The development of war technique called forth the expert and specialized officer; the differentiation of legal procedure called forth the trained jurist. In these three areas—finance, war, and law —expert officialdom in the more advanced states was definitely triumphant during the sixteenth century. With the ascendancy of princely absolutism over the estates, there was simultaneously a gradual abdication of the prince's autocratic rule in favor of an expert officialdom. These very officials had only facilitated the prince's victory over the estates.

The development of the "leading politicians" was realized along with the ascendancy of the specially trained officialdom, even if in far less noticeable transitions. Of course, such really decisive advisers of the princes have existed at all times and all over the world. In the Orient, the need for relieving the Sultan as far as possible from personal responsibility for the success of the government has created the typical figure of the "Grand Vizier." In the Occident, influenced above all by the reports of the Venetian legates, diplomacy first became a *consciously* cultivated art in the age of Charles V, in Machiavelli's time. The reports of the Venetian legates were read with passionate zeal in expert diplomatic circles. The adepts of this art, who were in the main educated humanistically, treated one another as trained initiates, similar to the humanist Chinese statesmen in the last period of the warring states. The necessity of a formally unified guidance of the whole policy, including that of home affairs, by a leading statesman finally and compellingly arose only through constitutional development. Of course, individual personalities, such as advisers of the princes, or rather, in actuality, leaders, had again and again existed before then. But the organization of administrative agencies, even in the most advanced states, first proceeded along other avenues. Top collegial administrative agencies had emerged. In theory, and to a gradually decreasing extent in fact, they met under the personal chairmanship of the prince who rendered the decision. This collegial system led to memoranda, countermemoranda, and reasoned votes of the majority and the minority. In addition to the official and highest authorities, the prince surrounded himself with purely personal confidants— the "cabinet"—and through them rendered his decisions, after considering the resolutions of the state counsel, or whatever else the highest state agency was called. The prince, coming more and more into the position of a dilettante, sought to extricate himself from the unavoidably increasing weight of the expertly trained officials through the collegial system and the cabinet. He sought to retain the highest leadership in his own hands. This latent struggle between expert officialdom and autocratic rule existed everywhere; only in the face of parliaments and the power aspirations of party leaders did the situation change. Very different conditions led to the externally identical result, though, to be sure, with certain differences. Wherever the dynasties retained actual power in their hands—as was especially the case in Germany—the interests of the prince were joined with those of officialdom *against* parliament and its claims for power. The officials were also interested in having leading positions, that is, ministerial positions, occupied by their own ranks, thus making these positions an object of the official career. The monarch, for his part, was interested in being able to appoint the ministers from the ranks of devoted officials according to his own discretion. Both parties, however, were interested in seeing the political leadership confront parliament in a unified and solidary fashion, and hence in seeing the collegial system replaced by a single cabinet head. Furthermore, in order to be removed in a purely formal way from the struggle of parties and from party attacks, the monarch needed a single personality to cover him and to assume responsibility, that is, to answer to parliament and to negotiate with the parties. All these interests worked together and in the same direction: a minister emerged to direct the officialdom in a unified way.

Where parliament gained supremacy over the monarch—as in England—the development of parliamentary power worked even more strongly in the direction of a unification of the state apparatus. In England, the "cabinet," with the single head of Parliament as its "leader," developed as a committee of the party which at the time controlled the majority. This party power was ignored by official law but, in fact, it alone was politically decisive. The official collegial bodies, as such, were not organs of the actual ruling power, the party, and hence could not be the bearers of real government. The ruling party required an ever-ready organization composed *only* of its actually leading men, who would confidentially discuss matters in order to maintain power within and be capable of engaging in grand politics outside. The cabinet is simply this organization. However, in relation to the public, especially the parliamentary public, the party needed a leader responsible for all decisions— the cabinet head. The English system has been taken over on the Continent in the form of parliamentary ministries. In America alone, and in the democracies influenced by America, a quite heterogeneous system was placed into opposition with this system. The American system placed the directly and popularly elected leader of the victorious party at the head of the apparatus of officials appointed by him and bound him to the consent of "parliament" only in budgetary and legislative matters.

The development of politics into an organization which demanded training in the struggle for power, and in the methods of this struggle as developed by modern party policies, determined the separation of public functionaries into two categories, which, however, are by no means rigidly, but nevertheless distinctly, separated. These categories are "administrative" officials on the one hand, and "political" officials on the other. The "political" officials, in the genuine sense of the word, can regularly and externally be recognized by the fact that they can be transferred any time at will, that they can be dismissed, or at least temporarily withdrawn. They are like the French prefects and the comparable officials of other countries, and this is in sharp contrast to the "independence" of officials with judicial functions. In England, officials who, according to fixed convention, retire from office when there is a change in the parliamentary majority, and hence a change in the cabinet, belong to this category. There are usually among them some whose competence includes the management of the general "inner administration." The political element consists, above all, in the task of maintaining "law and order" in the country, hence maintaining the existing power relations. In Prussia, these officials, in accordance with Puttkamer's decree and in order to avoid censure, were obliged to "represent the policy of the government." And, like the prefects in France, they were used as an official apparatus for influencing elections. Most of the "political" officials of the German system— in contrast to other countries—were equally qualified insofar as access to these offices required a university education, special examinations, and special preparatory service. In Germany, only the heads of the political apparatus, the ministers, lack this specific characteristic of modern civil service. Even under the old regime, one could be the Prussian minister of education without ever having attended an institution of higher learning; whereas one could become *Vortragender Rat,** in principle, only on the basis of a prescribed examination. The specialist and trained *Dezernent*† and *Vortragender Rat* were of course infinitely better informed about the real technical problems of the division than was their respective chief—for instance, under Althoff in the Prussian ministry of education. In England it was not different. Consequently, in all routine demands the divisional head was more powerful than the minister, which was not without reason. The minister was simply the representative of the political power constellation; he had to represent these powerful political staffs and he had to take measure of the proposals of his subordinate expert officials or give them directive orders of a political nature.

After all, things in a private economic enterprise are quite similar: the real "sovereign," the assembled shareholders, is just as little influential in the business management as is a "people" ruled by expert offi-

---

* A high ministerial official in charge of a special division concerning which he had to give regular reports.

† Head of an administrative division in a ministry.

cials. The personages who decide the policy of the enterprise, the bank-controlled "directorate," give only directive economic orders, and select persons for the management, without themselves being capable of technically directing the enterprise. Thus, the present structure of the revolutionary state signifies nothing new in principle. It places power over the administration into the hands of absolute dilettantes, who, by virtue of their control of the machine guns, would like to use expert officials only as executive heads and hands. The difficulties of the present system lie elsewhere than here, but today these difficulties shall not concern us. We shall, rather, ask for the typical peculiarity of the professional politicians, of the "leaders" as well as their followings. Their nature has changed and, today, varies greatly from one case to another.

We have seen that in the past "professional politicians" developed through the struggle of the princes with the estates and that they served the princes. Let us briefly review the major types of these professional politicians.

Confronting the estates, the prince found support in politically exploitable strata outside of the order of the estates. Among the latter, there was, first, the clergy in Western and Eastern India, in Buddhist China and Japan, and in Lamaist Mongolia, just as in the Christian territories of the Middle Ages. The clergy were technically useful because they were literate. The importation of Brahmins, Buddhist priests, Lamas, and the employment of bishops and priests as political counselors, occurred with an eye to obtaining administrative forces who could read and write and who could be used in the struggle of the emperor, prince, or khan against the aristocracy. Unlike the vassal who confronted his overlord, the cleric, especially the celibate cleric, stood outside the machinery of normal political and economic interests and was not tempted by the struggle for political power, for himself or for his descendants. By virtue of his own status, the cleric was "separated" from the managerial implements of princely administration.

The humanistically educated literati comprised a second such stratum. There was a time when one learned to produce Latin speeches and Greek verses in order to become a political adviser to a prince and, above all things, to become a memorialist. This was the time of the first flowering of the humanist schools and of the princely foundations of professorships for "poetics." This was, for us, a transitory epoch which has had a quite persistent influence on our educational system, yet no deeper results politically. In East Asia, it has been different. The Chinese mandarin is, or rather originally was, what the humanist of our Renaissance period approximately was: a literator humanistically trained and tested in the language monuments of the remote past. When you read the diaries of Li Hung Chang you will find that he is most proud of having composed poems and of being a good calligrapher. This stratum, with its con-

ventions developed and modeled after Chinese antiquity, has determined
the whole destiny of China; and, perhaps, our fate would have been similar if the humanists, in their time, had had the slightest chance of gaining
a similar influence.

The third stratum was the court nobility. After the princes had succeeded in expropriating political power from the nobility as an estate,
they drew the nobles to the court and used them in their political and
diplomatic service. The transformation of our educational system in the
seventeenth century was partly determined by the fact that court nobles
as professional politicians displaced the humanist literati and entered
the service of the princes.

The fourth category was a specifically English institution. A patrician
stratum developed there which was comprised of the petty nobility and
the urban *rentiers*; technically they are called the "gentry." The English
gentry represents a stratum that the prince originally attracted in order
to counter the barons. The prince placed the stratum in possession of the
offices of "self-government," and later he himself became increasingly
dependent on them. The gentry maintained the possession of all offices
of local administration by taking them over without compensation in the
interest of their own social power. The gentry has saved England from
the bureaucratization which has been the fate of all continental states.

A fifth stratum, the university-trained jurist, is peculiar to the Occident, especially to the European continent, and has been of decisive significance for the Continent's whole political structure. The tremendous after-
effect of Roman law, as transformed by the late Roman bureaucratic state,
stands out in nothing more clearly than the fact that, everywhere, the
revolution of political management in the direction of the evolving rational state has been borne by trained jurists; this also occurred in England, although there the great national guilds of jurists hindered the reception of Roman law. There is no analogy to this process to be found
in any area of the world.

All beginnings of rational juristic thinking in the Indian Mimamsa
School and all further cultivation of the ancient juristic thinking in Islam
have been unable to prevent the idea of rational law from being over-
grown by theological forms of thought. Above all, legal trial procedure
has not been fully rationalized in the cases of India and of Islamism.
Such rationalization has been brought about on the Continent only
through the borrowing of ancient Roman jurisprudence by the Italian
jurists. Roman jurisprudence is the product of a political structure arising
from the city state to world domination—a product of quite unique nature.
The *usus modernus* of the late medieval pandect [codifier] jurists and
canonists was blended with theories of natural law, which were born
from juristic and Christian thought and which were later secularized.
This juristic rationalism has had its great representatives among the Italian
podesta, the French crown jurists (who created the formal means for the

undermining of the rule of seigneurs by royal power), among the canonists and the theologians of the ecclesiastic councils (thinking in terms of natural law), among the court jurists and academic judges of the continental princes, among the Netherland teachers of natural law and the monarchomachists,* among the English crown and parliamentary jurists, among the *noblesse de robe* of the French Parliament, and finally, among the lawyers of the age of the French Revolution.

Without this juristic rationalism, the rise of the absolute state is just as little imaginable as is the Revolution. If you look through the remonstrances of the French Parliaments or through the *cahiers* of the French Estates-General from the sixteenth century to the year 1789, you will find everywhere the spirit of the jurists. And if you go over the occupational composition of the members of the French Assembly, you will find there—although the members of the Assembly were elected through equal franchise—a single proletarian, very few bourgeois enterprisers, but jurists of all sorts, *en masse*. Without them, the specific mentality that inspired these radical intellectuals and their projects would be quite inconceivable. Since the French Revolution, the modern lawyer and modern democracy absolutely belong together. And lawyers, in our sense of an independent status group, also exist only in the Occident. They have developed since the Middle Ages from the *Fürsprech* of the formalistic Germanic legal procedure under the impact of the rationalization of the trial.

The significance of the lawyer in Occidental politics since the rise of parties is not accidental. The management of politics through parties simply means management through interest groups. We shall soon see what that means. The craft of the trained lawyer is to plead effectively the cause of interested clients. In this, the lawyer is superior to any "official," as the superiority of enemy propaganda [(Allied propaganda 1914–1918)] could teach us. Certainly he can advocate and win a cause supported by logically weak arguments and one which, in this sense, is a "weak" cause. Yet he wins it because technically he makes a "strong case" for it. But only the lawyer successfully pleads a cause that can be supported by logically strong arguments, thus handling a "good" cause "well." All too often the civil servant as a politician turns a cause that is good in every sense into a "weak" cause, through technically "weak" pleading. This is what we have had to experience. To an outstanding degree, politics today is in fact conducted in public by means of the spoken or written word. To weigh the effect of the word properly falls within the range of the lawyer's task, but not at all into that of the civil servant. The latter is no demagogue, nor is it his purpose to be one. If he nevertheless tries to become a demagogue, he usually becomes a very poor one.

According to his proper vocation, the genuine official—and this is

* Supporters of monarchical principle in government.

decisive for the evaluation of our former regime—will not engage in politics. Rather, he should engage in impartial "administration." This also holds for the so-called political administrator, at least officially, insofar as the *raison d'état,* that is, the vital interests of the ruling order, are not in question. *Sine ira et studio,* "without scorn and bias," he shall administer his office. Hence, he shall not do precisely what the politician, the leader as well as his following, must always and necessarily do, namely, *fight.*

To take a stand, to be passionate—*ira et studium*—is the politician's element, and above all the element of the political *leader.* His conduct is subject to quite a different, indeed, exactly the opposite, principle of responsibility from that of the civil servant. The honor of the civil servant is vested in his ability to execute conscientiously the order of the superior authorities, exactly as if the order agreed with his own conviction. This holds even if the order appears wrong to him and if, despite the civil servant's remonstrances, the authority insists on the order. Without this moral discipline and self-denial, in the highest sense, the whole apparatus would fall to pieces. The honor of the political leader, of the leading statesman, however, lies precisely in an exclusive *personal* responsibility for what he does, a responsibility he cannot and must not reject or transfer. It is in the nature of officials of high moral standing to be poor politicians, and, above all, in the political sense of the word, to be irresponsible politicians. In this sense, they are politicians of low moral standing, such as we unfortunately have had again and again in leading positions. This is what we have called *Beamtenherrschaft* [(civil-service rule)], and truly no spot soils the honor of our officialdom if we reveal what is politically wrong with the system from the standpoint of success. But let us return once more to the types of political figures.

Since the time of the constitutional state, and definitely since democracy has been established, the demagogue has been the typical political leader in the Occident. The distasteful flavor of the word must not make us forget that not Cleon but Pericles was the first to bear the name of demagogue. In contrast to the offices of ancient democracy that were filled by lot, Pericles, led the sovereign *Ecclesia* of the demos of Athens as a supreme strategist holding the only elective office, or without holding any office at all. Modern demagoguery also makes use of oratory, even to a tremendous extent, if one considers the election speeches a modern candidate has to deliver. But the use of the printed word is more enduring. The political publicist, and above all the journalist, is nowadays the most important representative of the demagogic species.

Within the limits of this lecture, it is quite impossible even to sketch the sociology of modern political journalism, which in every respect constitutes a chapter in itself. Certainly, only a few things concerning it are in place here. In common with all demagogues and, by the way, with the lawyer (and the artist), the journalist shares the fate of lacking a fixed social classification. At least, this is the case on the Continent, in contrast to the English, and, by the way, also to former conditions in Prussia. The journalist belongs to a sort of pariah caste, which is always estimated by society in terms of its ethically lowest representative. Hence, the strangest notions about journalists and their work are abroad. Not everybody realizes that a really good journalistic accomplishment requires at least as much genius as any scholarly accomplishment, especially because of the necessity of producing at once and on order, and because of the necessity of being effective, to be sure, under quite different conditions of production. It is almost never acknowledged that the responsibility of the journalist is far greater and that the sense of responsibility of every honorable journalist is, on the average, not a bit lower than that of the scholar, but rather, as the war has shown, higher. This is because, in the very nature of the case, irresponsible journalistic accomplishments and their often terrible effects are remembered.

Nobody believes that the discretion of any able journalist ranks above the average of other people, and yet that is the case. The quite incomparably graver temptations, and the other conditions that accompany journalistic work at the present time, produce those results which have conditioned the public to regard the press with a mixture of disdain and pitiful cowardice. Today, we cannot discuss what is to be done. Here we are interested in the question of the occupational destiny of the political journalist and of his chance to attain a position of political leadership. Thus far, the journalist has had favorable chances only in the Social Democratic party. Within the party, editorial positions have been predominantly in the nature of official positions, but editorial positions have not been the basis for positions of leadership.

In the bourgeois parties, on the whole, the chances for ascent to political power along this avenue have become worse, as compared with those of the previous generation. Naturally, every politician of consequence has needed influence over the press and, hence, has needed relations with the press. But, that party leaders would emerge from the ranks of the press has been an absolute exception, and one should not have expected it. The reason for this lies in the strongly increased "indispensability" of the journalist, above all, of the propertyless and consequently professionally bound journalist, an indispensability which is determined by the tremendously increased intensity and tempo of journalistic operations. The necessity of gaining one's livelihood by the writing of daily, or at least weekly, articles is like lead on the feet of the politicians. I know of cases in which natural leaders have been permanently paralyzed in their ascent to power, externally and, above all, internally, by this compulsion. The relations of the press to the ruling powers in the state and in the parties, under the old regime [(of the Kaiser)], were as detrimental as they could be to the level of journalism; but that is a chapter in itself. These conditions were different in the countries of our opponents [(the Allies)]; but there, also, and for all modern states, apparently the journalist worker gains less and less as the capitalist lord of the press, of the sort of "Lord" Northcliffe, for instance, gains more and more political influence.

Thus far, however, our great capitalist newspaper concerns, which attained control, especially over the "chain newspapers," with "want ads," have been regularly and typically the breeders of political indifference. For no profits could be made in an independent policy; especially, no profitable benevolence of the politically dominant powers could be obtained. The advertising business is also the avenue along which, during the war, the attempt was made to influence the press politically in a grand style—an attempt that, apparently, it is regarded as desirable to continue now. Although one may expect the great papers to escape this pressure, the situation of the small ones will be far more difficult. In any case, for the time being, the journalist career is not, among us, a normal avenue for the ascent of political leaders, whatever attraction journalism may otherwise have and whatever measure of influence, range of activity, and, especially, political responsiblity it may yield. One has to wait and see. Perhaps journalism does not have this function any longer, or perhaps journalism does not yet have it. Whether the renunciation of the principle of anonymity would mean a change in this, is difficult to say. Some journalists—not all—believe in dropping principled anonymity. What we have experienced during the war in the German press, and in the "management" of newspapers by especially hired personages and talented writers who always expressly figured under their names, has unfortunately shown, in some of the better known cases, that an increased awareness of responsibility is not so certain to be bred as might be believed. Some of the papers were, without regard to party, precisely the notoriously worst boulevard sheets; by dropping anonymity they strove for and attained greater sales. The publishers as well as the journalists of sensationalism have gained fortunes, but certainly not honor. Nothing is here being said against the principle of promoting sales; the question is indeed an intricate one, and the phenomenon of irresponsible sensationalism does not hold in general. But, thus far, sensationalism has not been the road to genuine leadership or to the responsible management of politics. How conditions will further develop remains to be seen. Yet the journalist career remains under all circumstances one of the most important avenues of professional political activity. It is not a road for everybody, least of all for weak characters, especially not for people who can maintain their inner balance only with a secure status position. If the life of a young scholar is a gamble, still he is walled in by firm status conventions that prevent him from slipping. But the journalist's life is an absolute gamble in every respect, and under conditions that test one's inner security in a way that scarcely occurs in any other situation. The often bitter experiences in occupational life are perhaps not even the worst. The inner demands that are directed precisely at the successful journalist are especially difficult. It is, indeed, no small matter to frequent the salons of the powerful on this earth on a seemingly equal footing and often to be flattered by all because one is feared, yet knowing all the time that having hardly closed the door the host has perhaps to justify before his guests his association with the "scavengers from the press." Moreover, it is no small matter that one must express oneself promptly and convincingly about this and that, on all conceivable problems of life—whatever the "market" happens to demand—and this without becoming absolutely shallow and, above all, without losing one's dignity by baring oneself—a thing which has merciless results. It is not astonishing that there are many journalists who have become human failures and worthless men. Rather, it is astonishing that, despite all this, this very stratum includes such a great number of valuable and quite genuine men, a fact that outsiders would not so easily guess.

If the journalist as a type of professional politician harks back to a rather considerable past, the figure of the party official belongs only to the development of the last decades and, in part, only to recent years. In order to comprehend the position of this figure in historical evolution, we shall have to turn to a consideration of parties and party organizations.

In all political associations which are somehow extensive, that is, associations going beyond the sphere and range of the tasks of small rural districts where power-holders are periodically elected, political organization is necessarily managed by men interested in the management of politics. This is to say that a relatively small number of men are primarily interested in political life and, hence, interested in sharing political power. They provide themselves with a following through free recruitment, present themselves or their protégés as candidates for election, collect the financial means, and go out for vote-grabbing. It is unimaginable how, in large associations, elections could function at all without this managerial pattern. In practice, this means the division of the citizens with the right to vote into politically active and politically passive elements. This difference is based on voluntary attitudes, hence it cannot be abolished through measures like obligatory voting, occupational status group representation, or similar measures that are expressly or actually directed against this state of affairs and the rule of professional politicians. The active leadership and their freely recruited following are the necessary elements in the life of any party. The following, and through it the passive electorate, are necessary for the election of the leader. But the structure of parties varies. For instance, the "parties" of the medieval cities, such as those of the Guelfs and the Ghibellines, were purely personal followings. If one considers various things about these medieval parties, one is reminded of Bolshevism and its soviets. Consider the *Statuta della perta Guelfa,* the confiscations of the Nobili's estates—which originally meant all those families who lived a chivalrous life and who thus qualified for fiefs—consider the ex-clusion from office-holding and the denial of the right to vote, the inter-local party committees, the strictly military organizations and the premi-ums for informers. Then consider Bolshevism with its strictly sieved military and, in Russia especially, informer organizations, the disarmament and denial of the political rights of the bourgeois, that is, of the entrepreneur, trader, *rentier,* clergyman, descendants of the dynasty, police agents, as well as the confiscation policy.

This analogy is still more striking when one considers that, on the one hand, the military organization of the medieval party constituted a pure army of knights organized on the basis of the registered feudal estates and that nobles occupied almost all leading positions, and, on the other hand, that the soviets have preserved, or rather reintroduced, the highly paid enterpriser, the group wage, the Taylor system, military and workshop discipline, and a search for foreign capital. In a word, the soviets have had to accept again absolutely *all* the things that Bolshevism had been fighting as bourgeois class institutions. They have had to do this in order to keep the state and the economy going at all. Moreover, the soviets have reinstituted the agents of the former Ochrana [(tsarist secret po-lice)] as the main instrument of their state power. Here, we do not have to deal with such organizations for violence, but rather with professional politicians who strive for power through sober and peaceful party cam-paigns in the market of election votes.

Parties, in the sense usual with us, were at first, for instance in Eng-land, pure following of the aristocracy. If, for any reason whatever, a peer changed his party, everybody dependent on him likewise changed. Up to the Reform Bill [(of 1832)], the great noble families and, last but not least, the king controlled the patronage of an immense number of election boroughs. Close to these aristocratic parties were the parties of notables, which develop everywhere with the rising power of the bourgeois. Under the spiritual leadership of the typical intellectual strata of the Occident, the propertied and cultured circles differentiated themselves into parties and followed them. These parties were formed partly according to class interest, partly according to family traditions, and partly for ideological reasons. Clergymen, teachers, professors, lawyers, doctors, apothecaries, prosperous farmers, manufacturers—in England the whole stratum that considered itself as belonging to the class of gentlemen—formed, as first, occasional associations at most local political clubs. In times of unrest, the petty bourgeoisie raised its voice, and, once in a while, the proletariat, if leaders arose who, however, as a rule did not stem from their midst. In this phase, parties organized as permanent associations between localities do not yet exist in the open country. Only the parliamentary delegates create the cohesion, and the local notables are decisive for the selection of candidates. The election programs originate partly in the election appeals of the candidates and partly in the meetings of the notables, or they originate as resolutions of the parliamentary party. Leadership of the clubs is an avocation and an honorific pursuit, as demanded by the occasion.

Where clubs are absent (as is mostly the case), the quite formless management of politics in normal times lies in the hands of the few people constantly interested in it. Only the journalist is a paid professional politician; only the management of the newspaper is a continuous political organization. Besides the newspaper, there is only the parliamentary session. The parliamentary delegates and the parliamentary party leaders know to which local notables one turns if a political action seems desirable. But permanent associations of the parties exist only in the large cities with moderate contributions of the members and periodical conferences and public meetings where the delegate gives account of the parliamentary activities. The party is alive only during election periods.

The members of parliament are interested in the possibility of interlocal electoral compromises, in vigorous and unified programs endorsed by broad circles and in a unified agitation throughout the country. In general, these interests form the driving force of a party organization which becomes more and more strict. In principle, however, the nature of a party apparatus as an association of notables remains unchanged. This is so, even though a network of local party affiliations and agents is spread over the whole country, including middle-sized cities. A member of the parliamentary party acts as the leader of the central party office and maintains constant correspondence with the local organizations. Outside of the central bureau, paid officials are still absent; thoroughly respectable people head the local organizations for the sake of the deference which they enjoy anyway. They form the extra-parliamentary notables who exert influence alongside the stratum of political notables who happen to sit in parliament. However, the party correspondence, edited by the party, increasingly provides intellectual nourishment for the press and for the local meetings. Regular contributions of the members become indispensable; a part of these must cover the expenses of headquarters.

Not so long ago most of the German party organizations were still in this stage of development. In France, the first stage of party development was, at least in part, still predominant, and the organization of the members of parliament was quite unstable. In the open country, we find a small number of local notables and programs drafted by the candidates or set up for them by their patrons in specific campaigns for office. To be sure, these platforms constitute more or less local adaptations to the resolutions and programs of the members of parliament. This system was only partially punctured. The number of full-time professional politicians was small, consisting in the main of the elected deputies, the few employees of headquarters, and the journalists. In France, the system has also included those job hunters who held political office or, at the moment, strove for one. Politics was formally, and by far predominantly, an avocation. The number of delegates qualifying for ministerial office was also very restricted and, because of their position as notables, so was the number of election candidates.

However, the number of those who indirectly had a stake in the management of politics, especially a material one, was very large. For, all administrative measures of a ministerial department, and especially all decisions in matters of personnel, were made partly with a view to their influence upon electoral chances. The realization of each and every kind of wish was sought through the local delegate's mediation. For better or for worse, the minister had to lend his ear to this delegate, especially if the delegate belonged to the minister's majority. Hence, everybody strove for such influence. The single deputy controlled the patronage of office and, in general, any kind of patronage in his election district. In order to be re-elected, the deputy, in turn, maintained connections with the local notables.

Now then, the most modern forms of party organizations stand in sharp contrast to this idyllic state in which circles of notables and, above all, members of parliament rule. These modern forms are the children of democracy, of mass franchise, of the necessity to woo and organize the masses and develop the utmost unity of direction and the strictest discipline. The rule of notables and guidance by members of parliament ceases. Professional politicians *outside* the parliaments take the organization in hand. They do so either as "entrepreneurs"—the American boss and the English election agent are, in fact, such entrepreneurs—or, as officials with a fixed salary. Formally, a fargoing democratization takes place. The parliamentary party no longer creates the authoritative programs, and the local notables no longer decide the selection of candidates. Rather, assemblies of the organized party members select the candidates and delegate members to the assemblies of a higher order. Possibly there are several such conventions leading up to the national convention of the party. Naturally, power actually rests in the hands of those who, within the organization, handle the work *continuously*. Otherwise, power rests in the hands of those on whom the organization in its processes depends financially or personally—for instance, on the Maecenases [generous patrons] or the directors of powerful political clubs of interested persons (Tammany Hall). It is decisive that this whole apparatus of people—characteristically called a "machine" in Anglo-Saxon countries—or, rather, those who direct the machine, keep the members of the parliament in check. They are in a position to impose their will to a rather far-reaching extent, and that is of special significance for the selection of the party leader. The man whom the machine follows now becomes the leader, even over the head of the parliamentary party. In other words, the creation of such machines signifies the advent of *plebiscitarian* democracy.

The party following—above all the party official and party entrepreneur—naturally expects personal compensation from the victory of their leader, that is, offices or other advantages. It is decisive that they expect such advantages from their leader and not merely from the individual member of parliament. They expect that the demagogic effect of the leader's *personality* during the election fight of the party will increase votes and mandates and thereby power and, thereby, as far as possible, will extend opportunities to their followers to find the compensation for which they hope. Ideally, one of their mainsprings is the satisfaction of working with loyal personal devotion for a man and not merely for an abstract program of a party consisting of mediocrities. In this respect, the charismatic element of all leadership is at work in the party system.

In very different degrees, this system made headway, although it was in constant, latent struggle with local notables and the members of parliament who wrangled for influence. This was the case in the bourgeois parties, first, in the United States, and, then, in the Social Democratic party, especially of Germany. Constant setbacks occur as soon as no generally recognized leader exists, and, even when he is found, concessions of all sorts must be made to the vanity and the personal interest of the party notables. The machine may also be brought under the domination of the party officials in whose hands the regular business rests. According to the view of some Social Democratic circles, their party had succumbed to this bureaucratization. But officials submit relatively easily to a leader's personality if it has a strong demagogic appeal. The material and the ideal interests of the officials are intimately connected with the effects of party power which are expected from the leader's appeal, and, besides, inwardly it is per se more satisfying to work for a leader. The ascent of leaders is far more difficult where the notables, along with the officials, control the party, as is usually the case in the bourgeois parties. For, ideally, the notables make their way of life out of the petty chairmanships or committee memberships they hold. Resentment against the demagogue as a *homo novus,* the conviction of the superiority of political party experience (which, as a matter of fact, actually is of considerable importance), and the ideological concern for the crumbling of the old party traditions— these factors determine the conduct of the notables. They can count on all the traditionalist elements within the party. Above all, the rural, but also the petty bourgeois, voter looks for the name of the notable familiar to him. He distrusts the man who is unknown to him. However, once this man has become successful, he clings to him the more unwaveringly. Let us now consider, by some major examples, the struggle of the two structural forms—of the notables and of the party—and, especially, let us consider the ascendancy of the plebiscitarian form as described by Ostrogorsky.*

* M. Ostrogorsky, *Democracy and the Organization of Political Parties* (New York: Macmillan Co., 1922).

First England: there, until 1868, the party organization was almost purely an organization of notables. The Tories in the country found support, for instance, from the Anglican parson, and from the schoolmaster, and, above all, from the large landlords of the respective county. The Whigs found support mostly from such people as the nonconformist preacher (when there was one), the postmaster, the blacksmith, the tailor, the ropemaker—that is, from such artisans who could disseminate political influence because they could chat with people most frequently. In the city, the parties differed, partly according to economics, partly according to religion, and partly simply according to the party opinions handed down in the families. But, always, the notables were the pillars of the political organization.

Above all these arrangements stood Parliament, the parties with the cabinet, and the leader, who was the chairman of the council of ministers or the leader of the opposition. This leader had beside him the "whip"— the most important professional politician of the party organization. Patronage of office was vested in the hands of the whip; thus, the job hunter had to turn to him, and he arranged an understanding with the deputies of the individual election boroughs. A stratum of professional politicians gradually began to develop in the boroughs. At first, the locally recruited agents were not paid; they occupied approximately the same position as our *Vertrauensmänner*.* However, along with them, a capitalist entrepreneurial type developed in the boroughs. This was the "election agent," whose existence was unavoidable under England's modern legislation which guaranteed fair elections.

This legislation aimed at controlling the campaign costs of elections and sought to check the power of money by making it obligatory for the candidate to state the costs of his campaign. For, in England, the candidate, besides straining his voice—far more so than was formerly the case with us [(in Germany)]—enjoyed stretching his purse. The election agent made the candidate pay a lump sum, which usually meant a good deal for the agent. In the distribution of power in Parliament and the country between the leader and the party notables, the leader in England used to hold a very eminent position. This position was based on the compelling fact of making possible a grand, and thereby steady, political strategy. Nevertheless, the influence of the parliamentary party, and of party notables, was still considerable.

That is about what the old party organization looked like. It was half an affair of notables and half an entrepreneurial organization with salaried employees. Since 1868, however, the caucus system developed, first for local elections in Birmingham, then all over the country. A nonconformist parson, and, along with him, Joseph Chamberlain, brought this system to life. The occasion for this development was the democratization of the

* "Local agents" of the party.

franchise. In order to win the masses, it became necessary to call into being a tremendous apparatus of apparently democratic associations. An electoral association had to be formed in every city district to help keep the organization incessantly in motion and to bureaucratize everything rigidly. Hired and paid officials of the local electoral committees increased numerically; and, on the whole, perhaps 10 per cent of the voters were organized in these local committees. The elected party managers had the right to co-opt others and were the formal bearers of party politics. The driving force was the local circle, which was, above all, composed of those interested in municipal politics—from which the fattest material opportunities always spring. These local circles were also first to call on the world of finance. This newly emerging machine, no longer led by members of Parliament, very soon had to struggle with the previous power-holders, especially with the whip. Being supported by locally interested persons, the machine came out of the fight so victoriously that the whip had to submit and compromise with the machine. The result was a centralization of all power in the hands of the few and, ultimately, of the one person who stood at the top of the party. The whole system had arisen in the Liberal party in connection with Gladstone's ascent to power. What brought this machine to such swift triumph over the notables was the fascination of Gladstone's grand demagogy, the firm belief of the masses in the ethical substance of his policy, and, most important, their belief in the ethical character of his personality. It soon became obvious that a Caesarist plebiscitarian element in politics—the dictator of the battlefield of elections—had appeared on the plain. In 1877, the caucus became active for the first time in national elections, and with brilliant success, for the result was Disraeli's fall at the height of his great achievements. In 1866, the machine was already so completely oriented to the charismatic personality that when the question of home rule was raised the whole apparatus from top to bottom did not question whether it actually stood on Gladstone's ground; it simply, on his word, fell in line with him. They said, Gladstone right or wrong, we follow him. Thus the machine deserted [1866] its own creator, [Joseph] Chamberlain.

Such machinery requires a considerable personnel. In England, there are about 2,000 persons who live directly off party politics. To be sure, those who are active in politics purely as job seekers or as interested persons are far more numerous, especially in municipal politics. In addition to economic opportunities for the useful caucus politician, there are the opportunities to satisfy his vanity. To become "J.P." or even "M.P." is, of course, in line with the greatest (and normal) ambition; and such people, who are of demonstrably good breeding, that is, "gentlemen," attain their goal. The highest goal is, of course, a peerage, especially for the great financial Maecenases. About 50 per cent of the finances of the party depend on contributions of donors who remained anonymous.

Now then, what has been the effect of this whole system? Nowadays, the members of Parliament, with the exception of the few cabinet members (and a few insurgents), are normally nothing better than well-disciplined yes men. With us, in the Reichstag, one used at least to take care of one's private correspondence, thus indicating that one was active in the weal of the country. Such gestures are not demanded in England; the member of Parliament must only vote, not commit party treason. He must appear when the whips call him and do what the cabinet or the leader of the opposition orders. The caucus machine in the open country is almost completely unprincipled if a strong leader exists who has the machine absolutely in hand. Therewith, the plebiscitarian dictator actually stands above Parliament. He brings the masses behind him by means of the machine, and the members of Parliament are, for him, merely political spoilsmen enrolled in his following.

How does the selection of these strong leaders take place? First, in terms of what ability are they selected? Next to the qualities of will—decisive all over the world—naturally, the force of demagogic speech is above all decisive. Its character has changed since the time such speakers as Cobden* addressed themselves to the intellect and Gladstone mastered the technique of apparently "letting sober facts speak for themselves." At the present time, often purely emotional means are used—the means the Salvation Army also exploits in order to set the masses in motion. One may call the existing state of affairs a "dictatorship resting on the exploitation of mass emotionality." Yet, the highly developed system of committee work in the English Parliament makes it possible and compelling for every politician who counts on a share in leadership to cooperate in committee work. All important ministers of recent decades have this very real and effective work-training as a background. The practice of committee reports and public criticism of these deliberations is a condition for training, for really selecting leaders and eliminating mere demagogues.

Thus it is in England. The caucus system there, however, has been a weak form, compared with the American party organization, which brought the plebiscitarian principle to an especially early and an especially pure expression.

According to Washington's idea, America was to be a commonwealth administered by gentlemen. In his time, in America, a gentleman was also a landlord, or a man with a college education; this was the case at first. In the beginning, when parties began to organize, the members of the House of Representatives claimed to be leaders, just as in England at the time when notables ruled. The party organization was quite loose and continued to be until 1824. In some communities, where modern development first took place, the party machine was in the making even before the eighteen-twenties. But when Andrew Jackson was first elected Presi-

---

* Richard Cobden (1804–1865), English political economist apostle of free trade.

dent—the election of the western farmers' candidate—the old traditions were overthrown. Formal party leadership by leading members of Congress came to an end soon after 1840, when the great parliamentarians, Calhoun and Webster, retired from political life, because Congress had lost almost all of its power to the party machine in the open country. That the plebiscitarian machine has developed so early in America is due to the fact that there, and there alone, the executive—this is what mattered—the chief of office-patronage, was a president elected by plebiscite. By virtue of the separation of powers, he was almost independent of parliament in his conduct of office. Hence, as the price of victory, the true booty object of the office-prebend was held out precisely at the presidential election. Through Andrew Jackson, the spoils system was quite systematically raised to a principle, and the conclusions were drawn.

What does this spoils system, the turning over of federal offices to the following of the victorious candidate, mean for the party formations of today? It means that quite unprincipled parties oppose one another; they are purely organizations of job hunters drafting their changing platforms according to the chances of vote-grabbing, changing their colors to a degree which, despite all analogies, is not yet to be found elsewhere. The parties are simply and absolutely fashioned for the election campaign that is most important for office patronage: the fight for the presidency and for the governorships of the separate states. Platforms and candidates are selected at the national conventions of the parties without intervention by congressmen; hence, they emerge from party conventions, the delegates of which are formally, very democratically elected. These delegates are determined by meetings of other delegates, who, in turn, owe their mandate to the primaries, the assembling of the direct voters of the party. In the primaries, the delegates are already elected in the name of the candidate for the nation's leadership. Within the parties, the most embittered fight rages about the question of nomination. After all, 300,000 to 400,-000 official appointments lie in the hands of the President, appointments which are executed by him only with the approval of the senators from the separate states. Hence the senators are powerful politicians. By comparison, however, the House of Representatives is, politically, quite impotent, because patronage of office is removed from it and because the cabinet members, simply assistants to the President, can conduct office apart from the confidence or lack of confidence of the people. The President, who is legitimatized by the people, confronts everybody, even Congress; this is a result of the separation of powers.

In America, the spoils system, supported in this fashion, has been technically possible because American culture with its youth could afford purely dilettante management. With 300,000 to 400,000 such party men, who have no qualifications to their credit other than the fact of having performed good services for their party, this state of affairs could not exist without enormous evils. A corruption and wastefulness second to none could be tolerated only by a country with as yet unlimited economic opportunities.

Now then, the boss is the figure who appears in the picture of this system of the plebiscitarian party machine. Who is the boss? He is a political capitalist entrepreneur who, on his own account and at his own risk, provides votes. He may have established his first relations as a lawyer, or a saloonkeeper, or as a proprietor of similar establishments, or perhaps as a creditor. From here, he spins his threads out until he is able to control a certain number of votes. When he has come this far, he establishes contact with the neighboring bosses, and, through zeal, skill, and above all discretion, he attracts the attention of those who have already further advanced in the career; and then he climbs. The boss is indispensable to the organization of the party, and the organization is centralized in his hands. He substantially provides the financial means. How does he get them? Well, partly by the contributions of the members and, especially, by taxing the salaries of those officials who came into office through him and his party. Furthermore, there are bribes and tips. He who wishes to trespass with impunity one of the many laws needs the boss's connivance and must pay for it, or else he will get into trouble. But this, alone, is not enough to accumulate the necessary capital for political enterprises. The boss is indispensable as the direct recipient of the money of great financial magnates who would not entrust their money for election purposes to a paid party official or to anyone else giving public account of his affairs.

The boss, with his judicious discretion in financial matters, is the natural man for those capitalist circles who finance the election. The typical boss is an absolutely sober man. He does not seek social honor; the professional is despised in respectable society. He seeks power alone, power as a source of money, but, also, power for power's sake. In contrast to the English leader, the American boss works in the dark. He is not heard speaking in public; he suggests to the speakers what they must say in expedient fashion. He, himself, however, keeps silent. As a rule, he accepts no office, except that of senator; for, since the senators, by virtue of the Constitution, participate in office patronage, the leading bosses often sit in person in this body. The distribution of offices is carried out, in the first place, according to services done for the party. Also, auctioning offices on financial bids often occurs, and there are certain rates for individual offices; a system of selling offices exists which, after all, has often been known also to the monarchies, the church-state included, of the seventeenth and eighteenth centuries.

The boss has no firm political principles; he is completely unprincipled in attitude and asks merely: What will capture votes? Frequently, he is a rather poorly educated man. But, as a rule, he leads an inoffensive and correct private life. In his political morals, however, he naturally adjusts to the average ethical standards of political conduct, as a great many of us also may have done during the boarding period in the field of economic ethics. That, as a professional politician, the boss is socially despised, does not worry him. That he personally does not attain high federal offices, and does not wish to do so, has the frequent advantage that extraparty intellects, thus notables, may come into candidacy when the bosses believe they will have great appeal value at the polls; the same old party notables do not run again and again, as is the case in Germany. Thus, the structure of these unprincipled parties with their socially despised power-holders has aided able men to attain the presidency—men who, with us, never would have come to the top. To be sure, the bosses resist an outsider who might jeopardize their sources of money and power. Yet in the competitive struggle to win the favor of the voters, the bosses frequently have had to condescend and accept candidates known to be opponents of corruption.

Thus, there exists a strong capitalist party machine, strictly and thoroughly organized from top to bottom, and supported by clubs of extraordinary stability. These clubs, such as Tammany Hall, are like Knight orders. They seek profits solely through political control, especially of the municipal government, which is the most important object of booty. This structure of party life was made possible by the high degree of democracy in the United States—a "New Country." This connection, in turn, is the basis for the fact that the system is gradually dying out. America can no longer be governed only by dilettantes. Scarcely fifteen years ago, when American workers were asked why they allowed themselves to be governed by politicians whom they admitted they despised, the answer was: "We prefer having people in office whom we can spit upon, rather than a caste of officials who spit upon us, as is the case with you." This was the old point of view of American democracy. Even then, the socialists had entirely different ideas, and now the situation is no longer bearable. The dilettante administration does not suffice, and the Civil Service Reform establishes an ever-increasing number of positions for life with pension rights. The reform works out in such a way that university-trained officials, just as incorruptible and quite as capable as our officials, get into office. Even now [1918], about 100,000 offices have ceased being objects of booty to be turned over after elections. Rather, the offices qualify their holders for pensions and are based on tested qualifications. The spoils system will thus gradually recede into the background, and the nature of party leadership is then likely to be transformed also—but as yet, we do not know in what way.

In Germany, until now [1918], the decisive conditions of political management have been, in essence, as follows:

First, the parliaments have been impotent. The result has been that no man with the qualities of a leader would enter Parliament permanently.

If one wished to enter Parliament, what could one achieve there? When a chancellery position was open, one could tell the administrative chief: "I have a very able man in my election district who would be suitable; take him." And he would have concurred with pleasure; but that was about all that a German member of Parliament could do to satisfy his instincts for power—if he possessed any.

To this must be added the tremendous importance of the trained expert officialdom in Germany. This factor determined the impotence of Parliament. Our officialdom was second to none in the world. This importance of the officialdom was accompanied by the fact that the officials claimed not only official positions but also cabinet positions for themselves. In the Bavarian state legislature, when the introduction of parliamentary government was debated last year, it was said that, if members of the legislature were to be placed in cabinet positions, talented people would no longer seek official careers. Moreover the civil-service administration systematically escaped such control as is signified by the English committee discussions. The administration thus made it impossible for parliaments —with a few exceptions—to train really useful administrative chiefs from their own ranks.

A third factor is that in Germany, in contrast to America, we have had parties with principled political views who have maintained that their members, at least subjectively, represented bona fide *Weltanschauungen* [ideology]. Now then, the two most important of these parties, the Catholic Center party and the Social Democratic party, have, from their inceptions, been minority parties and have meant to be minority parties. The leading circles of the Center party in the Reich have never concealed their opposition to parliamentarian democracy, because of fear of remaining in the minority and thus facing great difficulties in placing their job hunters in office, as they have done by exerting pressure on the government. The Social Democratic party was a principled minority party and a handicap to the introduction of parliamentary government because the party did not wish to stain itself by participating in the existing bourgeois political order. The fact that both parties dissociated themselves from the parliamentary system made parliamentary government impossible.

Considering all this, what then became of the professional politicians in Germany? They have had no power, no responsibility, and could play only a rather subordinate role as notables. In consequence, they have been animated anew by the guild instincts, which are typical everywhere. It has been impossible for a man who was not of their hue to climb high in the circle of those notables who made their petty positions their lives. I could mention many names from every party, the Social Democratic party, of course, not excepted, that spell tragedies of political careers because the persons had leadership qualities and, precisely because of these qualities, were not tolerated by the notables. All our parties have taken this course of development and have become guilds of notables. Bebel,* for instance, was still a leader through temperament and purity of character, however modest his intellect. The fact that he was a martyr, that he never betrayed confidence in the eyes of the masses, resulted in his having the masses absolutely behind him. There was no power in the party that could have seriously challenged him. Such leadership came to an end, after his death, and the rule of officials began. Trade-union officials, party secretaries, and journalists came to the top. The instincts of officialdom dominated the party—a highly respectable officialdom, of rare respectability one may say, compared to conditions in other countries, especially the often corruptible trade-union officials in America. But the results of control by officialdom, which we discussed above, also began in the party.

Since the 1880's, the bourgeois parties have completely become guilds of notables. To be sure, occasionally the parties had to draw on extra-party intellects for advertising purposes, so that they could say, "We have such and such names." So far as possible, they avoided letting these names run for election; only when it was unavoidable and the person insisted could he run for election. The same spirit prevailed in Parliament. Our parliamentary parties were, and are, guilds. Every speech delivered from the floor of the Reichstag is thoroughly censored in the party before it is delivered. This is obvious from their unheard-of boredom. Only he who is summoned to speak can have the word. One can hardly conceive of a stronger contrast to the English, and also—for quite opposite reasons— the French usage.

Now, in consequence of the enormous collapse, which is customarily called the Revolution, perhaps a transformation is under way. Perhaps— but not for certain. In the beginning there were new kinds of party apparatuses emerging. First, there were amateur apparatuses. They are especially often represented by students of the various universities, who tell a man to whom they ascribe leadership qualities: We want to do the necessary work for you; carry it out. Secondly, there are apparatuses of businessmen. It happened that men to whom leadership qualities were ascribed were approached by people willing to take over the propaganda, at fixed rates for every vote. If you were to ask me honestly which of these two apparatuses I think the more reliable, from the purely technical-political point of view, I believe I would prefer the latter; but, both apparatuses were fast-emerging bubbles, which swiftly vanished again. The existing apparatuses transformed themselves, but they continued to work. The phenomena are only symptoms of the fact that new apparatuses would come about if there were only leaders. But even the technical peculiarity of proportionate representation precluded their ascendancy. Only a few dictators of the street crowds arose and fell again. And only the following

* August Bebel (1840–1913), instrumental in founding the German Social Democratic party.

of a mob dictatorship is organized in a strictly disciplined fashion; whence the power of these vanishing minorities.

Let us assume that all this were to change; then, after what has been said above, it has to be clearly realized that the plebiscitarian leadership of parties entails the "soullessness" of the following, their intellectual proletarianization, one might say. In order to be a useful apparatus, a machine in the American sense—undisturbed either by the vanity of notables or pretensions to independent views—the following of such a leader must obey him blindly. Lincoln's election was possible only through this character of party organization, and, with Gladstone, as mentioned before, the same happened in the caucus. This is simply the price paid for guidance by leaders. However, there is only the choice between leadership democracy with a machine and leaderless democracy, namely, the rule of professional politicians without a calling, without the inner charismatic qualities that make a leader; this means what the party insurgents in the situation usually designate as "the rule of the clique." For the time being, we in Germany have only the latter. For the future, the permanence of this situation, at least in the Reich, is primarily facilitated by the fact that the *Bundesrat** will rise again and will of necessity restrict the power of the Reichstag and therewith its significance as a selective agency of leaders. Moreover, in its present form, proportional representation is a typical phenomenon of leaderless democracy. This is the case not only because it facilitates the horse-trading of the notables of placement on the ticket, but also because in the future it will give organized interest groups the possibility of compelling parties to include their officials in the list of candidates, thus creating an unpolitical Parliament in which genuine leadership finds no place. Only the President of the Reich could become the safety valve of the demand for leadership if he were elected in a plebiscitarian way and not by Parliament. Leadership on the basis of proved work could emerge and selection could take place, especially if, in great municipalities, the plebiscitarian city manager were to appear on the scene with the right to organize his bureaus independently. Such is the case in the U.S.A. whenever one wishes to tackle corruption seriously. It requires a party organization fashioned for such elections. But the very petty-bourgeois hostility of all parties to leaders, the Social Democratic party certainly included, leaves the future formation of parties and all these chances still completely in the dark.

Therefore, today, one cannot yet see in any way how the management of politics as a vocation will shape itself. Even less can one see along what avenue opportunities are opening to which political talents can be put for satisfactory political tasks. He who, by his material circumstances, is compelled to "live off" politics will almost always have to consider the

---

* Formerly a federal legislative council of representatives from the twenty-six states of the German Empire; now the upper house of the West German parliament.

alternative positions of the journalist or the party official as the typical direct avenues. Or, he must consider a position as representative of interest groups—such as a trade union, a chamber of commerce, a farm bureau, a craft association, a labor board, an employer's association, et cetera, or else a suitable municipal position. Nothing more than this can be said about this external aspect; in common with the journalist, the party official bears the odium of being *déclassé*. "Wage writer" or "wage speaker" will unfortunately always resound in his ears, even though the words remain unexpressed. He who is inwardly defenseless and unable to find the proper answer for himself had better stay away from this career; for, in any case, besides grave temptations, it is an avenue that may constantly lead to disappointments. Now then, what inner enjoyments can this career offer and what personal conditions are presupposed for one who enters this avenue?

Well, first of all, the career of politics grants a feeling of power. The knowledge of influencing men, of participating in power over them, and, above all, the feeling of holding in one's hands a nerve fiber of historically important events can elevate the professional politician above everyday routine even when he is placed in formally modest positions. But now the question for him is: Through what qualities can I hope to do justice to this power (however narrowly circumscribed it may be in the individual case)? How can he hope to do justice to the responsibility that power imposes upon him? With this, we enter the field of ethical questions, for that is where the problem belongs: What kind of a man must one be if he is to be allowed to put his hand on the wheel of history?

One can say that three pre-eminent qualities are decisive for the politician: passion, a feeling of responsibility, and a sense of proportion.

This means passion in the sense of *matter-of-factness*, of passionate devotion to a cause, to the god or demon who is its overlord. It is not passion in the sense of that inner bearing which my late friend Georg Simmel used to designate as "sterile excitation" and which was peculiar especially to a certain type of Russian intellectual (by no means all of them!). It is an excitation that plays so great a part with our intellectuals in this carnival we decorate with the proud name of "revolution." It is a romanticism of the intellectually interesting, running into emptiness devoid of all feeling of objective responsibility.

To be sure, mere passion, however genuinely felt, is not enough. It does not make a politician, unless passion as devotion to a cause also makes responsibility to this cause the guiding star of action. And for this, a sense of proportion is needed. This is the decisive psychological quality of the politician: his ability to let realities work on him with inner concentration and calmness; hence his *distance* to things and men. Lack of distance per se is one of the deadly sins of every politician. It is one of those qualities the breeding of which will condemn the progeny of our intellectuals to political incapacity. For the problem is, simply: How can warm passion and a cool sense of proportion be forged together in one and the same soul? Politics is made with the head, not with other parts of the body or soul. Yet, devotion to politics, if it is not to be frivolous intellectual play, but rather genuinely human conduct, can be born and nourished from passion alone. However, that firm taming of the soul, which distinguishes the passionate politician and differentiates him from the sterilely excited and mere political dilettante, is possible only through habituation to detachment in every sense of the word. The strength of a political personality means, in the first place, the possession of these qualities of passion, responsibility, and proportion.

Therefore, daily and hourly, the politician inwardly has to overcome a quite trivial and all-too-human enemy: a quite vulgar vanity, the deadly enemy of all matter-of-fact devotion to a cause, and of all distance, in this case, of distance toward one's self.

Vanity is a very widespread quality and perhaps nobody is entirely free from it. In academic and scholarly circles, vanity is a sort of occupational disease, but precisely with the scholar, vanity—however disagreeably it may express itself—is relatively harmless, in the sense that as a rule it does not disturb scientific enterprise. With the politician, the case is quite different. He works with the striving for power as an unavoidable means. Therefore, power instinct, as is usually said, belongs indeed to his normal qualities. The sin against the lofty spirit of his vocation, however, begins where this striving for power ceases to be *objective* and becomes purely personal self-intoxication, instead of exclusively entering the service of the cause. For, ultimately, there are only two kinds of deadly sins in the field of politics: lack of objectivity and—often but not always identical with it—irresponsibility. Vanity, the need personally to stand in the foreground as clearly as possible, strongly tempts the politician to commit one or both of these sins. This is more truly the case as the demagogue is compelled to count on effect. He, therefore, is constantly in danger of becoming an actor, as well as taking lightly the responsibility for the outcome of his actions and of being concerned merely with the impression he makes. His lack of objectivity tempts him to strive for the glamorous semblance of power rather than for actual power. His irresponsibility, however, suggests that he enjoys power merely for power's sake without a substantive purpose. Although, or rather just because, power is the unavoidable means, and striving for power is one of the driving forces of all politics, there is no more harmful distortion of political force than the parvenulike braggart with power, and the vain self-reflection in the feeling of power, and, in general, every worship of power per se. The mere power politician may get strong effects, but actually his work leads nowhere and is senseless. (Among us, too, an ardently promoted cult seeks to glorify him.) In this, the critics of power politics are absolutely right.

From the sudden inner collapse of typical representatives of this mentality, we can see what inner weakness and impotence hides behind this boastful but entirely empty gesture. It is a product of a shoddy and superficially blasé attitude toward the meaning of human conduct; and, it has no relation whatsoever to the knowledge of tragedy with which all action, but especially political action, is truly interwoven.

The final result of political action often, no, even regularly, stands in completely inadequate, and often even paradoxical, relation to its original meaning. This is fundamental to all history, a point not to be proved in detail here. But, because of this fact, the serving of a cause must not be absent if action is to have inner strength. Exactly what the cause, in the service of which the politician strives for power and uses power, looks like is a matter of faith. The politician may serve national, humanitarian, social, ethical, cultural, worldly, or religious ends. The politician may be sustained by a strong belief in "progress"—no matter in which sense—or he may coolly reject this kind of belief. He may claim to stand in the service of an idea or, rejecting this in principle, he may want to serve external ends of everyday life. However, some kind of faith must always exist. Otherwise, it is absolutely true that the curse of the creature's worthlessness overshadows even the externally strongest political successes.

With the statement above, we are already engaged in discussing the last problem that concerns us tonight: the *ethos* of politics as a cause. What calling can politics fulfill quite independently of its goals within the total ethical economy of human conduct—which is, so to speak, the ethical locus where politics is at home? Here, to be sure, ultimate *Weltanschauungen* clash, world views among which, in the end, one has to make a choice. Let us resolutely tackle this problem, which recently has been opened again, in my view in a very wrong way.

But first, let us free ourselves from a quite trivial falsification: namely, that ethics may first appear in a morally highly compromised role. Let us consider examples. Rarely will you find that a man whose love turns from one woman to another feels no need to legitimize this before himself by saying: she was not worthy of my love, or, she has disappointed me, or whatever other like reasons exist. This is an attitude that, with a profound lack of chivalry, adds a fancied legitimacy to the plain fact that he no longer loves her and that the woman has to bear it. By virtue of this legitimation, the man claims a right for himself, and, besides causing the misfortune, seeks to put her in the wrong. The successful amatory competitor proceeds exactly in the same way, namely, the opponent must be less worthy, otherwise he would not have lost out. It is no different, of course, if, after a victorious war, the victor in undignified self-righteousness claims, "I have won because I was right." Or, if somebody under the frightfulness of war collapses psychologically, and instead of simply saying it was just too much, he feels the need of legitimizing his war weariness to himself by substituting the feeling, "I could not bear it because I had to fight for a morally bad cause." And likewise with the defeated in war. Instead of searching like old women for the guilty one after the war—in a situation in which the structure of society produced the war —everyone with a manly and controlled attitude would tell the enemy, "We lost the war. You have won it. That is now all over. Now let us discuss what conclusions must be drawn according to the *objective* interests that came into play and what is the main thing in view of the responsibility toward the *future* that, above all, burdens the victor." Anything else is undignified and will become a boomerang. A nation forgives if its interests have been damaged, but no nation forgives if its honor has been offended, especially by a bigoted self-righteousness. Every new document that comes to light after decades revives the undignified lamentations, the hatred and scorn, instead of allowing the war at its end to be buried, at least morally. This is possible only through objectivity and chivalry and, most important, only through dignity. But never is it possible through an ethic, which in truth signifies a lack of dignity on both sides. Instead of being concerned about what the politician is interested in, the future and the responsibility toward the future, this ethic is concerned about politically sterile questions of past guilt, which are not to be settled politically. To act in this way is politically guilty, if such guilt exists at all. And it overlooks the unavoidable falsification of the whole problem, through very material interests: namely, the victor's interest in the greatest possible moral and material gain; the hopes of the defeated to trade in advantages through confessions of guilt. If anything is vulgar, then, this is, and it is the result of this fashion of exploiting ethics as a means of "being in the right."

Now then, what relations do ethics and politics actually have? Have the two nothing whatever to do with one another, as has occasionally been said? Or, is the reverse true: that the ethic of political conduct is identical with that of any other conduct? Occasionally an exclusive choice has been believed to exist between the two propositions—either the one or the other proposition must be correct. But is it true that any ethic of the world could establish commandments of identical content for erotic, business, familial, and official relations—for the relations to one's wife, to the greengrocer, the son, the competitor, the friend, the defendant? Should it really matter so little for the ethical demands on politics that politics operates with very special means, namely, power backed up by *violence*? Do we not see that the Bolshevik and the Spartacist* ideologists bring about exactly the same results as any militaristic dictator just because they use this political means? In what but the persons of the power-holders and their dilettantism does the rule of the workers' and soldiers'

* The Spadacus party was founded circa 1916 by a radical group of German Socialists. It officially became the German Communist party in 1918.

councils differ from the rule of any power-holder of the old regime? In what way does the polemic of most representatives of the presumably new ethic differ from that of the opponents which they criticized, or the ethic of any other demagogues? In their noble intention, people will say "Good!" But it is the means about which we speak here, and the adversaries, in complete subjective sincerity, claim, in the very same way, that their ultimate intentions are of lofty character. "All they that take the sword shall perish with the sword," and fighting is, everywhere, fighting. Hence, the ethic of the Sermon on the Mount.

By the Sermon on the Mount, we mean the absolute ethic of the gospel—which is a more serious matter than those who are fond of quoting these commandments today believe. This ethic is no joking matter. The same holds for this ethic as has been said of causality in science: it is not a cab, which one can have stopped at one's pleasure; it is all or nothing. This is precisely the meaning of the gospel, if trivialities are not to result. Hence, for instance, it was said of the wealthy young man, "He went away sorrowful: for he had great possessions." The evangelist commandment, however, is unconditional and unambiguous: give what thou hast—absolutely everything. The politician will say that this is a socially senseless imposition as long as it is not carried out everywhere. Thus the politician upholds taxation, confiscatory taxation, outright confiscation; in a word, compulsion and regulation for all. The ethical commandment, however, is not at all concerned about that, and this unconcern is its essence. Or, take the example, "turn the other cheek." This command is unconditional and does not question the source of the other's authority to strike. Except for a saint, it is an ethic of indignity. This is it: One must be saintly in everything; at least in intention, one must live like Jesus, the apostles, St. Francis, and their like. *Then,* this ethic makes sense and expresses a kind of dignity; otherwise it does not. For if it is said, in line with the acosmic [unworldly] ethic of love, "Resist not him that is evil with force," for the politician the reverse proposition holds, "thou *shalt* resist evil by force," or else you are responsible for the evil winning out. He who wishes to follow the ethic of the gospel should abstain from strikes, for strikes mean compulsion; he may join the company unions. Above all things, he should not talk of revolution. After all, the ethic of the gospel does not wish to teach that civil war is the only legitimate war. The pacifist who follows the gospel will refuse to bear arms or will throw them down; in Germany, this was the recommended ethical duty to end the war and, therewith, all wars. The politician would say the only sure means to discredit the war for all foreseeable time would have been a *status quo* peace. Then the nations would have questioned, "What was this war for?" And then the war would have been argued *ad absurdum,* which is now impossible. For the victors, at least for part of them, the war will have been politically profitable. And the responsibility for this rests on behavior that made all resistance impossible for us. Now, as a result of the ethics of absolutism, when the period of exhaustion will have passed, *the peace will be discredited, not the war.*

Finally, let us consider the duty of truthfulness. For the absolute ethic, it holds unconditionally. Hence, the conclusion was reached to publish all documents, especially those placing blame on one's own country. On the basis of these one-sided publications, the confessions of guilt followed—and they were one-sided, unconditional, and without regard to consequences. The politician will find that, as a result, truth will not be furthered but certainly obscured through abuse and unleashing of passion; only an all-around methodical investigation by nonpartisans could bear fruit; any other procedure may have consequences for a nation that cannot be remedied for decades. But the absolute ethic just does not *ask* for consequences. That is the decisive point.

We must be clear about the fact that all ethically oriented conduct may be guided by one of two fundamentally differing and irreconcilably opposed maxims: conduct can be oriented to an "ethic of ultimate ends" or to an "ethic of responsibility." This is not to say that an ethic of ultimate ends is identical with irresponsibility or that an ethic of responsibility is identical with unprincipled opportunism. Naturally, nobody says that. However, there is an abysmal contrast between conduct that follows the maxim of an ethic of ultimate ends—that is, in religious terms, "The Christian does rightly and leaves the results with the Lord"—and conduct that follows the maxim of an ethic of responsibility, in which case one has to give an account of the foreseeable results of one's action.

You may demonstrate to a convinced syndicalist,* believing in an ethic of ultimate ends, that his action will result in increasing the opportunities of reaction, in increasing the oppression of his class and obstructing its ascent, and you will not make the slightest impression on him. If an action of good intent leads to bad results, then, in the actor's eyes, not he but the world, or the stupidity of other men, or God's will who made them thus, is responsible for the evil. However, a man who believes in an ethic of responsibility takes account of precisely the average deficiences of people; as Fichte† has correctly said, he does not even have the right to presuppose their goodness and perfection. He does not feel in a position to burden others with the results of his own actions, so far as he was able to foresee them; he will say: "These results are ascribed to my action." The believer in an ethic of ultimate ends feels responsible only for seeing to it that the flame of pure intentions is not quenched: for example, the flame of protesting against the injustice of the social order. To rekindle

---

* A syndicalist believes that any form of state is an instrument of oppression and, consequently, should be abolished. Syndicalism stresses the function of productive labor and regards the trade union as the essential unit of production and government.

† Johann Gottlieb Fichte (1762–1814), German philosopher.

the flame ever anew is the purpose of his quite irrational deeds, judged in view of their possible success. They are acts that can, and shall, have only exemplary value.

But, even herewith, the problem is not yet exhausted. No ethics in the world can dodge the fact that in numerous instances the attainment of good ends is bound to the fact that one must be willing to pay the price of using morally dubious means, or at least dangerous ones, and facing the possibility or even the probability of evil ramifications. From no ethics in the world can it be concluded when, and to what extent, the ethically good purpose justifies the ethically dangerous means and ramifications.

The decisive means for politics is violence. You may see the extent of the tension between means and ends, when viewed ethically, from the following: as is generally known, even during the war the revolutionary socialists (Zimmerwald faction)* professed a principle that one might strikingly formulate: "If we face the choice either of some more years of war and then revolution, or peace now and no revolution, we choose some more years of war!" Upon the further question: "What can this revolution bring about?" every scientifically trained socialist would have had the answer: "One cannot speak of a transition to an economy that in our sense could be called socialist; a bourgeois economy will re-emerge, merely stripped of the feudal elements and the dynastic vestiges." For this very modest result, they are willing to face "some more years of war." One may well say that even with a very robust socialist conviction one might reject a purpose that demands such means. With Bolshevism and Spartacism, and, in general, with any kind of revolutionary socialism, it is precisely the same thing. It is, of course, utterly ridiculous if the power politicians of the old regime are morally denounced for their use of the same means, however justified the rejection of their *aims* may be.

The ethic of ultimate ends apparently must go to pieces on the problem of the justification of means by ends. As a matter of fact, logically it has only the possibility of rejecting all action that employs morally dangerous means—in theory! In the world of realities, as a rule, we encounter the ever-renewed experience that the adherent of an ethic of ultimate ends suddenly turns into a chiliastic prophet. Those, for example, who have just preached "love against violence" now call for the use of force for the *last* violent deed, which would then lead to a state of affairs in which *all* violence is annihilated. In the same manner, our officers told the soldiers before every offensive: "This will be the last one; this one will bring victory and therewith peace." The proponent of an ethic of absolute ends cannot stand up under the ethical irrationality of the world. He is a cosmic-ethical rationalist. Those of you who know Dostoievski will remember the scene of the Grand Inquisitor, where the problem is poign-

* Circa 1915–1917, an anti-war splinter minority group in the French Socialist movement, which espoused extreme socialism.

antly unfolded. If one makes any concessions at all to the principle that the end justifies the means, it is not possible to bring an ethic of ultimate ends and an ethic of responsibility under one roof, or to decree ethically which end should justify which means.

My colleague Mr. F. W. Förster, whom personally I highly esteem for his undoubted sincerity, but whom I reject unreservedly as a politician, believes it is possible to get around this difficulty by the simple thesis: "From good comes only good; but from evil only evil follows." In that case, this whole complex of questions would not exist. But it is rather astonishing that such a thesis could come to light two thousand five hundred years after the Upanishads. Not only the whole course of world history, but every frank examination of everyday experience points to the very opposite. The development of religions all over the world is determined by the fact that the opposite is true. The age-old problem of theodicy consists of the very question of how it is that a power which is said to be at once omnipotent and kind could have created such an irrational world of undeserved suffering, unpunished injustice, and hopeless stupidity. Either this power is not omnipotent or not kind or entirely different principles of compensation and reward govern our life—principles we may interpret metaphysically, or even principles that forever escape our comprehension.

This problem—the experience of the irrationality of the world— has been the driving force of all religious evolution. The Indian doctrine of karma, Persian dualism, the doctrine of original sin, predestination and the *deus absconditus* [doctrine of "hiddenness of God"], all these have grown out of this experience. Also, the early Christians knew full well that the world is governed by demons and that he who lets himself in for politics, that is, for power and force as means, contracts with diabolical powers and for his action it is *not* true that good can follow only from good and evil only from evil, but that often the opposite is true. Anyone who fails to see this is, indeed, a political infant.

We are placed into various life spheres, each of which is governed by different laws. Religious ethics have settled with this fact in different ways. Hellenic polytheism made sacrifices to Aphrodite and Hera alike, to Dionysus and to Apollo, and knew these gods were frequently in conflict with each other. The Hindu order of life made each of the different occupations an object of a specific ethical code, a Dharma, and forever segregated one from the other as castes, thereby placing them into a fixed hierarchy of rank; for the man born into it, there was no escape from it, lest he be twice-born in another life. The occupations were thus placed at varying distances from the highest religious goods of salvation. In this way, the caste order allowed for the possibility of fashioning the Dharma of each single caste, from those of the ascetics and Brahmins to those of the rogues and harlots, in accordance with the immanent and autonomous laws of their respective occupations. War and politics were also included. You will find war integrated into the totality of life spheres in the *Bhagavad-Gita* [Song of the Lord, the major devotional book of Hinduism], in the conversation between Krishna and Arduna. "Do what must be done," i.e., do that work that, according to the Dharma of the warrior caste and its rules, is obligatory and that, according to the purpose of the war, is objectively necessary. Hinduism believes that such conduct does not damage religious salvation but, rather, promotes it. When he faced the hero's death, the Indian warrior was always sure of Indra's heaven, just as was the Teuton warrior of Valhalla. The Indian hero would have despised nirvana just as much as the Teuton would have sneered at the Christian paradise with its angels' choirs. This specialization of ethics allowed for the Indian ethic's quite unbroken treatment of politics by following politics' own laws and even radically enhancing this royal art.

A really radical Machiavellianism, in the popuar sense of this word, is classically represented in Indian literature, in the *Kautaliya Arthasastra** (long before Christ, allegedly dating from Chandragupta's time). In contrast with this document, Machiavelli's *The Prince* is harmless. As is known in Catholic ethics—to which, otherwise, Professor Förster stands close—the *consilia evangelica* are a special ethic for those endowed with the charisma of a holy life. There stands the monk who must not shed blood or strive for gain, and beside him stand the pious knight and the burgher, who are allowed to do so, the one to shed blood, the other to pursue gain. The gradation of ethics and its organic integration into the doctrine of salvation is less consistent than in India. According to the presuppositions of Christian faith, this could and had to be the case. The wickedness of the world, stemming from original sin, allowed with relative ease the integration of violence into ethics as a disciplinary means against sin and against the heretics who endangered the soul. However, the demands of the Sermon on the Mount, an acosmic ethic of ultimate ends, implied a natural law of absolute imperatives based on religion. These absolute imperatives retained their revolutionizing force, and they came on the scene with elemental vigor during almost all periods of social upheaval. They produced, especially, the radical pacifist sects, one of which, in Pennsylvania, experimented in establishing a polity that renounced violence toward the outside. This experiment took a tragic course, inasmuch as with the outbreak of the War of Independence the Quakers could not stand up arms-in-hand for their ideals, which were those of the war.

Normally, Protestantism absolutely legitimated the state as a divine institution and, hence, violence as a means. Protestantism, especially, le-

* A Sanskrit treatise on Hindu polity advocating unscrupulous measures. The author, Kautilya, has been identified with the minister of the Maurya king, Chandragupta (322–298 B.C.).

gitimated the authoritarian state. Luther relieved the individual of the ethical responsibility for war and transferred it to the authorities. To obey
the authorities in matters other than those of faith could never constitute
guilt. Calvinism, in turn, knew principled violence as a means of defending the faith; thus Calvinism knew the crusade, which was for Islam an
element of life from the beginning. One sees that it is by no means a modern disbelief, born from the hero worship of the Renaissance, which poses
the problem of political ethics. All religions have wrestled with it, with
highly differing success, and, after what has been said, it could not be otherwise. It is the specific means of legitimate violence, as such, in the hand
of human associations which determines the peculiarity of all ethical problems of politics.

Whosoever contracts with violent means for whatever ends—and
every politician does—is exposed to its specific consequences. This holds
especially for the crusader, religious and revolutionary alike. Let us confi-
dently take the present as an example. He who wants to establish absolute justice on earth by force requires a following, a human machine. He
must hold out the necessary internal and external premiums, heavenly or
worldly reward, to this machine or else the machine will not function.
Under the conditions of the modern class struggle, the internal premiums
consist of the satisfying of hatred and the craving for revenge; above all,
resentment and the need for pseudo-ethical self-righteousness: the opponents must be slandered and accused of heresy. The external rewards are
adventure, victory, booty, power, and spoils. The leader and his success
are completely dependent on the functioning of his machine and not on
his own motives. Therefore, he also depends on whether or not the premiums can be *permanently* granted to the following, that is, to the Red
Guard, the informers, the agitators, whom he needs. What he actually attains under the conditions of his work is, therefore, not in his hand, but is
prescribed to him by the following's motives, which, if viewed ethically,
are predominantly base. The following can be harnessed only so long as
an honest belief in his person and his cause inspires at least part of the
following; probably, never on earth [will it inspire] even the majority.
This belief, even when subjectively sincere, is in a very great number of
cases really no more than an ethical legitimization of cravings for revenge, power, booty, and spoils. We shall not be deceived about this by
verbiage; the materialist interpretation of history is no cab to be taken at
will; it does not stop short of the promoters of revolutions. Emotional
revolutionism is followed by the traditionalist routine of everyday life;
the crusading leader and the faith itself fade away, or, what is even more
effective, the faith becomes part of the conventional phraseology of political Philistines and banausic technicians. This development is especially
rapid with struggles of faith because they are usually led or inspired by
genuine leaders, that is, prophets of revolution. For here, as with every

leader's machine, one of the conditions for success is the depersonalization and routinization, in short, the psychic proletarianization, in the interests of discipline. After coming to power, the following of a crusader usually degenerates very easily into a quite common stratum of spoilsmen.

Whoever wants to engage in politics at all, and especially in politics as a vocation, has to realize these ethical paradoxes. He must know that he is responsible for what may become of himself under the impact of these paradoxes. I repeat, he lets himself in for the diabolic forces lurking in all violence. The great *virtuosi* of acosmic love of humanity and goodness, whether stemming from Nazareth or Assisi or from Indian royal castles, have not operated with the political means of violence. Their kingdom was not of this world, and yet they worked and still work in this world. The figures of Platon Karatajev [the philosophical peasant in Tolstoy's *War and Peace*] and the saints of Dostoievski still remain their most adequate reconstructions. He who seeks the salvation of the soul, of his own and of others, should not seek it along the avenue of politics, for the quite different tasks of politics can only be solved by violence. The genius or demon of politics lives in an inner tension with the god of love, as well as with the Christian God as expressed by the church. This tension can at any time lead to an irreconcilable conflict. Men knew this even in the times of church rule. Time and again the papal interdict was placed on Florence, and, at the time, it meant a far more robust power for men and their salvation of soul than (to speak with Fichte) the cool approbation of the Kantian ethical judgment. The burghers, however, fought the church-state. It is with reference to such situations that Machiavelli in a beautiful passage, if I am not mistaken, of the *History of Florence,* has one of his heroes praise those citizens who deemed the greatness of their native city higher than the salvation of their souls.

If one says "the future of socialism" or "international peace," instead of "native city" or "fatherland" (which at present may be a dubious value to some), then you face the problem as it stands now. Everything that is striven for through political action operating with violent means and following an ethic of responsibility endangers the salvation of the soul. If, however, one chases after the ultimate good in a war of beliefs, following a pure ethic of absolute ends, then the goals may be damaged and discredited for generations, because responsibility for *consequences* is lacking, and two diabolic forces which enter the play remain unknown to the actor. These are inexorable and produce consequences for his action and even for his inner self, to which he must helplessly submit, unless he perceives them. The sentence "The devil is old; grow old to understand him!" does not refer to age in terms of chronological years. I have never permitted myself to lose out in a discussion through a reference to a date registered on a birth certificate; but the mere fact that someone is twenty years of age and that I am over fifty is no cause for me to think that this alone is an achievement before which I am overawed. Age is not decisive; what is decisive is the trained relentlessness in viewing the realities of life and the ability to face such realities and to measure up to them inwardly.

Surely, politics is made with the head, but it is certainly not made with the head alone. In this, the proponents of an ethic of ultimate ends are right. One cannot prescribe to anyone whether he should follow an ethic of absolute ends or an ethic of responsibility or when the one and when the other. One can say only this much: If in these times, which, in your opinion, are not times of "sterile" excitation—excitation is not, after all, genuine passion—if now, suddenly, the *Weltanschauungs*-politicians crop up *en masse* and pass the watchword—"The world is stupid and base, not I," "The responsibility for the consequences does not fall on me but on the others whom I serve and whose stupidity or baseness I shall eradicate"— then, I declare frankly that I would first inquire into the degree of inner poise backing this ethic of ultimate ends. I am under the impression that in nine out of ten cases I deal with windbags who do not fully realize what they take upon themselves but who intoxicate themselves with romantic sensations. From a human point of view, this is not very interesting to me nor does it move me profoundly. However, it is immensely moving when a *mature* man—no matter whether old or young in years—is aware of a responsibility for the consequences of his conduct and really feels such responsibility with heart and soul. He then acts by following an ethic of responsibility, and, somewhere, he reaches the point where he says: "Here I stand; I can do no other." That is something genuinely human and moving. And every one of us who is not spiritually dead must realize the possibility of finding himself at some time in that position. Insofar as this is true, an ethic of ultimate ends and an ethic of responsibility are not absolute contrasts but rather supplements, which only in unison constitute a genuine man—a man who *can* have the "calling for politics."

[L]et us debate this matter once more ten years from now [1928]. Unfortunately, for a whole series of reasons, I fear that by then the period of reaction will have long since broken over us. It is very probable that little of what many of you, and (I candidly confess) I, too, have wished and hoped for will be fulfilled; little—perhaps not exactly nothing, but what to us at least seems little. This will not crush me, but surely it is an inner burden to realize it. Then, I wish I could see what has become of those of you who now feel yourselves to be genuinely principled politicians and who share in the intoxication signified by this revolution. It would be nice if matters turned out in such a way that Shakespeare's Sonnet 102 should hold true:

> Our love was new, and then but in the spring,
> When I was wont to greet it with my lays;
> As Philomel in summer's front doth sing,
> And stops her pipe in growth of riper days.

But such is not the case. Not summer's bloom lies ahead of us, but rather a polar night of icy darkness and hardness, no matter which group may triumph externally now. Where there is nothing, not only the Kaiser but also the proletarian has lost his rights. When this night shall have slowly receded, who of those for whom spring apparently has bloomed so luxuriously will be alive? What will have become of all of you by then? Will you be bitter or banausic? Will you simply and dully accept world and occupation? Or, will the third, and by no means the least frequent, possibility be your lot: mystic flight from reality for those who are gifted for it or—as is both frequent and unpleasant—for those who belabor themselves to follow this fashion? In every one of such cases, I shall draw the conclusion that they have not measured up to their own doings. They have not measured up to the world as it really is in its everyday routine. Objectively and actually, they have not experienced the vocation for politics in its deepest meaning that they thought they had. They would have have done better in simply cultivating plain brotherliness in personal relations. And for the rest—they should have gone soberly about their daily work.

Politics is a strong and slow boring of hard boards. It takes both passion and perspective. Certainly all historical experience confirms the truth —that man would not have attained the possible unless time and again he had reached out for the impossible. But, to do that a man must be a leader, and not only a leader but a hero as well, in a very sober sense of the word. And even those who are neither leaders nor heroes must arm themselves with that steadfastness of heart which can brave even the crumbling of all hopes. This is necessary right now, or else men will not be able to attain even that which is possible today. Only he has the calling for politics who is sure that he shall not crumble when the world, from his point of view, is too stupid or too base for what he wants to offer. Only he who in the face of all this can say "In spite of all!" has the calling for politics.

2

THE PURSUIT OF VIRTUE

Aristotle

Aristotle's (384–322 B.C.) Politics represents one of the earliest known steps toward the study of man in his social environment. It is an attempt to treat man as he is, not simply as he might be. Man in a social, political setting is in his natural habitat; he can know no other. Thus, participation in the civic life of the community is a necessary part of the life of virtue.

*

THERE REMAINS TO BE DISCUSSED the question, Whether the happiness of the individual is the same as that of the state, or different? Here again there can be no doubt—no one denies that they are the same. For those who hold that the well-being of the individual consists in his wealth, also think that riches make the happiness of the whole state; and those who value most highly the life of a tyrant deem that city the happiest which rules over the greatest number; while they who approve an individual for his virtue say that the more virtuous a city is, the happier it is. Two points here present themselves for consideration: first (1), which is the more eligible life, that of a citizen who is a member of a state, or that of an alien who has no political ties; and again (2), which is the best form of constitution or the best condition of a state, either on the supposition that political privileges are desirable for all, or for a majority only? Since the good of the state and not of the individual is the proper subject of political thought and speculation, and we are engaged in a political discussion, while the first of these two points has a secondary interest for us, the latter will be the main subject of our inquiry.

From *Aristotle, Politics,* translated by D. W. Ross. By permission of the Clarendon Press, Oxford.

Now it is evident that the form of government is best in which every man, whoever he is, can act best and live happily. But even those who agree in thinking that the life of virtue is the most eligible raise a question, whether the life of business and politics is or is not more eligible than one which is wholly independent of external goods, I mean than a contemplative life, which, by some, is maintained to be the only one worthy of a philosopher. For these two lives—the life of the philosopher and the life of the statesman—appear to have been preferred by those who have been most keen in the pursuit of virtue, both in our own and in other ages. Which is the better, is a question of no small moment; for the wise man, like the wise state, will necessarily regulate his life according to the best end. There are some who think that while a despotic rule over others is the greatest injustice, to exercise a constitutional rule over them, even though not unjust, is a great impediment to a man's individual well-being. Others take an opposite view; they maintain that the true life of man is the practical and political, and that every virtue admits of being practiced, quite as much by statesmen and rulers as by private individuals. Others, again, are of opinion that arbitrary and tyrannical rule alone consists with happiness; indeed, in some states the entire aim both of the laws and of the constitution is to give men despotic power over their neighbors. And, therefore, although in most cities the laws may be said generally to be in a chaotic state, still, if they aim at anything, they aim at the maintenance of power; thus in Lacedaemon and Crete the system of education and the greater part of the laws are framed with a view to war. And in all nations which are able to gratify their ambition, military power is held in esteem, for example among the Scythians and Persians and Thracians and Celts. In some nations, there are even laws tending to stimulate the warlike virtues, as at Carthage, where we are told that men obtain the honor of wearing as many armlets as they have served campaigns. There was once a law in Macedonia that he who had not killed an enemy should wear a halter, and among the Scythians no one who had not slain his man was allowed to drink out of the cup which was handed round at a certain feast. Among the Iberians, a warlike nation, the number of enemies whom a man has slain is indicated by the number of obelisks which are fixed in the earth round his tomb; and there are numerous practices among other nations of a like kind, some of them established by law and others by custom. Yet to a reflecting mind it must appear very strange that the statesman should always be considering how he can dominate and tyrannize over others, whether they will or not. How can that which is not even lawful be the business of the statesman or the legislator? Unlawful it certainly is to rule without regard to justice, for there may be might where there is no right. The other arts and sciences offer no parallel; a physician is not expected to persuade or coerce his patients, nor a pilot the passengers in his ship. Yet most men appear to think that the art of despotic government is statesmanship, and what men affirm to be unjust and inexpedient in their own case they are not ashamed of practicing toward others; they demand just rule for themselves, but where other men are concerned they care nothing about it. Such behavior is irrational; unless the one party is, and the other is not, born to serve, in which case men have a right to command, not indeed all their fellows, but only those who are intended to be subjects; just as we ought not to hunt mankind, whether for food or sacrifice, but only the animals which may be hunted for food or sacrifice, this is to say, such wild animals as are eatable. And surely there may be a city happy in isolation, which we will assume to be well-governed (for it is quite possible that a city thus isolated might be well-administered and have good laws); but such a city would not be constituted with any view to war or the conquest of enemies—all that sort of thing must be excluded. Hence we see very plainly that warlike pursuits, although generally to be deemed honorable, are not the supreme end of all things, but only means. And the good lawgiver should inquire how states and races of men and communities may participate in a good life, and in the happiness which is attainable by them. His enactments will not be always the same; and where there are neighbors he will have to see what sort of studies should be practiced in relation to their several characters, or how the measures appropriate in relation to each are to be adopted. The end at which the best form of government should aim may be properly made a matter of future consideration.

Let us now address those who, while they agree that the life of virtue is the most eligible, differ about the manner of practicing it. For some renounce political power, and think that the life of the freeman is different from the life of the statesman and the best of all; but others think the life of the statesman best. The argument of the latter is that he who does nothing cannot do well, and that virtuous activity is identical with happiness. To both we say: "You are partly right and partly wrong." The first class are right in affirming that the life of the freeman is better than the life of the despot; for there is nothing grand or noble in having the use of a slave, insofar as he is a slave; or, in issuing commands about necessary things. But it is an error to suppose that every sort of rule is despotic like that of a master over slaves, for there is as great a difference between the rule over freemen and the rule over slaves as there is between slavery by nature and freedom by nature, about which I have said enough at the commencement of this treatise. And it is equally a mistake to place inactivity above action, for happiness is activity, and the actions of the just and wise are the realization of much that is noble.

But perhaps someone, accepting these premises, may still maintain that supreme power is the best of all things, because the possessors of it are able to perform the greatest number of noble actions. If so, the man who is able to rule, instead of giving up anything to his neighbor, ought rather to take away his power; and the father should make no account of his son, nor the son of his father, nor friend of friend; they should not bestow a thought on one another in comparison with this higher object, for the best is the most eligible and "doing well" is the best. There might be some truth in such a view if we assume that robbers and plunderers attain the chief good. But this can never be; their hypothesis is false. For the actions of a ruler cannot really be honorable, unless he is as much superior to other men as a husband is to a wife, or a father to his children, or a master to his slaves. And therefore, he who violates the law can never recover by any success, however great, what he has already lost in departing from virtue. For equals, the honorable and the just consist in sharing alike, as is just and equal. But that the unequal should be given to equals, and the unlike to those who are like, is contrary to nature, and nothing which is contrary to nature is good. If, therefore, there is any one superior in virtue and in the power of performing the best actions, him we ought to follow and obey, but he must have the capacity for action as well as virtue.

If we are right in our view, and happiness is assumed to be virtuous activity, the active life will be the best, both for every city collectively, and for individuals. Not that a life of action must necessarily have relation to others, as some persons think, nor are those ideas only to be regarded as practical which are pursued for the sake of practical results, but much more the thoughts and contemplations which are independent and complete in themselves; since virtuous activity, and therefore a certain kind of action, is an end, and even in the case of external actions the directing mind is most truly said to act. Neither, again, is it necessary that states which are cut off from others and choose to live alone should be inactive; for activity, as well as other things, may take place by sections; there are many ways in which the sections of a state act on one another. The same thing is equally true of every individual. If this were otherwise, God and the universe, who have no external actions over and above their own energies, would be far enough from perfection. Hence, it is evident that the same life is best for each individual, and for states and for mankind collectively.

.　　　.　　　.

Since every political society is composed of rulers and subjects, let us consider whether the relations of one to the other should interchange or be permanent. For the education of the citizens will necessarily vary with the answer given to this question. Now, if some men excelled others in the same degree in which gods and heroes are supposed to excel mankind in general (having in the first place a great advantage even in their bodies, and secondly in their minds), so that the superiority of the governors was undisputed and patent to their subjects, it would clearly be better that once and for all the one class should rule and the others serve. But, since this is unattainable, and kings have no marked superiority over their subjects, such as Scylax* affirms to be found among the Indians, it is obviously necessary on many grounds that all the citizens alike should take their turn of governing and being governed. Equality consists in the same treatment of similar persons, and no government can stand which is not founded on justice. For if the government be unjust everyone in the country unites with the governed in the desire to have a revolution, and it is an impossibility that the members of the government can be so numerous as to be stronger than all their enemies put together. Yet that governors should excel their subjects is undeniable. How all this is to be effected, and in what way they will respectively share in the government, the legislator has to consider. The subject has been already mentioned. Nature herself has provided the distinction when she made a difference between old and young within the same species, of whom she fitted the one to govern and the other to be governed. No one takes offense at being governed when he is young, nor does he think himself better than his governors, especially if he will enjoy the same privilege when he reaches the required age.

We conclude that from one point of view governors and governed are identical, and from another different. And therefore their education must be the same and also different. For he who would learn to command well must, as men say, first of all learn to obey. As I observed in the first part of this treatise, there is one rule which is for the sake of the rulers and another rule which is for the sake of the ruled; the former is a despotic, the latter a free government. Some commands differ not in the thing commanded, but in the intention with which they are imposed. Wherefore, many apparently menial offices are an honor to the free youth by whom they are performed; for actions do not differ as honorable or dishonorable in themselves so much as in the end and intention of them. But since we say that the virtue of the citizen and ruler is the same as that of the good man, and that the same person must first be a subject and then a ruler, the legislator has to see that they become good men, and by what means this may be accomplished, and what is the end of the perfect life.

Now the soul of man is divided into two parts, one of which has a rational principle in itself, and the other, not having a rational principle in itself, is able to obey such a principle. And we call a man in any way good because he has the virtues of these two parts. In which of them the end is more likely to be found is no matter of doubt to those who adopt our division; for in the world both of nature and of art the inferior always exists for the sake of the better or superior, and the better or superior is that which has a rational principle. This principle, too, in our ordinary way of speaking, is divided into two kinds, for there is a practical and a

---

* Scylax of Caryandra, a Greek historian in the time of Dorius Hystapis (521–485 B.C.), who commissioned him to explore the course of the Indus.

speculative principle. This [better or superior] part, then, must evidently be similarly divided. And there must be a corresponding division of actions; the actions of the naturally better part are to be preferred by those who have it in their power to attain to two out of the three or to all, for that is always to everyone the most eligible which is the highest attainable by him. The whole of life is further divided into two parts, business and leisure, war and peace, and of actions, some aim at what is necessary and useful, and some at what is honorable. The preference given to one or the other class of actions must necessarily be like the preference given to one or other part of the soul and its actions over the other; there must be war for the sake of peace, business for the sake of leisure, things useful and necessary for the sake of things honorable. All these points the statesman should keep in view when he frames his laws; he should consider the parts of the soul and their functions and above all, the better and the end; he should also remember the diversities of human lives and actions. For men must be able to engage in business and go to war, but leisure and peace are better; they must do what is necessary and indeed what is useful, but what is honorable is better. On such principles children and persons of every age which requires education should be trained. Whereas even the Hellenes of the present day who are reputed to be best governed, and the legislators who gave them their constitutions, do not appear to have framed their governments with a regard to the best end, or to have given them laws and education with a view to all the virtues, but in a vulgar spirit, have fallen back on those which promised to be more useful and profitable. Many modern writers have taken a similar view: they commend the Lacedaemonian constitution,* and praise the legislator for making conquest and war his sole aim, a doctrine that may be refuted by argument and has long ago been refuted by fact. For most men desire empire in the hope of accumulating the goods of fortune; and on this ground Thibron and all those who have written about the Lacedaemonian constitution have praised their legislator, because the Lacedaemonians, by being trained to meet dangers, gained great power. But surely they are not a happy people now that their empire has passed away, nor was their legislator right. How ridiculous is the result, if, while they are continuing in the observance of his laws and no one interferes with them, they have lost the better part of life! These writers further err about the sort of government that the legislator should approve, for the government of freemen is nobler and implies more virtue than despotic government. Neither is a city to be deemed happy or a legislator to be praised because he trains his citizens to conquer and obtain dominion over their neighbors, for there is great evil in this. On a similar principle any citizen who could, should obviously try to

---

* After the historical name of Laconia. The Laconian or Spartan constitution kept the individual subordinate to the state. Obedience, endurance, and military success were its primary ends.

obtain the power in his own state—the crime that the Lacedaemonians accuse King Pausanias of attempting, although he had so great honor already. No such principle and no law having this object is either statesmanlike or useful or right. For the same things are best both for individuals and for states, and these are the things which the legislator ought to implant in the minds of his citizens. Neither should men study war with a view to the enslavement of those who do not deserve to be enslaved; but first of all, they should provide against their own enslavement, and in the second place obtain empire for the good of the governed, and not for the sake of exercising a general despotism, and in the third place they should seek to be masters only over those who deserve to be slaves. Facts, as well as arguments, prove that the legislator should direct all his military and other measures to the provision of leisure and the establishment of peace. For most of these military states are safe only while they are at war, but fall when they have acquired their empire; like unused iron they lose their temper in time of peace. And for this the legislator is to blame, he never having taught them how to lead the life of peace.

3

THE CONSCIENCE OF A STATESMAN

Henry Taylor

Henry Taylor (1800–1886) served as a public official in Great Britain from the years of deep corruption to the beginnings of the modern civil service, which is, properly, a source of pride.

    Oscar Wilde's flippant epigram—"nature imitates art"—was rarely better illustrated than by the widening gap between the intention and the reception of The Statesman. *Its author thought that he "ran no risk of being understood to recommend seriously the arts I expounded."* * *His Victorian readers were dismayed, and the edition of 750 to 1,000 copies printed in 1836 was not exhausted until 1873.†*

    In the mid-twentieth century, The Statesman *was republished, in the United States in a paperback edition. The spirit of the organization man is so much with us that we appreciate the irony, while acknowledging what is said as sober truth. Ironically intended or not, Taylor's distinction between the "strong conscience" and the "tender conscience" addresses itself sensitively to the situation of the modern politico-bureaucrat.*

*

THE CONSCIENCE OF A STATESMAN should be a strong conscience rather than a tender conscience. For a conscience of more tenderness than strength will be liable in public life to be perverted in two ways: first, by reflecting responsibilities disproportionately to their magnitude and missing

---

From Henry Taylor, *The Statesman* (Cambridge, Eng.: W. Heffer and Sons, Ltd., 1957).
  * Henry Taylor, *Autobiography,* Vol. I, p. 206, as quoted in C. Northcote Parkinson, "Introduction to the Mentor Edition." Henry Taylor, *The Statesman* (New York: The New American Library, 1958), p. 11.
  † C. Northcote Parkinson, *ibid.,* p. 20.

of the large responsibilities whilst it is occupied with the small; second, by losing, in a too lively apprehension of the responsibilities of action, the sense of responsibility for inaction.

No doubt the most perfect conscience would be that which should have all strength in its tenderness, all tenderness in its strength, and be equally adapted to public and private occasions. But, I speak of the consciences of men as they exist, with their imperfect capacities, bearing in mind the truth, *"ut multæ virtutes in vitia degenerant, et quod magis est, sæpe videas eosdem affectus, pro temporum sorte, nunc virtutes esse, nunc vitia."** These dilemmas of virtue duly considered, it will be found to be better for the public interests that a statesman should have some hardihood, than much weak sensibility of conscience.

As to the *mismeasurements* of a conscience tender to weakness, take the case of a sentence of death to be executed or remitted, according to the decision to be adopted by a statesman under the direction of this kind of conscience. The responsibility as regards the criminal, and the responsibility as regards the public, will each of them lie as a serious burden on a sore back. But the former of them will, with such a conscience, have an undue preponderance. To decide erroneously that a man had better die will appear a worse thing than to decide, more erroneously, that he had better live; and, human guilt and misery, which are to be the consequence of the error miscalled merciful, will appear of less account than human life; though to a strong conscience and a just judgment mere human life would be of less account, human innocence and happiness of more [account]. Moreover, whilst this question of an individual's life or death swings backward and forward in the conscience of the statesman, it probably keeps off from his conscience other questions, which, though not of the same immediate and tangible character, may nevertheless involve in their consequences numerous lives and deaths, numerous crimes and punishments. So difficult it is, in situations where the duties are diverse and momentous, for a very susceptible conscience to be true to itself.

As to the conscience becoming, from an exceeding tenderness as to acts and deeds, too insensible on the point of inaction or delay, it is very certain that there may be met with, in public life, a species of conscience which is all bridle and no spurs. A statesman whose conscience is of the finest texture as to everything which he does, will sometimes make no conscience of doing nothing. His conscience will be liable to become to him as a quagmire, in which the faculty of action shall stick fast at every step. And, to this tendency of the conscience, the worldly interests of a

* "Since many virtues degenerate in vices and what is more, you often seem attached to them, they may according to the moment be virtues or be vices"—trans. by P.T.

statesman will pander. Conscience is, in most men, an anticipation of the opinions of others; and, whatever the moral responsibility may be, official responsibility is much less apt to be brought home to a statesman in cases of error by inaction than in the contrary cases. What men might have done is less known than what they have actually done, and the world thinks so much less of it and with so much less definiteness and confidence of opinion that the sins of omission are sins on the safe side as to this world's responsibilities.

Above all, it is to be wished that the conscience of a statesman should be an intelligent and perspicacious conscience—not the conscience of the heart only, but the conscience of the understanding—that wheresoever the understanding should be enabled to foresee distant consequences or comprehend wide ones, there the conscience should be enabled to follow, not failing in quickness because the good or evil results in question are less palpable and perhaps less certain than in private life, are not seen with the eyes and heard with the ears, but only known through meditation and foresight. Many magnify in words the importance of public duties, but few appreciate them in feeling and that not so much for want of feeling as for want of carrying it out to whatever results the understanding reaches. It is impossible that the feeling in regard to public objects should be *proportionate* to the feeling for private ones, because the human heart is not large enough; and, it is too often found that when the conscience is not sustained by a sense of due proportion, it gets thrown out altogether. It sometimes happens that he who would not hurt a fly will hurt a nation.

4

THE PROBLEM OF MEANS

Jacques Maritain

Jacques Maritain (b. 1882), a French Neo-Thomist, became a convert to Catholicism and has devoted his life to the study of the application of Thomism to every part of modern life. His deep concern is with the role of reason in life. He served as Ambassador from France to the Vatican, 1945–1948, and is Professor Emeritus of Philosophy at Princeton University.

*

THE PROBLEM OF MEANS is, as I see it, a twofold problem: first, the problem of *end and means;* second, the problem of *the people and the state,* that is, of the means by which the people can supervise or control the state.

END AND MEANS

The problem of end and means is a basic, *the* basic problem in political philosophy. Despite the difficulties involved, its solution is clear and inescapable in the philosophical field; yet, to be applied in the practical field, that solution demanded by truth demands in return from man a kind of heroism and hurls him into anguish and hardship.

What is the final aim and most essential task of the body politic or political society? It is not to ensure the material convenience of scattered individuals, each absorbed in his own well-being and in enriching himself. Nor is it to bring about either industrial mastery over nature or political mastery over other men.

Reprinted from *Man and the State* by Jacques Maritain by permission of The University of Chicago Press. Copyright 1951 by The University of Chicago.

It is, rather, to better the conditions of human life itself or to procure the common good of the multitude, in such a manner that each concrete person, not only in a privileged class, but throughout the whole mass, may truly reach that measure of independence that is proper to civilized life and that is ensured alike by the economic guarantees of work and property, political rights, civil virtues, and the cultivation of the mind.

This means that the political task is essentially a task of civilization and culture, of helping man to conquer his genuine freedom of expansion or autonomy, or, as Professor Nef put it, of "making faith, righteousness, wisdom and beauty ends of civilization"; a task of progress in an order which is essentially human or moral, for morality is concerned with nothing else than the true human good.

I should like to add that such a task requires historic achievements on so large a scale and is confronted with such obstacles in human nature that it cannot conceivably succeed—once the good tidings of the gospel have been announced—without the impact of Christianity on the political life of mankind and the penetration of the gospel inspiration in the substance of the body politic. As a result, we are entitled to state that the end of the body politic is by nature something substantially good and ethical, implying, at least among peoples in whom Christianity has taken root, an actual—though doubtless always imperfect—materialization of the gospel principles in terrestrial existence and social behavior.

And now, what about the means? Do we not know, as a universal and inviolable axiom, an obvious primary principle, that means must be proportioned and appropriate to the end, since they are *ways to the end* and, so to speak, the end itself in its very process of coming to existence? So that applying intrinsically evil means to attain an intrinsically good end is simply nonsense and a blunder. Yes, we know that, even without the help of Aldous Huxley's remarkable writings. And we know that men in their practical behavior do not fail, as a rule, to make fun of that obvious and venerable axiom, especially in all that concerns politics. At this point, we are faced with the question of the *rationalization of political life.*

It is quite difficult for the rational animal to submit his own life to the yardstick of reason. It is quite difficult in our individual lives. It is terribly, almost insuperably, difficult in the life of the body politic. As regards the rational management of collective and political life, we are still in a prehistoric age indeed.

There are two opposite ways of understanding the rationalization of political life. The easiest one—it comes to a bad end—is the *technical* or *artistic*[1] one. The most exacting one—but a constructive and progressive one—is the *moral* one. *Technical rationalization,* through means external

---

[1] Artistic in the Aristotelian sense, pertaining to the realm and intellectual virtue of art, in contradistinction to morality.

to man, versus *moral rationalization,* through means that are man himself, his freedom and virtue—such is the drama which human history is
facing.

THE TECHNICAL RATIONALIZATION
OF POLITICAL LIFE

At the dawn of modern science and history, Machiavelli, in his *The
Prince,* offered us a philosophy of the merely technical rationalization of
politics: in other words, he made a rational system out of the manner in
which men most often behave in fact, by submitting that behavior to a
merely artistic form and merely artistic rules. Thus, good politics became
by definition nonmoral and successful politics: the art of conquering and
keeping power by any means whatsoever—even good, should an opportunity offer, a rare opportunity—on the sole condition that they be fit
to ensure success.

. . . I should like only to point out that the great strength of
Machiavellianism comes from the incessant victories gained by evil means
in the political achievements of mankind and from the idea that if a
prince or a nation respects justice, he or it is doomed to enslavement by
other princes or nations trusting only in power, violence, perfidy, and
lawless greed.

The answer is, first, that one can respect justice and have brains at
the same time and manage to be strong (I shall return to this point in a
moment); second, that in reality Machiavellianism does not succeed. For,
the power of evil is only, in reality, the power of corruption—the
squandering and dissipation of the substance and energy of Being and of
Good. Such a power destroys itself, in destroying that good which is its
subject; so, the inner dialectic of the successes of evil condemn them not
to be lasting. Let us take into account the dimension of time, the duration
proper to the historical turns of nations and states, which considerably
exceeds the duration of a man's life. According to the duration thus required by political reality to mature and fructify, I do not say that a just
politics will, even in a distant future, always actually succeed, nor that
Machiavellianism will, even in a distant future, always actually fail. For,
with nations and states and civilizations, we are in the order of nature
where mortality is natural and where life and death depend on physical as
well as moral causes. I say that justice works through its own causality
toward welfare and success in the future, as a healthy sap works toward
the perfect fruit, and that Machiavellianism works through its own causality for ruin and bankruptcy, as poison in the sap works for the illness
and death of the tree.

The illusion proper to Machiavellianism is the illusion of *immediate
success.* The duration of the life of a man, or rather the duration of the

activity of the prince, of the political man, circumscribes the maximum length of time required by what I call *immediate success.* Now, immediate success is success for a man, it is not success for a state or a nation, according to the duration proper to state-vicissitudes and nation-vicissitudes. The more dreadful in intensity the power of evil appears, the weaker in historic duration are the internal improvements and the vigor of life that have been gained by a state using this power.

The more perfect and ruthless become the techniques of oppression, universal mutual spying, forced labor, mass deportation and mass destruction peculiar to the totalitarian states, the more difficult also becomes any attempt to change or overcome from the outside those gigantic Machiavellian robots. But they do not possess lasting inner force; their huge machinery of violence is a token of their inner human weakness. The breaking down of human freedom and conscience, because it engenders everywhere fear and insecurity, is in itself a process of self-destruction for the body politic. How long, then, can the power of a state endure, which becomes more and more of a giant as regards the external or technical forces and more and more of a dwarf as regards the internal, human, actually vital forces? It will do during some generations the job it has been assigned or permitted. I doubt that it can take root in the historical duration of nations.

Thus, it is true that, politics being something intrinsically moral, the first political condition of good politics is that it be just. And it is true at the same time that justice and virtue do not, as a rule, lead men to success in this world, within that short time which separates the cradle from the grave and in which success makes sense for them. But the antimony is solved, as regards human societies, because the achievement of the common good, with the conditions of material prosperity which it involves, cannot be put in jeopardy or destroyed by the use of justice, if historical duration is taken into account and if the specific effect of the use of justice is considered in itself, apart from the effects of the other factors at play.

THE MORAL RATIONALIZATION
OF POLITICAL LIFE

There is another kind of rationalization of political life, not an artistic or technical, but a moral rationalization. This means the recognition of the essentially human ends of political life and of its deepest springs: justice, law, and mutual friendship; it also means a ceaseless effort to make the living, moving structures and organs of the body politic serve the common good, the dignity of the human person, and the sense of fraternal love—to submit the huge material conditioning, both natural and technical, and the heavy setting up of conflicting interests, power and coercion inherent in social life, to the form and regulations of human reason spurring human freedom—and to base political activity not on childish greed, jealousy, selfishness, pride, and guile, claims to prestige and domination transformed into sacred rules of the most serious game, but, instead, on a grown-up awareness of the innermost needs of mankind's life, of the real requirements of peace and love, and of the moral and spiritual energies of man.

That way of rationalizing politics was shown us by Aristotle and the great philosophers of antiquity, then, by the great medieval thinkers. After a rationalistic stage, in which some basic errors preyed upon it and vast illusions fostered genuine human hopes, it resulted in the democratic conception put into force during the last century.

Something particularly significant must be stressed at this point: democracy is the only way of bringing about a *moral rationalization* of politics, because democracy is a rational organization of freedoms founded on law.

We may appreciate from this point of view the crucial importance of the survival and improvement of democracy for the evolution and earthly destiny of mankind. With democracy, mankind has entered the road to the only genuine, that is *moral* rationalization, of political life: in other terms, to the highest terrestrial achievement of which the rational animal is capable. Democracy carries in a fragile vessel the terrestrial hope, I would say the biological hope, of humanity. Of course, the vessel is fragile. Of course, we still are at the very first steps in the process. Of course, we have paid and we are paying heavily for grave errors and moral failures. Democracy can be awkward, clumsy, defective. It can deserve the severe judgment passed on its capacities in foreign policy by the French jurist Émile Giraud, former juridical counselor of the League of Nations, when he wrote, concerning the period 1919–1939, a book entitled *The Nothingness of the International Policy of Great Democracies.* Yet, democracy is the only way through which the progressive energies in human history do pass.

By the same token, we may also appreciate the responsibility with which democracy is burdened. We may appreciate the unique, dramatic importance of the problem of end and means for democracy. In the process of moral rationalization of political life, the means must necessarily be moral. The end, for democracy, is both justice and freedom. The use, by democracy, of means basically incompatible with justice and freedom, would be to that very extent an operation of self-destruction.

Let us not be deceived, moreover, by the Machiavellian sophistries; they say that justice and respect for moral values spell weakness and doom and that strength is strong only if raised to the supreme standard of political existence. That is a lie. Not only, as we have seen, is evil incapable of succeeding in the long run, and not only does strength without justice weaken in the long run, but here and now strength *can exist* together with justice; and, the power of nations struggling for freedom can be even greater than that of nations struggling to enslave. The second world war was a proof of that. Yet, the strength itself of a democratic body politic supposes justice, because it uses human energies as energies of free men, not of slaves. Nay, more: a supreme effort of all the energies of freedom, in their own spiritual realm, is needed to compensate for the momentary increase in physical strength that is given Machiavellian powers by their determination to use any means whatsoever. And such a supreme effort cannot arise if the body politic ignores moral values and standards. In reality, strength is supremely strong only if not strength, but justice, is the supreme standard.

We know that the flesh is weak. It would be nonsense to require perfection and impeccability from anyone who seeks justice. We must forgive democracies for their accidental weaknesses and deficiencies. If, however, their exertions toward uprooting injustice from their own lives and toward making their means worthy of their ends were decidedly insufficient, then might history perhaps be less lenient with them than we would wish.

It is possible that the present and future course of human history will confront democracies with fearful trials and fateful alternatives. They might then be tempted to lose their reasons for living for their very lives' sake. As Henri Bergson put it, the democratic feeling and philosophy has its deepest root in the gospel. To try to reduce democracy to technocracy, and to expel from it the gospel inspiration together with all faith in the supramaterial, supramathematical, and suprasensory realities, would be to try to deprive it of its very blood. Democracy can only live on gospel inspiration. It is by virtue of the gospel inspiration that democracy can overcome its direst trials and temptations. It is by virtue of the gospel inspiration that democracy can progressively carry out its momentous task of the moral rationalization of political life.

Now, my analysis would be incomplete if I did not observe that political hypermoralism is not better than political amoralism and, in the last analysis, answers the very purpose of political cynicism. Politics is a branch of ethics, but a branch specifically distinct from the other branches of the same stem. For human life has two ultimate ends, the one subordinate to the other: an ultimate end *in a given order,* which is the terrestrial common good, or the *bonum vitae civilis*; and, an *absolute* ultimate end, which is the transcendent, eternal common good. Individual ethics takes into account the subordinate ultimate end, but *directly aims* at the absolute ultimate one; whereas political ethics takes into account the absolute ultimate end, but its *direct aim* is the subordinate ultimate end, the good of the rational nature in its temporal achievement. Hence a specific difference of perspective between those two branches of ethics.

Thus it is that many patterns of conduct of the body politic, which the pessimists of Machiavellianism turn to the advantage of political amorality—such as the use by the state of coercive force (even of means of war in case of absolute necessity against an unjust aggressor), the use of intelligence services and methods which should never corrupt people but cannot help utilizing corrupted people, the use of police methods which should never violate the human rights of people but cannot help being rough with them, a lot of selfishness and self-assertion which would be blamed in individuals, a permanent distrust and suspicion, a cleverness not necessarily mischievous but yet not candid with regard to the other states, or the toleration of certain evil deeds by the law, the recognition of the principle of the lesser evil and the recognition of the *fait accompli* (the so-called "statute of limitations") which permits the retention of gains ill-gotten long ago, because new human ties and vital relationships have infused them with new-born rights—all of these things are in reality ethically grounded.

The fear of soiling ourselves by entering the context of history is not virtue, but a way of escaping virtue. Some seem to think that to put our hands to the real, to this concrete universe of human things and human relations where sin exists and circulates, is in itself to contract sin, as if sin were contracted from without, not from within. This is pharisaical purism; it is not the doctrine of the purification of the means.

This doctrine primarily relates to the question of the *hierarchy of means*. It rests on the axiom that *the order of the means corresponds to that of ends*. It asks that an end worthy of man be pursued with means worthy of man. It insists first and foremost on the positive will to raise up means not only good in general, but truly proportionate to their end, truly bearing on them the stamp and imprint of their end, means in which that very justice which pertains to the essence of the common good and that very sanctification of secular life which pertains to its perfection shall be embodied.

A final remark must be made, which deals with a particularly sad aspect of human collective life. When the social group is in a process of regression or perversion and its moral level is sinking, then the precepts of morality do not change in themselves, of course, but the manner in which they must apply sinks also to a lower level, for our moral acts are concrete acts, the moral nature or specification of which can be changed by the nature of the situation which one has to face. I am quarreling with a man: suppose I kill him, this will be a murder. Now, suppose that this same man attacks me to kill me; it is a case of self-defense. I kill him, and this will not be murder. Suppose we live in a completely barbarous social group, a tribe of bandits, in which no law, no tribunals, no public order exists. Then we should have to take the law into our own hands;

which means that we might be placed in the position of justly killing some offender and that in such a case the physical act of putting that man to death would not morally constitute a murder. For the moral essence of murder is to kill a man on one's own merely human authority, whereas in such a case we should not act on our own authority, but in the performance of a judicial function to which mankind in general is virtually yet really entitled and which derives in mankind from the creator of being. Though, in civilized life, this judicial authority must be held and exercised only by those who have been invested with judicial powers in the state, nevertheless, even in civilized life, a quite exceptional case of emergency, like the case of self-defense to which I just alluded, can call any man whatever to participate in it by defending his own right to live against an unjust aggressor.

5

THE CHRISTIAN IN POLITICS

Reinhold Niebuhr

In his own lifetime, Reinhold Niebuhr (b. 1892) has moved from the pulpit to the lecture hall, from pastoral guidance to political activism. For about thirty years, he was Professor of Applied Christianity at Union Theological Seminary. From this post, he stimulated a clerical revolution —an activist social gospel, a concern with the here-and-now that is based on a conviction of man's sinfulness, a skeptical view of society, and an ironic attitude toward progress. Some of these qualities are evident in the excerpt included here as well as the ultimately conservative realism that has characterized his later writings.

*

IDEALISM, REALISM, AND CHRISTIAN RESPONSIBILITY

We can approach a solution of the problem of relating religious commitments to political decisions by excluding two answers. . . . The one wrong answer is to find no relevance at all between our faith and our political actions. This answer is wrong because it denies the seriousness of our political decisions and obscures our Christian responsibilities for the good order and justice of our civil community.

The other wrong answer stands at the opposite extreme. It is to equate religious and political commitments and to regard every political decision as simply derived from our faith. This is a wrong answer because political issues deal with complex problems of justice, every solution for which contains morally ambiguous elements. All political positions are morally ambiguous because, in the realm of politics and economics, self-interest and power must be harnessed and beguiled, rather than eliminated. In other words, forces that are morally dangerous must be used despite their peril. Politics always aims at some kind of a harmony or balance of interest, and such a harmony cannot be regarded as directly related to the final harmony of love of the Kingdom of God. All men are naturally inclined to obscure the morally ambiguous element in their political cause by investing it with religious sanctity. This is why religion is more frequently a source of confusion than of light in the political realm. The tendency to equate our political with our Christian convictions causes politics to generate idolatry.

An action in the field of politics may be prompted by Christian motives and viewpoints, but it never overcomes the ambiguities indicated and can, therefore, never be regarded as clearly right or clearly wrong. It is the action which we believe to be relevant at the moment in order to bear our Christian witness in the cause of justice. There are no absolutely clear witnesses of faith and love in the political sphere, though there may be highly significant testimonies. It would seem, then, that the first duty of Christian faith is to preserve a certain distance between the sanctities of faith and the ambiguities of politics. This is to say that it is the duty of a Christian in politics to have no specific "Christian politics."

Of course, Christians have been tempted by one or the other of the two wrong answers. There have always been orthodox Christians who have tended to accept the necessities of politics as practically normative and to elaborate a political ethic not very different from that of the cynics. (Thus, there are similarities between Lutheran and Machiavellian politics.) On the other hand, moralistic Christians tend to be irresponsible toward any political problem in which the realities of sin make coercion and resistance a requirement of justice. Either, they give themselves to the illusion that they are seeking to make love prevail in the complex collective behavior of mankind, or they wash their hands of the task of achieving justice because they realize that love does not prevail.

If we rule out these two extremes, we still face the primary question of how politics is to be related to faith. We can advance a little farther toward a solution of the problem if we recognize that political issues represent various grades and levels which range all the way from clear moral issues to problems of strategy and means.

It is obvious, for instance, that the Christian churches of America have, with a fair degree of consistency, espoused the idea of America's responsibility to a world community and have resisted nationalist and isolationist politics in the name of the Christian faith. They have been right in doing so. But, this broad moral purpose must be distinguished from problems of strategy. Various strategic devices will be advanced as the best ways of fulfilling our responsibilities. Such devices can never be invested with full religious sanctity. It would be impossible to claim, for instance, that the Christian faith requires that America give preference to either the European or the Asiatic field of strategy, or that we should defend the free world primarily by air rather than by land power.

In the same fashion, the commandment "Thou shalt love thy neighbor as thyself" brings us under religious and moral compulsions to eliminate the violations of brotherhood in the field of race relations. But, it can hardly compel us to choose between the efficacy of a state, as against a federal, Fair Employment Practices Act. In such questions of strategy, there are reasons for honest differences of opinion.

In actual life, however, no clear distinction between moral principles and strategy can be made. This is why Christian convictions that deal only with ultimate principle and exclude strategic issues tend to become wholly irrelevant. Yet, the farther one moves from a principle that is clearly related to the love commandment to detailed applications in particular situations, the more hazardous the decision becomes and the more impossible it is to compel others to a similar conviction by appeal to a common faith.

But, the exclusion of the religious element from pragmatic decisions is only another negative answer to the problem of defining a Christian approach to the economic and political order. How shall we find the positive answer? The basic presupposition of a positive answer must lie in a Christian understanding of the realities of man's social life. We must, then, find a way of dealing with these realities which makes justice something more than the prostitute of power, on the one hand, and something more than sentimental daydreams, on the other. We must find an understanding of life which is deep enough to save us from vacillating between sentimentality and cynicism, or from compounding the two when we are tired of one or the other.

It is wrong to interpret these realities in purely cynical or in purely sentimental terms. It is important to recognize an admixture of self-seeking in every form of human togetherness and, also, in every strategy of government required to prevent competitive self-seeking from degenerating into anarchy. We cannot (as does classical liberalism) regard the self-seeking that a bourgeois-liberal economy permits as completely harmless; and we cannot, as does orthodox Protestantism, particularly Lutheranism, be uncritical toward the coercive power of government on the ground that God ordained it to prevent anarchy; for, both the economic power that competes in the market place and the political power that sets restraints on the competition are tainted by motives other than the desire for justice. On the other hand, it would be wrong to be too cynical about this admixture of self-interest in all the vital forces of society. Men do have a residual capacity for justice. Government does express the desire of a community for order and justice and not merely the will-to-power of the oligarchy that controls the engines of power in government. An attitude that avoids both sentimentality and cynicism must obviously be grounded in a Christian view of human nature that is schooled by the gospel not to take the pretensions of men at their face value, on the one hand, and, on the other, not to deny the residual capacity for justice among even sinful men.

Thus, the real problem of a Christian social ethic is to derive from the gospel a clear view of the realities with which we must deal in our common or social life and also to preserve a sense of responsibility for achieving the highest measure of order, freedom, and justice, despite the hazards of man's collective life. Once again, the necessary idealism and the equally necessary realism can be held together only in terms of a Christian faith which refuses to make sin and self-interest normative, but which also understands that human history offers no simple way out to the kingdom of pure love and complete disinterestedness. Nothing is quite so difficult, yet so genuinely Christian, as to remember that in all political struggles there are no saints but only sinners fighting one another and to remember at the same time that history from man's, rather than God's, perspective is constituted of significant distinctions between types and degrees of sin. It is well to know that God judges all men, and that in His sight no man living is justified; but, we are men and not God. We must make historic choices.

Christians ought to be able to analyze a given situation more realistically than moralists and idealists, because they are not under the necessity of having illusions about human nature in order to avert despair and preserve their faith in the meaning of life. But, it is equally true that they are unable to regard any of the pragmatic policies of politics, by which relative justice is achieved in history, as ultimately normative. This means that Christians always live in a deeper dimension than the realm in which the political struggle takes place; but, they cannot simply flee the world of political contention into a realm of mystic eternity or moralistic illusion.

If the tension between Christian realism, and faith in love as the law of life, is not to be broken, the Christian must become immersed in the claims and counterclaims, the tension, conflict, and the risk of overt hostilities which characterize all attempts at justice, while refusing to regard any relative justice so achieved as exhausting his obligations. He must, as a Christian, participate responsibly in the struggle for justice, constantly making significant moral and political decisions amidst and upon perplexing issues and hazardous ventures. He must even make them "with might" and not half-heartedly. But, the Christian faith gives him no warrant to lift himself above the world's perplexities and to seek or to claim absolute validity for the stand he takes. It does, instead, encourage him to the charity which is born of humility and contrition. If he claims to possess overtly what remains hidden, he turns the mercy of Christ into an inhuman fanaticism.

In summary, an adequate political morality must do justice to the insights of both idealists and political realists. It must include a political policy that will reduce coercive power to the minimum and bring the most effective social check on conflicting egoistic impulses in society; it must generate a moral idealism which will make for a moral and rational adjustment of life to life and exploit every available resource of altruistic impulse and reason to extend life from selfish to social ends; and, it must encompass a religious world view that will do justice to the ideals of the spirit which reach beyond the possibilities of historic achievement.

International peace, political and economic justice, and every form of social achievement represent precarious constructs in which the egoism of man is checked and yet taken for granted and in which human sympathy and love must be exploited to the full and yet discounted. The field of politics is not helpfully tilled by pure moralists nor by moral cynics. Community must be built by men and nations sufficiently mature and robust to understand that political justice is achieved, not merely by destroying, but also by deflecting, beguiling, and harnessing residual self-interest and by finding the greatest possible concurrence between self-interest and the general welfare. They must also be humble enough to understand that the forces of self-interest to be deflected are not always those of the opponent or competitor. They are frequently those of the self, individual, or collective, including the interests of the idealist who erroneously imagines himself above the battle.

Since all political and moral striving results in frustration as well as fulfillment, the task of building community requires a faith that is not too easily destroyed by frustration. Such a faith must understand the moral ambiguities of history and know them not merely as accidents or as the consequence of the malevolence of this man or that nation; it must understand them as permanent characteristics of man's historic existence.

6

ETHICAL PROBLEMS OF
POLITICIANS

Paul H. Douglas

*An abiding desire to uplift the ethical tone of the United States Senate and
a deserved reputation as an untouchable make Paul H. Douglas (b.
1892) of Illinois stand out among his colleagues. He has publicly announced that he would return any gift with a value above $2.50 and has
thereby successfully discouraged well-wishers and would-be influencers. A
professional economist before entering the Senate in 1948, he wrote
several books and served in the Marine Corps 1942–1946. In the Senate,
he took a leading role in the Kefauver investigation of organized crime
and in the studies instituted by Congress to improve ethical standards of
public service. His book,* Ethics in Government, *was published in 1952.
Its basic recommendations are summarized here.*

*

THE MAGNITUDE OF THE PROBLEM

As summarized by the subcommittee,[1] the factors contributing to the
over-all problem may be stated in this way:

(1) In this day of big government, there is much at stake in public policies which directly affects the income and welfare of individuals, industries, and groups.

From Paul H. Douglas, "Improvement of Ethical Standards in the Federal Government:
Problems and Proposals," *The Annals of the American Academy of Political and Social
Science,* 280 (1952). Copyright © 1952 by The American Academy of Political and
Social Science.
    [1] The members of the subcommittee were Matthew M. Neely, Hubert H. Hum-
phrey, George D. Aiken, Wayne Morse, and the present author, who was chairman.

(2) Members of Congress have almost free discretion in making these policies, and administrative officials have great discretion in administering them.

(3) The great authority vested in elected officials is justified by the principle that they, as representatives of the public, will exercise their authority in the public interest and for public purposes; similarly, the discretionary authority delegated to administrators is based on the assumption that they will exercise it reasonably in accordance with public policies and for the furtherance of public purposes.

(4) Although the importance of the issues, the breadth of discretion involved, and the basic nature of responsible government make it necessary that, as far as humanly possible, issues shall be decided on their merits, interested parties are not willing to let the wheels of government turn unassisted, but in a great variety of ways bring pressure to bear on legislators and administrators in order to secure favorable decisions.

From these basic factors emerge special problems, most of which, in the opinion of the witnesses, call for affirmative and corrective action by the government.

PROBLEMS OF PRIOR EMPLOYMENT

One of the most pressing problems is that the government is employing mature, well-established businessmen, especially in numerous positions in defense agencies that deal directly with the very industries from which they recently came. These men are needed, and their work for the government, like that of every other public servant, must be considered a patriotic service. The employment of these men in defense agencies nevertheless creates ethical problems and hazards. Can they be perfectly fair if cases come before them which directly or indirectly involve the company from which they came? Can they be completely objective in decisions which affect their industry—for example, where the industry favors a policy divergent from public policy or from proposed public policy? Can these men be completely detached in determining what the public interest requires?

The basis of their employment may affect the perspective of exbusinessmen. Are they employed without compensation (WOC) or at a dollar a year, continuing to draw a corporation salary while on leave for public service? Some believe that these men should be as dependent on the government as salary can make them and that a WOC status is improper. Others say, however, that many able businessmen of middle age without accumulated savings and with heavy fixed obligations for insurance, house payments, education of children, etc. cannot afford to come into the government (short of an all-out emergency) if they have to drop from the industrial to the governmental scale of compensation for executives.

PROBLEMS OF SUBSEQUENT EMPLOYMENT

Another situation fraught with danger is the later affiliation of government servants with business concerns with which they have had official dealings. Public employees who place or settle contracts, recommend loans, award subsidies, or make similar decisions directly touching persons or firms which do business with the government and then leave the government to take positions with these same firms inevitably raise doubts as to how impartial they were when they decided these issues while in the government. If their new salary is out of line with the old (after allowing for differences in the business scale), this doubt is further strengthened. These circumstances are in fact inherently so suspicious that a public employee who values his reputation for integrity should feel himself disqualified for employment with a firm to which he has made valuable awards until a considerable period (e.g., two years) has elapsed after that business has been completed. Governmental employers should discourage such transfers by all possible means.

Coming events cast their shadows before and, if the possibility of lucrative employment with a private concern should be raised in any way, directly or indirectly, while the public servant is negotiating or doing business with that concern, it also casts doubts on the merits of the pending business. If public employees were under a standing order to report such improprieties and to ask to be relieved of the assignment in question, it might help to avert untimely offers.

Even when direct monetary payments or similar valuable privileges are not involved, a public employee who enters the employ of a concern that regularly does business with his former governmental employer creates an ethical problem. All agree that, in this new employment, he should not handle specific matters for which he was formerly responsible or which he officially knew about. The consensus is for disqualification in all such cases, and agency regulations more or less approximate this rule. The problem arises most frequently in the tax and regulatory functions, where public servants become expert in the law and the economics of the taxed or regulated industries, and their services are then demanded by business concerns.

PROBLEMS OF BECOMING UNDULY INVOLVED THROUGH INVESTMENTS, GIFTS, AND ENTERTAINMENT

A recognized problem of long standing is that of public officials becoming unduly involved with persons, concerns, or industries which are affected by their decisions. There is a strong presumption that a substantial economic involvement will create either a bias or an emotional problem through fear of bias. It is generally agreed, therefore, that any such involvement should be avoided. This is the purpose of the conflict-of-interest statutes and of the law of incompatible offices.

Involvements which it is generally agreed must be avoided include salaries, fees, and other compensation from business concerns, direct or indirect ownership of concerns doing business with the government, and speculation in securities or commodities in a field touching that in which the public servant has official functions. Somewhat less clear but also coming under the taboo for administrators is substantial investment in an industry affected by his official functions. How much is "substantial"? That probably depends in part on its ratio to the individual's total investments. On these points, there is not much disagreement. There is some feeling that public officials should be permitted to own businesses which do not concern their official function in any way and which they can operate through an agent or employee. But this, too, is frequently forbidden by law, perhaps to make sure that his official duties will have a public servant's full attention.

The recent disclosures have also shown that one of the most common ways in which interested parties seduce public officials is through costly gifts and expensive entertainment. Many men profess to see nothing wrong in this and state that it will not affect the attitude of the official. This is excessively naïve. What frequently happens is that the loyalties of the public official are shifted gradually from single-minded devotion to the public interest to a friendship for and loyalty toward the donor and patron. Then, when decisions are made, it is easy for the official to be influenced by considerations of friendship and personal obligation. Many public officials have gone wrong in this fashion and have shifted their loyalties so slowly and imperceptibly that they were not fully conscious of what was happening.

PROBLEMS OF ECONOMIC INVOLVEMENT: CONGRESS

The pressures on members of Congress which create ethical problems are of several varieties. One is financial pressure. Campaigning is costly. Where shall the candidate seek funds to help with his primary or his final campaign? Politics is not classifiable as philanthropy for tax purposes, and the average voters, including those who are most harsh in their judgment of politicians, do not contribute to campaign funds. The normal candidate's only recourse is to the more actively interested persons or to groups which are in politics to protect their interests. From which of these shall a candidate seek funds and support? Is it possible for him to retain some degree of independence if he does so? How much dare he obligate himself to a single group? Diversification is a good principle, as in investments, but frequently it is not possible.

Being the nominee of his party places the candidate under some obligation to the party; but who has a right to define its policy—the candidate or the professional workers below decks who run the "machine"? Assuming that some consideration of each for the other is normal, how far shall a successful candidate go in honoring obligations which the machine has assumed? In a complex industrial society, these questions get rather complex. No wonder the old system of finding a financial "angel" and then of sending him on a flight to the embassy in Graustark has its attractions, even from an ethical point of view. It has its advantages, even though it still pains the foreign service officers who would like these posts for themselves.

The financial pressure does not end with the campaign. The senator or representative has abnormal expenses. Maintaining a residence in Washington, in addition to keeping his roots in his home soil, is expensive. To keep in touch, he also generally needs to come home frequently for short visits. Travel is costly, and the government pays only for one trip per session. A senator or representative is a public figure and fair game for solicitors for all worthy causes. Even small contributions add up. Some members, particularly from the more populous states, find the allowances for clerk hire insufficient to cover the cost of maintaining their offices.

The upshot is that a majority of the members of Congress find it necessary to supplement their salary in some way. Were Congress meeting but six months or less a year, as it once did, there would be no serious difficulty, but membership is now practically a year-round activity, which, with the duties of campaigning, leaves little time to engage in business or professional activities. Members who are lawyers may accept fees or retainers for giving advice and counsel or for other legal services. But they have little time for very extensive service, and, if their duties become perfunctory, the question always arises; are they being paid for their influence and to influence their perspective? Men who pay legal retainers expect to get something for their money.

Members who are not lawyers have no device as well established as the legal retainer, but fortunately many of them are quite articulate and enjoy speaking. Since their function is one of educating the public as well as themselves on public issues, a good many public speeches can be considered in the line of duty. But there are other questions. To what groups should one speak? At what point does a large fee become payment for something more than the speech? How can adequate diversification be maintained?

Men of property in Congress, as well as the impecunious, also have their problems. If their investments are concentrated in one or a few industries, how can they avoid becoming protagonists of those industries, at the expense of a genuinely public perspective on issues of policy? What steps can they take to protect the public from their own bias?

ECONOMIC INVOLVEMENT VERSUS VENALITY

Differences of degree, usually accompanied by differences in motivation, change the character of improprieties. Gifts and favors which may begin as entirely innocent practices become improper when they begin to affect the public servant's ability to act for the public as agent or representative, fairly and objectively. They are improper as subtle influences on his point of view.

If carried further, they become ends in themselves, a way of increasing the public servant's income. At some point, the receiver becomes venal. He is, in effect, taking bribes and graft to enrich himself. This has been recognized to be wrong as long as "Western" civilization has existed. One can find it vividly depicted and scornfully denounced in the pages of the Old Testament. It is always a problem, but it is a less important problem today in its effect on the conduct of public affairs than subtle economic involvement.

When gifts, favors, and lavish entertainment begin to be evident in the relations of contractors with the government, it is prima-facie evidence of something wrong and time for corrective action.

PROBLEMS OF POLITICAL INVOLVEMENTS

Politics itself can give rise to embarrassing conflicts of interest. When men are appointed to important administrative positions, often with the clearance and approval of county and state political organizations or national committees or members of the Senate and House of Representatives, should they feel especially obligated to their political sponsors? If so, to what extent? Is there any obligation touching specific administrative decisions? If there is no obligation to the sponsor which can affect handling of administrative issues strictly on their merits, how can political sponsors be induced to accept this role of impartiality? Often political sponsors take a proprietary interest in departments or agencies in which they have helped to place men in key positions, and, if their interest is pushed aggressively, it creates serious ethical problems for the administrator.

PROBLEMS OF "REFERENCE"

The so-called function of reference is well established in the federal government. Members of Congress receive a large number of requests from constituents asking for their assistance in dealing with federal departments and agencies. Job-hunters, contractors and would-be contractors, applicants for loans, applicants for privileges in the public domain, men who want to get into the armed forces usually as commissioned officers and others who want to get out, veterans whose benefits have been delayed or denied, and many others, such as those seeking naturalization, come to their senator or congressman or write to him for help in getting a favorable decision from administrators. There is so much of this business that a member of Congress could spend his entire time on it.

It is, indeed, desirable that legislators perform this function provided they observe proper restraints in doing so, for civil servants frequently become perfunctory in their work and careless of the people whom they are presumed to serve. Legislators can, therefore, legitimately serve as an informal board of inspectors. They can prevent the administrators from flagging in their zeal and can detect and check abuses in the conduct of public business. From another point of view, legislators can serve as informal ambassadors for their states, which often seem to constituents to be rather far removed from the center of power in Washington.

PROBLEMS OF EXECUTIVE APPOINTMENTS

One of the most obvious influences on the conduct of public business is the selection of persons for top administrative posts. The president in his nominations, the Senate in its votes on confirmation, citizens who are invited to accept key positions, and the groups that seek to influence the selection or approval of nominees have great power to raise or lower the levels of public service.

Despite government's difficulties in competing with more remunerative or more peaceful occupations for top-grade talent, their enlistment must be a constant aim of every administration.

Refusal of able citizens to accept the responsibilities of public life; nomination of mediocre persons or those who are subservient to private interests; denial of confirmation to nominees who have been outspoken champions of the public interest; and sniping, unsupported attacks on various public officials are bound to result in depressing the morale and the practices of various government agencies.

On the other hand, the zeal to protect the public interest and the competence that is brought to government work at all levels are greatly strengthened when persons of high caliber receive appointments to leading positions and when able officers have the full support of the president, the Congress, and the people.

ADMINISTRATIVE FAULTS

Certain institutional tendencies or failures of administration tend to defeat public policies. One is the tendency of independent regulatory agencies to surrender their regulatory zeal as they age and to become more and more the protagonists of a clientele industry and less and less the vigilant defenders of the welfare of consumers or the general public. All too often, those who are supposedly being regulated actually regulate their nominal regulators.

A related fault in public administration is "tiredness" and a routine performance of public duties. This generally becomes worse as the agency grows older and as it tends to lose its initial zeal. It is unfortunately characteristic of all-too-many government departments at present.

Criticisms are also heard that the administrative interpretation and enforcement of statutes are unduly flexible and variable. Heads of agencies commonly turn to legal officers whom they appoint for rulings as to whether they can proceed in a given manner. The resulting opinions are not unbiased. They commonly tell the administrators what they want to hear. Undoubtedly, they are leading to an undue expansion of administrative power under which administrators are changing or creating law and hence usurping legislative functions. Administrators argue in their defense, however, that, in addition to the language of substantive acts of Congress, they receive instructions from the appropriation acts, the two appropriations committees, at least two legislative committees in each house, and sometimes also from individual committee members. They say that part of the problem is that these instructions are not always consistent. In those circumstances, any interpretation of public policy may seem to some to be improper. In any case, the consistent and equal application of the law is an objective that seems not yet fully attained.

CAMPAIGN METHODS

Just as serious as the problem of campaign finance is that of campaign methods. Here, the root of the problem is a tendency in campaigning to disregard the truth. The worth of the election system in representative government depends upon its being an extension of the legislative discussion of issues and policies. This is intended to be a process of revealing and of weighing the facts. If mendacity, misrepresentation, and irresponsible statements characterize electioneering, the mind and emotions of the public are immediately exploited, and, in the long run, the whole electoral process is discredited. These facts are apparent to members of Congress, and, from the testimony we received, it is evident that the public is also beginning to be aware of and concerned about the trend of campaigning. The level of responsibility and truthtelling is below that which the public in its heart approves. The fact that violators of reasonable standards may win an election is not evidence to the contrary. The European dictators demonstrated that it is possible to exploit the democratic tradition—a tradition of responsibility and reasonableness—by ruthless methods. As with monetary inflation, those who deliberately depreciate the currency of language can keep one step ahead of the rate of exchange. Cheating is unethical in any system, and cheating the public is more serious than cheating a rival.

The problem of equitable electioneering is complicated by the subtle campaigning which can be undertaken by advisers, business sales organizations, labor organizations, and farm organizations. Thorough exploration of the problem will doubtless lead also to the reconsideration of tax allowances and of the political activity of organized groups.

SUMMARY OF RECOMMENDATIONS

As a result of these complaints and disclosures, the subcommittee concluded that:

A Commission on Ethics in Government

A Commission on Ethics in Government should be established by joint resolution of Congress. The commission's function should be twofold. First, it would investigate and report to the president and Congress on the moral standards of the official conduct of persons and groups doing business with the government or seeking to influence public policy and administration. And, second, it would report on the moral standards generally prevailing in society which condition the conduct of public affairs or which affect the strength and unity of the nation. The commission's inquiry should focus primarily on the legislative and executive branches, but should not exclude the administration of justice; federally supported activities of the states; and such ideas, attitudes, habits, practices, and standards of American society as are relevant to the commission's functions.

The second function of the commission should be to recommend measures to improve and maintain at a high level moral standards of official conduct in the federal government and of all persons who participate in or are responsible for the conduct of public affairs. It should be noted that the commission would not be concerned with the morals of individuals —governmental personnel or private citizens—except as they are involved in the conduct of public affairs.

The commission should consist of fifteen members, five appointed by the president, five by the president of the Senate (i.e., the vice-president), and five by the Speaker of the House. All members should be persons of recognized integrity, judgment, and experience in public or civic affairs. Of the members appointed by the president, two should be public employees, one a career civil servant holding a position not above GS-16, and one holding an office of higher rank. Of the members appointed by the president of the Senate and speaker of the House, in each case two should be members of the respective legislative body of the appointing officer, one a Democrat and one a Republican.

The commission should have power to hold hearings and secure testimony and evidence, authority to employ staff, and funds to carry on its work. It should have two years in which to complete its investigation and report, but should place its major recommendations before the president and Congress during the first session of the Eighty-third Congress. It should terminate thirty days after submitting its final report.

Amendments to the Administrative Procedure Act

The Administrative Procedure Act should be amended to provide that the following practices shall be improper for federal officials and employees and shall be grounds for summary dismissal from the federal service:

(1) Engaging in any personal business transaction or private arrangement for personal profit which accrues from or is based upon the official position, authority, or confidential information of the official or employee.

(2) Accepting any valuable gift, favor, or service directly or indirectly from any person or organization with which the official or employee transacts business for the government.

(3) Discussing future employment outside the government with a person or organization with which there is pending official business.

(4) Divulging valuable commercial or economic information of a confidential character to unauthorized persons or releasing such information in advance of its authorized release date.

(5) Becoming unduly involved—for example, through frequent luncheons, dinners, parties, or other expensive social engagements—with persons outside the government with whom they do official business.

The Administrative Procedure Act should also be amended to prohibit federal officials who participate in the making of loans, granting of subsidies, negotiation of contracts, fixing of rates, or the issuance of valuable permits or certificates from acting in any official transaction or decision which chiefly concerns a person or organization by which they have been employed in the preceding two years or with which they have a valuable economic interest. Any violation of this prohibition should be grounds for summary dismissal.

The Administrative Procedure Act should be further amended:

(1) To provide that former federal officials and employees shall not appear before agencies in which they were formerly employed in cases which they previously handled or of which they had some direct knowledge as federal officials or employees and that they shall not participate in the preparation of such cases.

(2) To provide that, for a period of two years following the termination of their employment, federal officials and employees of the ranks GS-15 and above—that is, those in policy-making posts—who leave the government shall not appear before the federal agencies in which they

were formerly employed as the representative of a person or organization doing business with the government.

The penalties of disbarment from practice before a federal agency and of cancellation of contract in appropriate cases should be authorized to discourage those who would corrupt as well as those who allow themselves to be corrupted. Publicity for findings of improper practices would serve as a further deterrent.

Mandatory Disclosure of Income, etc.

Legislation should be enacted requiring all members of Congress, all federal officials receiving a salary of $10,000 or more or who are in positions of GS-15 and above or of equivalent rank, and the principal officials of national political parties to disclose their incomes, assets, and all dealings in securities and commodities. The disclosures should be made by filing reports with the comptroller general on forms provided by him to show income by source and amounts and to identify assets and show their value. These reports should be annual.

The revelation of such information will tend to deter individuals from accepting any income, holding any assets, or making any transactions which they believe are questionable. It will encourage public officials and political leaders to judge their own conduct with greater care. It will also provide for the public and for the great majority of such public servants and party officials whose actions and motives rise above personal considerations the strong ground of truth on which to stand against unfair charges and innuendo.

Thorough Study of Proposed Changes in Criminal Law

The laws governing conflicts of interest and bribery should be amended to extend their coverage, correct inconsistencies, and close loopholes. The proposed amendments, which the subcommittee recommends for thorough study by executive agencies and appropriate congressional committees would, if enacted, effect changes which can be made quickly and which are obviously needed. This action should not preclude a more exhaustive examination of the law governing illegal practices by the Commission on Ethics in Government and more extensive revision which the commission may recommend.

Creation of a Citizens' Organization to Work for Better Government on the National Level

Congress should encourage private citizens to establish a nonpartisan, national citizens organization to formulate suggestions and support affirmative programs for the improvement of government service. The successes of many reforms in local and national government stem from the activity of well-organized citizens groups. To win public understanding of the recommendations of a commission on ethics and to serve as an effective watchdog over the administration of approved measures, such a national organization can be a most effective force.

In addition, the subcommittee recommended that certain other measures receive further study looking to further positive action. These measures include corrupt-practices acts, financing of election campaigns, voluntary ethical codes for functional and professional groups, enforcement of existing ethical standards and codes, rewards for high standards of conduct, the strengthening of personnel administration, improvement of departmental management, clarification of the purposes of public policies, questioning of department heads on the Senate floor, fair play toward administrators and private citizens in congressional debates, and fair treatment of committee witnesses. . . .

7

PROFESSIONAL ETHICS

Émile Durkheim

Pioneering studies of The Division of Labor in Society *and* Suicide *won Émile Durkheim (1858–1917) his reputation as the first French sociologist after Auguste Comte. At first blush, those works may seem far removed from the interests of professional ethics as reflected in politics. Yet, in his work as a whole, there is the organizing theme of the influence of the collective social conscience as the source of standards of religion, morality, and ethics. That theme is reflected brilliantly here in his insistence that a profession is distinguished by its collectively formulated and enforced code of ethics.*

*

.   .   .

WE MIGHT SAY that there are as many forms of morals as there are different callings, and since, in theory, each individual carries on only one calling, the result is that these different forms of morals apply to entirely different groups of individuals. These differences may even go so far as to present a clear contrast. Of these morals, not only is one kind distinct from the other, but between some kinds there is real opposition. The scientist has the duty of developing his critical sense, of submitting his judgment to no authority other than reason; he must school himself to have an open mind. The priest and the soldier, in some respects, have a wholly different duty. Passive obedience, within prescribed limits, may for them be obligatory. It is the doctor's duty on occasion to lie, or to not tell the truth he

Reprinted with permission of the publisher from *Professional Ethics and Civic Morals* by Émile Durkheim. First published in the U.S.A. in 1958. © by The Free Press, a corporation.

knows. A man of the other professions has a contrary duty. Here, then, we find within every society a plurality of morals that operate on parallel lines. It is with this part of ethics we shall be concerned. The place we assign to it in the course of this study is thus exactly in line with those features we have just identified. This moral particularism—if we may call it so—which has no place in individual morals, makes an appearance in the domestic morals of the family, goes on to reach its climax in professional ethics, to decline with civic morals and to pass away once more with the morals that govern the relations of men as human beings. In this respect, then, professional ethics find their right place between the family morals already mentioned and civic morals that we shall speak of later. We shall therefore have a few words to say about professional ethics.

We shall only touch on them briefly, for it is obviously impossible to describe the code of morals proper to each calling and to expound them— their description alone would be a vast undertaking. It only remains to make a few comments on the more important aspects of the subject. We may reduce these to two: (1) What is the general nature of professional ethics compared with any other province of ethics? (2) What are the general conditions necessary for establishing any professional ethics and for their normal working?

The distinctive feature of this kind of morals, and what differentiates it from other branches of ethics, is the sort of unconcern with which the public consciousness regards it. There are no moral rules whose infringement, in general at least, is looked on with so much indulgence by public opinion. The transgressions which have only to do with the practice of the profession come in merely for a rather vague censure outside the strictly professional field. They count as venial. A penalty by way of discipline, for instance, imposed on a public servant by his official superiors or by the special tribunals to which he is responsible, never sullies the good name of the culprit seriously, unless, of course, it were at the same time an offense against common morality. A tax collector who commits some unscrupulous action is treated as any other perpetrator of such actions; but a bookkeeper who is complacent about the rules of scrupulous accounting, or an official who as a rule lacks energy in carrying out his duties, does not give the impression of a guilty person, although he is treated as such in the organization to which he belongs. The fact of not honoring one's signature is a disgrace, almost the supremely shameful act, in business. Elsewhere it is looked on with a very different eye. We do not think of withholding respect from a bankrupt who is only bankrupt. This feature of professional ethics can moreover easily be explained. They cannot be of deep concern to the common consciousness precisely because they are not common to all members of the society and because, to put it in another way, they are rather outside the common consciousness. It is exactly because they govern functions not performed by everyone, that not everyone is able to have a sense of what these functions are, of what they ought to be, or of what special relations should exist between the individuals concerned with applying them. All this escapes public opinion in a greater or lesser degree or is at least partly outside its immediate sphere of action. This is why public sentiment is only mildly shocked by transgression of this kind. This sentiment is stirred only by transgressions so grave that they are likely to have wide general repercussions.

It is this very fact that is a pointer to the fundamental condition without which no professional ethics can exist. A system of morals is always the affair of a group and can operate only if this group protects them by its authority. It is made up of rules that govern individuals, that compel them to act in such and such a way, and that impose limits to their inclinations and forbid them to go beyond. There is only one moral power —moral, and hence common to all—that stands above the individual and that can legitimately make laws for him, and that is collective power. To the extent the individual is left to his own devices and freed from all social constraint, he is unfettered, too, by all moral constraint. It is not possible for professional ethics to escape this fundamental condition of any system of morals. Since then, the society as a whole feels no concern in professional ethics, it is imperative that there be special groups in the society, within which these morals may be evolved and whose business it is to see they be observed. Such groups are and can only be formed by bringing together individuals of the same profession or professional groups. Furthermore, while common morality has the mass of society as its sole substratum and only organ, the organs of professional ethics are manifold. There are as many of these as there are professions; each of these organs—in relation to one another as well as in relation to society as a whole—enjoys a comparative autonomy, since each alone is competent to deal with the relations it is appointed to regulate. And thus the peculiar characteristic of this kind of morals shows up with even greater point than any so far made: we see in it a real decentralization of the moral life. While public opinion, which lies at the base of common morality, is diffused throughout society, without our being able to say exactly that it lies in one place rather than another, the ethics of each profession are localized within a limited region. Thus, centers of a moral life are formed which, although bound up together, are distinct, and the differentiation in function amounts to a kind of moral polymorphism.

From this proposition another follows at once, by way of corollary. Each branch of professional ethics being the product of the professional group, its nature will be that of the group. In general, all things being equal, the greater the strength of the group structure, the more numerous are the moral rules appropriate to it and the greater the authority they have over their members; for, the more closely the group coheres, the closer and more frequent the contact of the individuals, and, the more frequent and intimate these contacts, and the more exchange there is of ideas and sentiments, the more does a public opinion spread to cover a greater number of things. This is precisely because a greater number of things is placed at the disposal of all. Imagine, on the other hand, a population scattered over a vast area, without the different elements being able to communicate easily; each man would live for himself alone and public opinion would develop only in rare cases entailing a laborious calling together of these scattered sections. But when the group is strong, its authority communicates itself to the moral discipline it establishes, and this, it follows, is respected to the same degree. On the other hand, a society lacking in stability, whose discipline it is easy to escape and whose existence is not always felt, can communicate only a very feeble influence to the precepts it lays down. Accordingly, it can be said that professional ethics will be the more developed, and the more advanced in their operation, the greater the stability and the better the organization of the professional groups themselves.

That condition is adequately fulfilled by a number of the professions. This applies, above all, to those more or less directly connected with the state, that is, those having a public character, such as the army, education, the law, the government and so on. . . . Each one of these groups of functions forms a clearly defined body having its own unity and its own particular regulations, special agencies being instructed to see these are enforced. These agencies are sometimes officials appointed to supervise the work of their subordinates (inspectors, directors, seniors of all kinds in the official hierarchy). Sometimes they are regular tribunals, nominated by election or otherwise, and charged with preventing any serious defections from professional duty (supreme councils of the law, of public education, disciplinary boards of all kinds). Besides these callings there is one which is not of an official kind in the same degree but which has, however, an organization of a certain similarity: this is the advocates' association. The association (or "order," to use the recognized term) is in fact an organized corporate body that holds regular meetings and is subject to an elected council, whose business it is to enforce the traditional rules applying to the group. In all these instances, the cohesion of the group is clearly seen and assured by its very organization. There is also to be found a pervading discipline that regulates all details of the functional activity and is capable of enforcing it if needs be. . . .

PART TWO

Standards of Public Conduct

HONEST GRAFT AND DISHONEST GRAFT

William L. Riordan

Plunkitt of Tammany Hall, *from which the selection on "Honest Graft and Dishonest Graft" is taken, has become a minor American classic. It has turned the arguments of the reformers against themselves, and echoes of its wisdom are to be found in latter-day defenses of the professional against the reformer in metropolitan politics. But is there a satisfying distinction between honest and dishonest graft? Or is the opportunity for getting rich on the former precisely what the citizen resents when he mumbles and complains about "politics"?*

*

EVERYBODY IS TALKIN' THESE days about Tammany men growin' rich on graft, but nobody thinks of drawin' the distinction between honest graft and dishonest graft. There's all the difference in the world between the two. Yes, many of our men have grown rich in politics. I have myself. I've made a big fortune out of the game, and I'm gettin' richer every day, but I've not gone in for dishonest graft—blackmailin' gamblers, saloon-keepers, disorderly people, etc.—and neither has any of the men who have made big fortunes in politics.

There's an honest graft, and I'm an example of how it works. I might sum up the whole thing by sayin': "I seen my opportunities and I took 'em."

Just let me explain by examples. My party's in power in the city,

Reprinted from *Plunkitt of Tammany Hall* by William L. Riordan, by permission of Alfred A. Knopf, Inc. Published 1948 by Alfred A. Knopf, Inc.

and it's goin' to undertake a lot of public improvements. Well, I'm tipped off, say, that they're going to lay out a new park at a certain place.

I see my opportunity, and I take it. I go to that place, and I buy up all the land I can in the neighborhood. Then the board of this or that makes its plan public, and there is a rush to get my land, which nobody cared particular for before.

Ain't it perfectly honest to charge a good price and make a profit on my investment and foresight? Of course, it is. Well, that's honest graft.

Or, supposin' it's a new bridge they're goin' to build. I get tipped off, and I buy as much property as I can that has to be taken for approaches. I sell at my own price later on and drop some more money in the bank.

Wouldn't you? It's just like lookin' ahead in Wall Street or in the coffee or cotton market. It's honest graft, and I'm lookin' for it every day in the year. I will tell you frankly that I've got a good lot of it, too.

I'll tell you of one case. They were goin' to fix up a big park, no matter where. I got on to it, and went lookin' about for land in that neighborhood.

I could get nothin' at a bargain but a big piece of swamp, but I took it fast enough and held on to it. What turned out was just what I counted on. They couldn't make the park complete without Plunkitt's swamp, and they had to pay a good price for it. Anything dishonest in that?

Up in the watershed I made some money, too. I bought up several bits of land there some years ago and made a pretty good guess that they would be bought up for water purposes later by the city.

Somehow, I always guessed about right, and shouldn't I enjoy the profit of my foresight? It was rather amusin' when the condemnation commissioners came along and found piece after piece of the land in the name of George Plunkitt of the Fifteenth Assembly District, New York City. They wondered how I knew just what to buy. The answer is, I seen my opportunity and I took it. I haven't confined myself to land; anything that pays is in my line.

For instance, the city is repavin' a street and has several hundred thousand old granite blocks to sell. I am on hand to buy, and I know just what they are worth.

How? Never mind that. I had a sort of monopoly of this business for a while, but once a newspaper tried to do me. It got some outside men to come over from Brooklyn and New Jersey to bid against me.

Was I done? Not much. I went to each of the men and said: "How many of these 250,000 stones do you want?" One said 20,000, and another wanted 15,000, and another wanted 10,000. I said: "All right, let me bid for the lot, and I'll give each of you all you want for nothin'."

They agreed, of course. Then the auctioneer yelled: "How much am I bid for these 250,000 fine pavin' stones?"

"Two dollars and fifty cents," says I.

"Two dollars and fifty cents!" screamed the auctioneer. "Oh, that's a joke! Give me a real bid."

He found the bid was real enough. My rivals stood silent. I got the lot for $2.50 and gave them their share. That's how the attempt to do Plunkitt ended, and that's how all such attempts end.

I've told you how I got rich by honest graft. Now, let me tell you that most politicians who are accused of robbin' the city get rich the same way.

They didn't steal a dollar from the city treasury. They just seen their opportunities and took them. That is why, when a reform administration comes in and spends a half million dollars in tryin' to find the public robberies they talked about in the campaign, they don't find them.

The books are always all right. The money in the city treasury is all right. Everything is all right. All they can show is that the Tammany heads of departments looked after their friends, within the law, and gave them what opportunities they could to make honest graft. Now, let me tell you that's never goin' to hurt Tammany with the people. Every good man looks after his friends, and any man who doesn't isn't likely to be popular. If I have a good thing to hand out in private life, I give it to a friend. Why shouldn't I do the same in public life?

Another kind of honest graft: Tammany has raised a good many salaries. There was an awful howl by the reformers, but don't you know that Tammany gains ten votes for every one it lost by salary raisin'?

The Wall Street banker thinks it shameful to raise a department clerk's salary from $1500 to $1800 a year, but every man who draws a salary himself says: "That's all right. I wish it was me." And he feels very much like votin' the Tammany ticket on election day, just out of sympathy.

Tammany was beat in 1901 because the people were deceived into believin' that it worked dishonest graft. They didn't draw a distinction between dishonest and honest graft, but they saw that some Tammany men grew rich and supposed they had been robbin' the city treasury or levyin' blackmail on disorderly houses, or workin' in with the gamblers and lawbreakers.

As a matter of policy, if nothing else, why should the Tammany leaders go into such dirty business, when there is so much honest graft lyin' around when they are in power? Did you ever consider that?

Now, in conclusion, I want to say that I don't own a dishonest dollar. If my worst enemy was given the job of writin' my epitaph when I'm gone, he couldn't do more than write:

GEORGE W. PLUNKITT
HE SEEN HIS OPPORTUNITIES,
AND HE TOOK 'EM.

9

PUBLIC OFFICIALS OWE A POSITIVE DUTY TO THE COMMUNITY

Franklin D. Roosevelt

During the famed Seabury investigations into Tammany Hall in the early 1930's, Franklin Delano Roosevelt (1882–1945), a Democrat, occupied the Governor's chair in Albany, New York. As Governor, he held hearings on charges brought by Judge Samuel Seabury against certain public officers, including New York City Mayor, James J. Walker, and the Sheriff of the County of New York, Thomas A. Farley. At the hearing in the Executive Chamber, Sheriff Farley refused to explain the presence of large sums in his bank account. After the hearing, Governor Roosevelt prepared the memorandum that is reproduced here in part.

*

. . .

[When] the total of his bank deposits far exceeds the public salary which he is known to receive, he, the elected public official, owes a positive public duty to the community to give a reasonable or credible explanation of the sources of the deposits, or the source which enables him to maintain a scale of living beyond the amount of his salary.

While this rule may seem to be an enlargement of any previous ruling by a Governor of this State, it is time, I believe, that the standard of the conduct of public officer be put on a plane of personal as well as official honesty and that, therefore, there is a positive duty on the part of the public official to explain matters which arise on an inquiry which involves the expenditure or the depositing of large sums of money.*

Passive acquiescence by unthinking people in the actions of those who shrewdly turn to personal advantage the opportunities offered by public office is out of step with modern ideals of government and with political morality. Such personal gain is not to be excused because it is accompanied by the respondent's popularity of person and great public generosity. Public office should inspire private financial integrity.

The stewardship of public officers is a serious and sacred trust. They are so close to the means for private gain that, in a sense not at all true of private citizens, their personal possessions are invested with a public importance in the event that their stewardship is questioned. One of their deep obligations is to recognize this, not reluctantly or with resistance, but freely. It is in the true spirit of a public trust to give, when personally called on, public proof of the nature, source, and extent of their financial affairs.

It is true that this is not always pleasant. Public service makes many exacting demands. It does not offer large material compensation; often it takes more than it gives. But the truly worthy steward of the public is not affected by this. His ultimate satisfaction always must be a personal sense of a service well done, and done in a spirit of unselfishness. Standards of public service must be measured in this way. The state must expect compliance with these standards because if popular government is to continue to exist it must in such matters hold its stewards to a stern and uncompromising rectitude. It must be a just but a jealous master.

Public office means serving the public and nobody else.

Since the hearing before me, I have carefully examined the evidence given by Sheriff Farley, the argument of his counsel, together with further analyses of Sheriff Farley's bank accounts submitted to me subsequent to the date of hearing. I am compelled to hold that the charge relates to transactions arising before and continuing during the sheriff's term of office. I am not satisfied with the explanation of the sources of a large portion of the sums of money involved; and I hold that Sheriff Farley has not complied with the spirit or the letter of the rule which should guide public officers.

An order will issue removing Thomas M. Farley as Sheriff of the County of New York.

* Franklin D. Roosevelt at the hearing; he is quoting himself.

10

ROTATION—A LEADING
REPUBLICAN PRINCIPLE

Andrew Jackson

Elected President in 1828 and 1832 by a coalition of the frontiersmen, seaboard farmers, and factory workers, Andrew Jackson (1767–1845) championed the cause of the "common man" in politics and government. This concern was forthrightly expressed in his First Annual Message to Congress, December 8, 1829, along with an equally intense interest in building institutional barriers against abuse of power. The evils of long tenure—indifference to public interests and a tendency to look on office as a kind of property—fortunately could be overcome by frequent turnover without harm to the common good because public office required no great skill. In modern times, "rotation in office" has become tantamount to "spoils" and a synonym for inefficiency and corruption. Even so, the virtues of civil service may be exaggerated.

*

. . .

THERE ARE, PERHAPS, a few men who can for any great length of time enjoy office and power without being more or less under the influence of feelings unfavorable to the faithful discharge of their public duties. Their integrity may be proof against improper considerations immediately addressed to themselves, but they are apt to acquire a habit of looking with indifference upon the public interests and of tolerating conduct from which an unpracticed man would revolt. Office is considered as a species of prop-

---

From President Andrew Jackson's First Annual Message to Congress, December 8, 1829.

erty, and government rather as a means of promoting individual interests than as an instrument created solely for the service of the people. Corruption in some, and in others a perversion of correct feelings and principles, divert government from its legitimate ends and make it an engine for the support of the few at the expense of the many. The duties of all public officers are, or at least admit of being made, so plain and simple that men of intelligence may readily qualify themselves for their performance; and I cannot but believe that more is lost by the long continuance of men in office than is generally to be gained by their experience. I submit, therefore, to your consideration whether the efficiency of the Government would not be promoted and official industry and integrity better secured by a general extension of the law which limits appointments to four years.

In a country where offices are created solely for the benefit of the people no one man has any more intrinsic right to official station than another. Offices were not established to give support to particular men at the public expense. No individual wrong is, therefore, done by removal, since neither appointment to nor continuance in office is a matter of right. The incumbent became an officer with a view to public benefits, and when these require his removal they are not to be sacrificed to private interests. It is the people, and they alone, who have a right to complain when a bad officer is substituted for a good one. He who is removed has the same means of obtaining a living that are enjoyed by the millions who never held office. The proposed limitation would destroy the idea of property now so generally connected with official station, and although individual distress may be sometimes produced, it would, by promoting that rotation which constitutes a leading principle in the republican creed, give healthful action to the system. . . .

11

I TOOK A CHANCE

Welburn S. Mayock

These excerpts from the testimony of Welburn S. Mayock, one-time counsel to the Democratic National Committee, followed testimony by William S. Lasdon, president, Nepera Chemical Company, that he had spent $32,000 in legal fees in an attempt to obtain from the Bureau of Internal Revenue a tax ruling his lawyers advised him he was entitled to under the law. After many fruitless conferences with Bureau officials, he was introduced to Mr. Mayock as one who "could be helpful." Although four other cases presenting the same question of law were presented to the Bureau, only Mr. Lasdon's received a favorable ruling. Mr. Mayock was questioned by John E. Tobin, Chief Counsel, Subcommittee on Administration of the Internal Revenue Laws, with occasional assists from Representatives Robert W. Kean (R.—N.J.), Subcommittee Chairman; John W. Byrnes (R.—Wisc.); and Cecil R. King (D.—Calif.).

*

. . .

MR. TOBIN: Were you counsel for the Democratic National Committee in the year 1948?

MR. MAYOCK: Well, there seems to be some doubt about that now. I thought I was. I did the legal work for the committee during the campaign without compensation.

MR. TOBIN: On a volunteer basis?

From Hearings before a Subcommittee of the Committee on Ways and Means, House of Representatives, 83rd Congress, First Session, "Administration of the Internal Revenue Laws," Part D, May 25–26, August 3–7, 1953.

MR. MAYOCK: That is right.

MR. TOBIN: During the year 1948, did you meet a man named William S. Lasdon?

MR. MAYOCK: I did.

MR. TOBIN: How did you meet him?

MR. MAYOCK: He was introduced to me by a friend.

MR. TOBIN: And who was the friend, Mr. Mayock?

MR. MAYOCK: It was Mr. Solomon.

MR. TOBIN: How do you happen to know Mr. William Solomon?

MR. MAYOCK: Oh, I have known him for a number of years. He was a friend of one of my clients, and I used to meet him in the office when I went to see my client in New York City.

MR. TOBIN: Was this client Mr. Louis Markus?

MR. MAYOCK: Yes. The client was his company, the Mifflinburg Body Works, but Mr. Louis Markus was the president and I believe the sole stockholder besides qualifying shares.

MR. TOBIN: Was your relationship with Mr. Solomon one between friends rather than business associates?

MR. MAYOCK: Yes.

MR. TOBIN: And Mr. Solomon introduced you to Mr. Lasdon; is that right?

MR. MAYOCK: Yes.

MR. TOBIN: Previous to this introduction, had Mr. Solomon discussed with you Mr. Lasdon's problems?

MR. MAYOCK: Yes.

MR. TOBIN: How did that come about, Mr. Mayock?

MR. MAYOCK: Well, I was endeavoring to raise money which was so desperately needed in the campaign, and he stated that he thought he knew a way where I could raise money; that there was a man who had a tax problem in Washington, and he thought that he would raise a substantial amount of money if I could be of any service to him.

MR. TOBIN: In connection with his tax problem?

MR. MAYOCK: That is right; in Washington.

MR. TOBIN: What was the amount of money discussed at that time between Mr. Solomon and yourself?

MR. MAYOCK: It was way up; I think it was around $100,000 at that time.

MR. TOBIN: Did Mr. Solomon indicate to you, at that time, the nature of Mr. Lasdon's problem?

MR. MAYOCK: No; he said it was a tax problem.

MR. TOBIN: And you said you would be willing to talk to Mr. Lasdon about it; is that about it?

MR. MAYOCK: Yes; concerning employment to assist him in that, for a consideration.

MR. TOBIN: At that time was it your notion that this consideration would be paid solely to the national committee and not to yourself?

MR. MAYOCK: That was the original idea.

.   .   .

MR. TOBIN: Mr. Mayock, in response to several questions just asked you by Congressman Byrnes, I think you gave the impression, perhaps I misunderstood you, that Mr. Lasdon was unaware that he was making a political contribution, is that right?

MR. MAYOCK: Well, as far as I was concerned, my thought was he at all times considered that the money he was passing over was for that purpose, although I did not discuss it with him, and I cannot testify to his subjective event; that is, what was in his mind.

MR. TOBIN: I realize that. Had you led him in any way to believe that he was hiring you as his private attorney in this matter?

MR. MAYOCK: I would say no to that. I don't think that I led him to believe anything except that I might be able to help him, and if so, he was going to have to pay $65,000.

MR. BYRNES: To you or to somebody else?

MR. MAYOCK: To me.

MR. BYRNES: To whom would he pay the $65,000?

MR. MAYOCK: It was paid to me, sir. That would be about the best answer.

MR. BYRNES: That was the understanding in the first instance?

MR. MAYOCK: I didn't think it was going to be paid to anybody else at all, sir, I thought it was going to be paid to me.

MR. BYRNES: You had no discussions with him as to the purpose of the payment, whether it was to pay you a fee or to reimburse you or to be in turn turned over by you to the Democratic National Committee?

MR. MAYOCK: I don't think, sir, as I recall it, that that matter was ever discussed with Mr. Lasdon. It was discussed with Mr. Solomon and with Mr. Markus.

MR. TOBIN: Before turning to that point, I would like to read an excerpt from your staff interview the other day. I asked you (reading):

As far as you are concerned, you are quite clear Mr. Lasdon didn't think he was paying you any money for your services?

You responded:

I am quite sure.

MR. MAYOCK: That is right.

MR. TOBIN: I then asked you:

You are quite clear he understood the money was to go to the Democratic National Committee?

to which you replied:

Well, that is an opinion you are asking for, young man. Isn't what you are asking me the subjective events of Mr. Lasdon? I don't know what was in the man's mind, but so far as I know, that was the situation.

Then I asked you:

Certainly you had done nothing to give him any contrary impression?

Your response was:

No, sir.

MR. MAYOCK: That is right. I so testified or I so stated with you.

MR. TOBIN: You testified also, I believe, that you had stressed to Mr. Solomon your desire to raise $30,000 for the national committee?

MR. MAYOCK: For the campaign, yes.

MR. TOBIN: That was your object?

MR. MAYOCK: That was the original objective of the whole matter.

MR. TOBIN: Did Mr. Solomon then ask you if it was all right with you if he made some money on this transaction?

MR. MAYOCK: Yes. That was after the $25,000 episode. He said, "Well, if we raise more than the $30,000, have you any objection to splitting it?", and I said, "No."

MR. TOBIN: When did you first learn that Mr. Lasdon would offer $65,000?

MR. MAYOCK: When he told me.

MR. TOBIN: Mr. Solomon had never intimated that, and you accepted the $65,000 offer?

MR. MAYOCK: I did, sir. I didn't accept it at the time. I said, "I will see what I can do." My reason for that, if you will permit me to explain, was that I wanted to be certain in my own mind that the ruling he was seeking was justified as a matter of law before I endeavored to help, and if I thought that it was, then I would try to help him.

MR. TOBIN: So that when he offered you $65,000, he then told you that he was seeking a ruling?

MR. MAYOCK: I wanted to talk to his attorney and get the details of what the legal situation was, and that I did subsequently.

MR. TOBIN: Then you agreed to undertake this matter?

MR. MAYOCK: That is right, sir.

MR. TOBIN: Who was the contemplated escrow agent in this matter?

MR. MAYOCK: Well, I don't think there was any person named, but I have a recollection, and I don't know who I was talking to now whether it was Solomon or Lasdon or Mr. Markus, that I did have a telephone conversation where Lasdon's brother was suggested, and I laughed.

MR. TOBIN: That would not be your idea of a satisfactory escrow arrangement?

MR. MAYOCK: Why, no; Mr. Lasdon would probably himself be just as effective.

MR. TOBIN: In any event that idea was dropped?

MR. MAYOCK: It was abandoned. As far as I know, there was no escrow.

MR. TOBIN: You had no agreement with Mr. Lasdon in writing?

MR. MAYOCK: Certainly not.

MR. TOBIN: Why not?

MR. MAYOCK: Well, because I was hopeful that the matter would never become a matter of public knowledge, and writings have a way of turning up after many years and in peculiar places.

MR. TOBIN: Why did you want to conceal this transaction, Mr. Mayock?

MR. MAYOCK: I wanted to avoid the appearance of evil.

MR. TOBIN: Was it only the appearance you were afraid of, the substance did not exist?

MR. MAYOCK: I took a chance, sir, at that time. It was a considered chance. I have no right to whine about it. I needed the money for the party, and they were in desperate straits, and I took a chance, and if what I did was illegal, the blood be on my head.

MR. TOBIN: Was the reason for insisting on payment in currency also to avoid leaving any trace of this transaction?

MR. MAYOCK: Well, you again in your question bring in my insistence as though that were a fact, and I have not testified to it. I stated that it was just generally understood, and I don't think the matter was discussed with Mr. Lasdon, but that was the reason for the cash transaction and not a check transaction, because it is currently known that a cash transaction is not as easily traced as normal transactions through bank accounts.

MR. TOBIN: Well, you will agree, will you not, that the cash idea was your idea?

MR. MAYOCK: It probably was, but I don't recall the statement.

MR. TOBIN: But you do not want to say that you insisted on being paid in cash?

MR. MAYOCK: I don't recall of any insistence. It is not any reluctance on my part to tell everything that occurred and try in any way to forgive or avoid any of the consequences of my conduct.

MR. TOBIN: When I asked you the other day:

Did you request payment be made in cash?

you said,

Yes, I think I did.

MR. MAYOCK: I think that is probably true, but I just don't have a recollection of any insistence of any kind. I think it is more generally understood. Anyway, it was made that way, and probably at my suggestion, but I don't recall the conversation wherein that specific matter was referred to.

MR. TOBIN: You said the other day in answer to my question why you had asked for cash:

Well, because I didn't want any checks floating around that might complicate matters.

MR. MAYOCK: Well, that is in substance what I said again today. I have not seen my testimony. I submit to the committee that in substance that is what I have said today.

MR. TOBIN: I was just trying to get at whose idea it was, Mr. Mayock.

MR. MAYOCK: I have said as clearly as I can that I believe it was mine, but you are asking me to recall something that I don't recall, and I can't do that.

MR. TOBIN: I see. Why was it that you only wanted to give $30,000 to the party?

MR. MAYOCK: That was the original amount that I wanted.

MR. TOBIN: I see.

MR. MAYOCK: Then later when they said, "If we get some more, can we split it?" that was all right, too. That was a deviation from the original character motive of the transaction.

CHAIRMAN KEAN: Why was it $30,000? Was it because the Democratic party at that time was pretty hard up and certainly would have appreciated getting $30,000? Was there some reason to be in a position where perhaps you could get some future favors?

MR. MAYOCK: I am not able as far as I recall to get any favors out of the party any time anywhere.

CHAIRMAN KEAN: The $30,000, was there some special reason for it?

MR. MAYOCK: Yes, there was. I was on the finance committee and they had tried to get individuals to raise certain amounts, and I said I would try to raise $30,000.

CHAIRMAN KEAN: That was your quota with them?

MR. MAYOCK: Sort of my quota, yes, and I tried to do it.

MR. TOBIN: Mr. Mayock, after you had this conference with Mr. Lasdon and Mr. Cann, and you had become familiar with the nature of the problem, and you had undertaken to do what you could, what did you do to assist Mr. Lasdon?

MR. MAYOCK: Well, now let me see. As I recall it, the conversation with Mr. Cann and with Mr. Lasdon was in the early part of July, I would say the 5th or 6th, some place in there. I don't know the exact date, but I think I have it in my diary here. If you want I will try to look it up and get the exact date for you.

MR. TOBIN: We would appreciate that.

MR. MAYOCK: My diary is not complete but is a number of—sometimes it goes on for quite a while and then I miss up on it for some time. I wasn't as good as Mr. Pepys or Mr. Boswell.

I have it as Tuesday, July 6. Would you like the entry?

MR. TOBIN: If you like, go ahead.

MR. MAYOCK (reading):

Conference 1:30 to 3 P.M., Norman Cann and Mr. Lasdon re internal revenue matter. They agreed to give me power of attorney and to give me copy of brief submitted.

That is all there to the notation. Then the next—I was very busy at this time, sir. This was the days just before the convention, and I was in charge of the fiscal affairs of the convention, and I was just overwhelmed with detail.

CHAIRMAN KEAN: You were in charge of all the fiscal affairs of the convention?

MR. MAYOCK: Yes, sir.

CHAIRMAN KEAN: That is quite a responsible position.

MR. MAYOCK: Well, there was a reason for it.

MR. BYRNES: Do you want to explain that?

MR. MAYOCK: Yes. That is, you asked me if I wanted to. The answer is "No" to that.

MR. BYRNES: Well, since you brought it up maybe it would be helpful if you gave us an explanation in the record.

MR. MAYOCK: I had advised, and this was before I returned to any legal duty, I had advised that in my opinion the Democratic National Committee was acting unlawfully in that it did not have a treasurer, and my understanding of the law was that no political committee can receive a contribution or make an expenditure unless the positions of chairman and treasurer are filled, and I think that is in the Corrupt Practices Act.

And so I volunteered that legal advice to a gentleman who had been Solicitor General of the United States and was then United States Senator and the chairman of the committee. Shortly thereafter they filled the position, I have always believed because of my suggestion, with Senator Blythe of North Carolina. He sent for me and said that he knew me from 1944 and that I had—I think he used the words "kept the nose of the treasurer clean during that campaign" and he wondered if I would do the same for him. I said I would but on a volunteer basis; that I would accept no compensation.

He said that that was fine. I said, "The first thing I think you ought to look into is the fact that there is $200,000 here in your treasury that I don't think ought to be in there." I referred to the $200,000 which the Chamber of Commerce of Philadelphia had given to both the Republican party and the Democratic party in payment for bringing the convention to their city.

I pointed out that the sum of $200,000 exceeded $5,000, which was the limit under the Hatch Act, and that it was money from a corporation, which was a violation of the Corrupt Practices Act. I suggested, therefore, that the money be returned to the committee, that is, to the chamber of commerce in Philadelphia, and that a local committee in Philadelphia be appointed to whom the money would be paid and which committee would pay the bills of the convention, which is the current practice in conventions, well, from time immemorial, I think.

He agreed that that should be done. Thereupon he caused a check for $200,000 to be written to the Chamber of Commerce of Philadelphia. I took it and went to Philadelphia. I should say that he asked me what committee should be appointed and I said, "The smaller the better."

He said, "How small can it be?"

I said, "Two. You have to have a chairman, and you have to have a treasurer."

So I was appointed the chairman, and my secretary at that time was appointed the treasurer. We organized the local Democratic Political Committee of Pennsylvania. I had the check endorsed by the Chamber of Commerce of Philadelphia to the local Democratic Political Committee of Pennsylvania, and I deposited the money in the bank and proceeded to pay all the bills.

Is that a complete explanation, sir?

MR. TOBIN: You were looking for another diary item, I believe, Mr. Mayock?

MR. MAYOCK: Yes. Yes, I have an entry here on the 9th; that is, 3 days later (reading):

Lasdon sent power of attorney and letter re tax matter. I can't give it attention until after convention.

That is the note in the diary.

MR. TOBIN: At this conference in Mr. Cann's office, had you made any statements to either Mr. Cann or Mr. Lasdon as to how you would proceed in this Lasdon matter?

MR. MAYOCK: I don't believe I did, sir.

MR. TOBIN: The reason why I ask you that, Mr. Mayock, is this: Mr. Cann when he drew up this memorandum for submission to you and when he drew up the power of attorney from Mr. Lasdon to you and revoking the power of attorney previously issued to Mr. Cann, sent a letter to Lasdon to this effect:

We are forwarding herewith a letter drafted for your signature addressed to Welburn Mayock. As I told you over the telephone, we have tried to make the letter simple but adequate. For the character of presentation Mr. Mayock cares to make, I believe the material supplied is entirely adequate.

That leads me to believe that you had outlined in some fashion what it was you planned to do.

MR. MAYOCK: I don't recall, but there certainly was no secret of what I intended to do.

MR. TOBIN: What did you intend to do?

MR. MAYOCK: I intended to go to the Secretary of the Treasury and ask him to cause this case to be investigated, and if Mr. Lasdon was entitled to his ruling that I thought he ought to get it, and if he wasn't, why, then they should do their duty.

MR. TOBIN: Did you tell Mr. Lasdon that?

MR. MAYOCK: I don't think I did.

MR. TOBIN: Did you tell Mr. Cann that?

MR. MAYOCK: I don't think I did.

MR. TOBIN: Or Mr. Solomon?

MR. MAYOCK: I don't think I did.

MR. TOBIN: You just said you did not think it was any secret what you intended to do?

MR. MAYOCK: Well, Mr. Tobin, I knew and I think they knew as reasonable men that they were going or at least trying to purchase my services as a political figure rather than my skill as a lawyer, and I think anybody who had occasion to regard all the facts and circumstances would come to the same conclusion even though it were not blueprinted and specified.

MR. TOBIN: I see. Did you go to Mr. Snyder, the Secretary of the Treasury?

MR. MAYOCK: I did.

MR. TOBIN: When did you go, Mr. Mayock?

MR. MAYOCK: As I recall, it was some time in August. These books are not very orderly.

MR. TOBIN: Take your time.

MR. MAYOCK: Monday, August 16.

MR. TOBIN: Monday, August what?

MR. MAYOCK: The 16th.

MR. TOBIN: Would you mind reading your diary entry, Mr. Mayock?

MR. MAYOCK (reading):

Made appointment with Secretary Snyder.

That is when I made the appointment, but I didn't see him on that day.

MR. TOBIN: What day did you see him on?

MR. MAYOCK: Tuesday, August the 17th.

MR. TOBIN: What was the substance of your conversation with the Secretary?

MR. MAYOCK: Well, my diary account I guess would be as good as anything; it is better than my recollection. It says here (reading):

Went to Secretary Snyder. Good meeting. I was a little abrupt, but I can't be too diplomatic in a legal discussion. His Department is wrong in their attitude. It is admitted apparently that I am sound legally, but I have no power to force them to do their duty. This is one of difficulties of the administrative process.

.   .   .

MR. TOBIN: Well, the inference which I think is fair to draw, Mr. Mayock, from all this is that on August 20 the Secretary of the Treasury told you you were going to get this ruling. Would you quarrel with that?

MR. MAYOCK: You have the right, as I understand it, as the court to draw any inferences that you wish from anything that I have said. You infer, sir; I did not imply.

MR. TOBIN: You have read the memorandum in Mr. Cann's file which indicates that as of the day you saw the Secretary you told Mr. Cann's office the ruling would be out?

MR. MAYOCK: And I have no independent recollection of it, but it may be so; that is what I said, but I am not drawing any inferences from facts. As I understand it, that is the function of the court.

MR. BYRNES: Would you tell Mr. Cann that unless somebody told you or had given you reason?

MR. MAYOCK: No, I said that I had reason to be encouraged and I conveyed the encouragement. That is the only significance that I have, Mr. Byrnes, concerning it.

MR. BYRNES: And there is only one place you can get that, and that would be from the Secretary himself; is that right?

MR. MAYOCK: Or his office.

MR. BYRNES: Is that right?

MR. MAYOCK: Yes. That is the only contact that I can recall that I made on this matter.

CHAIRMAN KEAN: Mr. Mayock, I just wondered. It seems rather beyond comprehension to me that in the midst of a political campaign, and a political campaign in which it was well known that the party which you favored and the Secretary favored was having trouble raising funds; that when you talked to the Secretary you just did not mention the fact that this man looking for this decision might be a contributor. You are sure you did not mention that?

MR. MAYOCK: I am.

CHAIRMAN KEAN: Because to me it would seem the perfectly logical thing for you to do.

MR. MAYOCK: If it were a private matter and he were not a public official, what you say is quite correct, but many things, sir, are left unsaid in dealing with public officials, and I think that I had sufficient common sense not to go in and make any such statement as that. Like Mr. Tobin, people can infer; I did not imply.

MR. KING: Some people would like to have that spelled out.

MR. MAYOCK: What?

MR. KING: It would be nice for certain people to have that spelled out clearly, but as I understand, you felt that it would prejudice your case if you had come in on a purely political basis; is that correct? Is that true?

MR. MAYOCK: Yes.

MR. KING: Some would and others would not?

MR. MAYOCK: Yes.

MR. KING: In this case you felt the better part of wisdom was to let it go?

MR. MAYOCK: That is true, and I think I would have failed if I had come in and made any blunt statement of that kind. I think, sir—I will take no credit for anything—that it was a matter of skill on my part rather than character which caused me to make the presentation which I did.

MR. BYRNES: It was your legal skill; did you say?

MR. MAYOCK: That is right; my skill.

MR. BYRNES: Legal skill?

MR. MAYOCK: That is the only thing I have, sir, and not much of that.

MR. BYRNES: I thought you told us that you had considerable political skill and political appeal.

MR. MAYOCK: I never said anything about my political appeal. The fact of the matter is I have just exactly none, and that has been demonstrated, as Mr. King can tell you, in my own State where I achieved the distinction for the first time of uniting the Democratic party on a single issue, the first time in my generation they unanimously decided they did not want me for their governor.

·   ·   ·

MR. TOBIN: Did you have any other clients in 1948 from whom you received income in that year?

MR. MAYOCK: 1948?

CHAIRMAN KEAN: That was election year.

MR. MAYOCK: Not very many. Mr. Markus was the principal one. I think I received between $7,000 and $8,000 from him, and the balance of my income was only about $5,000 or $6,000. I remember $3,000 of it came from my practice in Arizona, $1,000 for conducting the negotiations on the sale of some junk in the Aleutian Islands.

MR. TOBIN: You did not enjoy that, then?

MR. MAYOCK: For the most part, sir, from the latter part of May through December, I didn't engage in private practice except that I took care of certain things that were pending, and Mr. Markus was my principal source of income.

MR. TOBIN: He did not pay you this regular weekly retainer all during the year?

MR. MAYOCK: I don't remember when he started, but I think it was in May. He had been paying it, and then there was a lapse, and then I think it started up again in May and then went through the year and on up from that, I think, every week, until about June or July— some time in 1950. Then, as I say, he was unable to pay any more.

MR. TOBIN: You had no income in that year which was unreported?

MR. MAYOCK: Not that I know of, sir.

MR. TOBIN: What did you do with the other $30,000, Mr. Mayock?

MR. MAYOCK: Well, I put it in my briefcase and went to the Democratic National Committee and unloaded it on Louis Johnson's desk.

MR. TOBIN: This is at the Biltmore, in New York?

MR. MAYOCK: That is right; and he was the director of finance.

MR. TOBIN: And did you tell him where you had gotten it?

MR. MAYOCK: I did not. I said, "Here is the $30,000 I have been trying to raise for the campaign," and he said, "Judge, this is magnificent." And it was, too.

MR. TOBIN: I certainly agree with you, Mr. Mayock.

Did you tell him anything about where you had obtained the money?

MR. MAYOCK: No; and I didn't like to answer "No" to questions, but it is sort of an implication on my ordinary good sense. I kept the matter as quiet as I could, and the implication there is that I am a fool.

MR. TOBIN: I am sorry if you think that. It was not suggested.

MR. MAYOCK: That is a characteristic for which I have no desire to be distinguished.

MR. TOBIN: I doubt very much whether anybody would so distinguish you, Mr. Mayock.

What did Mr. Johnson do with this money?

MR. MAYOCK: Well, he kept it for three to four minutes, and then he shipped it back to me.

MR. TOBIN: Why?

MR. MAYOCK: Well, it was not in the form that it could be taken by the Democratic National Committee.

MR. TOBIN: Why not?

MR. MAYOCK: Well, I hadn't submitted any names and addresses of the donors, and it was in such form as to indicate it all came from one place, which would have violated the Hatch Act, because $30,000 is in excess of $5,000. And so he handed it or sent it back to me. I don't think he had it four minutes.

CHAIRMAN KEAN: That was after he said it was magnificent?

MR. MAYOCK: Yes. Then he thought a little and realized that he couldn't take it; and he is a man of legal punctilio, and he passed it back to me.

CHAIRMAN KEAN: What did he say when he passed it back?

MR. MAYOCK: He sent it back to me by his secretary.

CHAIRMAN KEAN: You had gone?

MR. MAYOCK: I had gone, yes. I had gone down the hall into another office.

CHAIRMAN KEAN: And his secretary chased after you with a big bundle of money?

MR. MAYOCK: That is right, sir, just exactly, and put it down on my desk. I put it back in my briefcase.

CHAIRMAN KEAN: You had a desk there?

MR. MAYOCK: Yes, sir. As I say, there seems to be some difficulty now with what my title was. I was actually doing the legal chores for the Democratic National Committee, among other things.

CHAIRMAN KEAN: You had this pile of money put on your desk there?

MR. MAYOCK: That is right, sir.

CHAIRMAN KEAN: What did you do with it?

MR. MAYOCK: I put it in my briefcase immediately, sir.

CHAIRMAN KEAN: What did you do then?

MR. MAYOCK: Put it in a safe deposit box, as I recall.

MR. BYRNES: You were doing legal chores? You were the legal adviser to the Democratic National Committee at that time?

MR. MAYOCK: I advised everybody beautifully except myself.

MR. BYRNES: I was wondering if you had also been very acquainted with the proper handling of funds, as far as the convention was concerned?

MR. MAYOCK: That is right.

MR. BYRNES: You naturally would be well acquainted with how funds had to be handled?

MR. MAYOCK: Yes.

MR. BYRNES: How is it that you, as a legal counsel, should go to Louis Johnson and say "Here is $30,000. It is illegal for me to do it this way and it is illegal for you to get it, but this is how we are going to do it"?

MR. MAYOCK: That is not what I said.

MR. BYRNES: You did not say anything?

MR. MAYOCK: I said "Here is the $30,000 I said I was going to raise."

MR. BYRNES: You were the legal adviser and you knew that that was illegal?

MR. MAYOCK: I was probably showing off a little, a little vanity, for which I wouldn't be vain. I did know it was wrong. That is why I made no demur when in about four minutes it came back into my possession again.

MR. TOBIN: Then what did you do?

MR. MAYOCK: I knew it was illegal to do that, sir. I knew it probably better than anybody I have ever talked to, because, as far as I have ever been able to ascertain, I am the only man that has ever read the Hatch Act or the Corrupt Practices Act.

MR. KING: That is in either party or just one?

MR. MAYOCK: Both parties, sir. I recall very, very well, Congressman King, how in the 1940 campaign, with a ceiling of $3,000,000 as the top amount that a political committee could expend, the Republicans spent $18,000,000 not to elect Willkie, and reported it.

CHAIRMAN KEAN: At least they reported it.

MR. MAYOCK: We reported everything, too. The way you do it, sir, is to organize other committees, and then each committee has a $3,000,-000 limit and you don't run out of $3,000,000 gifts unless you run out of names.

MR. TOBIN: I believe, Mr. Mayock, that I asked you what did you do with the $30,000, after you got it back from Mr. Johnson?

MR. MAYOCK: Well, I was traveling around the United States a good deal and I funneled it back into the committee as contributions from various individuals and institutions around the United States, and I did it in this way: By asking them to make a contribution to the Democratic National Committee of a certain amount, and agreed to pay them in cash the amount of their contribution if they would do so. In that way money came in from various places that the committee knew nothing about, in checks of individuals, and I and the individuals strutted as great contributors, and I got rid of the $30,000 and got the money where it was supposed to go.

MR. TOBIN: And these amounts were also the customarily "less than $3,000" amounts?

MR. MAYOCK: Yes. I advised that, sir, and for the reason that if they are $3,000 or over, under the tax law, there is an informative return that has to be made, and to keep the matter nice and quiet we put the amounts at less than $3,000 so that no one had to make any informative returns.

CHAIRMAN KEAN: Do you believe that action was legal? Do you think that that action was legal?

MR. MAYOCK: I think it was a very close avoidance of the Hatch Act, sir. I would not have asked anyone else to do it. I killed my own Chinaman, and today I am suffering the consequences of it, which will probably destroy me. But I am not asking for any mercy from anybody. I did it and I can't turn back history.

MR. TOBIN: Who were the people who assisted you in funneling this money back into the national committee?

MR. MAYOCK: You mean the individuals around the country?

MR. TOBIN: Yes.

MR. MAYOCK: That I am going to refuse to answer. I will not re-fuse to answer any question that involves my conduct or which in any way extenuates my conduct, but individuals around the United States who may innocently, and in this case with no knowledge of the background of the transaction, suffer the punishment of publicity for my conduct, I think I should protect, and I am going to do it, and, if that be contempt, gentle-men, I want you to know there is none in my heart, but I will take the consequences.

CHAIRMAN KEAN: Do you think it was innocent for them to make a fake contribution to the party? Of course it was not innocent. They were guilty.

MR. MAYOCK: Well, my dear man, I beg your pardon, Mr. Congress-man.

Congress has seen fit to make politics difficult, dangerous, and com-plex, and has made it practically impossible to carry on the functions of the democracy in a proper manner by what I consider a very hypocritical law. I am referring to the Hatch Act. It is a case of an act being *malum* prohibition, bad merely because prohibited and not bad in itself.

CHAIRMAN KEAN: Do you go on the theory that if you do not agree with the law that it is all right to break it?

MR. MAYOCK: No, sir; that is why I am telling the truth, though it destroy me, this afternoon. I don't believe in that, but I was in the midst of a campaign. The Democratic party was in battle. It was an institution for which I had the highest regard and loyalty, and, in a war, sir, you tend to adopt the Devil's ethics, rather than normal human ethics. That is why, though it is in normal human ethics, wrong to kill a man, in war, why, to kill people wholesale becomes a great virtue and to deceive people by fraud in common practice becomes very wrong, but to do so by a mili-tary leader becomes superb diversionary military tactics. It is just the inver-sion, sir, of human ethics, and this was a war, as far as I was concerned, and I paid for my conduct in a deviation of character. That is the fact.

CHAIRMAN KEAN: I am not talking about you.

MR. MAYOCK: Well, you are talking about me.

CHAIRMAN KEAN: I am talking about these other people who per-jured themselves.

MR. MAYOCK: They didn't perjure themselves.

CHAIRMAN KEAN: They sent in a contribution as their contribution which was listed in the files of the Democratic Committee, in the files of Congress, as their contribution, when, in truth, it was not their contribu-tion. Were they not perjuring themselves?

MR. MAYOCK: As I understand perjury, there must be an oath, and you have left out all the oaths, as far as they are concerned.

CHAIRMAN KEAN: I did not mean legal perjury. I meant moral perjury.

MR. MAYOCK: I don't know that there is such a thing as moral perjury. That is a circumlocution that I think is inaccurate. That they were deceitful is true. That they held themselves out as making contributions which they did not in fact make, is true. But, Mr. Kean, as I understand my duty, it is to see to it that I receive—I am groping for a word—the just consequences of my own acts, and, as far as they are concerned, that is a matter of their consciences. If they want to come forward now to substantiate my story and tell the truth, they can do so. I hope they will. I am going to give them an opportunity to do so, but in my oblique sense of ethics, I don't think that having enticed them into the twilight of political practice, I have a right now to disclose their names. That is my position. I may be wrong.

MR. BYRNES: Of this $65,000 fee——

MR. MAYOCK: Yes, sir.

MR. BYRNES: There is no question in your mind, is there, but what $35,000 was a fee paid to somebody?

MR. MAYOCK: No, sir.

MR. BYRNES: It was a fee paid?

MR. MAYOCK: That was taken by three individuals, and I reported mine. I suppose, being honorable men, they reported theirs, too.

MR. BYRNES: It was a fee for performing a service?

MR. MAYOCK: That is right, sir.

MR. BYRNES: So that would be ended?

MR. MAYOCK: That is right.

MR. BYRNES: We have a question, apparently, as to the $30,000. Do you consider that $30,000 as paid by Mr. Lasdon as a fee or a political contribution?

MR. MAYOCK: I considered it a political contribution and operated under that theory.

MR. BYRNES: And you accepted it as a political contribution?

MR. MAYOCK: That is right, sir.

MR. BYRNES: To use as an officer?

MR. MAYOCK: I was not an officer or anything.

MR. BYRNES: As an employee?

MR. MAYOCK: I was not an employee of anybody.

MR. BYRNES: What were you in connection with the Democratic National Committee at that time?

MR. MAYOCK: I was a volunteer worker.

MR. BYRNES: All right. As a worker for the Democratic National Committee, you accepted a $30,000 contribution from a single individual. There is no question about that?

MR. MAYOCK: That is right, sir.

MR. BYRNES: And I do not suppose there would be any question in your mind that that is a violation of the Hatch Act?

MR. MAYOCK: There is no question in my mind about that.

.   .   .

MR. TOBIN: But your position, Mr. Mayock, is that you will decline to furnish the committee with the identity of those persons or institutions who assisted you in distributing this $30,000?

MR. MAYOCK: That is right. That is right, and, remember, an institution only acts through human beings.

MR. TOBIN: May I hear that answer?

(The record was read by the reporter.)

MR. TOBIN: And did you on your transfer of funds to this institution, file a gift-tax return?

MR. MAYOCK: I did not.

MR. TOBIN: In your judgment, no gift-tax return was required to be filed?

MR. MAYOCK: I didn't consider it my money, sir.

MR. TOBIN: If it had been your money a gift-tax return would have had to be filed?

MR. MAYOCK: I suppose so, yes, sir, but I didn't file a gift-tax return for the reason that I didn't consider it my money. I was just, in an indirect and a devious manner and I am using as objectionable a term as I can think of getting the money legally where it belonged.

CHAIRMAN KEAN: Whose money was it?

MR. MAYOCK: It belonged to be used in the campaign, sir.

CHAIRMAN KEAN: Whose money was it?

MR. MAYOCK: I considered it belonged to the Democratic party, sir.

CHAIRMAN KEAN: Because you had already given it to them?

MR. MAYOCK: Well, yes, I collected it for that purpose, sir. The whole genesis of all this sorry matter that I am revealing today was an attempt to get $30,000 to my party, and I did it, God help me.

.   .   .

MR. MAYOCK: . . . I gave you my recollections, and they were accurate when I made them. I think you would find it very difficult if I were to ask you, with accuracy, where you were on the 27th day of August in 1948.

CHAIRMAN KEAN: I certainly would.

MR. MAYOCK: Well, you are asking me that.

CHAIRMAN KEAN: No, I am not.

MR. MAYOCK: Yes, you are.

CHAIRMAN KEAN: I am asking you about whether you went to see certain people on a certain case.

MR. MAYOCK: And I said I didn't recall it.

CHAIRMAN KEAN: Or in a certain period, and I feel pretty certain that I would remember whom I had been to see if it was suggested that I might have been to see a certain person with reference to a certain matter, even though it was five years ago.

MR. MAYOCK: Yes, but Mr. Kean, you are placing the memory of a great statesman against that of a furtive little lawyer.

MR. KING: Mr. Mayock, I am going to have to leave the committee for ten minutes, and it is possible that you will no longer be on the stand at the time I return.

I recollect that earlier in the testimony today you evidently were a bit miffed about the fact that you were being disowned. I took it that way.

MR. MAYOCK: Disowned?

MR. KING: By the Democratic National Committee. Did I misunderstand your remark earlier in your testimony?

MR. MAYOCK: Yes, I was a little disappointed that, having received my services, a subsequent chairman denied that I was doing what I actually did, and I was a little put out at that.

I never expected any glory or scroll or anything of that sort, but, having received my services, I think that the denial of my activity on behalf of my party was a trifle below the belt. That was all. But I don't object to it now, because contempt and disillusionment and ingratitude are the price that an individual ought to know he has to pay for the luxury of engaging in political management.

MR. KING: You, I understand, Mr. Mayock, have said that you were never formally retained by the national committee?

MR. MAYOCK: That is correct, sir, and I never received any money for services from the national committee in either the 1944 campaign or the 1948 campaign, although in the 1944 campaign I got my scroll and acknowledgment and letter of thanks and all those things which are supposed to be ample consideration for the blood, sweat, and tears of a campaign.

MR. KING: I further recollect that just about in the middle of the afternoon, you did not want to be identified as an employee of the national committee.

MR. MAYOCK: That is right. I wasn't.

MR. KING: You were strictly a volunteer?

MR. MAYOCK: That is right, sir.

MR. KING: You had volunteered your services to them for whatever they may be worth?

MR. MAYOCK: That is right, sir, and they seemed to be worth a good deal at that time. As I sit here today, I am pondering whether I didn't do them more harm than good. If so, it was a mistake of the head and not the heart.

MR. KING: Mr. Mayock, in view of this one association with Mr.

Lasdon, would it not be more accurate to identify your association with the committee as being on a commission basis?

MR. MAYOCK: Well, sir, it is possible, by metonymy to refer to a complexity by a part. Thus some people can refer to a dirty diaper as the baby, but it is not. That is the one instance, sir—and I say that with regret.

·   ·   ·

MR. BYRNES: Mr. Mayock, have you had a rather extensive practice in tax cases?

MR. MAYOCK: Not extensive. I haven't had an extensive practice in anything, sir. I am one of those dying organisms in the practice of law, known as a general practitioner.

MR. BYRNES: Up to 1948, how many tax cases would you estimate that you had handled before the Treasury or the Bureau?

·   ·   ·

MR. MAYOCK: Well, as I say, I have been before it about thirteen times in various capacities, and I have advised clients on tax matters over a period of my professional life. I am not a novice, but I have not specialized.

MR. BYRNES: The workings of the Internal Revenue Bureau are not a mystery to you, either?

MR. MAYOCK: Sometimes it is.

MR. BYRNES: The administrative procedures?

MR. MAYOCK: Yes, it is, sometimes, sir, a mystery to all of us, how the rulings are made.

MR. BYRNES: You know the procedure that is followed, do you not?

MR. MAYOCK: I know the procedure I follow in trying to get a ruling, that is, try to get as high as I can and go down.

MR. BYRNES: You do not believe in dealing——

MR. MAYOCK: I don't believe seeing——

MR. BYRNES: You do not believe in dealing with the Bureau itself, if the ruling has to come from the Bureau?

MR. MAYOCK: I don't believe in seeing the janitor first and working up. I haven't been effective that way. I try to do the best job I can.

MR. BYRNES: May I ask you this, as a tax lawyer: Are rulings on tax cases matters of the Bureau of Internal Revenue or are they matters of the operations of the Treasury Department?

MR. MAYOCK: Well, I would say both. The Treasury Department is above the internal revenue service, but the internal revenue service has a right to make rulings and interpret them, by statute.

MR. BYRNES: But you never bother with going to the Bureau of Internal Revenue, as I gather? You just go to the Secretary of the Treasury?

MR. MAYOCK: That is not true. If I had a matter before the Bureau I would try to file it in the proper way, and then I would try to go as high as I could and come down.

. . .

MR. TOBIN: Why would you tell Mr. Lynch when you were appearing in your capacity as an attorney seeking a ruling, why would you tell him at such a meeting, that you were counsel for the Democratic National Committee?

MR. MAYOCK: I guess I have said that so many times, sir, that it is almost a formula.

When I was representing a private client, that is the first thing I always said when I went in, that "I am counsel for the Democratic National Committee, but I am representing a private client at this time and don't hold it against me."

MR. KING: It would not be presumed to do you any harm, would it, Mr. Mayock?

MR. MAYOCK: It wouldn't be presumed, but I wanted to make it clear in their minds, and, if this committee is so naïve as to believe that throughout government expedition hasn't been made at one time or another, why, they are more naïve than their duties. . . .

12

ONE DISHONEST OFFICIAL IS
ONE TOO MANY

Adlai E. Stevenson

In 1952 and 1956, the Democratic presidential candidate, Adlai E. Steven-son (1900–1965), brought a rare elegance, wit, and grace to campaign speeches. He also brought a fine understanding of the human demands of modern public life. He gave this address, "On Political Morality," to the Town Hall Luncheon, Los Angeles, California, September 11, 1952.

*

.　　　.　　　.

AS A DEMOCRAT, as an officeholder, an aspirant for the greatest office on earth, I do not, I have not, I will not condone, excuse, or explain away wrongdoing or moral obliquity in public office, whoever the guilty or wher-ever they are stationed. What's more, I have had the satisfaction of firing and prosecuting a good many. One dishonest public official is one too many. A dishonest official is as faithless to his party as he is to his office, and our political parties must never founder on the rocks of moral equivo-cation.

There have been cases of corruption, of bribery, and of venality in-volving a minute fraction of all of the tens of thousands of people in fed-eral service. Many of these cases have been discovered and exposed—I am happy to say, by Democrats—especially by Democratic senators and congressmen keeping watch over the spending of the public funds. I need only mention here such names as Senator Kefauver, Senator Douglas,

Senator Fulbright, Stuart Symington, your own Congressman Cecil King of Inglewood, Congressman Frank Chelf of Kentucky, and many others. In fact, I induced an old personal friend of mine, Steve Mitchell, who as a public service—one of many—has lately been counsel to the Chelf Committee conducting the investigation of the Department of Justice, to let me nominate him for Chairman of the Democratic National Committee.

And I am reminded of what Justice Charles Evans Hughes said during the Harding era scandals. He said this: "Neither political party has a monopoly of virtue or of rascality. Let wrong be exposed and punished, but let no partisan Pecksniffs affect a 'holier than thou' attitude. Guilt is personal and knows no party."

But there is a great danger in this very healthy public discussion of corruption in government which I hope gentlemen like you do not overlook. The problem of government is the problem of recruiting first-rate personnel. Basically, that is the problem, just as it is the major problem in your business. The reward for honest, able public service is too often complaint, criticism, abuse, and ingratitude. It would be a tragic disaster if we forgot the tens of thousands of honest, conscientious public servants. Generalities about crime and corruption in government, which embrace the many good with the few bad, can only make it harder to induce good people to enter public service. We do not lose faith in the banking system because a few bankers turn out to be embezzlers. When you realize that American private business is swindled out of more than $1,000,000 each year by its employees, from clerks to executives, it is not too remarkable, however deplorable, that government should occasionally be swindled.

For the information of the public and the morale of the multitude of decent, faithful men and women on whom government depends, it is just as important to recognize and support the good as it is to root out and to punish the bad. It bodes no good for the public service where recruitment is none too easy anyway, what with the salary competition of private business, when honest, conscientious public servants quit because they don't care to be abused and ridiculed any longer. I know what I am talking about. I am the governor of one of the largest states in the Union, and I have had my recruitment problems.

Only last week a very good friend of mine—a Republican from Chicago—told me that a revenue agent had been in to audit his return. He fell into conversation with him, and this able young lawyer, a recent graduate from a well-known law school who was doing this work for experience, said, "I am going to quit. I have been treated by businessmen and taxpayers as though I might be a thief, not they."

Look at it not alone from the point of view of its mischievous effect on a gullible public, but also from the point of view of the consequences to the public service as a whole. I wonder how much the people know of the stifling, the choking effect of irresponsible witch hunting, the paralysis of initiative, the hesitancy and the intimidation that follow in the wake of broad, generalized accusations and inhibit the bold, imaginative thought and discussion which is the anvil of public policy.

I'm frank to say I get a little confused about corruption in politics. We tend to think of it as something so simple, in the unsophisticated terms of graft—of cash on the barrelhead. But its forms are many, and I think of another, which we witness every day and to which I have become acutely sensitive in my brief experience in public service.

Perhaps the proper description is not "corrupt" but "expedient" for the legislator, be he in Sacramento, in Springfield, Illinois, or in Washington, D.C., who will vote for all kinds of special-interest bill to catch or to hold some votes while he prates piously about economy, and indignantly about waste.

Call that what you will, condone it as you please, even profit from it as you do now and then, its cost to you is infinitely greater than the thievery and rascality that capture the headlines.

Have you ever heard of a candidate who was against economy and efficiency? Of course not. It is part of the standard repertoire. Everybody is for economy, efficiency, and honesty and against waste, sin, corruption, and communism. But how about the log-rolling, the lobbying for laws or their repeal to serve the interest of some group at the public expense? To catch some votes, or for fear of losing some, many things are done which seem to me hard to distinguish from outright bribery. Yet, we will condone the one and condemn the other. I have seen many legislators vote for every appropriation during a legislative session and against every tax and babble about economy and fiscal responsibility at the very same time, and so have you.

And, what's more, they will be elected over and over again.

In the last session of my legislature in Illinois, I presented a very tight budget that called for no tax increases, in spite of all the cost increases in the previous two years. And, I called on the legislature to not add to that budget without subtracting from it in order to keep it in balance. What do you think they did? They subtracted $300,000 and added $50,000,000. I hope it isn't indelicate to advise you that it was an overwhelmingly Republican legislature in both houses.

The Republican leader, in that session, sponsored and passed a bill to increase all old-age pension allotments 10 per cent automatically, although we have a system of automatic adjustments in accordance with living costs. The cost of that measure we estimated at roughly $14,000,000, but he made no effort whatever to provide any of the money with which to pay for it.

I noted in my veto message that they had omitted from the bill the dependent children and the recipients of general relief—I suppose because they were not organized politically.

I could entertain you at some length with the difficulty I had to get one Republican vote to cut a large appropriation and thereby balance the budget at all, in the previous session. Indeed, if I recounted all my experiences of this kind I am afraid you might get the impression that I am slightly partisan. But I am sure you will forgive me if I say that from where I sit the carefully cultivated impression that Democrats are all extravagant and Republicans are all provident is a fairy tale and part of the phony folklore that a careful citizen will examine carefully.

And perhaps you will also, on closer consideration of the performance —timid, expedient, demagogic, or worse—of a lot of people in public office, share with me the growing confusion about ethics and morals and corruption in our public life. Surely there must be some higher standard and some better test than simple bribery for cash.

I daresay that the only way that we will attain some higher standard of ethics, and of responsibility and courage in public life will be compounded heavily of forbearance yourselves from exerting pressures for selfish ends, plus some positive applause and tangible support for the guy who is playing it straight, morally and ethically, as well as legally, in spite of the fact that you will probably not agree with him on the merits of issues and actions, many times. Indeed, sometimes he may not even bear your party label.

And, bear in mind too, that the special-interest people, especially what we call the hoodlums and the gangsters, are always very free with campaign contributions for the right candidates at the right time.

But, enough of this. Just remember that all that's gold to a politician does not glitter and that to be good and stay in office he needs a lot of help—from people who don't want anything from him except to be good. . . .

13

A SENATOR'S SWIMMING POOL
BECOMES A CAMPAIGN ISSUE

H. H. Wilson

H. H. Wilson (b. 1908), *Professor of Politics, Princeton University, made a careful comparative study of the treatment of corruption in Congress and the House of Commons in the book in which this selection appears. In the United States, it would seem, acceptance of gifts, bribes, and favors may become campaign issues, but not the subjects of disciplinary action in the Congress. By contrast, British legislators have their own standards and enforce them on each other. Professor Wilson argues that this course alone holds the promise of defining and maintaining appropriate ethical standards for legislators.*

*

> *What public official does not accept courtesies? Who objects to a friend befriending a friend? This is Southern hospitality.*
> "Letters to the Editors,"
> LOUISVILLE COURIER JOURNAL.

IN THE COURSE of a warmly contested senatorial primary contest in Kentucky in 1942, John Young Brown, a rival candidate, made public charges that the incumbent senator, Albert B. Chandler, had been the recipient of a swimming pool at his home in Versailles, Kentucky, for services rendered to a government contractor. Mr. Brown first revealed what was to become the theme of his campaign a few hours before meeting the deadline for primary papers to be filed. Then, on July 3, he opened his attack over Louisville radio station WHAS:

> Mr. Chandler attempts to laugh away his swimming pool. With an air of injured innocence he admits that it was nothing more than stupid. I wonder. Can you, as reasoning citizens, believe that stupidity is all that is involved here? There is not a business man in Kentucky who does not know that you cannot use steel, brass, rubber, without a permit. Those stocks were frozen. Was it stupidity? Or was it cupidity? . . .
>
> If a United States senator can, with your approval, accept a $10,000 gift from one doing business with the government, then you have no right to complain if all of your public officials share in future profits of governmental contracts.

Although such charges are not unusual in American political campaigns, Senator Chandler's response was out of the ordinary. On July 1, 1942, he requested Senator Harry S. Truman, chairman of the Senate Special Committee to Investigate the National Defense Program, to conduct an investigation into the charges. This somewhat unusual sensitivity to campaign vilification may have been a by-product of Mr. Chandler's position as President Roosevelt's candidate in this contest. Mr. Brown, indeed, had taken the trouble of sending pictures of the pool and "statements of fact" to the President.

Presumably because the charges involved matters related to the defense program, the Truman Committee assumed jurisdiction and, on July 7, announced that its chief investigator, Matthew J. Connelly, would conduct an investigation in Kentucky and report the facts for committee action. On behalf of Mr. Truman, the following explanation of the committee's action was given to the press:

> Last week, Senator Chandler informed me that an issue was being raised in Kentucky concerning his swimming pool and that he desired to have the matter investigated by the committee. Subsequently I received a similar request from Mr. John Y. Brown, Mr. Chandler's opponent in the forthcoming primaries.

The *Louisville Courier-Journal* had taken a keen interest in the affair from the start and, in an editorial headed, "This Is Important Senator Truman," congratulated Mr. Chandler for his prompt action:

> Judged by this, the Senator apparently wants the people of Kentucky to know the whole truth; they are imperatively entitled to that, and nothing less. The condition of the Republican Party in this State makes it appear almost certain now that the nominee in the Democratic primary in August will represent Kentucky during the next six years. . . .

This same editorial called attention to the fact that in just twenty-four days, votes would be cast in the primary, and the paper therefore urged Majority Leader Barkley to press Senator Truman for prompt action.

Whether as a result of this editorial recommendation or not, on July 10, the senior senator from Kentucky reinforced Chandler's original request to the Truman Committee with a letter to the chairman urging

. . . that the investigation be made as speedily as is consistent with thoroughness, and that the report be made public at the earliest possible date so that the people of Kentucky will know the facts. It is only about three weeks until the date of the primary. . . .

On July 9, Matthew J. Connelly, chief investigator, went out to inspect the pool at Versailles. In public speeches and in the press, it was asserted that Chandler had used his position as senator to obtain contracts for, or to assist in directing the awards to, Ben H. Collings, Louisville contractor, a holder of both prime war contracts and subcontracts. Feeling deeply grateful, Mr. Collings had allegedly built a $10,000 swimming pool at the former governor's home, and, in the process, had violated War Production Board priority regulations pertaining to the use of steel and brass, as well as ignoring WPB Order L-41, which prohibited certain types of construction after April 9, 1942.

The Truman Committee's investigator discovered that Senator Chandler's political opponent Mr. Brown was unwilling to set forth, in an affidavit, the charges which he had made orally and in writing. Nevertheless, Mr. Connelly examined the operation of all the companies involved in the charges against the senator. He stated his procedure, upon returning from an inspection of the pool:

I'm going to get a complete list of all Mr. Collings' contracts obtained since July 1, 1940. Then I'll check the manner in which they were obtained—by bid, negotiation or lump sum. Finally, I'm going to get a complete breakdown of the quantity and types of materials that went into Senator Chandler's pool.

To the Senate, on July 16, Senator Carl A. Hatch, New Mexico, submitted the committee's report of the Chandler investigation.

It appeared that Mr. Collings, the contractor involved, denied all the charges and asserted:

. . . [On] no occasion had Senator Chandler, either gratuitously or otherwise, interceded in his behalf, directly or indirectly, to obtain any contracts involving Government work for any of the companies in which he had a financial interest, and that he had never approached Senator Chandler directly or indirectly to solicit his assistance in obtaining such contracts.

The committee was also informed by the E. I. du Pont de Nemours Company, for whom Collings had provided materials, that Senator Chandler never at any time interceded on behalf of Mr. Collings or his companies. And, from the War and Navy departments, the committee received assurance that "they have no knowledge of intercession or attempted intercession by Senator Chandler in behalf of Mr. Collings or his companies."

As for the swimming pool, the construction of which was the source of most of the charges against Senator Chandler's integrity, Mr. Collings said he had built this for the Senator's family as a token of a long-sustained and intimate friendship. Furthermore, he assured the committee that Chandler had "nothing to do with the construction of the pool" and that its total cost was less than $3,500. (Apparently building swimming pools for Kentucky politicians was a well-established habit of Ben Collings. Lieutenant Governor Rodes K. Myers said that a mere chance remark of his, following the Kentucky Derby of 1941, had caused Collings to build him a pool—he made clear—July, August, and September 1941.)

Moreover, Senator Chandler was accustomed to receiving gifts. After he resigned as governor and was appointed to the Senate in October, 1939, state employees and friends built in the backyard of his Versailles home a gift "cabin" which the *Louisville Courier-Journal* described as "a luxurious clubhouse, panelled in old walnut and rosewood." According to Lieutenant Governor Myers, it was another chance remark of his to Ben Collings that brought forth this controversial pool for Mr. Chandler. He reported the following exchange of comments with Collings:

MYERS: Ben, Happy and Mildred are jealous of my pool. They would like to have one to go with their cabin.
COLLINGS: Is that so? Well, I'll just build them one.

So Happy acquired a pool ten feet longer than the Lieutenant Governor's, surpassing it with a blue tiled top and elevated sundecks at both ends!

John Lord O'Brian, general counsel of the War Production Board, notified Senator Truman on July 21, 1942, that "on the facts disclosed in this investigation (a separate one by the WPB) there is no evidence that Senator Chandler violated the provision of the priority statutes or any priority order of the War Production Board."

Presumably because the "jurisdiction of this committee is limited to matters involving the war effort," no consideration was given to the propriety of a United States senator's accepting a gift from a businessman, the bulk of whose business was with government contractors. But this aspect of the incident was most severely condemned by the newspapers and even by Mr. Chandler's political supporters. It also appears to have had some effect on the Senator's vote-drawing power, and may have influenced his eventual decision to abandon a political career.

The report concludes, "The committee has found no evidence and Mr. Brown has supplied no evidence in any way indicating that Senator Chandler interceded with anyone to assist Mr. Collings or his companies to obtain any contracts." All members of the committee, regardless of politics, were agreed on the report, said Senator Hatch:

There was no dissension or discussion, or anything of that nature which sometimes enters into what might be called a partisan matter. All Members of the committee united in giving to the Senate the facts as we found them.

The Senate accepted the committee's findings without discussion, and the matter was closed, so far as that body was concerned, when Senator Alben W. Barkley concluded with words of praise for the committee:

I think that the committee has rendered a service to the Senate and to the people of my State by the thoroughness with which they seem to have gone into the question, because not only my State but the whole United States would be interested in knowing whether any Senator from any State could intercede in behalf of a contractor who wanted contracts, and by the use of his influence could obtain for a contractor concessions not justified under the rules of the War Department and not in accordance with competitive bidding.

Naturally, Senator Chandler was well pleased with the committee's work; "The report . . . clearly shows that the charges made against me were malicious and false and wholly unsupported by fact." And it is not surprising that Mr. Brown found that the "report reads like a prepared alibi for Mr. Chandler."

Although the *Courier-Journal* accepted the report without illusions —"The Truman Committee did about all that could have been expected in the circumstances and in the time allowed by the late date at which John Young Brown discovered Senator Chandler's swimming pool"—the paper plainly was not satisfied that Chandler had been exonerated. This, generally, was the attitude throughout the remaining weeks of the primary. Mr. Chandler did not strengthen his position when he used pressure of duties on the Military Affairs Committee as a reason for not campaigning to answer Brown's allegations, especially since he had been a frequent visitor to the state and had been able to spend three weeks supervising construction of his pool. In his one primary campaign speech, a radio address from Louisville on July 22, the senator stressed his own morale-building value to the administration: "The president earnestly desires my re-election, Senator Barkley earnestly desires my re-election . . . when you have given me on August 1st a rousing vote of confidence, it will encourage the President and Senator Barkley."

On this occasion Senator Chandler dramatized his role by announcing that he might not be able to make another statement before the election, because he was to leave in a few days on "an important secret military affairs mission for the United States." This might have moved the populace to admiration, had it not been front-page news for several days that Mr. Chandler was going to Alaska with three of his colleagues!

The Senator had been warned by an able Kentucky political reporter, J. Howard Henderson, that his acceptance of Collings' gift had ruined his political future. Chandler's dreams of the presidency, or even the vice-presidency as a stepping-stone, were dispelled by a contractor's gift. "No political party would dare entrust him with a place on a presidential ticket." This conclusion was partially substantiated by the primary results, even though Chandler won 70 per cent of the vote. In the lightest vote since women had received the franchise, the Senator received approximately 134,000 votes to Mr. Brown's 53,000.

Senator Chandler was strongly advised not to misconstrue the results of the primary vote "as a vindication of a public officer's accepting a gift of value from a private individual doing business with the government."

Politically sensitive Kentucky Democrats were in something of a quandary. Should they elect a slightly tarnished nominal supporter of the administration or a presumably honest Republican candidate of the most conservative, isolationist, anti-Willkie wing of that party? Respected Senator Barkley strongly supported Chandler because he felt that the swimming-pool episode, "whatever interpretation may be placed upon it," did not outweigh the senator's usefulness in supporting vital legislation. Although the editor, Barry Bingham, had refused to support Chandler in the August primary and had shown no enthusiasm for Brown, on October 19, he decided he could not support Richard J. Colbert, the Republican opponent. In an editorial, "Chandler the Only Possible Choice," the *Courier-Journal* made it clear that "we neither take back nor attempt to soften one word which we said" before the primary, but now it had to advocate re-election for Mr. Chandler. This was a situation designed to confound advocates of neat black-and-white answers. Which was the lesser evil—to elect a candidate avowedly hostile to the administration or to elect one of questionable integrity on whom pressure could be exerted to support urgent measures? The voters decided that support for a war administration was vital. Senator Chandler was returned with a majority of 43,760 votes.

At no time did Chandler display any evidence of embarrassment or any awareness of impropriety involved in accepting a government contractor's gift. However, it is possible that his political intuition warned him that the Senate marked the pinnacle of his government career. At any rate, he resigned, after four years, to accept an appointment as major league baseball commissioner, after drawing salaries from both positions for six months.

14

A SENATORIAL DISCUSSION

Everett M. Dirksen et al.

As is well known, few rules restrict discussion of public issues on the floor of the United States Senate. The following colloquy took place July 23, 1959, because the Honorable Everett M. Dirksen, (b. 1896), Republican of Illinois, had something he wanted to get off his chest. Evidently, he struck a responsive chord, for he was joined by several Democrats—Senators Herman Talmadge (b. 1913), Georgia, Warren Magnuson (b. 1905), Washington, and Mike Mansfield (b. 1903), Montana—without a discernible trace of partisan disagreement. This dialogue should be referred to again when Senator Clifford Case's proposals (see Chapter 60) are considered.

*

.   .   .

MR. DIRKSEN: [A] hearing is taking place at the present time before a subcommittee of the Senate Judiciary Committee, of which I happen to be a member. One of the bills before that committee is Senate Bill 2374. It was introduced, on request, by the very distinguished senator from Colorado (Mr. Carroll). The title of the bill is, "A bill to establish standards of conduct for agency hearing proceedings of record."

It contains an interesting section, to which I gave a great deal of attention yesterday in connection with one of the witnesses before the subcommittee. I wish to read that section into the *Congressional Record*:

Sec. 5. *ex parte* Influence, Responsibilities of Litigants and Others, (a) It shall be unlawful after a proceeding subject to section 2(a) of this

From a discussion in the United States Senate on Senate Bill 2374: "A Bill to Establish Standards of Conduct for Agency Hearing Proceedings of Record," July 23, 1959, *Congressional Record*, Vol. 105, pp. 140–159.

Act has been noticed for hearing for any person, with intent to influence the consideration or decision of a proceeding, to communicate *ex parte,* directly or indirectly, with any agency member or hearing officer concerning a proceeding which is pending before the agency, except in circumstances authorized by law or upon reasonable notice to all parties of record.

(b) A willful violation of section 5(a) shall be subject to a fine of not more than $10,000 or imprisonment of not more than one year, or both.

Mr. President, when that section is stripped down what it means is that if any person, with intent to influence, telephones and make an *ex parte* communication to an agency member or a hearing examiner regarding an adversary proceeding which is pending, and there is no legal authority to do so under the circumstances, he may be put in jail and fined $10,000.

To me, that is very intriguing mainly because of the testimony of the General Counsel of the Navy before a committee of the House of Representatives, who in his testimony, which I read into the *Record,* said that in our system, even a casual inquiry by a member of Congress has great weight. The words "great weight" in my book can have no other connotation than being considered as influence.

Mr. President, the inference of all this inquiry and this search for ethical standards raises several questions. The first one is this. I wonder whether there are people who think we live in a vacuum in Washington, D.C. I have been calling agencies for twenty-five years. I make no apology for it. I do not know how, otherwise, a member of Congress can serve his constituents in a big, baffling, labyrinthian government in which even senators and representatives in Congress get lost and cannot find where the authority in a certain field rests. What shall the average citizen do? Are we to be put on the carpet because we represent out constituents, make inquiries, and find out what the status of matters is, and so serve our constituents?

I mention this because of what I said in committee yesterday. There are nearly 10,000,000 people in the State of Illinois. The matters in which they are interested are numberless. As a matter of fact, it is almost impossible for a finite mind to spell out the diversity of interests that are affected by and impressed by governmental action, particularly in the agencies. It is said that there are 102 agencies and subagencies in Government that have courtlike powers and powers to adjudicate.

In all the years that I have been a member of Congress, particularly in calling up an agency, I have called up persons whom I know. That is the natural thing to do. If one knows somebody in an agency, he calls him up and asks, "What is the score? What is this all about? What is the status of this case?"

That is the first question I raise. It was not answered at the hearing. A distinguished lawyer was there as a witness. He is a member of a committee of the American Bar Association. A number of lawyers have come to my office in the past twenty-five years who have asked me to make inquiry. The list is so long it would almost be equal to a Martindale directory.

Mr. President, some persons may think we live in a vacuum here in Washington, D.C. But there is not a vacuum, and we are made of flesh and blood. If a constituent from Illinois comes to Washington and asks for information, I am not going to plead the fifth amendment and say, "I have no comment." That is what it amounts to when a member of Congress talks to his constituents and does not try to ascertain the information they seek.

Mr. President, that is the first implication of this issue. The reason for my talking about it today is to forestall this kind of legislation, which will be on the floor of the Senate later, when many questions may be asked and no answers will be forthcoming. I could not get an answer from the witnesses as to whether in a matter before the Interstate Commerce Commission I would come under the purview of Section 5 of the bill in an adversary proceeding, if no one urged me to make a call, but I picked up the telephone on my own volition and made an inquiry. It was stated there were no exceptions. I would be subject to fine and imprisonment. If that is the score, I want to know about it, and I want to know about it now.

Then, Mr. President, I have something to say to the American Bar Association, because there have been many lawyers in my office during these many years, and there have been many members of bar associations. I, too, am a member of a flock of bar associations. I want to know what circumscription there might be of me in my representative capacity.

MR. MAGNUSON: And the lawyers get paid for their services.

MR. DIRKSEN: The senator from Washington is so right.

MR. MAGNUSON: Well, let us put it in the record, Mr. President. I suggested that they get paid.

MR. DIRKSEN: That might have a bearing on the situation. I do not know. But the more vicious implication and inference is the reflection on many officials who work in the executive branch of the government in judicatory positions. Sometimes when there is an airplane accident, as my colleague from Washington can testify, and a search is made for the reasons for the accident, it is said, "There was some kind of pilot failure." Well, we have a pilot failure around here, too.

When we consider the molds in which human beings are cast, we must admit that there are failures under stress. Ministers fail. Bankers fail and embezzle funds of their own banks. Those facts are merely testimony to the frailties and weaknesses God has left in us. They are vestigial things that will disappear through the chastening effect of civilization, but it will take a long time. By and large, those in the regulatory agencies are uninfluenced, and nobody knows it any better than does the senator from Washington, who has handled the independent offices appropriation bill and has seen representatives of various agencies march before his committee year after year and testify. They do a good job. I think it is a frightful reflection upon the ICC or the FTC or the FCC or any other regulatory agency to imply that when a senator calls up and asks an official about the status of a case, the official is going to cave in and consider it as influence. That is a serious reflection on the character of government officers, I must say. They are decent people. They are honorable people. I have always found them to be so.

· · ·

I was in the Congress when the Legislative Reorganization Act was drafted. There were six senators and six members of the House of Representatives on the committee. That was in 1945. The very distinguished senator from Oklahoma (Mr. Monroney), then a representative in the House, was the co-chairman of that committee. I served on the committee. Senator La Follette served on the committee. So did many others. We worked for two long years. Finally, we enacted the Legislative Reorganization Act.

What a to-do there was about incorporating in it an antilobbying title. We did so. For months we searched for language in order to make it effective and enforcible, and, at long last, we put the antilobbying provision on the books. We required, among other things, that under certain circumstances those who come to impress themselves on members of the House of Representatives and members of the Senate—to persuade them, to seek to influence them in matters of legislation—had to register. They do so now. They not only register, but they put down how much they receive by way of expenses and compensation.

It was 1946 when that law became effective. Every quarter, a report is filed. It is printed in the *Congressional Record*. In nearly every other issue the *Congressional Quarterly* features the antilobbying business.

· · ·

Yet I have not heard a speech on the Senate floor on the antilobbying statute from the day it was put on the books, and I have no knowledge that any such speech was ever made on the floor of the House of Representatives.

All of those engaged in lobbying line up. They all register. They all indicate how much money they receive for their services. We take it in stride. Nobody is concerned about it. Nothing is changed. The individuals concerned were not sinister before. We do not regard them as sinister now. We do not have any hesitation about going to the reception room and talking to representatives of labor unions, of farm organizations, of chambers of commerce, or of the National Association of Manufacturers.

What kind of creatures would we be if we listened to them and then let somebody say that we had been influenced, that our decisions had been modified or changed or molded by such interviews? Nobody in these halls ever gets such an impression. A man would not be worthy of his salt, in this body or in any other body, if he could not talk to the legitimate representatives of various interests, have them lay their cases before him as persuasively as they can, and still preserve his independence in dealing with any matter involved.

If we arrogate that kind of attribute to ourselves, then why should we not say as much for those who sit on regulatory benches and adjudicate adversary proceedings day after day? I see them around. I go to parties, as anybody else does. I have a cocktail, as anybody else does. I might see the commissioner of this agency or of that agency at some party. Probably, at times I have asked, at these social functions, about certain cases. I might say, "You have this matter over in your shop. What is its present status?" Is there anything so heinous or horrendous about that? It is the most natural thing in the world, but that does not mean the administrator caves in under any suggestion I may make. If he did, he should not be in the position he occupies today.

Is it necessary to constantly emphasize the fact that we have to have something on the statute books with respect to ethical standards of conduct? People had a chance to appraise our qualities before we came to Congress. They usually take us apart pretty well in any campaign. If there is anything wrong or weak about a candidate, it will be discovered, and our opponents will find it out and will dress it up so that people can understand. We are pretty well screened before we come to Congress.

Mr. President, those who sit in judgment on questions coming before government agencies have been screened, too.

My real purpose in rising today was to say a kind word for those who sit in adjudicatory positions in the executive branch of the government. There will be failures; that is only natural in the whole human scheme. However, taking them by and large, I am proud of what they do. I am proud that they do not cave in simpy because we lift a telephone and say, "Joe, there is a case pending in your shop. Can you give me the facts about it?" They respond. They cooperate, but at the same time they preserve the integrity and independence of character for which they were selected in the first instance.

So we have this matter to deal with in a committee. I have freely expressed myself already with regard to the bill, and I have freely expressed myself to my people. I made a television and radio speech a few weeks ago, carried by fifteen television stations and sixty radio stations. It was at the time when a proceeding was pending before a committee of the House of Representatives. I said, "I want to make clear to you, the people of Illinois, how I feel about the matter. Do not be dismayed, and do not be deterred about sending your problems to my shop if I can be of help. You sent me to Congress. I am one of your intermediaries, one of your liaison agents, as well as a lawmaker. I desire to help you in this big government, which is so colossal, so gigantic, so gargantuan that sometimes it simply baffles all description."

It is no wonder that the citizen gets lost. I want to take him by the hand and help him. Until there is a mandate in the law which says it is wrong and that I will be put in jail for doing it, I am going to continue to do so; and, whenever we put such a law on the statute books, I feel that I shall have outlived my usefulness in the public life of this country.

   .   .   .

MR. MANSFIELD: Mr. President, if such a mandate is put in the law it will mean there will be many new senators and new representatives in Congress. We will not be able to carry out our duties because we will be tying our own hands.

I feel no compunction whatever about calling an agency downtown on behalf of a constitutent of mine who has a legitimate request or complaint. I do not exert any pressure. I have been treated very favorably and fairly by those who administer the agencies, and this applies to both Democratic and Republican administrations.

I would be remiss in my duty if I did not try to do for my constituents everything I possibly could to comply with their legitimate requests. I certainly think this is a part of the job of being a senator. I would be opposed to having any inhibition placed on us in the carrying out of our functions in this respect, because in all too many instances we are in effect a court of last resort, and our constituents have no one else to whom to turn.

I think the senator from Illinois is to be commended for what he has said. I assure him that I stand shoulder to shoulder with him in looking after the interests of my constituents in the calling up of executive agencies on their behalf at any time when I can be of legitimate assistance to them.

MR. DIRKSEN: Mr. President, the assistant majority leader has spoken well. I can add to his remarks by recounting that even in the New Deal and Fair Deal days, when one of my principal functions was to sit on the House Committee on Appropriations and try to chop back the appropriations, which would never make the agencies happy, they were still always very cooperative, even knowing I was on the other side of the fence. That did not mean they caved in. It did not mean they were susceptible to influence. They did not regard an inquiry from me as a deliberate effort to influence them, but they were fair and cooperative in advising me of the status of different matters.

   .   .   .

MR. TALMADGE: Mr. President, first I should like to commend the distinguished minority leader for the comments he has made. I also wish to agree with the comments of the distinguished senator from Montana. I fully concur in those sentiments.

I feel that the constitutents in our respective states send us to the U.S. Senate to represent them in matters of government. If their affairs concern some regulatory agency, I think it is the duty of a senator to represent his constituents before that regulatory agency. So long as I remain a member of the U.S. Senate, I intend to do so.

. . .

MR. MAGNUSON: Mr. President, I wish to commend the senator from Illinois for his statement, and I should like to add something further, so that my position will be clear in this matter.

As the senator from Illinois knows, I happen to be the chairman of a committee that handles most of the affairs of the regulatory agencies and the chairman of the Subcommittee of Appropriations that handles the appropriations.

Many senators have constituents who have problems with the various agencies. Many senators come to me and ask me what they should do. I have no hesitation in helping them out and finding out what their constituents need to know. I shall continue to do so. Some days I think I am a senator's senator. Many of the problems are varied and difficult.

I commend the senator from Illinois for what he has said. Like himself, if I did not do as I have been doing, I would have no reason to be here. I try to help my people and the people of the country when they have problems connected with the great agencies of government.

Our role is difficult. I do not believe that we receive any favors from the agencies. Perhaps they may be a little more considerate in expediting consideration of a case because some senator may have called; but, as to their decisions, I have had as many "noes" as "yeas." I hope that it will continue to be that way and that the heads of the various agencies will call the shots as they see them. . . .

15

CONGRESSMEN WHO CHEAT

An enterprising reporter, Mr. Jack Anderson, wrote an article entitled "Congressmen Who Cheat" for a widely distributed Sunday magazine supplement. His article attracted great attention among congressmen, with the results disclosed in the following transcript of testimony.

*

THE COMMITTEE MET, pursuant to call, at 10:40 A.M., room H-329, U. S. Capitol Building. Hon. Omar Burleson presiding.

Members present: Chairman Burleson, Congressmen Friedel, Ashmore, Hays, Rhodes, Thompson, Abbitt, Everett, McFall, Waggonner, Dent, Schenck, Lipscomb, Chamberlain, Goodell, Kyl, Curtin, Skubitz, and Devine. Also present: Committee Clerks Julian P. Langston and Marjorie Savage.

THE CHAIRMAN: The committee will come to order.

It is likely we will have more members here in the next few minutes but we will proceed.

May I say to the members of the committee that it would seem proper for the Chair to recite the events leading up to this hearing and at the same time, as best I can, put into perspective matters of interest to us.

Information in an article in *Parade* magazine of March 24, 1963, entitled "Congressmen Who Cheat," was allegedly provided by an "anonymous" congressman to a Mr. Jack Anderson, the author. Three or four

From a Hearing before the Committee on House Administration, House of Representatives, 88th Congress, First Session, April 9, 1963, in connection with the *Parade* magazine article by Jack Anderson entitled "Congressmen Who Cheat," dated March 24, 1963.

alleged offenses could, in the opinion of the Chair, constitute felonious acts.

I have the article before me. The first accusation from the "anonymous" source says:

I remember one colleague pulling out a fat roll of francs upon his return from Paris. He turned them in at an Idlewild exchange counter for a sheaf of $100 bills which he regarded as a bonus for the hardship of visiting Paris.

Obviously this "anonymous" congressman purportedly witnessed this transaction.

It is entirely possible that this allegation would constitute a theft by conversion.

Another possible felonious allegation is that certain members of Congress have had salesmen of various equipment concerns on their payrolls in order to pay for items the salesmen sold. This would be a form of "kickback," in my opinion.

Then another allegation in the article refers to a member of Congress who, having prior knowledge of the purchase of certain lands on which the New House Office Building is now being constructed, coming out of committee, telephoned his broker and ordered him to buy the property. It is alleged that within sixty days he made a profit of $4,000. This obviously would constitute an act of fraudulent misconduct.

At a regular meeting of this committee on March 27, the chairman was requested, and in fact directed, to invite the author of the article entitled "Congressmen Who Cheat" appearing in *Parade* magazine on March 24, to appear before this committee and reveal the name of the "anonymous" congressman in order that he or she may be invited to give firsthand information to this committee. Incidentally, the record should show at this point that this committee is not charged by law or under the rules of the House of Representatives with making this type investigation. It is not charged with the responsibility or the authority of overseeing the conduct of members of Congress. In this instance, however, the charges appeared so serious it was decided by the committee that if a member of this or the other body had information as alleged in the aforementioned article, the committee should do what it could to produce the truth.

Under the Constitution there is provision for censure and expulsion of a member of Congress. Article I, section 5, of the Constitution prescribes the conditions and procedure. It is my understanding that any member who has information as to the misconduct or wrongdoing of a member of Congress may in open session prefer his charges then and there. There is no provision in the rules or under law which, as far as I know, specifically refers charges to a committee for a hearing.

May I continue with the sequence of events:

On March 28 the chairman of this committee on the floor of the House extended the invitation by direction of the committee to Mr. Anderson and joined with him were other members on both sides of the aisle. In addition, the "anonymous" member of Congress, as the alleged source of the information for the article, was at the same time invited to appear in order that the "best evidence" rule of law be applied. Now, as all lawyers know, the "best evidence" rule of law is that which requires the person having direct knowledge of facts to give direct testimony. When it is obvious that one with personal knowledge is available hearsay testimony is not admissible. This is true in all legal jurisdictions with which I am familiar. In other words, hearsay evidence is not admissible in a court of law under circumstances in which the witness with personal knowledge is available. Certain exceptions are provided. In this instance, it is per se [admissible because] the "anonymous" Congressman is [not] available.

At this point, if it is agreeable with the committee, I would like to reserve the right to insert the entire article in the records of the hearing, although I have pointed out the more serious charges which, in the Chair's opinion, would probably constitute a felony. I also would like to reserve the right to include in the hearings by reference the Congressional Record of March 28, pages 4663 through 4667.

Following the appearance on the floor of the House, where other members joined me in the invitation to the author of the article referred to, on March 30, as chairman of this committee I received a reproduced copy of a letter dated March 29 showing the signature of Mr. Jack Anderson who accepted the invitation but which placed certain conditions on his appearance.

.   .   .

THE CHAIRMAN: With an intervening telephone call from Mr. Anderson who advised he would appear without the qualification contained in his communication of March 29, he was asked to confirm his acceptance by letter, which he did by letter dated April 5. The letter says:

I accept your invitation to testify under oath before the House Administration Committee on Tuesday morning, April 9, beginning at 10:30 A.M. I understand I will be expected in room H–329.

With the permission of the committee the letter is introduced for the record.

(The letter from which the chairman read follows:)

Parade Publications, Inc.,
Washington, D.C., April 5, 1963.

Hon. Omar Burleson,
U. S. Congress, Washington, D.C.

DEAR CONGRESSMAN BURLESON: I accept your invitation to testify under oath before the House Administration Committee on Tuesday morning,

April 9, beginning at 10:30 A.M. I understand I will be expected in room H–329.

Sincerely yours,

JACK ANDERSON

THE CHAIRMAN: Now, this is the sequence of events leading up to this hearing. As far as I am aware it is a complete record of everything which relates to the matter under consideration.

Are there comments or questions from any member of the committee at this point?

If not, we will proceed. Mr. Anderson, will you please stand and be sworn.

Do you solemnly swear the testimony you are about to give before this committee will be the truth, the whole truth, and nothing but the truth, so help you God?

MR. ANDERSON: I do.

TESTIMONY OF JACK ANDERSON, WASHINGTON CORRESPONDENT FOR *Parade* MAGAZINE, WASHINGTON, D.C.

THE CHAIRMAN: Will you state your name, your occupation, and address?

MR. ANDERSON: My name is Jack Anderson. I am the Washington correspondent for *Parade* magazine, with offices at 1612 K Street NW., Washington, D.C.

THE CHAIRMAN: Are you also an associate of the writer, Mr. Drew Pearson?

MR. ANDERSON: I am.

THE CHAIRMAN: Do you appear before this committee voluntarily?

MR. ANDERSON: I do.

THE CHAIRMAN: Are you the same Jack Anderson who authored the article in *Parade* magazine of March 24, 1963, entitled "Congressmen Who Cheat"?

MR. ANDERSON: Yes, I wrote the article about congressmen who cheat.

THE CHAIRMAN: Mr. Anderson, did a member of Congress, either of the House of Representatives or the U. S. Senate, furnish the information as the basis of your article of March 24 in *Parade* magazine?

MR. ANDERSON: Mr. Chairman, in answer to that question I submit the following statement for the record. With your permission, I would like to read it.

THE CHAIRMAN: Will you please answer the question, Mr. Anderson. Did a member——

MR. ANDERSON: My answer to the question, Mr. Chairman, is contained in the following statement. With your permission, I would like to read it.

THE CHAIRMAN: You can answer the question "yes" or "no." I ask you the second time, did a member of Congress, either of the House of Representatives or the U. S. Senate furnish you the information as a basis of your article in *Parade* magazine of March 24, 1963?

MR. ANDERSON: The answer to the question is a little more complex than "yes" or "no."

THE CHAIRMAN: The question is simple and calls for a "yes" or "no" answer, Mr. Anderson. If you care to answer, all right.

MR. ANDERSON: I think it needs some amplification. I think the press understands it needs amplification, and I think the public does.

THE CHAIRMAN: It is a simple question, Mr. Anderson. For the third time, did a member of Congress furnish you the information on which you based your article in *Parade* magazine? You should have no difficulty in answering "yes" or "no."

MR. ANDERSON: Mr. Chairman, a member of Congress, of course, furnished me with information but there are a number of other sources and I would like to go into those.

THE CHAIRMAN: Your answer is that a member of Congress furnished you the information as a basis of your article of March 24——

MR. ANDERSON: Yes.

THE CHAIRMAN: ——1963, in *Parade* magazine?

MR. ANDERSON: Yes, and there are a number of other sources which I will discuss in full in this statement.

THE CHAIRMAN: Will you name the member of Congress who was the "anonymous" source of your information for the article in question, whether of the House of Representatives or the U. S. Senate?

MR. ANDERSON: Well, Mr. Chairman, I will be pleased to identify for this committee a number of sources who can back up the article that appeared in *Parade* magazine.

THE CHAIRMAN: That is not the question, sir. Will you identify the member of Congress?

MR. ANDERSON: I have at my side and I would like to introduce to the committee the editor of *Parade* magazine, Mr. Jess Gorkin.

THE CHAIRMAN: We are not questioning the editor of *Parade* magazine; we are questioning you, Mr. Anderson. Will you name the member of Congress who gave you the information as a basis of your article we are discussing?

MR. ANDERSON: Mr. Chairman, I will be happy to give all the names if you will just be patient.

THE CHAIRMAN: Will you now give this one name? This is within the rule of law of "best evidence" and this committee is entitled to this character of testimony before proceeding further.

MR. ANDERSON: Mr. Chairman——

THE CHAIRMAN: Will you name the member of Congress?

MR. ANDERSON: You said in the record that you have just cited:

We all have the responsibility as members of this great body to find the truth. My committee is willing and ready on short notice to convene itself for public hearing on these matters. I feel it will meet the approval of this House to say that it is the responsibility not only legally but morally for any person who has knowledge and who can support the accusations in this article to come forth and make it known.

And you were asked by Mr. Avery:

Is it proper to inquire of the chairman what his view is or what the innuendo is if the author of this article declines the invitation——

and your answer:

Mr. Burleson. I would conclude either that there is no fact or else that he did not respond to the call to exhibit good citizenship, and responsibility to come before this committee and tell us what he may actually be able to prove.

THE CHAIRMAN: That is correct and that is now our purpose. Now, Mr. Anderson, I ask you again to name the person who purportedly has firsthand knowledge of alleged acts of misconduct on the part of certain members of Congress.

MR. ANDERSON: In response to your question I am ready to read this statement. The statement does contain the names and the sources.

THE CHAIRMAN: Does it contain the name of this one individual? I have asked you repeatedly the simple question, to name the member of Congress whom you alleged to be the source of information for your article. Per se, it is one individual. Will you name that individual?

MR. ANDERSON: No, there are several individuals, and I will be glad to name them.

THE CHAIRMAN: We ask you to name the anonymous congressman; will you name him?

MR. ANDERSON: I said there are several individuals and I will be happy to name them if you will just be patient.

THE CHAIRMAN: Just name this one. This is the question I am asking now and I don't intend to argue about it longer. It is a simple matter for you to name your source of information and we will proceed from there.

MR. ANDERSON: Well, Mr. Chairman——

THE CHAIRMAN: Will you name the member of Congress?

MR. ANDERSON: Well, Mr. Chairman, it seems pretty obvious that you are backing down on your public challenge.

THE CHAIRMAN: I am backing down?

MR. ANDERSON: Yes.

THE CHAIRMAN: Surely you understood this question before you came before this committee. I ask you again: Will you name this member of Congress? I have a telephone here in front of me. It has been specially installed and is not, as my committee members will understand, regular equipment on this committee table. I am ready to call the member of the House or the Senate whom you name as your informer in order that he or she may confront you here and now.

Will you name that member of Congress?

MR. ANDERSON: Well, Mr. Chairman, it isn't the name of the particular source that matters, it is whether or not what he said is true.

THE CHAIRMAN: That is exactly what we wish to determine. The individual himself should be the witness and not yourself who obviously, from your article, can only produce hearsay testimony. Your article says you were told these things by an anonymous congressman. That means one and only one individual. Will you name that member of Congress?

MR. ANDERSON: What is it that you want to do to him?

THE CHAIRMAN: We wish to immediately invite him before this committee in a confrontation with you. Again, you will name that member of Congress?

MR. ANDERSON: What do you want to do to him, turn him into a pumpkin—poke him in the nose?

THE CHAIRMAN: It could be difficult to punch something which may not exist. Will you name that member of Congress? It is a simple question. Will you name him?

MR. ANDERSON: Mr. Chairman, under the first amendment members of the press are entitled to freedom of the press. That is a great and important right that we have.

THE CHAIRMAN: I do not question your position on this point, Mr. Anderson. If you claim that freedom we recognize it and that is all there is to it. But, Mr. Anderson, let me make it clear again the rule of "best evidence" calls for the person himself who has personal knowledge to testify. I repeat, it is the person himself and when that person is available, which is obvious if there is an informer, under all rules of jurisprudence that person is the person to testify, and it is not for us to accept hearsay testimony.

Now, if you want to name that member of Congress, well and good. If you do not, your position under the Constitution in not naming him is considered by the Chair to be valid.

Let me further say, as you doubtless have been advised and know firsthand—since I understand you have appeared before congressional committees previously—you know you are in a privileged position here in this committee hearing. Although you are here on your own volition, at our invitation and under oath, nevertheless you are privileged, for libel as I understand it. Whereas, in your column or in magazine articles you are not privileged. And so this committee does not intend to furnish a forum for hearsay testimony in which members of Congress who are not here cannot defend themselves. They are indicted in the press when they are accused. Even a criminal is considered to be innocent until his guilt is established by legal and competent evidence.

Now, I understand you decline to name the member of Congress under constitutional privilege of freedom of the press. Is that correct?

MR. ANDERSON: I decline to name the anonymous member, but I am glad to name for the committee several other sources with better information. I am glad to give the committee evidence that is far better.

THE CHAIRMAN: Your article certainly made no such distinction. You, by this admission, used a low-grade source of information. What you have just said indicates you were willing to indict the entire Congress on a source of second class and rumored reports.

This committee is adjourned.

MR. ANDERSON: I decline to name the anonymous member, but I

THE CHAIRMAN: If you wish to pursue this matter I suggest you take your hearsay testimony to the district grand jury. Grand juries are secret bodies and can receive whatever information they deem necessary for an investigation of whatever nature.

We shall continue our inquiry through the Justice Department and General Accounting Office, to determine any transactions of record which may cast any light on charges made in the article heretofore identified.

This committee is adjourned.

(Thereupon, the hearing was concluded.)

16

THE INIQUITY OF PRINCIPAL MEN

Henry St. John Bolingbroke

Henry St. John, Viscount Bolingbroke (1698–1751), was a Tory leader and favorite of the Duke of Marlborough. He was implicated in a plot to restore a Stuart to the throne of England and, on the death of Queen Anne, impeached. He fled to France before trial and attainder by Parliament. Pardoned by George I in 1723, with the assistance of a bribe, he returned to England and political influence. He retired from politics in 1735 to write. One aspect of his view of a "Tory Democracy," later admired by Disraeli, is presented in the discussion of the true iniquity of the corrupt public servant. What he wrote gained a certain authenticity from his own career, which earned him a reputation as a profligate who could not be trusted.

*

THE INIQUITY OF ALL the principal men in any community, of kings and ministers especially, does not consist alone in the crimes they commit and in the immediate consequence of these crimes; and therefore their guilt is not to be measured by these alone. Such men sin against posterity, as well as against their own age; and, when the consequences of their crimes are over, the consequences of their example remain. I think, and every wise and honest man in generations yet unborn will think if the history of ————'s administration descends to blacken our annals that the greatest iniquity of the minister, on whom the whole iniquity ought to be charged —since he has been so long in possession of the whole power—is the constant endeavor he has employed to corrupt the morals of men. I say, thus

---

From "Letters on the Spirit of Patriotism: On the Idea of a Patriot King: And on the State of Parties at the Accession of King George I" (London, Eng.: 1749).

generally, the morals, because he who abandons or betrays his country will abandon or betray his friends and because he who is prevailed on to act in parliament, without any regard for truth or justice, will easily prevail on himself to act in the same manner everywhere else.

A wiser and more honest administration may relieve our trade from that oppression and the public from that load of debt under which it must be supposed that he has industriously kept it; because we are able, by bare calculations, that he might have provided effectually for the payment of it, since he came to the head of the treasury. A wiser and more honest administration may draw us back to our former credit and influence abroad, from that state of contempt to which we have sunk among our neighbors. But will the minds of men, which this minister has narrowed to personal regards alone, will their views, which he has confined to the present moment—as if nations were mortal like the men who compose them and Britain were to perish with her degenerate children—will these, I say, be so easily or so soon enlarged? Will their sentiments— which are debased from the love of liberty, from zeal for the honor and prosperity of their country, and from a desire of honest fame, to an absolute unconcernedness for all these, to an abject submission, and to a rapacious eagerness after wealth that may sate their avarice and exceed the profusion of their luxury—will these, I say again, be so easily, or so soon elevated? In a word, will the British spirit, that spirit which has preserved liberty hitherto in one corner of the world at least, be so easily or so soon reinfused into the British nation? I think not.

We have been long coming to this point of depravation; and the progress from confirmed habits of evil is much slower than the progress to them. Virtue is not placed on a rugged mountain of difficult and dangerous access, as they who would excuse the indolence of their temper or the perverseness of their will desire to have it believed; but she is seated, however, on an eminence. We may go up to her with ease, but we must go up gradually, according to the natural progression of reason, which is to lead the way and to guide our steps. On the other hand, if we fall from thence, we are sure to be hurried down the hill with a blind impetuosity, according to the natural balance of those appetites and passions that caused our fall at first, and urged on the faster the further they are removed from the control that before restrained them.

To perform, therefore, so great a work as to reinfuse the spirit of liberty, to reform the morals, to raise the sentiments of a people, much time is required; and a work which requires so much time may too probably be never completed, considering how unsteadily and how unsystematically even the best of men are apt often to proceed and how this reformation is to be carried forward in opposition to public fashion and private inclination, to the authority of the men in power, and to the secret bent on many of those who are out of power. Let us not flatter ourselves; I did so too long. It is more to be wished than to be hoped that the contagion should spread no further than that leprous race who carry on their skins, exposed to public sight, the scabs and blotches of their distemper. The minister preaches corruption aloud and constantly, like an impudent missionary of vice, and some there are who not only insinuate, but teach the same occasionally. I say some, because I am as far from thinking that all those who join with him as that any of those who oppose him wait only to be more authorized that they may propagate it with greater success and apply it to their own use, in their turn.

It seems to me, on the whole matter, that to say he will redeem a nation under such circumstances from perdition, nothing less is necessary than some great, some extraordinary conjuncture of ill fortune, or of good, which may purge, yet so as by fire. Distress from abroad, bankruptcy at home, and other circumstances of like nature and tendency may beget universal confusion. Out of confusion, order may arise; but it may be the order of a wicked tyranny, instead of the order of a just monarchy. Either may happen, and such an alternative, at the disposition of fortune, is sufficient to make a stoic tremble! We may be saved, indeed, by means of a very different kind; but these means will not offer themselves, this way of salvation will not be open to us, without the concurrence and the influence of a patriot king, the most uncommon of all phenomena in the physical or moral world. . . .

17

THE GARDEN IN THE MOUNTAINS

Ignatius Donnelly

Ignatius Donnelly (1831–1901) had an extensive political career in the Minnesota legislature and in Congress and was a founder of the Populist party. An ardent reformer, his reaction to the lack of success attending his efforts on behalf of the underdog is reflected in the general tone of his popular utopian novel, Caesar's Column: A Story of the Twentieth Century, *published in 1890. The fragment presented here, however, is from a description of an ideal community in Africa to which the narrator retreats when the civilized world collapses in destructive horror.*

*

THE HIGHEST OFFENSE known to our laws is treason against the state, and this consists not only in levying war against the government, but in corrupting the voter or the officeholder; or in the voter or the officeholder selling his vote or his services. For these crimes the penalty is death. But, as they are in their very nature secret offenses, we provide, in these cases only, for three forms of verdict: *guilty, not guilty,* and *suspected.* This latter verdict applies to cases where the jury are morally satisfied, from the surrounding circumstances, that the man is guilty, although there is not enough direct and positive testimony to convict him. The jury then has the power—not as a punishment to the man, but for the safety of the community—to declare him incapable of voting or holding office for a period of not less than one, nor more than five, years. We rank bribery and corruption as high treason, because experience has demonstrated that they are more deadly in their consequences to a people than open war against the government, and many times more so than murder.

PART THREE

Political Motives

18

POLITICS

H. L. Mencken

In H. L. Mencken's (1880–1956) reckoning, politicians were deserving of even less respect than authors. On the whole, he expressed views of politics and politicians that were nearly as conventional as apple pie. Occasionally, his random broadsides hit targets worthy of his skill. As late as 1964, the senatorial candidacies of Robert F. Kennedy in New York and Pierre Salinger in California raised cries of "carpetbagger," reminding us that political parochialism has by no means disappeared, and making Mr. Mencken's discussion of the issue relevant.

*

> No person shall be a Representative who . . . shall not, when elected, be an inhabitant of that State in which he shall be chosen. . . . No person shall be a Senator who . . . shall not, when elected, be an inhabitant of that State for which he shall be chosen.

SPECIALISTS in political archaeology will recognize these sentences; they are from Article I, sections 2 and 3, of the constitution of the United States. I have heard and forgotten how they got there; no doubt the cause lay in the fierce jealousy of the states. But whatever the fact, I have a notion that there are few provisions of the constitution that have had a more profound effect on the character of practical politics in the Republic, or, indirectly, on the general color of American thinking in the political department. They have made steadily for parochialism in legislation, for

From H. L. Mencken's "Politics" in *Civilization in the United States,* edited by Harold E. Stearns. Reprinted by permission of Harcourt Brace & World, Inc.

the security and prosperity of petty local bosses and machines, for the multiplication of pocket and rotten boroughs of the worst sort, and, above all, for the progressive degeneration of the honesty and honor of representatives. They have greased the ways for the trashy and ignoble fellow who aspires to get into Congress, and they have blocked them for the man of sense, dignity, and self-respect. More, perhaps, than any other single influence they have been responsible for the present debauched and degraded condition of the two houses, and particularly of the lower one. Find me the worst ass in Congress, and I'll show you a man they have helped to get there and to stay there. Find me the most shameless scoundrel, and I'll show you another.

No such centripedal mandate, as far as I have been able to discover, is in the fundamental law of any other country practicing the representative system. An Englishman, if ambition heads him toward St. Stephen's,* may go hunting for a willing constituency wherever the hunting looks best, and if he fails in the Midlands he may try again in the South, or in the North, or in Scotland or Wales. A Frenchman of like dreams has the same privilege; the only condition, added after nineteen years of the Third Republic, is that he may not be a candidate in two or more *arrondissements* at once. And so with a German, an Italian, or a Spaniard; but, not so with an American. He must be an actual inhabitant of the state he aspires to represent at Washington. More, he must be, in all save extraordinary cases, an actual inhabitant of the congressional district— for here, by a characteristic American process, the fundamental law is sharpened by custom. True enough, this last requirement is not laid down by the constitution. It would be perfectly legal for the thirty-fifth New York district, centering at Syracuse, to seek its congressman in Manhattan or even at Sing Sing. In various iconoclastic states, in fact, the thing has been occasionally done. But not often; not often enough to produce any appreciable effect. The typical congressman remains a purely local magnifico, the gaudy cock of some small and usually far from appetizing barnyard. His rank and dignity as a man are measured by provincial standards of the most puerile sort, and his capacity to discharge the various and onerous duties of his office is reckoned almost exclusively in terms of his ability to hold his grip on the local party machine.

If he has genuine ability, it is a sort of accident. If he is thoroughly honest, it is next door to a miracle. Of the 430-odd representatives who carry on so diligently and obscenely at Washington, making laws and determining policies for the largest free nation ever seen in the world, there are not two dozen whose views on any subject under the sun carry any weight whatsoever outside their own bailiwicks, and there are not a dozen who rise to anything approaching unmistakable force and origi-

* A chapel at Westminster Palace used from 1547 to 1834 for meetings of the House of Commons; hence, a synonym for House of Commons.

nality. They are, in the overwhelming main, shallow fellows, ignorant of the grave matters they deal with and too stupid to learn. If, as is often proposed, the United States should adopt the plan of parliamentary responsibility and the ministry should be recruited from the lower house, then it would be difficult, without a radical change in election methods, to fetch up even such pale talents and modest decencies as were assembled for their cabinets by Wilson and Harding. The better sort of congressmen, to be sure, acquire after long service a good deal of technical proficiency. They know the traditions and precedents of the two houses; they can find their way in and out of every rathole in the Capitol; they may be trusted to carry on the legislative routine in a more or less shipshape manner. Of such sort are the specialists paraded in the newspapers—on the tariff, on military affairs, on foreign relations, and so on. They come to know, in time, almost as much as a Washington correspondent or one of their own committee clerks. But the average congressman lifts himself to no such heights of sagacity. He is content to be led by the fuglemen and bell-wethers. Examine him at leisure, and you will find that he is incompetent and imbecile [and] also incurably dishonest. The first principles of civilized law-making are quite beyond him; he ends, as he began, a local politician, interested only in jobs. His knowledge is that of a third-rate country lawyer—which he often is in fact. His intelligence is that of a country newspaper editor or evangelical divine. His standards of honor are those of a country banker—which he also often is. To demand sense of such a man, or wide and accurate information, or a delicate feeling for the public and private proprieties, is to strain his parts beyond endurance.

The constitution, of course, stops with Congress, but its influence is naturally powerful within the states, and one finds proofs of the fact on all sides. It is taking an herculean effort everywhere to break down even the worst effects of this influence; the prevailing tendency is still to discover a mysterious virtue in the officeholder who was born and raised in the state, or county, or city, or ward. The judge must come from the bar of the court he is to adorn; the mayor must be part and parcel of the local machine; even technical officers, such as engineers and health commissioners, lie under the constitutional blight. The thing began as a belief in local self-government, the oldest of all the sure cures for despotism. But it has gradually taken on the character of government by local politicians, which is to say, by persons quite unable to comprehend the most elemental problems of state and nation and unfitted by nature to deal with them honestly and patriotically, even if they could comprehend them. Just as prohibition was forced on the civilized minorities collected in the great cities against their most vigorous and persistent opposition, so the same minorities, when it comes to intrastate affairs, are constantly at the mercy of predatory bands of rural politicians. If there is any large American city whose peculiar problems are dealt with competently and justly by its state legislature, then I must confess that twenty years in journalism have left me ignorant of it. An unending struggle for fairer dealing goes on in every state that has large cities, and every concession to their welfare is won only at the cost of gigantic effort. The state legislature is never intelligent; it represents only the average mind of the county bosses, whose sole concern is with jobs. The machines that they represent are wholly political, but they have no political principles in any rational sense. Their one purpose and function is to maintain their adherents in the public offices or to obtain for them in some other way a share of the state funds. They are quite willing to embrace any new doctrine, however fantastic, or to abandon any old one, however long supported, if only the business will promote their trade and so secure their power.

This concentration of the ultimate governmental authority in the hands of small groups of narrow, ignorant, and unconscionable manipulators tends inevitably to degrade the actual officeholder, or, what is the same thing, to make office-holding prohibitive to all men not already degraded. It is almost impossible to imagine a man of genuine self-respect and dignity offering himself as a candidate for the lower house—or, since the direct primary and direct elections brought it down to the common level, for the upper house—in the average American constituency. His necessary dealings with the electors themselves and with the idiots who try more or less honestly to lead them would be revolting enough, but even worse would be his need of making terms with the professional politicians of his party—the bosses of the local machine. These bosses naturally make the most of the constitutional limitation; it works powerfully in their favor. A local notable, in open revolt against them, may occasionally beat them by appealing directly to the voters, but nine times out of ten, when there is any sign of such a catastrophe, they are prompt to perfume the ticket by bringing forth another local notable who is safe and sane, which is to say, subservient and reliable. The thing is done constantly; it is a matter of routine; it accounts for most of the country bankers, newspaper owners, railroad lawyers, proprietors of cement works, and other such village bigwigs in the lower house. Here, everything runs to the advantage of the bosses. It is not often that the notable in rebellion is gaudy enough to blind the plain people to the high merits of his more docile opponent. They see him too closely and know him too well. He shows none of that exotic charm which accounts, on a different plane, for exogamy. There is no strangeness, no mysteriousness, above all, no novelty about him.

It is my contention that this strangle hold of the local machines would be vastly less firm if it could be challenged, not only by rebels within the constituency, but also by salient men from outside. The presidential campaigns, indeed, offer plenty of direct proof of it. In these campaigns, it is a commonplace for strange doctrines and strange men to force themselves on the practical politicians in whole sections of the country, despite their constant effort to keep their followers faithful to the known. All changes, of whatever sort, whether in leaders or in ideas, are opposed by such politicians at the start, but time after time they are compelled to acquiesce and to hurrah. Bryan, as every one knows, forced himself on the Democratic party by appealing directly to the people; the politicians, in the main, were bitterly against him until further resistance was seen to be useless, and they attacked him again the moment he began to weaken and finally disposed of him. So with Wilson. It would be absurd to say that the politicians of his party—and especially the bosses of the old machines in the congressional districts—were in favor of him in 1912. They were actually against him almost unanimously. He got past their guard and broke down their resolution to nominate some more trustworthy candidate by operating directly on the emotions of the voters. For some reason never sufficiently explained, he became the heir of the spirit of rebellion raised by Bryan sixteen years before and was given direct and very effective aid by Bryan himself. [Theodore] Roosevelt saddled himself on the Republican party in exactly the same way. The bosses made heroic efforts to sidetrack him, to shelve him, to get rid of him by any means short of homicide, but his bold enterprises and picturesque personality enchanted the people, and, if it had not been for the extravagant liberties that he took with his popularity in later years, he might have retained it until his death.

The same possibility of unhorsing the machine politicians, I believe, exists in even the smallest electoral unit. All that is needed is the chance to bring in the man. Podunk cannot produce him herself, save by a sort of miracle. If she has actually hatched him, he is far away by the time he has come to his full stature and glitter—in the nearest big city, in Chicago or New York. Podunk is proud of him, and many other Podunks, perhaps, are stirred by his ideas, his attitudes, his fine phrases, but he lives, say, in some Manhattan congressional district which has the Hon. Patrick Googan as its representative by divine right, and so there is no way to get him into the halls of Congress. In his place goes the Hon. John P. Balderdash, state's attorney for five years, state senator for two terms, and county judge for a brief space—and always a snide and petty fellow, always on the best of terms with the local bosses, always eager for a job on any terms they lay down. The yokels vote for the Hon. [John P.] Balderdash, not because they admire him, but because their only choice is between him and the Hon. James Bosh. If anything even remotely resembling a first-rate man could come into the contest, if it were lawful for them to rid themselves of their recurrent dilemma by soliciting the interest of such a man, then they would often enough rise in their might and compel their parish overlords, as the English put it, to adopt him. But the constitution protects these overlords in their business, and, in the long run, the voters resign all thought of deliverance. Thus, the combat remains one between small men, and interest in it dies out. Most of the men who go to the lower house are third-raters, even in their own narrow bailiwicks. In my own congressional district, part of a large city, there has never been a candidate of any party, during the twenty years that I have voted, who was above the intellectual level of a corner grocer. No successful candidate of that district has ever made a speech in Congress (or out of it) worth hearing or contributed a single sound idea otherwise to the solution of any public problem. One and all, they have confined themselves exclusively to the trade in jobs. One and all, they have been ciphers in the house and before the country. . . .

19

GLORY AND POWER

Saint Augustine

Augustine (354–430) is perhaps best known for his Confessions, *a classic of Christianity. But in his* City of God, *from which the following selection was made, he expounded a Christian view of history. It was his belief that God was preparing two cities for all mankind: one of God and one of the Devil. In the selection presented here, he has attempted to distinguish between a desire for glory and a desire for domination, implying that the choice of ends has consequences for choice of means as well. The interested student may wish to compare Augustine's observations with those of latterday students of politics.**

*

. . .

THERE IS ASSUREDLY a difference between the desire of human glory and the desire of domination; for, though he who has an overweening delight in human glory will be also very prone to aspire earnestly after domination, nevertheless they who desire the true glory even of human praise strive not to displease those who judge well of them. For there are many good moral qualities, of which many are competent judges, although they are not possessed by many; and, by those good moral qualities, those men press on to glory, honor, and domination, of whom Sallust says, "But they press on by the true way."

From Henry Paolucci, ed., *The Political Writings of St. Augustine* (Chicago, Ill.: Henry Regnery Co., 1962), *City of God,* v, 15–22. Introduction and organization of text copyright 1962 by Henry Regnery Co.

　* See, for example, Arnold A. Rogow and Harold D. Lasswell, *Power, Corruption, and Rectitude* (Englewood Cliffs, N.J.: Prentice-Hall, Inc., 1963).

But whosoever, without possessing that desire of glory which makes one fear to displease those who judge his conduct, desires domination and power, very often seeks to obtain what he loves by most open crimes. Therefore, he who desires glory presses on to obtain it either by the true way, or certainly by deceit and artifice, wishing to appear good when he is not. Therefore, to him who possesses virtues, it is a great virtue to despise glory; for contempt of it is seen by God, but is not manifest to human judgment. For whatever anyone does before the eyes of men in order to show himself to be a despiser of glory, if they suspect that he is doing it in order to get greater praise—that is, greater glory—he has no means of demonstrating to the perceptions of those who suspect him that the case is really otherwise than they suspect it to be. But he who despises the judgment of praisers, despises also the rashness of suspectors. Their salvation, indeed, he does not despise, if he is truly good; for so great is the righteousness of that man who receives his virtues from the spirit of God, that he loves his very enemies and so loves them that he desires that his haters and detractors may be turned to righteousness and become his associates, and that not in an earthly but in a heavenly country. But with respect to his praisers, though he sets little value on their praise, he does not set little value on their love; neither does he elude their praise, lest he should forfeit their love. And, therefore, he strives earnestly to have their praises directed to Him from whom everyone receives whatever in him is truly praiseworthy. But he who is a despiser of glory, but is greedy of domination, exceeds the beasts in the vices of cruelty and luxuriousness. Such, indeed, were certain of the Romans, who, wanting the love of esteem, wanted not the thirst for domination; and that there were many such, history testifies. But it was Nero Caesar who was the first to reach the summit, and, as it were, the citadel, of this vice; for so great was his luxuriousness that one would have thought there was nothing manly to be dreaded in him, and such his cruelty that, had not the contrary been known, no one would have thought there was anything effeminate in his character. Nevertheless, power and domination are not given even to such men save by the providence of the most high God, when He judges that the state of human affairs is worthy of such lords. The divine utterance is clear on this matter; for the wisdom of God thus speaks: "By me kings reign, and tyrants possess the land." But, that it may not be thought that by "tyrants" is meant, not wicked and impious kings, but brave men, in accordance with the ancient use of the word, as when Virgil says,

> For know that treaty may not stand
> Where king greets king and joins not hand

in another place it is most unambiguously said of God, that He "maketh the man who is an hypocrite to reign on account of the perversity of the people." Wherefore, though I have, according to my ability, shown for what reason God, who alone is true and just, helped forward the Romans, who were good according to a certain standard of an earthly state, to the acquirement of the glory of so great an empire, there may be, nevertheless, a more hidden cause, known better to God than to us, depending on the diversity of the merits of the human race. Among all who are truly pious, it is at all events agreed that no one without true piety—that is, true worship of the true God—can have true virtue; and that it is not true virtue which is the slave of human praise. Though, nevertheless, they who are not citizens of the eternal city, which is called the city of God in the sacred scriptures, are more useful to the earthly city when they possess even that virtue than if they had not even that. But there could be nothing more fortunate for human affairs than that, by the mercy of God, they who are endowed with true piety of life, if they have the skill for ruling people, should also have the power. But such men, however great virtues they possess in this life, attribute it solely to the grace of God that He has bestowed it on them—willing, believing, seeking. And, at the same time, they understand how far they are short of that perfection of righteousness which exists in the society of those holy angels for which they are striving to fit themselves. But, however much that virtue may be praised and cried up, which without true piety is the slave of human glory, it is not at all to be compared even to the feeble beginnings of the virtue of the saints, whose hope is placed in the grace and mercy of the true God.

20

EGO AND COMMONWEAL

Jacob Burckhardt

From the vantage point of his beloved city-state of Basel, in Europe, but not of it, the Swiss historian, Jacob Burckhardt (1818–1897), watched the post-Napoleonic turmoil with increasing horror. Before 1846, he had been a liberal standing for limited suffrage and limited governmental power over the individual. After that year, he withdrew from politics declaring, "I will be a good private man," and explaining, "I hate democracy because I love liberty." * His view of history found little to support the aspirations of democratic idealists—great men, exempt from the ordinary moral code because they acted for the community, committed crimes with impunity. So long as they were successful, their crimes were condoned. The great man, the hero of the age, he argues, is really the great criminal.

*

. . .

THE VOCATION OF GREATNESS seems to be to fulfill a will that is greater than the individual will and is denoted, according to its point of departure, as the will of God, the will of a nation or a community, the will of an epoch. Thus, the will of a certain epoch seems to have been supremely fulfilled in the work of Alexander, namely the opening up and Hellenization of Asia, for durable conditions of life and long-lived civilizations were to

From Jacob Burckhardt, *Force and Freedom: An Interpretation of History.* Copyright 1943 by Pantheon Books, Inc.; reprinted by permission of Random House, Inc. Published in England by George Allen & Unwin, Ltd. Footnotes omitted.

   * James Hastings Nichols, ed., Jacob Burckhardt, *Force and Freedom: An Interpretation of History* (New York: Pantheon Books, Inc., 1943), pp. 7–8.

be founded on that work. A whole nation, a whole age, seems to have looked to him for life and security. But achievements of such a magnitude require a man in whom the strength and ability of infinitely many are united.

Now, the common purpose which the individual serves may be a conscious one; he carries out those enterprises, wars and acts of retribution which the nation or the time demands. Alexander took Persia, and Bismarck united Germany. It may, on the other hand, be an unconscious one. The individual knows what the purpose of the nation ought to be and fulfills that. The nation, however, later realizes that what was fulfilled was right and great. Caesar subjected Gaul; Charlemagne, Saxony.

There would seem to be a mysterious concidence between the egoism of the individual and the thing we call the commonweal, or the greatness, the glory of the community.

Here we become aware of the great man's strange exemption from the ordinary moral code. Since that exemption is allowed by convention to nations and other great communities, it is, by an inevitable logic, also granted to those individuals who act for the community. Now, in actual fact, no power has ever yet been founded without crime, yet the most vital spiritual and material possessions of the nations can only grow when existence is safeguarded by power. The "man after God's heart" then appears—a David, a Constantine, a Clovis; his utter ruthlessness is generally condoned for the sake of some service rendered to religion, but also where there has been none. Richard III, it is true, met with no such indulgence, for all his crimes were mere simplifications of his personal situation.

The crimes of the man, therefore, who bestows on a community greatness, power, and glory, are condoned, in particular the breach of forced political treaties, since the advantage of the whole, the state or the people, is absolutely inalienable and may not be permanently prejudiced by anything whatever; but he must then continue to be great and to realize that he will bequeath to his successors a fateful legacy, the necessity of genius, if what has been won by force is to be preserved until the world regards it as a right.

Here, everything depends on success. The same man, endowed with the same personality, would find no such condonation for crimes which entailed no such results. Only because he has achieved great things does he find indulgence even for his private crimes.

As regards the latter, he is not condemned for yielding to his passions, because men feel that life works more violently, more greatly, in him than in ordinary natures. Great temptation and impunity may also in part excuse him. Nor must we forget the indubitable kinship of genius with madness. Alexander may have shown the first signs of madness when, in his sorrow for Hephaestion, he tried to give it visible expression by ordering all the horses' tails to be docked and all the city battlements to be demolished.

There would be no objection to that exemption if nations were really absolute entities, entitled a priori to permanent and powerful existence. But they are not, and the condonation of a great criminal has its shady side for them, too, in that his misdeeds are not confined to acts which make the community great, that the delimitation of praiseworthy or necessary crime after the fashion of the *Principe* is a fallacy, and that the methods a man uses recoil on his own head and, in the long run, may destroy his taste for greatness.

A secondary justification for the crimes of great men seems to lie in the fact that, by them, an end is put to the crimes of countless others. When crime is thus monopolized by a communal criminal in the seat of government, the security of the community may prosper greatly. Before he came on to the scene, the powers of a brilliantly gifted nation may have been employed in a permanent and internecine war of destruction, which prevented the rise of everything which can flourish only in peace and security. The great individual, however, destroys, domesticates or employs unbridled individual egoisms. They suddenly gather into a power which continues to serve his purpose. In such cases—we might think of Ferdinand and Isabella—we are sometimes astonished by the rapid and brilliant bloom of culture till then retarded. Later, it bears the name of the great man—the age of so-and-so.

Finally, political crime profits by the familiar doctrine: "If we do not do it, others will." People would think themselves at a disadvantage if they acted morally. Indeed, some dreadful deed may be on the way, in the air; whoever performs it will secure, or obtain, dominion or an increase of power, and the existing government, for fear of being set aside, perpetrates the crime. Thus Catherine de'Medici usurped the massacre of St. Bartholomew from the Guises. If, in the sequel, she had given proof of greatness and genuine political capacity, the French nation would have entirely overlooked the horror. But she was later drawn completely into the Guises' wake, and a profitless condemnation was her portion. The *coup d'état* of 1851 might also be mentioned here.

As for the inner spur of the great man, we generally place first the sense of glory, or its common form, ambition, that is, the desire of fame in the contemporary world, a fame which actually consists more in a feeling of dependence than in admiration of an ideal. Ambition, however, is not a primary motive, and the thought of posterity still less so, however crass its expression may look at times, as when Napoleon said on Elba: "My name will live as long as God's." * There must have been a very great

* Fleury de Chaboulon, *Mémoires,* Vol. I, p. 116.

thirst for that glory of Alexander, but there have been other great men whose minds have not demonstrably dwelt on the thought of posterity. They may have been satisfied if their action contributed to settling the fate of posterity. Powerful men, moreover, may prefer flattery to fame, since the latter only pays homage to their genius while the former confirms their power.

The decisive impulse which matures and disciplines the great man is far more than the sense of power. It is that which irresistibly urges him into the light. As a rule, it is combined with so low an estimate of mankind that he no longer aims at that consensus of their opinion which is fame, but at their subjection and exploitation.

But fame, which flees the man that seeks it, overtakes the man who is heedless of it.

And it overtakes him with little regard to detached or expert opinion; for, in tradition, in popular judgment, the notion of greatness is not based exclusively on services rendered to the greater prosperity of the community, nor even on a nice appraisal of ability, nor yet on historical importance. In the last resort, the deciding factor is "personality," whose image is propagated by a sort of magic. This process is well illustrated by the Hohenstaufens. Henry VI Hohenstaufen, who was extremely important, is quite forgotten, not even the names of Conrad III and Conrad IV are remembered (the pathos of Conradin is of very recent growth), while Frederick I, on the other hand, is merged in Frederick II, who has faded into the distance. And now men look for the return of the man whose chief purpose in life, the subjection of Italy, had come to grief, and whose system of government in the Empire was of very doubtful value. His personality must have far outweighed his achievements, but the real object of men's expectations was indubitably Frederick I.

A peculiar phenomenon is the transformation and coloring undergone by those once acknowledged great. *On ne prête qu'aux riches.* Men lend of their own free will to the great, and thus great men are invested by their nations and partisans not only with certain qualities, but also with legend and anecdote, in which some aspect of the national type is expressed. An example illumined by the full light of history is Henry IV. Even the later historian cannot always remain impartial here. His very sources may be unconsciously contaminated, and a general truth is nevertheless hidden in these fictitious ingredients.

Posterity, on the other hand, tends to be rather severe with men who were once merely powerful, such as Louis XIV, and imagines them worse than they really were.

Apart from the symbolization of the national temperament or the development of the personality into a type, an idealization also sets in. For in time great men are liberated from all doubt of their value, from every effect of the hatred of those who suffered under them, and their idealization can then proceed in many senses at once—for instance, that of Charlemagne as hero, king, and saint.

Between the pines of the high Jura we see in the distance a famous peak shrouded in eternal snow. It can be seen in other ways from many other places at the same time, from vine arbors, or across a great lake, enframed in church windows or along the narrow arcaded streets of Upper Italy. Yet it is for ever the same Mont Blanc.

The great men who survive as ideals are of great value for the world, and more especially for their own countries. They are, for the latter, a source of emotion, an object of enthusiasm, and stimulate the minds even of the lowest classes by a vague sense of greatness. They maintain a high standard of things; they help to restore self-respect. All the evils that Napoleon brought down upon France are outweighed by his incalculable value to her as a national possession.

In our own day, we must first eliminate a class of men who declare themselves and the age emancipated from the need of great men. They declare that the present wants to look after its own affairs and imagine that with no great men to commit great crimes the reign of virtue will set in. As if little men did not turn evil at the slightest opposition, not to speak of their greed and mutual envy!

Others actually achieve that emancipation (n.b., as a rule in the intellectual sphere only) by a general guarantee of mediocrity, the ensurance of second-rate talents and false reputations, recognizable as such by the speed and noise of their rise. Such reputations, however, are very quickly exploded. The rest is done by the official suppression of all splendid spontaneity. Powerful governments have a repugnance to genius. In the state, it is hardly of use except by supreme compromise, for in the life of the state everything is judged by its "utility." Even in the other walks of life, men prefer great talents, i.e., the capacity for making the most of what is to hand, to the great, i.e., the new.

From time to time, however, there is an outcry for great men, and that mainly in the state, because in all countries matters have taken such a turn that ordinary dynasts and higher officials no longer suffice. Great men should be there. (Prussia, for instance, to maintain her position and increase her power, could do with a whole series of Frederick the Greats.)

Yet, even though the great man should come and survive his beginnings, the question still remains whether he would not be talked out of existence or overcome by contempt. Our age has a great power of attrition.

On the other hand, our age is very apt to be imposed upon now and again by adventurers and visionaries.

We can still remember how, in 1848, Europe sighed for a great man and who was later accepted as such.

Not every age finds its great man, and not every great endowment finds its time. There may now exist great men for things that do not exist. In any case, the dominating feeling of our age, the desire of the masses for a higher standard of living, cannot possibly become concentrated in one great figure. What we see before us is a general leveling down, and we might declare the rise of great individuals an impossibility if our prophetic souls did not warn us that the crisis may suddenly pass from the contemptible field of "property and gain" on to quite another and that then the "right man" may appear overnight—and all the world will follow in his train.

For great men are necessary to our life, in order that the movement of history may periodically wrest itself free from antiquated forms of life and empty argument.

And, for the thinking man, reviewing the whole course of history hitherto, one of the few certain premises of a higher spiritual happiness is an open mind for all greatness.

21

THE POLITICAL ACT AS AN
ACT OF WILL

Norton E. Long

Norton E. Long (b. 1910), peripatetic professor of political science, gad-fly to his profession, and possibly the only living American political theory-maker, was chairman of the Department of Political Science at Brandeis University in 1965. Besides teaching and writing, Mr. Long has broad ex-perience as an administrator, consultant, and political adviser. The view taken here of the essential nature of the political act may be compared profitably with Reinhold Niebuhr's "The Christian in Politics" (see Chapter 5) and Bertrand de Jouvenel's The Pure Theory of Politics.*

*

.   .   .

HOW PROFOUNDLY UNCERTAIN the knowledge of everyday life is, is hidden by the rarity of reflection concerning the adequacy of common sense, the rationalization of the course of events, and the literary con-ventions of the plausible narrative. The abyss beneath one's feet must be ignored if sanity and balance are to be maintained amid the depths of the multiple unknowns, the informational voids, and the normative uncer-tainties that surround us but of which we are routinely blissfully ignorant. Only those who have toyed with the world of the psychiatrist and the psychologist, or those with the artistic imagination, appreciate the thin

Reprinted from "The Political Act as an Act of Will" by Norton E. Long, *The American Journal of Sociology,* Vol. LXIX, No. 1 (July 1963), by permission of the University of Chicago Press. Copyright 1963 by the University of Chicago.
    * Cambridge, Eng.: University Press, 1963.

line of sanity that seems so certainly and monotonously to be neither thin
nor in danger. The doings of the Organisation Armée Secret, the stolid
English capacity for deteriorative violence in Kenya [Mau Mau] seem
alien to the [ordinary people we seem to long to be, although not at all to]
the contingent savage Hobbes saw in all of us.

The actors in the world of politics are neither the rational calculators
of economic man nor the uncultured savages of Hobbes's state of nature
but are born into a political culture, albeit frequently an ambiguous one,
and are socialized to a range of response patterns that may be invoked
by diverse stimuli. With this equipment, they confront a reality that seems,
to each public, one-dimensional common sense but, in fact, through the
differing glasses that it is viewed, presents widely differing perspectives.
The actors possess a repertory of responses that are articulated into roles
and interacting patterns of roles much like the repertory of plays of a
stock company. Given what seems to each the appropriate stimulus, a
given play is called for on the stage in which persons perceive themselves
as having a defined role or, as members of the audience, have an expectation as to how the performance on the stage will be presented. The
existence of these patterned sets of roles is part of the technology of the
political culture and permits the actors to function with the same ease as a
ballplayer playing his position.

Ambiguity lies in the differing stimuli that are simultaneously present,
differing interpretations of the same stimuli because of differences in the
equipment and perceptions of the actors and the fit of the plays to the
objective situation.

A governor, confronted with the necessity of deciding whether to call
a special session of the legislature to raise taxes to meet a fiscal emergency,
might use a decision-making model in which he would "game" the actors
to see how they might rationally weigh the ranges of possible and probable outcomes. While such a calculus is not without value, it is in most
cases less relevant than a consideration of the repertory of plays with
which the actors are equipped and those they can be made to consider, the
occasion, and the audience demands. Thus, there are objectively a number of possible pieces of theater that range from "let's choose up sides
and clobber each other and the governor" to "let's rally round the flag,
boys, and rise to the statesman-like task of saving the state." At critical
points, there is considerable leverage for leaders to manage the stimuli
that they are publicly expected to produce so that they can determine the
play considered appropriate by both actors and audience. Leaders are not
working with empty-headed malevolent savages or disembodied calculators, but with culture-bound actors whose political-art tradition is rich
in materials to which the ordinary imagination is conditioned.

The most significant political act is that of innovation through
which the existing materials are recombined and developed in such a way

as to unlock new human potentialities and overcome problems in physical and human nature. For example, the alteration of value patterns, operative political philosophy, is a major task in the political job of racial accommodation in a swiftly changing environment.

Were Hobbes's act of will, or the innovative, creative art of political art, writing new plays for the actors to perform, a constant necessity, rather than an intermittent and contingent one, the psychic cost might well be more than human nature and its systems of action could bear. Fortunately, custom, habit, and bureaucratization provide a framework of systemically functional routine that gives society a built-in automatic pilot that permits relaxation into common sense and the segmental rationality of the highly structured role and atmosphere of the laboratory and the office. Indeed, for the most part, the innovative and adaptive process by which the human system solves its problem is not through the self-conscious role of leadership, but through the random responses of individual and institutional actors to challenges in the environment that, when successful like the wheel and the union, are imitated and diffused within the common culture.

While one can and must lay great stress on the working of the social and political system as a system, as an ecology of institutions and actors where interaction produces unintended but systematically functional outcomes, one must not ignore the voluntary elements that maintain the culture. In the most dramatic case, missionaries undermine the native beliefs and, unsuccessful in replacing them with others, produce a condition that results in even biological decline. One may know this as a matter of scientific knowledge without possessing any cookbook recipe for the creation of an effective religion to meet social requirements. But quite beneath the great questions of political theory, the moral architecture, constructed like religions to give form and warmth and cooperative possibility to the life of men, there are the everyday acts of political will that signal the traffic of affairs and permit it to move.

President, governor, and mayor are called on to provide programs, acts of will, that focus the attention of public and legislature on some of the myriad things to which they might attend. They are called on to select from the currently acceptable diagnoses of social problems or, more rarely, to create their own and present them to the public. Their definitions of the situation, ranging from the fertility problems of prosperity and depression to the hostility problems of peace and war, not only create the conditions for cooperation among the bureaucracies of government but among the public at large.

In this broad field of symbolic manipulation exist deep-rooted public and individual behaviors going back in history to prehistory and to tribal patterns, and in childhood development to the deeply etched patterns of juvenile behavior.

Responses are ready to be triggered, and while, even from the special vantage points of political leadership, many stimuli fail to connect, these vantage points are the publicly expected sources of direction. Even the opposition requires a definition of the situation from the leadership in power to permit it to effectively play its role of adversary cooperation. Press and public, elite and mass, need a score card against which to follow the game. In the absence of some sufficient lead in defining the situation, the complex cooperation of the actors that rests on a sufficiently common definition of the situation for even adversary cooperation breaks down into stalemate and anarchy.

This is an ever-present danger where use and wont and the great stabilizing force of bureaucracy have not replaced the unstructured or partially structured situation with a realm of commonly accepted, largely unquestioned definitions. But the very motor of change is the unstructured, partially structured, structuring situation where possibilities are many and things are "up for grabs." Uncertainty, risk, amorality, and profit coexist and powerfully motivate the actors to explore an expanding and radically unknown and unexplored universe. The universe becomes known as the game to be played, it emerges, is created, and its rules are known, enforced, and accepted. At any time the players may fall out, become bored, wish to innovate, feel the pinch of its inadequacy, and in a thousand ways present difficulties to the maintenance of a smoothly functioning order. Both socialized habits and acts of political will are necessary to preserve the system.

In the everyday routine of life, the problematic nature of reality is made up of a multiplicity of potentially applicable norms cutting in different ways, a fragmentary state of information, an absence of any relevant substantial amount of scientific knowledge, and a pressure of time flooding by constraining decision on the most precarious definition of the situation. No certain rule exists as to whether to invoke the norms of loyalty to the chief, personal loyalty of friends, loyalty of institutional identification, professional loyalty, loyalty to a conception of the public interest with all its ramifications of city, state, national, and international publics and their variant interpretations, loyalty to geographic community, loyalty to party and part of party, loyalty to race or nationality, loyalty to religion or religious groups or to many more.

The multiplicity of norms, as well as the fragmentary and multiple nature of the perceived facts, contributes to the widely varying definitions of the situation that determine what Lippmann called the pictures in our heads.* The cognitive problem can at best be partially solved in its own terms. As Saint Augustine pointed out, the will focuses the attention and the norms invoked determine the interpretation of the relevant reality.

* Walter Lippmann, *Public Opinion* (New York: Harcourt, Brace & World, Inc., 1922, 1957).

The selection of the norms and the creation of a stable definition of the situation out of the manifold uncertainties of the reality masked by common sense is an act of political will. It cannot be escaped by resort to science or to the expert. It is the problem of choice, the choice of a possible order in a world that provides no substitute for the human act of moral will.

22

MY EARLY LIFE

James A. Farley

In another decade, James A. Farley (b. 1888), politician par excellence, may be seen as a transitional figure in politics and for the Irish in America. He rose from the lowly beginnings described in this selection to become the architect of Franklin D. Roosevelt's electoral triumphs of 1932 and 1936; then, breaking with FDR when the President sought an unprecedented third term, he went on to new heights as president of Coca-Cola, International. How does such a man begin? What does he seek in politics? Here are the answers of a master.

*

.   .   .

IN THE FALL of 1905, I enrolled in the Packard Commercial School of New York City to study bookkeeping, commuting each day by train from Grassy Point, which consumed about an hour's time each way.

After the bookkeeping course was completed late in the following spring, the business of looking for a permanent job began in earnest. After two or three days of pavement pounding, during which I walked untold miles, the Merlin Keiholtz Paper Company, 192 W. Broadway, hired a new and industrious bookkeeper by the name of James A. Farley. The salary was eight dollars per week, out of which, of course, had to be paid the daily train fare from Grassy Point and other incidentals such as lunch money. The net return was hardly great enough to suggest riotous living on the part of a young man seventeen years of age, but I was glad enough to get it. It was some time before the firm saw its way clear to increasing the weekly stipend to ten dollars. Even then I left because the chances for advancement seemed too slight and not primarily because the pay was too low. The pay envelope was always turned over to Mother to help the family budget.

My next job was with the United States Gypsum Company, a position obtained through the good offices of the Packard Commercial School. Advised in advance that an opening was available, I practiced long and carefully on a brief talk, outlining my qualifications, to the new boss. It must have been duly impressive because he decided to try me. When he mentioned that the salary would be eighteen dollars a week, the sum seemed almost unbelievably large. The United States Gypsum Company was my employer for fourteen or fifteen years during which I went up the lower rungs of the ladder, acting successively as bookkeeper, company correspondent, and, finally, as salesman. The last-named job suited me best because it provided an opportunity for me to travel about the state and meet people—an invaluable asset to a young gentleman who had his heart set on a political career.

PLAYING BASEBALL

Baseball was practically the only form of recreation which interested me after leaving school. Like so many American youngsters, I had started playing at an early age when my fingers were barely able to grasp the ball. There was the usual succession of neighborhood and schoolboy nines. Later, after I was grown, a local team at Grassy Point called the "Alphas" gave me a job as regular first baseman. The ball players got a lot of attention, and it was considered quite a distinction to play on the team. The spirit of rivalry between Haverstraw, Stony Point, Tompkins Cove, and other near-by communities was very keen, and the crowds turned out in large numbers for the Saturday and Sunday afternoon games. At various times, I played with Haverstraw, Verplanck's Point, and on a few occasions with the Peekskill team, for which the managements rewarded me with sums ranging from two or three up to five dollars a game. The last was considered rather a fancy figure to fork over, and the fellow who got it was supposed to be good. The local newspapers covered the games in ample fashion, and, for a long time after baseball had become a thing of the past for me, I preserved a newspaper which carried the banner sports headline, "Farley's double clears the bases."

In those days I considered myself quite a performer on the diamond, but looking back now I'm not so sure. The truth is, I was about the average player found in amateur and semiprofessional ranks. Being long and lank, I could reach for thrown balls and do a fairly good job otherwise of covering the bag. I was also a fair hitter and, because of my size, sometimes connected in lusty fashion and gave the ball quite a ride. But I wasn't very fast and I hated to slide. Because of my height, the fans nick-named me "Stretch," and even to this day, if I happen to be visiting the neighborhood, some old-time fan will come along and greet me by that nickname.

ENTERING POLITICS

The decade between the ages of twenty years and thirty years was swallowed up, except for the time given to business, by a constant study of the art of practical politics in local affairs. At the age of twenty, the Democratic leaders had enlisted me for electioneering work, especially for the role of hauling straight-voting but lazy citizens to the polling booths, an important factor in minor contests. In my twenty-first year, before I had cast my first ballot, the neighboring Democrats elected me as a member of the county committee. Frankly, I was burning with ambition for political preferment, although in retrospect the extent of that ambition seems curiously modest. The highest office to which I then looked forward was to be a member of the New York State Senate. Dancing and other forms of social activity were thrust aside while I devoted the daylight hours to business and commuting and the nights to studying whatever paths might be open to political success.

Confiding my hopes to a very limited circle of relatives and acquaint-ances, I met with discouragement at every hand. My mother, especially, was disturbed over the possibility of seeing me immersed in politics, be-lieving that it would lead to nothing but disappointment and failure. Time and again in her own quiet way, she advised me to forget about public life, to enjoy myself like other young men, and to concentrate on the chances for advancement in business.

There was one friend, whose advice I sought, who was far more dis-turbed than my mother in advising me against a political career and far more emphatic in expressing his views. He was Pat Morrissey, whose cousins ran a grocery store in Grassy Point. Like many others of its kind, the Morrissey store had developed into a combined loafing place and vil-lage forum for the men of the community who liked to sit around and ex-pound their views on public questions. In summer, the informal meetings took place on the spacious front porch, or "front stoop" as we called it; in winter they were adjourned to the back of the store where a full-bellied stove of old-fashioned design made things comfortable.

One night I called at the store and asked to see Pat in private. He went out to the porch where I revealed my intention to run for the job of town clerk—in a Republican community—and asked his opinion. Pat gave it to me. He said that of all the men he had ever known personally in Rockland County who had entered politics, not one had made a success of it. He said the only Republican he had ever known in Rockland County who was really successful was a Republican Supreme Court judge, who had dominated the affairs of the G.O.P. locally for almost thirty years, and even he had been disappointed in his great ambition to be nominated for governor. Morrissey gave me a truthful warning: that men are inclined to neglect other interests and duties after becoming mixed up in politics and then, when success has passed them by, to become disappointed and embittered. Then he concluded:

"However, no matter what advice I am giving you, if you have made up your mind that you want to run, then run you will and nothing can be done about it. So run and get it out of your system. If you win, good luck to you."

The fact is that my mind was made up, and, while I appreciated the viewpoint of those who disagreed, nothing in the world could have induced me to abandon the urge to take a fling at politics. The possibility of defeat, and the means that could be used to ensure a victory, had been carefully weighed in my own mind. Stony Point was a Republican township, and the gentleman who held the job of town clerk was a man of substance who wielded a wide degree of influence and commanded a great deal of respect in the community. On the surface, it hardly seemed probable that an "upstart of twenty-two years" belonging to the Democratic party could take the job away from him.

But it seemed to me that some of the old-timers were taking things too much for granted, that they were overlooking a good many opportunities for making friends and thus making votes. I got the Democratic nomination without any trouble and then started about the task of winning the election, something made considerably easier by the fact that my distinguished opponent wasn't inclined to take me seriously and did very little campaigning on his own account.

Playing first base on the Alpha baseball team had given me the chance to become known pretty generally, and, with that as a foundation, I started out to become personally acquainted with every voter in the town, or at least with as many as I could. A great many of the young people, even though they were normally Republicans, were red-hot baseball fans, and they came to my support in large numbers. The result was that on election day the town political seers almost fell over backward when they learned that young James A. Farley, Democrat, had taken over the eminent position of town clerk. Baseball had given me a modest start. I had made a good beginning, and it whetted my appetite for more.

Having won out unexpectedly, I set to work in deadly earnest to make good and to build a place for myself in the Democratic party. The town was still Republican, and the change of a few votes would have been sufficient to swing control back to that party at the next election. But that never happened. The voters of Stony Point re-elected me on three successive occasions; and, during those eight years in the town clerkship, I discovered a great many invaluable facts about public officeholding and what makes for success in running for office.

The daily commuting back and forth to New York City was a wearisome grind. I left home every morning about seven o'clock and failed to arrive home until after seven in the evening. After having dinner with the family, it was my usual routine to walk from Grassy Point to the town hall at Stony Point, where the town clerk's office was located, a distance of about one mile. This was done at least four or five nights a week, although such faithful attendance was not required by law. Even if there was nothing to be done, I went there anyway, because the job overshadowed all other interests. Frequently, a few cronies would drop in and we would chew over politics for hours on end. Always in winter, the place would be stone cold on my arrival because there was no janitor, and I would have to build a fire myself. It was usually a wood fire scraped together from whatever was available because the town furnished only a limited supply of coal.

The town clerk was not a salaried official; he got his pay in the form of fees for services rendered. For example, he got a fixed amount for serving as secretary to the Board of Health, another sum for serving as clerk to the Board of Assessors, and four dollars a day for attending the town board meetings. The town board frequently concluded its business in fifteen or twenty minutes and then "reconvened," with exactly the same members, as the Board of Health. The fact that they got paid separately for each service may have had something to do with this strange procedure.

There were other fees also. A license for fishing or hunting cost $1.10 of which amount $1.00 was forwarded to the state treasury at Albany and the other ten cents was for the town clerk. A dog license brought twenty-five cents to the town clerk, and for issuing a marriage license the fee was $1.00. The aggregate amounted in the course of a year to a pretty sizable sum.

This fee business offered just the right opportunity to build up a little "good-will." Although my job in New York paid me barely enough to get along, and the added funds would have been most welcome, I was far more concerned about building a political future than I was about cash on hand. Bearing that fact in mind, I never accepted the ten-cent fee from the hunters and fishermen of the community, who numbered more than two hundred, and as a result they remembered me on election day. The dog owners also got off without paying the twenty-five-cent fee and they were likewise kindly disposed toward the new town clerk.

And of course it would be unthinkable to take a dollar from a young man and his bride-to-be who were about to set up housekeeping. I learned also that young ladies about to enter the married state were as a rule very bashful about coming to the town hall to apply for the necessary license. In that case, it was a good idea to bring the license to the bride's home or to the home of the bridegroom. I performed that service on occasions without number, sometimes delivering a couple of licenses on the same night. It did me no harm on election day.

The years in the town clerkship also marked my beginning as a letter-writer, a form of electioneering which came to occupy an extremely important place in my later career. I never overlooked an opportunity to send a letter to the voters of the town, informing them about the state of the public business or giving other information which they were entitled to have. Individuals who wanted information or help also got it in the quickest time possible with a note from me explaining what was being done and why. The result was that every voter in the community got a letter from me at some time or other, and it was clearly apparent that this had created a very favorable impression. I never forgot the lesson.

The first contest for the town clerkship was won by a margin of twenty-odd votes. I was re-elected by a plurality of 288 votes out of 680 cast, or better than two to one. Commenting upon the election results and the unprecedented vote, a local newspaper said:

> This is unquestionably the result of Mr. Farley's courteous treatment of all the citizens of the town whose business takes them to the town clerk's office. Farley can be found morning, noon and night always ready to oblige a citizen of the town no matter what the inconvenience, and it would seem that his activities in this direction are gladly appreciated.

After serving as town clerk, I was also elected as town supervisor for a couple of terms. I recall sitting with a few friends in a Haverstraw restaurant the night before the balloting was to take place the first time. It was a three-cornered race. We started arguing about the outcome and, during the course of the discussion, I marked down the total vote each candidate would probably receive. When the returns were in the next day, it was shown that my estimates were only fifteen or twenty votes out of the way. Even in those early days, I had learned the value of careful checking in figuring results.

During this period, a few friends induced me to branch out and to seek the office of County Superintendent of the Poor, a position that paid $1,500 annually and which put the holder in a position to be known all over the county. I agreed to enter only after a careful check-up of the leaders disclosed the fact that my chances of getting the party nomination were excellent. The meeting was held in the firehouse at West Nyack, New York. Shortly after the meeting opened, someone proposed that the nomination should be voted on by ballot, instead of by a show of hands as was formerly done. I became suspicious. Those present voted fifteen to ten in favor of paper ballots, and later I lost the nomination by the same vote —because a certain leader who had pledged me his support went back on his word. It was the first time that I had been the victim of the "double cross" in politics, and the thing hurt for a long time. However, I learned afterward that men who do those things never get anywhere because no one trusts them. They dig their own political graves by deception and treachery. If there is one type of man who can't succeed in politics, it's the man who habitually lies.

The first really important political position I ever filled was the office of Democratic county chairman for Rockland County, to which I was elected early in 1918. This fulfilled a secret ambition of many years' standing because the county chairmanship was a handy steppingstone for an individual who wished to become active in state political affairs. It offered an opportunity to mingle with the leaders who picked the party candidates for office, and to attend the state conventions with a good deal of authority.

BOOMING AL SMITH

I entered upon the duties of the chairmanship with a rush of zeal because it was my intention to build the county organization into a stronger force than it ever had been before and to make it a real factor in NewYork State politics. Having had a good deal of experience in local politics by that time, I had acquired a few ideas on what could be done to improve the county organization. Being duly impressed with the importance of the new post, I did something in the spring of 1918 which, to a more experienced person, might have seemed a bit presumptuous on the part of a mere county chairman serving his first time.

I paid a visit to the offices of the New York City Board of Aldermen to urge the President of the Board, Alfred E. Smith, to become a candidate for the Democratic nomination for governor. Being admitted to his presence, I told Smith that he would get an unprecedented vote in New York City, that he would get an unusually large vote upstate because his long years of service in the legislature had made him popular with Republicans and Democrats alike, and that no other candidate could hope to run as well in the fall election. I added that my private business and my activity in the Benevolent and Protective Order of Elks caused me to travel about the state constantly and afforded me a good chance to judge political sentiment.

Smith said little or nothing but sat there looking me over in quizzical fashion while the speech was in progress. He was apparently trying to decide in his mind how much this newcomer from upstate knew about politics and how much of what he said could be relied upon. Finally, he got up from his chair, thanked me for calling, and said:

"You go over and give that information to Commissioner Murphy and then come back and tell me what he said."

The pleasant manner in which Smith received me on my first entry into "big-time" affairs was exceptionally pleasing, but his instructions to see "Commissioner Murphy" made me nervous and ill at ease. He was referring, of course, to Charles F. Murphy, leader of Tammany Hall, who was always given the title of commissioner by his fellow leaders in Democratic politics. Calling on Al Smith didn't faze me for a moment, but the idea of actually telling the great Murphy whom he should nominate for governor left me almost breathless.

It took me some little time to get up the necessary courage, but I went to see Mr. Murphy and urged the case for Smith to the best of my ability. At the time, there was a well-defined belief that no Tammany Hall Democrat could hope to be elected chief executive of New York State and that it was only wasting time and money to try it. Inasmuch as Murphy was a realist who always endeavored to see things as they were, and seldom bothered about making useless gestures, it was generally assumed that he was cold, or at best lukewarm, on the proposition of nominating Smith for the governorship. However, the latter had made an excellent record during his years in the State Assembly and a number of leaders were of the opinion that he could break the old prejudice against a Tammany man. I pleaded with Murphy to give Smith a chance, insisting that he would run well upstate despite opinions to the contrary. He listened in courteous fashion and, without committing himself one way or another, asked me to call again whenever I was in a position to give him more information about probable sentiment upstate. A few days later, I went back and related the entire conversation to Smith.

At the state convention, held in the early fall, I was in attendance as a delegate and got a thrill out of voting to nominate Al Smith who was subsequently elected—the first boy from the "sidewalks of New York" to make the grade. We came together in party meetings several times that year and, like a great many others, I fell under the spell of his powerful personality. He had a knowledge of the business of New York State that gave him an advantage over all opponents in debate, and he had an ability to explain campaign issues in simple homely phrases unrivaled by any stump orator of the day. He was at his best in hostile surroundings, and, whenever anyone tried to heckle him or place him at disadvantage, he always came out on top. It was only natural that his fame should gradually become nationwide.

When Smith went to Albany as governor, I thought there was a pretty good chance of getting appointed to a position which had appealed to me for a long time. It was the post of secretary to the State Industrial Commission. While not one of the better-known state offices, or one sought after generally, the position was important because the commission had a great deal to do with the enforcement of laws and regulations relating to labor. At that time, and earlier, the Democratic party was making an enviable record in New York State because of its efforts to put on the statute books humane legislation for the benefit and protection of working men and women. Having come from a family of laboring people and having earned a living that way myself on occasions, I was extremely anxious to know more about the subject, to become acquainted with what had been done to promote better working and sanitary conditions, and to learn what more could be done by government action along the same lines.

When I revealed what was in my mind to a few friends, they suggested that I pay a visit to Charles F. Murphy for the dual purpose of getting his opinion and finding out what were the probable chances of getting such an appointment. I called on Murphy in the office at Tammany Hall where all his callers were received. I put the proposition before him and asked for some advice. Murphy was a very courteous man but slow-spoken and noted for always saying what was on his mind in the fewest possible words. He said that the man who was appointed secretary to the State Industrial Commission should be acquainted with the details of the labor laws already on the statute books and also have a broad knowledge of New York City itself and its complicated problems. While he was impressed with my earnestness and ability, he felt that I was too inexperienced for the place and that it should go to someone else. He added that Governor Smith had given a great deal of thought to the matter, and they were casting about for a man qualified to do the job and do it well.

My talk with Murphy was about as pleasant as a wetting in a cold rainstorm. It dampened all my enthusiasm for politics for the time being and left me a bit embittered. Murphy's attitude seemed unreasonable. I had worked very hard for the success of the party and if given the place on the industrial commission would have made the whole business thoroughly familiar by long hours of study and work. But the more I thought it over, after the first disappointment had died down, the more reasonable Murphy's attitude seemed to be. He could very easily have put me off by saying that the post was already promised to someone else or he could have promised to help and then done nothing about it or secretly recommended someone else. Instead of that he had chosen the forthright course by plainly saying that I was unqualified and that he intended to back someone else. It gave me a new respect for Murphy and once again taught me the all-important fact that to be successful in party politics a man must keep his word. No matter how unpleasant it may be, the only course is to give the facts straight from the shoulder. There is an old saying that truth-telling saves a lot of embarrassing situations later on. That is especially true in public life. I have had literally thousands of men come to me asking for support for this place or that, and, in every case, it has been my policy to relate the situation exactly as it was. Very often the truth was distasteful, but the individuals always appreciated the fact that they were not being deceived. There is nothing baser than to promise help to a man looking for an appointment, knowing that you have no intention of giving it.

A few months later, a friend of Governor Smith's advised me that the governor wanted to appoint me as one of the port wardens of New York City. There were several port wardens in those days, and their principal duty was to survey the cargoes on boats coming into the harbor to see if damage had been done by water or shifting cargo. The place paid approximately $5,000, but the wardens for the most part employed assistants who did the actual work and were paid out of additional fees received from the shipowners. The place was a sinecure, and Governor Smith had urged its abolition, but the legislature up to that time had failed to act. As the work could be done without interfering with my private business, I agreed to take it, and Governor Smith made the nomination. The place was always a political football, and the Republican members of the State Legislature held up confirmation until the closing day of the session, when Smith forced the nomination through. I performed the duties or port warden for about a year, during which time it was evident to me that there was no real necessity for the place. When Nathan Miller, a Republican governor, came into office, I was legislated out of office by a bill reducing the number of port wardens. Only the Republicans were allowed to remain in. As a matter of fact, the number should have been reduced even further.

My energies were devoted mostly to business during this period, although politics was still a favorite hobby and got perhaps a lot of attention that should have been directed to private affairs. I was re-elected county chairman with gratifying regularity, and through that office was able to keep in close touch and to get better acquainted with the state Democratic leaders. . . .

23

WHY DID YOU RUN FOR CONGRESS?

Jerry Voorhis

*Representative Jerry Voorhis (b. 1904) served five terms as a congress-
man from California and was the first victim of Richard Nixon's political
style of spraying a faint pink haze around his opponent and claiming
there was more to it than met the eye. After his defeat in 1946, Mr.
Voorhis wrote the book from which this excerpt was taken. He has been
general secretary to the Cooperative League of the United States of
America since 1947.*

*

EVER SINCE I can remember I have been interested in politics. I recall
asking my mother when I was a small boy why some people were so rich
and others so poor and why something wasn't done to help the poor people have a more equal chance in life. She told me there were some men
and women—not very many, she said—who were trying to bring this
about. Ever since then I have been "for" those men and women. I guess
that has been my main political motivation.

In college, I experienced a very profound religious awakening, for
which I shall be humbly thankful as long as I live. Out of this there developed the very disturbing and impelling idea that the Christian Gospel
is to be taken seriously and that needless poverty and suffering, on the one
hand, and special privilege and inordinate power, on the other, are entirely contrary to its precepts.

All during my years at college, the barriers between "town and
gown" as they existed in New Haven were a terrible thing to me. I know

now, though I lacked the confidence in my own judgment to know it then, that I should have left school at some point along the way, gone out and found a worthwhile job, and gained a little of the knowledge that does not come from books, and then returned to finish my course. As it was, I felt it my duty to continue through the four years in the traditional manner and I did so, at the expense of great emotional strain. I felt all the time that I was not so much living as only "preparing for life" and that the real world lay among the people beyond the college walls.

Consequently, once the diplomas had been distributed to our class, I did the thing I had wanted to do for so many years. I found a boarding-house room and a factory job at thirty-nine cents an hour. After a period of months during which we worked a great deal of overtime (and were paid straight-time wages for it), I reported for work one morning only to find that I was one of the 2,000 employees of the company who had been "laid off" indefinitely. I got another job, this time handling freight in the railroad yards. I caught the work train at six o'clock those winter mornings and almost became accustomed to the unlighted cars and to the ride to work in complete darkness. It was hard, hazardous work. I shall never forget having seen two of my fellow workers killed one day when a huge cogwheel, which they were attempting to move from one car to another, slipped and pinned them under it. I wondered what would happen to their families.

I left the freight handler's job to make a trip to Europe. It was planned as a sort of good-will mission for the Student Friendship Fund of the YMCA. I went to England first, then to Germany. It was at the height of the postwar inflation. Postage stamps were selling for billions of marks and people could be seen on the streets clutching great bundles of bills which they were desperate to turn into goods before prices doubled again. There was very little food in Germany then. Students were in almost universal distress. In each city, I stayed in the home of someone to whom I had a letter of introduction. In Dortmund, it was with an unemployed miner, father of ten children. There was no food except a little cabbage soup and some sort of substitute for coffee. In Hamburg, I spent three days and nights in the home of a schoolteacher who could afford neither light nor heat in his rooms.

Everywhere people were having meetings and talking about "hunger" and "no more war."

Finally, I contracted pneumonia, managed somehow to get back to England, and spent six weeks in a nursing home. That was all of the European trip.

Back in the United States, I met a young lady doing social service work and promptly fell deeply in love with her. Then I went off to work for six months on a western ranch, partly, at least, for the purpose of re-building the physical strength I had lost during my illness. I learned to plant and harvest grain, to "put up" hay, to handle a team, and to build fences (not the political kind). I found out how ranchers in that section drove their cattle and sheep to the railroad in the fall of the year, figuratively kissed them good-by, and then waited for a check from an Omaha commission house for whatever "the market" had allowed on the particular day when the stock was sold. That check represented in most cases almost the entire cash income of the rancher for a year's labor.

Louise Livingston and I were married that fall and we went to North Carolina where I hoped to secure work in a textile mill. But that proved impossible. Strangers were simply not hired by the Southern mills in those days. I discovered, also, that I could not have supported the two of us on what I would have earned at such a job. So I tried elsewhere, and one day was lucky enough to be picked out of a milling crowd outside the Ford assembly plant and given a job on one of the "lines."

I started at five dollars a day, which seemed like big money at that particular point. After two months I made six dollars a day and we had saved enough to buy a second-hand Ford by the time spring came. The assembly-line job was the hardest one that I have ever held. The monotony was almost unbearable. I solved the problem tolerably by two devices. I memorized poetry and repeated it over and over during the long days— most of which consisted of twelve-hour shifts, with no overtime pay. Our line was adjacent to the freight siding and I could see the cars as they were backed in and pulled out. The names of the various railroads on the freight cars served to quicken my imagination and to conjure up thoughts about the parts of the country through which these railroads passed. This helped too.

When I left my job at the Ford factory I had not the least conscious idea of ever running for Congress or any other office. But I was quite sure I wanted to try to do something about the things I had seen and experienced, about low wages and long hours, arbitrary dismissals, inflation and deflation, the insecurity of farmers' incomes.

Our move from North Carolina was to a jack-of-all-trades job at Allendale Farm School in northern Illinois. This was both a home and a training school for boys, a sort of "boys' town." I taught the social science subjects in all grades, conducted chapel services, helped coach athletics, worked with the boys on the farm, and did anything else that needed doing. During this year our first baby was born. I was glad it was a girl.

The next year found us in Wyoming, at the call of the Episcopal bishop of that state. The job was that of getting the first church home for orphan boys started. It was a tough assignment, principally because there was apparently almost no money to support such an institution in the state and I proved none too adept at raising even what there was. I traveled over the state for this purpose, but everywhere I went I got boys to take care of and very little money to do it with.

Finally, the idea occurred to me of writing to people in all parts of the country asking them to sponsor—at three hundred dollars a year—one orphan boy in the projected home. This worked and our "family," some thirty-six boys, a big colored woman who was our cook and entire "staff," my wife, our baby girl, and I began living together in the fall of 1926. We had only one building and it was surrounded by red clay which in wet weather became red mud and was generously transferred to the interior of the building by everybody's shoes. The board of directors was principally concerned with good housekeeping, to the neglect, as it seemed to me, of the happy development of the boys. A variety of conflicts arose over this difference in point of view. Nevertheless, we lived a happy year with our boys in Laramie.

By this time my father was ready to retire from active business and anxious to make an investment in something far more worthwhile than stocks and bonds. He proposed that we found an institution which would be both a home and a school for boys who had lost their parents by death or separation. He preferred to do this in California and so, in the fall of 1927, with a dozen of the Wyoming boys for whom there seemed no other satisfactory solution, we moved to Claremont, California, and started constructing the Voorhis School for Boys at San Dimas, a few miles distant.

We rented, from Pomona College, a big old house that shook vigorously every time a Santa Fe train roared by, a block away. The boys attended school in Claremont, little Alice passed her second birthday, and I took my master's degree in education at Claremont College.

By the next summer our school at San Dimas was ready, and the first thirty boys had been selected to form our nucleus. By the end of our first year sixty-five boys were living there—our capacity. The "school" was, first of all, a home. All our boys were orphans, boys with but one living parent, or lads from broken homes. They lived the year around at our school and usually remained with us until they had been graduated from high school. Our chapel was the center from which a truly religious spirit pervaded our community. We taught the sixth, seventh, eighth, and ninth grades at the Voorhis School, and the older boys went to the regular public high school in San Dimas. We worked together in our fruit groves and our vegetable garden, in the chicken houses and rabbitry, the auto shop, the print shop, and the kitchen. These were happy years. The day began very early and didn't end till I had told the younger boys good night after they had gone to bed. But we compassed the whole gamut of life and made it something altogether worth while. Moreover, to bring an even greater fullness to our family life, our first son was born in the summer of 1931.

Not only did I teach the social sciences to our boys at the school, but for several years I gave a special lecture course at Pomona College. I was always telling the boys that we should put into practice the principles in which we believed. As time went on, therefore, the feeling grew that the time might sometime come for me to attempt some practical contribution toward carrying out the principles of government I had been teaching.

Just how it would ever be possible for me to do this through active politics was a question I did not then attempt to face, much less to answer. Certainly I would have at least two strikes on me if I tried, for I had been a political maverick ever since I was old enough to vote.

I cast my first vote for president in 1924. But I did not vote for John W. Davis, or for Calvin Coolidge. I voted for "Old Bob" La Follette. To make matters worse, in 1928 I voted for Norman Thomas and was, in fact, at that time a registered Socialist, since I could find no evidence that either of the old parties was genuinely concerned with the problems of the people. With the coming of the 1929 depression, those problems became nothing short of desperate, and my own concern markedly deepened.

It was virtually impossible for the graduates of our school to find worthwhile employment. Through intensive effort and the kindness of personal friends, we managed to find some sort of employment for many of them. But seldom indeed was it the type of work for which the boys were so well qualified by their training and ability. On the wages and salaries that they were able to earn hardly any of them could look forward to the possibility of supporting a wife and children. To them and to millions of other young men and women, America was saying, "We have no need for your talents and abilities. There are too many workers already. If you were put to work you would produce too much and it could not be sold, since the people, including yourselves, have so little money." To tell a young man you will not give him something he desires may make him angry; but to deny him the opportunity to make any worthwhile contribution to the society to which he belongs is a profound insult and a telling blow at his very hold on life. Not only did I believe this situation cruel to the individual young men, but I also suspected that it reflected some cockeyed economics and serious neglect on the part of those supposedly responsible for the health of the nation's economy.

Yet I found nothing on the political horizon which seemed to offer hope for a better future. President Hoover appealed to business to stop the disastrous downward spiral. But the effect of his appeal was to cause the very executives to whom he appealed to decide it was wise to lay off even more men and to curtail still further what little production was going on. The government's fiscal policies were exactly the opposite of those likely to lead to a checking of the depression. True, the RFC was established, and made a few loans to wealthy borrowers. But, in a feverish attempt to keep the budget balanced, government expenditures were severely curtailed, which circumstance undoubtedly contributed measurably to the fact that revenues fell off even faster. The Democrats, meanwhile, apparently sensing their first opportunity for political victory in many years, emphasized, as well they might, the mistakes and shortcomings of the Republican Administration but offered little which appeared particularly constructive in its place. From a purely political standpoint they were undoubtedly correct; but to a citizen as deeply distressed as I then was, little cause for encouragement was given.

It came time for the campaign of 1932. I remember with great vividness coming out of a moving picture theater with Mrs. Voorhis and hearing the newsboys crying "Extra." We bought a paper and saw in the middle of the front page of the extra edition a large picture of the Democratic nominee for president. He was Franklin D. Roosevelt. I can still feel the poignant sense of being left out of the main stream of American political life which came over me at that moment. There was something in the expression around the eyes of the man whose picture appeared on those papers which made one sure that he would not be afraid to act in the crisis which the nation faced. His action might not be 100 per cent correct in every instance, but at least there would be movement.

The presidential campaign which followed was, however, a disappointment to me. Mr. Roosevelt gave us little inkling of his program for overcoming the depression and relieving the distress which stalked the country. But his victory in November 1932 was overwhelming and perhaps this proved the wisdom of his political tactics.

The new president was inaugurated on March 4, 1933, and, within an hour, the American nation knew that it was once more blessed with the vital type of leadership that, in time of trouble, has again and again brought new hope to our country. From the beginning there were features of his program which raised some serious questions for the future. But the president was telling us that mass unemployment must always be a matter of national concern and a cause for national action; and, as his plans unfolded, they evidently deserved the support of all Americans who, like myself, sought first and foremost an immediate answer to our nation's most critical problems.

For a variety of reasons, California was ready to move somewhat faster than was the nation as a whole. Upton Sinclair, the author, became the symbol of this spirit.

In the fall of 1933, more than a year before the next California elections, he launched his campaign for the Democratic nomination for governor of California. His "EPIC plan" (End Poverty in California) was simple. It was this: that unemployed people be given an opportunity to produce for their own needs instead of being "cared for" by direct relief. The state was to buy or lease lands on which food products would be grown by some of the unemployed. Factories were to be erected where others among them would turn out such essential manufactured articles as clothing, furniture, and processed foods. The people were to be paid in scrip money, expendable only for goods produced within their cooperative "production-for-use" system.

Neither his nature nor his experience equipped Mr. Sinclair particularly well for the position of California's chief executive. But there were hundreds of thousands still unemployed in Los Angeles County alone; and national "recovery" appeared a long way off. Therefore, to many Californians, the hope in the EPIC proposal—hope of an end to destitution and the "relief" system, hope of a return to dignified self-support— seemed the one important consideration.

So it was that I decided to enter the Democratic primaries as a candidate for the nomination for state assemblyman from the Forty-ninth Assembly District. I was an avowed EPIC candidate and as such I shared in what was unquestionably one of the most bitterly fought campaigns in all the history of American politics.

On our side it was a crusade for what we believed was the best available solution for the profound problems of the great depression. Equally sincere, I now suspect, were our opponents who believed the EPIC plan would spell the end of the capitalistic system in America.

The primary results in August 1934 were, on the whole, a victory for the EPIC candidates. Mr. Sinclair was nominated for governor by a comfortable margin, and many of the candidates for the legislature, myself included, were likewise successful in winning their nominations. But thereafter it was a different story. Many Democrats joined forces with the Republicans to defeat the EPIC plan and candidates. Millions of dollars were spent against us and in the final event we lost. I was defeated by a margin that was not exactly overwhelming but was nonetheless decisive. I thought my political career was over.

But it wasn't.

The EPIC followers were terribly let down by Upton Sinclair's defeat. Tears were shed without shame or attempt at excuse in the postmortem meetings held in the various communities. In many instances the people decided they would go ahead anyway and organize cooperative production ventures. We tried one in our town—a tomato cannery—which did give work to a number of people for a while but which eventually failed—primarily, as I now realize, for want of a skilled manager.

Time passed, and the period approached for filing as candidates for office in the elections of 1936. I will say, as all politicians will, and generally with truth, that a good many people urged me to become a candidate for Congress. In the background, however, were the experiences in the factories and on the ranch, the problems the boys of our school had faced in the worst years of the depression, the failure of our cooperative and the reasons for it, the things I had seen in Europe—all the important events of my life. I believed there were answers to these problems. I saw that legislation passed by Congress was already getting the best of some of them. I believed the answers to more of them could be developed, in part at least, through wise action on the part of government.

It was essential that those basic American principles of opposition to concentrated economic power, equality of opportunity for the worker and the small farmer, and the preservation of the hopes of the common man should find practical political expression. I saw clearly then, as I have seen more and more clearly as the years passed, that the highest values in human life can be preserved only under a government which guarantees to its people a full measure of liberty—religious, personal, political, and economic. But the point was—and is—that the very existence of liberty depends directly on the maintenance of at least a reasonable degree of hope for economic betterment in the minds and hearts of the masses of people. Dictators have succeeded in destroying free political institutions only in nations riddled by economic chaos and despair. They have acquired power only through the willingness of a defeated people to sacrifice their liberty for the promise of employment and security. Ever since I was a boy I have had an abhorrence of the arrogance of power and every sort of totalitarianism—corporate, communist, fascist, or any other kind. Under dictatorship there can be no freedom of conscience. And without freedom of conscience, true religious faith cannot flourish. And without such faith no people can be great, since the best single expression of human life is not present to drive them on.

For all these reasons, I filed my name as a candidate for the Democratic nomination for Congress in the twelfth district of California in the spring of 1936.

When I did so, I had little idea that I would be elected. Of course I knew that, should I be, I would have to be away from our school during a considerable part of each year. But I hoped and believed that the school would go on anyway, and that during periods when Congress was not in session I could come back and take up my work with the boys where I had left it a few months before. Through the years the school had been not so much a job as an all-embracing life. It was a dynamic little community with its industry and agriculture, its education and its athletics, its newspaper and its library, its homes and its church. Had I known in 1936 that only two years later the Voorhis School for Boys was to become only a bright memory, and its property a gift to the state of California, I am doubtful that I would have ever run for Congress.

24

EVERY POLITICIAN IS SUBJECT
TO A GREAT FEAR

John T. Salter

Biography is an important, though neglected, technique in social science. An institution, Emerson once observed, is the lengthened shadow of a man. Most of us, on hearing this dictum, smile knowingly and go on collating impersonal data, feeding them into machines where, untouched by human hands, they will be turned into books. But Prof. John T. Salter (b. 1898) has made his lifelong work the study of individual politicians. He has combined the biographer's techniques with those of the diligent social scientist. Out of his researches has come the composite portrait of the politician presented here.

*

.   .   .

EVERY POLITICIAN IS SUBJECT to a great fear. This fear conditions the basic processes of democracy. Sometimes the politician does not do what he wants to do, but does what he must do, or thinks he must do, in order to keep power. The member of Congress, for example, nine times out of ten, does not vote or speak without weighing possible repercussions and recriminations. If he does not or cannot judge correctly the probable reaction of his constituents, he will not survive as their alter ego.

Theoretically, a member of Congress is free to vote as his own mind and conscience dictate. Actually, however, and on any number of important measures, his mind and conscience cannot dictate until some individ-

From the "Introduction," by John T. Salter, editor, to *The American Politician* (Chapel Hill, N.C.: The University of North Carolina Press, 1938).

ual organization, newspaper, or pressure group dictates to them. On other measures, the legislator may have a very definite opinion as to how he wants to vote, and (1) he votes that way, or (2) he does not vote at all, or (3) he votes contrary to his personal preference in the matter.

First, he votes according to his own preference when there is no particular reason why he shouldn't—that is, when any powerful force that he is amenable to, such as the president, or a newspaper, or some organization has either not advised him on the matter, or has expressed an opinion that coincides with his own. In the second case, we may think of the legislator at bay; he may look out on his constituency and hear such a jarring discord of voices, one group urging him to vote for the measure, another fraction promising punishment if he does, that he cannot vote either way without feeling that he will alienate support. And, in the third place, he may vote against his own conviction when he finds that to do otherwise would cost him support.

A congressman recently told me that he certainly wanted to vote for the reorganization bill that has just been defeated.* I asked him why he had not favored it then, instead of voting against it. He said, "Because of Bill Johnson's big stick!" (Johnson is the editor of a very powerful newspaper in the congressman's constituency.) Another congressman that I know voted for the reorganization bill. He said to me, "I could not have voted any other way without being ridiculous in my own eyes." He added, however, that he had received ten times as many letters against the reorganization plan as he had for it. Yet, he felt so strongly on this matter himself that he had no choice. He happens, however, to be one of the two or three strongest and most forthright men in Congress. Unfortunately, he is not so strong in his own constituency, and whether or not he is returned this November will depend on the personal campaigning that he does between now and then, as well as on the nature of his opposition at that time. . . .

* The reference is to the bills FDR submitted in 1937–1938 for the reorganization of the executive branch on the recommendation of the President's Committee on Administrative Management (the Brownlow committee). The bill had multi-intellectual support and competent thinkers, but it became mixed up with the court reform proposals, served to strengthen President vis-à-vis Congress, and the committee wanted to show FDR a thing or two. For these reasons, the package was defeated. In 1939, another, drastically watered, version passed.

25

A CAUSE CÉLÈBRE

George W. Pepper

Politics, in the sense of officeholding, was hardly more than an interlude in the long life of George Wharton Pepper (1867–1961), who practiced law and taught law for many years before and after his appointment to the United States Senate in 1922 to succeed the Republican "boss," Boies Penrose, deceased. At bottom, Mr. Pepper expressed in his autobiography a distaste for politics that is reflected in the selection reprinted here. Was he any the less partisan than the fellow senators he condemns —all, incidentally, of the Progressive stamp?

*

. . .

THE BIG QUESTION before the Senate when I took the oath of office [1922] was whether or not to unseat Senator Truman H. Newberry of Michigan. He had been nominated in an open state-wide primary in the course of which his friends had raised and spent about $195,000. Immediately thereafter, he and 134 others had been charged with conspiracy to violate the Corrupt Practices Act of Congress. A jury had been permitted by a federal judge to regard it a crime for a candidate to acquiesce in the expenditure of more than his own permissible contribution of $3750. Under this preposterous interpretation of the statute, Newberry and others had been convicted. On appeal, the Supreme Court set aside the conviction, the majority being of opinion that the Act of Congress did not extend to primary elections. Of course, no Justice approved the interpretation given to the statute by the lower court. Meanwhile, in a hotly contested campaign, in which the expenditure in the primary was the principal argument against Newberry, the people of Michigan voted him into office, thus expressing the judgment that there had been nothing unreasonable in the expenditure. There never was any evidence of fraudulent use of money. Senator Newberry having thus been fairly elected by the people, the question was whether the Senate should deny him a seat.

The Senate debate proceeded with fire and fury. As I listened with all the rapt attention of a new member, I became convinced of two things: first that in the absence of fraud it was not the Senate's business to set aside the deliberate judgment of the people of Michigan; and, second, that the talk of a majority of the senators who were attacking Newberry was hollow and unreal. A few of the attackers sounded fanatical and seemed quite unfit to discharge a delicate judicial duty. This was particularly true of Senator Kenyon of Iowa who clothed himself with self-righteousness as with a garment. Senator Walsh of Montana seemed to me to forget the big outlines of the case and to lose himself in details. "Joe" Robinson, "Jim" Reed, and a lot of others talked too good and looked too wise. "Tom" Heflin seemed more impressed by the fact that Newberry had been silent under accusation than by anything else in the case. It was fairly obvious why silence was incomprehensible to him.

It was a disillusioning debate, but was like many I was to hear later. Newspaper correspondents, sitting day after day in the press gallery, develop a cynicism about senators which, on the whole, is justifiable. These trained observers know perfectly well that a large percentage of noble utterances have no real relation either to the merits of the case or to the moral standards of the speaker.

The resolution to unseat Senator Newberry was lost. I voted against it. Nothing was thereby settled, for the prosecutors kept threatening to renew the attack at a later session; and under this sort of pressure, Senator Newberry finally resigned. The whole proceeding shocked me at the time, and I get angry whenever I think of it. Four years later, campaign expenditures were to become an issue in a Pennsylvania primary and I, personally, was to suffer from the use of funds ostensibly expended in my behalf.

26

I NEVER MET AN HONEST
POLITICIAN

M. R. Werner

After the exposé of the infamous Tweed Ring, the reform administration of New York City made half-hearted efforts to recover the sums swindled from the city treasury. In the course of the Tweed Ring investigations conducted by the city fathers, Alderman Cowing asked the assistant Ring paymaster, Mr. Woodward, the following questions and received the following replies.*

*

. . .

ONE ALDERMAN, Cowing, asked Mr. Woodward, the assistant paymaster of the Tweed Ring, the following questions and received the following replies:

Q. Now, how much more could you restore if compelled by a moral conviction of the necessity of dealing with the city with perfect honesty?

A. I couldn't restore another dollar. The $150,000 was all I could restore, and I don't think you have any right to ask me those questions.

Q. I wish to see if you are reformed?

A. I am not a reformer.

Q. And you would still do the same thing over again if you had a chance?

From M. R. Werner, *Tammany Hall* (New York: Doubleday Doran & Co., 1928), by permission of the author.

* See also *Tweed Ring Investigation: Report of the Special Committee of the Board of Aldermen Appointed to Investigate the "Ring" Frauds, Together with the Testimony Elicited During the Investigation.* Board of Aldermen, January 4, 1878, Document No. 8, New York, 1878.

A. I don't think there's one in this room who wouldn't do it if they had a chance.

Q. That is not complimentary to the people in this room. Do you include yourself?

A. Oh, yes, of course I do.

Q. Then the city's compromising with you has not made any better man and citizen of you?

A. I am not a citizen of New York and have got nothing to do with it. [He was then a resident of Connecticut.]

Q. I am trying to get at your idea of what might honestly be expected of you.

A. You have no right to ask me those questions, Alderman, but if you ask my opinion of politicians, I can only say I never met an honest one, and I don't believe there's an honest politician in the world. . . .

Q. You don't estimate the honesty of your fellow men very highly?

A. I never saw an honest politician in my life.

Q. Never did?

A. Never, sir; my experience is about as good as anybody's in this room.

Q. Have you met all politicians?

A. I have met all stripes of them.

Q. And never found an honest one?

A. Never.

Q. What do you predicate that on?

A. On my intimacy with them. . . . I may have been more unfortunate than others, but I don't think so.

27

MY CONNECTION WITH
MRS. REYNOLDS

Alexander Hamilton

Alexander Hamilton (1757–1804) was serving as Secretary of the Treasury when he formed his connection with Mrs. Maria Reynolds. In that period, rumors of an improper pecuniary relationship between himself and Mrs. Reynolds began to circulate. Hamilton was called to account, privately, by several congressmen who proposed to investigate his conduct, but he satisfied them that his alliance with Mrs. Reynolds had not impaired the credit of the United States. He resigned his cabinet post in 1795, but remained an influential figure in the Federalist party. In 1796, the old rumors took a more open form with the publication of a pamphlet, "The History of the United States for 1796," an attack on Hamilton that took the position that his interest in Mrs. Reynolds was not an affair of the heart, but of the purse. A portion of Hamilton's forthright answer is reprinted here.

*

.   .   .

I PROCEED . . . to offer a frank and plain solution of the enigma by giving a history of the origin and progress of my connection with Mrs. Reynolds, of its discovery, real or pretended by the husband, and of the disagreeable embarrassments to which it exposed me. This history will be

From Alexander Hamilton, *Observations on Certain Documents Contained in V and VI of "History of the United States for the Year 1796," in which the Charge of Speculation against Alexander Hamilton, late Secretary of the Treasury, Is Fully Refuted* (Philadelphia: 1797).

supported by the letters of Mr. and Mrs. Reynolds, which leave no room for doubt of the principal facts, and at the same time explain with precision the objects of the little notes from me which have been published, showing clearly that such even as have related to money had no reference to any concern in speculation. As the situation which will be disclosed will fully explain every ambiguous appearance and meet satisfactorily the written documents, nothing more can be requisite to my justification. For frail indeed will be the tenure by which the most blameless man will hold his reputation if the assertations of three of the most abandoned characters in the community, two of them stigmatized by the discrediting crime which has been mentioned, are sufficient to blast it; the business of accusation would soon become in such a case, a regular trade, and men's reputations would be bought and sold like any marketable commodity.

Some time in the summer of the year 1791, a woman called at my house in the city of Philadelphia and asked to speak with me in private. I attended her into a room apart from the family. With a seeming air of affliction, she informed me that she was a daughter of a Mr. Lewis, sister to a Mr. G. Livingston of the state of New York, and wife to Mr. Reynolds whose father was in the commissary department during the war with Great Britain, that her husband, who for a long time had treated her very cruelly, had lately left her to live with another woman, and in so destitute a condition, that though desirous of returning to her friends she had not the means; that knowing I was a citizen of New York, she had taken the liberty to apply to my humanity for assistance.

I replied, that her situation was a very interesting one—that I was disposed to afford her assistance to convey her to her friends, but this at the moment not being convenient to me (which was the fact) I must request the place of her residence, to which I should bring or send a small supply of money. She told me the street and the number of the house where she lodged. In the evening I put a bank bill in my pocket and went to the house. I inquired for Mrs. Reynolds and was shown up the stairs, at the head of which she met me and conducted me into her bedroom. I took the bill out of my pocket and gave it to her. Some conversation ensued from which it was quickly apparent that other than pecuniary consolation would be acceptable.

At meetings with her, most of them at my own house—Mrs. Hamilton with her children being absent on a visit to her father—in the course of a short time, she mentioned to me that her husband had solicited a reconciliation, and affected to consult me about it. I advised to it, and was soon after informed by her that it had taken place. She told me, besides, that her husband had been engaged in speculation, and she believed could give some information respecting the conduct of some persons in the department which would be useful. I sent for Reynolds who came to me accordingly.

In the course of our interview, he confessed he had obtained a list of claims from a person in my department which he had made use of in his speculations. I invited him, by the expectation of my friendship and good offices, to disclose the person. After some affectation of scruple, he pretended to yield, and ascribed the infidelity to Mr. Duer, from whom he said he had obtained the list in New York, while he (Duer) was in the department.

As Mr. Duer had resigned his office some time before the seat of government was removed to Philadelphia, this discovery, if it had been true, was not very important—yet it was the interest of my passions to appear to set value on it and to continue the expectation of friendship and good offices. Mr. Reynolds told me he was going to Virginia, and on his return would point something in which I could serve him. I do not know but he said something about employment in a public office.

On his return he asked employment as a clerk in the Treasury Department. The knowledge I had acquired of him was decisive against such a request. I parried it by telling him, what was true, that there was no vacancy in my immediate office and that the appointment of clerks in the other branches of the department was left to the chiefs of the respective branches. Reynolds alleged . . . as a topic of complaint against me that I had promised him employment and had disappointed him. The situation with the wife would naturally incline me to conciliate this man. It is possible I may have used vague expressions which raised expectations; but the more I learned of the person, the more inadmissible his employment in a public office became. Some material reflections will occur here to a discerning mind. Could I have preferred my private gratification to the public interest, should I not have found the employment he desired for a man, whom it was so convenient to me, on my own statement, to lay under obligations? Had I any such connection with him, as he has since pretended, is it likely that he would have wanted other employment? Or is it likely that wanting it, I should have hazarded his resentment by persevering refusal? This little circumstance shows at once the delicacy of my conduct, in its public relations, and the impossibility of my having the connection pretended with Reynolds.

The intercourse with Mrs. Reynolds, in the meantime, continued; and, through various reflections (in which a further knowledge of Reynolds' character and suspicion of some concert between the husband and wife bore a part), induced me to wish a cessation of it; yet, her conduct, made it extremely difficult to disentangle myself. All the appearances of violent attachment, and of agonizing distress of the idea of a relinquishment, were played off with a most imposing art. This, though it did not make me entirely the dupe of the plot, yet kept me in a state of irresolution. My sensibility, perhaps my vanity, admitted the possibility of a real fondness, and led me to adopt a plan of a gradual discontinuance rather than of a sudden interruption, as least calculated to give pain, if a real partiality existed.

Mrs. Reynolds, on the other hand, employed every effort to keep up my attention and visits. Her pen was freely employed, and her letters were filled with those tender and pathetic effusions which would have been natural for a woman truly fond and neglected.

One day, I received a letter from her . . . intimating discovery by her husband. It was a matter of doubt with me whether there had been really a discovery by accident, or whether the time for the catastrophe of the plot was arrived.

[Hamilton met Reynolds and paid him, in two installments, a thousand dollars as "the plaster for his wounded honor." Later he received a letter "by which Reynolds invites me to *renew my visits to his wife*. He had before requested that I should see her no more. The motive to this step appears in the conclusion of the letter, 'I rely upon your befriending me, *if there should anything offer which should be to my advantage*, as you express a wish to befriend me.' Is the pre-existence of a speculating connection reconcilable with this mode of expression?"]

[The affair resumed.] Mrs. Reynolds more than once communicated to me that Reynolds would occasionally relapse into discontent at his situation—would treat her very ill—hint at the assassination of me—and more openly threaten, by way of revenge, to inform Mrs. Hamilton—all this naturally gave some uneasiness. I could not be absolutely certain whether it was artifice or reality. In the workings of human inconsistency, it was very possible that the same man might be corrupt enough to compound for his wife's chastity and yet have sensibility enough to be restless in the situation and to hate the cause of it.

Reflections like these induced me for some time to use palatives with the ill humors which were announced to me.

.   .   .

But it is observed that the dread of the disclosure of an amorous connection was not a sufficient cause for my humility and that I have nothing to lose as to my reputation for chastity concerning which the world had affixed a previous opinion.

I shall not enter into the question what was the previous opinion entertained of me in this particular, nor how well founded, if it was indeed such as it is represented to have been. It is sufficient to say that there is a wide difference between the vague rumors and suspicions and the evidence of a positive fact—no man not indelicately unprincipled, with the state of manners in this country, would be willing to have a conjugal infidelity fixed on him with positive certainty. He would know that it would justly injure him with a considerable and respectable portion of the society, and especially no man tender of the happiness of an excellent wife could, without extreme pain, look forward to the affliction which she might endure from the disclosure, especially a *public disclosure,* of the fact. Those best acquainted with the interior of my domestic life will best appreciate the force of such a consideration on me.

The truth was, I dreaded extremely a disclosure, and was willing to make large sacrifices to avoid it. It is true that from the acquiescence of Reynolds, I had strong ties on his secrecy, but how could I rely on any tie upon so base a character? How could I know, but that from moment to moment he might, at the expense of his own disgrace, become the *mercenary* of a party, with whom to blast my character in *any way* as a favored object!

.   .   .

If, after the recent confession of the gentlemen themselves, it could be useful to fortify the proof of the full conviction my explanation had brought, I might appeal to the total silence concerning this charge when, at a subsequent period, in the year 1793, there was such an active legislative persecution of me. It might not even perhaps be difficult to establish that it came under the eye of Mr. Giles and that he discarded it as a plain case of a private amour unconnected with anything that was the proper subject for public attack.

Thus, has my desire to destroy this slander, completely, led me to a more copious and particular examination of it than, I am sure, was necessary. The bare perusal of the letters from Reynolds and his wife is sufficient to convince my greatest enemy that there is nothing worse in the affair than irregular and indelicate amour. For this, I bow to the just censure that it merits. I have paid pretty severely for the folly and can never recollect it without disgust and self-condemnation; it might seem affectation to say more.

PART FOUR

Civic Courage

28

CIVIC COURAGE

William James

This selection is from an oration by William James (1842–1910) at exercises in the Boston Music Hall, May 31, 1897, upon the unveiling of the monument to Robert Gould Shaw. Colonel Shaw led a regiment of Negro troops during the Civil War in the assault on Fort Wagner, their first serious engagement. In that battle, two-thirds of the officers and five-twelfths of the common soldiers of the regiment were killed. Colonel Shaw's body and those of his Negro comrades were buried in a common trench, an unmarked grave. As James observes, their burial, as had their lives, "bore witness to the brotherhood of man."

*

. . .

THE GREAT WAR for the Union will be like the siege of Troy; it will have taken its place amongst all other "old, unhappy, far-off things and battles long ago."

In all such events two things must be distinguished: the moral service of them, from the fortitude which they display. War has been much praised and celebrated among us of late as a school of manly virtue; but it is easy to exaggerate on this point. Ages ago, war was the gory cradle of mankind, the grim-featured nurse that alone could train our savage progenitors into some semblance of social virtue, teach them to be faithful one to another, and force them to sink their selfishness in wider tribal ends. War still excels in this prerogative; and whether it be paid in years of service, in treasure, or in life-blood, the war tax is still the only tax

Memories and Studies, Copyright © 1934 by William James. Reprinted by permission of Paul R. Reynolds, Inc., 599 Fifth Avenue, New York 17, N.Y.

that men ungrudgingly will pay. How could it be otherwise, when the survivors of one successful massacre after another are the beings from whose loins we and all our contemporary races spring? Man is once [and] for all a fighting animal; centuries of peaceful history could not breed the battle-instinct out of us; and our pugnacity is the virtue least in need of reinforcement by reflection, least in need of orator's or poet's help.

What we really need the poet's and orator's help to keep alive in us is not, then, the common and gregarious courage which Robert Shaw showed when he marched with you, men of the Seventh Regiment. It is that more lonely courage which he showed when he dropped his warm commission in the glorious Second to head your dubious fortunes, Negroes of the Fifty-fourth. That lonely kind of courage (civic courage as we call it in times of peace) is the kind of valor to which the monuments of nations should most of all be reared, for the survival of the fittest has not bred it into the bone of human beings as it has bred military valor; and of five hundred of us who could storm a battery side by side with others, perhaps not one would be found ready to risk his worldly fortunes all alone in resisting an enthroned abuse. The deadliest enemies of nations are not their foreign foes; they always dwell within their borders. And from these internal enemies, civilization is always in need of being saved. The nation blest above all nations is she in whom the civic genius of the people does the saving day by day, by acts without external picturesqueness; by speaking, writing, voting reasonably; by smiting corruption swiftly; by good temper between parties; by the people knowing true men when they see them, and preferring them as leaders to rabid partisans or empty quacks. Such nations have no need of wars to save them. Their accounts with righteousness are always even; and God's judgments do not have to overtake them fitfully in bloody spasms and convulsions of the race.

The lesson that our war ought most of all to teach us is the lesson that evils must be checked in time, before they grow so great. The Almighty cannot love such long-postponed accounts, or such tremendous settlements. And surely He hates all settlements that do such quantities of incidental devils' work. Our present situation, with its rancors and delusions, what is it but the direct outcome of the added powers of government, the corruptions and inflations of the war? Every war leaves such miserable legacies, fatal seeds of future war and revolution, unless the civic virtues of the people save the state in time.

Robert Shaw had both kinds of virtue. As he then led his regiment against Fort Wagner, so surely would he now be leading us against all lesser powers of darkness had his sweet young life been spared. You think of many as I speak of one. For, North and South, how many lives as sweet, unmonumented for the most part, commemorated solely in the hearts of mourning mothers, widowed brides, or friends did the inexorable war mow down! Instead of the full years of natural service from so many of her children, our country counts but their poor memories, "the tender grace of a day that is dead," lingering like echoes of past music on the vacant air.

But so and so only was it written that she should grow sound again. From that fatal earlier unsoundness, those lives have brought for North and South together permanent release. The warfare is accomplished; the iniquity is pardoned. No future problem can be like that problem. No task laid on our children can compare in difficulty with the task with which their fathers had to deal. Yet, as we face the future, tasks enough await us. The republic to which Robert Shaw and a quarter of a million like him were faithful unto death is no republic that can live at ease hereafter on the interest of what they have won. Democracy is still upon its trial. The civic genius of our people is its only bulwark, and neither laws nor monuments, neither battleships nor public libraries, nor great newspapers nor booming stocks, neither mechanical invention nor political adroitness, nor churches nor universities nor civil service examinations can save us from degeneration if the inner mystery be lost. That mystery, at once the secret and the glory of our English-speaking race, consists in nothing but two common habits, two inveterate habits carried into public life— habits so homely that they lend themselves to no rhetorical expression, yet habits more precious, perhaps, than any that the human race has gained. They can never be too often pointed out or praised. One of them is the habit of trained and disciplined good temper toward the opposite party when it fairly wins its innings. It was by breaking away from this habit that the slave states nearly wrecked our nation. The other is that of fierce and merciless resentment toward every man or set of men who breaks the public peace. By holding to this habit the free states saved her life.

O my countrymen, southern and northern, brothers hereafter, masters, slaves, and enemies no more, let us see to it that both of those heirlooms are preserved. So may our ransomed country, like the city of the promise, lie forever foursquare under Heaven, and the ways of all the nations be lit up by its light.

29

EXCERPT FROM *ANTIGONE*

Sophocles

Should a citizen, a politician, a ruler respond to human law or divine law —prefer order in human affairs or obedience to the gods? In this excerpt from Antigone, *Creon has declared that Polynices, who warred against Thebes, shall not be buried or mourned. He decrees death as the penalty for violation. Polynices' sister, Antigone, disobeys, is captured, and is brought before Creon who carries out his decree. To Creon, "whoso greater than his country's cause esteems a friend, I count him nothing worth." Antigone replies that, "a mortal's bidding," such as Creon's edict, could not override "unwritten laws, eternal in the heavens."*

In the confrontation between Creon and Antigone, we discern the now familiar idea that men live under contradictory imperatives—politicians more than most. Can we do more than clarify the alternatives?

*

. . .

CREON: Sirs, it hath pleased the gods to right again
Our Theban fortunes, by sore tempest tossed:
And by my messenger I summoned hither
You out of all the state; first, as I knew you
To the might o' the throne of Laïus loyal ever:
Also, when Oedipus upheld the state,
And when he perished, to their children still
Ye with a constant mind were faithful found:
Now they are gone: both on one fatal field

From Robert Whitelaw, trans., "Sophocles, *Antigone*," in *Fifteen Greek Plays* (New York: Oxford University Press, 1943), by permission of Clarendon Press, Oxford.

An equal guilt atoned with equal doom,
Slayers of each other, by each other slain:
And I am left, the nearest to their blood,
To wield alone the scepter and the realm.
There is no way to know of any man
The spirit and the wisdom and the will,
Till he stands proved, ruler and lawgiver.
For who, with a whole city to direct,
Yet cleaves not to those counsels that are best,
But locks his lips in silence, being afraid,
I held and hold him ever of men most base:
And whoso greater than his country's cause
Esteems a friend, I count him nothing worth.
For, Zeus who seeth all be witness now,
Nor for the safety's sake would I keep silence,
And see the ruin on my country fall,
Nor would I deem an enemy to the state
Friend to myself; remembering still that she,
She only brings us safe: on board of her
Our friends we make—no friends, if she be lost.
So for the good of Thebes her laws I frame:
And such the proclamation I set forth,
Touching the sons of Oedipus, ev'n now—
Eteocles, who fighting for this land
In battle has fall'n, more valiant none than he,
To bury, and no funeral rite omit
To brave men paid—their solace in the grave:
Not so his brother, Polynices: he,
From exile back returning, utterly
With fire his country and his fathers' gods
Would fain have burnt, fain would with kinsmen's blood
Have slaked his thirst, or dragged us captive hence:
Therefore to all this city it is proclaimed
That none may bury, none make moan for him,
But leave him lying all ghastly where he fell,
Till fowls o' the air and dogs have picked his bones.
So am I purposed: not at least by me
Shall traitors be preferred to honest men:
But, whoso loves this city, him indeed
I shall not cease to honor, alive or dead.
     CHORUS: Creon, son of Menoeceus, 'tis thy pleasure
The friend and foe of Thebes so to requite:
And, whatso pleases thee, that same is law,
Both for our Theban dead and us who live.

CREON: Look to it, then, my bidding is performed.
CHORUS: Upon some younger man impose this burden.
CREON: To watch the body, sentinels are set.
CHORUS: What service more then wouldst thou lay on us?
CREON: That ye resist whoever disobeys.
CHORUS: Who is so senseless that desires to die?
CREON: The penalty is death: yet hopes deceive,
And men wax foolish oft through greed of gain.

.   .   .

CREON: Where, on what manner, was your captive taken?
SENTINEL: Burying the man, we took her: all is told.

.   .   .

CREON: Speak thou, who bendest on the earth thy gaze,
Are these things, which are witnessed, true or false?
ANTIGONE: I say I did it; I deny it not.
CREON: So, sirrah, thou art free; go where thou wilt,
Loosed from the burden of this heavy charge.
But tell me thou—and let thy speech be brief—
The edict hadst thou heard, which this forbade?
ANTIGONE: I could not choose but hear what all men heard.
CREON: And didst thou dare to disobey the law?
ANTIGONE: Nowise from Zeus, me thought, this edict came,
Nor Justice, that abides among the gods
In Hades, who ordained these laws for men.
Nor did I deem *thine* edicts of such force
That they, a mortal's bidding, should o'erride
Unwritten laws, eternal in the heavens.
Not of to-day or yesterday are these,
But live from everlasting, and from whence
They sprang, none knoweth. I would not, for the breach
Of these, through fear of any human pride,
To heaven atone. I knew that I must die:
How else? Without thine edict, that were so.
And if before my time, why, this were gain.
Compassed about with ills, who lives, as I,
Death, to such life as his, must needs be gain.
So is it to me to undergo this doom
No grief at all: but had I left my brother,
My mother's child, unburied where he lay,
Then I had grieved; but now this grieves me not.
Senseless I seem to thee, so doing? Belike
A senseless judgment finds me void of sense. . . .

30

THE POLICY OF "DON'T CARE"

Abraham Lincoln

*At Cooper Institute, in his address to the Young Men's Republican Union,
February 27, 1860, Abraham Lincoln (1809–1865) explained how he
thought a determined and aggressive opposition should be met. His
speech had been carefully thought out, reflecting perhaps the difficulty he
experienced personally in coming to grips with the issue of slavery. In
the face of his declaration that "right makes might," his position seems
cautious and politic. Are those qualities simply the vacillations of a
presidential aspirant, or do they suggest a way of dealing sensibly with
irreconcilables?*

*

.　　.　　.

A FEW WORDS now to Republicans. It is exceedingly desirable that all
parts of this great confederacy shall be at peace, and in harmony, one
with another. Let us Republicans do our part to have it so. Even though
much provoked, let us do nothing through passion and ill temper. Even
though the Southern people will not so much as listen to us, let us calmly
consider their demands, and yield to them if, in our deliberate view of our
duty, we possibly can. Judging by all they say and do, and by the subject
and nature of their controversy with us, let us determine, if we can, what
will satisfy them.

Will they be satisfied if the territories be unconditionally surrendered
to them? We know they will not. In all their present complaints against
us, the territories are scarcely mentioned. Invasions and insurrections are

From Abraham Lincoln's address at Cooper Institute, February 27, 1860, in response to
an invitation from the Young Men's Republican Union.

the rage now. Will it satisfy them, if, in the future, we have nothing to do with invasions and insurrections? We know it will not. We so know, because we know we never had anything to do with invasions and insurrections; and yet this total abstaining does not exempt us from the charge and the denunciation.

The question recurs, what will satisfy them? Simply this: We must not only let them alone, but we must, somehow, convince them that we do let them alone. This, we know by experience, is no easy task. We have been so trying to convince them from the very beginning of our organization, but with no success. In all our platforms and speeches we have constantly protested our purpose to let them alone; but this has had no tendency to convince them. Alike unavailing to convince them, is the fact that they have never detected a man of us in any attempt to disturb them.

These natural, and apparently adequate means all failing, what will convince them? This, and this only: cease to call slavery *wrong,* and join them in calling it *right*. And this must be done thoroughly—done in *acts* as well as in *words*. Silence will not be tolerated—we must place ourselves avowedly with them. Senator Douglas' new sedition law must be enacted and enforced, suppressing all declarations that slavery is wrong, whether made in politics, in presses, in pulpits, or in private. We must arrest and return their fugitive slaves with greedy pleasure. We must pull down our free-state constitutions. The whole atmosphere must be disinfected from all taint of opposition to slavery, before they will cease to believe that all their troubles proceed from us.

I am quite aware they do not state their case precisely in this way. Most of them would probably say to us, "Let us alone, *do* nothing to us, and *say* what you please about slavery." But we do let them alone—have never disturbed them—so that, after all, it is what we say, which dissatisfies them. They will continue to accuse us of doing, until we cease saying.

I am also aware they have not, as yet, in terms, demanded the overthrow of our free-state constitutions. Yet those constitutions declare the wrong of slavery, with more solemn emphasis than do all other sayings against it; and when all these other sayings shall have been silenced, the overthrow of these constitutions will be demanded, and nothing be left to resist the demand. It is nothing to the contrary, that they do not demand the whole of this just now. Demanding what they do, and for the reason they do, they can voluntarily stop nowhere short of this consummation. Holding, as they do, that slavery is morally right and socially elevating, they cannot cease to demand a full national recognition of it, as a legal right, and a social blessing.

Nor can we justifiably withhold this, on any ground save our conviction that slavery is wrong. If slavery is right, all words, acts, laws, and constitutions against it are themselves wrong and should be silenced and swept away. If it is right, we cannot justly object to its nationality—its universality; if it is wrong, they cannot justly insist on its extension—its enlargement. All they ask, we could readily grant, if we thought slavery right; all we ask, they could as readily grant, if they thought it wrong. Their thinking it right, and our thinking it wrong, is the precise fact on which depends the whole controversy. Thinking it right, as they do, they are not to blame for desiring its full recognition, as being right; but, thinking it wrong, as we do, can we yield to them? Can we cast our votes with their view, and against our own? In view of our moral, social, and political responsibilities, can we do this?

Wrong as we think slavery is, we can yet afford to let it alone where it is, because that much is due to the necessity arising from its actual presence in the nation; but can we, while our votes will prevent it, allow it to spread into the national territories, and to overrun us here in these free states? If our sense of duty forbids this, then let us stand by our duty, fearlessly and effectively. Let us be diverted by none of those sophistical contrivances wherewith we are so industriously plied and belabored —contrivances such as groping for some middle ground between the right and the wrong, vain as the search for a man who should be neither a living man nor a dead man—such as a policy of "don't care" on a question about which all true men do care—such as Union appeals beseeching true Union men to yield to Disunionists, reversing the divine rule, and calling, not the sinners, but the righteous to repentance—such as invocations to Washington, imploring men to unsay what Washington said and undo what Washington did.

Neither let us be slandered from our duty by false accusations against us, nor frightened from it by menaces of destruction to the government nor of dungeons to ourselves.

Let us have faith that right makes might, and in that faith, let us, to the end, dare to do our duty as we understand it.

31

MORAL COURAGE

Mark Twain

During the "Great Barbecue," as Mark Twain (Samuel Clemens, 1835–1910) dubbed the era after the Civil War, few resisted the opportunity to share the "common oil," land for farmer-soldiers, pensions for their widows, public bounty for energetic railroad magnates. Mark Twain saw in all this two conditions of Roman decline: "stupendous wealth with its inevitable corruptions" and "vote bribes, which have taken away the pride of thousands of tempted men and turned them into willing alms receivers and unashamed."* Why, he asks in this selection, is the kind of courage required to oppose civic evil in such short supply?

*

. .

IT IS CURIOUS—curious that physical courage should be so common in the world, and moral courage so rare. A year or two ago a veteran of the Civil War asked me if I did not sometimes have a longing to attend the annual great Convention of the Grand Army of the Republic and make a speech. I was obliged to confess that I wouldn't have the necessary moral courage for the venture, for I would want to reproach the old soldiers for not rising up in indignant protest against our government's vote-purchasing additions to the pension list, which is making of the remnant of their brave lives one long blush. I might try to say the words but would lack the guts and would fail. It would be one tottering moral coward trying

* *Mark Twain in Eruption*, p. 69.

to rebuke a houseful of like breed—men nearly as timid as himself but not any more so.

Well, there it is—I am a moral coward like the rest; and yet it is amazing to me that out of the hundreds of thousands of physically dauntless men who faced death without a quiver of the nerves on a hundred bloody fields, not one solitary individual of them all has had courage enough to rise up and bravely curse the congresses which have degraded him to the level of the bounty-jumper and the bastards of the same. Everybody laughs at the grotesque additions to the pension fund; everybody laughs at the most grotesque of them all, the most shameless of them all, the most transparent of them all, the only frankly lawless one of them all—the immortal Executive Order 78.* Everybody laughs—privately; everybody scoffs—privately; everybody is indignant—privately; everybody is ashamed to look a real soldier in the face—but none of them exposes his feelings publicly. This is perfectly natural, and wholly inevitable, for it is the nature of man to hate to say the disagreeable thing. It is his character, his nature; it has always been so; his character cannot change; while he continues to exist it will never change by a shade. . . .

* Executive Order 78 amended the civil-service rules so as to remove upper age limits for examination.

32

POLITICAL TRICKERY

Joyce Cary

Joyce Cary (1888–1957), the British novelist, is probably best known in the United States for his character, Gully Jimson, the outrageous egoist-artist of The Horse's Mouth. *A traditional liberal in politics, Cary was disturbed by the incompatibility of liberal thought and modern experience. Toward the end of the 1930's, he tried his hand at the reformulation of liberal doctrine. The result, a book of rather unsystematic (though carefully numbered) paragraphs, was published in 1939 as* Power in Men. *From this work the following excerpt on political trickery was taken.*

*

PUBLIC CORRUPTION is probably greater and much more dangerous, because less easily discovered, in autarchies than democracies. But in one special form it appears, at first sight, to belong only to democracy. Democratic statesmen are continually reproached or despised by idealist critics for suggesting a lie, or hiding behind some ambiguity.

This trickery has perplexed even democrats. It has produced in the free countries a great body of literature in which the politician is always a liar, traitor, and self-seeker.

The truth is that democratic statesmen, as party leaders, are obliged to play the part of the advocate. No one finds fault with a barrister for making a good case on behalf of his client. A party leader is under the same duty. For he represents a group; he is chosen to do so. Through him

From *Power in Men* (Seattle: University of Washington Press, 1963). Reprinted by permission of the authors; copyright © 1963 by A.L.M. Cary and D.A. Olgivie.

alone the group makes its will effective; and if he fails to represent that will, he deprives it of its liberty. This fact is obvious to a parliamentarian. It puzzles only laymen. But it has been responsible for much sincere contempt, by foreign critics, of democratic institutions. . . .

33

THE DAY WE PASSED THE OATH BILL

Richard L. Neuberger

*The late Senator from Oregon, Richard L. Neuberger (1912–1960) was
a journalist, a scholar, and a politician. As the last, he attempted conscientiously to live up to the standards he had set for politicians in his
writings. He also kept up a stream of commentary on American politics
—its opportunities, frustrations, glories, and dilemmas. How he felt about
his vocation is suggested by the title of the book from which this selection
has been chosen—*Adventures in Politics. *In this chapter, he discusses what
can happen in a legislative chamber when its members are caught in the
no-man's land between their better judgment and extreme contrary pressures. His wife, Maurine, who is mentioned in the selection, succeeded
Mr. Neuberger as senator.*

*

THE DAY WE PASSED the teachers' oath bill in the Oregon Senate was the
most uncomfortable day I ever have spent during my service in minor
political posts, which includes membership as an Oregon state representative before the war and now as a state senator.

It was unlike any other issue. An atmosphere of tension prevailed
from the start. Ordinarily, the senators gossiped and bantered with one
another before a day's session, trading opinions about the bills on the calendar for that particular date.

But on this day there was no swapping of early-morning views. A strange and ominous silence hung over most of us. A member of a veterans' organization to which I belong had come to my desk and said he hoped I would "vote for America." I told my veteran friend that according to the best of my poor lights I always voted for America. Aside from this, no one mentioned Senate Bill 323. Curiously, however, I did overhear some minor observations about trivial bills on the docket.

A grim nervousness troubled me. It was a feeling I never had experienced when we debated a sales tax, or highway standards, or old-age assistance, or any other public question; but, on what other question before a state legislature might your vote result in doubts about your patriotism? I even had sent to Portland for a copy of a letter of commendation from my wartime commanding officer, General O'Connor. I looked it over and the phrases reassured me: ". . . a person of integrity, loyalty and ability . . . faithful and diligent. . . ."

I thought of the General standing in the clawing Arctic cold at Whitehorse and Big Delta, with the temperature at 66° below zero, exhorting his troops to build the wilderness highway and clear the tundra airfields. The General's muskrat-skin cap, I remembered, was always at a jaunty angle, no matter what the difficulties. Surely approval from such a man—West Point, '07—would stand me in good stead that day if my vote aroused the kind of unfounded suspicions we had been led to expect.

Perhaps some of our anxiety stemmed from the fact that we were so unprepared to endure the kind of political pressure endemic to this issue. There we sat on the Senate floor, in front of God and everybody. We did not even have offices to which we could go for sanctuary and meditation. All our whispered presession discussions were as public as a football game. On top of all this, we virtually were serving without pay. Yet we were expected to stand up to a question as full of bitterness and hostility as any before the national Congress.

Several of my colleagues had tried hard to bottle up the bill in committee. They were opposed to a teachers' oath, felt it was bad legislation. Yet, now that the measure had been forced to the floor, I knew they intended to cast a yea vote. They had brilliant careers ahead of them in the Republican party. They could not afford to have their patriotism and loyalty impugned.

There was some advantage, I reflected sadly, to being in the minority party in a one-party state. At least, you probably weren't going anywhere. You could vote your own convictions without fearing you had cost yourself the governorship and political glory.

The first speeches for the bill were reasonably calm and logical. Why should anyone hesitate to sign such an oath in a period of national crisis? But, then, the speeches began to take on fire and brimstone. Hearst editorials were quoted, and so were statements by U. S. Senator McCarthy.

Some of the most zealous promoters of loyalty oaths for schoolteachers turned out to be senators who had sponsored bills calling for greater financial returns to the operators of pari-mutuel racetracks, to promoters of irrigation districts and to fly-by-night stock salesmen.

As I mused on the irony of this, a Republican senator strolled over and sat beside me at my walnut desk. "How are you going to vote?" he asked.

"I believe against the bill," I said somewhat tentatively.

"Then I will, too," he said and returned to his own chair.

This had never happened before. On many measures a senator often was willing to cast a solitary nay vote. Indeed, it could be a sign of independence. But this was not the case on the oath bill. No one desired to be without partners on such an issue. In fact, the brief visit from my Republican colleague helped considerably to fortify my own attitude. Truth compels me to admit that I still am uncertain how I would have voted had I been completely alone in opposition to the bill. His visit bolstered my courage.

As the speeches went on, it was evident that only a comparatively few members of the Senate felt strongly on the issue. They were making all the noise. The great majority sat in silence. In my opinion, they were ill at ease. A demagogic speech, with much flag-waving, was made by a so-called New Deal Democrat. It provoked some embarrassed glances, but no applause. I knew he had been elected to the Senate with endorsements from both the AF of L and CIO. I looked up at the gallery where sat the gray-haired retired teacher who represented the Teachers Union at the legislature. Her usually serene face was drawn and taut. Some of labor's chickens were coming home to roost.

Finally, the first talk was made against the bill. A youthful radio station manager who served on the Senate Education Committee wanted to know why teachers had been singled out. Bob Holmes asked for specific evidence of disloyalty among Oregon schoolteachers. I may have been mistaken, but I thought his speech stirred some admiration on the floor.

My own remarks were relatively short. I called to the attention of my fellow Democrats the fact that President Truman had vetoed the McCarran Bill. I reminded the Republicans that their most popular public figure, Dwight D. Eisenhower, had taken a positive position against teacher oaths when he was president of Columbia University. I pointed out that only a few days earlier the Senate had set the oath to be taken by circuit judges *pro tem.* It was the standard oath of allegiance to the state and national constitutions—no test oath at all. In other words, the Senate was alarmed about the loyalty of schoolteachers but evidently not about that of a man who would wield life-and-death powers on the bench. Was Earl Warren unpatriotic? As Governor of California, he had opposed the faculty oath at the State University. I closed with a quotation from Paul G. Hoffman which warned against the hysteria of witch-hunting.

The speeches resumed and at last we voted. The bill passed 25 to 5.

Of twelve members of the Oregon senate who were originally elected with the endorsement of organized labor, only three voted against the oath bill. In view of the fact that the national policy of both the CIO and the AF of L is emphatically against this type of legislation, the record would seem to confirm a recent claim in Portland by U. S. Senator Wayne L. Morse to the effect that trade unions have not been sufficiently "selective and discriminating" about whom they back for public office. Furthermore, at least three of labor's endorsees delivered vehement speeches for the bill. Indeed, they were the main orators on the issue!

The five who voted nay were a diverse lot. Three were Democrats, two Republicans. One was a Union Pacific railroad brakeman, a Mormon, from the rugged Blue Mountains of Oregon. Another was the manager of radio station KAST. A third was a wealthy logging-equipment wholesaler who drove a big tan Cadillac and was lay head of the Presbyterian Church synod in the state. Another was a quiet, earthy farmer who was a bell-wether of the most conservative wing of the GOP, although he told me after the vote that he was pleased to learn that Mr. Eisenhower opposed teacher oaths. And there was I, a journalist.

After we had adjourned for the day, a group of war veterans clustered at the rear of the chamber. They asked the reason for my vote. I reminded them that the lobbyists for some of the veterans organizations had spent many hours trying to lobby through the oath bill. Then I showed these veterans a bill from the U. S. Veterans Administration, a model act in force in most of the states. This bill proposed to limit the fee that a bank or lawyer could assess for administering the estate of a veteran who was in a mental institution. While the lobbyists for the veterans' groups had been spending their time on teachers' oaths, the banks had destroyed the effectiveness of the model bill to safeguard the finances of veterans who had lost their sanity. I had protested as a member of the Military Affairs Committee but received no backing. The protest had failed. I said to the assembled veterans in the Senate chamber:

"I may be wrong, but I should think that spokesmen for veterans' organizations ought to be more concerned about the welfare of men who have been mentally damaged fighting on the field of battle for the United States than in foisting special oaths on schoolteachers."

The veterans stayed on a long time. The heat and anger were gone. No further resentment was voiced. The contrast of the two bills had made an impression. I felt sure that the rank and file of these war veterans had no real personal interest in the question of a teachers' oath.

Lunch that day in the Senate lounge was a dismal occasion. One or two of the speakers for the oath bill ate their sandwiches with gusto and talked of the victory. But most of the Senators munched and said little. As I looked around me in the lounge, I could see that the so-called normal measurements of liberalism and conservatism were no gauge in such a fight. The oath bill had been supported by men who regularly voiced the aphorisms of the New Deal, who always voted against the corporations and with the "common people." On the other hand, one of the adversaries of the oath bill was a Hoover Republican who made a fetish of governmental economy and who talked frequently for "the old-fashioned virtues."

Suddenly, I realized that there was a whole lot to the old-fashioned virtues, after all—particularly when a citizen believed in them with sufficient faith to brave political perils in their defense. All at once, integrity seemed more important to me than ideology. As one of the youngest members of the Senate, I fear that this was a comparatively new set of values. In the past, zeal had dictated otherwise.

One of the conservatives said to me, "I am glad you and I voted together against the oath bill. It shows that freedom is more important than the budget." Perhaps he knew what I had been thinking, for his words paraphrased my thoughts.

It was not an historic or world-shaking episode, and it occurred in a state with 1 per cent of the national population. Yet it told me many things. Liberalism may have more to do with the heart than with the stomach. And we do not tread the trail of Jefferson just because we may remark occasionally that Jefferson was a great man. Did not the president buried at Monticello tell us that "each generation must make its own fight for liberty"?

Looking back, I have decided that the day we passed Senate Bill 323 was one brief sortie in that fight. But there was no clear division as to sides, and this will make me more circumspect in my political judgments during the future.

Yet, I must add the auspicious footnote that the teachers' oath never became law. Our brief fight, however futile in terms of Senate votes, alerted many forces in the state. This included not only schoolteachers but also the faculties of the University and State College, who saw that they would be next. The woman lobbying for the Teachers Union helped to enlist the intervention of two influential editors, Charles Sprague of the *Salem Statesman* and William M. Tugman of the *Eugene Register-Guard*.

But not even this combination could have beaten the bill had it reached the floor. Political fright and ambition would have prevailed over reason. The liberals triumphed by a stratagem frequently used by the reactionaries. They kept the bill locked in committee until the clock ran out at adjournment time.

"I don't necessarily approve of the tactic of denying a vote on the floor," Maurine [Neuberger] later told a group of Parent–Teacher leaders. "Yet," she continued, "I believe many members of the House were grateful for it. They did not like the teachers' oath bill, but they were afraid to vote against it. By holding the bill in committee, we saved their consciences and also saved the state."

This tenuous victory may yet prove to be permanent. The American Legion soon had a new state commander, Karl Wagner, who said that no Oregon schoolteachers had been shown to be Communistic and subversive, and that the Legion would not humiliate loyal teachers by forcing an oath upon them. He said that the standard oath to support the Constitutions of the state and nation had proved sufficient.

And so Oregon today, for all its conservatism, is one of the few states in the country without special test oath legislation. Never again will I regard a lost fight in the Senate as valueless. Had we sat silent when the oath bill passed our arm of the legislature 25 to 5, it probably would have been law long before this.

34

THE BIG DILEMMA: CONSCIENCE OR VOTES

William L. Benton

William L. Benton (b. 1900), chairman of the board of Encyclopaedia Britannica, *served as United States Senator from Connecticut, 1950–1952. He has kept up a lively interest in politics and the behavior of his former colleagues. Mr. Benton writes with considerable authority on "The Big Dilemma." It is said that his motion to have the Senate expel the late Senator Joseph McCarthy for abusing American citizens and for taking advantage of his position as a senator led to Benton's defeat in 1952.*

*

. . .

SHOULD A LEGISLATOR compromise his principles in order to be a successful politician? How far should he go in order to be elected? Is it enough to be right most of the time, but to yield, on occasion, to the predilections or even the prejudices of his constituents?

Many people have asked me about the dilemma implicit in these questions that has puzzled students of politics since representative government began. But, paradoxically, I have found that legislators themselves are much less puzzled—and not because they are morally insensitive. The problems they actually confront, either as candidates or as lawmakers, are rarely black-and-white issues of conscience. Almost always, they are questions of prudence and judgment—the height of a tariff or a subsidy,

From *The New York Times Magazine,* April 26, 1959. Copyright by The New York Times. Reprinted by permission.

the size of a budget item, or, more particularly, the best tactics for advancing a particular cause in the face of opposition from colleagues or from constituents at home.

Nevertheless, the classic dilemma has a new relevance. Issues of civil and human rights—for example, segregation—tend to fall in the category of conscience, and these are critically important today. We had a dramatic example last November [1958] in the write-in, paste-in blitz that unseated representative Brooks Hays in the Little Rock district [of Arkansas] because his record, his campaign and his conscience had classified him as a "moderate" on race issues.

It has been said that I was myself defeated in 1952 on an issue of conscience because I had insisted on denouncing Senator McCarthy and on demanding his expulsion from the Senate. The parallel is valid only in that I was willing, on principle, to take publicly a position that seemed politically dangerous at the time. As it turned out, I lost because 1952 was an Eisenhower year, not on the McCarthy issue, and I ran well ahead of the national ticket.

In the corridors of the Capitol in Washington, one hears it said occasionally that if a congressman votes "right" 95 per cent of the time—that is, in accordance with his own best judgment—he can afford to be "wrong" on 5 per cent of his votes—that is, against his own judgment or conscience—in seeking to serve some particular end, including his reelection. (He is supposed to console himself that his defeated opponent would doubtless have done worse.) The same formula has been said to apply to a campaign in which the candidate is forced to take controversial stands.

Is this attitude justifiable? Can such "wrong" votes be defended?

I invited some of my former colleagues to share in this discussion. They tend to focus on the question, should a legislator, once elected, compromise as a matter of practical politics in order to push necessary legislation through? They see this as closely intertwined with the question, Should a legislator compromise his principles in order to be elected?

None of these colleagues will openly admit that a principle should ever be abandoned, under any circumstance. Almost all would agree with the formulation of Prof. T. V. Smith, the philosopher-politician, who wrote: "A politician is a man who can compromise an issue without compromising himself, and who can in a pinch give an issue away without giving himself away."

Two thoughtful Republicans who have just retired—voluntarily—after distinguished careers in Congress come to different conclusions about the issue of conscience and compromise as applied to segregation. I have worked intimately with both. They are men of high principle. Senator Ralph Flanders of Vermont, who seemingly does not want to see Governor Faubus in the Senate, writes me:

There is a saying to the effect that a Senator's first duty is to get re-elected. This sounds a bit cynical, but there is a real vein of truth in it.

If I were a Southern Senator and were facing the Little Rock situation,* I would be strongly moved to avoid the extreme segregationist position, but would also avoid crusading for anti-segregation. I would join the moderates so far as seemed safe and hope for re-election, knowing that if I were defeated in the primaries my place would be taken by a rabid segregationist.

Representative John Vorys of Ohio, who was the intellectual leader of the Republican minority interested in foreign policy in the House, says:

I am extremely cautious about calling political decisions moral issues. On the other hand, I think that Congressmen and Senators are expendable rather than indispensable, and no Congressman or Senator should cast a vote he knows is wrong in order to be re-elected. It makes no difference whether the wrongness is on a moral, legal, economic, or other issue.

As Edmund Burke said: "Your representative owes you, not his industry only, but his judgment; and he betrays instead of serving you, if he sacrifices it to your opinion."

Taking the example you mention, I think that if a Southern Senator is opposed morally to segregation he should vote his convictions and take his medicine. For one thing, he might be surprised to find how many people admire that kind of courage.

Two of my correspondents cited the vote on the 1957 Civil Rights Bill and reached opposite conclusions. Senator Wayne Morse of Oregon, never one to shirk an unpopular cause and one of the most courageous men in the history of the Senate, argues that the politician's "dilemma" can usually be resolved if he works hard enough at informing his constituents. He writes:

Too often and too readily politicians—when they vote against something they know is in the public interest—fall back upon the excuse that "I know it is right, but people don't understand it."

What these politicians don't understand themselves is that it is part of their function in representative government to get the facts across to the people so they will understand. Instead, they become panhandlers for votes. We have many in public life who are afraid or unwilling to be defeated. Winning is their only goal, not true public service.

Senator Morse is certain he could not have been re-elected to the Senate in 1956, in the face of the Eisenhower landslide, if public opinion, which had opposed some of his votes when he cast them, had not later swung over to his view.

Having battled for civil rights throughout his career, he was never-

* In 1957, Governor Orville Faubus of Arkansas attempted by various means to prevent the admission of Negro children to the Little Rock High School pursuant to court order. President Eisenhower sent federal troops to Little Rock to enforce the mandate of the judiciary. Feelings ran high among white citizens and segregationists withheld votes from politicians who did not support their hard line against integration. Representative Brooks Hays was a victim of this political backlash.

theless the only senator outside the south who voted against the 1957 Civil Rights bill. Here is an example of his individuality and his spirit. He says:

Of course, I recognize the need for compromise in legislation; but, the Civil Rights bill of 1957 was passed because members of Congress wanted to be on record as having voted for something with that title; their bill actually compromised the civil rights guarantee of the Fourteenth Amendment. I do not accept the view that such a compromise of principle is ever justified. When a principle is compromised it is destroyed, and all that is left is a statement of expediency.

"But," says the doubter, "when does the legislator know when he is dealing with a matter of principle?" The answer is that his brains and conscience always tell him so, and he always knows when he has compromised a principle.

Senator Clinton P. Anderson of New Mexico, one of the most able, experienced, and humble men in public life, reached a different conclusion about the same measure:

The house had passed a Civil Rights bill. It came to the Senate. The Judiciary Committee was bypassed and the bill came at once to the Senate floor. Some Senators were determined to try to pass a Civil Rights bill with the strongest possible language and the most drastic provisions. They could have adopted all their amendments, perhaps, but could never have passed the bill. . . .

I became disturbed at the situation because I wanted a Civil Rights bill passed. . . . I talked it over with Senator [now President] Lyndon Johnson and out of our conference came my approach to Senator George Aiken of Vermont, whom I greatly admire. We developed an amendment and were subsequently joined in it by a third co-sponsor, Senator Francis Case of South Dakota. That amendment to Section III was not pleasing to those who preferred defeat of the bill to any compromise, but it was adopted by the Senate and paved the way for adoption of another amendment previously offered by Senator O'Mahoney and others. When the amending process was finished, the Southerners realized they could not successfully filibuster against the revised bill. . . .

Maybe the Civil Rights bill was not everything it ought to be; maybe it will need to be amended in view of Little Rock and other spots. That will, however, come easier because of abuses which followed the passage of civil rights legislation by the Eighty-fifth Congress and will be much easier than would have been the case had the no-compromise faction had its way and no bill resulted.

Senator Johnson of Texas, widely admired as majority leader of the Senate, writes me:

The real issue is not whether a man should compromise—because I do not believe in compromising a principle—but whether he should insist on asserting his position aggressively on every single issue that comes along.

Everybody is fond of quoting Clausewitz' dictum, "War is politics carried on by other means." The reverse is also true that politics is war carried on by other means. When it is viewed in that perspective, the answer becomes somewhat more readily apparent. It would be ridiculous to say that a captain of infantry out on a scouting expedition should charge into a regiment that he meets unexpectedly.

Nobody would expect him to do so. In fact, he would be court-martialed if he did anything other than the sensible thing, which is to fall back to the main body of troops and gather his forces so he can be ready for action when action is feasible.

The captain of infantry has not "compromised" his position because he refused to sacrifice his men or his followers by fighting under impossible circumstances. Similarly, I do not think that the political leader should be accused of "compromising" his position because he, too, refused to fight on impossible terrain. It is essential for a political leader to be able to pick the terrain and the time upon which he will give battle.

Representative John W. McCormack of Massachusetts, majority leader of the House of Representatives, whose job requires him to steer legislation through the House, seems to agree with Senator Johnson. He writes:

As between partial progress and no progress, it seems to me that the constructive mind takes the road of progress.

I never place myself mentally in the position of compromising principle and conscience. But there are times when I might harmonize differences in order to make progress, or maintain unity, and then start the journey from there.

The extent of "compromise" or "harmonization" depends upon the circumstances of each case, the atmosphere, the strength of the opposition, as well as the support for a measure, and other factors. But sometimes there can be no "compromise" or "harmonization," such as the etxension of the Selective Service Act in 1941, three months before Pearl Harbor.

Senator [and late President] John F. Kennedy's book, *Profiles in Courage,** written in 1955, consists of case studies of political courage in the Senate going back to 1803. He finds that it sometimes takes courage to compromise. He writes in his book:

We shall need compromises in the days ahead, to be sure. But these will, or should be, compromises of issues, not of principles. We can resolve the clash of interest without conceding our ideals. . . . Compromise need not mean cowardice. Indeed, it is frequently the compromisers and conciliators who are faced with the severest tests of political courage as they oppose the extremist views of their constituents. It was because Daniel Webster conscientiously favored compromise in 1850 that he earned a condemnation unsurpassed in the annals of political history.

Senator Kennedy [wrote] me:

* New York: Harper, 1955, pp. 19–20.

I think even more now than I did in 1955 that the politician faces this dilemma more than the member of any other professional or occupational group. Others face different moral choices perhaps, wondering when a compromise is one of accommodation or one of principle—but no one else has to do it in such a glare of publicity, or in such an irretrievable manner, on a permanent record, and with only the answer of an "aye" or "nay" to choose between.

This last point is of high importance. There are no footnotes in the voting record; each vote is the monosyllable "aye" or "nay." The business executive seldom faces such dilemmas. His mistakes tend to be buried in the over-all record of profit and loss—or at least they can be explained in his annual report.

In my opinion, these statements by senators and congressmen (and other comments I have not quoted) deserve the highest respect, even from those who may disagree.

Further, my own experience as a legislator persuades me that congressmen are fully justified in intermingling the question of campaign policies and tactics with the question of legislative policies and tactics. The two are inseparable. The great majority of legislators who are elected in a given year in the United States—federal, state and local—have been re-elected. From the moment they were first sworn in as legislators, they were running for re-election, and this is seldom out of their thoughts. Each must run on his legislative record, he knows his next opponent will scrutinize that record with a magnifying glass.

Finally, the issues that actually confront a legislator are rarely simple. When a major bill reaches the floor it is a long, complex document. If a congressman or senator disagrees with some aspect of it, he may seek to amend that aspect from the floor—but it is usually an exercise in futility. Generally he must cast his "aye" or "nay" on its net value.

In my judgment it is often impossible for a legislator clearly to separate considerations of prudence from moral principles. Indeed, he must frequently fall back on prudence if he is to advance his moral principles.

One of America's greatest social thinkers, the late Prof. Robert Redfield,* discussing progress toward race equality, pointed out that a right and moral action may in some circumstances defeat or postpone the social end it is intended to serve.

Abraham Lincoln never doubted that slavery was wrong. Yet, in December, 1860, a month after his election as president, he offered to guarantee to the Southern states, in perpetuity, their right to a slave system, providing they agreed there should be no extension of slavery in the territories.

---

* American anthropologist, known especially for his studies of Mexican villages and his interest in integrating social science and the humanities.

Lincoln hoped that this offer might avert civil war; and undoubtedly he hoped also that the slave system would in time dissolve and disappear.

The danger in the argument for prudence is that, for those of us who are less than Lincolns, it can be an excuse for weakness. Like most other men, politicians too often underestimate the long-range values of boldness and stubbornness in defense of an ideal. Gandhi can be an example as well as Lincoln. Gandhi won because he was bold and stubborn and preferred jail to compromise.

I am so impressed with this danger that I cannot personally agree with any argument to the effect that a legislator need be morally right only 95 per cent of the time—and can thus give away the other 5 per cent even if it involves an affront to his conscience.

Ultimately, each member of Congress must make his own decision each time a matter of principle arises—to compromise or not to compromise, to stand fast or to yield ground in the belief that his action will help achieve the desired final goal. His burden is that he must make the decision again and again and again—and not just once in a moment of emotional intensity—for there may be some 200 aye or nay roll-call votes each year, plus hundreds of votes in committee or elsewhere, any one of which may involve a moral choice.

A whole nation will be watching; but, for each member of Congress the decisions, whatever they may be, must be taken in the solitude of heart and mind and conscience.

35

LIABILITIES

Stimson Bullitt

The public knows that politics has its rewards, and, intuitively, some of the pains and penalties are also known. Stimson Bullitt ran unsuccessfully for Congress in 1952 and has been active in politics in the State of Washington. He knows something of both the elation and the depression that can come from political participation. "My intention," he wrote in the foreword of To Be a Politician, *"is not to encourage those who consider entering politics either to go in or stay out. It is to give them comprehension with which to make their choice." As his first line in this selection says, to be a politician is to "live dangerously."*

*

ONE WHO ENTERS politics must realize that he is to live dangerously. In business, the line between the red and the black divides anxiety and comfort, but a businessman can survive a bad year; in politics .1 per cent of one's biennial gross vote can mean the difference between prosperity and ruin. Some politicians would say it is the difference between anxiety and ruin.

Between politics and other professions runs a deep crack. At the bottom are a lot of nice fellows. A defeated candidate, conscious of this hazard, often resumes his former work with desperation rather than enthusiasm as he hustles to make up for lost time.

For a man of active intellect, the most severe condition of politics is to abstain from the full and constant use of his powers. He must be willing to submit to boredom and make the effort to conceal it. Insofar as a politician works in his party organization, his patience is taxed by tedium such as service on committees engaged in administration (e.g., organizing a dinner meeting or picnic), a function suited to a single person. Most political meetings are dull enough to spur the ambition of impatient men. By custom, a private has to sit through them in silence, an officer is allowed to speak, and a general may arrive at the end to make the main oration during which he may while away the time by listening to his own voice.

To converse on public affairs is often stimulating. To compose a speech on some important issue is satisfying. To deliver it sometimes is exhilarating. Those occasions on which one is able to entertain or amuse a responsive audience are great fun. But much of the public relations work, in and out of campaigns, is a pattern of sitting through long meetings where the business transacted and the ceremonies performed are almost identical with what took place at the meeting the evening before, which was dull the first time; then, at the end, one must circulate within the group as it breaks up and greet strangers or acquaintances with a cordial handshake. Politics, like parenthood, is less paternal than it used to be, but it resembles parenthood in the drudgery which is a part of both.

In politics, the rate of pay is modest, although not as low as one might think from the complaints of some. Expense is high and much is not tax deductible. Because, unlike happiness, money-making can be best achieved by direct approach, politics is no place for anyone who wants to make big money, or, unless he has it already, to live on a scale of comfort which requires it. The main loss of income caused by politics is not the drop, if any, in actual net income on entering public office. It is rather that following a period of political activity the long-run level of private income tends to be below what it would have been if the person had stayed where he was and "polished the handle of the big front door." Although having done time in politics is likely to reduce a person's total lifetime income, this loss, because evenly spread and deferred to future years, is a weaker deterrent than the conditions, say, of becoming a physician, where the austerity comes at the start.

Some other lines of work take as much effort, but, except for some kinds of medical practice, none allows less time free from the cares of the job. The hours are too irregular and long to permit a satisfactory family life, although extensive political activity can be postponed until the children are of such an age that no one suffers much from your absence except your wife. After sundown, far from home, a politician may remind himself that "I have promises to keep, and miles to go before I sleep."

Cirrhosis of the liver has been called an occupational disease of newspapermen, and the same could be said of politicians. Drinking often becomes a problem because of long meetings and conferences under conditions which encourage it, in hotels, lodge halls, restaurants, and homes; social conventions permit it, and exacting thought is not required. Artificial aid seems almost imperative to men who feel they must be as genial as Santa Claus in conversation with the fiftieth stranger they have met that day. It is hard not to tire of playing the cheery friend to all the world, and the devoted slave of one's constituents; but in this profession are some teetotalers and few drunkards, because ambition is to politics what hope of profit is to business, and it is strong enough in most politicians to protect them from the allurements of drink.

It would be less perplexing to be a politician if one did not have to learn to make, and practice making, a living in two ways, as a politician and in some private work. In order to live, and also to acquire the respected status which will help him to be elected, he must apply much of his time to acquiring knowledge and practicing skills not directly connected with public affairs, and which may not be easy for him or of special interest to him. For success in most lines of work, a person's choices of activity in other, unconnected fields and his failures or successes in them are irrelevant. A physician's practice is not impaired by the fact that stocks always drop as soon as he buys them, nor is it assisted by the fact that he is a renowned poet. But a politician is measured to some extent by the nature and quality of his work performance outside politics. In politics, as elsewhere, nothing succeeds like success; but success in another field is often a condition to making a successful jump from private to public life.

A politician is helped or hurt in politics by both the choice of his private work activity and the level of his private success, which has less effect on his political success than does the nature of the private work itself. He may be shunned as unsound if he is known as an artist, good or bad, and some voters may doubt his interest in the public welfare if he has shown himself to be a gifted speculator, no matter how legitimate. For him to excel in certain fields may handicap him more than if he failed. Having gone broke as a storekeeper did not cost Lincoln or Truman many votes, but either man might have found it hard to reach the White House through the needle's eye of the Board Chairmanship of Montgomery Ward.

In many constituencies it tends to be harder to acquire the public respect and confidence necessary for election if one does not wear the mantle of the man of affairs. Some people suspect the ideas and proposals of one who does not accept tradesmen's values. Having "met a payroll" has lost some of its appeal, but long-sustained effort in the management of affairs continues to be an important asset in earning the respect of one's fellow men. Some teachers who enter politics surmount this handicap by superior knowledge of the subject matter in politics and by skill in presenting it to their audience. However, some experience acquired in the management of affairs is not merely relevant to questions of public policy but is an essential condition to political competence. Also, because a person's political ideas or abilities to apply them may be worthless, the practice of his private profession can serve as a useful end and a safe hedge to the bets on which part of his life is committed.

Because life is too short for him to master two trades, a politician sometimes learns little more about public office than how to attain it, like a student who fails to get an education because he concentrates on grades to keep his scholarship. Few men are frustrated for long by this thinly spread application of their time. Most either do not mind it, become resigned to it, or quit. Even if a politician's main interest is politics, so long as he enjoys people and the busy life of affairs, in or out of government, he is not much discontented by the differences in subject matter between his public and private callings. Also, if he prefers politically unacceptable work, this fact may prove to him and others his lack of fitness for politics.

Mendès-France* said, "To govern is to choose," but a politician's choices give offense. He does not coldly call them as he sees them. No one thinks him a mechanism which makes automatic choices as an agent of the Law, a brooding presence overhead. Everyone knows he cares about his decisions. As both referee and advocate, he plays in a game for which he makes the rules, and the rules are the object of the game. He is less protected than unknown umpires or majestic, impersonal judges. Seldom are more than a few people at a time hurt by the ruling of a trial court, but a strong, revengeful group is ready for ignition by a governor's appointment or a legislator's vote. Because a politician estranges many people by what he does or fails to do, popularity, in contrast to notoriety or fame, is not as easy to attain or to keep in politics as in some other fields, although many politicians have a craving to be liked.

When public opinion about a policy issue is widely held and strongly in contradiction to what a politician thinks is wise or just, he has to yield in principle or power. He must choose between declining to run at the next election, conforming to the public wish, or disregarding the sentiment and inviting defeat. Like an actress asking a casting director for a part, his response to these distasteful conditions depends on the comparative pulls on him of his principles, his ambition, and his taste. The most public-spirited citizen has the right, sometimes the duty, to say for himself, "The public opinion be damned." But even if at times a politician does not follow public opinion, he always must give it respect.

Another hazard, less real than apparent, is the restraint on free speech. The argument goes like this: On most jobs your speech must be

* Pierre Mendès-France (b. 1907) is a French statesman, lawyer, and economist. He entered the Chamber of Deputies as a Radical Socialist in 1932 and became premier in 1954. His cabinet fell in 1955 on the issue of his liberal North African policy.

circumspect in the presence of employer, clients, and customers, but after work you may say what you please; a servant of the public, however, whether actual or aspirant, never can escape the agents of his employer; such continual discretion is an inconvenience requiring severe discipline until it becomes a habit. This overstates the difference between the speaking conditions of public and private life. The practical limits on un-popular speech are similar for a politician and any private person whose position is a responsible one in the conduct of affairs. A man's associations often compel him to be silent so as not to hurt others close to him in his business or his firm. The silence of business life is more absolute than the cautious reticence of politics. In general, compared with private life speech in politics is less free for casual conversation, yet more free for is-sues. A politician may feel he should refrain from complaining to a friend at lunch about the cost of haircuts because this remark might start a rumor that he is "against the barbers"; yet, without disloyalty to his as-sociates, he can lead a street march for one side of a disputed issue, while if he were not in public life he might feel ashamed to appear at his place of work the morning after such a performance.

To be a brave and useful politician it is not necessary to speak out boldly whenever you differ from your associates or party. Political ties have their loyalties, and there are occasions when a man must keep silent, or else blunt the thrusting edge of his convictions. Here comes the time for anxious study and balancing what is to be gained by speaking out, as against waiting his turn. Without sacrifice of the public interest, a com-promise can be struck between saying nothing about anything and letting the chips fly. A man's duty demands candor, while his survival demands discretion. As much as possible, a politician must refrain from criticism of individuals and groups, except by inference; such talk is the main source of antagonisms. The public interest does not obligate him to make truthful statements about the truthfulness of used car dealers or Hearst news-paper editors. When asked about a pending issue, he has the duty to speak out clear and straight; but, he may mitigate the rancor of those who feel the other way by phrasing his declaration in terms which accommodate the audience. General answers of opinion are more likely to inflame than specific answers of fact. Arguing the merits of a specific solution to a prob-lem is safer than asserting controversial principles—which may antagonize whether understood or misunderstood—and more useful than asserting principles on which everyone agrees.

Speech in politics is, on the whole, as free as it is in at least some im-portant walks of private life, and thought is more free. Of late we have been learning the falsity of the old assumption that everyone is unfettered in his thoughts, no matter what restrictions may be imposed on his rights to express them. Russia and China have shown by extreme examples that conditions imposed on the individual not only can silence him but can cramp his thinking as well. The practice is to invade his thoughts, compel him to chant a litany, and then when this becomes a routine so that he can ignore it, he is made to declare some new belief. No longer can a person under such conditions reassure himself, "Come what may, I shall be undisputed master in the castle of my skin." Although the forces operating on Americans in private life are weaker and less calculated, our private citizens often become so molded by their work that, after five o'clock, they think and speak the way they do while on the job. In 1940, an advertisement appeared in the Chicago *Tribune* declaring that: "In a last stand for democracy, every director and officer of this bank will vote for Wendell Willkie." Those labor union spokesmen who for a long time claimed that the Taft-Hartley Act had repealed the Thirteenth Amendment did not exemplify such frozen thought only because most of them either did not believe what they said, or erred from lack of knowledge; they were demagogues or ignorant, but not true believers.

A businessman, conformed by his eagerness for money, recognition, or power, becomes as empty as his counterpart in public life, even more so, because in many walks of private life thought is numbed by the pursuit of money, while in politics the strife, in part, is over ideas. The habit of expressing ideas, even if not one's own, is a help. Most conversations in which a politician takes part are the same as those of other people, confined to small talk, big talk, and shop talk. Among politicians, talk is often gossip, but despite the limits on their jurisdiction, the subject matter of their conversations with other people has an almost unlimited range.

It is no harder for a politician than for a private person to stand up for principle. In politics this action tends to be taken before a crowd. There a speaker's feelings may remain more protected within himself than when he confronts another individual, the more common situation in private life. Political communication's current shift from public meetings to the media makes even more impersonal the atmosphere in which a politician declares a position which may please or offend. His thinking can be more independent of the audience, more concentrated on the subject matter, when he is looking at a camera lens or speaking to a mike. Face to face with another person, you are exposed to his reaction to you as a person. A crowd, visible or invisible, may do you harm or help you, but it will not scowl or smile.

The actual choice of side on an issue is as perplexing for a politician as for a private person, and when the side is publicly taken the exposure to criticism is the same whether one is in or out of public life. But the decision to take a stand at all, preliminary to the decision of what stand to take, is easier for a politician than for a private person because by doing nothing a politician cannot escape criticism or shame. Like a driver approaching a fork in the road, he knows that if he falters cars behind will honk. The burden of effort to get up from the armchair or bed and start action is lighter for a politician; he cannot succumb to inertia; he is jarred loose from his resting place.

When a private person sees a hot public issue he can stay in the shadows without disapproval. Even when asked, the private man can safely say, "I pass," while politicians must explain their indecision. If they fail to fulfill their publicly recognized duty to take a position on important issues they suffer the consequences of showing themselves evasive or weak. They cannot excuse themselves by ignorance, either admitted or claimed. If they do not meet an issue they must pretend illness or claim that the issue does not exist. Frequent visits to the hospital are impractical, and it is uncomfortable to be scorned by both sides of a controversy for dodging it. Therefore, the decision to take a public stand on an issue requires less effort of a politician than of private persons, who are not goaded into action and who have little to lose by standing pat.

A politician is exposed to abuse by opponents, critics, and constituents. Anyone is free to attack him and his family with falsehood or with painful truth, and many do. The half-truth is a common device because of the low risk of either legal liability or public disapproval of the author. Some news reports of a campaign resemble the ship's log in which, after the mate had written, "Today the captain was drunk," the captain wrote, "Today the mate was sober."

There are two forms of assault: on a politician's principles or policies, and on his character. A man who calls for a tariff cut on certain goods is damned by their local producers as an assassin and a cad. It is not hard to get used to invective, just as a surgeon gets used to the flow of blood. A politician is consoled by the belief that he is right and that some others agree with him. Abuse based on the things he stands for is faced without concern by any sensible politician as a hazard of his job. After a local convention, I saw a leading member of the U.S. Senate pushed backward across a hotel lobby by a drunk who prodded him with one thumb and dropped cigar ashes on his tie while scolding him for his vote on a measure which had affected a commercial interest. The senator kept repeating gently that he certainly respected the man's opinion. At last he backed into an elevator which lifted him to a room filled with loyal adherents and smoke, where he could expect to be put upon again.

In the other form of attack, no matter how preposterous the charges may be, lies about a politician's character upset and embitter him if their nature so combines with the climate of the time as to make some of his fellow men accept them as true. Even for a veteran, the pain remains acute. He has no defense, he cannot prove his innocence; and there is no fair way to hit back except by ridicule, such as for example, Franklin Roosevelt's taunts at "Martin, Barton and Fish" and his defense of his "little dog Fala"; but, ridicule is effective only when the audience is not too distrustful, and it is available only to politicians with enough wit and commanding presence to put across their gay contempt.

An impersonal attitude toward personal attacks reduces the shock and helps a politician to react with more calm than a layman would, just as an athlete is not depressed or offended by bumps he takes from other players in the course of a game. At a Senate committee hearing a certain McCarthy told a cruel lie about the young colleague of a lawyer named Welch, whom he thereby drove to tears, although Welch had a cool head and long experience in courts. Not even such a thing as this would make many politicians cry. However, players in a body-contact sport need only keep in mind that their opponents feel no spite, while a politician must try, not to remember but to ignore a fact, that his assailants often mean their blows to hurt; and therefore his defenses can be pierced.

To a politician whose policies follow the middle of the political road, abuse is like a wind blowing across it. He may move to the position opposite his critic, drifting over to the lee side for refuge and a kind word, or else going there in anger like the man who took the pitcher to the cellar for his wife. After he tripped on the top step and tumbled to the floor below, his wife called down, "Did you break the pitcher?" "No," he replied with an oath, "but I'm going to break it now!" On the other hand, a politician with a keener sense of survival but no more courage may try to refute his accusers by moving to join them on the windward side of the road.

Men shrink from politics because they can be ruined by enemies. Friends are trouble, too. The truth is hidden from a politician to keep him cheerful, or twisted to make him a more fiercely aggressive campaigner. A license to cheat the public by deceiving its servants tends to be assumed by persons who are otherwise upright.

Friendship is difficult. A politician sees many people but few of them often and over a long period. He loses friends when he acts or speaks against their wishes or beliefs. His profession is small, and the turnover is high. Few among those of his companions who remain follow the pattern of his location as it shifts between home town, county seat, state capital, and Washington. He is like a professional baseball player who does not come home in the off season. Enduring friendship is difficult because "in the frequent jumble of political atoms, the hostile and the amicable ones often change places." A politician has few friends, and he is sure of hardly any except those he knew when he was still unknown. Yet loneliness is the fate of the well-differentiated man wherever he finds himself, save as it may be cushioned by family ties. Among lawyers there is more comradeship than in any other vocation, but fellowship is less than friendship. A man with a clear-cut personality is fairly sure to feel lonely, whenever he stops to think of it. In public life he may receive inspiring loyalty that goes far to justify his personal isolation; but along with heroism and hero worship, now less common and less strong, such loyalty is in decline.

A politician may be lonely but he cannot be alone. About public leadership, Montaigne wrote: "Ambition is of all others the most contrary humor to solitude; glory and repose are things that cannot possibly inhabit in one and the same place." Some kinds of ambition permit solitude, but ambition for power and glory during life does not.

Because politics is urban, a politician may frequently praise, but seldom enjoy, nature's beauties. The only exception is a part-time politician like the farmer who goes to the legislature in winter. On a summer afternoon a politician may attend a lodge picnic at a lakeside park but he cannot walk on mountain heather nor stroll alone among the green and rolling furrowed hills of cultivated land.

Recognition for accomplishment is passing and uncertain. "It's not what you've done, it's what you've done lately" (or probably will do). This political proverb describes a fact which is in the public interest though often disappointing to an individual, as it was to Churchill in 1945. Nor is full credit given for merit. Acts of generosity, conviction, or even courtesy, are discounted as done for political gain. In principle, the practice of virtue is as it is in private life. For external rewards one has to wait for heaven.

A politician may receive gratitude for his acts of public service, and he may be pitied for his misfortunes. In politics, both gratitude and pity vanish as quickly as these fleeting sentiments do when directed at some person in private life. The transience of gratitude is the same on the part of a politician as it is for others who feel it toward him—as any president knows when he appoints a judge. Pity toward politicians is more common than gratitude. Although it is almost never felt for a loser, pity is often felt for personal misfortunes unconnected with failure, such as a death in the family. This pity is genuine and, because the politician is so well known, is widespread. President Eisenhower's partially disabling illnesses increased his support from some voters as much as it reduced it from others. Because pity often is a substantial motivating force for votes, a politician is in luck if circumstances choose campaign time in which to do him harm.

The risks of becoming a megalomaniac or a cynic are not like Scylla and Charybdis, because one can succumb to both at once. Thus a politician may think politics nonsense, and at the same time refer to himself in the third person. The altitude of some offices encourages delusions of grandeur which are latent in many of the men attracted to politics. A politician who plays the big shot in order to meet the expectations of some constituents runs the danger of coming to believe his own pretense. Sometimes, encouraged by his wife, a man may dream that destiny has chosen him to legislate in marble halls. Others give less thought to whether their country's money is going to bear a graven image of their heads. A state senator told me, "How I hate to see my name in the papers. It's always something bad. I could be re-elected forever if I could only stay out."

If a politician reveals a touch of cynicism, humbugs in a swarm embrace him. Like everyone, he sees the world through his experience, and these companions confirm his cynicism. The pressure to be cynical is strong, and the withering effect of cynicism is hard to resist. He can be lonely and thick-skinned and discreet, yet remain himself. If he becomes a cynic he is an altered man, and a hollow one. He can escape this penalty, however, if he takes care not to expect an improbable rate of progress or level of goodness, and if he does not lose his nerve.

Under the temptation and pressure to respond to popular wishes and beliefs, a politician may become nothing but a suggestion box for pressure groups—like the Emperor Claudius, "who had neither partialities nor dislikes, but such as were suggested and dictated to him." This hazard has increased. The public will is stronger, and a politician need no longer fear that by obedience to it he may forfeit his colleagues' respect; many guiding rules have disappeared. A dreadful private evil of public life is this corruption of personality which produces men who have lost their savor and are "neither fit for the land, nor yet for the dunghill."

There are two ways to listen to what is said to you: to consider the content of the statement, or to try to discern the mind of the speaker and to determine what response would be most effective to achieve your wishes in respect to him. In conversation, most people combine the two approaches, but, like those theorists of teaching method who advise, "Teach the child, not the subject," these faceless men ignore the meaning of the content except as related to the feelings of their listeners. The crowd plays Hamlet to such a man's Polonius, prodding him on to shift his interpretations to please them. An echo board with nothing of himself to give, he may be addressed in the scornful words of Conrad's captain to the outcast, "What is there in you to provoke?"

A man can lose his soul anywhere, of course. In politics there are two protections from this risk: one is a moderate ambition, enough to maintain one's effort and purpose; the other is an alternative trade, as a hole card to remind the politician of a further chance for service in another worthy calling after his defeat.

A politician has to keep his place. He will be found at fault if he is either undignified or arrogant. The former sin is venial, the latter cardinal. As Tacitus once pointed out, men tend to "scrutinize with keen eyes the recent elevation of their fellows, and to demand a temperate use of prosperity from none more rigorously than from those whom they have seen on a level with themselves." The quality of a politician's bearing is measured against the background of his rank. Arrogance in a coroner is dignity in a governor.

Egotism is increased by the sweet music of applause, but humility is also induced by the conditions of a politician's life: to be told off and have to beg his daily bread from face to face. A successful politician has a strong ego, but he lacks that kind of pride which inhibits him from asking for help.

Sometimes men are driven back to private life by exasperation with their constituents. People often resent a politician for his failure to be both delicately responsive to public wishes and a self-sustaining leader who leads. He disappoints them if he is not at once a thistledown on the breeze and a game fish that swims upstream. Hiram Gill, a former waiter, was elected mayor of Seattle on a closed-town platform. He kept his promise and was dismissed from office at the next election. He ran again on an open-town platform, was elected, kept this promise, and was again defeated. This confused Gill, who just wanted to be mayor.

Another attitude which makes for disappointed citizens and exasperated politicians is people's dislike of a cocksure manner and their concurrent wish that a politician be sure he knows the answers, since they did not elect him to doubt and ponder. They want a humble messiah. To combine modesty and certainty is less contradictory than to join responsiveness and leadership but is nonetheless a difficult standard to meet. A politician also knows that many of his constituents wish him to perform the functions of his profession yet be "above politics"—where Eisenhower tried to be and where they think Lincoln was. For a politician's personality, still another aggravating paradox is the common wish that he be both subservient and dignified, that he run petty errands, and run them as though he were descending Sinai with tablets of stone.

Imperious negative demands by constituents, often opposed to each other, may discourage one who thinks of going into politics. These persons intimidate politicians and stifle their enterprise. Subdued by threats, politicians often stand pat in order to survive or else resort to "the usual substitute for wisdom in waiting for the folly of others." In dealing with one's supporters, and with other pressure groups, one could learn from the football coach who hoped his team would lose no more games than just enough to "keep the alumni sullen but not mutinous." Indifferent to anything beyond their single purpose, these bitter citizens are less offended by sins of omission than by one act which they regard as wrong, even though combined with a record of good deeds. Politicians well may say to one another, "Constituents do make cowards of us all," and tell their fellow citizens, "He that depends upon your favors swims with fins of lead."

The Way Things Are

PART FIVE

The Way Things Are

36

IN PRAISE OF THE LEGISLATIVE
WAY

T. V. Smith

The democratic legislature has had few champions in the twentieth century. The body has seemed unduly compliant when it has been popular and merely obstructive when it has taken an independent stand. T. V. Smith (1890–1964), author, teacher, state legislator, and congressman from Illinois (1938–1940), found much good in these representative assemblies. Professor Smith was for many years associated with the Maxwell School of Public Affairs of Syracuse University.

*

. . .

LET US REPAIR NOW to the place prepared for such a conflict, to the legislative assembly. A fit meeting place it is; for the legislature, by identification, is the organ of the function in question; it is the place where honest men meet to argue over and to adjust, if possible, their differences as to honesty, where just men meet to quarrel over justice. You will expect it to be a noisy place, for there honest men will at first stand aghast at the audacity of other men who claim to be equally honest. Such men aghast are not usually silent about it. It is, in the Anglo-Saxon tradition, not as noisy a place, however, as you might well expect. The noise is mitigated by the fact that it is not the honest men of the original differences who meet there; it is rather their agents. The distance from the original differences lends, from the outset, a certain dispassion to the scene. These agents are the elected representatives, altogether representing—if the system be just and wise—all citizens with their divided interests. Rising out of this noisy void of politics, our subject now achieves form and takes this shape for systematic discussion of the tragedy of reason in the domain of action. To contain this tragedy, we must first consider the relations of these agents, organized as the legislature. But since they are agents, not principals, we must consider the relations between them and their principals: "the people" in theory, "the party" in well regulated practice, and "the interests" in all too frequent suspicion. Since, furthermore, the conflicts which are so noisy between the agents are but the tighter-meshed conflicts that smolder behind the scenes in the interest-groups involved, our final discussion must be of the people themselves banded into competing groups and represented by historic parties.

We are lucky to begin with the most humanely pleasant of our interrelationships. In the legislative domain of life you will find human relations at their best. You may have thought differently upon your last visit to a legislative gallery. But what went ye for to see—good men all agreed on goodness, honest men all agreed on honesty, just men all agreed on justice, holy men all agreed on holiness? Such agreement is not on earth, not yet, not soon. What saw ye—articulate simpletons intent on minimum business, to the tune of maximum noise, in an atmosphere of partisan strife? Come, now! Go again! Look again from the legislative gallery!

Do you not notice how courteous the interruptions? Do you not notice that they go by protocol through the Speaker, that the interruptions are tended in courtliness and received with grace—whether accepted as interruptions or declined for lack of time or merely postponed, more likely, out of a sense of orderliness? Having looked again to see what you did not at first see, go again to hear what you did not at first hear. Go when great issues impend, when action upon issues is imminent. If you return at such a time, you will see the chamber packed, party lines marshaled, time fairly divided and carefully assigned, amendments efficiently argued and quickly voted up or down. You will see, for example, 435 orators and egoists behaving, as neither is popularly supposed to behave, as disciplined adults intent upon collective action.

Look closer still and you will isolate two elements in that impressive view: one, the individual component; the other, the traditional factor. Individually, the representatives are for the most part treating each other with respect, even with deference. The approach is seldom rude. Not "that so and so from such and such a district." It is usually all too urbane: "the distinguished representative of a great constituency from a noble state. . . ." When occasionally the approach is strident, you will see, if you stay to observe, the member attacked walk out arm in arm with the attacking member, as if they were close friends, which more than likely they are.

A "political apprentice" of mine once sat in the gallery of the Senate of Illinois to keep analytic tab on the pattern of all interpersonal relations, by charting every call of one member upon another member over several weeks. It was a beautiful chart, but I forget what it proved, if anything. Politics is more aesthetic than scientific, and more responsive to the synthetic than to the analytic approach. As one who has always enjoyed the game, whether fully understood or not, I here hazard only the main conclusion: that nowhere on earth is the inescapable human factor more fruitfully or more beautifully handled under conflict conditions than in legislative halls. Responsible men (but their responsibility is owed to different sections of the people) meet and mingle and enjoy each other as full plenipotentiaries—of the whole people.

The reason for all this both entrenches upon and transcends the personal factor. The rationale reaches into the traditional for its main support. Parliamentary usages are what make meetings possible from what would otherwise be mobs. "Rules of Order" are literally what give order to any and every effort to pool human insight, to each endeavor to compose adult differences. The rules for all sorts of public occasions have grown out of legislative procedures. Legislatures are both the source and the continuing beneficiaries of this marvelous invention whereby mind meets mind to ends constructive. In America, the rules of our national House of Representatives are built upon British experience in the House of Commons. Thomas Jefferson gave us our first systematic manual. This, as elaborated by experience and implemented through many volumes of decisions by the Speaker of the House upon "points of order," constitutes the seasoned wisdom of our race in collective procedure. The respect by each member for this priceless legacy, this supplement to his shortsightedness, makes progress in legislation possible because it makes order actual in deliberation. Those who have not learned that tradition is the backbone of all effective individualism are no good at the democratic process. This respect for procedural authority makes operative in each representative the great principle of liberty under law. . . .

37

WHAT MAKES A STATESMAN?

Boies Penrose

Boies Penrose (1860–1921), Senator from Pennsylvania (1896–1921) and Republican boss of this state after 1904, was a man of gargantuan appetites for food, liquor, women, and money. Coarse, crude, and vulgar, he was thought by many to be the archtype of the democratic politician. He might have served as a model for the politicians who disgusted Henry Adams—those portrayed in his satirical novel, Democracy.* *Yet that book was published in 1880, the year before Penrose graduated from Harvard and plunged enthusiastically into the political life Adams disdained. There is no evidence that the two even met, but Adams might well have served as the model for the sketch of the "statesman" drawn here by Penrose.*

*

. .

"AM I A STATESMAN?" [Boies Penrose, Republican senator from Pennsylvania] demanded.

One of the friends shook his head. The other did better.

"No, Senator, you're not," said he. "Not what the highbrows call a statesman anyway."

"Nor what anybody else calls a statesman," said Penrose, draining the bottle. "What makes a statesman? Talk. What ruins a politician? Talk. What does a statesman live on? Publicity. People don't read the record. They don't read anything. They'll listen to high-falutin' flap-

From Walter Davenport, *Power and Glory: The Life of Boies Penrose* (New York: G. P. Putnam's Sons, 1931). Copyright © 1931 by Walter Davenport.

* Henry Adams, *Democracy* (New York: Henry Holt and Company, 1880).

doodle and if they're praised by it or promised something for nothing or if it contains a new bill of rights they never thought of having—that's a statesman. Take a cabinet officer—a secretary of state. There's a chance to be a statesman. All he has to do is to take everything from a weaker nation and what he can get from a stronger, announce it as a victory in phrases the ordinary man can't understand and—well, what it is? Statesmanship, b'God. That gin's rotten. Let's have another.

"Anybody can be a statesman—if he has the backing of his party. But who gives him the support of his party. The leader of the party. And who's the leader of the party? Why, the best politician in it. The test of a politician isn't in just hanging on to his job; it's hanging on to his party. However, I'm not against statesmen. Every party's got to have a few. They're the kept women of the politicians. They come in handy when the people get tired of you. Instead of nominating a politician you pick on a statesman, and the people take him like food and drink. The thing to do is to raise your statesmen in the way they should go, and when they're elected, they will not depart from it. Window dressing.

"Statesmen, hell! Why if this country went into the statescraft business we'd be bankrupt in a month. Europe would hog-tie and strangle us at that game. They've been at it for centuries—statescraft. And look at them. Statesmen, hell! Just orators who do what their betters tell them—weak sisters in a full dress suit.

"Listen here. Last week one of our statesmen who comes from the noble west came to me with tears in his voice. Seems he'd been devoting too much of his time to noble-mindedness. He had read all about England, France, Russia, Japan, and Germany and was telling the country all about it, while he should have been doing something for the railroads out his way. By God, they elected him—the railroads—and if you hire out to a man he has the right to expect something.

"Well they had told him that as senator he was about through, that, as long as he'd gone in for this statesman business, they'd have to look further for a hired man. Took all the wind out of our statesman, b'God. What was the use being a statesman if you hadn't any job to practice it in. Back home he's just a country lawyer. Six thousand dollars a year. See?

"I had a hell of a time with those people. Never met them in my life. Don't give a damn for them anyway. But finally I made them listen to reason. I had to tell them that I'd be responsible for their senator after this—for their statesman. I had to give them my word that he'd shut up and go to work and stop talking about Europe and Asia. So, when he came around to me next day with more tears, I told him it was all right, that he'd be re-elected. So we're shy one statesman now. S'all right. We got plenty more. How'd you like that gin? Good enough for me. Good enough for you. Or a statesman."

Presently he went off to sleep.

38

TALKING POLITICAL

Thomas L. Hughes

Thomas L. Hughes (b. 1925) observed behavior on floor and off on Capitol Hill from his vantage point, first, as legal counsel to the then Sen. Hubert H. Humphrey, and as aide to then Rep. Chester Bowles. Since 1963 Mr. Hughes has been director of Intelligence and Research for the State Department.

*

. . .

THERE HAS BEEN increasingly widespread acknowledgment inside Congress of the value of reducing cloakroom talk to the lowest common denominator when politicians get together. Senators and representatives find that life is much easier if they explain themselves to one another in terms of political opportunism. In this way a number of otherwise distasteful feelings about one another become palatable. Principles no longer get in the way of working relationships. Even friendships can result. "Talking political" takes everybody off the hook—at least in personal terms.

Naturally, a concerted depreciation of issues as issues is inevitable in this situation. If the southern hierarchy cannot abide a Humphrey and a Douglas because they appear to believe what they say on a thorny subject like civil rights, a mediator will intervene to explain that, after all, the Northern senators have to say it. And vice versa. The political explanation, even when it does violence to the character and personalities of the men involved, is acceptable and understandable, while an image of sincerity would be intolerable. There is general agreement that if everyone were sincere, and if sincerity were translated into real stubbornness, Congress simply could not operate. Nor could the principles of accommodation.

39

CONFLICTS OF INTEREST

Jesse M. Unruh

A powerful figure in California politics of the 1960's, Jesse M. Unruh (b. 1923) has earned the soubriquet "Big Daddie." He has lectured on a Chubb Fellowship at Yale University, and, next to Lyndon B. Johnson, he may be the most skillful legislative leader produced in the United States in this century. In his utterly uncluttered view, there is an inevitable conflict between the public and private roles of the politician. But there are also built-in safeguards.

*

. . .

OUR AMERICAN DEMOCRATIC form of government has from the start been committed to the principle of citizen participation in government. By this, I do not mean that citizens are expected simply to participate in the discussion of public policy nor simply to cast an intelligent vote; I am referring, rather, to our system of citizen-lawmakers, citizen-governors, and citizen-judges.

We take a man who more or less reflects that slice of the social fabric from which he is cut; he is more or less educated, ethical, financially independent and able as the segment of the populace from which he is drawn. We take him and elect him to office or put him on the bench, and we expect him to write our laws and enforce them—in short we expect him to govern us.

From an address before the Los Angeles Federal Bar Association, February 15, 1963, by The Honorable Jesse M. Unruh, Speaker of the Assembly, California Legislature. By permission.

When Mr. Common Man is elected or appointed to public office, he is thrown immediately into a crossfire of conflicts of interest. It is inevitable. After all his job can be described as one of balancing the interests of all the forces in society which seek representation. He is part and parcel of a certain number of those interests. There must, inescapably, be a conflict between his private and his public roles.

I say this is inevitable, but is it really? Perhaps the only safe way out of this dilemma—the only way for the public official to avoid the nagging fear that he may get caught up in such a conflict and the only safe way to avoid the constant public inference that the general interest has been sold out is to do as the Kennedy family has done (to choose an example on the federal level): One generation devotes its talents and energies to amassing a fortune; the fortune is put in trust for the second generation so that generation can be totally free of the burden of making a living or increasing its wealth. That second generation is then able to apply itself to public service without a guilty conscience. Milton Berle claims that Joseph Kennedy has referred to this phenomenon as "my sons the government."

[But] we are not content to restrict our government to an aristocracy of wealth. We regard this as too narrow a group from which to draw our public servants. Democracy does not lend itself to management by an elite.

The alternative is that the man who serves in office must also make a living. How can he do justice to both the public welfare and his own without doing violence to either?

Let us take the problem of the lawyer-legislator. He spends part of the year enacting or studying laws. The remainder of his time is spent in trying to make a living in the practice of law.

What about the whole matter of practicing before state commissions or boards—seeking information for his client from state agencies or departments?

If he calls on a state official and asks him to reverse the rules, or just to bend them, on behalf of his client, I think it is easy to agree that he is engaged in a conflict of interest, at least, and possibly a great deal more. But, what if he calls the director of a state agency and simpy asks for information on behalf of his client? He may have authored legislation which created the agency or amended its statutory authority. He may have influenced the governor in the selection of the incumbent director. If he is a committee chairman, he may have legislation important to that department pending before his committee. Is *he* engaged in a conflict? Can any lawyer-legislator practice before any state court without running the risk of conflict? Did he vote to create the very court in which he appears? Did he recommend the appointment of the judge? Will he, in the future, vote on the salary increase of that judge?

Some of the problems raised by the call from the legislator to the department or agency on behalf of his constituent exist even when he is *not* a lawyer. Occasionally, the state official will attempt to give the legislator a favorable reply in an effort to curry favor, when the legislator has not asked for this advantage. In short, there is virtually nothing one can do as a member of the legislature that does *not* constitute a conflict of interest—something that somebody, some day, can bring up to haunt him.

Some legislators attempt to meet this problem by a kind of scrupulous honesty which can best be described as saintly. I have known some who made it a standing practice to return every gift, no matter how small, to the sender. I have known others—attorneys—who made an honest effort to avoid taking on any clients who came to them because of their governmental connection. Some of these have left the legislature because they were unable to support their families on the combined legislative pay and legal fees.

Recently, I discussed this question with a colleague of mine who made what I considered to be the very telling point: Rarely—in this day and age—is a legislator's vote corrupted by the exchange of money; far more often the integrity of the vote is shattered by a commitment to a particular interest group, resulting from a lack of independence on the part of the legislator for a variety of reasons which go well beyond economics.

For example, for reasons of ideology or fear of antagonizing the voting strength of a particular group, one who is overly committed to labor or to management, or to any other interest group, whatever his reasons, is at least as guilty of selling out the public interest as the man who takes money for his vote, unless he votes the way he does because he believes it is right.

In an interesting and ironic sort of way the public has a certain amount of protection which is probably not recognized. I have in mind the fact that the more ambitious a public figure is the less susceptible he is of falling into these traps. In the first place, he is determined to create a record upon which to campaign for higher office. In the second place, the faster he moves the quicker the spotlight of public scrutiny is likely to fall upon his activities. Finally, the higher he wants to go the less likely he is to sacrifice that chance for any other personal advantage.

In the face of these complexities, I know many, many legislators and public officials who are trying desperately to do their jobs honorably and fairly. None of them will tell you that the question of conflicting interests does not disturb them. No one I know is confident he has the answer.

Perhaps we need something like a blue-ribbon commission composed of individuals in whom the public has confidence. To such a commission, one would be able to submit any problem which raises in his mind the question of a conflict of interest. This commission would then pass upon the issue of whether or not a conflict in fact exists. If such a method were used, a necessary condition would have to be that when a favorable judgment is rendered the individual who submits the question and agrees to abide by that decision would then be assured of freedom from challenge, abuse, or criticism on that specific issue. I do not know how good a solution this would be. I do know, however, that this kind of issue must be the subject of public discussion by groups such as this.

40

MEN ARE SUCH FOOLS

Christine Keeler

The first part of Lord Denning's Report, *from which the following excerpt is taken, deals with the circumstances leading to the resignation of the former Secretary of State for War, Mr. John D. Profumo.*

*

. . .

THE REPORTERS of the *Sunday Pictorial* prepared a proof of Miss Keeler's story. She signed every page as correct on February 8, 1963. It is the first signed statement she gave to anyone. (The police did not get a signed statement until April 4, 1963.) It is on that account instructive to see how she put it. It was in fact never published, but this is how it ran:

Men are such fools. But I like them. I have always liked them.

Unfortunately, the combination of these things has led me into a lot of trouble and may even have risked the security of this country. It certainly could have been harmful to the country.

You see, one man who was foolish enough and irresponsible enough to have an affair with me was a cabinet minister, a member of Her Majesty's Government.

And at the same time I was having an affair with another man—a Russian diplomat.

If that Russian or anyone else had placed a tape recorder or movie

From *Lord Denning's Report,* Command Paper No. 2152, presented to Parliament by the Prime Minister by the Command of Her Majesty, September 15, 1963.

camera or both in some hidden place in my bedroom it would have been very embarrassing for the minister, to say the least.

In fact, it would have left him open to the worst possible kind of blackmail—the blackmail of a spy.

I am not suggesting that he really would have given up state secrets to avoid a scandal. He might have been tough and refused.

But I do believe that any man in his position—particularly a married man—is both unwise and irresponsible to have an affair with some unknown girl like me.

More especially so in this case, because this minister has such knowledge of the military affairs of the Western world that he would be one of the most valuable men in the world for the Russians to have had in their power.

He is, in fact, the Secretary of State for War, Mr. John Profumo.

I believe now that a man in his position should not indulge in such pastimes as me. I suppose even cabinet ministers are only human, but I think they should curb their feelings when they take on the job.

One might think that, as a politician, he would have been particularly discreet in the affair. John Profumo was not. It is true he did not take me out much, but he did take me to his own home while his wife was away. And he did write letters to me.

One might also think that those responsible for state security would keep some sort of watch on men who hold as many secrets as he holds.

Yet, if that happened, he would never have been able to come and see me at the flat where I was being visited by the Russian.

And, believe me, the Russian was a man who would be very much aware of the value of the secrets which Profumo knew. He was not a civilian.

He was, in fact, a naval captain, Captain Eugene Ivanov.

Of course, at the time I did not realize the sinister implications behind my two affairs. I was only eighteen and knew nothing of politics or international matters. I was not interested.

I did not realize then that blackmail is one of the Russians' favorite weapons when they are trying to recruit traitors or discover secret information.

I am sure that Jack Profumo would not have allowed his harmless affair with me to be used as a lever to prise secrets from him. But a weaker man in his position might have allowed it to happen.

At the time, however, I saw no danger in the situation. It just seemed funny to me that I should be seeing the two men, sometimes on the same day. One might leave my flat only a few minutes before the other arrived.

I did find it worrying when someone asked me to try to get from Profumo the answer to a certain question,

That question was: "When, if ever, are the Americans going to give nuclear weapons to Germany?"

I am not prepared to say in public who asked me to find out the answer to that question. I am prepared to give it to the security officials. In fact, I believe now that I have a duty to do so. . . .

41

PERSONAL REFLECTIONS ON
BOSSES AND MACHINES

Edward J. Flynn

In this selection, Edward J. Flynn (1892–1953), boss of the Bronx, or Democratic leader, as he would have preferred to have been called, tells how an astute "boss" maintains control over his organization and explains the balanced ticket. Mr. Flynn served as chairman of the Democratic National Committee and led the party during Franklin D. Roosevelt's campaign for a third term. His appointment as Ambassador to Australia was withdrawn when the Senate refused to confirm.

*

"THE MEETING will come to order. The Chair recognizes Mr. Brown."

MR. BROWN: I offer the following resolution and move its adoption.

THE CHAIRMAN: The Secretary will read.

THE SECRETARY: *Resolved,* That the Executive Committee of the Democratic County Committee of Bronx County offer to the enrolled Democrats of Bronx County at the primary election to be held on July 31, 1945, the following named persons for the respective offices to be filled at the said primary:

For Mayor of the City of New York: William O'Dwyer.
For Comptroller of the City of New York: Lazarus Joseph.
For President of the Council: Vincent R. Impellitteri.
For President of the Borough of the Bronx: James J. Lyons.
For District Attorney, County of Bronx: Samuel J. Foley.

For Justices of the Municipal Court, 1st Municipal Court District, County
of Bronx: William Lyman, Christopher C. McGrath, Charles A. Loreto.
For Justices of the Municipal Court, 2nd Municipal Court District,
County of Bronx: Michael N. Delagi, Agnes M. Craig.

THE CHAIRMAN: All those in favor of the resolution will kindly so
signify by saying "Aye." The motion is carried and the resolution is
adopted. The Chair recognizes Mr. Buckley.

MR. BUCKLEY: I move that the meeting adjourn.

THE CHAIRMAN: All those in favor of the motion to adjourn kindly
so signify by saying "Aye." The meeting is adjourned.

These are the minutes of a meeting of the Executive Committee of
the Democratic party of Bronx County, New York. The meeting was
called to present, formally, the Democratic organization's slate to the enrolled Democrats of that county.

The executive committee of the Democratic party in Bronx County
consists of thirty-three men and women, who are executive members of
the county committee. They are the heart of the Democratic organization.
They are presided over by the chairman, who happens to be myself.
There you have, very simply, what is known as a "machine."

It took ten minutes (perhaps less) to hold the meeting. There were
no objections, for everything had been arranged in advance. The very
smoothness of the proceedings exemplifies practical politics in action; for,
within the periphery of that meeting may be found, one by one, the
axioms on which practical politics are based, beginning with the voter root
and extending to the highest political office—the presidency of the United
States.

In discussing mechanism, and in trying to arrive at just what makes a
political machine tick, I am calling on my own twenty-five years of political experience and the specific example of Bronx County. For more than
a quarter of a century, Bronx County has elected only Democratic county
officials. It has become, on percentage, the greatest Democratic county
north of the Mason and Dixon line.

Thus, by augmenting or reducing the model of Bronx County, and
with due allowance for variations in state laws, one can get a picture of
party workings in almost any part of the United States, for political divisions are substantially the same in fundamentals all over the country.

At the meeting described at the beginning of this chapter, the enrolled Democrats were being offered candidates for mayor, for comptroller,
and for president of the city council. They were also being presented with
candidates for president of the Borough of the Bronx, Bronx County district attorney, and five municipal court judgeships.

The nominations for the city-wide offices had already been agreed upon by the five county leaders of the City of New York. Nominations for Bronx County offices were agreed to after a series of conferences between the executive members and the chairman of the executive committee.

How, then, were these nominations actually arrived at? To deny that I, as chairman of the executive committee, am the dominant force in the Bronx Democratic organization would be foolish. And since I am the controlling force, any action I take must be one that I believe will benefit the people of the Bronx first, and enhance the prestige of the organization second. I mention the people first, because it is one of our political legends that bosses never pay any attention to the public. Of course, the legend will not stand up against any logical analysis, for it must be rather obvious that a political boss can survive only so long as he wins elections, and equally obvious that the only way to win elections year after year is to know what the voters want and give it to them.

The slate mentioned above is an example. James J. Lyons was renominated for president of the Borough of the Bronx. He had been elected three times and was looking toward his fourth term. From the standpoint of the people, generally he had done a good job. There had been no scandals connected with his office, and the people believed him to be an honest official; for that reason, it was expedient for the organization to renominate him. If, however, he had been a failure, or if there had been any scandals in his administration, the organization and I, without any qualms, would have turned him down for renomination; for, always, the primary purpose is to win an election.

In the same resolution Samuel J. Foley was offered as a candidate for re-election as Bronx County district attorney. His office had a splendid reputation. Foley, himself, had been praised highly in many New York newspapers for the conduct of his office. In fact, rackets had been stopped in Bronx County long before the term "racket-buster" was invented to dress up an obscure Republican. The criminal element knew that they could not exert political influence in the Bronx, and so they fought shy of the county. One instance illustrates my point. Terrenova, one of the most notorious racketeers of his time, lived in Westchester County. Now, one cannot reach Manhattan from Westchester without crossing the Bronx or crossing either the Hudson River twice or Long Island Sound and the East River. Yet Terrenova chose to cross the Hudson twice—over to New Jersey and back again—rather than to risk being picked up in the Bronx. So it was to the advantage of the organization to offer Foley to the people again.

Four of the five municipal court judges were also seeking re-election. The records of Lyman, McGrath, Delagi, and Craig were good, and they were renominated. The fifth, Charles A. Loreto, was being presented as a candidate for the first time. His nomination was agreed upon at a series of conferences between myself and some of the members of the executive committee. What factors were taken into consideration in this nomination?

The Bronx is a cosmopolitan place. The Jewish and Italian populations are large. There are also many Irish Catholics. These three groups make up the largest portions of the county. Therefore, when the organization is forming a ticket to present to the people, it is important that the candidates represent and come from these three large groups. It is curious how some "reformers" labor this point, arguing that it is "pandering to racial and religious blocs." Our whole system of government is based on proportional representation. But of course the "reformers" in question are not always consistent, for just now they see nothing wrong with special appeals to organized labor, to take just one example. (Neither do I, but the distinction is that I am consistent in my belief that special-interest groups have a perfect right to be represented in the bodies that govern us all.)

Today there are more Jewish than Irish Catholic voters in the Bronx. Yet there is no such thing as a "Jewish bloc"—as Governor Dewey discovered in the last New York mayoral election. Dewey thought that by nominating Judge Jonah Goldstein, a onetime Tammany Democrat, for mayor on the Republican ticket, he could ensure the Jewish vote of the city in his own gubernatorial race a year later. Goldstein had everything a Jewish candidate should have—except that not all Jews thought him the better qualified candidate. The Jew is a discriminating individualist.

In the vacancy Loreto was a candidate to fill, it was important to name a man of Italian extraction. This was so because Lazarus Joseph, candidate for comptroller, was Jewish and came from the Bronx. Beyond this, it was important that every geographical section of the Bronx be represented. Neighborhood feeling carries great weight with a political organization. Men and women who are prominent in their own localities are recognized by being placed in public office. Thus it was deemed necessary to have a man of Italian extraction from a particular sector of the Bronx.

Prior to the meeting described above, I consulted with members of the executive committee who were from that particular part of the county and asked them to suggest names. Various leaders suggested different persons. The abilities and political strengths of each were looked into. Finally, I, myself, decided that Loreto was the man.

Hence, our ticket shaped up as a well-rounded one: Lyons and Foley were Irish, Joseph and Lyman were Jewish, Delagi and Loreto were of Italian descent.

"Cynical!" the "reformers" will say. "Shocking!" "Calculating!" "So this is how a machine functions!"

Yes, this is the way a machine functions. And I would ask the reformers how else it could function in the interests of all the people. It should be remembered that we were offering these names to the enrolled Democrats of Bronx County in a Democratic primary. It did not mean that there could be no opposition to them. Any person who wished to dispute our judgment had that right in the primary polling booth, where none could see him.

True, scattered individuals cannot successfully challenge the decisions of a machine. But if the machine is a bad one, if it deserves to be beaten because of its offensive political activities or because of the caliber of the men it nominates, opposition can be organized to fight out the issues in the primaries. I'll admit it is not easy. It takes time, patience, and a lot of hard work to beat a machine in this way. Nor am I attempting to say that this is the best method. It just happens to be the only one provided under the election laws of the State of New York. The point is, machines have been successfully fought in the past, and they will be again.

I have been chairman of the Democratic executive committee of Bronx County for a quarter of a century. In order to remain in that position, I must always have the committee votes to support me. My control is entirely dependent upon this support. If a majority of the committee decided they no longer wanted me, they could call a meeting tomorrow and supplant me. But, during my entire service as chairman, there has never been any serious threat to my leadership. There has been occasional scattered opposition, but never any real danger.

How do I maintain the majority support of the executive committee? To begin with, I always see to it that the key party workers have some sort of exempt noncivil-service positions, if they want them. Some of the salaries are small (particularly those given to women). They run from twenty-five hundred to five thousand dollars, with only one at ten thousand. Still, to use political parlance, all the district leaders have been "taken care of" during my entire term as county leader. In New York County, by contrast, there have been many changes among the district leaders during the same period—because they were not put into exempt positions. The biggest turnover came about when the Democrats lost the county and borough offices in the Fusion heyday. Bronx County is the only county within the city that has never been defeated either for county or for borough offices.

The families, also—sons, daughters, husbands, wives—of the district leaders are taken care of in some way or other. Sometimes they are given exempt positions, and sometimes they get help from us in the line of civil service promotion. It is an exaggeration to say that this is the sole reason for which I have had their support down through the years, but I cannot deny that it has been extremely important to my remaining as leader.

There is one other important factor in retaining the support of the executive committee, and, although it has never been put to test, I am confident that it could be with perfect safety. I have the final word about who should be appointed to positions that control exempt jobs. The county committeemen who elect the executive members know this. Also, it is inevitable that during the years of my leadership I have come to know these committeemen well, and they in turn know me. I feel sure that should I express to them a desire to have a district leader removed, a new leader would be selected immediately. Thus, not only my long association with the party, but my absolute control of exempt positions, is a powerful influence in my control.

The importance of this business of patronage in the success of a party and a leader may be seen by studying the strengthening of the Democratic party during Roosevelt's terms as governor of New York and his first terms in the White House. Because he paid attention to his leaders and made the party appointments they recommended (always after previously investigating the candidate's abilities), Roosevelt built up the greatest vote-getting machine, both state and federal, that has ever been known. When he began to accept the recommendation of the New Dealers of "nonpolitical" appointments, there was a falling away of organization support. However, by that time Roosevelt's policies were so well known and his own name had such magic that he was able, notwithstanding, to maintain his leadership.

If the men and women who were delegates to the later national conventions, and who were in every instance organization Democrats, had felt that the president would continue the same policy, as far as the party was concerned, he had followed in his first term—that they would receive consideration at his hands—there would have been much less opposition by them to a third and fourth term.

Thus may be seen, in that one instance, how the principles, the axioms learned and used in a county committee, may apply in federal scope.

But this works both ways, for no matter what the effort, the machine, after so many years, has become a more or less personal one. For several years past I have seriously considered resigning. The detail work in a county organization no longer has any appeal to me. Financially, the job has been expensive. Naturally, I myself, contribute to the support of the party. But there is another item that can hardly be classed as a party contribution, but which goes hand in hand with the party job I hold. Whenever a member of the organization is in financial difficulty and comes to me for assistance, I usually lend him money. Some of these loans have even been paid back.

Because of my long association, however, I naturally feel responsible to men who have loyally supported me down through the years. If I resigned, these men would be left out in the cold. I do not say it in any spirit of vanity, but it is perfectly logical to suppose that an organization that has been kept so compact through all these years would tend to disintegrate if the moving spirit died or resigned. This did happen in the case of Tammany Hall after the death of Charles F. Murphy. Tammany has never since been able to occupy the place it did under his leadership. There has been constant change and constant squabbling for power among the leaders. Undoubtedly, the same situation would develop in the Bronx if I resigned.

It is possible, but not perhaps feasible, that I might, if I did resign, be able to help keep the machine together by giving the utmost support to whomever was elected in my place. This possibility is a hope, I'm afraid, rather than something I believe to be true. The old principle that an "ex" in politics is truly an "ex" is a verity. Once power has been relinquished, it is difficult either to regain it or to exercise authority through others. So that not only in the interests of the success of the party, but because of reciprocal loyalty, I am as truly bound to the machine as anyone else. . . .

42

HOW MUCH FORTUNE CAN DO
IN HUMAN AFFAIRS

Niccolò Machiavelli

*In common with most other authors in this book, Niccolò Machiavelli
(1469–1527) took an active part in the political life of his times. For
fourteen years, he served as Secretary to the Office of the Ten Magistrates
of Liberty and Peace; in effect, he was the principal adviser to the government of the Republic of Florence. Nowadays, his realism is trite, the all-
too-familiar attitude of a thoroughly disillusioned nation of idealists. It is
not for such qualities that a selection from* The Prince *is included here.
His observations on fortune and her influence on human affairs emphasize, not only that fully half our fate cannot be controlled, but that nearly
half can be controlled by thought and action. Fortune favors youth and
impetuosity, is kind to him who takes precipitating, resolving action. On
this matter, compare Machiavelli with Norton Long (see Chapter 21).
What the master adviser said about fortune may be tempered by latter-
day cautions. "We all know that half of the money spent on political campaigns is wasted," Vice President Hubert Humphrey has been heard to
say, "but we don't know which half." * And in counterpoint to the emphasis on youth, James Thurber paraphrased an old saw: "Youth will be
served: frequently stuffed with chestnuts."*

*

IT IS NOT UNKNOWN to me how many have been and are of opinion that
worldly events are so governed by fortune and by God, that men cannot

---

From Niccolò Machiavelli, *The Prince,* trans. Luigi Ricci (London: Oxford University
Press, 1903).
* In the presence of this writer, St. Louis, 1958.

by their prudence change them, and that on the contrary there is no remedy whatever, and for this they may judge it to be useless to toil much about them, but let things be ruled by chance. This opinion has been more held to in our day, from the great changes that have been seen, and are daily seen, beyond every human conjecture. When I think about them, at times I am partly inclined to share this opinion.

Nevertheless, that our free will may not be altogether extinguished, I think it may be true that fortune is the ruler of half our actions, but that she allows the other half or a little less to be governed by us. I would compare her to an impetuous river that, when turbulent, inundates the plains, ruins trees and buildings, removes earth from this side and places it on the other; every one flees before it, and everything yields to its fury without being able to oppose it; and yet, though it is of such a kind, still when it is quiet, men can make provision against it by dams and banks, so that when it rises it will either go into a canal or its rush will not be so wild and dangerous. So it is with fortune, which shows her power where no measures have been taken to resist her, and turns her fury where she knows that no dams or barriers have been made to hold her. If you regard Italy, which has been the seat of these changes, and who has given the impulse to them, you will see her to be a country without dams or banks of any kind. If she had been protected by proper measures, like Germany, Spain, and France, this inundation would not have caused the great changes that it has, or would not have happened at all.

This must suffice as regards opposition to fortune in general. Limiting myself more to particular cases, I would point out how one sees a certain prince today fortunate and tomorrow ruined, without seeing that he has changed in character or otherwise. I believe this arises in the first place from the causes that we have already discussed at length; that is to say, because the prince who bases himself entirely on fortune is ruined when fortune varies. I also believe that he is happy whose mode of proceeding accords with the needs of the times, and similarly he is unfortunate whose mode of proceeding is opposed to the times. For one sees that men, in those things which lead them to the aim that each one has in view, namely, glory and riches, proceed in various ways: one with circumspection, another with impetuosity, one by violence, another by cunning, one with patience, another with the reverse. Each, by these diverse ways, may arrive at his aim. One sees, also, two cautious men, one of whom succeeds in his designs, and the other not; and, in the same way, two men succeed equally by different methods, one being cautious, the other impetuous— which arises only from the nature of the times, which does or does not conform to their method of proceeding. From this it results, as I have said, that two men, acting differently, attain the same effect, and of two others acting in the same way, one attains his goal and not the other. On this depend also the changes in fortune; for if it happens that time and circumstances are favorable to one who acts with caution and prudence, he will be successful; but if time and circumstances change he will be ruined, because he does not change his mode of proceeding. No man is found so prudent as to be able to adapt himself to this, either because he cannot deviate from that to which his nature disposes him, or else because having always prospered by walking in one path, he cannot persuade himself that it is well to leave it; and, therefore, the cautious man, when it is time to act suddenly, does not know how to do so and is consequently ruined; for if one could change one's nature with time and circumstances, fortune would never change.

Pope Julius II acted impetuously in everything he did and found the times and conditions so in conformity with that mode of proceeding that he always obtained a good result. Consider the first war that he made against Bologna while Messer Giovanni Bentivogli was still living. The Venetians were not pleased with it; the kings of Spain and France likewise had objections to this enterprise, notwithstanding which, owing to his fierce and impetuous dispositions, he engaged personally in the expedition. This move caused both Spain and the Venetians to halt and hesitate, the latter through fear, the former through the desire to recover the entire kingdom of Naples. On the other hand, he engaged with him the King of France, because seeing him make this move, and desiring his friendship in order to put down the Venetians, that king judged that he could not refuse him his troops without manifest injury. Thus, Julius by his impetuous move achieved what no other pontiff with the utmost human prudence would have succeeded in doing, because, if he had waited till all arrangements had been made and everything settled before leaving Rome, as any other pontiff would have done, it would never have taken place. For, the king of France would have found a thousand excuses, and the others would have inspired him with a thousand fears. I will omit his other actions, which were all of this kind and which all succeeded well, and the shortness of his life did not suffer him to experience the contrary; for, had times followed in which it was necessary to act with caution, his ruin would have resulted, for he would never have deviated from these methods to which his nature disposed him.

I conclude then that fortune varying and men remaining fixed in their ways, they are successful so long as these ways conform to each other, but when they are opposed then they are unsuccessful. I certainly think that it is better to be impetuous than cautious, for fortune is a woman, and it is necessary, if you wish to master her, to conquer her by force; and it can be seen that she lets herself be overcome by the bold rather than by those who proceed coldly. Therefore, like a woman, she is a friend to the young, because they are less cautious, fiercer, and master her with great audacity.

PART SIX

Political Life

43

A RECENT TYPICAL DAY

Clem Miller

Clem Miller (1916–1962) wrote the collection of letters containing the following selection "simply for the people of my district to share what I was learning myself." Fortunately, Prof. John Baker, one of his constituents, saw to it that these letters were given permanent form and wider circulation. From the congressman's vantage, we get a vivid picture of everyday life in Congress.

Mr. Miller served as Representative from California from 1958 until his untimely death in an airplane accident in 1962.

*

THE CONGRESSIONAL RECESS is that period in the fall, after adjournment, which offers respite from the steady press of legislation. Congressmen, extremely weary of themselves and their fellows, are eager to be home—to see how things are.

Congress remains in session for longer and longer periods as the complexity of government mounts. In the early days of the republic, sessions lasted from one to three months. Today, a nine-or-ten-month session is routine.

Recess at home is traditionally a time for checking grass-roots reaction; it is also a time for public viewing of the congressman. Citizens have a right to see their representative, to talk to him and observe him.

In a city district, a central office with daily office hours is sufficient. In a district covering as much territory as the First California (if transplanted to the East Coast it would reach from Boston to Baltimore), this is impossible.

As soon as I know about when Congress will adjourn, my field representative and I frame in certain dates from the requests for appearances which come in to us. We spot invitations on the calendar, providing a schedule that will move us from one community to another, in a sequential manner. A great deal of time must be spent actually on the road. Our station wagon is loaded with files of research material, congressional reports to distribute to constituents, and all the personal paraphernalia we need for a two-month safari—including cookstove and stenographic recording equipment.

My home and office for two or three months is a series of motels. The pressure of the schedule and the distances involved make use of my real home in Corte Madera impossible.

We usually begin with three or four days in Marin County with headquarters in a San Rafael motel, ready for engagements in nearby towns.

From Marin, we move to my district office in Santa Rosa, in reach of various Sonoma County towns. Then, a swing north along Highway 101, from Ukiah to Cresent City. Returning, we tour through Lake County, in the Napa Valley, and back to Marin to prepare for a renewal of the cycle. Such a swing around the 300-mile-long district takes at least ten days, and preferably fifteen to eighteen days. Two such complete swings are made during a recess, with side forays into smaller communities. Time is set aside to talk to a dozen federal and state agencies in San Francisco and Sacramento.

We lay out the schedule with reasonable attention to population densities, and allot time for the ordinary continuing duties of a congressman. This time out for routine duties is important. The continuing duties of a member of Congress—answering the mail from constituents, seeing individuals on special problems, and keeping up with events—do not come to a halt simply because you are on the road. The press of the routine is insistent, and must somehow be sandwiched in between service-club speeches, church socials, local-group barbecues, and visits to defense installations.

When we first begin a tour, the commitments are well spaced out. But, as time goes on, the schedule becomes choked with a succession of extra events that make each day tighter and tighter. Telephone calls begin to follow us around from place to place. Can I spare a few minutes on this? Can I see that person for five minutes? Can I talk to the annual meeting of the soil conservation district directors? It may mean skimping on lunch, shaving travel time, and postponing bedtime, but we generally work them in.

A recent typical day went like this: At 7:00 or 8:00, breakfast with a small group to talk over a legislative program on dairy products for school lunches. The next engagement was set for 10:00 in a nearby town to talk to the high school civics class. The ample time allotted to get there was cut to ribbons by the fact that a constituent had driven up from San Rafael to see me about a harbor project. The worked-in appointment for twenty minutes took forty, so the daily rush was on—behind schedule already.

The civics class ended at 10:50; we had planned time for the drive to another town and time to collect my thoughts and make a few notes for a Rotary luncheon speech. However, the schedule did not provide for the senior problems class,* which blocked my exit from school with some very serious questions, demanding answers. The principal also wanted a word about science equipment available through the National Defense Education Act. According to the schedule I should have left at 11:30, but the final breakaway came fifteen minutes later.

Service club luncheons you can count on. They must be over by 1:30. This gave from 1:45 to 2:45 to work on the backlog of accumulated telephone calls. (They come from everywhere. Invariably, the caller begins, "Well, you *are* a hard man to track down . . .") While I was telephoning, a delegation of Indians arrived to talk to me about their reservation hospital. At 3:00 I accompanied the board of supervisors to inspect the site of a much needed river levee to keep back floods; this took longer than anticipated, so it was a strain to arrive clean and ready for a veterans' dinner at 6:30. I had been asked to speak for twenty minutes on veterans' legislation and national defense. A part of the meal was given over to reviewing that portion of my portable file pertaining to these subjects, and to formulating notes on my remarks. This was accompanied by frequent interruptions to shake hands and to be introduced to new friends. I had to finish the dinner, and the speech, and move on for an 8:30 meeting at the local farm center to discuss the farm bill. We arrived at 9:00, after a hectic nighttime drive over a strange road. The meeting lengthened with lively and forceful questions until 11:00; the room was hot and crowded. The tone of the meeting at the start had been quite hostile. At the end, as mutual understanding grew closer, the extra cake and twentieth cup of coffee (for the day) was hard to refuse. The relief of the group as tensions relaxed was obvious, and their friendly attention was hard to break away from. They followed us to the car and talked while the engine ran. Finally, we were off and down the road, with the necessity of driving to a neighboring town to position myself for the next day. Bedded down at last, the last half hour of the day was spent reading mail, a newspaper or two, and a memo from Washington in order to keep up with what was going on in my own office there, and in the world—and then lights out.

* A course in problems of American democracy.

This is the schedule for more than two months, seven days a week. It is a life of constant movement and relentless physical activity. It imposes a constant vigilance, unrelieved, hour upon hour. An inappropriate off-hand remark, misplaced flippancy, or a flash of irritation are not readily forgiven. People ask meaningful, serious questions on all conceivable subjects and they demand and are entitled to informed, thoughtful answers. This means an ever-active brain. Even a social evening is turned into a mental exercise. The time for solitude, for refueling of the machine, is nonexistent. As representative, I am constantly exposed to the represented —to our mutual education and benefit.

What the recess trip home also means is that my capacity, as any congressman's, is taxed to the limit. We are called on in this field of legislation one moment, in another the next moment, and a third shortly afterward. This is in the approved tradition of the United States. It is a kind of testing which Americans insist on. We use it as a yardstick for off-years as well as for election years. It's an exhilarating experience, but an exhausting one. The long hours of work in Washington, keeping oneself up to the mark on district and national and world affairs, pay off. When I return to Washington I know that I have been through the mill. I have sheaves of notes for action on new proposals: a mental health bill, an upgrading in priority of a proposed harbor project, a new outlook on the civil defense and shelter programs, the need for a new post office, and on and on. . . . A rest of several weeks is in order, then a new session of Congress, and I'm off again.

44

POLITICS CREEPS UP ON US

Marjorie M. Beach

In a speech to the Kansas City Lions Club, December 9, 1924, Mayor Albert Beach (1883–1939), the author's husband, said: "America's cities have developed few statesmen. Boss rule of cities is the reason for this. And boss rule is to blame for the surface interest of the people in the government of cities." Despite the efforts of the Beaches, who led the good government forces for more than twenty years, and a new charter form of government, organizational politics prevailed in Kansas City. It is not for imprecations against bosses and bossism, but for its simple appreciation of the qualities of everyday political life that this excerpt from The Mayor's Wife *is presented here.*

*

WE HAD a large rug in our living room which my husband and I had given each other as a Christmas present. The children named it "the pacing rug." It was up and down this rug that my husband walked when he was letting off steam. You could trace his path from one end to the other. The turn-about would have made a good home plate, had we played indoor baseball.

I kept hoping the salesman's claims of the wearing quality of the rug's fibers were not exaggerated.

Today my husband's pacing was unusually determined, and these fibers were really taking a beating.

"I'm all for the bonds," he exclaimed, as he paused for a moment, "and I'm all for women, but why do they have to cloud the issue of our most important election?"

From *The Mayor's Wife* (New York: Vantage Press, 1953).

"Are these the bonds for the ten-year plan?" I asked.

"Yes, and tremendously important to the city. The bond committee has done a good job preparing them."

"But you're not for them?"

"Of course I am," he exploded, "but there is nothing in Kansas City as important at this time as getting the machine out, and this can be done only by obtaining a majority of the council. Some people are not for the bonds and they may vote against the candidates who endorse them."

"I suppose that's why you don't want a woman to run on the ticket at this time."

"The only reason! Gosh, even if the Atheneum weren't the biggest woman's club in town, I'd still think them justified in putting a woman on the council; but, what if a lot of people—especially men—won't vote for a woman? Some will refuse; we don't know how many."

"You don't think it's safe to run a woman candidate now?"

"I don't think it is the time to try," he answered. "We don't know what the reaction would be. We should not take *any* chances, *now*. If one candidate was knocked out because she was a woman, we would have only five chances out of eight to get a majority in the council, instead of five out of nine.

"We must keep the people's minds on the fact that we must elect a majority," he continued. "Everyone must work toward that end, and that end alone."

"Did you get Dave Childs to act as mayor when we go on our jaunt tomorrow?" I asked.

"So you're trying to get me off my pet peeve?" he said, as he stopped at one end of the rug to face me.

"No, I'm just interested in carrying through our plans," I replied.

"You don't want to be anywhere around here when the Republicans hold their nominating convention, I believe," he continued.

"That's it," I admitted. "When we agreed you'd run last time, it was on the condition that it was to be for one term. I really don't trust Henry Ashly and those other men. They have plenty of good material to put up for mayor: Dave Childs, Ray Barnett, Matt Foster—just any number of men, but—"

"You haven't told me where we are going, have you?" He grinned.

"Nope," I muttered, "afraid someone would get it out of you. This is to be a real disappearance."

My friend, Frances Ricksecker, had told me we might have the Ricksecker summer cottage at their private lake in Grandview. I felt that no one would ever dream of our being out there. She had promised she wouldn't even tell her husband. It was a perfect hideout, and not even our son or our maid knew where we were going.

After the convention had chosen all of its candidates, we would re-turn and throw everything we had into electing them. It was very child-like of me, but my husband was willing to humor me in my great desire to disappear. He had already turned in to the nominating committee the names of the men he preferred as candidates.

And so the next day we found ourselves unlocking the door of the little cottage at Grandview, throwing its windows wide open and letting spring in to welcome us in our joy at this adventure. We hung our good clothes in the closet and put on old things which would give us a feeling of freedom. The lake, which lay blue and rippling in the sunlight, drew us at once. My husband got out his rod and reel and hooked on a special fly, while I took over the oars. So we began our circle of all the elbows of the lake.

The trees surrounding the lake shimmered with the thin green of their new leaves, and at times their branches dipped into the water. The wild grapevine swinging in the soft breeze which blew across the lake fell from tree branches and touched our heads as we wound in and out. The odor of flowers made us breathe deep in the exhilaration of being out-doors on this first day when it really seemed like spring.

My husband threw his line with the fly at its end under each projecting rock, seeking to tease the crappie and bass. And how they responded, with a flash of silver and a stout pull as they came flopping and shiny into the boat!

My husband would dip his hands into the water before he released the fish. He said a wet hand protected the scales from a fungus growth that came otherwise. He'd then throw them back into the lake with a "Cheerio! See you later." We needed only a few for dinner.

"Cornbread and crappie! Um—um-m-m!" he said, emphasizing his good appetite with an especially long cast of his line.

We had a wonderful day outdoors, and slept like logs that night.

The next day we were enjoying our crappie and cornbread on the screened-in porch of the cottage. The bullfrogs that had crept from their winter quarters to the lily pads on the lake were entertaining us with their chorus of nuptial "kerchugs."

"It's heaven on earth," my husband said. "You got a swell *do* on these fish. Don't believe I ever tasted better ones." He tilted his chair back and stretched with satisfaction.

"I have a hot apple pie—with cheese," I said, "for dessert."

"Jumping Juniper—and I'm full already! Think I can make it, though."

We heard the front gate creak on its hinges as it swung open, and looked up to see a car come through. We pushed back our chairs and stood up. Our first thought was to run, but there was no escape. There they came—Delano, Foster, Perry, Childs, and Ashly. No one needed to say a word. We knew. They had come with a demand from the convention.

My husband swore. Resentment boiled up in me. This was too much! Why couldn't we be allowed to live our own lives? I remembered what my father had said as he lay dying. Politics sneaks up on you and you cannot get rid of it. My knuckles hurt from the memory of the tightness with which he had held my hands.

"How could you do a thing like this, Beach?" Matt Foster spoke first. "This is a critical time in Kansas City's history."

My husband's words had a slight sting. "I have been telling you fellows this same thing over and over. It is the most critical time in her history. I wanted you to wait for two more years with the charter."

"We certainly are not for bringing the charter up now," Dave Childs said.

"No, but Ray is for bringing up the bonds, and you, Perry, have agreed there should be a woman on the ticket. None of you knows what the machine is really like. You haven't stood with me on any of these points, and I have told you over and over that I wasn't going to run again."

Ever since the men had come I had been turning the question over in my mind as to how they had discovered our hiding place. I couldn't stand it any longer. I had to ask them how.

"Your old chauffeur, George Lawson, told us that he had brought you out here, sometimes," Ray replied. "We had been every place else. This was a last resort."

"He would!" I looked at my husband in disgust. I glanced around. "Why don't we all sit down," I suggested. And so we did, with much scraping of chairs.

"How we were found doesn't matter too much," my husband said. "How we are going to make these men know they have to find another candidate for mayor is important. It's hardly fair to put us up again to take four more years."

"Come, come, Beach!" Henry Ashly smiled. "You have enjoyed this cutting of city expenses and making over a defunct city. Your time will be more your own under the new charter. The city manager has the responsibility, and you have only to advise him."

Ashly always found the most convincing reasons for everything.

"It is always so easy for you men to talk," my husband answered. "Mrs. Beach and I are the ones who have to live the stuff. Hell; if by chance we should get down there at city hall without a majority of the council—I'd rather be dead."

Matt Foster leaned across the table, pleading, "You've thrown the convention into turmoil. They had to adjourn until we could find you."

"Why insist on me, Matt," my husband replied. "You, and Dave Childs there, are equally well-equipped."

"Pish, posh!" Ray Delano spoke up. "There is only one man in Kansas City who is absolutely sure to win and carry the ticket with him, and that is Albert I. Beach."

"You flatter me, Ray—and unduly," was the answer. "The people know these other two men as well as they do me."

Henry Ashly had seated himself beside me. He looked at me with those cool, blue eyes and reached over to pat my hand. "I'd be willing to bet," he said softly, "that here's the one who tried to disappear. And one of the main obstacles."

"I know your smooth tactics, Mr. Ashly, from other times," I retorted. "I wanted to make certain you would not find us. We really have been pushovers in our desire to help our city. But we were afraid of just what is happening now. You assured us last time we would only be committed for two more years."

"Everyone will say that you ran out on your city, Beach," Dave Childs threw at us.

"Oh, hell!" my husband said, twisting his chair back. "You always develop perfectly wonderful pushers to shove us in." He stood up and began pacing the floor.

"Unbeknownst to you, Mr. Mayor, we have organized a 'demand dinner' for Friday night," J. W. Perry said, as he got out of his chair and began taking big steps beside him. "Five thousand Kansas citizens have subscribed to it, Democrats as well as Republicans. The people of Kansas City must have you, Beach."

My husband stopped dead in his tracks. "You can count me out— I'm not running!" he exploded.

I felt like shouting, "He really doesn't want it," but deep inside of me I knew it was hopeless. We were in a trap. There was a dead silence for several minutes, broken only by the deep-voiced frogs.

My husband resumed his pacing. Henry came up quietly and walked beside him without saying a word. Then he spoke up in that clear, vibrant voice.

"Should this election be lost, Beach, it will rest directly on your shoulders. You are the one man who can win, and we all know it."

My husband found his chair and dropped back into it. The tenseness of the men on the porch had reached its highest pitch.

"Pendergast has put up Ben Jaudon, his 'always win' candidate, to run for Mayor," Dave Childs revealed.

Angry tears welled up. They had us pinned down from every side. They would not let us escape.

My husband threw up his hands. "Hell! Once you offer yourself in service, there's no getting out." We looked at each other across the table. We understood without a word that there was no way out.

The mayor rose abruptly and faced them. "I want you fellows to know," he shouted, "it's up to you now to win this election. Damn you!" He pounded the table with his fist. "Get me a majority of that council!"

The five men stood as if ordered and held up their right hands. This Boy Scout gesture broke the tension for them, but not for me. They had a good laugh, but I burst into tears.

"I don't want congratulations," my husband said, as they rushed toward him with hands extended, "and I don't want tears," he continued, turning toward me.

"Go back and tell the convention that Mrs. Beach and I will run," he concluded.

When they had gone, we sat looking at each other in silence. The hot apple pie was cold, and, besides, we had no zest for it. The bullfrog chorus which had meant fun and freedom and fishing now sounded deep and foreboding.

Four more years! Four more years!

"Shall we stay out here until Friday?" I asked, breaking the silence.

"What's Friday?" he replied.

"The 'demand dinner' given to honor you—that Mr. Perry told us about."

"Hell, no!" I had never known my husband to swear so much. "I've got to go in this afternoon and thank the convention for choosing me to head its ticket. And talk them out of their overconfidence about winning this election."

We did the dishes, swept out the house, and closed the windows which he had opened so gleefully to let in the spring. With our city clothes on we went down to have a last look at the lake.

"Just think of all the crappie and bass lying out there under the rocks just waiting for a fly," my husband sighed.

"And just think—it's spring. How I love to find wild grapes and strawberries, and smell things growing," I said.

We turned our backs on the things we liked most and went back. Kansas City needed us.

45

THE CRUCIAL PERIOD IN MY
PUBLIC LIFE

Robert M. La Follette

*The most justly famous of the Progressives, Robert M. ("Fighting Bob")
La Follette (1855–1925), was known as an independent, courageous,
crusader even before he joined a stubborn few in the Senate to vote against
the declaration of war on Germany in 1917. Later, he opposed entrance
of the United States in the League of Nations. In 1924, he ran for
President on the Progressive party ticket and polled 5,000,000 votes. In
campaigns, his style was to choose one issue or theme and develop it
single-mindedly, dramatically, in unmistakable blacks and whites. This
selection from his autobiography tells of his temptation.*

*

IT WOULD be idle to say that the termination of my career as a congressman in March 1891 was not a bitter disappointment to me. It was. I had
not made a great many speeches in the six years of my service, but when I
did enter the debates it was with careful preparation; and I think I may
fairly say that I had attained to such a position as warranted me in looking
forward to a career of some distinction had I been permitted to remain in
the House. So the defeat came to me as a severe blow. But I had acquired a
very valuable experience in my public service and formed delightful and
valuable acquaintances. I had been in contact with the strong men of the
country, and as a result had, I think, grown in character and power.

I was but thirty-five years of age, and went back with firm resolutions
and good cheer to my law practice at Madison, Wisconsin. I was poor,

Reprinted with permission of the copyright owners, the Regents of the University of
Wisconsin, from Robert M. La Follette, *La Follette's Autobiography: A Personal Narrative,* 1960, the University of Wisconsin Press, pp. 60–76.

and the expenses attendant upon readjustment to the new life were matters of consequence. These matters were discussed from time to time by Mrs. La Follette and myself. Our little daughter Fola, very much impressed with frequently hearing these talks, came one day to her mother, and having in mind my recent failure of re-election, said, "Mama, will papa have to be elected before he can practice law and earn some money?"

I found that my public service, while it had been a serious interruption to my professional life, had extended my reputation materially and tended to draw to me a very substantial clientage. Any thought I had of returning to the public service was vague and remote. That I should continue to be interested in public questions and in matters political was inevitable. I knew that issues of great importance affecting the lives and homes of all the people of the country were coming rapidly forward. I had followed the great debate in the Senate and House on the Sherman Anti-Trust Law, had taken part in the debate in the House on the Interstate Commerce Law, had seen the manifestations of corporate power in the halls of Congress. I recognized, in a way, the evidences of the oncoming struggle. I had come to understand the power of Sawyer, Payne, and a few other prominent Republican politicians, closely associated with railroads and other corporate interests in national and state legislation. I was convinced that Payne had not been seriously disappointed with my defeat; that, in fact, whenever he could exert any influence against my political success, without leaving a trail as broad as a highway, he had for some time lost no opportunity of doing so.

Not so with Sawyer. I had disappointed him again and again, in my course, on legislation. But he was a loyal party man and believed in supporting party candidates, regardless of personal feeling. Furthermore, as I have said before, I always believed that Sawyer did not violate his standard of political ethics, in his course, on legislation. As did many politicians, he regarded Congress as a useful agency for the promotion of business enterprises in which he and his friends were identified or interested. If a man did not accept his point of view, he would argue the matter in a blunt, frank, simple way without any display of feeling. The only time I remember to have seen Senator Sawyer manifest the least show of temper was on the floor of the House in connection with the ship subsidy measure, which I have already reviewed. While I understood Senator Sawyer, I think rightly, and know that our standards were not the same and that we would always differ on questions where there was a conflict between corporate and public interests, yet I did not entertain any personal ill will toward him, and I am sure that he then entertained no feeling of personal hostility to me.

I might, therefore, have gone forward with my law practice quite contentedly, had it not been for an event which soon took place and changed my whole life. I shall deal with this event considerably at length because it was not only all-powerful in its effect upon me personally, but it will reveal to what lengths corrupt politicians are prepared to go. I had, of course, seen that sooner or later a conflict with the old leaders was inevitable; the people were already restive against the private-interest view of government, but if it had not been for the incident to which I refer—which brought the whole system home to me, personally, in its ugliest and most revolting form—I should not so soon have been forced into the fight.

One of the political grafts of Wisconsin, ancient and time honored, was the farming out of the public funds to favored banks. Excepting the office of governor, the state treasuryship was more sought after than any other place on the ticket. The reason for this lay in the fact that the state treasurer was able to deposit public moneys in such banks as he chose, on terms satisfactory to the bankers and profitable to himself. Interest on this money was regarded as a political perquisite.

One of the first acts of the Democratic state administration which came in on January 5, 1891, was to institute suit against all state treasurers of Wisconsin who had occupied that office during the preceding twenty years. The Wisconsin treasury cases became noted as pioneer cases for the enforcement of the correct principle in the discharge of duty regarding the custody of trust funds. The beginning of these cases produced a profound sensation in the state and attracted much attention throughout the nation. Suits were instituted against former treasurers Henry B. Harshaw, Edward C. McFettridge, Richard Guenther, Ferdinand Kuehn, and Henry Betz and their bondsmen. Senator Sawyer's wishes had largely controlled in the selection of several of these treasurers, and he was one of the principal bondsmen. Certain of the treasurers had little or no property to satisfy judgments of large amounts. Hence, Sawyer, as the wealthiest of all the bondsmen, stood to lose a large sum of money in the event of the state's recovery. The suits finally resulted in judgments in favor of the state aggregating $608,918.23. Of this amount, Sawyer was liable for nearly $300,000. The estate of Guido Pfister, a leading businessman of Milwaukee, was also liable as bondsman for former Treasurer Kuehn to the extent of something more than $100,000. The liability of this estate marks the advent into Wisconsin state politics of Charles F. Pfister of Milwaukee, one of the principal heirs of the Guido Pfister estate, who will figure hereafter in this narrative.

The ex-treasurers and their bondsmen employed a strong array of excellent counsel, among others S.U. Pinney, afterward Supreme Court Justice, and Joseph V. Quarles, afterward United States Senator. The state retained as counsel to assist Attorney-General O'Conner, Col. William F. Vilas, former member of Cleveland's cabinet, afterward United States Senator, and R.M. Bashford, afterward Supreme Court Justice.

Robert G. Siebecker, then one of the justices of the supreme court of

Wisconsin, was at that time judge of the circuit court for Dane County. He had been appointed to that office by Governor Hoard, in 1889, to fill a vacancy, and a telegram from Governor Hoard's secretary announcing Siebecker's selection was my first intimation that he had been considered. I was indeed surprised, because Siebecker was a Democrat and was appointed by Governor Hoard to succeed Judge Stuart, who was a Republican. I mention this point in this connection because insofar as the appointment was criticized at all, it was on the ground that Siebecker was a Democrat. This fact, and the further fact that he was my brother-in-law and my partner in the firm of La Follette, Siebecker & Harper was also the subject of newspaper comment at the time, and his appointment was ascribed to my known friendly relations with Governor Hoard. I have taken pains to state these facts somewhat in detail because of their important connection with the incident which I am about to relate.

Shortly before these cases were to come on for argument in the Circuit Court, I received a letter from Senator Sawyer—whose home was in Oshkosh, Wisconsin—of which the following is an exact copy:

Dictated.

Oshkosh, Wisconsin, September 14, 1891.
Hon. Robert M. La Follette, Madison, Wisconsin.

My dear La Follette:
    I will be in Milwaukee, at the state fair, on Thursday. I have some matters of importance that I would like to consult you about, that escaped my mind yesterday. If convenient can you be in Milwaukee on that day and meet me at the Plankinton House at 11 o'clock A.M.? If not on that day, what day would suit your convenience this week? Please answer by telegraph. All you need to say, if you can meet me that day, is merely telegraph me "yes." If not simply mention day you can meet me.

                                                   Yours truly,
                                                   PHILETUS SAWYER.

    The letter was typewritten on a single sheet of paper, letter size. The top part of the sheet had been torn off, down nearly to the date line, leaving only the printed words, "Dictated, Oshkosh." This fact did not impress me at the time I received the letter but led me to investigate the matter later and to discover that it was written on the office stationery of ex-Treasurer Harshaw, who afterward came to me with a message from Sawyer. The reference to his having seen me the day before it was written, related to our meeting on the 13th of September at Neenah, Wisconsin, on the occasion of the funeral of former congressman Charles B. Clark. During the services and afterward, until Mr. Sawyer left to take his train, other people had been constantly with us, so that Sawyer had had no opportunity for any private conversation with me.

    I conferred with my law partner Sam Harper, after receiving the letter, and, believing that the proposed interview concerned political matters, decided to meet Sawyer. I remember that the brief nature of the response which he requested to the letter impressed me as a precaution taken to forestall newspaper interviewers. And I filed a telegram in response, limited to the word "yes," as directed.

On the seventeenth of September, I went to Milwaukee and met Sawyer at the Plankinton House. The state fair was in progress at that time and the hotel was crowded. Sawyer said that he had been unable to secure a room and requested me to go with him to the hotel parlors on the second floor. The parlors were large, and he led me away to a portion of the room remote from the entrance—where we sat down. After some preliminary conversation in which he said, "I wanted to talk with you about Siebecker and the treasury matter," he finally came directly to the point and said:

"These cases are awfully important to us, and we cannot afford to lose them. They cost me a lot of anxiety. I don't want to have to pay——" naming a large sum of money—whether $100,000 or more, I am not certain. "Now I came down here to see you alone. No one knows I am to meet you here. I don't want to hire you as an attorney in the cases, La Follette, and don't want you to go into court. But here is fifty dollars, I will give you five hundred more or a thousand—or five hundred more and a thousand (I was never able to recall exactly the sums named) when Siebecker decides the cases right."

I said to him, "Senator Sawyer, you can't know what you are saying to me. If you struck me in the face you could not insult me as you insult me now."

He said, "Wait—hold on!"

I was then standing up. I said: "No, you don't want to employ me as an attorney. You want to hire me to talk to the judge about your case off the bench." He said, "I did not think you would take a retainer in the case. I did not think you would want to go into the case as an attorney. How much will you take as a retainer?"

I answered, "You haven't enough money to employ me as an attorney in your case, after what you have said to me."

"Well, perhaps I don't understand court rules. Anyway, let me pay you for coming down here."

I said, "Not a dollar, sir," and immediately left the room.

Nothing else ever came into my life that exerted such a powerful influence upon me as that affair. It was the turning point, in a way, of my career. Sooner or later, I probably would have done what I did in Wisconsin. But it would have been later. It would have been a matter of much slower evolution. But it shocked me into a complete realization of the extremes to which this power that Sawyer represented would go to secure the results it was after. But, in another way, its effect on me as an individual was most profound. I had always had a pride in my family—in my good name. It had been the one thing that my mother had worked into my character. It was the thing that she emphasized when she talked with me about my father, whom I never saw. One who has never been subject to an experience like that cannot realize just what comes over him.

There has always been uncertainty in my mind about the money he offered me—the amounts. He named different amounts. He was going to give me a sum right then, and more, conditioned on the case being decided "right." He had his pocketbook in one hand, and a roll of money in the other. For an instant I was dazed, and then the thing surged through me. I felt that I could not keep my hands off his throat—I stood over him, said the things to him that I have related, and then left him, blindly. I knew he followed me. I went rapidly downstairs, and out of the hotel. The state fair was on, and the hotel lobby was crowded with people. I saw nobody. I got out in the street and walked and walked.

Six or eight years afterward, when I was a candidate for governor, I stopped one day in the little town of Sheboygan Falls. Among those who called on me was former congressman Brickner. He had been on the Democratic side when I was on the Republican side of the House. He came into the hotel to greet me, and while he was sitting there he brought up the Sawyer affair. The state, of course, had been aflame after the interview had been published. Sawyer's power over the Republican press of the state was very great, and it was all turned against me. I was denounced as a liar and assassin of character, trying to destroy one of the great and good men of the state. Brickner said, "Mr. La Follette, I knew which one of you two told the truth about what took place in the Plankinton Hotel that day. I saw your face when you came down the stairs, with Sawyer following trying to catch up with you. I knew that there had been serious trouble."

After the interview with Sawyer at the Plankinton Hotel that day I disclosed what had transpired between him and me to a few close personal friends and told them I thought it my plain duty to report the matter to the court. Several of them took strong ground against this course. They pointed out the great power of Senator Sawyer, his corporation and political connections, his control of newspapers; they argued that he would utterly destroy me. I granted all that, but urged that as a member of the bar, an officer of the court, I could not be silent; that it was my duty to report to Judge Siebecker exactly what had occurred. Conferences of these friends were held from time to time, they urging their view and I contending that my course, though the harder one, must be followed.

It was finally agreed that the whole matter be submitted to Judge Romanzo Bunn, the federal judge for the western district of Wisconsin, whose home was in Madison, and who enjoyed the confidence and esteem of all who knew him. I remember the afternoon when I saw him by appointment at his chambers in the federal building in Madison. He listened with patience and understanding, his benign face expressing the utmost pain and sympathy. He did not speak until I had finished. Then he said,

"Robert, have you told Judge Siebecker?"

"No," I answered. "And on the advice of a few friends I came to tell you about it and to ask your counsel."

He said, "Well, you must tell Judge Siebecker. You cannot permit him to sit in the case without telling him all about it. I doubt very much whether he will feel that he can try the cases. That is for him to decide—but you must tell him."

I said to him, "Judge Bunn, I have insisted from the first that it was my duty to tell Judge Siebecker, but my friends have strongly urged against that course, because they realize that Sawyer will follow me relentlessly as long as he lives. I understand that well, for this thing has weighed on me every hour since it occurred."

On the evening of the same day on which I saw Judge Bunn, in the privacy of Judge Siebecker's home I told him exactly what had taken place. He was very much moved. He decided immediately, of course, that, with the knowledge of Sawyer's attempt to corrupt the court, he could not sit as judge in the cases. He said that if he caused Sawyer to be cited for contempt, the facts would necessarily become public with the result that it would prejudice the cases. So far as either of us knew, many of the defendants probably were ignorant of Sawyer's action. At any rate, it was important that they be given a fair and impartial trial. Before I left him he had determined that he would promptly call together the attorneys on both sides, tell them that he would not hear the cases for reasons which were controlling with him, but that he would call in any other circuit judge in the state upon whom they agreed. Siebecker was then a young man—he had been on the bench two years and was making an excellent record as judge. These cases were certain to be important, and if he rendered a judgment which should ultimately be sustained by the Supreme Court, it would make a record in which any trial court could take just pride, and might prove an important factor in his judicial career. Indeed, it transpired that Judge A.W. Newman, who was called in to try the cases after Siebecker's withdrawal, was elected to fill the first vacancy upon the supreme bench of Wisconsin.

I think it was on Friday that Judge Siebecker informed the attorneys on both sides that he could not try the treasury cases. They were amazed at his announcement, and the news quickly spread. The cases were of such great public interest, involving so many prominent men and such large sums of money, that the keenest speculation and indeed excitement followed Siebecker's withdrawal.

By the following day, newspaper correspondents, representing the principal papers of the state and leading dailies of Chicago, were rushed to Madison, keen on the scent for sensational news. Efforts were made to interview Judge Siebecker. And because of my relationship with the judge and my interest in political matters, every possible effort was made to extract something from me; but I did not regard it as incumbent upon me to make any public statement. Unable to ascertain any facts, a lot of newspaper stories were predicted upon guesses—some wide of the mark and some shrewdly direct in their shot at the facts.

On Sunday morning, October 25, 1891, the Chicago *Times* printed a sensational story with the startling query as to whether there had been an attempt made to "influence" the court in the Wisconsin Treasury cases, suggesting that if an effort had really been made to influence the court, causing Siebecker's withdrawal, that the guilty party was known, and stood in the shadow of the penitentiary. Here are the headings from the Chicago *Times:*

BRIBERY THEIR GAME

PERSONS INTERESTED IN THE WISCONSIN STATE TREASURY SUITS ATTEMPT DESPERATE MEANS.

AN EFFORT MADE TO "INFLUENCE" JUDGE SIEBECKER, OF MADISON, WHO WAS TO TRY THE CASES.

THE INDIGNANT OFFICIAL NOTIFIES THE LAWYERS THAT HE WILL NOT SIT DURING THE TRIAL.

HE REFUSES TO AT PRESENT MAKE PUBLIC THE DETAILS OF THE AFFAIR—STARTLING DISCLOSURES EXPECTED.

From what followed, I was led to believe that Senator Sawyer had read and been very greatly alarmed by the matter published in the *Times.* His home was in Oshkosh, where also lived former state treasurer Harshaw. Sunday evening I was surprised to receive a note from Harshaw brought to me by a bellboy from the Park Hotel, Madison. The note, which was written on the hotel stationery, indicating that Harshaw was then in Madison, requested an interview at my law office on the following morning at eight o'clock. I showed it to my law partner, Sam Harper, who happened to be with me at the time. I suggested that Harshaw probably desired to see me regarding the Sawyer matter; that as no witnesses were present when Sawyer made his proposal to me at the Plankinton Hotel in Milwaukee, the time might come when the question of veracity would be raised between us; that Harshaw's proposed interview with me might result in some disclosure which would show conclusively that Sawyer had endeavored to corrupt the court; and that I would consent to see Harshaw if he (Harper) would be present at the interview.

At eight o'clock the next morning, Harshaw came to my office, accompanied by Joseph V. Quarles, afterward United States Senator, one of the attorneys in the treasury cases. They were shown into my private room. After formal greetings, Mr. Quarles made inquiry about Judge Siebecker and said he wanted to see him. I told him where the Judge could be found and he thereupon withdrew. Harshaw remained. As Quarles left Sam accompanied him to the door of the outer office, leaving Harshaw in the private office with me.

The moment we were alone, Harshaw leaned across the desk, and said quickly:

"Bob, will you meet Sawyer at the Grand Pacific Hotel in Chicago tonight?"

I was incensed that he had succeeded in communicating to me privately a message from Sawyer, and rising to my feet I said in a tone of voice which immediately brought Sam back into the room.

"No, I will never meet Saywer or have any communication with him again as long as I live."

I was determined that Harper should know exactly what Harshaw had said to me during his absence, and so leaning across the desk, I repeated:

"You have just asked me if I will meet Sawyer tonight at the Grand Pacific Hotel in Chicago, and I answer you, no, so long as I live, I will never again meet Sawyer or have any communication with him."

Harshaw put up his hand in protest and said, "Don't, Bob, don't be angry with me. I have always respected you and always shall."

I then said to Harshaw that it was wrong for him to come to me with any such proposal; that he knew just what Sawyer had attempted at the Plankinton, and that he ought to have known that I would have nothing more to do with Sawyer. Harshaw said, "I do know what Sawyer did; but had I known beforehand what he intended to do when he met you at Milwaukee, it never would have occurred." This ended the interview, and Harshaw left the office.

From what occurred immediately thereafter, it was plain that Sawyer was then in Milwaukee awaiting Harshaw's return, prepared to go on to Chicago provided I consented to meet him at the Grand Pacific; that upon Harshaw's arrival in Milwaukee and his report to Sawyer of the failure of his mission, he (Sawyer) then, apprehensive that the truth might come out, decided that he would forestall any possible statement which I might make. Up to that time no public charge had been made connecting Sawyer with Judge Siebecker's retirement from the treasury cases; but Sawyer knew, and that knowledge impelled him to commit the folly of protesting his innocence in advance of any public charge of guilt. On that same (Monday) evening he personally gave to the *Sentinel,* in Milwaukee, an interview in which he stated that he had "telegraphed" me to meet him at the Plankinton Hotel in Milwaukee; that he had offered me a retainer of five hundred dollars, but no money was paid; that I thought it would not be advisable to take a retainer, as Judge Siebecker was my brother-in-law; that it was the first he knew that Siebecker was my brother-in-law, and that had he known that fact he would not have proposed to retain me; that if I had put any improper interpretation upon his conversation with me, I had misunderstood or misconstrued what he said; and that at the time of the conversation I certainly made no such intimation to him. The interview with Senator Sawyer was published Tuesday morning, October 27, 1891.

The publication of Sawyer's statement wholly misrepresenting the facts made it necessary that I should make public the truth regarding that interview, and, in the Milwaukee *Sentinel* of Wednesday morning, October 28th, in a signed statement, I set forth in detail just what actually did occur between Senator Sawyer and myself. I requested Judge Siebecker's sanction to speak, and received it. I did not point out the weakness and inconsistency of Sawyer's statement; I did not note the fact that he could not be ignorant of the relation existing between Siebecker and myself, which everybody knew, and which had been the subject of public discussion and comment when Siebecker was appointed circuit judge; I made no mention of the fact that I was constantly practicing my profession in Siebecker's court and that there could be no impropriety in my accepting a retainer had it been offered upon honorable terms. In that interview I stated only the naked facts required to make public record of the exact truth.

I believed I fully realized what this would cost me. Sawyer was the power in Wisconsin politics. He was many times a millionaire. His wish was law—his rule unquestioned. His organization extended to every county, town and village. I knew that within twenty-four hours after giving my signed statement to the Milwaukee *Sentinel,* his agents would be actively in communication with newspapers, with political committees, with the representatives of prominent business interests throughout the commonwealth.

Party feeling and party loyalty were still strong, and partook in some measure of the zeal and fervor of the days following the war. My veracity had never been questioned by any man. I was confident that the truth of my statement would be accepted. I did anticipate that men who loved the Republican party would resent as an attack upon it a statement which must impeach the honesty and integrity of its leader and, that while members of my party and all men generally would approve of my refusing a bribe, men devoted to the success of the Republican party would say that I might have suppressed the facts, though Sawyer had falsified them; that I might indeed have withheld information from the Court and, for the good of the party, have kept secret all knowledge of the fact that its leader had attempted to corrupt even the courts. This may seem strange in these times [1913] of growing independence and keener civic conscience; it was vastly different twenty years ago.

Prepared as I was to meet criticism, no one could have anticipated the violence with which the storm broke upon me. In my own party there was no newspaper that dared to brook Sawyer's disapproval. Besides a little group of personal friends, there was no one to raise his voice in my defense. Prominent politicians denounced me. I was shunned and avoided everywhere by men who feared or sought the favor of Senator Sawyer and his organization. At every turn, the way seemed barred to me. No one can ever know what I suffered. As I recall the fearful depression of those months, I wonder where I found strength to endure them. But I went about my work determined that no one should see in my face or daily habit any sign of what I was going through. But the thing gnawed all the while. I went from my office to my house, from my house to my office, and did my work as it came to me day by day. Fortunately, I found clients who wanted the services of a man who could not be tempted by money. They came to me with their cases, and I found plenty to do. But I could not shake off or be indifferent to the relentless attacks on my veracity which came in a steady onset from the Republican press of the state. Anonymous, threatening letters crowded my mail with warnings that if I dared to show my head in politics I would do well to arrange in advance for a lot in the cemetery. I did not know it at the time, nor indeed until after Harper's death, but Mrs. La Follette has since told me that there was a long period following the Sawyer affair when Sam was so apprehensive for my personal safety that he scarcely permitted me to be out of his sight.

But I was resolved that I would not let it break me down. The winter of 1891–1892 proved an ordeal. Sam Harper, General Bryant, Charles Van Hise, my classmate, then at the head of the Department of Geology of the University of Wisconsin, and a few friends stayed by me. These friends and the immediate family knew what I suffered during that time, but on the street, in my office and in the courtroom, I carried myself so that no one should know how keenly I felt it all. I slept very little and there was fear that my health would give way. But it did not.

Fourteen years afterward, when I first came to the Senate of the United States, I was placed in a somewhat similar position. I was again alone. When I entered the cloakroom, men turned their backs upon me and conversation ceased. Members left their seats when I began to speak. My amendments to bills were treated with derision and turned down with a lofty wave of the hand. For nearly two years I went through an experience that had seldom failed to bring a fresh, independent member to terms. It was said that I would soon be "eating out of their hands." They did not know the iron that had been driven into me years before.

During that winter of 1891–1892 I spent much time alone, in the private room at my law offices, and in the little study at my home in the long hours of the night. I went back over my political experiences. I thought over many things that had occurred during my service in the House. I began to understand their relation. I had seen the evils singly—here and there a manifest wrong, against which I had instinctively revolted. But I had been subjected to a terrible shock that opened my eyes, and I began to see really for the first time. I find now no bitterness and little resentment left in me against individuals. The men of that time filled their places in a system of things, in some measure the outgrowth of the wealth of our resources and the eagerness of the public for their development. Corporations, and individuals allied with corporations, were invited to come in and take what they would, if only the country might be developed, railroads and factories constructed, towns and cities built up. Against this organized power it had been my misfortune—perhaps my fortune—to be thrown by circumstances. The experiences of my congressional life now came back to me with new meaning—the ship subsidy bill, the oleomargarine bill, the Nicaraguan Canal, the railroad rate bill, the Sioux Indian land grant and the Menomonie timber steal.

So, out of this awful ordeal came understanding; and out of understanding came resolution. I determined that the power of this corrupt influence, which was undermining and destroying every semblance of representative government in Wisconsin, should be broken.

I felt that I had few friends; I knew I had no money—could command the support of no newspaper. And yet I grew strong in the conviction that in the end Wisconsin would be made free.

And in the end it was so. That Sawyer incident had a tremendous effect on the young men of the state. Three years afterward, in the campaign of 1894, they came into the state convention, standing together and taking defeat like veterans. The ten years' fight was on.

I did not underrate the power of the opposition. I had been made to feel its full force. I knew that Sawyer and those with him were allied with the railroads, the big business interests, the press, the leading politicians of every community. I knew the struggle would be a long one; that I would have to encounter defeat again and again. But my resolution never faltered.

I well understood that I must take time to develop my plan; that the first encounter with the organization in Wisconsin must be one which should compel their respect, even though it resulted in temporary defeat for the reform movement. First of all, I must make it manifest that I had not been destroyed as an individual. To do this it was necessary to go out and meet men wherever they were gathered together on political occasions.

The national Republican convention was called to meet in Minneapolis, June 7, 1892. There was no serious contest for the presidential nomination. Harrison's administration was generally popular throughout the country. The country was prosperous, and when the country is prosperous a presidential administration is popular.

Harrison, himself, was a man of superior ability. On a trip across the country, in 1891, he accomplished a remarkable feat. It is generally said of these presidential "swings around the circle" that you get substantially all the man has to say in the first three or four days; after that he repeats his thought in varied form. Harrison's speeches, however, made on this trip to the Pacific coast, were a notable series of daily addresses covering a wide range of important subjects, treated broadly and thoughtfully. They aroused a great deal of enthusiasm and were eagerly read by the public. Reserved, undemonstrative, a bit austere in manner, direct, quick to grasp a proposition and decide on its merits, Harrison was a strong executive, commanding the respect and confidence of all with whom he came in contact. He was conservative but not what we would call, today, reactionary. His state papers were noteworthy for the ability and directness with which he discussed public questions. He stood for integrity in every branch of the government; he strengthened, supported, and extended the civil service law; he was not in favor with the spoilsman and the jobster. After his retirement from the presidency, he delivered many important addresses throughout the country, one of which in particular was markedly progressive in thought. This address was made to the Union League Club of Chicago, February 22, 1898, on the "Obligations of Wealth." We were then in the midst of our struggle in Wisconsin, and I found his views as expressed therein of great help to me in the speeches I was making in support of reforms in taxation.

I made no attempt to be elected as a delegate to the convention; but I determined, nevertheless, to attend as a spectator. Sam Harper went with me. Of course the delegates elected to the convention by the Wisconsin machine were bitterly hostile to me. My trouble with Sawyer had been given wide publicity and was well known to all prominent politicians in that great gathering. I knew that generally they would not judge the matter upon its real merit, but strictly with reference to its effect upon the political situation in Wisconsin. To the extent that it injured Sawyer, the party leader in the state, it lessened the chances of Republican success; and the delegates to a national convention are looking, above all things, for immediate political victory. So, to that extent, I anticipated disapproval even among those who had been my personal friends in public life at Washington. It taxed my resolution severely to meet these former political friends. I found all that I had anticipated in the way of coldness and hostility. One encounter which cut me to the quick will illustrate my meaning:

I had served for six years in Congress with David B. Henderson of Iowa (afterward, Speaker of the House of Representatives) upon terms of personal intimacy. When the roll was called in the 49th Congress for the allotment of seats, mine chanced to fall almost within touch of Henderson, who was already in the seat which he had chosen—a sturdy figure he was, square face, fine head, covered with thick iron-gray hair. He turned on me a keen, searching, yet withal a kindly look; our eyes met for a moment, and then putting out his hand, he said, "Well, my boy, I think you'll do." That was the beginning, and we were always good friends. We represented adjoining districts, the Mississippi River between. He had called me across the state line to speak for him in the campaign of 1890 when he feared that he was losing, and had often declared that I was a material help in saving him from defeat in that landslide year. When I met him at Minneapolis he came at me quickly with "What are you fighting Sawyer for, and tearing things all to pieces in Wisconsin?" I told him that if he knew the truth he would not ask me such a question. And then the jostling crowd swept between us, and I saw him no more. A few old-time friends, Major McKinley among them, greeted me cordially with a warm hand and an understanding look in the eye, though in the main I was made to feel that they regarded me a political outcast. But it was good training; it was seasoning me for the hard struggle ahead.

With Harrison's nomination, the Wisconsin machine selected its candidates for the state campaign. Former Senator Spooner was its candidate for governor. The rank and file of the party had nothing to say— Sawyer, Payne, and a few others made the plans.

I was not yet ready to offer opposition, and decided to wait until two years later; but it was obvious that I must insist on keeping my place as a factor in the Republican campaign of that year.

The defeat of Governor William D. Hoard, two years before, had seriously divided the party. Hoard's friends felt that he had not been loyally supported by Payne in conducting the state campaign of 1890. In order to mollify Hoard's friends, and they were legion among the farmers of Wisconsin, and to bring about the desired party harmony, Payne withdrew as chairman of the Republican State Central Committee, and H.C. Thom, a warm personal friend of Hoard was elected in his place.

During my four congressional campaigns I had been called each time by the chairman of the State Central Committee to speak outside of my district and over the state. The facts warrant me in saying, I think, that there was a general demand in campaigns for my work as a speaker; but, in the campaign of 1892, I was not invited to speak. This, I understood, was by the orders of the machine.

I had well considered the wisdom of making my fight against the corrupt organization in Wisconsin politics in the Republican party rather than out in the field as an independent. I believed in the integrity of the rank and file of the party. I could see no valid reason why I should stand apart from the great body of men with whom I had been affiliated politically since coming to my majority, so long as I was in substantial agreement with the ideas about which that party was organized; for these reasons, briefly stated, I had settled it in my own mind that I would fight within the ranks. I did not propose that those nominally in control of the party organization should for any reason blacklist and put me outside of the party lines. If I chose at any time to leave the party, it would be because my convictions compelled me to do so. But I would not recognize the authority of any man or any set of men to decide my party status.

After waiting until it became quite apparent that I should not be invited, I wrote to the chairman of the State Central Committee tendering my services as a speaker in the campaign. He came to see me at my law office in Madison and suggested that in view of the feeling existing against me on the part of Senator Sawyer and his many friends, it would be inadvisable for me to take part in the campaign. We were personal friends and discussed the matter frankly. He suggested that Senator Sawyer was an old man and that if I ever wished to take any part in political matters in Wisconsin, the easier course for me would be to wait until he had passed away. He suggested that the feeling against me was very intense and that my appearance on the platform might be resented with violence. I answered that that would not deter me from entering the campaign; that I proposed to maintain my relations with the party and would not consent to be turned out to pasture to wait for my opponents to die off; that I was opposed to the corrupt machine methods of those in control and intended to stay on the firing line. I furthermore stated that if it was not desired that I should speak under the auspices of the State Central Committee, I would make my own announcements and speak under my own auspices; that I was deeply interested in Harrison's election and wanted to do all in my power for him; and that I was reasonably confident that I would have as good meetings in numbers and results as any managed by the State Central Committee. Chairman Thom thereupon decided that if I was going to speak anyway, he preferred that I should speak under the direction of the State Central Committee.

This I told him would be perfectly agreeable to me, but that I should designate the places where I was to speak. He desired to know what my attitude would be regarding the state ticket. I told him that I should discuss national issues.

I never held better meetings in any political campaign. I found every town placarded with great posters in flaming red, urging that I be called upon in my meetings to discuss the Sawyer affair. These posters contained a list of questions which it was urged should be put up to me for answer. I had little doubt that they emanated from Democratic sources, and it was their purpose to force that issue into my campaign.

Strange as it may seem, in no instance throughout that campaign was there a single unfriendly interruption from the audience, and never

was I given a more respectful and attentive hearing. I was greatly encouraged and firmly convinced that whatever the attitude of the politicians, I still had many friends among the people.

In the next campaign, that of 1894, I began my fight on the Wisconsin machine which continued for ten years and resulted in the complete
reorganization of the Republican party of the state. . . .

46

POLITICS AND THE SAME OLD STUFF

Maury Maverick

Plainspun, forthright, impatient of cant, disrespectful of pomp, and heed-less of ceremony—the frontier man, Maury Maverick (1895–1954), Rep-resentative from the San Antonio area of Texas in the New Deal years, was all of those things. He was, these memoirs suggest, something more, however, than a mere tintype cowboy-politician. He was a self-conscious, reflecting human being of considerable sensitivity and great human warmth. The humor does not hurt, either.

*

DEMAGOGING IS NOTHING NEW; Demosthenes was a demagogue, him-self. But some have been cured; and this is the story of my own cure. I have read Hamlet, and remember where the Dane with the morbid Freudian complex says that players should not "split the ears of the groundlings" which will only pain sensible people or make "the judicious grieve." But, in my campaign technique, I owe no debt either to Hamlet or to Shakespeare. I reformed myself!

Out in Texas I used to be rated a pretty good stump speaker. I drew fair crowds, really good-sized ones, even when I was a raw recruit. But I was no rosebud. When the man who is now "the gentleman from Texas" took the stump he was hell-bent for election, roaring down the alley, and the devil take the hindmost. I always ascribed evil motives to my op-ponents and enemies, and I could see a political sin ten miles off without field glasses. I would call an opponent a rascal and a thief, and ascribe

From *A Maverick American* (New York: Covici, Friede Publishers, 1937).

to him all the crimes, misdemeanors, and felonies in the judicial catalogue. Word would get around that Maury was going to skin somebody alive. In fact, I would see to it that word got around. The crowds would gather. I would take the hide off. Even in local campaigns, the crowds would sometimes number two or three thousand; my good friends of the citizens' league would stomp, roar, and pitch.

I don't do that any more. And yet, I get elected. The thing that converted me, more than anything else, was the Steffler affair. Paul Steffler was my political enemy then, and he is my political enemy now, but by the time I had got through calling him names in a certain city campaign in San Antonio, I got religion, though it was only political religion. Ever since then I have left the demagoguery to others—at least I never start it myself.

Steffler was street commissioner in San Antonio. He was running for re-election to that office, and I was a speaker on the other side. I suspected that all was not well with the handling of the city's funds, and, after a lot of verbal scalping, my colleagues and I forced an audit of the books. Discrepancies were found, and I was absolutely convinced it was a clear case of thievery. In Steffler's department, there was a large sum unaccounted for, or not properly receipted—as much as $50,000 or $75,000. It concerned a sewer line. That gave me the irresistible opportunity of crying out that there was indeed a bad odor in the city sewer system. Moreover, I had been reading about the sewer scandals of the Borough of Queens in New York, and I became a ruthless zealot for reform.

I was scheduled to give a speech on the evening of the day when that audit came out. I had no time for more than a cursory study of the facts. But with undiminished zeal, I got up before a large crowd and accused Paul of all manner of crookedness. I harangued about the large apartment house he had built—"with the taxpayers' money." I undertook to prove— and didn't fall far short of it—that he was a rascal and a thief.

The crowd ate it up. But Steffler, backed by a strong political machine, won his election just the same.

About two months after this, my statements began to eat on my conscience. I finally came to the conclusion that the procedure of the city was entirely innocent and that it was merely a case of slipshod books. I realized that out of several million dollars of money expended, some $50,000 had not been properly authenticated. But there was no evidence of felony and no proof of graft. Padding the payrolls and stealing the people's money had not been practiced; in other words, I had made a story which though technically true was really false. It kept eating and eating on me, so finally I went to see the man I had blackened.

I told him that I was very sorry, and I apologized. Then I learned some things that made me suffer in my turn. He told me that his wife had suffered a great deal over it, and that my attack had done his family injury. I had gone there in a mood of penitence, but I went away more troubled than before. I made up my mind then that I was going to abandon tar-brush methods forever.

I went home and sat myself down in a chair. Then I put myself way over in a corner and argued with myself. I indulged in a severe course of critical self-examination. I called myself a demagogue and a slanderer. After I had given myself a good bawling out, I let the Maury over in the corner have a chance to defend himself. He had no defense. So then and there I agreed I would indulge in no more demagoguery and no more accusations unless I was sure of my facts.

My campaign methods changed. And the crowds reacted. After I began to make speeches about the tariff, world trade, the Constitution, throwing in a good ballast of facts, crowds dropped off from a thousand or two, to a hundred or two. Everybody said that there was something the matter with me. But the next time I ran for office, although many of my friends were worried about the small crowds at the meetings, there was nothing wrong with the crowds at the polls, and I got a bigger majority than ever before.

Since that time I have never tried to get big crowds. After I came to Congress I saw Huey Long getting huge audiences all over the country, but I was acquainted with Huey and I knew it didn't mean anything. And, long before the national election in 1936, I knew that old Doctor Townsend and Father Coughlin really had no substantial influence with the people because they were merely eccentrics or clowns, and though the people would come out and make a great lot of noise listening to them, this kind of emotionalism was only temporary and as unstable as the crazy panaceas that aroused it.

I have found that you can shock the people with the truth, and they can take it. By this, I do not mean to tell a lady voter that her baby is pie-faced and a nuisance. That is neither good manners nor sensible.

But you can tell them that a certain petition is pie-faced and a nuisance, if you give them a rational explanation. And no politician need be frightened by petitions. You can get a wagon-load, and upon investigation you can find that thousands signed without reading, or signed just to get rid of the promoter. "Prominent citizens" often sign petitions to get the worst criminals out of jail and then write you confidentially not to pay any attention to their signatures. The soundest and most conservative citizen will also sign petitions showing the most crack-pot ideas.

For instance, take the Townsend craze. I got thousands and thousands of letters and petitions. When I went back to Texas for the campaign, I made a simple explanation that the plan was suicidal, and I gave my reasons. I lost no votes. Sometimes big corporations rib their employees and friends to write letters against progressive measures such as the Social Security Act, the TVA and the holding company bill. This is what the politicians called "inspired stuff," and I don't swallow it.

If you give reasons to your people, they will generally stand by you, though sometimes they do not. Another thing is that our American wants you to talk in plain language. He has a horror of European "isms"—but TVA is all right, because it works. Nor does he want to take political medicine in one big dose. He will not gulp down the whole of any philosophy. His idea of independence forbids him following any program blindly, and he wants to do as we do in Congress—"reserve the right to object."

Even on the Constitution, you can tell the people the truth. For a hundred and fifty years they have been misled on the subject. But if you hammer hard enough, they will kick over all the propaganda and lies that have been told them by the press which is prostitute and lawyers that are kept.

I would not have anyone believe, however, that the people don't get off the track once in a while. Neither would I have anyone believe that I live in any rarefied atmosphere, and wholly abstain from being a first-class politician when I can. I am not beyond using sarcasm, ridicule, spectacular language, and sometimes working up a little hate. However, I do try to start out as a gentleman, and never use the rough and tumble stuff until my opponent starts something.

One time, running for Congress, I delivered radio talks on the tariff, which is about the most important subject for Texas; I spoke on our trade relations with Mexico, and kept to the field of economics, with language which had a touch of the University. At the same time my opponent was spending all of his time saying that I was a Communist because I belonged to the American Civil Liberties Union. I then delivered a dissertation on freedom of thought, conscience, and religion: but the old Communist gag went on.

I finally got tired of it. About that time a friend of mine, a gentleman who had two notches on his gun, came to me and told me quite indignantly that he had been insulted by my opponent. He said this opponent of mine had tried to buy his vote by offering him a bottle of beer at a cockfight on Sunday. The two-notch man was horrified.

So I got up on the stump and said my most worthy opponent was two-faced and double-dealing. "Upon Sunday morning," I said, "with reverend tread and pious mug, diked out in whitewash tie and the habiliments of the elder, he pompously enters the church, and sits in the front row. But, sir, what else does he do? That afternoon, in flashy suit and familiar smile, he swaggers (which, my fellow citizens, is unnatural to him, and all a pose) into where? Where, my fellow citizens? (Pause.) Into a cockfight, held in violation of the law, against the peace and dignity of the mighty state of Texas.

"And, then, he attempts to purchase the vote of a murderer with a bottle of beer!"

The rest of my language was quite lurid and unrestrained. It cannot be said that this was very lofty campaigning. But enough is enough, and no man who goes into politics can sit on Mount Olympus, talking sweet philosophy, and get elected.

The truth is, what I did was not in malice. Everyone enjoyed it. I won, too.

The last time I ran, in 1936, it was the same old stuff, the same old accusations, the same old lies. But it was worse, being so very old, and so very tiresome. My opponent was a very nice fellow and a schoolmate, named Seeligson. He was a first cousin to John Dos Passos. But he and his co-spielers let themselves in for a lot of talk about the flag being torn down and more stupidity about the Constitution. I was in no danger of losing, but my friends all wanted me to answer, so I gave them what they wanted.

One night I pictured my opponent as a "country club communist." I said that a country club communist was one that sits on the front porch of the country club, speaks loftily of the common people, gets all the advantages of monopoly and communism, and gives people none. Mr. John Dos Passos, his first cousin, was a bona fide, Red Russian Communist, I said, intent on overthrowing capitalism; but there was a difference between the two: Dos Passos had brains.

Then, I accused my opponent of being a political Little Lord Fauntleroy, and, while speaking, I mixed Fauntleroy with Little Boy Blue, and pictured him as one dressed in blue silk, ribbon on knee and frills around his lordly collar. I said he would be a society congressman, flying up to Wilmington in his big airplane to be entertained by the Du Ponts.

That night my opponent's camp was in consternation. They decided that he should enter the lists as a demagogue. He did. He got personal in what he thought would be a devastating attack on my ownership of property. He accused me of having paid for my house, while he was so poor that he had not been able to pay for his. He went on to accuse me of living in a brick house.

Thus, the issue of the campaign came to be whether Maverick lived in a brick house or not. Some of my supporters were worried. They thought I was in a bad hole—convicted of being rich, for to live in a house of brick, or at least a decent one, is admittedly something of a sin. But I told them General Sam Houston never revealed his plans of battle until the last moment and that night I would make a spectacular speech, destroying my opponent.

Since I have been a Congressman, I have seen many meetings reported. So I shall tell you the story just as it happened, as a respectable court reporter would tell it. Here goes:

Scene: San Pedro Springs.

Platform properly decorated. Flags. Crowd. Children playing under trees. A microphone.

MR. MAVERICK: Friends and fellow Americans. . . . My friends, I have had a serious and grave charge made against me. I am accused of being a communist. That is not all. My opponent says I live in a brick house. (Pause.) So what? (Pause by the people, slight laughter.) Who in this crowd would refuse to live in a brick house? (Stony silence.) He who would not live in a brick house, send his children to school, educate them and have a high standard of living, let him stand up. (Pause by Maverick. No one rises.) Do you agree that I can live in a brick house? All those that agree say "aye." (Chorus of loud ayes.)

All right, my fellow citizens, I shall tell you a great secret. It is one of the secrets that statesmen must tell their people. The issue is, does Maverick live in a brick house? That is the issue red-blooded Americans want to know. Now I shall let you in on a secret. (Long pause.)

I do not even live in a brick house! My house is of plaster—and plaster is of dirt, or earth, and from earth we come and to earth we go! (Incredulous laughter, shouts of Aw! aw!)

Now, my fellow Americans, let us go into this matter. My statisticians and my great staff of brain-trusters have made a thorough study. My opponent lives three blocks from my house, much nearer the country club of which he is the revered vice-president, and in which great humanitarian institution I hope he will be appointed president, where he can get his promotion, so that I may return to Congress. (Mock interest shown by the audience.) But my statisticians have told me, fellow citizens, that my opponent has passed my house 7,862 times in the ten years he has lived near me. Every day as he passes my house (Aside: for indeed it is a house where a sinner lives, since he aspires for office and he lives in a brick house) (laughter) he looks out. He looks at the plaster. He cranes his neck, like this. (Maverick indicates method.) And when he looks at the plaster, he sees brick, red brick, I presume.

Now, my fellow citizens, I say to you that a man who has no better eyes than that, or that isn't smart enough to tell plaster from brick, hasn't got sense enough to go to Congress. He might do the same in Congress—(Applause in extenso, or possibly cum laude). Now he says he didn't pay for his poor humble peasant cottage. But, my fellow citizens, he paid for that airplane of his (boos for my opponent); he has his ranch paid for; his stocks and bonds (groans) (groans in extenso).

Yes, my fellow citizens, I am criticized because I have a house which I have paid for. Of course I have paid for it. It is the proper thing to do. Every American should have a house and he should pay for it if he can. I also pay my butcher, my baker, and if I had a candlestick maker I would pay him also. But I do pay my electric light bill in lieu of my candlestick maker's bill, and the light costs twice as much as it should, and yet, like you, I pay for my electricity. That is the reason that I stand well in this community. I pay my bills. Let any of my countrymen among you raise his hand who can say I owe any man a dime. (Marked attention by the audience.) (Extended applause.)

Now, my gentle reader, you may say with good reason, and impeccable logic, that all this is undignified, and quite demagogic. For the sake of modern politics, I am going to argue this out.

As to dignity, I wonder if the rumble-mouth politicians of the past, wooly-hatted and frock-coated, perspiring and redundant, were really any more dignified than those of today. In Congress, now, not 1 per cent of its members dress as the politicians of old. Most of them are neat-looking fellows and cannot be distinguished from any other citizen walking down the street. Many still have the mental hangover of old-time politics, but these are on the way out; for politics is now a cold, fast game to the man who is in it.

Members of the old "dignified" school used to make the same speech over and over again; a copy was given the newspapers; it was printed in one paper, and possibly copied by others days and weeks later. But now the press is more alert, and the press associations have a nationwide coverage. You can make a speech or issue a statement at three in the afternoon; it will be in all the night editions within two or three hours. The very next morning's mail seems to indicate that people sat up during the night writing letters, and went to the post office to catch the last train, to be the first to call you a Fascist, Communist, demagogue, or statesman, as it touches their prejudices.

Moreover, the modern politician must work. He is tied to his political lathe, being messenger boy and statesman, letter writer and business representative, and a jack-of-all-trades. It takes all of his time, energy and intelligence to keep his head above water.

All of our present-day politicians have a better sense of humor; at least they express it more openly. I can remember the windjamming politicians of old, roaring to the clouds about absolutely nothing. As to the direct charge that the kind of speech I made is undignified or silly, my only answer is that there is no excuse in boring the public with long and unnecessary denials simply because your opponent is a bore and makes statements which are not true. It is better to jump on him, and let him do the running.

As for being demagogic—and I am still talking about my Little-Lord-Fauntleroy-does-Maverick-live-in-a-brick-house speech—my attitude might be so interpreted, but it is not laborious, nor is it the tedious answer of the professors. The politician of today cannot afford to be a bore, and, by the same token, he cannot afford to affect the incomprehensible, jargon of the professor. Modern politics demands the man who can think on his feet like a prizefighter, and who can give and take hard punches. The old-timer is as definitely out as the old Shakespearean actor; for the audience is no longer half slave and half Rube, and they will accept neither the old-time actor nor the new-time professor.

Modern American politics, however, have a background thrilling and brave. We have probably read too much of the Lincoln–Douglas debates and of the sayings of some of our politicians. But we do not know enough of the real struggles of our own people, so that we may translate all this into a way of living today. Everybody knows that Patrick Henry said "Give me Liberty or give me Death," but few know he went up and down the State of Virginia, saying "He is the greatest patriot who stops the most gullies."

It is better that we go into the gullies and ground, and see what we have there.

47

MARRIAGE AND POLITICS

Finley Peter Dunne

Finley Peter Dunne (1867–1936), newspaperman, writer, and, on the evidence here, humorist, has merged with the personality of his principal creation, the loquacious Irish-American saloon-keeper, Mr. Martin Dooley. The dissertations of Mr. Dooley on all aspects of American public life have been collected in book form beginning in 1898 with Mr. Dooley in Peace and War.*

*

"I SEE," said Mr. Hennessy, "that wan iv thim New York joods says a man in pollytics oughtn't to be marrid."

"Oh, does he?" said Mr. Dooley. "Well, 'tis little he knows about it. A man in pollytics has got to be marrid. If he ain't marrid where'll he go f'r another kind iv throuble? An' where'll he find people to support? An unmarrid man don't get along in pollytics because he don't need th' money. Whin he's in th' middle iv a prim'ry, with maybe twinty or thirty iv th' opposite party on top iv him, thinks he to himsilf: 'What's th' good iv fightin' f'r a job? They'se no wan dependant on me f'r support,' an' he surrinders. But a marrid man says: 'What'll happen to me wife an' twelve small childher if I don't win out here today?' an' he bites his way to th' top iv th' pile an' breaks open th' ballot box f'r home and fireside. That's th' thruth iv it, Hinnissy. Ye'll find all th' big jobs held be marrid men an' all th' timpry clerkships be bachelors.

"Th' reason th' New York jood thinks marrid men oughtn't to be

From Finley Peter Dunne, Mr. Dooley's Philosophy (New York: R. H. Russell, 1900).
* *Mr. Dooley in Peace and War* (Boston: Small, Maynard & Co., 1898).

in pollytics is because he thinks pollytics is spoort. An' so it is. But it ain't amachoor spoort, Hinnissy. They don't give ye a pewter mug with ye'er name on it f'r takin' a chanst on bein' kilt. 'Tis a profissional spoort, like playin' baseball f'r a livin', or wheelin' a thruck. Ye niver see an amachoor at annything that was as good as a profissional. Th' best amachoor ball team is beat be a bad profissional team; a profissional boxer that thrains on bock beer an' Swiss cheese can lan the head off a goold medal amachoor champeen that's been atin' moldy bread an' dhrinkin' wather f'r six months; an' th' Dago that blows th' cornet on th' sthreet f'r what annywan 'll throw him can cut the figure eight around Dinnis Finn, that's been takin' lessons f'r twinty year. No, sir, pollytics ain't dhroppin' into tea, an' it ain't wurrukin' a scroll saw, or makin' a garden in a back yard. 'Tis gettin' up at six o'clock in th' mornin' an' r-rushin' off to wurruk, an' comin' home at night tired an' dusty. Double wages f'r overtime an' Sundahs.

"So a man's got to be marrid to do it well. He's got to have a wife at home to make him oncomfortable if he comes in dhrunk, he's got to have little prattlin' childher that he can't sind to th' Young Ladies' academy onless he stuffs a ballot-box properly, an' he's got to have a sthrong desire f'r to live in th' av'noo an' be seen dhrivin' downtown in an open carredge with his wife settin' beside him undher a r-red parasol. If he hasn't these things he won't succeed in pollytics—or packin' pork. Ye niver see a big man in pollytics that dhrank hard, did ye? Ye never will. An' that's because they're all marrid. Th' timptation's sthrong, but fear is sthronger.

"Th' most domestic men in th' wurruld ar-re pollyticians, an' they always marry early. An' that's th' sad part iv it, Hinnissy. A pollytician always marries above his own station. That's wan sign that he'll be a successful pollytician. Th' throuble is, th' good woman stays planted just where she was, an' he goes by like a fast thrain by a whistlin' station. D'ye mind O'Leary, him that's a retired capitalist now, him that was aldherman, an' dhrainage thrustee, an' state sinitor f'r wan term? Well, whin I first knew O'Leary he wurruked down on a railroad section tampin' th' thrack at wan-fifty a day. He was a sthrong, willin' young fellow, with a stiff right-hand punch an' a schamin' brain, an' anny wan cud see that he was intinded to go to th' fr-ront. Th' aristocracy iv th' camp was Mrs. Cassidy, th' widdy lady that kept th' boordin'-house. Aristocracy, Hinnissy, is like rale estate, a matther iv location. I'm aristocracy to th' poor O'Briens back in th' alley, th' brewery agent's aristocracy to me, his boss is aristocracy to him, an' so it goes, up to the tsar of Rooshia. He's th' pick iv th' bunch, th' high man iv all, th' pope not goin' in society. Well, Mrs. Cassidy was aristocracy to O'Leary. He niver see such a stylish woman as she was whin she turned out iv a Sundah afthernoon in her horse an' buggy. He'd think to himsilf, 'If I iver can win that I'm settled f'r life'; an' iv coorse he did.

'Twas a gran' weddin'; manny iv th' guests didn't show up at wurruk f'r weeks.

"O'Leary done well, an' she was a good wife to him. She made money an' kept him sthraight an' started him for constable. He won out, bein' a sthrong man. Thin she got him to r-run f'r aldherman, an' ye shud've seen her th' night he was inaugurated! Be hivins, Hinnissy, she looked like a fire in a pawnshop, fair covered with dimons an' goold watches an' chains. She was cut out to be an aldherman's wife, and it was worth goin' miles to watch her leadin' th' gran' march at th' Ar-rchy Road Dimmycratic Fife an' Dhrum Corps ball.

"But there she stopped. A good woman an' a kind wan, she cudden't go th' distance. She had th' house an' th' childher to care f'r an' her eddy-cation was through with. They isn't much a woman can learn afther she begins to raise a fam'ly. But with O'Leary 'twas diff'rent. I say 'twas dif-f'rent with O'Leary. Ye talk about ye'er colleges, Hinnissy, but pollytics is th' poor man's college. A la-ad without enough book larnin' to r-read a meal-ticket, if ye give him tin years iv polly-tical life, has th' air iv a statesman an' th' manner iv a jook, an' cud take anny job fr'm dalin' faro bank to r-runnin th' threasury iv th' United States. His business brings him up again' th' best men iv th' com-munity, an' their customs an' ways iv speakin' an' thinkin' an' robbin' sticks to him. Th' good woman is at home all day. Th' on'y people she sees is th' childher an' th' neighbors. While th' good man in a swallow-tail coat is addhressin' th' Commercial club on what we shud do f'r to reform pollytics, she's discussin' th' price iv groceries with th' plumber's wife an' talkin' over th' back fince to the milkman. Thin O'Leary moves up on th' boolyvard. He knows he'll get along all r-right on th' boolyvard. Th' men'll say: 'They'se a good deal of rugged common sinse in that O'Leary. He may be a robber, but they's mighty little that escapes him.' But no wan speaks to Mrs. O'Leary. No wan asts her opinion about our foreign policy. She sets day in an' day out behind th' dhrawn curtains iv her three-story brownstone risidence prayin' that somewan'll come in an' see her, an' if annywan comes she's frozen with fear. An' 'tis on'y whin she slips out to Ar-rchey r-road an' finds th' plumber's wife, an' sets in th' kitchen over a cup iv tay, that peace comes to her. By an' by they offer O'Leary th' nommynation f'r Congress. He knows he's fit for it. He's sthronger thin th' young lawyer they have now. People'll lis-ten to him in Wash'nton as they do in Chicago. He says: 'I'll take it.' An' thin he thinks iv th' wife an' they's no Wash'nton f'r him. His pollytical career is over. He wud niver have been constable if he hadn't marrid, but he might have been sinitor if he was a widower.

"Mrs. O'Leary was in to see th' Dargans th' other day. 'Ye mus' be very happy in ye'er gran' house, with Mr. O'Leary doin' so well,' says Mrs. Dargan. An' th' on'y answer th' foolish woman give was to break down an' weep on Mrs. Dargan's neck."

"Yet ye say a pollytician oughtn't to get marrid," said Mr. Hennessy.

"Up to a certain point," said Mr. Dooley, "he must be marrid. Afther that—well, I on'y say that, though pollytics is a gran' career f'r a man, 'tis a tough wan f'r his wife."

48

COMMUTING CONGRESSMEN

The New York Times

Politicians are like other men, as this piece shows, if proof were needed. But if being a Representative from New York is serious business, what about all those other members of the "Tuesday-to-Thursday Club"?

*

THE CONGRESSIONAL "Tuesday-to-Thursday Club" [has] lost a New Yorker. . . .

Representative Benjamin S. Rosenthal, a second-term Democrat, moved his wife, two children, mother-in-law and political career from the Queens district he represents to a suburban Washington home.

As a result, Mr. Rosenthal can no longer qualify for membership in the unofficial, but very real, group of House transients who commute to Capitol Hill and rarely spend more than two nights and three days a week in Washington.

Mr. Rosenthal is the first New York City Democrat to take this step, as far as anyone in the state delegation can recall. Traditionally, New York House members of both parties—together with many other congressmen from states near Washington—fly into the capital Tuesday morning, attend sessions on three days, and fly home Thursday afternoon.

COMMUTERS CRITICIZED

Although there are notable exceptions, New York City congressmen have popularly been considered the hard core of this "Tuesday-to-

From *The New York Times,* March 16, 1964. © 1949, 1959, 1964 by The New York Times Company.

Thursday club," and been accordingly criticized for lack of attention to their elective responsibilities.

It took Mr. Rosenthal, a forty-year-old lawyer, two years to decide that he couldn't do justice to either Congress or his family by commuting back and forth to Queens. His family life was disrupted even more because he worked at being a Monday-to-Friday man as often as possible.

Mr. Rosenthal engaged in considerable soul-searching before making the move. These were some of the factors that convinced him:

Congress now meets twelve months a year, instead of five or six as in the past, and there is no prospect that the working season will get any shorter.

Unlike many New York City Democrats who have accepted a House nomination as a political stepping stone, Mr. Rosenthal has decided—the voters willing—to make a career in Congress.

With a Washington home, he should be able to see his eleven-year-old daughter, Debra, and his three-year-old son, Edward, four or five nights a week, instead of one or two.

WILL STILL VISIT QUEENS

Under the new schedule, Mr. Rosenthal expects to spend Friday, Saturday and part of Sunday in Queens, at his congressional office serving constituents, at his Woodside law office and on the political speaking circuit.

He will retain his apartment in Elmhurst as a legal residence and lodging when he works in the district.

The Rosenthal move is not without precedent. Representative John V. Lindsay, Manhattan Republican, moved his family to Washington two years ago.

Members of the House from the eastern and southern states within commuting distance of the capital do not like references to the "Tuesday-to-Thursday club." They consider this a slur on the time and effort they devote to Congressional activity.

For the New York delegation, at least, the existence of a three-day week on Capitol Hill is not very difficult to document. There is a quorum call, if not a roll-call, almost every day the House is in session, and a study of absentees' names over recent months shows a clear pattern.

The week of August 4, 1963, for example, there were thirteen New York representatives absent on Monday, but only three on Tuesday, six on Wednesday and eight on Thursday. The following week there were sixteen New Yorkers absent on Monday but only four for the Wednesday roll-call.

Establishing that any given congressman is not in Washington on

Friday is difficult to do after the fact. The House almost never sits on Fridays, and, when it does, the few members present charitably omit any request for a quorum call.

Many of the members, particularly the more recent arrivals, insist there is no point in their spending more time in the capital since the leaders rarely schedule any important business for Monday and almost never for Friday.

The leaders maintain that they have been forced to conform to this pattern by the refusal of representatives to show up on Mondays and Fridays.

The question whether a House member should live in his district or in Washington is not a simple, one-sided matter. A number of representatives would take issue with Mr. Rosenthal's decision, arguing that a congressman is seriously limiting the degree to which he represents his constituents if he moves away.

Others argue that many House members are dependent on the income they earn at home and cannot afford to serve if they must live in Washington.

On the other side, one can argue that a reasonably dedicated representative can see little of his constituents under the present working schedule no matter where he lives and his salary should cushion reliance on home-earned income.

PART SEVEN

Social Science Assays the Politicians

49

THE PRECINCT WORKER

Sonya Forthal

Sonya Forthal (1899–1963) is the author of Cogwheels of Democracy: A Study of the Precinct Captain. *The work on which that book and the following selection were based was done in Chicago in the 1920's. Hers is one of the pioneering field studies, and she can actually claim to have scrutinized political action at its most fundamental level.*

*

. . .

THE PRECINCT WORKER himself varies in type according to the kind of district which he serves. One is an uncouth laborer, with unofficial headquarters in the corner tavern, and catering to a poverty-ridden community. In another instance, the worker is a retired farmer who lives in the best house in a respectable residential neighborhood, and serves a middle-class income group. In still another case, he is a university graduate and a practicing attorney, a resident of a first-class community, and guiding an educated public. The worker who operates in a neighborhood with a transient population is still another type. He may be a truckman, for example, ready with small kindnesses to help the floaters who drift through his bailiwick, whether his benevolence takes the form of handing out small gifts of money or a night's lodging in his garage.

Naturally, the more picturesque of the petty politicians are to be found in the poorer districts. Wherever the necessity for gaining a livelihood, however meager or precarious, is sharpest, there the precinct worker, with his allotment of jobs or favors, is an important overlord.

From Sonya Forthal, "The Precinct Worker," *The Annals* of the American Academy of Political and Social Science, 259 (1948).

The outstanding characteristic of the precinct captain in each of the residential areas is his vocational interest. Politics, in a vague way, constitutes his profession, a profession subsidized by an administrative task he performs in a governmental agency.

These political handy men are remarkably frank in their attitude toward the position which they hold. None of them pretends that he is in the game for other than personal ends. One—captain in an Italian neighborhood—complained bitterly that he was required to report daily on a municipal job and received only two hundred dollars a month. He was dickering for a political post which would require no attendance and pay three hundred a month. The party which would meet this figure would have his services in the next campaign. This elementary reasoning is typical of this semiprofessional group. Statistics have shown that in Chicago more than 80 per cent of the ward committeemen, elected party agents in the next rung of the political ladder, were making their livelihood from government jobs; 70 per cent of the precinct captains, also presumably serving gratis, were likewise maintained at public expense. In most cities, official appointments are made through the party machine. The jobs are dealt out by the boss, acting through the nominal official and the mayor's patronage secretary. The boss, in his turn, consults with local leaders, who present their claims on the plum basket.

The numerous studies made of precinct workers corroborate the findings of the writer in her study of these agents in Chicago. In general, the precinct workers in major proportion are native Americans of foreign-born parents, and the larger proportion of them are of Protestant faiths. They are mostly married men of long residence in the city and the precinct.

Although the precinct workers generally come from poor or middle-class economic and social circles, there is less illiteracy among them than among the voters they represent; there are among them considerably more college and professional school graduates. However, more than half of them, and the great majority of the voters, in the Chicago area have gone no further than grammar school. The officials living in the poor areas are predominantly of grammar school training; those in middle-class localities, usually high school grades; those in the good residential districts usually have been educated in colleges or in professional schools.

In most instances, local party functionaries tend to settle in localities occupied by their own racial [ethnic] groups. The precinct workers, in the main, resemble their constituents in education and in economic and social status; as an occupational class they are stamped with the common characteristics of friendliness and informality in their relations with the constituents of their bailiwicks.

HIS STOCK IN TRADE

The precinct worker, or, as he is known in Chicago, the precinct captain, holds his power not because of the swagger of his personality or because of his economic interest in government, but because he daily performs services useful to his neighbors and indispensable to his party's success.

The miscellany of duties which falls to the precinct worker includes many activities normally given over to organization secretaries in other countries, such as canvassing and spreading of propaganda. He has likewise the responsibility for a certain amount of "entertaining," as witness the neighborhood club, the picnics and clambakes, and the free beer. Moreover, he will be found tampering endlessly with the various agencies of local government, for the benefit, real or supposed, of his constituents; and his tender mercies toward the unfortunate (who are also empowered to cast votes) are demonstrated by innumerable benevolences, less expertly performed than those of the trained social worker, but sometimes urgently sought by his constituents.

KINDNESS TO THE POOR

There is constant kindness of the poor to each other, and an unfailing response to the distresses of their poorer neighbors, even when the benefactors themselves are in danger of bankruptcy. The kindness which a poor man shows his neighbor is doubtless heightened by the consciousness that he himself may be in distress next week; he therefore stands by his friend when he gets too drunk to care for himself, when he loses his wife or child, when he is evicted for nonpayment of rent, or when he is arrested for a petty offense.

In a locality where political standards are undeveloped and plastic, where the practice of self-government is new, the poor expect the same kind of favors from their political representatives, irrespective of the justice or ethics involved. The precinct captain living in the poorer locality is merely adhering to the moral code set by his neighbors; but he has greater power than they have because of his position in the political machine and his "way-about" in the government agencies of his community.

The precinct worker may be thoroughly sincere in his deeds of kindness; he may enjoy the pleasure of being spoken of as a "good fellow," he may humanely desire to alleviate distress. This impulse may, however, gradually change into the desire to put his people under obligation. On the other hand, the person who receives aid gives in return a commodity prized highly by the local party agent. He is not a beggar asking for help, but an independent human being with a marketable vote. As far as the community is concerned, the demoralizing aspect appears when kindly impulse is made a cloak for the satisfaction of personal ambitions, and when the primitive and plastic ethics of an immature locality gradually conform to the standards of the precinct philanthropist.

EXTENT OF BENEVOLENCES

The extent of the basic benevolences of the party official in a large metropolis is not too easily measurable; they are frequently given in secrecy. But the fact of such beneficence is well corroborated by the many writers on the subject, and by the classic success of Tammany Hall in New York, the Thompson and Kelly-Nash machines in Chicago, and the Vare machine in Philadelphia. The Chicago studies show roughly that three-fifths of the precinct workers acknowledge the granting of such services, that there was a decrease in benevolences during the depression or lean years, and that the extent of these services is contingent on the power of the ward committeeman.

It is the precinct worker who calls upon the ward committeeman, the alderman, or even the county agent, whenever he alone is unable to furnish the necessary service. Whenever a constituent applies directly to any of the higher officials he is referred to his local party agent, or else information about him is procured from the precinct worker, and the recommendation he makes is followed. This is the standard etiquette. There are times when the precinct captain individually raises funds to meet the needs of his district, and other times when he is too poor or too insignificant to have personal power.

FAMILY SERVICES

The precinct worker provides food, clothing, coal, and rent or lodging to his needy constituent. He manifests an interest in children by helping widowed mothers secure pensions, by arranging for the adoption of children, by procuring birth certificates or work certificates, or, if the situation demands it, by preventing the under-age child from securing an employment permit; also by obtaining the transfer of a child from one school to another.

The precinct worker also steps in as family adjuster, especially when the ways of the foreign-born parent clash with those of his American-born child. Some precinct workers adjust misdemeanors and thefts which sometimes start as children's fun. The kindness showered upon the child frequently serves to gain the captain the confidence of the adults in the family and eventually their votes. He also functions as an adjuster in difficulties between husband and wife. In one instance the captain was asked to prevent an Italian from beating his wife; in another, he helped a mother of ten children secure a divorce from a drunkard; and in still another, he secured the release of a workingman, father of two children, from Bridewell, a penal institution, where he had been sent because, crazed by liquor, he had attempted to slash his wife's throat.

To be family conciliator requires much tact. If the party agent favors one member of the family in preference to another, he is likely to create enmity which is registered unfavorably against him on election day.

In illness and bereavement, warm sympathy and good fellowship place individuals and families under a long indebtedness to their local political agent. "To visit the poor, sick, and bury the dead" is an established political axiom. Many precinct workers secure some form of aid for those needing medical care. Most frequently this help is provided with the assistance of public agencies. Sending flowers to the sick is a frequent occurrence and providing adequate burial with flowers, even paying funeral expenses, is not an unusual service.

As the precinct worker mourns with his neighbors, so he rejoices with them by attending weddings and sometimes christenings. On holidays, and especially at the Christmas season, the successful precinct worker sends baskets of food or greeting cards. Usually the ward organization provides the baskets distributed. Four thousand baskets were distributed one year in a ward of Chicago.

JOBS AND LEGAL AID

A precinct worker may supply his constituency with locally situated governmental jobs, jobs in semipublic concerns and with private firms. The faction or party in power inevitably determines the extent of the ward committeeman's and the precinct worker's patronage in the local levels of government, and at times in the National Government. If the precinct agent holds a political job and is in a position to employ other men, his constituents have first consideration.

Of the nongovernmental jobs which the precinct worker provides his friends, the range is wide. Frequently the ward committeeman or the alderman or the party secretary assists him in making such placements. Among the private concerns cooperating with the precinct workers are the public utility companies, taxicab companies, large mail-order houses, and friends of the party. The jobs supplied are usually clerical and unskilled.

The precinct workers at times also provide legal aid to their potential "reliables." Most of those seeking such help live in the poorer areas of the large cities. Most frequently this service consists of directing the voters needing such help to see an attorney friendly to the party.

MISCELLANEOUS SERVICES

There are also many miscellaneous services which place the precinct worker in the category of the voter's friend. He lends money or tools, he acts as a matchmaker, he cares for his neighbor's baby, he helps build a garage, he gets a dog out of the dog pound.

In some localities the party worker is also a special local community agent; he intervenes to remedy the unsatisfactory conditions in his precinct. He induces the men in the various administrative agencies of the city to collect the garbage in his neighborhood, to light dark streets and alleys, to mend torn-up pavements, to clean sewers stuffed with refuse, to provide adequate police protection at unsafe crossings.

Sometimes the party worker intervenes between his neighbors as well as between the individual and the larger community. One cautions a neighbor against throwing mattresses into an alley, one prevents the owner of a pie factory from disposing of refuse in the streets, one intervenes between querulous women who throw ashes in front of each other's doorsteps when they quarrel, one restrains an apartment builder from disobeying building laws.

THE SOCIAL WORKER

Sometimes the precinct worker utilizes the public or private social service agencies in the kindly deeds he performs. Several of the executives of the public social service agencies in Chicago said that they knew precinct officials referred cases to their workers.

From the viewpoint of organized society, the activities of the precinct worker may not be classified as positive beneficence; they are not the conscious effort to adapt individuals to society—usually the objective of the professional social worker. Yet the outgoing friendliness of the precinct mediary cannot be considered a negative quality. Surely there are times in the lives of those with limited opportunities, living in squalor and need, when a friendly smile or the respect of an equal may be more valuable than a loaf of bread. The standardized kindness of a young social worker may sometimes lack human qualities and may fail to furnish the sympathy and heartfelt understanding which is so essential. The motives or ideals of the precinct worker may be questionable, but the technique he has developed for treating the people in his locality, his geniality, kindness, and sympathy, are noteworthy.

Nor are the precinct worker's good deeds limited to satisfying immediate economic or social wants. He intercedes for the individual in the application of the law. This is especially true in the districts where newly naturalized Americans make their homes, although the same condition is found in traditionally American localities.

Is it any wonder that many foreigners in the large municipalities, unaccustomed to American institutions, look upon the politician, who shakes hands warmly and speaks English, as their friend and interpreter of American life? It is not surprising that when he gets into trouble with the government, the newcomer seeks the help and advice of the man who is ready to give this help. It would be surprising if the meagerly educated American did not lean on his political representative when he is in need or in trouble. Men living near the masses of the people recognize the value of the simple and more primitive human interests and ways. They realize that the people clamor for the informal, for the warm human qualities of social interrelationship. The people misinterpret the harsher, more formal governmental and private agencies.

HUMANIZING THE LAW

Every great American city has an elaborate organization concerned with humanizing the law. This organization thrives within the government and constitutes the nonbureaucratic manipulator of governmental institutions. Favors, graft, and protection are its mainstay. Its chief resources include the manipulation of the taxing machinery, the placement of public funds with anticipation of splitting the profits, the letting of contracts, the protection and defense of . . . various . . . types of criminals. Tax fixing and adjusting, sundry payments for enactment and blocking of legislation, control of machinery, perquisites and miscellaneous adjustments—all are important cogs in this machine.

The more glaringly inefficient governmental agencies are, the more are they subject to pressure from party officials. Because of the antiquated tax machinery in the state of Illinois, the precinct workers have been in a favorable position. The personal property tax lends itself to easy "fixing." In some cases, the party agent merely gives advice on the making out of schedules; in others, he may encourage his constituents to ignore the schedules or he may take the forms and hand them to an official, who conveniently disposes of them. The assessor, the board of tax appeals, the county judge, the county treasurer, and the state's attorney all have some responsibility in connection with the assessment and payment of taxes; it is very easy for a slip to be made somewhere along the line beneficial to some precinct worker's adherent.

Political intervention of workers is further found to affect city government and finance in a variety of ways. The trail of the party worker leads to many city agencies, such as building, health, police, fire, weights and measures, and such activities as the enforcement of ordinances or franchises and the issuance or withdrawal of licenses and permits. The permits secured include peddler's, milk, garage, basket,* building, and so on.

* Probably a reference to a permit for selling goods out of a basket on the street.

"FIXING" THE LAW AGENCIES

The judicial system, especially the machinery of criminal justice, is also subject to "fixing" by political agents. The direct responsibility for the enforcement of the criminal law generally is divided between the police and the office of prosecuting attorney. Though the prosecuting attorney is responsible for trying criminals, he is largely dependent upon the police for the detection of crime and the arrest of offenders, and for securing the evidence upon which successful prosecution rests. In the larger cities, and especially in Chicago, the municipal court has jurisdiction in criminal matters. In all cases of felony it is limited to binding over for the grand jury. The prosecuting attorney has absolute power to nol-pros; furthermore, he can ignore the municipal court by procuring indictments directly before the grand jury. In the higher state courts, archaic methods of procedure obtain, with the result that conviction is secured in only a small fraction of the cases.

Responsibility for the enforcement of the criminal law is diffused instead of concentrated. The practice of choosing judges by election tends also to throw the court into politics and obligation to the party. Like most elective offices, the judgeships, the clerkships, and the office of sheriff are accompanied by many additional jobs which are distributed among party henchmen, with avenues open for fixing.

One of the most difficult problems connected with prosecution has to do with bail, a matter particularly subject to fixing. Many of the precinct workers furnish bail. The charges for which bail is given vary from drunkenness to grand larceny, including murder, gambling, and carrying concealed weapons. Three to four calls a day from the police station are not unusual for many of the local "fixers" in some of the poorer areas. A few keep cash on hand for such emergencies.

The "fix" sometimes starts with the police officers, the janitors of the court, the clerks, or bailiffs. The trail may lead through the ward committeeman to the judge, in all cases depending upon the influence of the fixer and the power of his party. For minor offenses, in the local police station, some precinct workers find the promise of a few dollars to an official, or the assurance of a job to an ordinary cop, sufficient to do the trick. When more serious offenses are involved, the judge is reached through the bailiff, or by a party representative higher in the hierarchy who has power to threaten the defeat of the judge in the next election if the fix does not go through.

Traffic fixes are requested by the best citizens, sometimes. The offenses are usually parking or speeding. Party workers are delighted to oblige.

Precinct workers also acknowledge fixing of jury personnel by securing the release of persons summoned to serve. Jury fixing is also a part of the activity of the precinct worker, but for obvious reasons this feat is usually accomplished through intermediaries and is rarely acknowledged by the party agent. The fixing of election cases, with henchmen of the precinct captains indicted for vote frauds, is also found to exist.

HELPING IN NATURALIZATION

The party worker also intervenes for his constituency in the federal agencies of the government, especially in the naturalization bureau. The federal law regarding naturalization presents many confusing details to a foreigner, and the precinct broker is very ready to help him out of the confusion. He fills out naturalization blanks, acts as witness, teaches the language, and coaches on the questionnaire. He not infrequently speaks to the naturalization examiner in behalf of the declarant, pays his fees, and provides every conceivable suggestion. A precinct worker who had assisted sixty-two aliens within fifteen years declared that he felt it was this service particularly that impressed the voters in his locality.

EFFECT ON LOCAL GOVERNMENT

The basic question concerns the effect of the captain's activities on the processes of local government. There may very well be cases in which it is essential that the precinct worker interpret the laws to the less educated and fortunate citizens or that he intercede when his client is placed at a disadvantage by some government agent, and even that he interfere in the functions of government in his constituents' interest. When such interference breeds corruption, inefficiency, and a weakened morale among the executives of the local government, it cannot be considered an unmitigated blessing.

PARTY ORGANIZATION

It is generally conceded that a political party is an association of individuals and groups who band together for the purpose of obtaining and retaining control of the political institutions of the community, the state, or the nation. With the precinct worker, participation in politics is mainly a vocation dependent on the success of his party machine.* Conversely, the success of his party depends on his activities and services. He is the party to the voter in his precinct. Good organization is essential to party success, and one of the cardinal principles of party structure is

* Seventy per cent of the precinct captains in Chicago were holding government jobs [1948].

that a definite organization be maintained within each electoral area. It has been estimated that about 1,125,000 party workers would be necessary if both of the major parties in the United States were to be completely organized. In Chicago there are approximately between 5,000 and 7,000 workers, depending on the amount of party factionalism and party patronage.

Both the major political parties function through a hierarchy of committees responsible for progressively smaller units; national, state central or executive, congressional, senatorial, county, city, and township or town. In the larger cities, the city committee functions through ward and precinct committees, the latter often consisting of one person, the precinct captain or . . . the precinct worker. Party leaders, bosses, and workers who may not belong to any committees also figure largely in politics.

All committees are charged with the management of party affairs in their geographical areas. Their power is often more formal than real, for the word of command most frequently comes from some individual on the outside who has come to be recognized as the party leader; nor are these committees dependent upon one another, except insofar as they have the common interest of winning elections for their party and insofar as they share campaign funds and patronage.

The local committees are influenced only indirectly by the national organization. The precinct worker is immediately concerned only with city, ward, and precinct committees. He is daily on the job in every election, however—congressional, senatorial, city, and ward—but is accountable only to the ward committeeman, who in turn is responsible to the city or county boss.

THE PRECINCT

Almost universally throughout our nation, the precinct is the unit cell of party organization. In 1940, the United States was politically divided into 127,245 precincts. On the basis of the presidential vote, there was one precinct for each 392 voters. New York City has approximately 5,000 precincts, Chicago about 3,000, Philadelphia 1,283, New Orleans 262, and Austin, Texas 21.

The size and number of precincts vary greatly throughout the nation, and also within any given city. In Chicago, the number of voters in a precinct varies from over 600, to 400 or less. The law of Illinois requires that a precinct be subdivided in case it has more than 600 voters, but the great mobility of Chicago's population has made equitable enforcement of this law virtually impossible. Although state laws, as a rule, provide for the size of precincts—which vary from a maximum of 250 voters each in Washington state to 2000 voters in the metropolitan districts of Massachusetts—the exact boundaries of these precincts are usually set by city ordinance, and, in some instances, the city council reapportions the precincts after each election.

In charge of the political organization in the precinct is the precinct captain, most frequently male, sometimes assisted by a woman or by other workers. The precinct captains may be elected by the voters as they are in Pennsylvania cities, selected by party caucus as in some cities, or appointed by the ward leaders as in New York, Chicago, New Orleans, and other cities.

WARD COMMITTEEMAN AND PRECINCT CAPTAIN

In Chicago, the ward committeeman is nominated by petition of at least ten voters belonging to his faction, and usually by as many more as he can secure. A plurality of votes in the next primary elects him for a term of four years.

The legal duties of the ward committeeman are varied. He is a delegate to the county convention which nominates candidates for the circuit and superior court benches, and which selects the delegates to the district convention where a candidate for the state supreme court bench is chosen. He picks representatives from his ward to attend the state convention which nominates candidates for presidential electors and trustees of the state university, adopts the state platform, and chooses members and alternates-at-large to the national convention and fills vacancies.

The ward committeemen in Chicago correspond to the precinct committeemen in the unit voting areas outside the city; their legal duties are the same. They both differ from the precinct captain, whose post is appointive. He serves on the city committee of his faction or party. He is, however, chosen by the ward committeeman and is accountable to him. His selection is contingent on the number of votes he controls in the party primary, especially.

The relation of the ward committeeman to the precinct captain is determined individually, within the tactical policies of the party. In the well-disciplined political machine, the ward committeeman is boss of the area, and the precinct captain does his bidding. Nor does he adhere implicitly and with unswerving loyalty to the ward committeeman, any more than the committeeman retains him if he does not produce the votes of his precinct. He is as much interested in jobs and favors as is the man at the top of the ladder.

Frequently, too, the man at the top started his career as a precinct official, and the tricks he learned serve him in good stead when he reaches the top. Anton Cermak, who was mayor of Chicago and target for the bullet aimed at the late Franklin Delano Roosevelt, climbed the ladder from precinct captain to state representative, alderman, bailiff of the municipal court, president of the county board, and mayor.

SOCIAL ACTIVITIES

The most significant fact about the precinct worker is that he is indispensable to the party machine, no matter what economic or political change fortune brings to the municipality. Besides the daily benevolences he showers on his constituents, and the amount of "fixing" he does, he performs political and social activities which benefit his party. Frequently, he engages in the spectacular mass meetings and personally conveys his constituents to them. More frequently, he organizes a club to cultivate sociability in his locale.

The ward club plays a more important role than the precinct club, partly because of the election of aldermen and ward committeemen. Even so, it is usually only temporary, lasting merely during the campaign. Public job holders, whose destinies are intimately related to those of the ward leader, are the nuclei of the ward club and finance it. In one ward, a captain earning $6,000 a year as assistant state's attorney was asked to contribute $15 a month to his ward organization. Others make contributions according to their earnings and their agreements with the ward committeemen.

The precinct club is similarly financed by the local party agent; it is found less frequently. The club adds continuity and sociability to party organization, but more than that, it serves as a vote-holding unit. Its duration is shortlived—only during campaigns. The meeting place is sometimes at the captain's home, at the ward headquarters, at a neighborhood confectionery, in a poolroom, or in a tavern.

It is in the poorer areas that these clubs are found most frequently. Gang feeling, and loyalty to a particular person, help to sustain them. Sometimes, the introduction of an athletic program binds the members closer. Often, too, misdemeanors committed by boys bring them into these clubs. The stanchest workers in one club were a group of boys who had been arrested one night for rough-housing. The precinct worker, aided by the alderman, secured their release. Out of gratitude they joined the club.

Social contacts are an extremely valuable adjunct to vote-getting. The precinct worker joins many clubs in his locality. Where there are no local clubs, he opens his home to entertain his neighbors. The social functions include smokers and stags for men; more frequently, card parties, and, in the middle-class and poorer localities, Bunco (especially for women), and mixed socials, including dances, picnics, and ice cream parties.

CANVASSING

The canvass is the most effective and extensive method used to solicit votes. The precinct functionary uses this "face to face" opportunity to influence and persuade the accessible voter to select the precinct worker's preference. The opportunities for such contacts are greater in the states which do not have permanent central registration of voters; but even in the thirty-two states which have such registration on a state-wide basis and the twelve which have it only for certain areas, the canvass is used extensively preceding and following the primary.* This procedure is used to ascertain the preferences of the voter and to persuade him to vote the ticket. An early canvass gives the trained party worker an index to the voters' preferences. Even though he may not convert skeptics, he gains information about the weak spots in his precinct.

The successful canvasser chats easily, takes a warm interest in the family, and, above all, makes himself a ready friend. The technique of the canvass is determined largely by the locality in which it is used. In the better middle-class and the first-class residential areas, the canvasser rarely gets beyond the front door; the only way he reaches the voter is through a social club or on the golf course. Sometimes the party worker engages quarters in a large apartment hotel, learns to know his neighbor, and then approaches him for his support; sometimes he picks his lieutenants from among the residents of these hotels and thus gains votes.

In the poorer districts, the canvasser uses sundry subterfuges; he buys inexpensive gifts for the children or he distributes calendars or otherwise ingratiates himself with the householder. He runs errands for him, pays a tax bill, gets a fishing permit, provides him with tickets for a prize fight or an amusement park, fixes a burned-out fuse, makes out his tax schedule, and so on.

When proffered generosities fail, the canvasser tries to engage the franchise-holder to work for him on election day, as a cover-over for outright buying of his vote, which in most states is illegal. If all his blandishments fail, he takes his defeat philosophically and makes a genial exit.

In lodginghouse areas, the strategy of the canvasser is again different. Votes are bargained for in blocks through the owners of the "hobo" hotels. Sometimes the precinct worker owns a lodginghouse, and, by allowing free lodging or special concessions in rent, he gains votes without canvassing; sometimes the clerks in the rooming houses are hired as canvassers.

The more ambitious local mediary, especially in the poor and middle-class areas, does his own canvassing twelve months a year; he thus keeps

* These are the current statistics. Source: Report of the President's Commission on Registration and Voting Participation, Appendix II, November 1963.

tab on the people as they move into and out of the precinct. The most effective appeal used during the canvass in the poorer areas is the "bread-and-butter" argument. The canvasser states that he is holding a governmental job which depends on the number of votes he can muster on primary or election day. In such localities, the vote is too frequently regarded less important than a friend's job.

A FAULTY SYSTEM

The precinct worker's influence in the party is contingent on the votes he controls. With these in hand, he is in a position to bargain for the job he personally desires or for the other emoluments he expects. It therefore goes without saying that the qualifications expected are related not so much to fitness for a particular job in a governmental agency which he may seek to fill, as to his power to control votes.

Within a spoils-conducted municipal, county, or state administration, inevitably, the results of selection on this basis must be largely unsatisfactory. Administrative officials work, not under the direction of their nominal superiors, but under the political sponsors who bring about their appointments. Such administrative office is subject to a division of authority which makes for inefficiency and demoralization. It is almost impossible for a department head to suspend a party worker, however valid may be his reasons, if the machine is behind the worker.

This substitution of party service for public service produces disastrous results in the administration of government, especially on the city level. Not only does it degrade the standards of government agencies, but its effect on the individual party worker is to burden him with a sense of insecurity. He can have no reasonable assurance of reward for laudable public service, and, on the other hand, he never knows at what moment factional or party defeat will cost him his job. It is small wonder that, under such a system, slackness, graft, and inefficiency flourish.

It should be apparent, then, that the methods of the party worker are not to be condemned in themselves. The captain of the precinct, under existing circumstances, is indispensable. He is a hard worker, and, even if his time and energy must frequently be expended upon activities not ethically above reproach, the fact remains that he fulfills a necessary function and hence deserves reward. The question is, What form should that reward take?

Disregarding for the moment the precinct worker's motives, we must grant him his place in the scheme of present-day democracy. The very drudgery involved in canvassing, entertaining, and convincing an indifferent public that it ought to vote entitles him to some recognition. His other activities, notably his tampering with government functions and playing the role of sister of charity, are open to question. If, however, these performances were removed from his repertoire, he would still remain a valuable factor, because of his close personal relations with his neighbors. He would still be the go-between, the interpreter of public affairs to the local citizenry, and, as such, an important party adjunct.

Obviously, then, the machine which engages the precinct worker should rightfully take the responsibility for rewarding him. The present situation, with the whole taxpaying public, regardless of party affiliations, contributing indirectly to his support, is wasteful and illogical.

ELECTION TECHNIQUE

For the precinct worker, the election is the showdown; his very livelihood depends upon it. After the convention, and throughout the campaign, his activities gather momentum, reaching out in every direction.

First, he makes certain that his henchmen constitute the election machinery in the voting area by having them appointed as judges or clerks of election, with the fee paid for the job. In Chicago, the precinct captain chooses the men and women he desires as election officials, then submits the list to the ward committeeman, who in turn conveys these lists to the bipartisan Board of Election Commissioners, which, after a perfunctory examination of these officials, appoints them. In the more congested or river areas, the election officials are not too infrequently pickpockets, card sharks, confidence-game men, or criminals, skilled in the art of manipulating, effacing, or miscounting ballots. Frequently, the election officials are directly related to the worker by blood or marriage, or they have many potential voters who can be depended upon to vote as he wishes.

The precinct worker also selects the polling place. In short, he manipulates the election machinery. The permanent central registration system and the voting machines, when and where used, have in recent years lessened his control but not abolished it.

The precinct worker then, smells out votes as a terrier hunts rats, his methods becoming more desperate as the day approaches when he must prove to the party that he has been working. He draws upon additional aides in his campaign, i.e., canvassers, party challengers, and, in malodorous precincts, impersonators, ballot-treaters, "floaters," or "repeaters." *
In an Illinois primary, $70,000 was spent in Cook County alone for watchers. In another primary, the precinct captains were allowed from $25 to $80 apiece. Assuming that they each receive only $25, Chicago's cost on that one item was about $75,000.

This, of course, does not include the expense of the city for the

---

* Ballot-treaters are those who mar a ballot in order to ruin it; "floaters" go from precinct to precinct voting illegally under others' names. One Chicagoan maintained that he has not succeeded in voting in five years; the impersonator always got to the polls first.

thirty- and sixty-day jobs in the administrative offices, or the money spent on publicity, radio broadcasting, courtesies such as cigars and drinks, maintaining headquarters, hiring strong-arm men to intimidate, or hiring extra workers, with or without legitimate functions, specifically to get their votes. It is evident that one-fourth to one-third of the campaign expenses are used for this purpose alone. The price for the vote ranges from three to five dollars or sometimes as little as twenty-five cents. This form of bribery, for some reason, appears more palatable, both to the giver and to the taker [than the outright buying of votes, which may be purchased for $3.00 to $5.00 and sometimes for as little as $.25]. Its odor is fully as unpleasant, however, and the net results equally demoralizing. Inevitably, it leads to the creation of a venal class of voters, and the principle of democratic government is hopelessly lost in the shuffle.

THE ALTERNATIVE

The point has been reached where a political group must either limit the effectiveness of its campaign by restricting its budget to the free-will offerings of the rank and file (which are practically nil) or else compromise with the business interests, assess office holders and the individual candidates, steal from the public funds, or even accept gratuities from the criminal element, considerably reduced in the past few years. The keeper of the disorderly house or the gambling house still depends on his stand-in with the dominant party to remain in business. Protection is still guaranteed and penalties fixed—at a price, and all the way along the political ladder; for, in the transfer of such moneys, the entrepreneur is quite as likely to be the precinct captain as the city boss.

The secrecy attending these transactions, and the many soiled hands through which they pass, make any estimate necessarily a matter of guesswork. They are nevertheless still the bulwark against party disintegration and defeat, shoddy and reprehensible though they may be. For, although there are a certain number of respectable citizens who, impelled by traditional loyalty or by principle, will contribute to their party when asked, the party has no assurance that it may rely on such support. Neither of the two parties has a dues-sustaining membership; the funds derived from "reputable" sources are so paltry as to be almost negligible. Legislation, to date, has been of a negative type and has failed to provide an effective method for meeting the party finance problem.

TO CORRECT THE SYSTEM

It must be remembered that the local party is merely a section of the general election machinery. The sins of the petty politician are not his own sins; they are the reflection, *in parvo,* of the defects of the larger whole. Considering the vast number of administrative jobs to be filled in a large city, one realizes that the precinct worker is a very busy man, especially with the inadequacies of selection on merit and the workings of the civil service. Moreover, it is the decentralized, bipartisan handling of the election that gives him his control over election officials and his opportunity to defraud. A reorganization of the system itself would appear far more logical than the perpetual criticism of this or that official or of this or that party.

The many small voting precincts in a city like Chicago overburden the machine with innumerable agents. Would it not be possible to enlarge the voting areas, so that the number of officials could be reduced? Fewer party agents would mean a curtailment of party expenses. For the payment of this smaller number of salaries, the money might come directly from the party's coffers, rather than indirectly from the public pocket.

Efficient election officials, apportioned to the polling places according to the number of voters in the area, ought to be able to handle the mechanics of the election without a great deal of trouble. To make the process of voting less tedious and the vote more safe, it is necessary to guard the system of permanent central registration against impersonators at the precinct level and to insist on persistent and intelligent prosecution of election frauds.

Notification of all potential voters about the details of the election, and cancellation of registration as a penalty for not voting, might be suggested as means of awakening the proverbially indifferent citizen to his electoral duties. Such measures would be valuable, too, in limiting the activities of the precinct worker.

SUMMARY

The precinct captain, as we see him today, is not an intrinsically corrupt and blameworthy individual, but the lowliest member of the party system. It has been shown that he is indispensable to the party, at least in an urban community where numbers are power. He adapts the form of our institutions to the human equation and conducts himself according to the mores of the group he serves.

His work as community agent will continue just as long as his community requires it, no matter how perfunctory and self-seeking the work may be. By the same token, it will be restricted wherever the merit system of personnel selection is rigidly applied to the administrative offices of the city. It will be restricted wherever his power to exchange favors is curtailed. Particularly will his activities be limited where the use of money is regulated in the conduct of elections, and where adequate funds are provided, by the party itself, for campaign management. His future, in any highly industrialized center, is dependent wholly on the type of electors to be found there.

50

THE JOB OF THE POLITICAL
EXECUTIVE

Marver H. Bernstein

Marver H. Bernstein (b. 1919) is Dean of the Woodrow Wilson School of Public and International Affairs, Princeton University, and an authority on public administration. The Job of the Federal Executive *grew out of discussions at The Brookings Institution, the so-called "Round Table" of the Federal Executive." Though relatively few in number, political executives, usually presidential appointees, play important roles in the federal bureaucracy. As much as precinct workers and party bosses, they are politicians.*

*

THE TERM "political executive," which has become important in the vocabulary of official Washington during the 1950's, was defined by the Round Table on the federal executive as any appointee, outside the civil service, who has policy-making duties.[1] The Round Table was concerned primarily with presidential appointees at the level of under secretary and assistant secretary; it confined itself mainly to executives in Washington

---

From *The Job of the Federal Executive* (Washington: The Brookings Institution, 1958).

[1] The second Hoover Commission preferred to use the term "non-career" rather than "political" in classifying political appointments outside the civil service. It apparently feared that "political" had an invidious connotation and should be avoided. It stated: "It is generally understood that the nation requires non-career executives who serve at the pleasure of the president and his immediate department and agency heads and who represent the political party in power and the measures to which it is committed." U.S. Commission on Organization of the Executive Branch of the Government, *Personnel and Civil Service*, A Report to the Congress (1955), p. 25.

and dealt only peripherally with executives in field offices. However, the category of federal political executives also includes heads of agencies, bureau chiefs appointed outside the civil service, and certain subordinate political appointees.

There are about 1,100 political executive positions in the federal government. About 100 of these positions have been created since 1954 when the Task Force on Personnel and Civil Service of the second Hoover Commission estimated the number as follows:

Heads of agencies and their deputies		230
Assistant agency heads		125
General managers of boards and commissions		10
Noncivil service bureau chiefs		250[2]
Subordinate executives		390
Heads of substantive staff offices	40	
Heads of departmental information offices	50	
Political aides and assistants	300	
	TOTAL	1,005

[2] The Task Force found that 190 of 266 bureau chiefs in 45 major agencies were exempt from civil service. If the same proportion of the bureau chiefs in all agencies (350) are appointed outside the civil service, their number would be 250.

WHAT POLITICAL EXECUTIVES DO

The second Hoover Commission tended to view the job of the political executive as a composite of tasks. The major ones include taking command of departments and agencies, developing policies and programs, defending these before Congress, the public, and presidential staff arms such as the Bureau of the Budget, making political speeches, and participating in political activities to promote his party's position. The Commission's Task Force on Personnel emphasized the functions of the political executive in providing political leadership:

In the National Government, it is the function of political executives to represent within the administration the policy purposes of the president, to bring the general public's point of view to bear upon administrative decisions, to provide leadership in developing national policy, to exercise statutory powers vested in them as public officials, and to act for the chief executive in seeing that all of the laws are faithfully executed; in short, to take the responsibility for governing.[3]

In November 1946, Donald C. Stone contributed to the Princeton University Bicentennial Conference on University Education and the Public Service an analysis of the setting in which the federal administrator works. Stone included in his category of "top managers" the heads of de-

[3] *Task Force Report on Personnel and Civil Service*, p. 1.

partments and agencies, their principal operating and staff assistants, and similar officials in the bureaus and other major subdivisions within agencies. These various executives, comprising presumably both political and nonpolitical appointees, were defined functionally in the following terms:

Their energies are devoted, broadly speaking, to defining the objectives of their agencies, planning the program, developing an organization properly staffed to carry out the program, scheduling and budgeting the program, developing the necessary interrelationships, channels of communication, work habits, and doctrine for the organization to move forward as a harmonious team, establishing devices for control and coordination, exercising oversight and guiding the operations of the establishment, and maintaining and reacting to many external relationships.[4]

It is clear from the context of Stone's description that no single executive performs all or most of these functions. Rather, the statement covers a range of tasks encompassing the entire sequence of command and direction within an organization. With this qualification in mind, the Round Table considered the validity of Stone's job description. A career executive commented:

My impression is that his definition indicates what somebody thought a political executive ought to do rather than what he usually does. For example, the first item is the defining of objectives. By and large, the objectives of agencies are spelled out in law and practice, prior to the appointment of executives who have to spend a good deal of their time finding out what these objectives are. Moreover, as quickly as political executives come into office, they have to resist pressures that would make them prisoners of their agencies. They have to meet so many demands, make so many contacts, process so much paper, and attend so many meetings all at once that they have little time for such matters as defining objectives. There is an inexorable Gresham's Law of public administration: Day-to-day problems tend to drive out long-range planning. Only the most astute executive is able to organize his time to fend off outside pressures and internal office routine sufficiently to leave adequate time to deal with longer range items.

Three other executives commented as follows:

This sounds like a definition of the job of an executive during World War II or the Korean War who faced the task of creating a new program and a new staff to administer it. The typical political executive comes into an established federal agency from private life. This statement is more applicable to an executive who did not have any predecessors.

The definition seems to apply primarily to career executives in staff positions. The last of the eight functions listed in the definition—maintaining and reacting to external relationships—seems to be an afterthought, although it is the one element of the definition that presumably identifies the political

[4] Donald C. Stone, "The Top Manager and His Environment," Joseph E. McLean, ed., *The Public Service and University Education* (1949), p. 51.

executive clearly, and distinguishes him from the corporation executive. All the other elements are focussed primarily inward. This is not a description of an executive who is responsible for some government activity. It fits better the political program or staff type of person who utilizes his time to develop a program, evaluate performance, set objectives, and so forth. The line operator wouldn't begin to have the time to do all the things in this definition.

In order to make this definition applicable to the political executive, it would have to include the task of harmonizing the programs of his agency with the political point of view and the aspirations of his party. The political executive has the task of assuring that his subordinates are loyally following that program. Instead of defining the objectives of his agency, he must make certain that the agency conforms to the policy of the administration.

There was general agreement that in any agency a number of people perform these functions, but the daily job of a single executive does not encompass all of them. A political executive has broad responsibility for all eight functions, but he is apt to devote a major part of his time to external relations and to rely in varying degrees on subordinates to perform the other functions. The definition indicates the range of his responsibility, but gives a misleading picture of the way he spends his time.

Once again, generalizations are hazardous. Political appointees come from a variety of occupational and professional backgrounds. They bring to the task of political leadership differing views toward government and their roles within the government. Executives drawn from corporate management, investment firms, law offices, universities, federal civil service, metropolitan government, and public service in predominantly rural states may have little in common beyond their temporary willingness to serve their government.

It is useful to keep in mind an obvious characteristic of the work of executives, both in business and government. Management can rarely achieve its aims by command alone. Men do not spring into action when buttons are pressed and orders go down the line. Authority is not automatically enforced. The task of management, both public and private, is to provide the kind of leadership that produces spontaneous and cooperative effort rather than to impose authoritative decisions. What the executive "achieves is largely the product of his influence rather than his command. Therefore, in long range terms, the job of an executive is to create an environment conducive to concerted effort in pursuit of the organization's objectives."

In a civil service system that makes employees relatively secure, and in an unstable environment that makes political executives relatively insecure, the obstacles confronting the executive seeking to maximize his influence on his organization are formidable and frustrating. They can be overcome only by executives who understand the governmental environment and who combine a capacity for popular leadership with a capacity for management of large-scale, complex enterprises.

Examples of How They Spend Their Time

Because of differences in departmental organization and functions and variations in personality and competence among political executives, it was not possible for the Round Table to draft a meaningful standard job description for federal political executives. But comments by various participants do suggest the range of the executive's activities. Even within the level of assistant secretary in a major department, jobs vary significantly.

Assistant Secretary A heads one of five bureaus in a large cabinet department. He, as well as the other four assistant secretaries, had considerable experience in private business relevant to his governmental assignment. Mr. A, who deals principally with personnel management, was active in general management and personnel administration in business. The enormous size of the working force of the department requires the assistant secretaries to devote a substantial percentage of their time to managerial activities. Mr. A described how he spent his time:

My day depends pretty heavily on whether Congress is in session. Assuming that Congress is in session, I spend about one third of my time in direct contact with members of Congress, committee staffs, and other governmental agencies. If I add the time I spend with other persons not engaged in departmental activities, the proportion of time spent with outsiders would probably rise at least to 40 per cent and perhaps as much as 50 per cent. The rest of my time is split between direct technical management of the bureau I head, and over-all departmental problems which involve meetings and conferences with the Secretary and the other assistant secretaries.

My normal working day is roughly nine hours. The time for thinking and planning is usually the first hour of the morning, because I happen to get to the office before anyone else does. I can also do some serious reflection and thinking between 5:15 and 6:15 in the afternoon after the phones stop ringing constantly, but that hour is not included in the nine hours.

I don't mean to leave the impression that most of my days can be divided into these time spans. If the department has an important bill up for consideration on the Hill, I may spend almost all of my time for several weeks on legislative matters, but taking the year as a whole, that is roughly how it goes.

I try to save time by delegating broad responsibilities to my division heads. Some of these tasks involve continuing relations with industrial groups on semi-technical matters. The daily contacts with these organized groups are handled mostly by the division heads. Most of the group contacts can be delegated downward in the organization.

Assistant Secretary B supervises a cluster of bureaus and offices in a department that employs about 50,000 persons. Before becoming a political executive, he served as a senior executive in a large corporation and had developed a consulting service in his technical field. He described his work as follows:

My work day is pretty long. I get to the office about 8:30 and leave about 6:00 or 6:30, and I take work home with me almost every evening. The distribution of my time depends upon Congress. If the department is subject to legislative pressure, I have to give that business top priority. During the last investigation that concerned me, I spent about 90 per cent of my time testifying before committees or else getting ready for the next day's appearance.

It is very difficult to prevent your work from becoming a succession of telephone calls, meetings, and documents. I try to screen my contacts as much as possible. Perhaps the best time I have for thinking is when I am shaving.

About 20 per cent of my time is spent talking with the heads of the bureaus under my supervision or reading their reports. That may be less time than other executives devote to this work, but I depend as much as I can on monthly and other reports to keep me informed about our activities. I often take these reports home with me in the evening when I can look at them leisurely.

I have always felt that an executive must have face-to-face contacts, and I encourage them. I try to screen them to avoid waste of time. A great volume of correspondence comes across my desk, but a lot of it is fortunately answered before it reaches me. I scrutinize it, see how many people have cleared it, and sign it. I do not have a great deal of personal dictation, but I try to write my own speeches in order to reflect my own ideas and personality. This takes an extraordinary amount of time, but it is rewarding. I have constant calls from senators and congressmen; I try to accommodate them on the phone. If necessary, I go to chat with them directly. All in all, these congressional contacts on individual matters probably take no more than 5 per cent of my time.

At least one third of my day is devoted to interdepartmental conferences and committee meetings on defense mobilization affairs, foreign economic policy, public policy toward certain domestic industries, and so forth. These meetings usually lead to important policy decisions; consequently, preparation for them requires a lot of time. I have such a meeting practically every day.

I try to delegate to the bureaus almost all contacts with industry, labor, and other nongovernmental groups. I feel it is important for the bureaus to have those contacts. I get my industry contacts when I attend a business convention, make a speech, and chat informally away from the office. Some of the bureaus I supervise are strictly scientific in their work; they have few industrial contacts that require my attention. But other bureaus active in economic affairs must maintain their industrial contacts. We have depended on this general area rather heavily upon industry advisory committees, and they have been very helpful to us. On the whole, delegation of nongovernmental contacts to the bureaus has worked well.

Factors Influencing Executive Behavior

The distribution of a political executive's time depends in part upon his disposition to dig deeply into some matters and to stay removed from others. As a career bureau chief remarked, an assistant secretary can usually make some choices about the depth of his direct participation in particular decisions:

> I have had some political executives as bosses who did not want to get into certain fields, and left those decisions to me. And I have had some who wanted to make all decisions. The job of the bureau chief is to find out where certain types of decisions are going to be made.

Organization factors also influence the job of the assistant secretary. In a department headed by a secretary, an under secretary, and one assistant secretary, the bureau chief usually exercises more discretion in making policy decisions. In departments with an under secretary and a corps of assistant secretaries, these officials are likely to maintain closer control over bureau policy. The relationship of an assistant secretary to his bureau chief depends on how well-informed the former is about the work of the bureaus, the degree of compatibility between the two levels of direction, and the competence and experience of the assistant secretary. To some extent, an assistant secretary serves as an appellate body, to whom outsiders may go if their wants are not satisfied by the bureau chief. If the assistant secretary frequently overrules his bureau chiefs in their dealings with outside groups, those groups will be tempted to come directly to the assistant secretary who will then become more involved in administrative details and nongovernmental contacts.

The budget process also takes considerable time. Emphasis upon budgeting varies greatly from agency to agency, but most political executives are exposed to a perpetual cycle of estimates, budget bureau clearances, appropriations hearings, allotments and allocation of appropriated funds, supplemental estimates, and deficiency estimates. An assistant secretary commented: "I was on the Hill this morning testifying on my estimates. I will be back tomorrow morning also. You no sooner finish with one appropriation matter than a new one comes."

As in other matters, however, the political executive may or may not, as he chooses, become involved in the details of the budget process. An assistant bureau chief noted:

> Quite often a lawyer without previous executive experience becomes an assistant secretary. He tends to bury himself in the details of budget estimates, just as if he were preparing a case for trial. When he realizes that he is swamped with work he cannot handle, he usually seeks assistance. On the other hand, an assistant secretary with previous executive experience will probably concentrate more on establishing program objectives and broad cost determinations and then rely on the bureau chiefs for detailed estimates. As long as the bureau officers are able to support the secrtary's program decisions, the assistant secretary does not get substantially involved in the budget process; but, if something goes wrong, he will step in quickly.

The budget process raises many interesting and relevant questions. For example, does it help an agency to have its estimate presented to Congress by a political executive who belongs to the same party as the chairman of the appropriations subcommittee? Or, is it better to have the estimate presented by the individual who is thoroughly familiar with its details? One participant, who has observed the appropriations process in Congress closely for many years, replied:

Generally speaking, in my experience the fellow who has fared best in presenting budget estimates to Congress is the one who knows what he is talking about and makes an impression on the committee as a good administrator. If such a fellow is utterly frank, lays his cards on the table, and impresses the committee with his competence and knowledge, he gets along well except in those cases where there is some special political aspect. It is tragic to see the political head of a department or bureau, in testimony before a committee, forced to turn to his career staff to answer simple questions about the operations of his agency. If a political executive doesn't know much about his agency, the committee will soon find it out. It is much better for that political executive to send somebody from his office who does know the details of operation to represent the bureau or department.

Executives who are deeply involved in negotiations with Congress, interdepartmental conferences, cabinet committees, interest groups, and internal managerial problems are not likely to have much time for leisurely thinking and analysis. Instead they have to rely on other people to help them do their thinking. The staff cannot do it all, but it can supply the background and framework. Frenzied activity to meet the deadlines of a congressional committee or to frustrate the appropriation-cutting objectives of the bureau of the budget may seem to make thoughtful consideration of problems and issues by political executives almost impossible. Nevertheless, their jobs make heavy demands on them for clarity of thought, analytical judgment and apt expression. A close observer stated:

Political executives in recent administrations have not usually been as expert in their subject matter fields as their technical staffs. But the fact remains that they were able, within their own departments, in interdepartmental committees, in the White House, and before committees on the Hill to think through some difficult problems. They have been able to come out with the kind of answer that is normally required in American politics: a backing away from the original position into a modified program that somehow blends with the desires of competing interests and the wishes of Congress.

However a political executive spends his time, much of his work is designed to protect his agency and the integrity of its programs. A career executive characterized this process as "defending the empire":

The field of federal activities today is finely fragmented across a very broad spectrum. There is scarcely a political executive in town whose jurisdiction does not overlap that of some other agency and some other executive. If he is going to do the job that the president and his secretary expect of him, he will have to develop a carefully calculated and highly polished belligerency in defense of his agency. In time this becomes almost a reflex action, and at that point it may lead to a dangerous overconfidence or aggressiveness. But the fact remains that the political environment is highly competitive as well as actually or potentially unstable. Active rather than passive defense is crucial to survival.

The political executive's social life presents some special problems and hazards in Washington. Opportunities for socializing at lunches, dinners, cocktail parties, and receptions are superabundant. For some executives, social activity within and outside of office hours represents a substantial part of their lives and those of their wives. The apparent "demands" of the social season in Washington may even make a significant dent in their personal incomes. However, success on the job need not depend on after-hours activities. Much depends on the attitude and fortitude of the individual executive and his wife. Some executives perform their jobs successfully although they are rarely seen at social affairs. The military departments have had a number of executives whose success was not dependent on their extracurricular activities. As secretary of war, Henry Stimson was quite austere. As assistant secretary of war for air and under secretary of state, Robert Lovett attended few social functions. Secretary of the Navy Forrestal, as a defense department official stated, "did pretty much as he pleased." As secretary of state, George C. Marshall accepted few invitations.

Dealing with Technical Matters

One of the most difficult recurrent problems facing the political executive is the extent to which he should deal with technical matters. There is general agreement that executives ought not to become deeply involved in them, but there is no accepted way of distinguishing policy making from technical work. The depth of policy tends to vary from agency to agency. In some agencies, the major tasks of the staff are related to the framing of decisions. In a few agencies, the overriding characteristic is management of routine, nondiscretionary activities. Occasionally some matters may appear deceptively technical. The internal revenue service, for example, may have to decide whether a particular group or individual comes within the meaning of the term "church" in order to determine tax liability, or whether a particular organization qualifies as a "charitable organization," thereby making contributions to it tax-exempt. The tax laws are general and offer administrators little guidance. While these matters appear to be technical details, they are likely to have marked political implications. If so, political executives may have to review the proposals or decisions of the career staff.

The tendency of technical staffs to resist executive control seems to be common to both government and business. A former federal executive said: "I used to think that only insurance actuaries said: 'Don't ask me why. Just take my word for it.' During the past few years I have spent time with oil companies. There the geologists behave the same way. The geologist says: 'Don't ask me why. Just drill where I say because I say so.' "

The tendency to dip into technical matters depends somewhat on previous technical and executive experience. An experienced executive is likely to be more aware of the importance of "operating on his proper level," that is, dealing with major matters of program, policy, and political involvement and avoiding technical work as much as possible. Moreover, an executive with a particular technical background may have an important advantage. One executive stated: "When a man comes into government in an executive post in a field in which he has some familiarity, he can ask the technicians questions earlier. The good executive starts out asking questions and is still asking questions."

If some executives have technical backgrounds, technicians are not necessarily devoid of political skills and instincts:

> The technician's political instinct may be only to protect a vested interest in the know-how of doing something. Sometimes it may be an effort to please by anticipating the information that an executive wants to have; and sometimes it may lead to action designed to sabotage the political purposes of the political executive. I was present once when a Secretary of Agriculture asked an economist for some statistics on burley tobacco. The economist stopped at the door and asked: "What do you want to prove, Mr. Secretary?" Every executive has a risky relationship with his technical staff, some of whom really resist his decisions and some of whom are so anxious to conform to it that they distort their technical competence. The fellow who becomes an executive in a department in which he has had a lot of technical experience is very fortunate, but the average federal executive doesn't have the advantage of being as well equipped technically as his subordinates. He has to define as best he can the point at which he feels safe in asking questions, using his own judgment, or imposing a decision about which the technicians have misgivings. This is one of the greatest challenges facing an executive.

The capacity of an executive to question and control his technical staff is most severely tested in the military departments. American experience suggests that the survival risks are high when a political executive questions the military officer-technicians in the Department of Defense.

One safeguard available to the political executive is to put qualified technicians on his own staff to review the staff work of the bureau technicians. Through the competition of the two technical staffs, the executive can be relatively assured of obtaining the benefit of completed staff work before decisions are made. . . .

51

THE AMBIVALENT SOCIAL STATUS
OF THE AMERICAN POLITICIAN

William C. Mitchell

In the following article, William C. Mitchell, a sociologist, argues that the contradictory attitudes of Americans toward politics and politicians are derived from contradictory attitudes toward power. On one hand, the need for power in public affairs is acknowledged, while on the other, power is thought to be evil. James Madison, as in so many other matters, may have encapsulated this aspect of the American dilemma when he observed in The Federalist, *No. 51: "If men were angels, no government would be necessary."*

*

. . .

IN 1946, a public opinion poll was conducted by the National Opinion Research Center. A representative sample of American people were asked to rate ninety occupations according to a scale provided them. The scale contained five general categories: excellent, good, average, below average, and poor in standing. The ratings were then scored so that any occupation which received excellent on every questionnaire would be given a total score of 100 points. Among the deficiencies of the poll, from the point of view of the political scientist, is the fact that many elective offices are not included. Among the most conspicuous exceptions are those of the president, senators, the vice president, and most of the state officials, not to mention local governmental officials. Nevertheless, four groups of politi-

From "The Ambivalent Social Status of the American Politician," *Western Political Quarterly,* XII (1959), No. 3, pp. 687–698.

cians are included, and two other groups of political leaders who are not elective, but generally have had political experience and are chosen on the basis of political considerations.

The interesting fact about the ratings is that the political roles are all rated within the top thirteen positions. Undoubtedly, if other officials were included in the list, many of them might be rated rather low, but some of them, including the president, vice president and senators, would surely be placed very high, judging by the high ratings given governors, mayors of large cities, and congressmen.

Here is the list and the ranking for the first thirteen occupations in terms of prestige.

TABLE 1

THIRTEEN HIGHEST RATED OCCUPATIONS IN THE UNITED STATES

Occupation	*Score*
1. U. S. Supreme Court justice	96
2. Physician	93
3. State governor	93
4. Cabinet member in the federal government	92
5. Diplomat in the U. S. Foreign Service	92
6. Mayor of a large city	90
7. College professor	89
8. Scientist	89
9. United States representative in Congress	89
10. Banker	88
11. Government scientist	88
12. County judge	87
13. Head of a department in the state government	87

It should be noted that in addition to the shortcoming mentioned above, there is a certain ambiguity in the titles used to describe the jobs. We are not certain how respondents might conceive of number 9; they might include senators. We do not know whether respondents think of county judges as being elected or not. Perhaps the most serious shortcoming is the distortion of results, at least from our point of view, by the inclusion of several nonelective officials in the list of occupations. We do not know, but it might be that nonelective officials are more highly considered than are the politicians.

Another limitation results from the investigators' decision not to correlate the respondent's evaluations with his own social status. Fortunately, we do have some information on this matter from another poll, and it will be considered shortly. But, to return to the first poll. When occupations are classified according to groups of a common type, we find that government officials, as listed in the poll, rate higher than any other single group. The following table contains the entire classification.

It must be remembered that the group classification of government officials includes several officials who either are or may be appointive, although we have no way of knowing from the poll. One might also speculate on the results if the term of approbrium, "politician," had been included in the list of occupations of the original poll.

TABLE 2

SOCIAL STATUS ACCORDING TO OCCUPATIONAL TYPE

Classification	Number of Occupations	Average Score
Government officials	8	90.8
Professional and semiprofessional	30	80.6
Proprietors, managers, and officials (except farm)	11	74.9
Clerical, sales, and kindred workers	6	68.2
Craftsmen, foremen, and kindred workers	7	68.0
Farmers and farm managers	3	61.3
Protective service workers	3	58.0
Operatives and kindred workers	8	52.8
Farm laborers	1	50.0
Service workers (except domestic and protective)	7	46.7
Laborers (except farm)	6	45.8

A quite different picture of the status of the politician is presented when the results of a different type of poll, conducted by the same organization, the National Opinion Research Center, are studied. In this study, "The Public Looks at Politics and the Politician," [1] a national sample of 2560 respondents were asked a series of questions to elicit their attitudes toward the general area of politics as a career, honesty in politics, and satisfaction with officeholders.

The first question put to the interviewees was as follows: "If you had a son just getting out of school, would you like to see him go into politics as a life work?" The responses indicate that 18 per cent would like to see their sons go into politics, while 69 per cent would not. Some 12 per cent said they were undecided, while 1 per cent said "It depends."

When the sample of those who said "no" is broken down into various groups according to education, economic level, occupation, and 1940 voting record in the presidential election, we get some interesting results. The preceding table summarizes the returns.

According to the investigators, the "undecided" vote varies considerably according to the group. Referring to the group, e.g., classified under educational attainments, 5 per cent of the college group were "undecided,"

[1] *Public Opinion News,* Vol. XX (March 1944).

TABLE 3

"I DIDN'T RAISE MY BOY TO BE A POLITICIAN"

	Percentage Answering "No"
Total Cross-section	69
By Education	
College	81
High School	76
Less	57
By Economic Level	
Upper	78
Middle	73
Lower	54
By Occupation	
Professional, business, and white collar workers	77
Farmers	70
Factory and construction	64
Service workers	51
By 1940 Voting Record	
Willkie voters	79
Roosevelt voters	73
Nonvoters	59

10 per cent of the high school group, while 18 per cent of the remainder were "undecided."

The low status of politics and politicians is also indicated by the reasons respondents gave for their attitudes. According to the report, almost half of the people believe that politics is fundamentally dishonest. A typical reply was "If he is a good Christian man, politics will ruin him. I believe no man in politics remains honest." Other respondents objected to many "unpleasant phases" of politics such as "mudslinging," "making enemies," "lack of independence," and other "headaches." Again, a typical expression quoted from the report: "My father was a politician for twenty-five years, and all he got out of it was bad luck and no friends." Still other interviewees felt that politics was insecure and unprofitable. "For the amount of work a politician does, it doesn't pay enough." Or, "Political jobs are too unstable. A person might lose his job every time the administration changes." As might be expected, some respondents considered politics to be a useless occupation. "I believe in work, not politics," said one person. Another claimed that "there are many types of work more useful than politics."

On the other hand, an idealistic strain in American thought was revealed in the answers of those who would like to see their son go into
politics. A few of the reasons are quoted, here: "He might be able to improve conditions in our country." "I think there is no public service better
than an honest politician." Still other persons betrayed a low estimate of
politics, but felt someone ought to clean up the situation. "It's a profession
that needs some good men in it."

The second question asked by the National Opinion Research Center
dealt with the honesty of politicians as conceived by the same respondents.
The question was as follows: "It has been said that it is almost impossible
for a man to stay honest if he goes into politics. Do you agree or disagree?"
The results, in general, showed 48 per cent agreed to the proposition, and
42 per cent disagreed, while 10 per cent were undecided. When the "undecided" vote was eliminated, according to the pollsters, opinion was
divided, regardless of population groups used in the study, with 53
per cent agreeing to the assertion and the remainder objecting.

Generally, the people who thought it almost impossible to stay honest, in politics, gave similar reasons as those who preferred not to have
their sons enter politics. The largest single group of respondents (over
one-third), placed emphasis upon graft, easy money, and other temptations that public office provides men. Some believed dishonesty was situa-
tional, blaming machines and the pressure brought to bear upon the
politician. The necessity of making campaign promises that could not be
kept bothered some. A desire for power was attributed by a number of
persons to the politicians. Others said they personally knew of dishonesty.
One respondent said, "I believe every man in politics has his price." Another claimed "the money spoils them. They get chances to get graft and
they can't resist taking it. I know; my husband was an alderman once."
And, still another retorted, "A politician is bound to make pledges that
he knows he cannot keep."

Of those who believed it possible to stay honest in politics, the ex-
planations given generally suggested there was no special reason why one
could not be honest. One response was: "Any man can stay honest if
he's honest at heart. We have more dumbbells than crooks in politics."

The last question asked of the respondents was concerned with determining attitudes on whether people were satisfied with the way in which
office-holders performed their jobs. Unfortunately, the question was restricted to attitudes toward only state and local officials. We are told that
slightly over half of the people are satisfied with the way these officials do
their work. One person in six, however, has doubts about local politicians.
The question put by the Center was as follows: "Are you satisfied with the
way most people who hold political offices in this state are doing their
jobs?" As stated above, 51 per cent of the people were satisfied, while 32
per cent were not. A total of 17 per cent were undecided. Subtracting those

without opinions on the subject from the totals, we get 68 per cent answering "yes" and 32 per cent, "no." According to the investigators, differences among the population groups were not great, but the lower elements of each grouping, education, economic level, and occupation were more satisfied than the more privileged groups. No significant difference was found between Roosevelt and Willkie voters. Sectionally, the West was better satisfied than the East and the South. Citizens in small towns were also more satisfied than were residents of the large cities.

The apparent contradictions in the data of the two polls suggest either deficiencies in the data, or that Americans hold ambivalent attitudes towards politics and those who make it an occupation. Admitting much of the former, I shall nevertheless argue for the latter theory as being relevant to our problem.

A THEORY OF AMBIVALENCE

Certain propositions seem warranted on the basis of the "evidence" presented. First, it is evident that the American people have varying attitudes about the politician and that these attitudes probably are related to the socioeconomic status of the person considered. Secondly, individuals have contradictory attitudes about politicians. Thirdly, political offices are not all attributed the same prestige; a hierarchy of status is to be found. These propositions are not, in themselves, very startling, yet an explanation for them is not easily arrived at for the simple reason that adequate testing of alternative theories is at present extremely difficult. Some type of explanation, is, however, better than none.

The evaluation of political offices and action poses a dilemma for many Americans because the criteria by which status is determined (functional significance or responsibility and training or knowledge), are not always easily measured, and in cases where measurement seems possible a position may be evaluated quite differently by each criterion. The problem here grows out of the Jacksonian tradition of democracy in which persons may wield great political power and responsibility, yet quite ordinary men are felt to be capable of handling that power. No special aristocracy nor training is held necessary. Thus, the highest office in the land in terms of responsibility may be, and has been, filled by men with little formal education. Before going on to apply the above criteria to specific offices, it will be necessary to consider the general status of political action or power in American history, because it is within a context of power that the elective public official acts.

Social status is a product of evaluation, and, as such, is intimately related to the values and standards of the people doing the evaluating. In order to understand the social status of the elective public official, it is imperative to understand the value system of the society; the value system being the source of the standards of the individuals who constitute that society. Since there is seldom complete uniformity in acceptance of the values, we can expect variations in the interpretation and application of the values. Occupying different positions themselves, men will tend to view other persons occupying still other positions from different perspectives, and, therefore, will accord them differing amounts of prestige. Nevertheless, the extent of agreement in the United States is impressive.

The element of the value system most relevant to judgments of the politician is that of power. Power, itself, in America, is regarded with quite mixed or contradictory feelings, not simply between groups of the population, but with the same person. On the one hand, power-holders tend to be admired for what they can accomplish, particularly in the economic sphere of action. On the other hand, power-holders are regarded with some fear and distrust for the deprivations they may inflict. Traditionally, the fear of power has been most closely connected with attitudes toward political power. It is a commonplace theory to suggest that the framework of the American government, itself, is a product of that fear of power. If power is depreciated and admired at the same time, the holders of power will also be treated with the same contradictory attitudes. Since the politician is among the most visible power-holders, attitudes are apt to be sharp and conflicting, and he is bound to be accorded an ambivalent status.

Occupational roles are, we have maintained, evaluated according to the assumed contribution (functional importance) they make to society, i.e., in terms of the value system which predominates in the society. Political functions have been disparaged in American history with the result that politicians are often regarded as not performing vital tasks. This was reflected in the replies of many of the respondents to the National Opinion Research Center question of why they did not want to see their sons go into politics. Common answers were, "I want my son to be a doctor and serve humanity. Politicians serve themselves"; and, "He wants to be a farmer. We need farmers more than politicians." Still another such reply was, "I believe in work, not politics." The American politician consequently appears superfluous to many Americans. As a society which has not had to concern itself, to the same extent as many others, with societal goals, the activities of government are often regarded as an unessential burden.

Because the norms and values of a society are often vague and sometimes contradictory, we can expect both ambiguity and contradictions in status assignment. Furthermore, large-scale societies are seldom so completely integrated that every member will make identical evaluations. Various social groups will evaluate the same object from different perspectives. The findings of the National Opinion Research Center, as shown in Table 3, would seem to indicate the same holds for the realm of politics and social status. The less well-endowed groups all tended to assign the politician a higher status than did their better-off fellows. Politics would not appear to the poor and less educated, at least under New Deal leadership, as a useless activity nor one requiring but little knowledge. For the wealthy, the reforms of the recent New Deal period would be regarded as threats to their social status. Thus, politics being identified with New Deal, politicians might be regarded with considerably less enthusiasm. For the educated, political functions might not appear to be intellectually demanding. For the poor and uneducated, politics might appear to offer attractive opportunities. James M. Curley* wrote in his autobiography that he "chose politics because conditions were deplorable and prospects of ever getting anywhere seemed remote."

Governor Curley would hardly appear to be the only politician who entered public office for personal advancement. In a unique little study conducted by Robert Rosenzweig on the motivation of some sixteen candidates for public office in the State of Massachusetts, seven said outright that they regarded political office as a means of social and/or financial advancement. The offices sought included the governor's council, United States representative, the state Senate and House of Representatives. Rosenzweig concluded that the candidates were "characterized by strong upward mobility." He also expressed the view that:

Prestige and respect are, after all, relative matters. The step from the ministry into politics may entail a loss of prestige, but the step from the factory into politics may carry with it a great deal of added prestige and respect. . . . For the individual concerned about prestige or respect, and considering a political career, the important question would seem to be not whether politics is a high or low prestige profession, but what it is higher than or lower than.

Again, as Table 3 indicates, the more highly educated, professionalized, and upper income groups had the highest percentage of respondents opposing a political career for their sons. In comparing statuses these groups of persons apparently feel that politics has little to offer. Certainly this is the case with respect to the monetary rewards most public offices offer. One exception to this tendency must be noted. Some extremely wealthy and/or high social status persons such as the late President Roosevelt, Governor Harriman, Governor Rockefeller, Senator [John F.] Kennedy, Governor Williams, to mention but a few, have made or are making political careers. All these men have inherited their wealth and social positions. It may be that for such individuals, politics is the only activity in which they find a challenge. But, we must be careful to remember that the decision of these men to enter politics was a personal decision and

* Curley (1874–1958), colorful, corrupt mayor of Boston, governor of Massachusetts, and congressman, was sentenced to the penitentiary following his election to a fourth term as mayor. Later, he was pardoned by President Truman. Curley is sometimes thought to have been the last of the old-style city bosses and is said to have been the model for Frank Skeffington in Edwin O'Connor's *The Last Hurrah* (New York: Little, Brown, 1956).

not necessarily the decision of their parents or similar people who may be represented in the poll. In any case, the wealthy men in American politics may constitute but a small percentage of the total group of high-income families. Certainly, they constitute but a small percentage of the total number of elective public officials in the nation. The wealthy politicians are conspicuous by their wealth.

Aside from class or group attitudes toward politics, it can be asserted that no individual is ever completely consistent in his evaluation of an object through time. Thus, a voter or citizen can alternately view the politician and his work with favor and disdain. Furthermore, it is quite possible to draw rather sharp distinctions between politics and the persons who practice it, valuing the one highly, or at least differently, from the other. . . . Americans appear to be cynical about politics and quite idealistic about certain politicians, especially dead ones, and about certain offices (the ones listed in Table 1, and the presidency). Cynicism and idealism may be logically incompatible, but psychologically they are mutually supporting, indeed, necessary to one another. The American tends to expect the worst in politics, but hopes for the best.

The polls cited above contain paradoxical evidence; but it may be that the responses of the interviewees were structured somewhat by the terminology of the questions. If, e.g., the pollsters had, in the second poll, asked people whether they would like to have their son become a governor, a senator, or president, rather than simply entering politics, it is at least conceivable that the results would be quite different and more consistent with the poll on occupational rating. No doubt, the same divergent results might be had if respondents were asked whether they would like to see their sons become "shysters" rather than lawyers, or "quacks" rather than physicians. Each profession has its presumed seamy side with an appropriate set of labels to describe the activities and their practitioners. In government, the seamy side is "politics," and the practitioners are "politicians" as contrasted with "statesmen" who serve the public and not themselves.

While our ideal statesman is selfless, we also have a pronounced tendency to apply the assumptions of the economic system to political behavior, i.e., to assume that political action is motivated by the same forces that presumably govern man in his economic activities. Thus, while we may hope that the politician will act selflessly we really expect and interpret his behavior as we would our competitors in the marketplace.

DIFFERENTIAL STATUS AMONG OFFICES

The data in Table 1 make it readily apparent that even among the offices listed there are differences in social status. How these differences would be affected by the inclusion of many offices, other than those noted, cannot be determined solely by logic. In any case, we may observe that among the offices listed, three (state governor, mayor of a large city, and head of a department in state government) are executive offices while only one, congressman, is legislative; and the remaining office, county judge, is judicial in nature. I am, of course, not considering the nonelective positions (U. S. Supreme Court justice, cabinet member in the federal government, diplomat in the U. S. foreign service). It should also be noted that the two highest ranked elective offices are executive (state governor, and mayor of a large city).

Looked at in another way, the data indicates that two of the offices (mayor, and county judge) are both local offices, while two are state (governor, and department head), and one (congressman) may be considered both local and national. How he may be seen by his constituents is an open question. When the nonelective positions are considered, three are on the national level (Supreme Court justice, cabinet member, and diplomat), in that order, and ranked first, third, and fourth. The relative prominence of local offices in this hierarchy is probably a reflection of the fact that only the more important ones were included in the list, while the absence of the offices of president, vice president, and senator minimizes the number of national and state officials with high status. This recitation of facts, however, is of little value unless provided an explanation.

. . . [There] are vast differentials in the functional importance of the several offices constituting the government, and the number of persons qualified for political office varies directly with the number of such offices. Thus, the presidency is a unique office in that it is the only such office in the American system, that the span of its responsibility is greater than any other single office or position in our society, that it requires a fairly unique set of skills and information. As a result, Sidney Hyman can assert and probably with confidence that "not more than 100 men now possess the combination of traits that qualify them for the 'natural aristocracy' from which presidents are chosen." On the other hand, local offices are in plentiful supply, their range of discretion and responsibility is exceedingly narrow, the amount of knowledge and skill required to fill them effectively is small; therefore, many citizens would experience little difficulty in satisfying their requirements. The supply and demand of office and talent operate in the political arena as in the market, placing a high value on the presidency, a low one on most local offices, and some intermediary value upon other offices.

The fact that Americans have tended to regard political offices as not requiring any special training, and the fact that political office has been so accessible to the poor and formally uneducated, has, in turn, attracted persons whose performances in office have not always been very exemplary. Thus, a vicious circle developed in which offices with low status attracted less desirable officeholders, and their inadequate or corrupt actions further confirmed the low status of public office. The very success of the economy in making room for the ambitious to succeed made a political career less attractive, a place for the economically unsuccessful. Since the standards by which political performances were judged were economic, politics and politicians suffered. Yet, both the poor politician and the "apolitical" rich profited; they did so by an "alliance," especially during the period around the turn of the century when the poor politicians could do the bidding of the capitalists.

AN AGENDA FOR RESEARCH

The materials introduced here are incomplete, and perhaps misleading. As in most areas of the social sciences, we need more and better research; in this case, research specifically oriented to the issues raised concerning the social status of the politician. We also are in need of information and theories relating social status to certain other variables. I should like now to merely suggest some of these other variables or areas of interest. They may be classified under three headings: (1) the recruitment of politicians; (2) behavior of politicians; and (3) effects on personality.

The Recruitment of Politicians

Here we are concerned with the effect of the social status of various offices upon the selection of candidates, i.e., of persons who offer themselves for public office. A number of studies on the social origins of politicians have already been made but, unfortunately, the authors seemed to have restricted their interest to the higher ranking elective offices. Thus, we need more studies of the type done by Rosenzweig on motivations,* particularly in the comparison of social statuses by the candidate; and we need more of the social origins type of analysis, but applied to state and local officials. If possible, a time dimension ought to be included since it is highly probable that the social origins of politicians have changed and will continue to change as their social status has and probably will continue to change.

The Behavior of Politicians

The problems involved in relating behavior with social status will no doubt be much more difficult to specify and convert into operational terms than are those of determining social origins. We may as well speculate upon the matter. If, for example, a person occupies, or thinks he occupies, an ambivalent social status he may behave quite differently from persons who are characterized either by an unambiguous high or low status position. Perhaps his behavior will be less certain, more defensive, and less

* Robert M. Rosenzweig, "The Politician and the Career in Politics," *Midwest Journal of Political Science*, I (1957), 163–172.

consistent. Perhaps his attitudes toward others will also contain ambivalent elements. Some politicians, as Rosenzweig has shown, clearly manifested ambivalence in their attitudes towards the electorate. In Rosenzweig's words:

. . . it is not surprising that the politician's view of the people contains an element of conflict. The conflict arises when "the people" become the "electorate." It is noticeable in some responses that an euphoric, almost sentimental, view of people as constituents or as friends is translated into a hearty cynicism of people as voters.

We need more information on the ways in which politicians view the entire situations in which they are involved. Social status may constitute an important variable in such analyses.

Effects on Personality

What has been said about the possible relationships between social status and political behavior is not without importance in the matter of personality. Yet, the two concerns are quite different; the behavior of the politician means his political behavior while personality refers to all of his behavior whether it has political relevance or not. The social status of a politician poses a number of different problems depending upon that status. The high status of a president, e.g., undoubtedly causes a new incumbent a trying period of adjustment, especially if his previous status was much lower. President Truman has written rather feelingly about the period of transition in his diaries. On the other hand, a politician occupying an office of much lower prestige might have to suffer some indignities he would not have to endure were he not in politics. In any case, politicians even on the highest levels tend to believe that they deserve more appreciation. The fact of their subjective uncertainty concerning status is an interesting fact in itself. What its implications are for the development of personality, as well as for political behavior and for the recruitment of politicians, are fruitful areas for further research.

52

POLITICALS AND APOLITICALS

Bernard C. Hennessy

How are politicians different from other men and women? Stereotypes of the pols have them avid for power, yet prone to compromise, disinterested in issues and avoiding moralizing. Prof. Bernard C. Hennessy (b. 1924), Director of the National Center for Education in Politics, subjected a group of activists to tests on these and other dimensions of personality with results summarized in his article "Politicals and Apoliticals."

*

.　.　.

THIS . . . IS A work-in-progress report of research designed to raise some questions about the political personality, to state some propositions (and hypotheses), and to isolate, if possible, some of the perhaps measurable traits of the political personality. The data come from 138 interviews with Arizona adults, mainly in the Tucson metropolitan area, but also involving legislators throughout the state. The interview consisted of a questionnaire, filled out by the respondent in the presence of the interviewer, and another sheet on which biographical information was gathered. The interviewer also recorded answers to a number of open-ended attitude and projective questions. The total interview time averaged about forty-five minutes.

The questionnaire itself was the source of our "scales." These were devised to measure six personality characteristics about which hypotheses

From "Politicals and Apoliticals: Some Measurements of Personality Traits," *Midwest Journal of Political Science*, III (1959), 339–355. Copyright © 1959 by Wayne State University Press. Reprinted by permission of the Wayne State University Press.

Footnotes renumbered, mere citations omitted.

were advanced relative to expected differences between politicals and apoliticals. The questions were of three kinds: (1) hypothetical problem-solving or role-playing situations, (2) direct questions measuring attitudes or opinions, and (3) statements with which the respondent indicated degrees of agreement or disagreement. Some sample questions follows:

Type 1:
 You are on a project team. Which of the following positions on the team would you prefer?
  —The head of the group
  —The idea man respected for his suggestions
  —A good guy, well liked, who helps the group work smoothly
  —The man who contacts outsiders about the group's work.

There were eight questions of Type 1.

Type 2:
 Which of the following do you think is most important in getting ahead in our society?
  —Brains
  —Good connections
  —Money.

There were nine questions of Type 2.

Type 3:
 When you come right down to it, human beings never do anything without an eye to their own advancement.
  —Strongly agree
  —Agree
  —Uncertain
  —Disagree
  —Strongly disagree.

There were thirty statements of Type 3.

 A number of the questions used in this instrument were specially constructed for the questionnaire. The rest—possibly two-thirds of the total—had been used before, in slightly different form, by U.S. and British psychologists, social psychologists, and political scientists.

 The responses to the questions were scored, weighted, and grouped into the six scales. These are not true scales, but rather summary indices of questions assumed to tap the same personality characteristics. The numbers of questions making up the scales ranged from five for the risk scale, to ten each for the toughmindedness and authoritarianism scales.

 A listing of the scales, and some of the relevant hypotheses, follow:

(1) Power Orientation

 This we defined as the desire to exercise control over persons and things. It was expected that the political would have a higher score here than the apolitical. He would be more aware of, and calculating toward, power differentials in interpersonal and intergroup relations.

(2) Willingness to Compromise
The expectation was that the political would be more willing to compromise, and/or that, having compromised, he would be less resentful of his compromising than the apolitical. The political personality comes to the bargaining more concerned with strategy and power than does the apolitical, and less concerned with ideals as such.

(3) Willingness to Risk
The hypotheses here were not as simple as those on the first two scales. The "enthusiast-politician" . . . may be more willing to risk in the name of the cause; the "bureaucrat-politician" less willing. The political, we expected, would be more willing to risk in the power game than the apolitical. But, on economic risk we expected to find no difference; our questions included both power-risk and economic-risk, and our scale, being an aggregate of both types might (if a difference should be shown to exist) wash out any distinction between politicals and apoliticals.

(4) Toughmindedness
This is a personality variable of Eysenck's. From a large number of factor-analysis studies he concludes that toughmindedness is an aggregate of traits which represents the "social projection of extroverted personality traits" (the opposite, tendermindedness, is the social projection of introverted personality traits). Our expectation was that the politicals would not differ from the apoliticals on this; our hypothesis disagreed not with Eysenck's view that toughmindedness reflects extroversion, but with the folklore that says politicians are extroverts.

(5) Authoritarianism
This is a much discussed and much studied personality variable. In general, our working definition of authoritarianism is that of Adorno. No studies of authoritarianism to our knowledge have specifically dealt with politicals. We expected, in spite of McConaughy's pertinent but highly tentative findings, that there would be no important differences between the politicals and the apoliticals in our sample on authoritarianism.

(6) Liberalism
This for our purposes was to be considered as a willingness to accept social change, and, in the contemporary use of the term, willingness to accept governmental activity in social and economic life as the vehicle of this change. Here, again, we advanced a null hypothesis—that politicals would not differ significantly from apoliticals on our liberalism scale.

The sample for this pilot project consisted of 138 voting-age Arizonans, most of them from the Tucson metropolitan area. The sample is not representative of Tucsonans, or Arizonans. Nor is the subsample of 72 politicals representative of all those who are active in partisan politics in Arizona or elsewhere. Our hope was to draw two groups of people— one of partisan activists, the other of adults whose political activity in many cases extends no further than fairly regular voting—and to match them on two or three possibly significant variables, especially those of socio-economic status and of education. This matching of samples was fairly successful. We have, on the one hand, 72 people who are active as party workers, officials and candidates and, on the other hand, 66 people who have, generally speaking, equal educational, economic and social opportunity to be active politicals, but are not. The apoliticals, on these *objective* criteria, *might* be politicals. Our question, therefore, is whether personality characteristics may be one of the *non*objective or *less*-objective factors which tend to prevent them from becoming politicals.

Our subsamples compare, in a gross way, as follows:

(1) The average age for the politicals is 41.78; for the apoliticals 38.26.

(2) The average number of years of formal education for the politicals is 15.58 (slightly less than the bachelors degree); for the apoliticals 15.33.

(3) The political group included 30 professionals, and the apoliticals 21 professionals; 17 politicals were in business (not necessarily their own), compared with 13 such apoliticals. There were 14 housewives among the politicals and 20 among the apoliticals (67 per cent of the political women and 61 per cent of the apolitical); a majority of the housewives in both groups had a bachelors degree and professional or business experience. Three people whose occupations were labeled as clerical were found in each group; and there were three skilled workers among the apoliticals and two among the politicals. Two retired persons were found in each group. The only important (but hardly surprising) differences were the presence of 24 lawyers among the politicals (only one among the apoliticals), and six state or local government employees among the politicals (none in the apolitical group).

The two samples were, on these and other grounds, quite evenly matched at the middle and upper-middle class levels. Our estimation (we did not ask for the information) of the average family income for each group was about $8,000–9,000, with the apolitical average being possibly slightly higher.

FINDINGS ON THE SIX SCALES

Power Scale

Table 1 indicates that the politicals, as a whole, are significantly higher than the apoliticals on the power scale.

The ranges in Table 1, and in subsequent tables, are to be read, as

TABLE 1

POLITICALS AND APOLITICALS ON POWER SCALE

| | Politicals | | | Apoliticals | | |
	All (N72)	Male (N51)	Female (N21)	All (N66)	Male (N33)	Female (N33)
Range	13/−2	13/−1	8/−2	12/−3	12/−1	10/−3
Mean	4.736	5.412	3.095	3.107	3.758	2.455
St. Dev.	3.202	3.126	2.759	3.260	3.273	3.114

Differences	Level of Significance
All pols and all apols	.01
Male pols and male apols	.05

in the case of all politicals above, "plus thirteen to minus two." Thus, of the 72 political activists, at least one person scored as high as + 13 on the power scale and at least one as low as −2. The mean, or average, score of the 72 politicals on the power scale was + 4.736, and the standard deviation, as one measurement of the spread of scores in this particular distribution, was 3.202.

The test of significance applied here is the standard error of the difference of the means. In nontechnical language, it is a test designed to measure whether or not two groups of figures (scores, percentages, measurements, etc.—called "populations") could reasonably be said to have come from the same source. Here we have scores for a particular psychological, or personality, quality—orientation to power, or power drive, defined as the desire for direct influence over persons and things—and we are asking whether the difference between the average scores made by 72 people categorized as politicals and those made by 66 other people (apoliticals) could happen by chance and, if so, how often such a difference could happen by chance. We find, applying this test, that the difference shown by our scores probably could not happen purely by chance more than once in 100 times.

No one will be surprised to find that our politicals appear to be more concerned with power than do our apoliticals; but, within this overall confirmation of the politicians-power association, an interesting sex difference seems to be indicated. It is, no doubt, the effect of cultural factors that accounts for the lower power aspirations of women, whether political or apolitical. The male apolitical mean-score, significantly lower than that of the male political, is nevertheless higher than that of the female political.[1] There is obviously a sex differential here, but not one which

[1] It is, of course, not possible to be confident about any conclusions based on a sample of 21 cases (the number of female politicals studied here). Two things should be said, however: (1) the test of significance used here is conservative in dealing with small samples, and there are other tests which will generally make the same difference

could account for the gross differences between whole political and whole apolitical scores.

Our score-analysis of the female respondents alone indicates this last point. We had postulated, at the beginning of this study, two types of political activists; among the females we were able to distinguish between these two types. Those who have active roles in public decision-making (our rough definition of politicals) may be divided into two major kinds: (1) party politicals (Ps), and (2) pressure-group politicals (PPs) who, by elimination, are all political activists not identified primarily with party associations.

It is apparent that there are many marginal cases in which the same individual is both a party and a pressure-group activist. A number of our women politicals had been, or were at the time of interviewing, officers or core-members of the League of Women Voters; but, in practice, there was no difficulty, on the basis of the biographical material and our knowledge of Arizona politics, in separating these into categories of *major* effort. We find that the officers and core-members of "nonpartisan" political interest groups take seriously their obligations, to appear and to perform within the group's organizational framework, in a genuinely nonpartisan way— even though their personal sympathies, and sometimes a part of their own energy and money, are channeled into the Republican or Democratic camp. Even when there are two (or more) hats to be worn, it is in every case fairly easy to identify the big hat and to categorize the person under that label. Thus, one of our male respondents came from a political family, had been active in party politics, and had even once run for an important county office; but his principal connection, and the one for which he was widely known, was as an officer—local, state and national—of an important veterans organization. Because we had too few pressure-group politicals among the males to warrant breaking them into the two kinds of political activists, this case was submerged in the over-all category of political; otherwise, he would clearly have been among the PPs.

Although our total number of female respondents was rather small (54) we were able to divide the thirty-one politicals into partisan politicals and pressure-group politicals. Our Ns, then, became *very* small— 16 Ps, 15 PPs, and 23 apoliticals (APs). Because of this small number of cases the three-way breakdown of females produces only a few *significant* differences; but the differences in mean scores which do exist on several scales—some of them quite large—are instructive and illustrate the importance of distinguishing the Ps from the PPs.[2]

---

appear more significant; (2) all tests are such that the significance of the difference increases if the same difference between the means is maintained as the size of the two samples increases. Thus, as cases are added to the two samples, the difference between the means becomes more significant if it remains the same (or, of course, becomes larger).

[2] It should be noted that in the two-way breakdown only those who have clear

Table 2 discloses a rather large difference in power drive between the party politicals and the pressure-group politicals. The apolitical women, in fact, score higher on the power scale than do the PPs. These differences cannot be said to be statistically significant, but they suggest that, with greater sample size, they would become so. Psychologically, the PPs do not seem to need the personal power-involvement which goes with direct,

TABLE 2

FEMALE Ps, PPs, AND APs ON POWER

	Ps (N16)	PPs (N15)	APs (N23)
Range	8/−2	8/−3	10/−2
Mean	3.625	2.067	2.478
S.D.	2.571	3.295	2.903

No differences reach .05 level.

TABLE 3

POLITICALS AND APOLITICALS ON COMPROMISE SCALE

	Politicals			Apoliticals		
	All (N72)	Male (N51)	Female (N21)	All (N66)	Male (N33)	Female (N33)
Range	7/−8	5/−7	7/−8	7/−6	7/−6	6/−6
Mean	.181	.196	.142	.909	.303	1.515
S.D.	3.300	3.170	3.605	2.927	3.214	2.464

No differences reach .05 level.

party, organization of votes and voters; they appear to be more concerned with issues and the indirect effect of ideas upon public policy. This difference is perhaps summed up by one respondent, very active in the League of Women Voters, who had done some party work which she described as "stupid clerical stuff."

Willingness to Compromise Scale

Our hypotheses were not borne out on the compromise scale. Table 3 indicates that the apoliticals were uniformly more willing to compromise than the politicals. The difference between the political and apolitical

partisan connections are labeled politicals; in the three-way analysis this is not so. Thus, five of the female politicals in Table 1 appear in Table 2 as PPs. The other ten PPs appear in Table 1 as apoliticals because, although active in pressure groups, they were not active in political parties.

males would seem to be probably a chance matter, but, as Table 4 shows, the differences among the three female categories may be very significant.

Contrary to everything we expected, our pressure-group political women are much more willing to compromise (significant to the 99 per cent confidence level) than are our party-political women. Our tentative explanation for the differences disclosed in Table 4, based on other inter-

TABLE 4

FEMALE Ps, PPs, AND APs ON COMPROMISE

	Ps (N16)	PPs (N15)	APs (N23)
Range	4/−8	7/−2	6/−6
Mean	−.688	2.467	1.174
S.D.	3.406	2.498	2.461

Differences	Level of Significance
Ps and PPs	.01
Ps and APs	.06

view material and on our general knowledge of most of the respondents, is that the questions which made up our compromise scale had high salience for our party politicals; the questions tended to be more black and white politically, some of them with an ethnocentric flavor, and it seems possible that our party politicals experienced more direct ego-involvement here, and therefore held more strongly to their views. This overall difference, it seems to us, is related to what Riesman calls the "moralizing" type.

We had, as a matter of fact, built into our interview two questions relating to political "indignation," which Riesman describes as being part of the attitude-complex of his moralizers. On the direct questions "Do you think it does any good to be indignant about political happenings?" there seems to be no difference in the pattern of responses from our Ps and our PPs; the most common answer, in about the same ratio from each group, was that indignation was "good" only if it led to some action.

On the closely allied question, with a projective twist, "Do you think most people get indignant about political happenings?" the two groups responded somewhat differently. Four of the party politicals, but only one of the pressure-group politicals, gave an unqualified "yes." Three of the Ps, and six of the PPs gave a qualified "yes," but all of the PP's limited widespread political indignation to issues which were either dramatic or which personally affected most people in their purse or in their daily lives. There was, in short, practically no feeling among the PPs that political indignation was general and widespread; nearly half of the party politicals, when the question was framed in terms of *other* people, indicated some such feeling. Admittedly, no conclusions can be drawn on such few cases, but our not-wholly-subjective appraisal of these differences in willingness to compromise includes the possibility that female moralizers (we have no evidence of this in males) may tend to find satisfaction in party activity. We hope to test this hunch in the next of this series of studies.

Willingness to Risk Scale

Although none of the differences on our risk scale were statistically significant, the differences were all in the direction of men being more willing to risk than women and of political men being more willing to risk than apolitical men.

That women seem less willing to take political (and probably economic) risk than men among our middle-class American sample is consistent with the findings of Stouffer and others in recent years. Yet, when the female scores are analyzed alone, there is a decidedly greater (but still not statistically significant) willingness to risk on the part of Ps over both PPs and APs, and on the part of PPs over APs. It cannot be said, then, that the differences indicated in Table 5 are sex-differences alone; the tendency remains for political activists (of both kinds and irrespective of sex) to score higher than the apoliticals on willingness to risk.

Toughmindedness Scale

We found, on the whole, no significant differences between politicals and apoliticals on toughmindedness. The apolitical males, it turns out, are

TABLE 5

POLITICALS AND APOLITICALS ON RISK SCALE

	Politicals			Apoliticals		
	All (N72)	Male (N51)	Female (N21)	All (N66)	Male (N33)	Female (N33)
Range	10/−9	10/−9	7/−8	10/−7	10/−7	9/−7
Mean	2.181	2.588	1.190	1.409	1.939	.879
S.D.	4.017	3.882	4.172	4.192	4.150	4.168

No differences reach .05 level.

slightly *more* toughminded than the political males (and the apoliticals, as a whole, slightly more toughminded than the politicals), but these are probably chance differences of no importance.

The females on our scale, both political and apolitical, were less toughminded than the males. This was especially pronounced among the apoliticals, where our women were significantly less toughminded than our men. Eysenck finds this to be true in general that the "T-factor," as he calls

TABLE 6

FEMALE Ps, PPs, AND APs ON RISK

	Ps (N16)	PPs (N15)	APs (N23)
Range	7/−6	9/−8	8/−7
Mean	2.063	1.200	.130
S.D.	3.647	5.205	3.519

No differences reach .05 level.

TABLE 7

POLITICALS AND APOLITICALS ON TOUGHMINDEDNESS

	Politicals			Apoliticals		
	All (N72)	Male (N51)	Female (N21)	All (N66)	Male (N33)	Female (N33)
Range	10/−12	10/−12	7/−10	12/−11	12/−6	9/−11
Mean	.653	1.039	−.286	.697	1.818	−.424
S.D.	4.352	5.448	4.506	4.445	3.656	4.861

Differences	Level of Significance
Male apols and female apols	.05
No other differences reach .05 level.	

it, is "relatively independent of sex, age, and education, ([except that]) women showed a distinct tendency to be more tender-minded. . . ."

If subsequent study should bear out this first finding that tough-mindedness is not associated with the political more than with the apolitical —and if Eysenck can make good his claim that toughmindedness is the projection of the extrovert personality—then we will have, for the first time, empirical evidence challenging that item of folklore which describes "the politician" as an "extroverted" fellow.

When we asked our respondents "What kind of people do you think are interested in politics?" the stereotype of the extrovert appeared more frequently than that of any other personality type or trait. This is not surprising. The lay image of the politician (and to some extent the self-image of the practicing politician) is Nast's* cartoon of the city boss—a loud, forward, gregarious, outgoing, optimist. We suspect there is little or no truth in this stereotype. Our first, tentative, findings increase our suspicion.

* Thomas Nast (1840–1902), cartoonist and caricaturist, famed for political cartoons. It was he who created the tiger, the donkey, and the elephant as the symbols for Tammany, the Democratic party, and the Republican party.

Authoritarianism Scale

Our authoritarianism scale is essentially an adaptation of some of the items of the California F-Scale. Six items of our ten were taken more or less intact from that scale, and four were our own creations. The validity of the scale has not been established, but there is high surface correspondence between the scores and our expectations based on personal knowledge of about half of the respondents. The whole matter of validity of our scales is one which is, of course, open to question. Without minimizing its importance, it may be said that the matched-sample technique makes any absolute measurement of validity less critical, since the objective is to compare score distributions of two groups—alike in some respects and unlike in others—which have been given the same tests. The scales—whatever their nominal or even "real" validity—are the same for each group. This is not to deny the need for constant scale improvement through item analysis and substitution; it is only to say that tentative findings may be interesting, suggestive, and helpful to understanding, even when the measurements are far from being scientifically pure.

TABLE 8

POLITICALS AND APOLITICALS ON AUTHORITARIANISM

| | Politicals | | | Apoliticals | | |
	All (N72)	Male (N51)	Female (N21)	All (N66)	Male (N33)	Female (N33)
Range	12/−15	10/−15	12/−13	6/−12	6/−10	3/−12
Mean	−1.903	−2.039	−1.571	−3.531	−3.061	−4.000
S.D.	5.481	5.448	5.542	4.302	4.113	4.435

Differences	Level of Significance
All pols and all apols	.06
Female pols and female apols	.10

Table 8 indicates that on the authoritarianism scale there were no differences which reached the .05 level of significance. The politicals, however, were higher in every case than the apoliticals. In fact, the difference between all the politicals and all the apoliticals very nearly reached the .05 level, and it is perhaps a quibble to say that this is not significant in view of the margin of error known to be associated with probability tests.

On the three-way breakdown of female respondents into the party political, pressure-group political, and apolitical categories, the party politicals score highest (−1.750), with the pressure-group politicals (−2.733) and the apoliticals (−4.154) following. These may well be chance differences, although the ordering of mean scores is consistent with Table 8 and arouses further interest.

If it is true that middle-class American politicals tend to have higher authoritarianism scores than other middle-class Americans, what do we make of it? Authoritarianism as a personality variable has been associated in the minds of western social scientists with "the bad guys." Notwithstanding the ritualistic affirmations of "objectivity" and "science," authoritarian personality traits, since the Iowa studies of the thirties, and especially since the Adorno work, are conceived to be destructive of both healthy personal adjustment and vital democratic practices.

It is no doubt true that individuals who score extraordinarily high on the F-scale tend to be incapable of friendly and satisfying personal relations and to be, in the aggregate, poor risks for democracy. But we are concerned here not with extremely high authoritarians, but only with a group which, on one test of authoritarianism, scored relatively higher than another group.

It is possible that people with low authoritarianism scores may be dull, passive, and unimaginative people, and that those who have higher (but not extremely high) authoritarianism scores may be more positive and self-reliant personally, and better prepared, on the whole, to be participants in the democratic process. It seems to have been something of this sort which was discovered by Ithiel Pool in a study of college-age summer tourists to Europe. As part of the International Communications Project of the M.I.T. Center for International Study, Pool interviewed a number of Americans on their way to Europe and, three months later, on their return voyage. He gave them measurements of both xenophilia and authoritarianism and found: (1) those who were low on both scores tended to be steady and dependable, but unexciting and sometimes even dull people, (2) those who were low on authoritarianism and high on xenophilia were romantics, high in aggressive traits, highly independent and imaginative, but more willing to entertain fantasy; (3) those who were low in xenophilia and high in authoritarianism were object oriented, like authority figures; and (4) those who were high in both showed greater self-discipline, tended to establish more effective relations with Europeans, and in a number of ways had better balanced and more attractive personalities.[3]

If Pool's study suggests—as it does—that medium high authoritarianism scores, in combination with other traits, may be desirable, rather than detrimental, to effective social adjustment, then we need perhaps to think of authoritarianism as one of a number of personality traits in pattern,

[3] Some of the findings of Pool's study were reported by him in a paper, "The Prediction of Attitudes of Foreign Travellers," at the May 1957 meeting of the American Association of Public Opinion Research. It should be said, of course, that the interpretation of these results is mine and not necessarily Dr. Pool's.

rather than as one with special and separate meaning for the democratic society.[4]

Liberalism Scale

We found, as we expected and as Table 9 shows, no significant difference between the politicals and the apoliticals on liberalism. The apo-

TABLE 9

POLITICALS AND APOLITICALS ON LIBERALISM

| | Politicals | | | Apoliticals | | |
	All (N72)	Male (N51)	Female (N21)	All (N66)	Male (N33)	Female (N33)
Range	11/−7	11/−7	6/−5	10/−3	7/−2	10/−3
Mean	1.236	1.359	.952	1.834	1.667	2.000
S.D.	3.204	3.242	3.048	2.485	2.291	2.697

No differences reach .05 level.

liticals as a group and by sex are consistently higher than the politicals, but these differences are so small as to be probably attributable to chance.

There are, further, no significant differences to be seen in the three-way breakdown of the females into party politicals, pressure-group politicals, and apoliticals.

When we arranged the liberalism scores of our whole sample by the self-identification of the respondents (as liberal, middle-road, or conservative) we found that the liberals had identified themselves accurately, according to our scale, but that the middle-roaders and conservatives had not sorted themselves out very well. We suspect that a number of our apolitical Republicans (there were 30 Republicans among our 66 apoliticals) thought they should call themselves conservatives regardless of the social and political attitudes they hold. In point of fact, as Table 10 shows, our apoliticals who described themselves as conservatives actually have a higher mean liberalism score than those apoliticals who said they were middle-roaders.

We did find, however, that the self-ranking of the politicals had a high overall correspondence to the score distribution which these politicals received on our scale. The politicals probably had a better understanding of what we meant by these terms, and were more skilled at self-categorizing.

---

[4] See, in this connection, Charles D. Farris's contention ("Authoritarianism as a Political Behavior Variable," *The Journal of Politics*, XVIII (February, 1956), 61–82) that authoritarianism as a single factor explanation for political behavior is no better than, perhaps not as good as, other variables.

TABLE 10

LIBERALISM SCORE OF POLITICALS AND APOLITICALS BY SELF IDENTIFICATION

| | *Liberals* | | | *Middle-Roaders* | | | *Conservatives* | | |
	All (N57)	Pols (N33)	Apols (N24)	All (N48)	Pols (N25)	Apols (N23)	All (N29)	Pols (N14)	Apols (N15)
Range	11/—2	11/—1	10/—2	8/—4	6/—4	8/—3	5/—7	5/—7	5/—2
Mean	2.754	2.909	2.542	.729	.360	1.130	.345	—1.071	1.667
S.D.	2.481	2.429	2.532	2.627	2.480	2.725	2.985	3.326	1.812

Differences	*Level of Significance*
All liberals and all middle-roaders	.01
Pol liberals and pol middle-roaders	.01
Apol liberals and apol middle-roaders	.10

SUMMARY

Our preliminary study indicates that politicals, as we anticipated, have greater "power drive." On willingness to compromise, contrary to our expectations, we found that our apoliticals had somewhat higher (but not statistically significant) mean scores than our politicals; this was largely a result of pronounced (and this time significant) differences between the two categories (and among the categories in the three-way breakdown) of female respondents. Our tentative explanation for this difference in willingness to compromise is that female "moralizers" may be attracted to party activity rather than to pressure group, or nonpolitical, pursuits.

We found, on our assessment of willingness to risk, that men were more willing to risk than women and that our political men were more willing to risk than our apolitical men. These differences are not statistically significant, however, and may be chance results.

On our toughmindedness scale we found that the females are less toughminded. No difference, however, appears between politicals and apoliticals, although the T-factor is supposed to be the "social projection of the extrovert personality." If subsequent work should confirm this lack of difference we will have some quantitative evidence to refute the popular notion of the politician as the extrovert.

In our measurement of authoritarianism the differences between politicals and apoliticals did not reach the 95 per cent confidence level. But the politicals scored higher in every case than the apoliticals. This may offer some support to suggestions growing out of an earlier study by Ithiel Pool that low authoritarianism, per se, may not indicate as socially useful personality development as moderately higher authoritarianism in combination with other traits.

On our liberalism scale we found, as expected, no important differences between our matched politicals and apoliticals. As a check on our scale, and as a check on our respondents' skill at self-categorization, we arranged the mean liberalism scores by the classes of self-identification. We found, in general, that those who labeled themselves as liberals did in fact score more highly on our index, but that the self-proclaimed middle-roaders and conservatives among the apoliticals did not show the expected difference on their liberalism scores. The self-identification of our politicals, however, quite strikingly agreed with their mean scores on our liberalism scale.

53

THE POLITICAL SOCIALIZATION
OF AMERICAN STATE LEGISLATORS[1]

Heinz Eulau, William Buchanan,
Leroy Ferguson, and John C. Wahlke

The authors of this excerpt are among the rising generation of political scientists marked especially by their interest in the behavioral and quantitative aspects of the study of politics. Each is a professor at a leading university. Their collaboration is in itself an indication of the laborious, painstaking nature of the work of the behaviorists. Only with a division of labor could the elaborate data on which their conclusions rest be collected and analyzed.

*

As LONG AGO as 1925, Charles E. Merriam, viewing the promises of political research, proposed that "the examination of the rise and development of the political ideation and the political behavior of the child has in store for us much of value in the scientific understanding of the adult idea and conduct." [2] Yet, over thirty years later, we know next to nothing about

From Heinz Eulau, William Buchanan, Leroy Ferguson, and John C. Wahlke, "The Political Socialization of American State Legislators," *Midwest Journal of Political Science,* III (1959), 188–206. Copyright © 1959 by Wayne State University Press.

[1] This study was made possible by grants from the Political Behavior Committee of the Social Science Research Council. Neither the Committee nor the Council is responsible for the study. The data reported in the study come from interviews with 474 state legislators in California, New Jersey, Ohio and Tennessee, conducted by the authors and research assistants during the 1957 sessions of the four legislatures. The samples are 91 per cent [of the members of the legislature] in Tennessee, 94 per cent in California and Ohio, and 100 per cent in New Jersey.

[2] Charles E. Merriam, *New Aspects of Politics* (Chicago: University of Chicago Press, 1925), p. 85.

"political socialization"—the process by which people selectively acquire the values, attitudes, interests, or knowledge that fit them for particular political roles and make them take these roles in characteristic ways. Studies of voting behavior suggest that, under certain conditions, family tradition can be an important factor in a person's orientation toward politics, influencing the degree, kind, and direction of his political involvement. We also know that religious, ethnic, and class perceptions and attitudes are formed rather early and, through time, become integrated into a system of values which tends to shape a person's social outlook and changes only slowly when it comes into conflict with opposed social values.[3] But, these studies shed little light on the development pattern of a person's political socialization.

If little is known about the initiation to politics of the population at large, not much more is known about the initiation of those for whom politics is a matter of central concern—politicians. Biographies, of course, tell us a great deal about the political socialization of particular, usually distinguished, public figures, but they represent unique cases which cannot be generalized. On the other hand, what systematic analyses have been made of political elites, are limited to data about the social bases of political recruitment and changes in the composition of elites.[4] These studies do not include systematic information on questions such as these: When do politicians become interested in politics? How do they become oriented to politics? Who are the agents of political socialization? What political or social events seem to arouse attention to politics? What kind of predispositions seem to accompany the initial interest in politics? Are political or other social beliefs involved in the process of political socialization?

This study presents some data on the political socialization of a particular type of politician—the American state legislator. In soliciting recollections about these legislators' earliest interest in politics, we did not consider it appropriate to think in motivational terms. Motivational analysis would have required more intensive interviewing than our research design permitted.[5] Hence, even though some of our respondents might use motivational language in trying to explain "why" politics interested or attracted them, we are not prepared to take such comments at face value. It seems doubtful that even those with some sense of self-awareness could accurately tell the reasons or motives that directed them to politics. We are

[3] See Herbert Hyman, *Political Socialization* (Glencoe: The Free Press, 1959).

[4] See Morris Janowitz, "The Systematic Analysis of Political Biography," *World Politics,* VI (1954), 405–412, for a review of such studies.

[5] The interview question read: "How did you become interested in politics? What is your earliest recollection of being interested in it?" It should be pointed out that the problem of legislators' political socialization was only peripheral to our main research interest—the analysis of state legislatures as political role systems. We did not intend to collect as full a set of data as might be desirable—the story of politicians' socialization could be the subject of a full-scale research project in its own right. This study therefore aspires to nothing more than a descriptive presentation of state legislators' perception of their political socialization, and the analysis has not been guided by specific hypotheses.

therefore not concerned with "why" state legislators became interested in politics, but rather with "how" they perceive what happened in the course of their political socialization. Recollections of this kind, it seems to us, have a functional reality of their own in constituting a part of the situation in which state legislators define their political roles.[6]

TIME OF POLITICAL SOCIALIZATION

In a recent review of voting behavior studies, Lipset and his associates reported that "it is difficult, if not impossible, to make any reliable estimate, on the basis of empirical evidence, of the age at which politics becomes meaningful to children or youth." After examining the skimpy research evidence, they inclined to focus on the period of adolescence— "the period in the life cycle where the individual first encounters strong influences outside of his family and must proceed to define his adult role." [7] Assuming Lipset's conclusion to be correct, our data (summarized in Table 1) suggest that politicians see themselves as exposed to the po-

[6] It should also be pointed out that the open-ended character of the question makes it mandatory to consider the results of this study as suggestive rather than definitive. While open-ended questions have the advantage of making for spontaneity and a wide range of response, and of allowing the respondent himself to formulate or "structure" the topic under investigation, there are certain drawbacks which limit their usefulness in statistical analysis. Heterogeneous answers make statistical controls difficult, if not impossible, and they make statistical inference of doubtful validity. For instance, some respondents mentioned primary groups they considered instrumental in stimulating their first political interests; others referred to some form of activity, political or otherwise, as a source of their first interest; others described events or conditions with which they associated their political concerns; still others referred to personal predispositions accompanying their initiation to politics; and a few mentioned political beliefs. Moreover, many respondents gave more than one "reason" for their political socialization. This makes it difficult to single out any one factor as more important than any other.

The respondents differed a great deal in a number of personal characteristics which are significant in answering open-ended questions. A few were suspicious of the interview and gave minimum, if not evasive, answers, while others, more favorably inclined, were more candid. Some were genuinely pressed for time and failed to elaborate as fully as those who were willing to devote a great deal of time to the interview. Still others— especially those with relatively little education—were unable to articulate answers to a question about which they evidently had thought little prior to the interview. Fluctuations in mood, in attitude towards the interview, in verbal facility or in self-consciousness made undoubtedly for considerable variability in answer patterns.

These differences are inherent in the open-ended type of interview question and in the interview situation. They do not allow us, therefore, to make categorical statements about the actual distribution of perceptions of factors in political socialization which we might have found if we had asked direct, closed questions about the particular factors which we were able to code. For instance, the fact that a certain percentage of our respondents mentioned some form of primary group influence does not mean that others, who did not mention this, were not possibly affected by family or friends in the process of their political socialization. In other words, the percentages of responses occurring in any particular category are, at most, suggestive indices of the extent to which legislators recalled certain socializing influences.

[7] Seymour M. Lipset, Paul F. Lazarsfeld, Allen H. Barton, and Juan Linz, "The Psychology of Voting: An Analysis of Political Behavior," in Gardner Lindzey, ed., *The Handbook of Social Psychology* (Cambridge: Addison-Wesley, 1954), II, 1145.

TABLE 1

TIME OF STATE LEGISLATORS' EARLIEST RECOLLECTION
OF POLITICAL INTEREST

Time of Recollection	Cal. N=113	N.J. N=79	Ohio N=162	Tenn. N=120
Childhood/grammar school	39%	23%	35%	32%
Adolescence/high school	16	10	15	11
College/equivalent period	8	10	13	7
After college	17	14	11	18
Time of entry into politics	18	15	23	13
Time not specified/codable	2	28	3	19
Total	100%	100%	100%	100%

litical environment at an earlier stage of their personal development than the average citizen. With the exception of New Jersey,[8] about a third of state legislators recalled their childhood or the grammar school period as the time when they first became interested in or aware of politics. But only 10 to 16 per cent mentioned a period roughly coinciding with adolescence and high school. Altogether, almost one-half had recollections locating their first political interest in the pre-college or equivalent age period. The childhood-grammar school period is perceptually more salient for state legislators than the time of adolescence or any single later period.

Nevertheless, as Table 1 shows, a sizeable proportion of state legislators reported first paying attention to politics either after college and its equivalent period or at the very time of entry into active politics. As one legislator put it:

Well, this might come as a surprise to you, but I was never interested in politics. I first became interested in politics after I was elected.

The data suggest that the process of political socialization, even for those who are most active in politics, is not necessarily restricted to the early years of the life cycle. As Talcott Parsons has argued, socialization may occur at almost any phase of a person's development and is part of a continuous process of growth.[9]

[8] There is reason to believe that the low percentage figure for New Jersey legislators having political recollections from childhood is not too accurate. New Jersey legislators, more than those from at least two other states, mentioned family influence as an important factor in their political socialization. As Table 1 shows, the low percentage of New Jersey legislators recalling the childhood period must be accounted for by the fact that, compared with the other states, an inordinately large percentage could not be coded on the time dimension. In other words, it is unlikely that New Jersey represents a special case.

[9] "The term socialization in its current usage in the literature refers primarily to the process of child development. This is in fact a crucially important case of the opera-

If we look at the interstate differences with regard to the time of political socialization, no particular pattern emerges. The fluctuations from state to state in each time period are small. Apparently, the process of political socialization in the four states follows a relatively similar time scale.

What accounts for the fact that legislators are initiated into politics in different periods of the life cycle? The evidence suggests that differences in the time of political socialization would seem to be a function of different influences which come into play in different periods of an individual's personal development.

PRIMARY GROUP INFLUENCE IN POLITICAL SOCIALIZATION

An interest in politics is probably related to the opportunity to hear about it or directly experience it. The opportunity to become acquainted with political life is given when significant persons in an individual's most immediate social environment are themselves in close and continuing contact with politics. Having parents, relatives, or close friends in politics is likely to facilitate an individual's own awareness of and familiarity with public affairs. The strong influence exerted by primary groups on voting behavior, for instance, is a reasonably well-documented finding of recent social research.[10] Earlier research on nonpolitical social participation has also shown that family members tend to be either all participants or all nonparticipants.[11] While precise data concerning the general population are lacking, it is plain that state legislators tend to come from families which are much more involved in politics than the average American family. As Table 2 indicates, from 41 per cent, in the case of New Jersey legislators, to 59 per cent, in the case of Ohio and Tennessee legislators, reported that one or more of their family had been or were in politics, although in a few cases they went back several generations to find them.

State legislators, in recalling their earliest interest in politics, indi-

---

tion of what are here called the mechanisms of socialization, but it should be made clear that the term is here used in a broader sense than the current one to designate the learning of *any* orientations of functional significance to the operation of a system of complementary role-expectations. In this sense, socialization, like learning, goes on throughout life. The case of the development of the child is only the most dramatic because he has so far to go." Talcott Parsons, *The Social System* (Glencoe: The Free Press, 1951), pp. 207–208.

10 See Paul F. Lazarsfeld, Bernard Berelson, and Hazel Gaudet, *The People's Choice* (New York: Columbia University Press, 1948), pp. 140–145; Angus Campbell, Gerald Gurin, and Warren E. Miller, *The Voter Decides* (Evanston: Row, Peterson and Company, 1954), pp. 199–206; Bernard R. Berelson, Paul F. Lazarsfeld, and William N. McPhee, *Voting* (Chicago: University of Chicago Press, 1954), pp. 88–109.

11 W. A. Anderson, "The Family and Individual Social Participation." *American Sociological Review,* VIII (1943), 420–424.

TABLE 2

RELATIVES OF STATE LEGISLATORS IN POLITICS

Relatives in Politics	Cal. N=113	N.J. N=79	Ohio N=162	Tenn. N=120
One or more	43%	41%	59%	59%
None	57	59	41	41
Total	100%	100%	100%	100%

cated that they are sensitive to primary group influence and attributed their political awareness to parents, relatives, or friends and associates. Between 34 per cent, in the case of the California respondents, and 47 per cent, in the case of the New Jersey respondents, spontaneously mentioned members in their immediate circle as agents of their political socialization. If we look in more detail at those who attributed their political interest to persons with whom they were in direct and sustained relationship, we find that many more mentioned family members than friends and associates as having been instrumental in this respect (Table 3). Moreover, in the case of two states, New Jersey and Ohio, substantial pluralities of those who mentioned primary group influence as the source

TABLE 3

THE INFLUENCE OF PRIMARY GROUPS ON STATE LEGISLATORS' INTEREST IN POLITICS

Primary Group	Cal. N=113	N.J. N=79	Ohio N=162	Tenn. N=120
Family members/relatives *active* in politics	18%	32%	31%	19%
Family members/relatives interested in politics	12%	2%	8%	16%
Friends/associates active or interested in politics	7%	13%	4%	8%

of their political consciousness—32 per cent and 31 per cent, respectively —recalled that their family had been more than occasionally active, and attributed their own political awakening to this fact; and, in New Jersey, friends and associates were named more frequently than elsewhere. Whether the differences between Ohio and New Jersey, on the one hand, and California and Tennessee, on the other, are meaningful reflections of possibly differing functions of the nuclear family in the political socialization of youth in these states can only be a matter of conjecture.

Political interest is seen as a matter of family tradition or inheritance:

"I was born into a political family. . . . I grew up in politics"; or, "I guess it's pretty much a combination of environment and heredity. . . . We are all sort of involved in politics," were typical comments. Others were more explicit. Familiarity with political campaigning by his father, going hand in hand with earliest awareness, is illustrated in this comment.

> My first recollection of politics was when I was four years old and my father was a member of the House of Representatives. I played here in this room when I was a little boy. . . . Then, too, I experienced a brief congressional campaign when my father was a candidate. He was defeated, but the whole thing left a deep impression on me. I met lots of people in politics through my father.

The family as a source of the politician's early identification with a political party and awareness of a political issue is described as follows:

> My father was a member of the city council. He ran for Congress on the Republican ticket and was defeated. I went to political meetings with him, I was always interested in politics. I therefore always felt a close identification with the Republican party. On my mother's side the family was Democratic. . . . And my mother's mother was a suffragette. There was much discussion about the woman franchise.

The vividness of these and many other accounts testifies to the important role played by family members in shaping the politician's orientations. Ties with a political party, consciousness of public issues, knowledge of both the serious and pleasurable aspects of political behavior, or sense of public responsibility, appear as products of political socialization in the most intimate form of primary group life.

What strikes one in reading some of the comments is the casualness of the socialization process when the agents are friends or associates. As one respondent put it, "some of the boys I was going around with were interested in politics, so I just went along." Another put it this way:

> I would say that I was catapulted into politics without any approach. My law partner has been city councilman and had held other political jobs. So I went naturally to work in his behalf in these campaigns. This I did for a number of years. So from there I was asked to run for the legislature. I didn't seek the job, I was asked.

In the first case, political interest seemed to be a by-product of one's need to be socially acceptable; in the second case, it derived from activity on behalf of a politically involved professional associate. In both cases apparent political apathy is transformed into political awareness and participation as a result of primary group contact.

POLITICAL INTEREST AS RESULT OF PARTICIPATION

Political socialization does not necessarily precede some form of political activity. A person may participate in political action of one kind or another without any previously crystallized political affect. For instance, he may find himself involved in "school politics" because his political potentialities are sensed by his peers; he may become active in political campaigns because of other social ties with other campaign workers; or, he may even participate in low-level political party work, as an errand-boy or leaflet distributor, without really understanding the meaning of his activity. As Table 4 indicates, these types of participation are reported as

TABLE 4

POLITICAL INTEREST AS RESULT OF POLITICAL AND
NONPOLITICAL PARTICIPATION

Type of Participation	Cal. N=113	N.J. N=79	Ohio N=162	Tenn. N=120
Activity in school politics	12%	4%	4%	#%
Study of politics	20%	9%	14%	8%
Political work: general (campaigns, meetings)	20%	6%	10%	13%
Party work	12%	32%	10%	7%
Civic/community work	11%	8%	6%	8%
Activity in occupational/ professional groups	8%	4%	6%	#%
Activity in ethnic/religious groups	#%	3%	—	—
Legislative lobbying	3%	1%	—	2%
Politically-related job (teaching civics; journalism; law; etc.)	8%	4%	3%	7%

Less than 1 per cent.

stimulants of political interest. California respondents, in particular, mentioned these directly political forms of activity as sources of their political involvement, though New Jersey legislators exceed the Californians in the "party work" category.

Secondly, a person may become exposed to politics by experiences which are themselves nonpolitical in character, but which are close enough to politics to serve as agencies of political socialization. For instance, formal education, or even self-education, may stimulate political awareness; so may participation in civic or community affairs, as well as activity in occupational, professional, or minority groups. A person may come to be politically conscious by performing professional tasks which are relatively close to politics, like lobbying, newspaper work, law practice, teaching of civics, or public employment. As Table 4 shows, some of these forms of nonpolitical participation were recalled by state legislators as avenues of their political socialization. These forms of activity seem to play a somewhat more important role in California than in the other states, though interstate differences are consistently small.

Two aspects of the distributions in Table 4 deserve special mention. First, the study of civics, politics, or related subjects in school does not seem to serve as a potent lubricant of political consciousness or interest. With the exception of California, where a fifth of the legislators pointed to their formal schooling as having had relevance to their political interest, a surprisingly small percentage gave responses such as: "I guess it started with my getting interested in the study of civics in grade school and high school. I suppose this study of civics was my first inspiration."

Secondly, it seems that, for a number of the politicians who populate the four state legislatures, political or party work itself was the source of their political initiation. This seems to be particularly the case in New Jersey, and might be due, in part, to the highly politicized atmosphere characteristic of that state's metropolitan areas. In other words, party politics operates as its own socializing agent. Involvement in political work, either occasionally in connection with a campaign, or by doing regular party work, seems for some of these politicians to have been a first stimulus of a more permanent dedication to public life. Running errands, handing out leaflets, or door-to-door canvassing work was given by some as their earliest recollection of interest in politics, usually among those whose family had been active or interested in politics before them. For others, being recruited by a party to run for party or public office seems to have been the source of a political orientation. As one legislator put it, "I got politically interested in 1938 when I became involved in county and state politics. I then became the chairman of the county committee."

Among nonpolitical forms of participation mentioned by legislators as decisive in their political socialization, activity in civic affairs or community work ranks first in all four states. That such activity served as a direct incentive to political interest might be expressed as follows:

> This is actually an extension of my activities in the school and community. I was interested in service clubs, civic progress and community problem-solving. It was getting so I was going to meetings ten nights a week. It's only a short step from this to public office.

Activity in occupational and professional groups, or contact with politics as a result of actually nonpolitical but politically-connected jobs, was recalled by a few legislators as influencing their interest in politics. A newspaperman would say that, of course, he became interested because of his profession. Another "became interested in political intrigue as a young cub reporter, and was hired to write publicity for a state senator." A former union leader recalled that his interest was aroused when politicians catered to him to win the support of his membership. A lawyer recalled his work for a property owners association before government bodies, or a teacher of civics suggested that his political interest was stimulated when he took his classes to visit the state capital. Contacts with politicians in service jobs were reported by some as having been instrumental in developing their political interest. A number of legislators mentioned having served as pages in the state legislature while in college. As one of them recalled, "I attribute my early interest in politics to my employment in the legislature." Public employment, in administrative departments of the state government or in the elected office of county trustee, was reported by some as a source of their first political interest.

The impression one gets from these recollections is one of the great variety of agents and activities which can operate as influential stimuli of political socialization. One is struck by the great heterogeneity of the sources which stimulate a political focus of attention. Most of those who mention these stimuli became interested in politics, at least in their own definition of what it means to be "politically interested," rather late in their personal development—in support of the notion that political socialization is not restricted to the earliest years of the life cycle, but that it is a process which takes place at later phases as well. While it is likely, of course, that the foundations of political interest were laid earlier, it is the later phases which apparently stand out in these legislators' perceptions of their political socialization.

POLITICAL INTEREST AS RESULT OF PUBLIC EVENTS

Great public events, either of a periodic character, like election campaigns, or of more singular though farreaching nature, like wars or economic depressions, may have a politically mobilizing impact on persons not previously concerned with public affairs. Similarly, relatively unimportant local or state problems become public issues which may involve people who before their occurrence had paid no attention to politics. Some 42 per cent of California, 25 per cent of New Jersey, 21 per cent of Ohio, and 18 per cent of Tennessee legislators recalled particular events or conditions as stimuli of their first political interest. While the percentages in particular categories are small (see Table 5), except in the case of California, in connection with political campaigns, and in New Jersey, in connection with local conditions or issues, the tenor of these recollections suggests that political socialization occasioned by public events may be ac-

TABLE 5

POLITICAL INTEREST AS RESULT OF PARTICULAR EVENTS OR CONDITIONS

Events or Conditions	Cal. N=113	N.J. N=79	Ohio N=162	Tenn. N=120
Presidential campaigns or administrations	14%	4%	11%	8%
Other political campaigns	19%	5%	2%	3%
War	2%	3%	2%	3%
Depression	5%	—	2%	—
Local conditions/issues	5%	15%	2%	4%
State conditions/issues	5%	—	1%	—

companied by a special intensity of feeling not generally experienced under other circumstances.

The presidential campaign, in particular, seems to have a latent socializing function in the American political system. It serves not only to activate voters, but the excitement, the turbulence, the color, the intrusion of the presidential campaign into the routine existence of a relatively little politicized society seem to make a profound impression, so that many years later a particular election or administration may be recalled with a good deal of relish as a source of political interest—as if the election had been held only yesterday:

In the Hughes campaign of 1916 my grandfather said to me: "My boy, I'll meet my maker. There's only one thing I regret, that I voted in the re-election campaign for Cleveland's second term." People streamed through the house to find out from the old man how to vote.

During the Bryan-McKinley campaign I hanged a picture of McKinley on my bedroom wall. My father took it off and I hanged it up again. He took it off and took me to the woodshed. I've been a Republican ever since.

Remarks made about gubernatorial, senatorial, or other election campaigns were less colorful than recollections of presidential contests. War, on the other hand, was recalled in more intensely personal terms by the few who ascribed their political interest to this experience. "Many of us, when we came back, had a new awakening, a new interest in civic affairs," or, "In prison camp I decided that we should do everything that we could on a local level instead of joining big organizations to influence grand policy."

Some California and Ohio legislators mentioned the depression as the origin of their political awakening. One respondent reported, for instance, that in the thirties, while he was employed in county agricultural work, "the plight of the farmers brought my interest." Another said that "during the depression everybody was politically conscious, and that interest stayed with me." For some of those who claimed to have become politically aware in the depression, politics seems to have meant a job. As one of them put it, "Well, during the depression, we weren't selling any automobiles. The situation was favorable for me to get on the ticket for county auditor." In this case, for instance, a first interest in politics seems to have coincided with the respondent's active entry into politics. Finally, state or local conditions were reported by a few legislators as having been instrumental in their political socialization.

PERSONAL PREDISPOSITIONS AND POLITICAL SOCIALIZATION

As we mentioned earlier, our research orientation was to find out "how" state legislators became interested in politics, not "why" they became interested. Nevertheless, it is noteworthy that half of the California, New Jersey, and Ohio legislators, and a third of the Tennesseans, seized our question of "how" they had become interested as an opportunity to reflect on certain personal predispositions that, they apparently felt, preceded or accompanied their political awakening. It is possible, of course, that these recollections are nothing more than current rationalizations. Yet,

TABLE 6

PERSONAL PREDISPOSITIONS AND POLITICAL SOCIALIZATION

Predispositions	Cal. N=113	N.J. N=79	Ohio N=162	Tenn. N=120
Political power	3%	6%	2%	3%
Admiration for politicians	19%	3%	5%	2%
Indignation	9%	8%	5%	2%
Sense of obligation: general	15%	5%	8%	#%
Sense of obligation: to special groups	3%	6%	#%	#%
Desire for sociability	2%	5%	1%	2%
Physical handicaps displaced	#%	—	#%	#%
Long interest: unspecified	14%	24%	33%	23%

Less than 1 per cent.

even if we are not prepared to interpret these responses as anything else, they are probably quite genuine perceptions and, as such, constitute significant elements in legislators' self-definitions as politicians.

Of course who expressed themselves in predispositional terms, a good many simply said that they had always been interested in politics, and left it at that. But perhaps the most interesting finding revealed in Table 6 is that only very few of these politicians spontaneously mentioned political power, influence, or authority as the kind of stimuli which predisposed them toward a political orientation. While it is, of course, impossible to say whether such power motives were really present or absent among those who admitted to them and those who did not, there is no reason to suppose that in a democratic society, where a large part of the community participates in the selection of public officials, politicians are necessarily (and only) recruited from power-motivated persons. Even if politicians differ from average citizens in the degree of their political involvement, values other than power are likely to bring would-be leaders to public attention.[12] The fact that only few of these legislators indicated power as a predispositional correlate of their political socialization is, therefore, quite understandable. Only a few were as explicit as the legislator who said that it was hard for him to explain what first interested him in politics, but continued:

I would say that I'm the sort of person interested in doing things. I feel I should contribute from the policy point of view. I'm not a good joiner. I feel the same sort of thing carries over into government and politics. I have always some desire not to be in the crowd. I'm never content to go to meetings and just listen and go home. I like to get my oar in.

Admiration for politicians—as ego-ideals—was suggested by others as having had some influence on their developing political interest. That favorable impressions of other politicians formed at an early age have an impact on political awareness seems plausible, as the following example illustrates:

I do remember that one summer I was staying with my uncle. I guess I was about thirteen. I attended an old-fashioned town meeting with him. My uncle was quite active at the meeting, and it made quite an impression on me.

While some legislators recalled having become politically interested as a result of admiring certain politicians, others reported having become interested for just the opposite reason—because they were dissatisfied with politicians or political situations:

This is a somewhat long story. I was an officer of a club, and in this capacity I had to call upon a city councilman to speak with him about getting the use of (some facility). He promised me to look into it and have my request heard before the commission, but he never did. He just ignored me.

Sense of obligation appears, not surprisingly, as a relatively frequent category of predispositional responses. This kind of answer is, of course,

---

[12] See Harold D. Lasswell, "The Selective Effect of Personality in Political Participation," in Richard Christie and Marie Jahoda, eds., *Studies in the Scope and Method of "The Authoritarian Personality"* (Glencoe: The Free Press, 1954), p. 221, for a discussion of political personality in democratic settings.

part and parcel of a politician's armor of rationalizations and can hardly be taken at face value:

> Well, it came about twelve or fourteen years ago when I decided I had spent all my life tending to our business and had done nothing for the community. I looked around to see how I could help out and decided to run for the legislature. I thought my business experience would be useful in the legislature.

Yet, there is an element of genuine commitment in this response that is in sharp contrast to mere political rhetoric. In other words, a distinction must be made between the politician for whom "public service" is a convenient device of deception, of himself, his audience, or both, and the politician who really feels a sense of obligation.

A few legislators suggested that their interest in politics was stimulated by the "social" possibilities which politics seemed to offer, as, for instance, the former school superintendent who upon retirement missed the chance to meet people which his occupation had given him and who, for this reason, claimed to have become interested in politics. Finally, three legislators attributed their initial interest in politics to the existence of a physical handicap and implied that politics offered them a compensatory opportunity. As one of these pointed out, "As a kid I had a bad leg, couldn't participate in sports and developed an interest in politics. I thought a legal background qualified a fellow for anything in public life."

It requires re-emphasis that our data do not tell us "why" these legislators were "moved" to seek a political career, while others in the general population, with similar ostensible experiences were not so moved. In other words, the perceptual data on legislators' prepolitical activities, or the events surrounding their earliest political interest, or even what they described as predispositional factors, cannot be interpreted in a motivational sense. If there is a personality syndrome of which one may think as "political man," the data do not and cannot reveal its existence among these state legislators.

IDEOLOGY AND POLITICAL SOCIALIZATION

Not unexpectedly in a society like the American, where politics is pragmatic rather than ideological, political beliefs seem to play a minor part in the process of political socialization. As Table 7 shows, only very small minorities in all four states linked our question of how they had become interested in politics with a discussion of political beliefs. This is all the more significant because the open-ended character of the question represented a perfect opportunity for ideological discourse if the respondent wished it. One can only guess, of course, that in a European country, where ideology constitutes a more important item of political culture, a

TABLE 7

SOCIO-ECONOMIC BELIEFS IN POLITICAL SOCIALIZATION

Beliefs	Cal. N=113	N.J. N=79	Ohio N=162	Tenn. N=120
Liberal	7%	1%	2%	—
Conservative	4%	1%	1%	2%
Probusiness	—	—	#%	—
Prolabor	3%	3%	#%	—
Profarmer	#%	1%	1%	—
Proreligious/ethnic groups	—	3%	#%	—

\# Less than 1 per cent.

legislator would probably have seized this opportunity to express political opinions or beliefs. [In our study,] those who did mention beliefs gave them only most cursory attention.

SUMMARY: MAJOR SOURCES OF POLITICAL INTEREST

If we look at a summary of the major sources of political interest as spontaneously reported by legislators themselves, some state-to-state patterns emerge. We cannot say absolutely that these patterns are not due purely to chance, but the very fact that patterns do occur suggests that interstate differences may be genuine expressions of political socialization processes among the four states. Table 8 summarizes the responses in our major categories. The most obvious difference to be noted is between California and the other states in regard to the influence of primary groups. One possible explanation of the relatively low percentage in the California column is that primary groups are less effective as political socializing agents in California because primary group influence is predicated on a reasonably stable population structure. But California is distinguished from the other three states by the fact that it is an immigrant state, and it may be that the population movement into the state has not permitted the formation of stable primary groups which can act as effective agents of political socialization. On the other hand, New Jersey, the oldest of these states in terms of admission to the Union, shows the greatest percentage in the primary group category, with Ohio and Tennessee in close middle positions.

What California may lack by way of primary group influence, it seems to make up in the categories of participation, and events or conditions, as stimulants of political interest. With regard to participation, it may be suggested that social and political activity is seized upon by an im-

TABLE 8

SUMMARY: MAJOR SOURCES OF POLITICAL INTEREST

Major Sources	Cal. N=113	N.J. N=79	Ohio N=162	Tenn. N=120
Primary groups	34%	47%	43%	42%
Participation	70%	60%	49%	43%
Events/conditions	42%	25%	21%	18%
Predispositions	52%	53%	52%	33%
Beliefs	16%	10%	6%	3%

migrant population to make itself feel at home in a new environment. In newly created communities, fewer legislators are "born into" politics, more become politically active in the process of community life. Similarly, political beliefs seem to play a slightly more important role in a state where stable political party patterns have had less of a chance to crystallize than in states characterized by very definite, if different, party-system structures. In both the participation and the event categories, as in the category of political beliefs, the pattern of responses ranks California first, New Jersey second, Ohio third, and Tennessee last. Moreover, Tennessee legislators were less likely to mention personal predispositions than the legislators from the other three states. Just why this should be the case, we cannot say.

What do our data tell us about the political socialization of state legislators? In general, it seems that a great many sources are operative in initiating political interest. Perhaps the most significant finding is tentative support for the hypothesis that political socialization—the process by which political interest is acquired—may occur at almost any phase of the life cycle, even among men and women whose concern with public affairs is presumably more intense and permanent than that of the average citizen. But, it seems to take place more often at a relatively early age. Whether the differences we found from state to state, either with regard to the agency or time of socialization, are significant as evidence of differing political subcultures would require more detailed and systematic inquiry than we were able to execute here.

54

HOOSIER REPUBLICANS IN
CHICAGO

David R. Derge

Prof. David Derge (b. 1928) attended the 1960 Republican National Convention as a Fellow of the National Center for Education in Politics and the Eagleton Institute of Politics. As a Fellow he lived with and worked with the Indiana delegation, at the same time observing their behavior from the perspective of the political scientist. He set himself the task of identifying and analyzing the phenomena of perception and adjustment among the delegates in order to understand how and why they behaved as they did. The results are reported here.

*

> "Why should I pay $500 for my seat as a delegate, and incur a total expense of probably $1200, only to come and have somebody tell me what do do?"—*Overheard in the Indiana delegation.*

. . .

THE INDIANA DELEGATION did not need to transport itself to Chicago to make decisions. The significant decisions either had been made before the convention started, or were made by others before the delegation had much chance to become involved. The delegation was committed to the nomination of Richard M. Nixon by a presidential primary and by personal preference, and this was known to all. Further, the delegation was committed to Nixon to the extent that it would accept his designee for the

From Paul Tillett, ed., *Inside Politics: The National Conventions 1960* (New York: Oceana Publications, Inc., 1962).

vice-presidential nomination even if he should be Henry Cabot Lodge. Finally, the delegation issued a statement about the forthcoming platform after its sole preconvention meeting in July. At this time the delegation went on record for a conservative platform which would not attempt to out-promise the Democrats, and one which would preserve the integrity of the states against what delegates viewed as a threat of federal encroachment. Most delegates could examine the final draft of the platform only a short time before they were asked to approve it by voice vote on the convention floor.

This is not to say that the Indiana delegation found all of these key decisions pleasing. Many in the delegation had hoped for a midwestern vice-presidential nominee and had little enthusiasm for Lodge. They reasoned that a midwesterner would strengthen state and national tickets in what Hoosiers have always considered the most important section of the country—the midwest and more specifically, Indiana. The conservative base of Indiana Republicans did not mix well with some features of the platform thought to be leaning too far to the left. Grumbling about the platform was heard in Indiana ranks throughout the convention. Ex-senator William Jenner came close to expressing the sentiment of the delegation when he commented in caucus that "the Republican party is just a little bit pregnant with New Dealism, and you ladies know you can't be just a little bit pregnant."

However, all of the talk within the delegation about a midwestern vice-presidential nominee and a conservative platform took place against the background of a strong and irrevocable commitment to Nixon. This commitment embraced, directly or indirectly, all convention decisions and emasculated Indiana's role, as it did that of most other states.

The Indiana delegation drifted into a something less than festive convention city on Sunday and Monday. The governor firmly presided over formal caucuses on Monday, Tuesday, and Wednesday. While some delegates may have thought that they were in Chicago to settle important questions, the atmosphere of the caucuses was not that of a deliberative body debating alternatives and reaching meaningful decisions. The first of the two open caucuses was called to hear a report from Indiana's representatives on the platform committee. Since the committee was still in session, and no one claimed to have seen a copy of the platform, there was only general discussion and no decision. The delegation did not take a decision on the vice-presidential nomination because Nixon had not revealed his preference.

The Tuesday caucus went in much the same way. After some general discussion about the platform, the governor stated that "the platform is to be one on which the presidential candidate can wage his campaign," committing the delegation to whatever the platform committee reported. The delegation agreed to postpone until Wednesday further discussion of

vice-presidential candidates since Nixon had still not revealed his preference.

The Wednesday caucus was closed, and each delegate and alternate
was given the opportunity to express his views on the vice-presidential
nomination. The purpose of the caucus was twofold: first, to allow the
delegation to let off steam on an issue which had been causing some dis-
comfort, and had left some delegates with a frustrated and powerless
feeling; second, to determine what the delegation would do in the unlikely
event of an "open" nomination, which few really thought would happen.
Nearly everyone spoke out. Discontent was expressed over the impending
nomination of Lodge, with various delegates urging support for Morton,
Judd, Goldwater, and others. This session produced the wistful statement
that, should the nomination be thrown open, the Indiana delegation would
conduct "lightning" caucuses on the floor of the convention to determine
where its thirty-two votes would go. When asked what would happen if
Nixon picked his running-mate, the governor publicly stated that "when
the decision is made, Indiana will accept it whatever it is. Indiana has been
in Nixon's corner for a long time and will continue to be."

Thus, the delegation as a group made no meaningful decisions
during its stay in Chicago. The governor was active during the convention
in support of a conservative platform and a midwestern vice-presidential
nominee. He attended governors' meetings, talked with Nixon and his
advisers, and made public statements; but it seemed to observers that all of
his efforts had the ubiquitous qualification that he, and the delegation,
would accept Nixon's decisions and would support them on the floor of the
convention. They did just that.

One Hoosier wryly appraised the delegation's deliberative and decision-making activities as follows: "Where did you go? Out. What did
you do? Nothing." But the Indiana delegation did more than fret about
the inexorable forces at work in the convention. Much as religious orders
retreat to a different environment to refurbish the soul, the Indiana
Republicans underwent a heartening reintegration in Chicago. It was not
a notably optimistic group of politicians in the first days of the convention,
but a spirit of optimism, conviction, and unity developed before the day
of adjournment.

The business of state politics went on unabated by the convention.
While Indiana Republicans became sincerely enthused about a national
victory in November, they were keenly aware that this happy event would
be a Pyrrhic victory if political fortunes within Indiana failed. There are
few Hoosiers with political ambitions extending beyond the state boundaries; and, to most, political surivival is measured in terms of maintaining
control in Indiana. The party loyal threw themselves into a state party
function. Numerous candidates for state executive offices and Congress
played no important role in delegation activities, but got in five good days

of campaigning. More than five hundred Hoosiers came to visit with one another and to attend convention sessions. The Indiana hospitality room at the Palmer House was well supplied with county chairmen, women's clubs, and candidates running for public office back home. These people generally discussed national nominees and platform in terms of what effect they would have on state and local Republican tickets. Political fence-mending kits were in evidence. Republicans were seen exchanging generous measures of cordiality which might have been in shorter supply had the encounters taken place back in Bippus, or Santa Claus, or Russiaville. This cannot be discounted in a state noted for its intraparty factional battles.

Most of the convention's formal business and social activities seemed calculated to truss up the sagging elements in the party and to send away uplifted and inspired delegates. Conservatives went away thinking that they had served warning on the prodigal factions of their party and had laid the groundwork for a renascence in coming years. Liberals went away feeling that the party is still in good hands. Practically everyone left with the conviction that Republicans had a good chance of staying in the White House. Such convention functions might be ridiculed by solemn editorial writers, but they were good for the party, and for Indiana Republicans.

CHARACTERISTICS OF THE INDIANA DELEGATION

Assuming that conventions may sometimes be called on to deliberate and make decisions, do delegates seem to be equipped by background and experience to perform these functions? A short analysis of the Indiana delegations to the 1960 conventions may provide some evidence on this question.[1]

As measured by occupation, both delegations were much alike—biased toward high socio-economic status. As indicated in Table 1, 61 per cent of the Republicans were professionals, managers, officials or proprietors, while 72 per cent of the Democrats fell into these high-status occupations. Entrepreneurial occupations were more heavily represented among Republicans; the professions among Democrats. There was more upward social mobility in evidence among the Democratic delegates. One fourth of the fathers of Democrats were professionals, managers, proprietors or officials in contrast to about one-half of the fathers of Republicans. One-fifth of the Democrats came from working class families, but this was the case for only about one-twentieth of the Republicans.

---

[1] Data on which statistics in this section and other parts of the paper are based were gathered on survey forms sent to delegates of both parties. The sample size for the Republicans is 57 per cent, and for the Democrats 65 per cent. Because of these sample sizes, the conclusions should be treated as tentative.

TABLE 1

OCCUPATIONS OF CONVENTION DELEGATES

	Republicans *Per cent*	*Democrats* *Per cent*	*Experienced labor force, Indiana 1950* *Per cent*
Professional	19	48	7
Manager, Official, Proprietor	42	24	8
Farmer and farm manager	6	5	9
All other occupations	33	23	76
Total	100	100	100

High status is also reflected in the educational backgrounds of the delegates. College attendance was reported by 85 per cent of the Republicans and 78 per cent of the Democrats. One-third of the Republicans and one-half of the Democrats held advanced or professional degrees. In a state where the median number of school years completed is 9.8, the delegates clearly came from the highly educated sector of the population.

Many delegates had extensive political experience in the management of party affairs, competition for public office, or both. In the Democratic delegation, 60 per cent had run for public office, 37 per cent successfully. Only 35 per cent of the Republicans had been candidates and 24 per cent had held office. Most of the running for office in both groups had been on the local and county level. Salaried political appointments to public office had been held by 21 per cent of the Republicans and 45 per cent of the Democrats. Thus, the Democratic group included more competitors for, and holders of, public office than the Republican group.[2]

The skeleton of Indiana's party system is the party committee structure—which manages most of the political activities in the state. Many of the delegates to both conventions had occupied key positions in this structure. One-fourth of the Democrats, and one-fifth of the Republicans, had served at least one term on the highest party council, the state central committee. Delegates who had served at least one term on a county committee made up 67 per cent of the Democratic delegation, and 56 per cent of the Republican delegation.[3]

A sharp contrast develops between the two delegations when party

[2] A significant minority in both delegations came from a family background of high political involvement. Parents of 45 per cent of the Democrats and 40 per cent of the Republicans had held either an elective public office, a party office, or both.

[3] This is in interesting contrast to another group of Indiana politicians, the members of the General Assembly. Only 29 per cent of the 1959 General Assembly had ever served on a party committee, 41 per cent on the state central committee. There is reason to believe that the party managers and office-seekers come from two different groups within the state, and that the overlap between the two is not great. Some delegates present interesting exceptions to this rule.

involvement is defined in terms of performance for the party during campaigns and the undertaking of the necessary chores of winning elections.

TABLE 2

WHICH ACTIVITIES HAVE YOU PERFORMED FOR YOUR PARTY?

	Republicans Per cent	Democrats Per cent
Managed Campaigns	35	73
Gave Speeches	35	85
Contacted Voters	71	90
Distributed Literature	50	73
Other	47	45

As Table 2 indicates, more than twice as many Democrats undertook management of campaigns and speech-making, and Democrats have a significant edge in routine work of contacting voters and distributing literature. Most of the "other" activities reported by Republicans related to the raising and soliciting of funds. The "other" activities reported by Democrats ranged widely but did not concentrate on fund raising. To the extent that the two delegations can be compared on political activities, it appears that the Democrats were more heavily involved in both party management and other facets of party work.

All the Democrats, and 85 per cent of the Republicans, had attended at least one state party convention (which, in Indiana, nominates candidates for state executive offices and the United States Senate, and writes the state party platform). About four out of ten in both delegations had been to at least one other national convention as delegate or alternate, and several more had attended as spectators. Thus, the mysteries of political conventions were not new to either group, and many members of both delegations went to the 1960 conventions with an extensive background in the lore and operation of nominating politics.

In summary, Indiana provided the two national conventions with more than ordinarily seasoned politicians. Many were experienced in the management of party affairs, and had themselves run for public office. On the whole, they were highly educated and were drawn from high socio-economic strata. These groups could hardly be called cross-sections of the citizenry. On the contrary, one might say that they had been skimmed off the top. Judged by personal background and political experience, the delegates to both conventions appear to be fully capable of any decision-making required of them. This is a tribute to Indiana's selection process which is firmly under party control. It seems doubtful whether any other method of selection would have produced a more comely group of politicians.

WHY DELEGATES GO TO CONVENTIONS

What causes an individual to undergo the considerable expense and lost time resulting from a national convention?[4] Indiana Republican and Democratic delegates were asked to explain why they chose to attend the 1960 convention, and, while each answer was different, the following general classification can be made.

TABLE 3

WHAT LED YOU TO BE A DELEGATE OR ALTERNATE TO THE 1960 NATIONAL CONVENTION?

	Republicans *Per cent*	*Democrats* *Per cent*
General interest in politics and desire to participate in as many phases as possible	35	45
Desire to have a part in nomination of party's candidates and/or writing of the platform	33	23
Desire to further the interests of a particular candidate designated by the respondent	9	18
Honor and recognition which derives from attending convention	6	5
All other responses	17	9
Total	100	100

Findings in Table 3 suggest that less than half of the respondents in both parties *specified* that they went to the conventions with the hope of playing a decisive part in the nomination of a particular candidate or, in general, to be instrumental in the convention's decisions. It seems reasonable to presume that more than half of both delegations would have made the trip even if they had the foreknowledge that the convention's important decisions would be made without benefit of consultation with delegates. Most of these people, in the words of one delegate, "have been hooked by the political habit." The writer is inclined to believe that less than half, and possibly only a fraction, of the Republican delegates expected that they might make a significant impact on decisions. If this is correct, most Republican delegates were not disappointed to discover that their job was to legitimize decisions made by others. . . .

[4] Indiana Republicans were assessed $500 by the party for a delegate's position, and $300 for an alternate's position. Furthermore, all delegates and alternates were required to meet all convention expenses without party assistance.

55

THE BUREAUCRAT AND
THE ENTHUSIAST

John P. Roche and Stephen Sachs

To Prof. John P. Roche and Stephen Sachs, both the enthusiast and the bureaucrat have essential roles in political organizations. The one lends moral tone and urgency to the matter of fact routine of the other. In this article, the authors do not concern themselves with "why" but rather attempt to describe the objective acts, the patterns of action and belief associated with these political types.

*

THE QUEST for historical uniformities is a dangerous game and one which generally reveals more about the preconceptions of the observer than about the historical process. The historian, alas, is denied even the camouflage of numbers, which so often permits the social psychologist to portray his hunches as "science," and he is fair game for countless safaris of cultural anthropologists who are prepared to fire instantly at any suggestion that, say, Zulus have anything in common with Japanese, or Americans with the British. Historical speculation, unless cloaked with the rites of numerology, has clearly been consigned to the province of journalists, mystics, and fakirs.

To say this is not to endorse for a moment all that has been done in the name of history. On the contrary, it is patent that historians have brought much of this obloquy on themselves by their oracular pretenses, by their unfortunate tendency to confuse insight with "fact." Yet, admitting

From "The Bureaucrat and the Enthusiast: An Exploration of the Leadership of Social Movements," *Western Political Quarterly*, VIII (1955), 248–261.

both the uncertain nature of the data and the imperfections of the analyst, the student of politics can learn much from the perusal of history. The specialist in public administration who neglects—to use but one example —Philip Woodruff's superb *The Men Who Ruled India,* deprives himself of an invaluable fund of information and insight, and the student of social theory can similarly find in historical and biographical studies an enormous body of significant data.

It is in this spirit that we have prepared this brief analysis of leadership types. The technique applied deserves explanation: we have in the text advanced a series of generalizations which are largely, though not exclusively, based on an intensive case-study of the history of the British Labour party. Because we have attempted to keep the generalizations in the text general, the footnotes are unusually elaborate—constituting, in effect, another article. We should like to make it clear that the hypotheses suggested here are not put forth under the *imprimatur* of science; although we feel that they may have utility in the examination of organizations as different as political parties, churches, and labor unions, we make no claim to universal validity. Furthermore, we assert no copyright on the ideas incorporated herein; other scholars, better equipped than we, have conducted forays of a similar type into the nature of organizational leadership, and we have profited from their explorations. Moreover, the classic exposition of our thesis is Dostoevski's symbolic *tour de force,* "The Grand Inquisitor."

The examination of social movements which seek public support for their political, social, or religious objectives suggests that there is a tendency for two major leadership types to emerge. Their specific characteristics may vary greatly with the cultural context or with the type of goal toward which the organization is oriented, so that precise definition is elusive. Yet, granted this elusiveness, we feel that a meaningful typological distinction can be made, and we have designated the two leadership types the "bureaucrat" and the "enthusiast."[1] To forestall the criticism that we are indulging in psychological monism, we should state at the outset that one individual can, in varying social situations, display the characteristics of both, i.e., he can perhaps be a bureaucrat in his union and an enthusiast in his religion. But, in any one context, the pattern of behavior tends to remain constant and is thus subject to generalization.

The bureaucrat, as his name implies, is concerned primarily with the organizational facet of the social movement, with its stability, growth, and tactics. To put it another way, he concentrates on the organizational means by which the group implements and consolidates its principles. He

---

[1] Our "bureaucrat" is a first cousin of Max Weber's bureaucrat, sharing many of the latter's characteristics. Our "enthusiast" is on loan from theological studies where he has had a long and tumultuous career; *cf.* Mgr. Ronald Knox, *Enthusiasm* (London: Oxford University Press, 1950).

will generally be either an officeholder in the organization or interested in holding office. While he may have strong ideological convictions, he will be preoccupied with the reconciliation of diverse elements in order to secure harmony within the organization and maximize its external appeal. He seeks communication, not excommunications.

In contrast, the enthusiast, seldom an officeholder,[2] and quite unhappy when in office, concerns himself primarily with what he deems to be the fundamental principles of the organization, the ideals and values which nourish the movement. No reconciler, he will concentrate on the advocacy of these principles at the risk of hard feelings or even of schism.[3] While the bureaucrat tends to regard the organization as an end in itself,[4] to the enthusiast it will always remain an imperfect vehicle for a greater purpose. Whereas the bureaucrat is likely to equate "The Cause" with its organizational expression, the enthusiast, with his fondness for abstraction, identifies it with a corpus of principles.[5]

[2] The British Labour party's bureaucrats generally center in the party Executive and the Parliamentary Labour party, notably in the contingents supplied to each of these bodies by the trade-union movement. The enthusiasts formerly rallied around the standard of the affiliated Independent Labour party (ILP) and, upon its disaffiliation, migrated to the Socialist League. Since the latter was disbanded, there has been no nesting place organizationally, but functionally the enthusiasts can always be located in the Constituency Labour parties and can be spotted ideologically by their vigorous support for Aneurin Bevan. They constitute the readership of the journal *Tribune* and of the *New Statesman & Nation,* and are at present busy learning Chinese.

[3] For instance, Stafford Cripps' work for the constitution of a popular front with the Communists and other "anti-fascist" organizations which led, in 1939, to his expulsion from the party. Cripps, of whom Churchill once observed: "There, but for the grace of God, goes God," never faltered for a second in his labors for this cause and, secure in his conviction that it was just, accepted expulsion as the stigma which proved it.

[4] The bureaucrat *par excellence* of the Labour party was Arthur Henderson, long-time party secretary and foreign minister in the 1929–1931 government. A good example of the bureaucratic preoccupation with organization and reconciliation was the preparation by Henderson of the 1918 party constitution, a masterpiece of organizational ingenuity; see G.D.H. Cole, *A History of the Labour Party from 1914* (London: Routledge & Kegan Paul, 1948), pp. 44 ff. Henderson was severely criticized for not leading opposition to Ramsay MacDonald during the 1929–1931 period, when it appeared to many that the prime minister was ignoring party policy, but to do so would have run contrary to Henderson's bureaucratic loyalty. As Cole puts it, Henderson "in that crisis . . . made . . . too many . . . concessions in the hope of holding the party together." Cole, *ibid.,* p. 305. Henderson, of course, never dreamed that MacDonald would desert the party. Postgate's description of Henderson after that sad event is illuminating in this context: "Henderson seemed shrivelled and bowed, and his usually ruddy face was yellow. Disloyalty was a thing he could not understand. He had given his most unswerving support to the handsome, eloquent leader who had helped him build up the movement; he had never allowed himself to be influenced by the fact that he had not in his heart liked MacDonald and had more than once received discourtesy from him. Now, that man had deserted the people in its greatest misery. He could not understand, though he would try to forgive; he looked like a man who had been given a mortal wound." Raymond Postgate, *George Lansbury* (London: Longmans, Green & Co., 1951), pp. 271–272. Cole elsewhere notes Henderson's identification of the cause and the organization, *op. cit.,* p. 305.

[5] To understand this approach, a reading of the various studies by Archibald Fenner Brockway is invaluable. See his *Socialism over Sixty Years* (London: George Allen &

Several other typical characteristics emerge from this fundamental difference in outlook. Outstanding among them is the varying attitude towards compromise in policy matters. The bureaucrat approaches a policy question with a predisposition towards harmony; he is prepared to compromise in order to promote unity and cohesion within the organization and to broaden its external appeal. He considers policy, if not a mere expedient with which to build up organizational strength, no more than a flexible expression of intentions which can be modified as required by "practical" needs.[6] However, to the enthusiast policy is far more than a "political formula" far more than a sonorous exposition of attractive, organization-building slogans; on the contrary, he insists that policy must be the undiluted expression of first principles.[7] The bureaucrat specializes in studied ambiguity; the enthusiast, in credal precision. In short, while the former looks upon policy statements as something less than ex cathedra pronouncements of the whole "Truth," the latter views policy as the living Word, and considers compromise as not only wrong, but also evil.[8]

The same approach to compromise is evident in attitudes towards membership: the bureaucrat is inclusionary, and holds a quantitative emphasis, while the enthusiast is exclusionary, desiring to limit the body of saints only to those full of grace.[9] That this problem of membership has plagued social movements from time immemorial hardly needs elaboration here; suffice it to say that the struggle between the inclusionists

Unwin, 1946); *Inside the Left* (London: The New Leader, 1942); and *Bermondsey Story* (London: George Allen & Unwin, 1949). Brockway was a paladin of enthusiasm and his various crusades, and those of the men he chronicles, against the party leadership make exciting reading. One is struck with the resemblance to *Pilgrim's Progress,* for he is transported to a world populated by moral "forms," and the perils of Socialist (the Christian of Brockway's epics) are frightful to behold.

[6] For an exhaustive treatment of this theme see Robert Michels, *Political Parties* (Glencoe, Ill.: The Free Press, 1949), and Gaetano Mosca, *The Ruling Class* (New York: McGraw-Hill, 1939). It is also discussed by Max Weber in his essay on "Bureaucracy" in H.H. Gerth & C.W. Mills, eds., *From Max Weber: Essays in Sociology* (New York: Oxford University Press, 1946).

[7] For example, George Lansbury's 1926 motion to "abolish the navy by discharging 100,000 men," Postgate, *op. cit.,* pp. 236–237 as distinct from the regular Labour motions in favor of disarmament in the abstract. See also the ILP position on "the cruiser issue" in 1924, Brockway, *Inside the Left,* p. 156.

[8] The ILP split from the Labour party on precisely this point. The ILP Members of Parliament demanded the right of private judgment, asserting that an M.P. should vote on the merits of a proposal rather than under party instruction. The Labour party, operating on the maxim *ex nihilo nihil,* refused to permit this and the ILP disaffiliated. Brockway, *Inside the Left,* p. 215; Postgate, *op. cit.,* p. 278. The ILP saw the MacDonald defection as the logical conclusion of moderation: "Truly the policy of compromise has brought its reward." Brockway, *Socialism over Sixty Years,* p. 294.

[9] This is a function of the perfectionism of the enthusiast and is a common feature of all enthusiastic political, social, or religious movements. A man can not be saved by "good works," but only by true inspiration, which may or may not lead him to good works. The bureaucrat, essentially Niebuhrian in outlook, is prepared to settle for less on the assumption that while good works may be badly motivated, they are still preferable to bad works, however motivated.

and the exclusionists, which inspired St. Augustine's polemics against the Donatists as it does those of the Bevanities against Attlee, is a constant feature in ideologically oriented groups.[10] In particular, it plagues political organizations, for the bureaucrat here is characterized by an acute hypersensitivity towards the marginal voter,[11] while the enthusiast, with full confidence in the truth of his convictions, operates on the principle that if the people refuse to share his vision, so much the worse for them. To the latter, defeat at the polls means nothing; a moral totalitarian, his slogan is "Damn the electorate! Full speed ahead!"[12]

It is perhaps, therefore, valid to suggest that the bureaucrat seeks to extend the area of compromise; the enthusiast, the area of principle.[13] Although we are not asserting that the bureaucrat always flees from principle, nor that the enthusiast is inevitably a moral totalitarian, there is in our view sufficient evidence to justify the establishment of these positions as typical.[14] David Riesman, drawing on the insights of Ortega y Gasset[15] and Erich Fromm,[16] has suggested a similar hypothesis in different lan-

[10] For a discussion of this aspect of the Donatist heresy, see Knox, *op. cit.,* chap. iv. Actually the Donatists were never officially ruled heretics, but they were treated as such by Augustine and his bureaucratic descendants.

[11] According to Cole, MacDonald objected to the ILP's "Socialism in Our Time" program because "it would only frighten the electorate and ensure a crushing Labour defeat." *Op. cit.,* p. 198. In contrast, the official 1929 program was, according to the same authority, "a moderate social reform program, in which socialism found neither place nor mention. It was evidently drafted in contemplation of a result to the election which, at best, might enable Labour to take minority office with a stronger backing than in 1924." *Ibid.,* p. 213. Following the 1931 defeat, Lansbury wrote Cripps that Henderson wanted "to trim our sails so as to catch the wind of disgust which will blow ([Mac-Donald]) and his friends out and that he is not anxious to be too definite about Socialist measures as our first objectives. Put them in our programme but be sure when we come to power we keep on the line of least resistance. . . ." Postgate, *op. cit.,* p. 280.

[12] For instance, in both 1924 and 1929, in each case when the Labour party became a minority government, the ILP sought to implement a radical program, knowing that it would bring defeat in Commons. Such a defeat, they urged, would put to the country in stark terms the issue of socialism versus capitalism, and would arouse the working class to full militancy in the class struggle. See Cole, *op. cit.,* pp. 157 ff., 210 ff., 218, 246, 281 ff.; Postgate, *op. cit.,* pp. 225–226, 224; Philip Snowden, *An Autobiography* (London: Nicholson & Watson, 1934), II, pp. 592 ff.; Brockway, *Socialism over Sixty Years,* pp. 206 ff., 214, 229 ff., 253, 259 ff.

[13] As, for instance, when Jowett and Wheatley, ministers in the 1924 government, refused to wear morning dress on a visit to the king; Brockway, *Socialism over Sixty Years, op. cit.,* pp. 208–210; or when Brockway himself, on principled grounds, refused to attend a party given by Lady Astor; *Inside the Left,* p. 201. Surely the high point of this symbolic rejection was achieved by Dr. Salter, a Republican, who kept his hat by his bed so he could quickly put it on when the chimes of a nearby church played "God Save the King" at seven in the morning. Brockway, *Bermondsey Story,* p. 14.

[14] That is to say, definable types. Obviously, a man may have a mixed personality, may be enthusiastic with respect to some things and passive about others. But this differentiation is not important for our purposes; we are solely concerned with the relationship of these types to the operation of social movements. How an individual integrates the different facets of his personality is a problem for the psychiatrist and psychoanalyst.

[15] The distinction between "mass man" and the "aristocrat" developed in *The Revolt of the Masses* (New York: W. W. Norton & Co., 1932).

[16] The quest for autonomous personality which is the central theme of *Escape from*

guage.[17] Following his typology, we might say that the bureaucrat, conditioned and molded by his intense awareness of, and concern for, the opinions of others, both within and without the organization, is "other directed"; whereas the enthusiast, whose actions and beliefs stem from a set of a priori principles, is "inner directed." In fact, bureaucratism and enthusiasm are the "other directed" and "inner directed" facets of the organizational personality.

However, there is one important qualification to the last generalization which, while it narrows the scope of the thesis, serves also to highlight the fundamental difference in orientation of the bureaucrat and the enthusiast. The bureaucrat, a genial eclectic with respect to policy questions, becomes an uncompromising fighter when he feels that the sovereignty or organizational integrity of the group is menaced. The enthusiast, in his pounding pursuit of principle, is often prepared to compromise organizational integrity, to form "Popular Fronts" or "United Fronts" with those who share his ideological assumptions. Against this form of eclecticism, the bureaucrat will wage ruthless war, as he will against the common tendency of the enthusiast to build a faction, a party within a party. As the history of the Catholic church's dealings with heresy will indicate, the bureaucrat is prepared to tolerate a wide range of viewpoints within the organization so long as the viewpoints do not become organized factions, but once the enthusiasts raise the standard of organizational autonomy and attempt to institutionalize their ideas, tolerance ends and is replaced by war to the knife.[18]

To say this is not to impugn the motives of the bureaucrat, to assert that he is a self-seeking Machiavellian who consciously manipulates men and ideas in the effort to gain and maintain power. On the contrary, the significance of this typology lies in large part, at least in our view, in the fact that the bureaucrat *does not* deliberately plan his course. In fact, he often plans very badly what little he does plan, permitting enthusiasts to put organizational integrity in great jeopardy before he realizes that a threat exists, and taking counter-action long after an effective Machiavellian would have gone into action. Thus, it is a cast of mind, a psychological

---

Freedom (New York: Rinehart & Co., 1941), and *Man for Himself* (New York: Rinehart & Co., 1947).

[17] *The Lonely Crowd* (New Haven: Yale University Press, 1950).

[18] This may be true even if the bureaucrat is in ideological agreement with the factionalists, a fact which greatly hindered certain CIO unions in their struggle against communist domination. When an anti-communist district or local decided that secession was their best program, no one could be more ruthless in fighting them than anti-communist bureaucrats who put their organizational loyalty above ideological considerations. See Vernon Jensen, *Nonferrous Metals Industry Unionism, 1932–1954* (Ithaca, N.Y.: Cornell University Press, 1954), *passim,* for some classic examples of this manifestation in the Mine, Mill & Smelter Workers. For a similar French experience, see Val R. Lorwin, *The French Labor Movement* (Cambridge: Harvard University Press, 1955), pp. 125–127.

pattern of reaction, rather than counsels of greed and guile that supplies the bureaucrat with his direction.

It is with this difference in fundamental attitudes that we must concern ourselves now. We make no attempt to discuss the factors that influence human behavior in the directions of enthusiasm and bureaucratism except to note a dissent from any monolithic theory, any rigid determinism. What we are concerned with is not the "Why?" but the "What?"—and we shall limit ourselves to an exploration of the objective aspects of the problem, i.e., the pattern of action and belief that seems to be associated with our two types. Again we must caution that our remarks and definitions will not be applicable to all situations; rather, we are making probability statements which, although they may not subsume each individual case, have aggregate validity.

"Respectable, conventional, orthodox religion," wrote Emrys Hughes, an outstanding Labourite enthusiast, "is something very different from the living faith. And that is also true of politics." [19] Following this line of demarcation, the bureaucrat is the "respectable, conventional," and "orthodox" churchman. The organizational structure, from which he gets profound satisfaction, and with which he identifies himself, exists concretely— he need only look about him or open his desk drawer to appreciate its reality. His patient, untiring, and probably publicly unrecognized labor has gone into its creation, and the stable security that it offers acts as an antidote to his insecurity. Like the men and women who refused to leave slum hovels during intense wartime bombing because these were "home," the bureaucrat has a psychological commitment to the organization that far outweighs any economic attachments. Thus, it may be predicted that the bureaucrat will be reluctant to depart from habitual and tested practices which have fostered the past growth of the organization; he will assuredly take a dim view of experiments, although he will seldom oppose them frontally. He is the past master of the motion "To Table."

In part because he is tradition-oriented, and in part because of the psychological make-up of his opposition, the bureaucrat tends to be antiintellectual. The proportion of intellectuals among enthusiasts is often quite high, although it must be added that in situations where organization and intellectualism have gone hand in hand, for example, in the Church of England, the enthusiasts may rally around anti-intellectualism and antirationalism of the crudest sort. But even given this qualification, the man who causes trouble in an organization must attempt a respectable intellectual case for his position—indeed, in the twentieth century we have seen the irony of intellectuals building an intellectual foundation for antiintellectualism! [20]—and so the bureaucrat grows to look with suspicion on

---

[19] Emrys Hughes, *Keir Hardie* (London: Lincolns-Prager, 1950), p. 5.

[20] Some of the German and Italian justifications for fascism, notably those of Schmitt and Gentile, fall into this category, as do certain contemporary French apologies for communism.

people who think too much, who are always popping up with new ideas. He is likewise suspicious of oratory and big meetings, where his hard-built discipline may tumble before the charismatic charm of an enthusiast-demagogue; his natural habitat is the committee room where even if a Messiah should reveal himself, he would not recruit more than half-a-dozen disciples. In short, the bureaucrat detests and fears unpredictability and the flamboyance with which the unpredictable often gird themselves; the road to his affection and trust is through hard work, patiently and undramatically executed, and acceptance of hierarchical decision-making.[21]

Unlike the bureaucrat, the enthusiast has no tangible symbols to supply him with satisfaction and security; almost by definition, he must believe in the ultimate value of things unseen, and he is likely to scorn institutions as snares set to draw men from the paths of righteousness.[22] While the bureaucrat is an instinctive collectivist, holding as he does an almost Burkean view of the presumptive validity of tradition, the enthusiast is a militant individualist, prepared like Nietzsche's "Super Man" to achieve self-fulfillment at whatever cost to the social fabric. If the bureaucratic personality is dominated by caution and fear of the unorthodox, the enthusiast is a captive of hubris, of cosmic egotism, and of blindness to the fact that "Humanity" is not humanity. He lives in a world peopled by abstractions rather than by human beings, and it is quite possible for him to contemplate, in Koestler's phrase, "sacrificing one generation in the interest of the next." [23]

The ideals which the enthusiast seeks to realize, whether a glorious vision of heaven on earth, the resurrection of a romanticized past, or less ambitious versions of both, are hardly capable of attainment in this imperfect world; indeed, such is the nature of ideals. Yet, gripped by his Promethean quest, the enthusiast never ceases in his effort to storm heaven. Against the skeptical patience of the bureaucrat, he pits his passion and his chiliastic dedication; his is indeed a "living faith." [24]

[21] The respect for "channels" is very great in bureaucratic circles; indeed, one of the main complaints made against the enthusiast is his disregard for them, his willingness to "appeal to the movement" or to the "people" against unpleasant decisions instead of patiently appealing to the various hierarchical bodies in the apparatus, through "channels," for recourse. Much of Aneurin Bevan's unpopularity in the Labour party, notably among the trade-union potentates, is an outgrowth of his lack of respect for decisions collectively made, and his effrontery, as they see it, in appealing these to the wider constituency.

[22] This is particularly true of religious enthusiasts, who generally distinguish between true religion and the church much as Jesus contrasted Judaism with the religion of the Pharisees. See Knox, *op. cit., passim,* and for some rather unfriendly polemics in this vein, *The Journal of George Fox* (Everyman ed.; New York: E. P. Dutton & Co., 1924).

[23] Koestler used this figure of speech in an address in New York some years ago. We have not seen it used in any of his works.

[24] Eric Hoffer observes: "It is the true believer's ability to 'shut his eyes and stop his ears' to facts that do not deserve to be either seen or heard, which is the source of his unequaled fortitude and constancy. He cannot be frightened by danger nor disheartened by obstacles nor baffled by contradictions because he denies their existence. Strength

In the light of this analysis of the two polar types, it might be suggested that each makes a major, and vital, contribution to the organization. Enthusiastic cadres supply it with its ideological dynamic, attempting to make it into a "living faith," while the bureaucrat injects organizational stability and a sense of realism. In the same sense that each type contributes its assets to the group, each also donates its liabilities. From the viewpoint of sound organization, let us now examine their respective contributions in the effort to ascertain what relationship between the enthusiast and the bureaucrat provides the firmest foundation for group success and organizational effectiveness.

The faith of the enthusiast may have negative consequences for an organization in two significant regards. First, his firm belief in the basic articles of his credo may lead him to be dogmatic and doctrinaire and into unfortunate excesses. He frequently offends his non-enthusiastic brethren by the rigidity of his viewpoint,[25] as well as by his semblance of sanctimonious piety.[26] The enthusiast specializes in denouncing organizational shortcomings—falls from grace, so to speak—and this role, no matter how reluctantly or humbly it is performed, creates in the minds of listeners the impression that the speaker considers himself pure and uncontaminated, a saint calling upon sinners to renounce the wicked and their ways. Such homilies can arouse great resentment, and sometimes lead to internecine conflict and schism.[27] Externally, the enthusiast's inability to compromise

---

of faith, as Bergson pointed out, manifests itself not in moving mountains but in not seeing mountains to move. And it is the certitude of his infallible doctrine that renders the true believer impervious to the uncertainties, surprises, and the unpleasant realities of the world around him." *The True Believer* (New York: Harper & Bros., 1951), pp. 78–79.

[25] When MacDonald entered the Dawes Plan negotiations, the ILP demanded that he insist on the total abolition of German reparations, and protested vigorously when all that emerged was a lightening of the German load. Brockway, *Inside the Left*, p. 152. Later, after MacDonald's defection while the regular Labour M.P.'s were seething with hatred towards their former leader, the ILP members aroused much indignation by their attitude of "good riddance." Brockway records that the others were "indignant [at the ILP] because we remained cool amidst their heated denunciations." *Ibid.*, p. 217. This attitude of "we knew it all along" is calculated to win few friends, particularly since there was good reason to believe that the ILP had been right for the wrong reasons.

[26] While Stafford Cripps was probably the leading candidate for canonization, Aneurin Bevan has also been characterized as a "Jeremiah, Cassandra, and guardian of the Holy Socialist tablets." Vincent Brome, *Aneurin Bevan* (London: Longmans, Green & Co., 1953), p. 202. The ILP's conspicuous asceticism and its refusal to participate in the gayer side of Parliament irked many Labour M.P.'s, who looked upon these enthusiasts much as a well-fed Benedictine monk probably reacted to a flagellant friar in an earlier epoch. Brockway, *Inside the Left,* chap. 22.

[27] Thus, the ILP attitude towards MacDonald, and their self-congratulatory pose when he "sold out," led to a hardening of relationships between the ILP and the Labour party. The fact that the enthusiasts had been objectively "right" in their analysis, far from bridging the schism that had been widening throughout the 1929–1931 Labour government, made them absolutely unbearable in the view of the average Labour member. Indeed, the ILP fought the 1931 election as a separate party, although it did not formally disaffiliate until 1932. See Brockway, *Socialism Over Sixty Years,* chaps. 15–17; *Inside the Left,* chaps. 20–22; Cole, *op. cit.,* pp. 274–275.

his principles, and the vigor with which he presses them, is likely to alienate potential organization supporters of moderate views, even if the organization does not accept his doctrines.[28]

A second unfortunate consequence of the enthusiast's "living faith"
is that it warps his own judgment. With his fervor and sense of righteousness, he can easily become a prisoner of his own presuppositions with the
result that the actual world becomes a handmaiden of his abstractions.[29]
Moreover, the more tenaciously the enthusiast embraces his a priori's, the
more he loses sight of the pluralism, the diversity, and the complexity of
the universe, and the more likely will he be to subscribe to a conspiracy
theory which will ascribe his failure in rallying public support to a sinister
plot, to a devil.[30] The consequences of such flights from reality can be
quite serious, for not only do they hinder the enthusiast from fulfilling
his proper calling, but they also lead to a weakening of public confidence
in the organization.[31]

But, while he creates great problems for an organization, the enthusiast can make an enormously significant positive contribution. In the first
place, he supplies a vigor, stemming from his convictions, which is the
sine qua non of effective organization. Paradoxically, it is this vigor and
willingness to work for "The Cause" which forms the foundation of the
bureaucratic apparatus. Beyond this, his originality, initiative, and flamboyance—the characteristics which frighten and unsettle the bureaucrat—
serve as a stimulant and tonic to the whole movement, and act as an effective and necessary antidote to the traditionalism of the bureaucrat.[32] His

[28] The Labour party Executive, for instance, went to great lengths in the late '30's
to "disassociate itself" from certain radical positions taken by the Socialist League which
the anti-Labour press had characterized "as revealing the 'real mind' of the Socialists."
Cole, *op. cit.,* p. 298.

[29] This is particularly true of the enthusiast's approach to war, and to international
relations in general. Rejecting concrete alternatives, he may generally be found clinging
to a "third position," which, if only implemented, would avoid the dangers of war,
oppression, starvation, misery, etc., latent in the other viewpoints. Thus, in recent years,
Labour enthusiasts have raised the slogan: "Neither Washington nor Moscow," and have
attempted to build "third force" sentiment around Jugoslavia and, more recently, India.
See Leon D. Epstein, *Britain: Uneasy Ally* (Chicago: University of Chicago Press, 1954),
passim.

[30] A classic instance of this devil theory in action was the enthusiast's explanation
for the failure of the General Strike of 1926. Although it is quite clear that the strike
was a failure because the average worker was unprepared to become a revolutionary, and,
absent a willingness to start a revolution, the strike had no place to go, the enthusiasts
claimed that the "revolutionary will of the Proletariat" had been betrayed by the union
leadership. Brockway, *Inside the Left,* pp. 192–193. MacDonald's 1931 defection was,
in similar fashion, attributed to Wall Street machinations. Postgate, *op. cit.,* pp. 270–272.

[31] See John P. Roche, "The Crisis in British Socialism," *Antioch Review,* Winter
1952–1953, for a discussion of the consequences of Bevanism on the public view of the
Labour party.

[32] The valuable function that the ILP played in creating and stimulating the
Labour party is emphasized by G.D.H. Cole, *British Working Class Politics, 1832–1914*
(London: Routledge & Kegan Paul, 1946), pp. 250 ff. Henry Pelling, in his excellent
study *The Origins of the Labour Party, 1880–1900* (London: Macmillan & Co., 1954),

idealism and faith contribute an *élan* and a courage, encouraging the movement to expand its horizon and to strike out boldly for new worlds to conquer. Indeed, if we believe with Max Weber that only by reaching out for the impossible has man attained the possible, it is the enthusiast who may bring the movement to the fullest realization of its own potentialities.[33] Thus, the enthusiast injects idealism into hard organizational reality and brings to the movement a priceless leaven.

The second, and equally significant, contribution of the enthusiast is the moral tone which his presence lends to organizational action. His fundamentalism, his very refusal to come to terms with immorality, his frequently prophetic assertion of basic values and aspirations, make him the conscience of the movement, the voice which calls it back to the ways of righteousness.[34] It is this Messianic function of the enthusiast which can serve to counteract the ideological myopia of the bureaucrat, and the latter's tendency to compromise his ideals to the point of extinction.[35] Furthermore, the spirit of self-sacrifice which is characteristic of the "true believer," to use Eric Hoffer's phrase, is a wholesome antidote to the opportunism of the bureaucrat.[36]

While anyone who has read widely in the history of enthusiasm tends to sympathize with the bureaucrat in his endless conflict with "wild men," it must be realized that the bureaucrat, too, has his limitations. Caution and moderation can easily become sluggishness and inaction, and the bureaucrat's dedication to the organizational structure can lead him to an almost paranoidal suspicion of all proposals which involve change.[37] In addition, the collective anonymity of the bureaucracy can encourage an

---

credits the energy of the Socialists with much of the success in creating an independent working class party.

[33] Max Weber in "Politics as a Vocation," *op. cit.*

[34] This was manifestly the outstanding contribution of George Lansbury to his beloved party, as Postgate's excellent biography makes clear.

[35] As, for instance, was the case with the French Socialist deputies who voted *pleins pouvoirs* to Pétain in 1940, or with the German Socialists who became militant chauvinists in 1914 and turned the *Freikorps* on the *Spartakusbund* after the war. See the bitter critique of the latter by Eduard Bernstein, discussed in Peter Gay, *The Dilemma of Democratic Socialism: Eduard Bernstein's Challenge to Marx* (New York: Columbia University Press, 1952). [The *Freikorps* were those German private armies after World War I that fought in the Baltic against the Bolsheviks. These armies were recruited and paid by the German generals who had been retired by the terms of the Armistice—P.T.]

[36] For a discussion of this spirit of self-sacrifice and its ramifications, see Hoffer, *op. cit.*, chap. 13.

[37] Robert Michels has given this ample treatment in his *Political Parties*, cited earlier. The German Social Democrats, who have always suffered from an acute case of over-bureaucratization, supply the best examples of this mentality in action. Of course, because he feels that the bureaucracy is not representative of the true feelings of the movement, the enthusiast is perpetually crusading for structural changes that "will increase grass-roots democracy." The French Socialists have been so successful in this that they have fallen off the other side of the bed; see Philip Williams, *Politics in Post-War France* (London: Longmans, Green & Co., 1954), pp. 60–76.

assembly-line approach to the problems of the membership, a depersonalization of the group's function which it is extremely difficult to counteract. "Rank and file" protests the bureaucrat dismisses scornfully as the work of disgruntled, disappointed office-seekers, because he is incapable of spontaneous action himself and projects his own personality on the organization.[38]

But, probably the bureaucrat's greatest drawback is his inability to dream the enthusiast's dreams, his fundamental lack of empathy. His concentration on organizational problems may lead him to ignore policy and particularly to overlook the relationship between policy and principle.[39] Although, as was suggested earlier, this attitude is seldom founded on conscious Machiavellianism, he often comes to the point where he considers a policy question essentially as an organizational gambit: "What do we stand to gain from it?" Similarly, his dislike for policy formulations which may offend potential supporters can lead to wishy-washy pronouncements which, far from assuaging discordant elements, only aggravate them further and leave nobody happy.[40] In short, the bureaucrat, preoccupied with organizational politics, may treat policy much too lightly and, in his willingness to compromise both policy and principle for the sake of organizational strength, may destroy the ideals and values which the movement was formed to advance, its very *raison d'être*.[41] If the dangers of enthusiasm stem largely from a rigid maintenance of principle regardless of organizational consequences, the abuses of bureaucratism flow from its hyperconcern for organizational consequences and its callous disregard for the movement's fundamental spiritual values.

[38] As is usually the case in a trade union under similar circumstances, the bureaucrat, faced with "rank and file" opposition, inquires cynically, "Whose rank and file?" Similarly, the possibility that two or three people could arrive spontaneously at the same viewpoint never enters his head; his immediate reaction is, "They have a caucus." As a projection of the bureaucratic personality, with all its paranoidal trappings, upon a society, the Moscow Trials have never been equaled. Arthur Koestler implicitly makes this point in *Darkness at Noon* (New York: The Macmillan Co., 1941) when Rubashov, a bureaucrat, is hoist by his own bureaucratic petard. See also Victor Serge, *The Case of Comrade Tulayev* (Garden City: Doubleday & Co., 1950).

[39] Cole suggests that the Labour government was deluded in its notion that it had triumphed in its defeat of the Mosley manifesto in 1930–1931; it might have given this statement far more serious consideration and profited from some of its suggestions. Cole, *op. cit.*, p. 258. As it was, the party's handling of the unemployment crisis bore no visible relationship to the principles advanced by socialists; a capitalist government would probably have acted no differently. See Adolf Sturmthal, *The Tragedy of European Labor* (New York: Columbia University Press, 1943), for a discussion of the socialist dilemma of whether to ameliorate or to eliminate capitalism.

[40] The history of the Italian Socialist party supplies superb examples of the failure of this tactic; the centrists, known variously as "integralists" or "unitarians," regularly worked out compromises which aggravated both the left and the right wings and, if anything, exacerbated internal tensions. See W. Hilton-Young, *The Italian Left* (London: Longmans, Green & Co., 1949).

[41] See, for instance, the flip-flops, rationalized in terms of principles, which various socialist leaders performed on the war issue in 1914; Merle Fainsod, *International Socialism and the World War* (Cambridge, Mass.: Harvard University Press, 1935).

Yet, with all his defects, the bureaucrat, too, makes a precious contribution to the success of the movement. First, by his skepticism about the authoritative nature of the enthusiast's revelation, he provides psychological ballast; his assumption, in George Orwell's brilliant phrase, "that saints must be presumed guilty until proven innocent" [42] helps to keep reason in control and to inhibit potential Peter the Hermit's from dragging the group into some disastrous charismatic crusade. Against the monism of the enthusiast, and the devil theories that so often accompany it, he raises the standard of common sense, asserting that men are men and not abstractions of good and evil. Where the enthusiast is optimistic about man in the abstract, but pessimistic about man in the concrete, the bureaucrat takes the world as he finds it and judges men as men, rather than as "Man," whom he has never met and, probably, never worried about.

Second, the bureaucrat's agnosticism and nominalism—his rejection of the enthusiast's true faith and abstract man—combine to make him profoundly suspicious of short-cuts; he is likely to be satisfied with piecemeal progress, scorning as fatuous and unrealistic the "all or nothing" approach which is so characteristic of the enthusiast. "Half a loaf is 50 per cent better than no loaf," he submits, "and tomorrow we can go after the other half." [43] To this end, he builds his cadres, convinced that ideals are no stronger than the organization engaged in institutionalizing them, and that organized pressure, not doctrinal purity, is the key to success.

Indeed, it is this dedication to technique, to means, which is the bureaucrat's supreme gift to a movement. It is he who builds the instruments of social action, the structural machinery necessary to channel, concretize, and implement the group's aspirations, and it is he who puts organizational flesh on the bones of theory. Denied the vision of the enthusiast, sneered at by the high-flying intellectual, he spends his life in the quagmire of detail, and in so doing renders a unique and invaluable service to his cause. While the enthusiast is out exploring the nature of the cosmos, the bureaucrat is repairing the mimeograph machine; yet, who will deny that a well-working mimeograph is as essential as correct doctrine to the effective operation of a social movement?

Thus, both the bureaucrat and the enthusiast supply a movement with vital components. Each by himself works badly; left alone, the bureaucrat simply goes in concentric circles around his precious organization, while the enthusiast rushes unbridled from one ideological orgasm to another. Consequently, a healthy vital social movement needs both, and profits from their complementary assets. True, there will always be con-

[42] In his "Reflections on Gandhi," in *Essays by George Orwell* (Garden City, N.Y.: Doubleday-Anchor Books, 1954).

[43] This conflict between the "possibilists" and the "impossibilists" has been endemic in socialist movements; see Sturmthal, *op. cit., passim;* as well as in religious organizations; see Knox, *op. cit., passim.*

flict; for, to the bureaucrat, the enthusiast—"impatient," "emotional," "dogmatic," "sanctimonious"—will always *ipso facto* remain a threat to the organization; and, to the enthusiast, the bureaucrat—"timid," "opportunistic," "cynical," "manipulative"—will always seem indifferent to, if not subversive of, the very ideals and values from which the enthusiast draws his inspiration. But this conflict, inevitable as it is, is by no means a mere disruptive influence; on the contrary, it is a life-giving dialectical process in which each force counters the weaknesses of the other, and from which a movement can emerge with both dynamism and stability.

The history of social movements is the history of this conflict. On the one hand, we find groups, such as the German Social Democratic party of 1900–1914, or the American Federation of Labor of 1900–1937, which have been stricken with bureaucratic paralysis and have lost all power to move. On the other, we see those movements, such as the French Socialist party of our era, or the Puritan left of Cromwell's time, which disintegrated or are in the process of disintegrating from the unchecked centrifugal force of enthusiasm triumphant. These are the extremes, for we can also find organizations which have moved on from generation to generation, expanding their horizons as they go, because they have attained a proper balance between these two forces. How this balance is struck is the subject of another analysis; suffice it here to conclude that the struggle between bureaucratism and enthusiasm is part of a larger canvas on which similar battles, between security and freedom, realism and idealism, means and ends, passion and perspective, are waged, and in which the outcome is likewise determined by the extent to which factors which are logically irreconcilable are reconciled.[44]

[44] "Passion and perspective" are the criteria submitted as central to political analysis by Max Weber in his "Politics as a Vocation," in Gerth and Mills, *op. cit.*

56

LEADERSHIP AND PSYCHOSOMATIC ANALYSIS

Alex Gottfried

Perhaps the true nature of the political personality lies in more basic traits than those associated with politics itself. Deeper channels of personality formation account for political styles, any number of which might prove successful in courthouse, statehouse, or on the hustings. At any rate, Prof. Alex Gottfried (b. 1919) has explored this possibility in recounting the political career of "Boss" Cermak, a Democratic Mayor of Chicago who was killed in 1932 in Miami by a bullet intended for President-elect Franklin D. Roosevelt.

*

THE DYNAMIC CONCEPT of personality as propounded by Freud and enlarged or elucidated by other psychologists and analysts, although it has scarcely begun to be exploited by political scientists, has to some degree affected the work of students of political leadership. It is true that most writers, faced with the problem of dealing with the relation between political power and personality, continue to fall back in the main upon describing the manifest traits of the successful politician; but there are few among the more serious students of leadership who do not give at least a passing glance at childhood circumstances, family relationships, and striking evidences of personality disorders in a subject, where these are available.

An additional avenue of insight into the relationship between power

From *Boss Cermak of Chicago* (Seattle, Washington: University of Washington Press, 1962).

and personality has been opened up by clinical research in the field of psychosomatic medicine. The theory underlying the psychosomatic approach to illness is that emotional factors play a causative role in disease. No valid correlation between personality types and diseases has been made; that is to say, there has been found no typical "asthmatic personality," "rheumatoid arthritic personality," etc. On the other hand, correlation does appear to exist between specific emotional conflicts and specific diseases; e.g., in the unconscious of asthmatics a typical conflict-situation will be found.

[I]n a study of the career of the Chicago politician Anton J. Cermak, the literature on psychological factors in disease was of great assistance in an effort to determine the emotional background of the subject's behavior. Among the most conspicuous of Cermak's characteristics were closemouthedness and the absence of personal friendships. He kept no diary, wrote few personal letters, and was the author, with assistance, of only one manuscript. Thus, while many descriptions of the overt features of personality were available from surviving associates and from contemporary newspaper articles, only the crudest sorts of inferences as to the interior organization of personality could be made.

Newspapers, some three weeks following Cermak's death, carried the story that the immediate cause of his death had not been, as had at first been given out, the bullet wound inflicted by Roosevelt's would-be assassin, but rather a case of ulcerative colitis fatally aggravated by the bullet injury. Reports of illnesses, recuperative trips, confinements to bed or hospital, begin to punctuate the record of Cermak's career consistently, beginning with the year 1925, when he was fifty-two years old. These illnesses, even in the more garbled newspaper reports, are described as "gastro-intestinal." Dr. Frank Jirka, Cermak's son-in-law and one of his physicians, stated that the politician's chronic ailment was colitis. These various bits of medical information, which at first appeared to be of no more than ordinary biographical interest, eventually provided a key to the specific emotional needs which had led the subject to seek, and to fight to maintain, political power; which influenced his conduct of political office; and which, to some degree, were responsible for his winning of a following, for his choice of political role, and for the extent and limitations of the power he achieved.

Cermak was born in Kladno, Czechoslovakia, the eldest son of Anton Cermak, a coal miner, and his wife Katherine. The couple emigrated to America in 1874 when Anton, Jr., was a year old, settling near Chicago in Braidwood, Illinois, a mining community heavily populated by Czechs. Moves from Braidwood to Chicago and back again, brought on by the instability of employment in the mines and in the city, recurred throughout Cermak's poverty-ridden childhood. His formal education amounted to a total of approximately three years of elementary school, attended sporadically in Braidwood and Chicago.

Both Cermak parents were physically vigorous, hard-working, and long-lived. The father was the more outstanding personality; he was remembered for his powerful physique even in his old age. The mother was most frequently described as "like everybody else," or "like any other mother." In his own marriage, Cermak repeated the pattern of his parents, choosing a shy, undistinguished partner who, by choice, played absolutely no role in his public life. Cermak's six siblings—four boys and two girls—like the parents were hard-working and reliable, but demonstrated none of the unusual aggressiveness or ambition of the eldest brother. Although his brothers were young men at the time when Cermak began to gain significant political power, none of them attempted to use his influence to any end beyond the retention of the minor public position Cermak obtained for them. Both sisters married within the ethnic group; their husbands were men of no special prominence.

The Bohemian-American family, like the Bohemian-American community, is a close-knit unit; and, in details of behavior relating to the family, Cermak was not atypical of his group. He maintained amicable relations with the members of his immediate family throughout his life. He saw to it that his brothers were put into positions as fortunate as their capabilities allowed; prior to his entrance into politics, he welcomed them into the wood-and-hauling business he established as a youth. As soon as he was able, he became the support of his father and mother; moreover, both parents lived under his roof in Chicago until their deaths. It is said that Katherine Cermak was often approached by friends to intercede with her son for favors and that he never refused a request made through her. With his own children, Cermak's indulgence—even overindulgence—was marked.

Very early—as early as elementary school age—the young Cermak began to exhibit an interest in leading his fellows. Although there was intense enmity between the Czechs and the second largest (and socially dominant) ethnic group in Braidwood, the Irish, Anton, Jr., not only established friendships with Irish boys, but became a ringleader among them. He appears to have accomplished this through a combination of brash derring-do, a quick wit, and a superior physical strength, which he did not hesitate to use in physical encounters. In the acts of vandalism and in the gang fights which occupied boys of his age and economic circumstances in Braidwood, his personal pugnaciousness as well as his strong, stocky physique stood him in good stead.

Cermak entered the Braidwood mines at the age of thirteen—not an unusual age, among Braidwood boys of that time, to leave school and become so employed. His social life, like that of his friends, now centered largely about the Braidwood saloons—although minors were presumably not allowed. In this period, Cermak continued to have a following of youths who regarded him as spirited, popular, and affable. Not all observers, however, were so impressed.

He didn't get along with people. He was always getting into fights. He thought he was a tough guy and could fight. He couldn't leave people alone, and most were afraid of him. Girls were very scared. He would always ask to take them home from dances, and they were afraid because he was mean and drunk, and would say "No." He would then "lay" for the girl and the boy who was walking her home, beat him up, and land in jail. The cop used to say that he never had to go into a tavern and haul him out. All he had to do was wait by the door, and soon he would be thrown out because he was making trouble.

At sixteen, Cermak went to live with a relative in Pilsen, a predominantly Czech neighborhood on Chicago's near southwest side. It was not long before he gained the leadership of one of Pilsen's gangs of young men—an ascendancy which was influential in securing for him his first petty job with the local Democratic organization. By the time he was nineteen he had purchased a horse and wagon and had launched an independent business. He had also become a busy ward heeler. Within two years, his business had prospered sufficiently to allow him to marry; and in two years more he had built a home that was the equal of any in his new neighborhood of Lawndale—the Czech community where he was to maintain residence to the end of his life.

In the years that followed, as his young family and his young business grew and flourished, Cermak was carefully working his way up the party ladder—always rationalizing his political activity on the ground that it was "good for my business"—going from the position of precinct election official to assistant precinct captain, to precinct captain, to bailiff in a justice-of-the-peace court. All the while, he was assiduously building a personal following among his own ethnic group, a following which eventually widened to include Chicago foreign-born in general. In 1902, at the age of twenty-nine, he reaped the rewards of his efforts in the form of nomination and election to his first elective office, that of state representative.

Thereafter, for the thirty-one remaining years of his life, Cermak held virtually uninterrupted elective office—legislative, executive, and administrative, in city, county, and state governments. He rose to the mayoralty in a city which for nearly a hundred years had not recruited a single one of its forty mayors from among the foreign born, and which has not done so again in the . . . years since his death. He died, according to Edward J. Kelly (his successor as mayor and, ultimately, as party chief) the most powerful figure in the State of Illinois and in the history of Chicago.

Needless to say, Cermak did not win his successive political laurels in the guise of the brawling, undisciplined "plug-ugly" he had been as a youth. At the same time, the traits which had characterized his adolescence did not utterly vanish.

His pugnaciousness survived as a dormant threat in his bearing and his manner, which intimidated many people. Even though, as an adult, he did not engage in fisticuffs, "People were afraid he would crack them one." [1] He was, moreover, capable of violent states of rage in which he hurled at those who had offended him not only verbal abuse, but whatever heavy objects happened to be handy.

In his maturity, he by no means took on charm, refinement, or suavity, nor did he learn to cultivate the gentler arts of diplomacy. In interviews with former associates and critics, the descriptive terms, "crude," "blunt," "outspoken," "bullying," "tough," "aggressive," regularly occurred. He appeared to take pride in his own absence of polish. "([The Mayor]) is sure of one thing and that is that it is not through any charm of personality that he has arrived" [2] is only one of many statements made in the same vein throughout his career.

For his success in impressing associates and followers, Cermak depended upon other qualities. A man without formal education, he showed an amazingly wide knowledge of governmental affairs. He was always thoroughly conversant with the remotest aspects of any public problem; he earned, and capitalized on, the title of "a master of detail." He was also a talented and effective party organizer and administrator. In the mayoralty campaign against Thompson, he ran as a "master public executive." In this campaign, as in others, he made little or no attempt to create for himself a "colorful" personality. Far from being jovial, hearty, or outgoing, he gave an impression of withdrawn, absorbed seriousness, even to lumpishness and melancholia—"You couldn't love him." [3]

He was described, even by enemies, as a "man of his word." He never made promises lightly or hastily, but once he had committed himself to a program he could be depended on to act decisively about it. He was frequently described as "courageous" or "fearless." Again, the facts seem to be that he was slow to espouse any public policy, and, in his political life, cannily wed himself only to issues whose popularity was assured. But he would fight all opposition to defend those measures in which he had come to "believe."

"He trusted no one"; he "permitted nothing to happen without his personal knowledge." Cermak's intimate acquaintance with the details of so many public matters was in part the result of his mistrust of co-workers

---

[1] Charles Eaton, who served on the city council with Cermak, in personal interview.
[2] Francis X. Busch, corporation counsel for the City of Chicago during Cermak's majority, in personal interview.
[3] Philip Kinsley, *Chicago Tribune*, March 22, 1931.

and subordinates, a mistrust which appears to have been compounded of the convictions (1) that no one could be trusted to do any given job so well as he; and (2) that no one could be trusted not to attempt to do him personal injury—he was "suspicious," "hostile." He did not like to rely on people. Since delegation was inevitable in the complicated hierarchy of governmental and party affairs, he did a prodigious amount of checking and overseeing. He is known to have employed espionage agents. In addition, he saturated himself with information on any subject with which he was concerned. Thus, he was much less at the mercy of the words and judgments of others.

Cermak is said to have "worked constantly." Journalists, co-workers, and other politicians, all commented on the phenomenon of his indefatigable attachment to work. Frequent illness was not allowed to interfere; even on his deathbed, five days after the shooting, in extreme pain and weakness, he said to Clara D. Beasley [his secretary]: "So you arrived all right . . . you've brought your typewriter, I hope, and plenty of stationery. We've got a lot to do. . . ."

Cermak's ability to work almost literally around the clock was made possible not only by his tremendous reserve of physical energy, but by his absolutely undivided concentration on gaining, maintaining, and expanding his political power and prestige. When persons interviewed compared him to contemporary or past political figures, they invariably assessed him as being, in their experience, the figure with the fewest "soft spots," the fewest extraneous demands upon his time and energies. With the exception of his doting affection for his three daughters, he appears to have had no life and no serious interests outside the political arena. His wife had little in common with him, and he was not in the habit of spending a great deal of leisure time with her—in fact, from the time he became president of the county board, he maintained a downtown hotel room in which it was his habit to work through the night, often not returning home. It was remarked again and again that "he had no personal friends." Such cronies as he did have were always men with whom there was a definite political or business tie; and even with these he "always talked business," he "confided in no one." His apparent indifference to sex was also commented upon: he did not attempt to be gallant, or even sociable, with women. During his long career, no breath of scandal relating to his sexual behavior ever touched him; and in the course of many interviews with enemies who would have been delighted to add to their criticisms of him the charge of sexual looseness, not one made this accusation. In short, Cermak indulged few human claims that could be considered a "waste" from the point of view of power. In line with this sort of orientation, it is notable that characteristically his strongest emotional reactions, in anger or in enthusiasm, were called forth by groups and stereotypes (as, the Czechs, the poor, the Irish), or by causes and ideas (as "personal liberty," World War I, America, the City of Chicago), rather than by particular individuals.

Cermak's attitudes toward wealth deserve some special attention because of the psychological significance of money in the illness from which he suffered. There is no doubt that he revered wealth and respected those who possessed it. He did not take to people who were cultured, but he stood in awe of culture and learning generally; and it may be conjectured that his respect for these was as symbols of wealth. This conjecture is strengthened by the fact that culture without wealth impressed him much less: his respect and deference went to such figures as wealthy banker Melvin A. Traylor, rather than to scholars Charles E. Merriam and Leonard D. White.

Cermak was an excellent businessman and a successful one. His business enterprises, quite apart from any money he made in politics, were sufficient to make him a well-to-do man: he was director of two banks and co-owner of a flourishing real estate business; his property-holdings and other investments were large. It seems clear that he regarded it as of the greatest importance to accumulate wealth. And yet, although he was described by one of his associates as "the most acquisitive man I know," it is significant that he never seriously considered deserting politics for business, even when his political fortunes were at their lowest.

Cermak seems to have had some genuine feeling of obligation to the "less fortunate." He was greatly preoccupied with the "deserving poor" in both his public and his private acts. His charitable activities began in the earliest stages of his career, with the founding and presidency of two organizations devoted to charity—the Bohemian Charitable Organization (1910) and the Bailiffs' Benevolent Association (1912). He also dispensed private charity. According to his eldest daughter, there were often foundlings in the Cermak home, whom Cermak supported until he found homes for them. Gifts were given to poor families every Christmas; and Mrs. Cermak did a great deal of sewing "for the poor." Cermak was very active in initiating, organizing, and supporting public welfare projects during his tenure as county board president—thus gaining, incidentally, a good deal of his support from Chicago "reform elements." Many unofficial charitable activities—such as the presidency of the All-Chicago Christmas Fund and the presidency of the United Charities of Chicago—also figured in this period. Efforts of the official sort in public welfare continued during the mayoralty, growing more prominent as the depression rolled on and the need for them increased. The unofficial charities also kept pace, with Cermak's realty firm donating money to twenty-eight charities, and "Mayor Revealed as Food Provider for Hundreds of Youngsters."

Cermak was often described as ruthless. He, himself, made no secret of his policy of overlooking both personal liking and personal enmity in

the conduct of his political affairs. He cooperated with enemies and attacked friends, as political necessity indicated—"You don't keep books in
politics," being his favorite and often stated maxim. He showed no
sentimentality about firing incompetent employees and eliminating party
rivals. Although neither his stated ethics nor any of his practices was at all
uncommon among his fellow-politicians and fellow-businessmen, the com-
pleteness of his dedication to protecting his position and his seeming im-
passivity in so doing impressed all observers.

Cermak's emotional stolidity, his apparent seriousness of purpose, his
intimidating manner, his absolute refusal to allow his authority to be
questioned in any of the various posts he held—all these doubtless contributed to a central impression of him, held by the greatest number of
observers—that of a dominating, autocratic, czar-like personality.

Having described, in brief, the traits of this political personality as
they appeared to others, the questions arise: what shaped this character;
what necessities lay behind the aggressiveness, painstakingness, ruthlessness,
personal coldness, hostility, and so on? It is insufficient to answer, as it is
often answered, that this man, "like most politicians," was formed by the
"love of power," or the "desire for financial gain." To have said this is
actually to have said very little, inasmuch as "power" and "money" are
not ends in themselves, but serve more deeply rooted complexes of
psychological needs which may vary greatly from individual to individual.

No answer could be anything but partial. Regardless of what psy-
chiatry has to say about the importance of infantile experiences in shaping personality, it cannot be doubted that certain later life experiences,
certain social and economic factors, play a determining part. The data
offered here are not intended to "explain" the life-behavior of the subject,
but only to suggest the category of psychological dynamisms into which
this behavior fits.

The literature on the influence of psychic factors in intestinal disturbances includes cases ranging from chronic diarrhea to cases of mucous
and spastic colitis. Ulcerative colitis, in which ulceration of the large
bowel develops, is the most extreme and dangerous form of the disease.
The symptoms of colitis are painful cramps and frequent evacuations. It
is not known to what extent the different forms of colitis are related.

The general theory underlying the investigations of the influence of
psychic factors on the gastrointestinal system is that those emotions which
cannot, for various reasons, be expressed in overt behavior or through
the sexual apparatus will express themselves through the only outlet left
to them, the internal organs. Diseases of these organs are referred to as
"organ neuroses." "Neurosis" as a general term has been conveniently defined as "the fixed repetition of inappropriate behavior in response to

conflict." In the case of an organ neurosis, this "inappropriate behavior" is not a matter of overt action, as it is in, for example, the case of a compulsion neurosis, but takes place within the body. It is the affected organ that behaves "inappropriately"; i.e., functions improperly, its dysfunction being the response of the individual to a conflict situation. Although inherent constitutional factors may play a part in vulnerability to the disease, certain individual experiences are nevertheless causative.

Three "elemental tendencies" in emotional life are of importance in dysfunctions of the gastrointestinal system. These are: (1) the wish to take or receive; (2) the wish to give or eliminate; (3) the wish to retain. Alexander associates these three emotional tendencies with three types of patients. They are, corresponding to the emotional tendencies just listed: (1) the gastric type; (2) the colitis type; and (3) the constipation type. We will here consider only the gastric and colitis types, in which the same conflict situation is typically found.

In the unconscious of both these types are found intense "oral-receptive" and "oral-aggressive" wishes, that is, exaggerated desires to be loved, to be taken care of, to be dependent and passive, as well as to take, to grab, even to rob. To these desires, the patient reacts with a sense of guilt and inferiority, because of the incompatibility of such longings with the aspirations of the adult ego for independence and activity. The unconscious dependent wishes are strongly repressed in the case of the gastric patient, whose conscious attitude is usually one of extreme independence, self-sufficiency, activity. Unable to gratify his unconscious longing for help, love, and passivity in his conscious behavior, the patient reverts to the infantile mode of gratifying these desires: "the wish to be loved becomes converted into the wish to be fed"; the stomach, under these conditions, "behaves all the time as if it were taking or about to take in food." [4] It is this chronic stimulation of the stomach which leads to such disturbances as epigastric distress, "heartburn," "nervous stomach," and in many cases, ulcer formation.

The colitis patient, like the gastric patient, wishes to overcompensate for his passive, dependent, in-taking wishes with great activity, with giving, and with independence. Where the two types usually differ is in their solutions to this conflict. While the gastric type overcompensates for his dependent receiving and taking desires by real activity and accomplishments, the typical colitis patient has a "violent reluctance to exert himself, to engage in systematic strenuous work, and to fulfill those obligations to which he feels compelled emotionally." [5] Unable to compensate for his dependent desires by real activity and accomplishment, he expresses these in the "tacit language of the body." Whereas the upper end of the

[4] Franz Alexander and T. M. French, *Studies in Psychosomatic Medicine* (New York: Ronald Press, 1948), pp. 116–117.
[5] Franz Alexander, *Psychosomatic Medicine* (New York: Norton, 1950), p. 119.

gastrointestinal tract is peculiarly suited for expressing thwarted desires for receiving, for taking, for dependence and passivity, the lower end of the intestinal tract is especially adapted for expressing thwarted desires, on the one hand, to give and accomplish, on the other hand, to attack. The colitis patient, then, overcompensates for his passive, dependent wishes not through actual efforts to accomplish, but by reverting to the infantile expression of achievement: that is, with attacks of diarrhea. The chronic eliminative pressure on the colon may result in colitis, in the same way that the chronic stimulation of the stomach may lead to ulcer.

Colitis, however, appears not only in patients who manifest this surface flight from activity and responsibility, but also in individuals who for most of their lives manifest the independent, "go-getting" attitudes of the typical ulcer patient. It appears that the desire to give and accomplish may be thwarted, not by the patient's neurotic inhibitions against exerting himself, but by external circumstances. The loss of material wealth figures very prominently among such external circumstances. Patients to whom the power to meet financial obligations is very necessary as a means of overcoming guilt over repressed receptive desires, once deprived of this means, often substitute the infantile "valuable possession." Thus, colitis appears not only in individuals whose dynamic formula is: "I have the right to take and demand, for I always give sufficiently. I do not need to feel inferior or guilty on account of my receptive and grasping wishes, because I am giving something in exchange"; but also in those with the typical gastric-type attitude, i.e., "I do not want to receive or to take. I have no such wishes. I am independent, active, and efficient."

Colitis frequently indicates the patient's fixation on the anal phase of his libidinal development; thus, many of the prevailing traits of the "anal character"—as they have been delineated by Freud, Abraham, Jones, Brill, and other writers—may be found in patients suffering from the disease.

Cermak's surface attitudes throughout his life were those most typical of the ulcer patient rather than of the colitis patient. He showed anything rather than a violent reluctance to exert himself, dependence, or direct demands for affection in most relationships. Occasionally, in illness, he articulated a desire to throw off responsibility ("I'm through, exhausted, and tired of it all"); in particular, Mayor Kelly recalls his having stated to him, not long before the shooting in Miami, when Cermak was in the most deplorable physical condition, that he had no desire "to be mayor or anything else." For the most part, however, even in illness, his active, aggressive, independent manner did not desert him. It is particularly noteworthy that, in spite of the inevitable publicity given his many periods of illness, he was never taunted by political enemies with the accusation of physical infirmity. Of all the people interviewed, only two seemed so much as aware that he was a sick man. One was his son-in-law and private physician, Dr. Frank Jirka; the other was the reporter, John Dienhart, a more than commonly acute observer, who accompanied Cermak on the trip he took to advertise the World's Fair to Europe, during one of his severest periods of illness.

A careful survey of Cermak's power situations at the time of his attacks reveals that the attacks occurred during crises of the kinds described by Alexander as being typical of situations precipitating the disease. The attacks of colitis began at the stage of his career when he had gained most and had most to lose; interestingly, up until this time, he had usually manifested gastric symptoms as well. His attacks occurred in situations where his leadership was being actively challenged; but they continued after he had firmly established his dominance over the party and had gained the mayoralty. It is notable that this period coincided with the worst phase of the depression, when he was continually preoccupied with financial worries, both public and personal. The period of the mayoralty, assumed as it was in 1931, was a time of unceasing anxiety, of public responsibilities that could not be met satisfactorily no matter what dogged efforts were made, of public problems that had no solution. In Cermak's final illness, he appears to have been haunted principally, both in delirium and in his clear moments, by the fear that Chicago's schoolteachers would not be paid.

The dynamic background of Cermak's illness, as formulated by Alexander and other writers, allows us to place this politician rather squarely in the category of power-seeking personalities suggested by Lasswell and a number of psychologists; viz.: those persons in whom the power-urge is a "compensatory reaction against low estimates of the self." Further, the formation of certain specific personality traits, although doubtless influenced by other factors, can be traced to the conflict-situation characteristic of gastrointestinal disturbances. Among these may be counted the propensity to "give to the poor," related to the hidden desires to take, to grab, or to rob, which can only be compensated for in "giving"—in this case, in acts of personal charity as well as through above-average performance in the sphere of public welfare. Again, Cermak's refusal to exert himself to be outgoing, charming, or colorful, his creation of the relatively uninteresting and austere role of the master public executive, his insistence upon relying on his record of dependability, hard work, and thorough acquaintance with any job undertaken, is of a piece with the preoccupation of some colitis patients with giving "real values."

Cermak demonstrated the characteristics of the "anal" person in a whole congeries of related traits: his hostility, suspiciousness, lack of warmth, reluctance to delegate responsibility, unswerving adherence to courses of action agreed upon; and finally, in the central characteristic of his personality, the demand for power.

Cermak's anal characteristics were of the sublimation type rather than of the reaction-formation type. In the former type of orientation, the infantile pleasure in the bowel function and resistance to interference with its control, instead of being repressed to the degree that entirely opposite surface attitudes are formed (i.e., cleanliness, orderliness, parsimony, gentleness, overcompliance, as in the case of a reaction-formation) simply pass over into other areas of life which are structurally analogous. Thus, the "sense of power that accompanies control of the sphincters . . . may be obtained through self-control or the control of other persons." [6] The more intense this infantile experience, the greater may be the subsequent need to satisfy the essentially sadistic urge to wield power.

The explanation of why Cermak should have sought to gratify his power-demands in the area of government must be sought elsewhere than in his individual infantile experiences. It may be said in passing that government in the modern urban environment, as has often been observed, offers opportunities for the exercise of as nearly naked control and power as is sanctioned in our society. Moreover, Cermak's own ethnic group, the Czechs, set an unusually high premium upon political power, their adulation and respect going first not to the businessman, the intellectual, or the artist, but to the politician.

The anal personality has been described as withdrawn from others; he seeks security by making himself an autarchic, self-sufficient system, and feels love or any other outgoing attitude as a threat to his security. Abraham explains the inability to love thus: the child will have the earlier-mentioned sense of pleasure and accomplishment in its bowel function if the period of training is not forced upon him before he is "psychically ready for it." This psychical preparedness only appears when the child begins to transfer to others—its mother, for example—the feelings that were originally bound narcissistically. If the child has acquired this capacity to identify with others, it will perform its function "for the sake of" others; but if the training is forced upon it too soon, it will acquire the habit through fear, its inner resistance remains; "its libido will continue in a tenacious narcissistic fixation, and a permanent disturbance of the capacity to love will result." [7]

It seems fair to assume, then, on the basis of the foregoing summary, that a number of related traits manifested by Cermak—his suspiciousness, his hostility, the apparent impoverishment of his personal relations, his seeming indifference to sex—had deeper roots than the conscious desire to protect his political position. It is significant, however, that all these traits, so negative from the point of view of human intercourse, should have proved useful in the career of a political power-seeker.

Cermak's desire to rely upon no one but himself, his insistence on

[6] Otto Fenichel, *Outline of Clinical Psychoanalysis,* trans. Bertram D. Lewin and Gregory Zilboorg (New York: Norton, 1934), p. 430.

[7] Karl Abraham, *Selected Papers* (New York: Basic Books, 1957), p. 374.

checking all personnel and all details of every operation, and his adherence to his "political word" are characteristics commonly found in certain types of anal personalities. Jones says that such persons are "equally hard to move to a given course of action as to bring them from it once they have started on it," and relates this stubborn persistence to the infantile pleasure in control of the sphincters. In all these traits there is manifest the "self-willed independence" of some anally fixated personalities, a confidence in personal powers which makes it difficult for the individual to believe that anyone delegated to do a task can do it properly. Jones cites the case of Napoleon as an example of the type who ". . . organizes an elaborate system which functions marvellously well while its author, with tireless energy, attends in person to every detail, but which runs the risk of collapse as soon as the master hand is inactive; for, having assumed it all himself, he has given no one else the chance of being trained in responsibility." [11] Cermak's career offers a microcosmic parallel here. He was responsible for the organization of the first cohesive, city-wide party machine, comparable to Tammany Hall, that Chicago had ever known. So complete was his grasp of the organization, so tirelessly had he eliminated possible pretenders, that on his death there was no one to step into his shoes.

As will be apparent from the material presented here, it should be possible, given an acquaintance with the literature of psychoanalysis, to form a working theory as to the psychological background of the behavior of a given political figure out of descriptions of his overt behavior or from direct observation of it. The presence of disease offers a slightly more reliable guide, in that the fact of disease—provided it is firmly established —is irrefutable, while the impressions of observers with regard to the behavior of any political subject are subject to certain biases. The literature on psychic factors in disease is as yet incomplete, but the material thus far published should prove valuable in many individual and comparative leadership studies.

[11] Ernest Jones, *Papers on Psychoanalysis* (Baltimore: Williams & Wilkins, 1938), pp. 415–416.

PART EIGHT

Some Practical Proposals

57

SUMMARY RECOMMENDATIONS

President's Commission on Campaign Costs

Money, the pressure of money, has long been thought by students as well as the cynic in the street to be the source of much that is evil in politics. Regulation, however, has tended to be unrealistic and unnecessarily stringent, perhaps out of misplaced moral concern. Statutes setting fixed, low limits of campaign expenditures are routinely honored by impudently innocuous reports that campaigns cost exactly what the laws allow. Loopholes so obvious that resort to them cannot rightly be called evasions permit the expenditure of nearly $200,000,000 in recent presidential campaigns. Fears are often expressed that politics will become a rich man's sport and that huge sums will buy elections. Wealth is an advantage, no doubt about it, especially when campaigning for the nomination; but even Kennedys and Rockefellers raise more money than they spend from personal sources. As for buying elections, it still happens, here and there, but participation and observation suggest that the evil lies more in promises made in raising funds than in those secured by its expenditure. The instruments of modern campaigning—pre-eminently television time, travel, and printed materials—are expensive. To reduce the hazards to the public interest, this commission appointed by President Kennedy recommended that the nation experiment with tax deductions for limited political contributions.

*

Members of the President's Commission on Campaign Costs

ALEXANDER HEARD, *Chairman*
 Dean of Graduate School, University of North Carolina
 Author, *Costs of Democracy,* Financing American Political Campaigns

From *Report of the President's Commission on Campaign Costs* (Washington: U. S. Government Printing Office, 1962).

V.O. KEY, JR.
Professor of Government, Harvard
Author, *Politics, Parties and Pressure Groups*

DAN A. KIMBALL
President, Aerojet-General Corporation
Secretary of Navy, 1951–1952
Chairman, Southern California Democratic Committee for Kennedy-Johnson, 1960

MALCOLM C. MOOS
Professor of Political Science, Johns Hopkins University
Adviser to Rockefeller Brothers on public affairs
Administrative assistant to President Eisenhower, 1958–1961

PAUL A. PORTER
Lawyer
Chairman, Federal Communications Commission 1944–1946
Director, campaign publicity for the Democratic National Committee, 1944

NEIL O. STAEBLER
Democratic national committeeman, Michigan

WALTER N. THAYER
President, New York Herald Tribune
Member, United Republican finance committee of New York, 1954–1960

JOHN M. VORYS
Lawyer
Member, U. S. House of Representatives 1939–1959 (Ohio–R.)

JAMES C. WORTHY
Lawyer
Assistant Secretary of Commerce, 1953–1955
Member, Republican National Finance Committee, 1959–

THE FAITH of the American people in constitutional government has been regularly renewed by an uninterrupted series of presidential elections. This testing of the popular will every four years has survived many periods of crisis and change. Presidential campaigns and elections over the decades have served as shining emblems of effective democracy, opening new doors of hope to people seeking freedom all around the world.

In 1960, approximately 150 foreign correspondents covered each of the two presidential nominating conventions. Some seventy-five of them accompanied each of the presidential and vice-presidential candidates during some portion of the campaign. On election day itself, 56 of 86 accredited embassies responded positively to President Eisenhower's suggestion that teams of observers be sent to view, at first hand, the manner of holding presidential elections in different parts of the United States. In addition, from at least twenty nations came groups composed primarily of scholars who studied the campaign in minute detail.

These observers saw a presidential campaign molded by the long heritage of American political life, a heritage consistently embracing two important elements: (1) a profound belief in widespread citizen participation; and (2) an equally deep belief in voluntary action—a belief that politics should be animated by the voluntary efforts of individuals, groups, and organizations rather than by government.

Many problems have been encountered in the long story of presidential campaigns, campaigns varying from that of 1860 when Abraham Lincoln never left Springfield nor made a single speech, to that of 1960 when John F. Kennedy made 360 speeches while traveling 44,000 miles in forty-three states, and Richard M. Nixon gave 212 speeches and journeyed 65,000 miles through fifty states.

No problem, however, has become more troublesome than that of providing adequate financial support for campaigns.

A chronic difficulty in maintaining adequate support has long been the lurking suspicion that contributing to political parties is somehow a shoddy business. This is unfortunate. Improvement of public understanding of campaign finance is essential. This commission hopes the American people will come to regard contributions to parties with the same sense of obligation they display toward contributions to educational and charitable institutions.

Active, widespread political participation is the key to successful democracy in the United States and voluntary effort is the great sustaining force of our political parties.

The rocketing costs of presidential campaigns, and the recurring difficulties parties encounter in meeting these costs, require us to seek new methods and incentives for financing our political parties.

We agree with [the late] President Kennedy, former President Eisenhower, and other leaders of both parties that the existing system of presidential campaign finance poses serious problems. It is not desirable to have candidates for high office, especially for president and vice president, dependent on individuals or organizations with special interests who are willing to make large contributions in the form of cash or campaign services. As President Kennedy has stated, "it is not healthy for the democratic process—or for the ethical standards in our government—to keep our national candidates in ([the present]) condition of dependence."

Many of the existing legal regulations of campaign finance have become a mockery. They are not realistic in light of today's campaign requirements. As a consequence, many provisions of the law are evaded or avoided, a condition contributing to the unfavorable climate that has surrounded fund-raising efforts.

In this climate, the political parties have found it increasingly difficult to meet satisfactorily the "great financial burdens" of presidential campaigns noted by the president. Further, the parties have lacked the continuity of leadership and the staff necessary for efficient fund raising and campaigning.

Mindful of these problems, we have sought to find ways that

presidential candidates, and the political parties supporting them, can be helped in raising funds;
public confidence in the ways these campaigns are financed can be increased;
public respect for the system of legal regulation can be instilled; and
presidential campaign costs can be reduced.

There is a wide range and diversity of opinion as to how the problems of financing presidential campaigns can best be solved. We have had the benefit of hundreds of suggestions from experienced individuals and organizations who are knowledgeable about financing political activities. We have considered these suggestions in the light of three basic beliefs shared by all members of the commission:

(1) In a strongly organized and effectively functioning two-party system;
(2) In widespread participation by citizens in the political system through the political party of their choice; and
(3) In the desirability of voluntary, private action—wherever such effort will suffice to meet the common needs of the society.

While our recommendations are directed toward problems of presidential and vice-presidential campaign finance, in accordance with our charge, our recommendations carry implications for campaigning for other offices. We are aware of the possibility of overemphasis of a presidential campaign to the detriment of congressional, state, and local races, but it is our view that the measures we propose would have a desirable effect on all political fund raising.

We recommend:

(1) That individuals and private organizations—including corporations, labor unions, farm organizations, civic societies, and other appropriate groups—be encouraged to take part in and to make expenditures for voluntary *bipartisan* political activities, and where an individual or organization is subject to taxation, that the reasonable costs of such activities be declared a deductible expense for tax purposes.

(2) That for an experimental period extending over two presidential campaigns:

Political contributors be given a credit against their federal income tax of 50 per cent of contributions, up to a maximum of $10 in credits per year;

Contributors be permitted, alternatively, to claim the full amount of their contributions as a deduction from taxable income up to a maximum of $1,000 per tax return per year;

The only contributions eligible for these benefits be ones made to the national committee of a party, and to a state political committee designated by such a national committee (provided that no more than one committee per state be designated by a national committee).

(3) That an effective system of public disclosure be adopted which requires that the principal sources and uses of money in presidential campaigns be reported to a Registry of Election Finance;

That, toward this end, periodic reports be submitted by all political parties, committees, and other campaign groups receiving or disbursing as much as $2,500 per year, any part of which aided a presidential or vice presidential candidate for nomination or election;

That such reports show total income and outgo, and itemize contributions that aggregate $250 or more from one source (including purchases of tickets to dinners or other fund-raising events), expenditures of $100 or over and transfers of funds and debts;

That candidates for nomination or election to those offices be required to submit similar reports;

That any individual or family (husband, wife, and dependent children) contributing to the above committees as much as $5,000 in the aggregate in a single year, or spending and contributing a combined total of that much on behalf of such a candidate or candidates, shall also submit reports of such disbursements;

That similar reports of both direct or indirect expenditures be required of individuals and groups taking part or spending money in bipartisan political activities as urged in our first recommendation, if such expenditures total $5,000 or more in a year; and

That the present meaningless ceilings on individual contributions and on total expenditures by political committees be abolished.

(4) That the present equal treatment of corporations and labor unions by Section 610, Title 18, *United States Code,* that prohibits direct, partisan campaign contributions and expenditures, be maintained and strictly enforced.

(5) That all other statutes regulating the financing of political parties and candidates be vigorously enforced.

(6) That the political parties take full advantage of opportunities to modernize and increase the effectiveness of their fund-raising practices.

(7) That research to increase campaign efficiency and help reduce campaign waste be encouraged among individuals and organizations, public and private.

(8) That the Congress provide funds to pay the reasonable and necessary costs of preparing and installing in office new administrations during the "transition" period between the election and inauguration of a new president.

(9) That a further temporary suspension of section 315 of the Federal Communications Act be enacted to permit broadcasters to make

their facilities available on an equal basis to the nominees of the major political parties for president and vice-president without the legal compulsion of doing likewise for minor party candidates for those offices.

(10) That a nonpartisan White House Conference on Campaign Finance be called by the president of the United States to launch broad solicitation programs by all parties following the adoption of measures to stimulate such giving, such a conference to include representatives designated by the important political parties, as well as representatives from various sectors of political life and the communications media, and to lay the groundwork for further continuing efforts to encourage voluntary, private action in meeting campaign costs.

(11) That the several states consider measures similar to those recommended in this report along with others that would help to reduce the costs of campaigning and make it easier for the parties and candidates to meet them, and that the Post Office Department make its change-of-address files available to the parties as well as to election boards as a way of assisting in local registration drives.

(12) That, after a trial period with the measures here proposed, the president should provide for another nonpartisan evaluation of presidential campaign finance, and that, if the objectives sought by our proposals have not been realized, study be given to additional measures to achieve them, especially a "matching incentive" system to stimulate party solicitation.

58

SUGGESTED REGULATIONS

The Association of the Bar of the City of New York

Under the direction of the remarkable and prestigious Association of the Bar of the City of New York, a study of conflicts of interest in federal service resulted in the recommendations presented here. While recognizing the danger of "over-reaction to an occasional instance of misconduct" among government employees, the lawyers went into considerable regulatory detail at the agency level and called for presidential promulgation of more general regulations.

*

.　　　.　　　.

NOT ALL AREAS of conduct calling for controls on conflicts of interest can be treated by statute. The program advanced here assumes particularized regulation at the agency level. It also calls for presidential promulgation of a body of general regulations under the statute [model suggested by the Bar Association]. One of the main functions of the proposed Administrator would be study and preparation of such regulations; but the subject and range of some of these regulations can be foreseen.

GENERAL INTERPRETATION

Several critical phrases in the statute have been drafted in anticipation that interpretative regulation will fill in detail.

Reprinted by permission of the publishers from The Association of the Bar of the City of New York, *Conflict of Interest and Federal Service*, Cambridge, Mass.: Harvard University Press. Copyright 1960 by The Association of the Bar of the City of New York Fund, Inc.

Under section 3, an official is required to disqualify himself from action where he has a "substantial economic interest." Supporting regulation should be drawn setting minimum standards, built upon the principle that an economic interest is not "substantial" unless it is such as to be likely to influence the action of a reasonable man—or to cause the public to think that it would. It is not likely that the regulations could set up standards in dollar or other numerical terms, but guidance could be provided by listing factors to be considered and indicating something of the weight to be given to different factors. The difficulty of drawing lines in this field should not lead the Administrator to yield to the temptation to interpret every economic interest, however trivial, as ground for necessary disqualification. The statutory use of the term "substantial" is important and deliberate.

PENSION AND GROUP SECURITY PLANS

Technical implementing regulations must be promulgated under the outside compensation section to spell out the details of the statutory scheme for permitting retention of certain pension, insurance, and other rights under security plans. The necessary general criteria are set forth in the statute.

JOINT CLAIMS

A technical problem, under sections 4 and 8, that has received no attention in the past should be mentioned as appropriate for regulatory action. These sections prevent an employee or former employee from assisting others in certain adversary situations vis-à-vis the government, but preserve to the employee himself his personal rights to protect his own interests and claims against the government (subject, of course, to the disqualification rule). The employee must be able to fight out his own income tax problems with the internal revenue service, for example. In some situations, however, certain conduct on the employee's part in support of his personal rights may not be acceptable. Consider, for instance, a government employee who owns a small part of a large tract of land being condemned by the government. Clearly he can press his claim for damages with full vigor. But ought he to assume a position of leadership in organizing all the other landholders and financing their activities to try to block the entire project—by court action, administrative process, and legislative lobbying? Or, consider a government employee with a real though relatively small interest in an oil company that is pressing for transfer of federal off-shore oil rights to state control. To what extent may he participate in the effort to bring about the transfer? Such questions cannot be answered in the statute. It is important to be aware that the necessary and legitimate statutory exclusion of personal claims of employees can, in some circumstances, be abused. Regulatory recognition of the problem in advance could do something to head it off.

GIFTS

The statute expressly calls for regulatory exceptions, and without such supplementation is unworkably stringent. These regulations are of special importance and should be accorded top priority by the administrator. In particular, the recurrent problem of the business lunch and the small gratuity should receive prompt regulatory attention.

SALE OF INFORMATION AND SPECULATION

Much of the private law on the question of the fiduciary loyalty of an employee to his employer has revolved about two situations. In the first, the employee acquires a useful piece of business information, such as a trade secret or a list of customers, and then either sells this information to a competitor or sets up business [in direct competition] on the basis of the information. In the second, the employee in the course of his work learns of information that can be turned to his personal economic advantage, whereupon he makes off with the business opportunity and does not turn it over to the employing company. For centuries, the courts have been seeking to work out the proper limits of the scope of duty of different kinds of employees in different kinds of situations to their employers.

These situations are not exactly analogous to the situation of most government employees, though in some cases the circumstances overlap. The reason is that normally the government is not itself looking for business opportunities; but, closely similar problems can arise. When they do, they are severely aggravated by the ingredient of public confidence that is involved when the parties are the government and an official. Suppose an employee of the air force learns that an air base is to be built in a particular location, and promptly runs out to buy up land in the area. Or, suppose he sells this information to some other person who buys up the land. He has clearly violated a confidence, used his office to line his own pocket, and probably has cost the government money. Or, consider another somewhat different case. An employee of the agriculture department learns that the department will soon announce that much of the wheat crop is infected with hay fever fungus, and, with this advance knowledge that the price of uninfected wheat will skyrocket, he plunges into wheat futures. Here, the government is not directly, economically, and adversely affected by the employee's action. Nonetheless, this is clearly intolerable behavior and inconsistent with the fundamental injunction not to mix up public and conflicting private interest.

Existing conflict of interest statutes do not treat either the sale or misuse of government information or speculation, though there are special statutes dealing with protection of agriculture statistics, trade secrets, and income tax data. No separate statutory provision on information sale is included in the new statute, primarily because of drafting problems. Some agencies have general regulations respecting speculation, but more carefully drawn and wider-ranging regulation is needed on this point.

Fundamentally, regulation should make it clear that no government employee shall sell or use for the purpose of personal economic advantage any information which he acquired solely by virtue of his official position and which is not public information; but, serious difficulties arise from such broad restrictions. The distinction between legitimate long-term investment, and speculation on the basis of a hot tip, is frequently hard to detect. Furthermore, information has a way of resisting compartmentation, and we often cannot avoid using information to which we have been exposed as it melds into what we call experience. In the case of the scientist who learns, while in government employment, something of a new technique, or a government lawyer who acquires extensive knowledge of the tax laws, what begins as information becomes fused into a body of professional knowledge and skill, and conflict of interest regulations must not be so broadly drawn as to prevent the use of such professional skill. Finally, regulations on sale of information pose delicate questions of freedom of speech, freedom of inquiry, and the importance to the public of keeping information channels open from inside government to the public outside. For example, the public interest requires that, subject only to security requirements, autobiographies, memoirs, and other writings of men who have retired from government be open to the public eye. Many observers feel that there are already too many muffles on the release of information from inside government.

Information control is difficult, but the difficulty of the job does not mean that the job itself must be abandoned. The principle is certainly clear: a government employee should not be able to use inside government information as a commodity for sale or as a device to hold up the government or as a basis for speculation.

CONTRACTING OUT

Earlier chapters have pointed out the extent to which the government looks to independent contractors for the performance of services. Such contracting out is essential to the government's operations. Specialists—whether for operating cafeterias, developing an engine, setting up a filing system, or designing war games—can, through the contracting-out arrangement, be brought in on an *ad hoc,* short-term basis to help the government where it needs help. These specialists are sometimes individuals; more often they are specialized professional or semi-professional institutions or companies. Often, the contracting-out arrangement makes it possible to attract the services of specialists who would not be willing to serve as direct employees of the government, mainly because of low salary scales, but also because of the generally more regulated environment.

The relationship of conflict-of-interest regulation and the contracting-out practice is ticklish. Legally, the party contracting to perform the services is an "independent contractor" and not an "employee." As such, he is not subject to the existing statutes and regulations respecting government employees. Yet, in particular cases, the work being performed by the specialist-contractor can be identical with that which he would perform if the legal arrangement between him and the government were that of employee and employer. In these functionally identical situations, all the conflict of interest problems of one are mirrored in the other. The only significant exception to this statement arises from the fact that there is less of an identification in the public's eye between the contractor and the government. Thus, in the public's view of appearances, the contractor is not in as sensitive a position with respect to conflicts of interest as is the employee.

An over-all statutory solution is impossible. As described earlier, the variety of different kinds of contractual relationships between outsiders and the government is endless. Especially in the case of the specialist organization, there can be no workable general rule defining the reach and scope of the possible particular conflict of interest restrictions. To use an admittedly extreme example, if General Motors contracts to design and develop a new rocket, which, if any, of the conflict of interest rules should be applied to which employees of General Motors? the limitations on outside compensation? or the restrictions on assisting outsiders? Would the rules include employees of subcontractors? General Motors as a corporation? all employees of General Motors? only those working in the project? only executive personnel working on the project? The questions multiply easily.

Again, the service contract, in which a private concern and government work closely together, illustrates the interpenetration of public and private, characteristic of this century. Yet, the normal and useful contracting-out arrangement can be abused for the purpose of evading conflict of interest regulation. How this can be prevented—in what circumstances and by what techniques—is another important problem facing the administrator.

Until the basic pattern of regulation of employees is settled, and until many more facts are in hand respecting the conflict of interest risks arising from contracting out, any effort to spell out rules applicable beyond the category of employees is premature. The statute, therefore, stops at the point of recognition of the problem, but specifically calls on the administrator to undertake and conduct, in conjunction with agency heads, a study of the extent to which principles of the statute should be made applicable to persons having contracts, subcontracts, licenses, or the like, with or from the United States, and to their employees.

ADVISORY COMMITTEES

As the use of advisory committees has increased, pressure to regularize the procedures of these committees has mounted. The Attorney General has been motivated by antitrust considerations to promulgate a government-wide code on the procedural practices to be followed by such committees. Similarly, legislation was introduced in the Congress, in 1957, proposing an over-all set of procedures designed to put more direct responsibility in the regular-employee members sitting with the committees.

The problem, as usual, is easier to state than to resolve. Advisers should advise, and the decisions should be made by the regular government employees: this, in general, is the right formula for the new era of government-private cooperation. Realistically, however, it is often a most difficult standard to apply. It assumes that the government has in its regular service men of a professional competence that enables them, regardless of the circumstances to make a reasonable choice among several alternatives presented to them by the private members of the advisory committee. Frequently, particularly in areas of the most advanced technology, the number of men able to deal with the particular problem is so limited, and the likelihood that one of them will be a permanent employee of the United States Government is so small, that as a practical matter the advice tendered by the private advisory committee can resolve the issue on the table, regardless of the form in which the meeting is conducted. Nonetheless, there are clear protections to the government in keeping the chairmanship of these committees in government hands, in requiring fixed agenda, and in making serious efforts to obtain several sides of controversial decisions.

One of the more difficult, and more interesting, tasks that would confront the administrator under the proposed statute would be a study of procedures of these advisory committees from the point of view of conflicts of interest. In the preparation of regulations, great effort must be made not to impose upon all agencies an identical pattern that may work well in some but be ill-adjusted to the needs of others. Flexibility at the agency level is essential. . . .

59

SPECIAL MESSAGE ON CONFLICTS OF INTEREST

John F. Kennedy

Early in his term, the late President John F. Kennedy (1917–1963) sent to Congress the following message concerning conflicts of interest among federal appointees. The message was based on a number of studies, including that by Senator Paul Douglas (see Chapter 6), but was most heavily influenced by the work of a panel appointed by President Kennedy immediately after his inauguration. His intense interest was stimulated no doubt by the acute difficulties inherent in finding men willing and able to take on important government assignments who did not possess large interests in business concerns doing government or government-related work. At the same time, the need for safeguards against the abuse of public trust for private gain were never more important. The President's recommendations emphasized recruiting from the "entire reservoir of talent and skill," and he took the position that "no web of statute or regulation" could cope adequately with the range of challenges to integrity actually offered in public life.

*

TO THE CONGRESS OF THE UNITED STATES

No responsibility of government is more fundamental than the responsibility of maintaining the highest standards of ethical behavior by

Text of President's message on conflicts of interest, submitted to Congress, April 27, 1961.

those who conduct the public business. There can be no dissent from the principle that all officials must act with unwavering integrity, absolute impartiality and complete devotion to the public interest. This principle must be followed not only in reality but in appearance; for the basis of effective government is public confidence, and that confidence is endangered when ethical standards falter or appear to falter.

I have firm confidence in the integrity and dedication of those who work for our government. Venal conduct by public officials in this country has been comparatively rare—and the few instances of official impropriety that have been uncovered have usually not suggested any widespread departure from high standards of ethics and moral conduct.

Nevertheless, in the past two decades, incidents have occurred to remind us that the laws and regulations governing ethics in government are not adequate to the changed role of the Federal Government, or to the changing conditions of our society. In addition, many of the ethical problems confronting our public servants have become so complex as to defy easy common sense solutions on the part of men of good will seeking to observe the highest standards of conduct, and solutions have been hindered by lack of general regulatory guidelines. As a result, many thoughtful observers have expressed concern about the moral tone of government, and about the need to restate basic principles in their application to contemporary facts.

Of course, public officials are not a group apart. They inevitably reflect the moral tone of the society in which they live. If that moral tone is injured—by fixed athletic contests or television quiz shows—by widespread business conspiracies to fix prices—by the collusion of businessmen and unions with organized crime—by cheating on expense accounts, by the ignoring of traffic laws, or by petty tax evasion—then the conduct of our government must be affected. Inevitably, the moral standards of a society influence the conduct of all who live within it—the governed and those who govern.

The ultimate answer to ethical problems in government is honest people in a good ethical environment. No web of statute or regulation, however intricately conceived, can hope to deal with the myriad possible challenges to a man's integrity or to his devotion to the public interest. Nevertheless, formal regulation is required—regulation which can lay down clear guidelines of policy, punish venality and double-dealing, and set a general ethical tone for the conduct of public business. Such regulation—while setting the highest moral standards—must not impair the ability of the government to recruit personnel of the highest quality and capacity. Today's government needs men and women with a broad range of experience, knowledge and ability. It needs increasing numbers of people with top-flight executive talent. It needs hundreds of occasional and intermittent consultants and part-time experts to help deal with problems of increasing complexity and technical difficulty. In short, we need to draw on America's entire reservoir of talent and skill to help conduct our generation's most important business—the public business.

This need to tap America's human resources for public purposes has blurred the distinctions between public and private life. It has led to a constant flow of people in and out of business, academic life, and government. It has required us to contract with private institutions and call on part-time consultants for important public work. It has resulted in a rapid rate of turnover among career government employees—as high as 20 per cent a year. As a result, it has gravely multiplied the risk of conflicts of interest while seriously complicating the problem of maintaining ethical standards.

These new difficulties and old problems led me to appoint, immediately after my inauguration, three distinguished lawyers to review our existing conflict of interest laws and regulations. This panel was composed of Judge Calvert Magruder, retired chief judge of the First Judicial Circuit; Dean Jefferson B. Fordham of the University of Pennsylvania Law School; and Professor Bayless Manning of the Yale Law School. The proposals put forward in this message are in large measure based on their work and that of others who have considered the problems in recent years.

The recommendations of this panel were arrived at after careful study and review of the work of other groups, particularly the 1958 staff report of the Anti-Trust Subcommittee of the House Judiciary Committee under Congressman Celler; the pioneering study in 1951 by a subcommittee of the Senate Committee on Labor and Public Welfare under Senator Douglas; the recent report of the staff of the Senate subcommittee on National Policy Machinery of the Committee on Government Operations headed by Senator Jackson; and valuable appraisals conducted during the last administration by the executive branch, and by the Association of the Bar of the City of New York.

All of these studies have emphasized the seriousness of the problem encountered. All have recommended that our outmoded and hodge-podge collection of statutes and regulations be amended, revised, and strengthened to take account of new problems. If the proposals have varied in their details, all have underscored the need for legislative and executive action in a commonly agreed direction.

Statutory Reform

There are seven statutes of general application termed "conflict-of-interest" statutes. Many others deal with particular offices or very limited categories of employees. These latter usually exempt officials from some or all of the general restrictions. Occasionally they impose additional obligations.

The seven statutes cover four basic problems:

The government employee who acts on behalf of the Government in a business transaction with an entity in which he has a personal economic stake.

The government employee who acts for an outside interest in certain dealings with the government.

The government employee who receives compensation from a private source for his government work.

The former government employee who acts in a representative capacity in certain transactions with the government during a two-year period after the termination of his government service.

Five of these statutes were enacted before 1873. Each was enacted without coordination with any of the others. No two of them use uniform terminology. All but one impose criminal penalties. There is both overlap and inconsistency. Every study of these laws has concluded that, while sound in principle, they are grossly deficient in form and substance.

The fundamental defect of these statutes as presently written is that: On the one hand, they permit an astonishing range of private interests and activities by public officials which are wholly incompatible with the duties of public office; on the other hand, they create wholly unnecessary obstacles to recruiting qualified people for government service. This latter deficiency is particularly serious in the case of consultants and other temporary employees and has been repeatedly recognized by Congress in its enactment of special exemption statutes.

Insofar as these statutes lay down the basic law restricting the private economic activities of public officers and employees, they constitute a sound and necessary standard of conduct. The principle which they embody in varying form—that a public servant owes undivided loyalty to the government—is as important today as when the first of these statutes was enacted more than a century ago. However, the statutory execution of this principle in the seven statutes of general application was often directed to specific existing evils which at the time of their enactment were important political issues. As a result, large areas of potential conflict of interest were left uncovered.

For example, where some of these conflict-of-interest statutes are restricted to "claims of money and property"—as the courts have said—they do not protect the government against the use of official position, influence, or inside information to aid private individuals or organizations in government proceedings which involve no claims for money or property. Yet the danger of abuses of government position exists to an equal if not greater degree in proceedings such as license applications for television or radio stations, airline routes, electric-power sites, and similar requests for government aid, assistance or approval.

Thus, literally read, it would be a crime punishable by fine or imprisonment under these statutes for a postal clerk to assist his mother in filing a routine claim for a tax refund, but it would be permissible for a cabinet officer to seek to influence an independent agency to award a license for a valuable television station to a business associate in a venture where he shared the profits.

There are many other technical inadequacies and statutory gaps. Section 434 of title 18, born of the Civil War procurement scandals, prohibits a government official interested in the pecuniary profits of a business entity from acting as an officer or agent of the United States for the transaction of business with that business entity. By limiting its scope to "business entities" the statute does not cover the many other organizations which deal with the government. In addition, the concept of "transacting business," if narrowly construed—as would be likely in a criminal prosecution—would exclude many dealings with the government, such as the clearance or rejection of license applications in the executive branch or before an independent agency.

Similar defects exist in the case of government officials who have left government service. Clearly such an official should be prohibited from resigning his position and "switching sides" in a matter which was before him in his official capacity; but, for technical reasons, the statutes aimed at this situation do not always hit the mark. There is nothing in the criminal statutes which would prevent the general counsel of the Federal Power Commission from resigning to represent an unsuccessful license applicant who is contesting the commission's decision in the courts (although such conduct might be grounds for disbarment). A commission employee who was not a lawyer could, in the present state of the law, unscrupulously benefit in such a case from his "inside information" without fear of sanctions.

But, if the statutes often leave important areas unregulated, they also often serve as a bar to securing important personal services for the government through excessive regulation when no ethical problem really exists. Fundamentally, this is because the statutes fail to take into account the role in our government of the part-time or intermittent advisors whose counsel has become essential but who cannot afford to be deprived of private benefits, or reasonably requested to deprive themselves, in the way now required by these laws. Wherever the government seeks the assistance of a highly skilled technician, be he scientist, accountant, lawyer, or economist, such problems are encountered.

In general, these difficulties stem from the fact that even occasional consultants can technically be regarded as either "officers or employees" of the government, whether or not compensated. If so, they are all within the prohibitions applicable to regular full-time personnel.

A few examples illustrate some of the difficulties:

Section 281 of the Criminal Code forbids public employees from providing services to outsiders for compensation in connection with any matter in which the United States is interested and which is before a department, agency or commission.

This section makes it almost impossible for a practicing lawyer to

accept a part-time position with the Government. He would be in violation of Section 281 if he continued to receive compensation for cases before government agencies, or even if his law partnership receives such
compensation, though he personally has no connection with any case. It
is usually impractical for the law firm to withdraw from all transactions involving the government; and almost all law firms have some tax
matters, for example, as part of their normal business. The same prohibition unfairly affects accountants.

In addition, the two existing postemployment statutes raise serious
problems in terms of recruiting noncareer personnel (particularly lawyers). Enacted at different times, they employ different terms and are totally uncoordinated in language or in policy.

The criminal statute (18 U.S.C. 284) forbids a former employee for
two years after his government employment ceases to prosecute in a
representative capacity any claim against the government involving a
"subject matter" directly connected with his government job. The civil
statute (5 U.S.C. 99) forbids employees of an executive department for
two years after the end of their government service from prosecuting in a
representative capacity any claim against the United States, if the claim
was pending before "any department" while he was an employee.

These prohibitions are unnecessarily broad. They should be confined
to "switching sides." For example, they now prohibit a lawyer who worked
for the Department of Labor from subsequently representing a client in a
wholly unrelated tax matter which had been before the Treasury during
his government service.

These restrictions prove an even more formidable barrier to the part-
time consultant who works in a partnership since he and his partners
would be excluded from participation in many, if not all, claims against
the government—a severe and unnecessary penalty for contributing to
public service. It is possible to cite many other examples of excessive restrictions which serve no ethical purpose, but effectively bar government
from using available talent.

It is true that a large number of statutory exemptions passed at various times over the years have mitigated some of the adverse effects of these
statutes on certain specific individuals and certain categories of employees. However, no uniform standard of exemption has ever been adopted by
the Congress in enacting these exemptions. Many of the exemptions are
inconsistent. Some exemptions are subject to so many limitations as practically to nullify them. Some statutes unqualifiedly exempt categories of
employees from all of the conflict statutes. Others exempt them from some
but not all of the restrictions. The resulting hodge-podge of exemptions
seriously weakens the integrity of the government personnel system.

To meet this need for statutory reform, I am transmitting to the
Congress a proposed Executive Employees' Standards Act—a comprehensive revision of existing conflict-of-interest statutes. I believe that this bill

maintains the highest possible standards of conduct, eliminates the technical deficiencies and anachronisms of existing law, and makes it possible for the government to mobilize a wide range of talent and skill.

First, the bill closes gaps in regulation, of the type discussed above, and eliminates many of the pointless differences in treatment. For example, no longer will some former government employees be subject to more severe restrictions simply because they once worked for one of the ten executive "departments" rather than in an agency which is not technically a department.

Second, the bill overrules existing judicial interpretation that only when a claim for money or property is involved is a former government employee prohibited from working for a private interest in a matter for which he once had governmental responsibility. The basic issue of integrity is the same if the matter relates to government regulation rather than to a property or money claim.

Third, the bill establishes special standards for skilled individuals whose primary activity is in private professional or business life, but whose skills are used by the government on a part-time or advisory basis. By permitting such individuals to carry on private business, even business with the government, as long as there is no direct conflict between their private and public work, ethical principles are maintained and a wide range of abilities are made available to government.

Fourth, this bill adds to the traditional criminal sanctions by permitting agency heads to adopt implementing regulation and impose disciplinary measures. Most of the existing laws are criminal statutes. As such, they have been strictly construed and, because of their harshness, infrequently invoked. By granting this added flexibility we help to ensure more effective enforcement. In addition, the regulations which are adopted will permit more specific adaptation of the general prohibitions tailored to the activities of particular agencies.

Fifth, the bill deals only with employees involved in executive, administrative, and regulatory functions. It does not apply to either the judicial or legislative branch of government. Existing laws relating to the judiciary are deemed adequate. The adequacy and effectiveness of laws regulating the conduct of members of Congress and Congressional employees should be left to strictly Congressional determination.

Sixth, the proposed bill covers the District of Columbia and its employees. However the District—essentially a municipal government—has its own distinctive problems. I will submit legislation dealing with these problems in the near future.

Ex Parte Contacts with Officials of Independent Agencies

Some of the most spectacular examples of official misconduct have involved *ex parte communication*—undisclosed, informal contact between an agency official and a party interested in a matter before that official.

Such covert influence on agency action often does basic injury to the fairness of agency proceedings, particularly when those proceedings are judicial in nature.

This problem is one of the most complex in the entire field of government regulation. It involves the elimination of ex parte contacts when those contacts are unjust to other parties, while preserving the capacity of an agency to avail itself of information necessary to decision. Much of the difficulty stems from the broad range of agency activities—ranging from judicial type adjudication to wide-ranging regulation of entire industries. This is a problem which can best be resolved in the context of the particular responsibilities and activities of each agency.

I therefore recommend that the Congress enact legislation requiring each agency, within 120 days, to promulgate a code of behavior governing ex parte contacts within the agency specifying the particular standard to be applied in each type of agency proceeding, and containing an absolute prohibition against ex parte contact in all proceedings between private parties in which law or agency regulation requires that a decision be made solely on the record of a formal hearing. Only in this manner can we assure fairness in quasi-judicial proceedings between private parties. The statute should make clear that such codes, when approved by Congress, will have the force of law, and will be subject to appropriate sanctions.

Executive Orders and Presidential Action

There are several problems of ethics in government which can be dealt with directly by Presidential Order, Memoranda or other form of action.

First, I intend to prohibit gifts to government personnel whenever (a) the employee has reason to believe that the gift would not have been made except for his official position; or (b) whenever a regular government employee has reason to believe that the donor's private interests are likely to be affected by actions of the employee or his agency. When it is impossible or inappropriate to refuse the gift it will be turned over to an appropriate public or charitable institution.

Such an order will embody the general principle that any gift which is, or appears to be, designed to influence official conduct is objectionable. Government employees are constantly bothered by offers of favors or gratuities and have been without any general regulation to guide their conduct. This order will attempt to supply such guidelines, while leaving special problems, including problems created by gifts from foreign governments, to agency regulation.

Second, I intend to prohibit government employees from using, for private gain, official information which is not available to the public. This regulation will be drawn with due regard for the public's right to proper access to public information. A government employee should not be able to transform official status into private gain, as is done, for example, if a government employee speculates in the stock market on the basis of advance knowledge of official action.

Third, I am directing that no government employee shall use the authority of his position to induce another to provide him with anything of economic value whenever the employee has reason to believe that the other person's private interests may be affected by the actions of the employee or his agency.

This regulation is an effort to deal with the subtler forms of extortion where an employee acquiesces in the gift of an economic benefit, or gives a delicate indication of receptivity. The criminal law deals with outright extortion. Beyond this, the problem is too elusive for the criminal law and must be dealt with by administrative regulation, and by the sound judgment of the administrator.

Fourth, I am directing that no government employee should engage in outside employment which is "incompatible" with his government employment. The outside employment of government employees is one of the most complex and difficult of all ethical problems. It is clear that some forms of employment may have benefits to the government or society (e.g., teaching in universities), or be beneficial to the employee and not inconsistent with his government work. On the other hand, some types of outside work may involve exploitation of official position or be incompatible with the best interests of the agency to which the employee owes his first allegiance.

Since "incompatibility" of employment will depend on many varied factors, its definition will be left to agency and department regulation and case-by-case rulings.

Fifth, I will shortly issue an Executive Order regulating in more detail the conduct of those officials who are appointed by the president. These high level officials owe a special responsibility to the government and to the employees of their departments to set a high standard of ethical and moral behavior. Therefore, the Executive Order (a) prohibits outside employment or activity of any sort incompatible with the proper discharge of official responsibility; (b) prohibits outside compensation for any activity within the scope of official duty; (c) prohibits the receipt of compensation for any lecture, article, public appearance, etc., devoted to the work of the department or based on official information not yet a matter of general knowledge.

Sixth, In carrying out the provision of law, I will apply government-wide standards to the continuance of property holdings by appointees to the executive branch. The law prohibits any conflict of the public and private interests of employees of the government. The Senate, in the exercise of its power of confirmation, has taken the lead in requiring that presidential appointees sell their property holdings in cases where retention of property might result in such a conflict of interest. The problem of property ownership by executive appointees is properly a matter of continuing congressional concern, and I welcome the initiative taken by the Jackson Subcommittee on Conflict of Interest. At the same time, the executive branch has an obligation to ensure that its appointees live up to the highest standard of behavior. It is to carry out this responsibility that I will apply general standards governing the ownership of property by presidential appointees—standards which will ensure that no conflict of interest can exist. It is my hope that these regulations will aid the Senate in the uniform exercise of its own responsibility.

The Administration of Ethical Standards

Criminal statutes and presidential orders, no matter how carefully conceived or meticulously drafted, cannot hope to deal effectively with every problem of ethical behavior or conflict of interest. Problems arise in infinite variation. They often involve subtle and difficult judgments, judgments which are not suited to generalization or government-wide application. And even the best of statutes or regulations will fail of their purpose if they are not vigorously and wisely administered.

Therefore, I am instructing each cabinet member and agency head to issue regulations designed to maintain high moral and ethical standards within his own department. These regulations will adapt general principles to the particular problems and activity of each agency. To aid in the administration of these regulations, each agency will establish an ad hoc committee to serve in an advisory capacity on ethical problems as they arise.

Although such agency regulation is essential, it cannot be allowed to dissolve into a welter of conflicting and haphazard rules and principles throughout the government. Regulation of ethical conduct must be coordinated in order to ensure that all employees are held to the same general standards of conduct.

Therefore I intend to designate, in the Executive Office of the President, a single officer charged with responsibility for coordinating ethics administration and reporting directly to the president. This officer will:

prepare, for presidential proclamation, general regulations as needed;
develop methods of informing government personnel about ethical standards;
conduct studies and accumulate experience leading to more effective regulation of ethical conduct, including the formulation of rules in areas which are not yet regulated, such as government use of outside advisers and the contracting of government services to private institutions or firms; and
clear and coordinate agency regulations to assure consistent executive policy.

Such an officer will not only provide central responsibility for coherent regulation, but will be a means through which the influence of the presidency can be exerted in this vital field.

Conclusion

Ultimately, high ethical standards can be maintained only if the leaders of government provide a personal example of dedication to the public service—and exercise their leadership to develop in all government employees an increasing sensitivity to the ethical and moral conditions imposed by public service. Their own conduct must be above reproach. And, they must go beyond the imposition of general regulations to deal with individual problems as they arise—offering informal advice and personal consideration. It will often be difficult to assess the propriety of particular actions. In such subtle cases, honest disclosure will often be the surest solution; for, the public will understand good faith efforts to avoid improper use of public office when they are kept informed.

I realize, too, that perhaps the gravest responsibility of all rests upon the office of president. No president can excuse or pardon the slightest deviation from irreproachable standards of behavior on the part of any member of the executive branch. For his firmness and determination is the ultimate source of public confidence in the government of the United States. And there is no consideration that can justify the undermining of that confidence.

60

PROMOTION OF PUBLIC CONFIDENCE IN THE INTEGRITY OF CONGRESS AND EXECUTIVE BRANCH

Clifford P. Case

Disclosure has long been a favored weapon of reformers. On its power, alone, all manner of public evil has been reduced or eradicated. Senator Clifford P. Case of New Jersey (b. 1904) has for some time sought to turn the clear light of publicity on the sources of income of major public servants and on the efforts of his fellow congressmen to influence the flow of business before federal regulatory agencies. Formally, his efforts have come to naught; the bills he has introduced lie, unattended, in the files of the committee of "appropriate reference." Yet, informally, there may be some headway. In 1964, each candidate for President and Vice President felt obligated to make public report on the extent of his personal fortune and the nature of his holdings. Good newspapers, active questioning, and the interest of voters' groups could do as much for other major offices. But, if disclosure is a good idea, it probably must become a matter of law to be effective.

*

MR. PRESIDENT, I introduce, for appropriate reference, a bill designed to improve the public service. This bill is the result of much concern and several years of thought on how best to maintain high standards in both Congress and in the executive branch of government.

Speech in the United States Senate, August 1, 1958.

The bill has four major provisions:

(1) The requirement that members of Congress, and all employees of the executive and legislative branches of the government earning in excess of $12,500 a year and candidates for federal office file an annual report of income, including reimbursement for any expenditure, gifts in excess of $100 in amount or value, fees or honorariums for speeches or articles, and the monetary value of subsistence, entertainment, travel, and other facilities received by an individual in kind, and all dealings in securities, commodities, or real property during the year. These reports would be filed with the comptroller general and would be open to the press and the public.

(2) The requirement that all communications, whether written or oral, including those from Congress and the executive branch, with respect to any case pending before a federal agency be made a part of the public record of such case.

(3) A requirement that committees of the Senate and the House file annually itemized expense accounts for all travel, subsistence, or accommodations used by members of such committees or staff members. The reports shall be published in the *Congressional Record*.

(4) The establishment of a commission on legislative standards to conduct a study of problems of conflicts of interest and of relations with executive agencies which confront members of Congress, with a view to devising and recommending measures and procedures to deal with such problems. This would include such problems as that of disqualification of particular votes and the often difficult determination of the line between adequate representation of constituent interest and attempted influence.

The key section of this bill is the first one. The requirement for disclosure of gifts and fees received by members of Congress or federal employees will serve as a brake on both those who would influence and those who would be influenced. When an individual realizes a gift will be a matter of public record, he is likely to give additional consideration to the propriety of the gift. The principle involved is similar to that employed in the Federal Lobbying Act and the proposed Federal Elections Act.

The mere existence of such a report will make it easier for the legislator and the policymaker to reject such gifts.

This bill would apply to all persons in the upper grades who are likely to be in a position to make or influence policy in the executive branch. It would also apply to persons at equivalent levels in the services and in the legislative branch. In fairness to incumbent members of Congress, it would also include candidates for Congress. It is possible that the scope of this bill is too large. I feel it is better to err on the side of inclusion, rather than to permit any important class of officials to be exempted. If experience indicates the need for amendments, they can be made.

Respect for privacy is deeply ingrained in Americans. I value it highly myself; but, reluctantly, I have concluded that in this instance an overriding public interest makes necessary the disclosure of information for which my bill would provide. Action is necessary, and I am convinced that it would be far more effective to turn the spotlight of publicity on all gifts and favors, than to attempt to draw a line between those which are proper and improper. My bill would require public officials to exercise their own judgment in acceptance of favors, and then would give the public the chance to decide whether the judgment exercised was sound.

61

REPORT OF THE SPECIAL
COMMITTEE ON ETHICS,
NEW YORK STATE LEGISLATURE

The disclosure that seven state legislators had taken a Caribbean cruise at the expense of the Association of New York State Savings Banks hastened the appointment by legislative leaders of a citizens' committee to study and recommend improvements in the New York State Legislature's code of ethics.

Cloyd Laporte, chairman of the New York City Board of Ethics and law partner of former Governor Thomas E. Dewey, was selected to head the committee composed of State Controller Arthur Levitt and Cornell University law professor Gray Thoron.

The reaction of a state senator who went on the cruise was: "Why bring it up now? These trips have been going on for seventeen years."

*

WE RECOGNIZE that members of the Legislature and legislative employees are required by the demands of their constituents to maintain frequent liaison with state agencies and to seek appropriate action with respect to countless administrative requests. We do not seek to discourage this traditional practice and consider it an essential part of their duties so long as it is done with propriety and without compensation.

We do, however, recommend that members of the Legislature and legislative employees be prohibited from practicing or appearing before most state agencies for compensation.

We would except from this prohibition practice before the Depart-

---

From *The New York Times*, March 9, 1964. Copyright © 1964 by The New York Times.

ment of Taxation and Finance, and the Division of Corporations and State Records in the Department of State, and practice involving claims for workmen's compensation, disability benefits and unemployment insurance. These exceptions seem necessary and appropriate to avoid impinging on the right of a large number of professional people to pursue important and normal aspects of their private callings.

We would also except representational activity which is incidental to a larger employment or in which the action of the agency is primarily ministerial.

Finally, to avoid hardship to clients as well as to their representatives, we are recommending a provision which would exempt pending matters from the prohibition.

We do not imply by our recommendations that the appearance of legislators before agencies of the Government in behalf of private interests necessarily involves the exercise of undue influence. We recognize, however, that state administrators are in many respects subject to the control of the Legislature, which approves their budgets, including their salaries, and may change or limit their jurisdiction. These circumstances provide an appearance of impropriety which is almost as damaging to public confidence as actual impropriety would be.

Practice before the Court of Claims

We recommend that members of the Legislature and legislative employees be prohibited from practicing before the court of claims.

The adoption of this recommendation would bring the practice in the State of New York into accord with the federal rule which for over a century, has prohibited members of Congress from practicing in the United States Court of Claims. The jurisdiction of the New York Court of Claims, like that of the United States Court of Claims, is limited to cases in which the government is the defendant and involves solely the award of public funds.

In the City of New York councilmen are prohibited from appearing as counsel or giving opinion evidence against the interests of the city in any litigation to which the city, or an agency thereof, is a party. Our recommendation in this respect, we believe, would counteract any impression on the part of the public, however unjustified it may be, that members of the legislative branch of government have a special advantage over others in representing claimants. This recommendation is in no way intended as a reflection on the integrity, fairness, or impartiality of any judge or any member of the Legislature.

As in the case of state agencies, we have suggested a provision which would exempt pending cases.

We believe that the recommendations relating to the prohibition of practice by members of the Legislature and legislative employees before state agencies and the court of claims, if adopted, would greatly enhance public confidence in the Legislature.

GIFTS, TRAVEL, ENTERTAINMENT, AND HOSPITALITY

We recommend that there be added to Section 73 of the Public Officers Law a new subdivision prohibiting members of the Legislature and legislative employees from soliciting or accepting gifts of substantial value, including loans, travel, entertainment and hospitality, under circumstances in which it could be reasonably inferred that the gifts were intended to influence, or could reasonably be expected to influence, the performance of official duties or were intended as a reward for official action. The recommended prohibition would extend to those who give as well as to those who receive.

DISCLOSURE

Financial Interests in Regulated Activities

We recommend that the provisions of Section 74(3)(j) of the Public Officers Law requiring the disclosure of direct or indirect financial interests in regulated activities be transferred to Section 73, which would make its violation punishable as a misdemeanor; that the $10,000 minimum interest requiring disclosure be eliminated; and that a requirement of annual filing be established.

Legislative Rule Concerning Disclosure of Financial Interests

We recommend adoption by the Legislature of a rule requiring any member having a substantial financial interest, not shared by the general public, in a legislative proposal to file a statement before promoting or opposing the proposal. The same requirement would apply where the interest is that of the legislator's client or of someone with whom the legislator has an employment, business, or family relationship and where the legislator is aware of the existence of such interest. These statements would be open to public inspection.

We considered the advisability of recommending disclosure as a condition precedent to voting on proposals before the Legislature. However, a large number of bills are introduced and voted upon in each session of the Legislature covering a wide variety of subject matter. In the closing days of a session a legislator must rely upon committee recommendations with respect to many bills; he may not be able to analyze every bill to be certain that no conflict exists. We therefore concluded that a requirement of disclosure prior to voting would place an undue burden on legislators.

We also considered whether there should be a rule prohibiting voting where a conflict of interest exists. This would not only be difficult for the reasons above stated, but it would preclude many classes of citizens such as farmers from being represented by persons who were sent to the Legislature partly for the purpose of voting in favor of their interests. Moreover, since a majority of all members is required to pass a bill, a failure to vote amounts to a vote against a bill. To prohibit voting would, therefore, in effect compel negative votes.

STATE ETHICS COMMISSION

We recommend the establishment of a State Ethics Commission consisting of six members, three appointed by the governor and three elected by the Legislature in joint session. The commission's function would be to render advisory opinions on request interpreting legislation and rules relating to ethics. The services of the commission would be available to all state officers and employees, so that uniformity of ethical standards may be achieved.

This proposal would provide machinery for continuing guidance on ethical standards and for the development of a meaningful body of case-by-case precedents. It would also provide a method by which persons, unjustly accused of improper conduct, could obtain vindication.

In 1954, the Legislature, recognizing the need for an agency to perform this function, established an advisory committee in the Department of Law. This advisory committee, composed of able and distinguished citizens, has made its services available to the attorney general. If the single centralized agency which we propose is established, the functions of the advisory committee will no longer be necessary.

OTHER PUBLIC OFFICERS

In accordance with the concurrent resolution, we have confined our proposals principally to ethical standards as they affect legislators and legislative employees. We believe that the principles underlying our recommendations are generally applicable to other public officers, and we suggest that this subject is a proper one for further legislative action.

62

LEGISLATORS VOTE OWN
ETHICS CODE

The New York Times

New York State lawmakers reacted sharply and promptly to the Laporte Committee report. For the most part, they reacted negatively. Despite the disclosures of questionable practices—representation of private interests before public bodies, for example—despite the fact that other legislative bodies prohibit such practices, the state legislators looked on the recommended code as an admission of guilt, when, as they saw it, the only thing required was an exercise in public relations. This news item from The New York Times *tells how they voted when the question was put to them.*

*

THE LEGISLATURE gave final approval tonight to its own version of an ethics code for legislators.

In doing so, it turned down the proposals of the Laporte committee, which the Republican legislative leaders appointed late last year to recommend ways of strengthening the existing code. The existing code was adopted ten years ago and has not been changed.

Tonight's action disposed of one of the top issues that remained to be resolved before adjournment, which is scheduled for Wednesday.

The Laporte committee, which was headed by Cloyd Laporte, chairman of the New York City Ethics Committee, was denounced in both houses. Legislators said the committee's report had left implications of wrongdoing by lawmakers.

The Senate, which acted first, had before it only the rules committee bill. It approved the measure, 54 to 1.

In the Assembly a companion bill, and two bills incorporating the recommendations of the Laporte committee, were debated together.

The Assembly approved the companion bill, 142 to 4, then recommitted the Laporte bills when a show of hands indicated overwhelming opposition to bills. However, twenty-one assemblymen were recorded against the motion to recommit the first of the bills and fifteen against recommitting the second.

While there were a number of differences between the proposed codes, the principal conflict was over a recommendation by the Laporte committee to prohibit lawyer-legislators from practicing before the court of claims and before most state agencies.

The Legislature's bill would permit such practice but would make it unlawful for legislators to accept cases on a contingent fee basis.

The approved bill also sets up restrictions for accepting . . . and tendering gifts, including entertainment, and expands the present legislative committee available to provide guidance on ethical questions.

The only vote against the bill in the senate was cast by Frank Glinski, Democrat of Buffalo, who explained:

"By voting for a code we ourselves are pleading guilty that maybe we need a code. I have the Ten Commandments, and I have my integrity, and as far as I am concerned that is enough."

He declared that the Legislature would be "losing the confidence of the public by voting for a code," and added, "if we have nothing to hide, why have we a code at all."

That was approximately the sentiment of the four assemblymen, all Republicans, who opposed the bill. They were Assemblymen Joseph C. Younglove of Johnston, Robert Hatch, Jr., of Onondaga, Verner M. Ingram of St. Lawrence, and Robert A. Blakeman of Nassau.

In addition to barring practice before state agencies and the court of claims on a contingent basis, the approved code would also do the following:

Make it a misdemeanor to accept any gift, including money, service, loan, travel entertainment, or hospitality having a value of $25 or more if it could reasonably be inferred that the gift was intended to influence official actions.

Require the disclosure of any stock interest in a business regulated by the state, instead of just amounts of $10,000 or more as is now required.

Bar companies in which any legislator has a stock interest of 10 per cent or more from providing goods or services of $25 or more to any state agency, except on a competitive bid basis.

Require legislators to list offices in any corporations and to disclose any other relationships that might reasonably be expected to be particularly affected by legislative action.

The expanded advisory committee will be comprised of the two standing committees on ethics, plus the dean of the Albany Law School and the president of the New York State Bar Association.

Also included in the bill are a list of "general standards" to help legislators avoid compromising situations. It admonishes them not to use their official positions to obtain special privileges, to avoid employment that could affect their independence, to avoid seeking advantage from the possession of confidential information, and to pursue a course of conduct that will not arouse public suspicion that a trust might be violated.

The bill, which will become effective December 31, if signed by Governor Rockefeller, applies also to employees of the Legislature.

John Hughes, Republican of Syracuse, spoke longest during the senate debate and devoted much of his remarks to an attack on *The New York Herald Tribune,* although he did not name the paper.

A series of articles in that newspaper concerning alleged conflicts of interest was among the developments that preceded the appointment of the Laporte committee.

"I don't think the members of the Legislature need anyone to tell them what their ethics should be," he said.

Senate Majority Leader Walter J. Mahoney did not speak. The minority leader, Joseph Zaretzki, said that possibly some members of the Senate had made mistakes in judgment "public relations-wise" and that the new code would be "a guide for public relations."

The assembly debate was led off by Assemblyman Donald Campbell of Amsterdam, chairman of the Assembly Ethics Committee.

Referring to newspapers, he declared that "the Legislature has been indicted by a forum from which there is no appeal." Urging defeat of the Laporte bills, he declared the Legislature should not be "coerced" into accepting them.

Eight other assemblymen participated in the attack, and only two, Daniel Kelly and Albert H. Blumenthal, both Democrats from Manhattan, defended the Laporte proposals.

Referring to these, a Brooklyn Democrat, Lawrence Murphy, declared: "I resent their report and if I could vote against it five times I would."

PART NINE

The Citizen as Politician

63

THE PRACTICAL REFORMER

Theodore Roosevelt

Theodore Roosevelt (1858–1919), twenty-sixth President of the United States, played politics with the same gusto that he gave to war and big game hunting. His disdain for those who kept their virtue in their hand-kerchiefs for use only on ideal occasions was rarely more apparent than when he encountered criticism of the "practical reformer" as an opportunist or dupe of the bosses. His argument that politics is not an impossible career for a man of intelligence, sensitivity, and integrity is more cogent and more valid now than when it was made.

*

.   .   .

ALL MEN in whose character there is not an element of hardened baseness must admit the need in our public life of those qualities which we somewhat vaguely group together when we speak of "reform," and all men of sound mind must also admit the need of efficiency. There are, of course, men of such low moral type, or of such ingrained cynicism, that they do not believe in the possibility of making anything better, or do not care to see things better. There are also men who are slightly disordered mentally, or who are cursed with a moral twist which makes them champion reforms less from a desire to do good to others than as a kind of tribute to their own righteousness, for the sake of emphasizing their own superiority. From neither of these classes can we get any real help in the unending struggle for righteousness. There remains the great body of the people, including the entire body of those through whom the salvation of

From Theodore Roosevelt, "Latitude and Longitude among Reformers," *The Strenuous Life: Essays and Addresses* (New York: The Century Company, 1901).

the people must ultimately be worked out. All these men combine or seek to combine in varying degrees the quality of striving after the ideal—that is, the quality which makes men reformers—and the quality of so striving through practical methods—the quality which makes men efficient. Both qualities are absolutely essential. The absence of either makes the presence of the other worthless or worse.

If there is one tendency of the day which more than any other is unhealthy and undesirable, it is the tendency to deify mere "smartness," unaccompanied by a sense of moral accountability. We shall never make our republic what it should be until as a people we thoroughly understand and put in practice the doctrine that success is abhorrent if attained by the sacrifice of the fundamental principles of morality. The successful man, whether in business or in politics, who has risen by conscienceless swindling of his neighbors, by deceit and chicanery, by unscrupulous boldness and unscrupulous cunning, stands toward society as a dangerous wild beast. The mean and cringing admiration which such a career commands among those who think crookedly, or not at all, makes this kind of success perhaps the most dangerous of all the influences that threaten our national life. Our standard of public and private conduct will never be raised to the proper level until we make the scoundrel who succeeds feel the weight of a hostile public opinion even more strongly than the scoundrel who fails.

On the other hand, mere beating the air, mere visionary adherence to a nebulous and possibly highly undesirable ideal, is utterly worthless. The cloistered virtue which timidly shrinks from all contact with the rough world of actual life, and the uneasy, self-conscious vanity which misnames itself virtue, and which declines to cooperate with whatever does not adopt its own fantastic standard, are rather worse than valueless, because they tend to rob the forces of good of elements on which they ought to be able to count in the ceaseless contest with the forces of evil. It is true that the impracticable idealist differs from the hard-working, sincere man who in practical fashion, and by deeds as well as by words, strives in some sort actually to realize his ideal; but the difference lies in the fact that the first is impracticable, and not in his having a high ideal, for the ideal of the other may be even higher. At times, a man must cut loose from his associates and stand alone for a great cause; but the necessity for such action is almost as rare as the necessity for a revolution; and to take such ground continually, in season and out of season, is the sign of an unhealthy nature. It is not possible to lay down an inflexible rule as to when compromise is right and when wrong; when it is a sign of the highest statesmanship to temporize, and when it is merely a proof of weakness. Now and then, one can stand uncompromisingly for a naked principle and force people up to it. This is always the attractive course; but in certain great crises it may be a very wrong course. Compromise, in the proper sense, merely means agreement; in the proper sense opportunism should merely mean doing the best possible with actual conditions as they exist. A compromise which results in a half-step toward evil is all wrong, just as the opportunist who saves himself for the moment by adopting a policy which is fraught with future disaster is all wrong; but no less wrong is the attitude of those who will not come to an agreement through which, or will not follow the course by which, it is alone possible to accomplish practical results for good.

These two attitudes, the attitude of deifying mere efficiency, mere success, without regard to the moral qualities lying behind it, and the attitude of disregarding efficiency, disregarding practical results, are the Scylla and Charybdis between which every earnest reformer, every politician who desires to make the name of his profession a term of honor instead of shame, must steer. He must avoid both under penalty of wreckage, and it avails him nothing to have avoided one, if he founders on the other. People are apt to speak as if in political life, public life, it ought to be a mere case of striving upward—striving toward a high peak. The simile is inexact. Every man who is striving to do good public work is traveling along a ridge crest, with the gulf of failure on each side —the gulf of inefficiency on the one side, the gulf of unrighteousness on the other. All kinds of forces are continually playing on him, to shove him first into one gulf and then into the other; and even a wise and good man, unless he braces himself with uncommon firmness and foresight, as he is pushed this way and that, will find that his course becomes a pronounced zigzag instead of a straight line; and if it becomes too pronounced he is lost, no matter to which side the zigzag may take him. Nor is he lost only as regards his own career; what is far more serious, his power of doing useful service to the public is at an end. He may still, if a mere politician, have political place, or, if a make-believe reformer, retain that notoriety on which his vanity feeds; but, in either case, his usefulness to the community has ceased.

The man who sacrifices everything to efficiency needs but a short shrift in a discussion like this. The abler he is, the more dangerous he is to the community. The master and typical representative of a great municipal political organization recently stated under oath that "he was in politics for his pocket every time." This put in its baldest and most cynically offensive shape the doctrine upon which certain public men act. It is not necessary to argue its iniquity with those who have advanced any great distance beyond the brigand theory of political life. Some years ago, another public man enunciated much the same doctrine in the phrase, "The Decalogue and the Golden Rule have no part in political life." Such statements, openly made, imply a belief that the public conscience is dull; and where the men who make them continue to be political leaders, the public has itself to thank for all shortcomings in public life.

The man who is constitutionally incapable of working for practical results ought not to need a much longer shrift. In every community there are little knots of fantastic extremists who loudly proclaim that they are striving for righteousness, and who, in reality, do their feeble best for unrighteousness. Just as the upright politician should hold in peculiar scorn the man who makes the name of politician a reproach and a shame, so the genuine reformer should realize that the cause he champions is especially jeopardized by the mock reformer who does what he can to make reform a laughing stock among decent men.

A caustic observer once remarked that when Dr. Johnson spoke of patriotism as the last refuge of a scoundrel, "he was ignorant of the infinite possibilities contained in the word 'reform.'" The sneer was discreditable to the man who uttered it, for it is no more possible to justify corruption by railing at those who by their conduct throw scandal upon the cause of reform than it is to justify treason by showing that men of shady character frequently try to cover their misconduct by fervent protestations of love of country. Nevertheless, the fact remains that exactly as true patriots should be especially jealous of any appeal to what is base, under the guise of patriotism, so men who strive for honesty, and for the cleansing of what is corrupt in the dark places of our politics, should emphatically disassociate themselves from the men whose antics throw discredit on the reforms they profess to advocate.

These little knots of extremists are found everywhere, one type flourishing chiefly in one locality and another type in another. In the particular objects they severally profess to champion, they are as far asunder as the poles, for one of their characteristics is that each little group has its own patent recipe for salvation and pays no attention whatever to the other little groups; but in mental and moral habit they are fundamentally alike. They may be socialists of twenty different types, from the followers of Tolstoi down and up, or they may ostensibly champion some cause in itself excellent, such as temperance or municipal reform, or they may merely with comprehensive vagueness announce themselves as the general enemies of what is bad, of corruption, machine politics, and the like. Their policies and principles are usually mutually exclusive; but that does not alter the conviction, which each feels or affects to feel, that his particular group is the real vanguard of the army of reform. Of course, as the particular groups are all marching in different directions, it is not possible for more than one of them to be the vanguard. The others, at best, must be off to one side, and may possibly be marching the wrong way in the rear; and, as a matter of fact, it is only occasionally that any one of them is in the front. There are in each group many entirely sincere and honest men, and because of the presence of these men we are too apt to pay some of their associates the unmerited compliment of speaking of them also as honest but impracticable. As a matter of fact, the typical extremist of this kind differs from the practical reformer, from the public man who strives in practical fashion for decency, not at all in superior morality, but in inferior sense. He is not more virtuous; he is less virtuous. He is merely more foolish. When Wendell Phillips denounced Abraham Lincoln as "the slave-hound of Illinois," he did not show himself more virtuous than Lincoln, but more foolish; neither did he advance the cause of human freedom. When the contest for the Union and against slavery took on definite shape, then he and his kind were swept aside by the statesmen and soldiers, like Lincoln and Seward, Grant and Farragut, who alone were able to ride the storm. Great as is the superiority in efficiency of the men who do things over those who do not, it may be no greater than their superiority in morality. In addition to the simple and sincere men who have a twist in their mental make-up, these knots of enthusiasts contain, especially among their leaders, men of morbid vanity, who thirst for notoriety, men who lack power to accomplish anything if they go in with their fellows to fight for results, and who prefer to sit outside and attract momentary attention by denouncing those who are really forces for good.

In every community in our land there are many hundreds of earnest and sincere men, clergymen and laymen, reformers who strive for reform in the field of politics, in the field of philanthropy, and in the field of social life; and we could count on the fingers of one hand the number of times these men have been really aided in their efforts by the men of the type referred to in the preceding paragraph. The socialist who raves against the existing order is not the man who ever lifts his hand practically to make our social life a little better, to make the conditions that bear upon the unfortunate a little easier; the man who demands the immediate impossible in temperance is not the man who ever aids in an effort to minimize the evils caused by the saloon; and those who work practically for political reform are hampered, so far as they are affected at all, by the strutting vanity of the professional impracticables.

It is not that these little knots of men accomplish much of a positive nature that is objectionable, for their direct influence is inconsiderable; but they do have an undoubted indirect effect for bad, and this of a double kind. They affect for evil a certain number of decent men in one way and a certain number of equally decent men in an entirely different way. Some decent men, following their lead, withdraw themselves from the active work of life, whether social, philanthropic, or political, and by the amount they thus withdraw from the side of the forces of good they strengthen the forces of evil, as, of course, it makes no difference whether we lessen the numerator or increase the denominator. Other decent men are so alienated by such conduct that in their turn they abandon all effort to fight for reform, believing reformers to be either hypocrites or fools. Both of these phenomena are perfectly familiar to every active politician who has striven for decency, and to every man who has studied history in an intelligent way. Few things hurt a good cause more than the excesses of its nominal friends.

Fortunately, most extremists lack the power to commit dangerous excesses. Their action is normally as abortive as that of the queer abolitionist group who, in 1864, nominated a candidate against Abraham Lincoln when he was running for re-election to the presidency. The men entering this movement represented all extremes, moral and mental. Nominally, they opposed Lincoln because they did not feel that he had gone far enough in what they deemed the right direction—had not been sufficiently extreme—and they objected to what they styled his opportunism, his tendency to compromise, his temporizing conduct, and his being a practical politician. In reality, of course, their opposition to Lincoln was conditioned, not on what Lincoln had done, but upon their own natures. They were incapable of supporting a great constructive statesman in a great crisis; and this, not because they were too virtuous, but because they lacked the necessary common sense and power of subordination of self to enable them to work disinterestedly with others for the common good. Their movement, however, proved utterly abortive, and they had no effect even for evil. The sound, wholesome common sense of the American people fortunately renders such movements, as a rule, innocuous; and this is, in reality, the prime reason why republican government prospers in America, as it does not prosper, for instance, in France. With us these little knots of impracticables have an insignificant effect upon the national life, and no representation to speak of in our governmental assemblies. In France, where the nation has not the habit of self-government, and where the national spirit is more volatile and less sane, each little group grows until it becomes a power for evil, and, taken together, all the little groups give to French political life its curious, and by no means elevating, kaleidoscopic character.

Macaulay's eminently sane and wholesome spirit and his knowledge of practical affairs give him a peculiar value among historians of political thought. In speaking of Scotland at the end of the seventeenth century he writes as follows:

It is a remarkable circumstance that the same country should have produced in the same age the most wonderful specimens of both extremes of human nature. Even in things indifferent, the Scotch Puritan would hear of no compromise; and he was but too ready to consider all who recommended prudence and charity as traitors to the cause of truth. On the other hand, the Scotchmen of that generation who made a figure in Parliament were the most dishonest and unblushing time-servers that the world has ever seen. Perhaps it is natural that the most callous and impudent vice should be found in the near neighborhood of unreasonable and impracticable virtue. Where enthusiasts are ready to destroy or be destroyed for trifles magnified into importance by a squeamish conscience, it is not strange that the very name of conscience should become a byword of contempt to cool and shrewd men of business.

What he says of Scotland in the time of King James and King William is true, word for word, of civic life in New York two centuries later. We see in New York sodden masses of voters manipulated by clever, unscrupulous, and utterly selfish masters of machine politics. Against them we see, it is true, masses of voters who both know how to, and do, strive for righteousness; but, we see also very many others in whom the capacity for self-government seems to have atrophied. They have lost the power to do practical work by ceasing to exercise it, by confining themselves to criticism and theorizing, to intemperate abuse and intemperate championship of what they but imperfectly understand. The analogues of the men whom Macaulay condemns exist in numbers in New York, and work evil in our public life for the very reason that Macaulay gives. They do not do practical work, and the extreme folly of their position makes them not infrequently the allies of scoundrels who cynically practice corruption. Too often, indeed, they actually alienate from the cause of decency keen and honest men, who grow to regard all movements for reform with contemptuous dislike because of the folly and vanity of the men who in the name of righteousness preach unwisdom and practice uncharitableness. These men thus do inestimable damage; for the reform spirit, the spirit of striving after high ideals, is the breath of life in our political institutions; and whatever weakens it by just so much lessens the chance of ultimate success under democratic government.

Discarding the two extremes, the men who deliberately work for evil, and the men who are unwilling or incapable of working for good, there remains the great mass of men who do desire to be efficient, who do desire to make this world a better place to live in, and to do what they can toward achieving cleaner minds and more wholesome bodies. To these, after all, we can only say: Strive manfully for righteousness, and strive so as to make your efforts for good count. You are not to be excused if you fail to try to make things better; and the very phrase "trying to make things better" implies trying in practical fashion. One man's capacity is for one kind of work, and another man's capacity for another kind of work. One affects certain methods, and another affects entirely different methods. All this is of little concern. What is of really vital importance is that something should be accomplished, and that this something should be worthy of accomplishment. The field is of vast size, and the laborers are always too few. There is not the slightest excuse for one sincere worker looking down on another because he chooses a different part of the field and different implements. It is inexcusable to refuse to work, to work slackly or perversely, or to mar the work of others.

No man is justified in doing evil on the ground of expediency. He is bound to do all the good possible. Yet he must consider the question of expediency, in order that he may do all the good possible, for otherwise he will do none. As soon as a politician gets to the point of thinking that in order to be "practical" he has got to be base, he has become a noxious member of the body politic. That species of practicability eats into the moral sense of the people like a cancer, and he who practices it can no more be excused than an editor who debauches public decency in order to sell his paper.

We need the worker in the fields of social and civic reform; the man who is keenly interested in some university settlement, some civic club or citizens' association which is striving to elevate the standard of life. We need clean, healthy newspapers, with clean, healthy criticism which shall be fearless and truthful. We need upright politicians who will take the time and trouble, and who possess the capacity, to manage caucuses, conventions, and public assemblies. We need men who try to be their poorer brothers' keepers to the extent of befriending them and working with them so far as they are willing; men who work in charitable associations, or, what is even better, strive to get into touch with the wage-workers, to understand them and to champion their cause when it is just. We need the sound and healthy idealist; the theoretic writer, preacher, or teacher; the Emerson or Phillips Brooks,* who helps to create the atmosphere of enthusiasm and practical endeavor. In public life, we need not only men who are able to work in and through their parties, but also upright, fearless, rational independents who will deal impartial justice to all men and all parties. We need men who are farsighted and resolute; men who combine sincerity with sanity. We need scholarly men, too—men who study all the difficult questions of our political life from the standpoint both of practice and of theory; men who thus study trusts, or municipal government, or finance, or taxation, or civil-service reform, as the authors of the "Federalist" studied the problems of federal government.

In closing, let me again dwell upon the point I am seeking to emphasize, so that there shall be no chance of honest misunderstanding of what I say. It is vital that every man who is in politics, as a man ought to be, with a disinterested purpose to serve the public, should strive steadily for reform, that he should have the highest ideals. He must lead, only he must lead in the right direction, and normally he must be in sight of his followers. Cynicism in public life is a curse, and when a man has lost the power of enthusiasm for righteousness it will be better for him and the country if he abandons public life.

Above all, the political reformer must not permit himself to be driven from his duty of supporting what is right by any irritation at the men who, while nominally supporting the same objects, and even ridiculing him as a backslider or an "opportunist," yet by their levity or fanati-

* Episcopal bishop of Massachusetts, preacher of great renown.

cism do damage to the cause which he really serves, and which they profess to serve. Let him disregard them; for though they are, according to their ability, the foes of decent politics, yet, after all, they are but weaklings, and the real and dangerous enemies of the cause he holds dear are those sinister beings who batten on the evil of our political system, and both profit by its existence and, by their own existence, tend to perpetuate and increase it. We must not be diverted from our warfare with these powerful and efficient corruptionists by irritation at the vain prattlers who think they are at the head of the reform forces, whereas they are really wandering in bypaths in the rear.

The professional impracticable, the man who sneers at the same and honest strivers after good, who sneers at the men who are following, however humbly, in the footsteps of those who worked for and secured practical results in the days of Washington, and again in the days of Lincoln, who denounces them as time-servers and compromisers, is, of course, an ally of corruption; but, after all, he can generally be disregarded, whereas the real and dangerous foe is the corrupt politician, whom we cannot afford to disregard. When one of these professional impracticables denounces the attitude of decent men as "a hodge-podge of the ideal and the practicable," he is amusingly unaware that he is writing his own condemnation, showing his own inability to do good work or to appreciate good work. The Constitutional Convention over which Washington presided, and which made us a nation, represented precisely and exactly this "hodge-podge," and was frantically denounced in its day by the men of the impracticable type. Lincoln's career throughout the Civil War was such a "hodge-podge," and was in its turn denounced in exactly the same way. Lincoln disregarded the jibes of these men who did their puny best to hurt the great cause for which he battled; and they never, by their pin-pricks, succeeded in diverting him from the real foe. The fanatical antislavery people wished to hurry him into unwise, extreme, and premature action, and denounced him as compromising with the forces of evil, as being a practical politician—which he was, if practicality is held to include wisdom and high purpose. He did not permit himself to be affected by their position. He did not yield to what they advised when it was impracticable, nor did he permit himself to become prejudiced against so much of what they championed as was right and practicable. His ideal was just as high as theirs. He did not lower it. He did not lose his temper at their conduct, or cease to strive for the abolition of slavery and the restoration of the Union; and, whereas their conduct foreboded disaster to both causes, his efforts secured the success of both. So, in our turn, we of today are bound to try to tread in the footsteps of those great Americans who in the past have held a high ideal and have striven mightily through practical methods to realize that ideal. There must be many compromises; but we cannot compromise with dishonesty, with sin. We must not be misled at any time by the cheap assertion that people get only what they want; that the editor of a degraded newspaper is to be excused because the public want the degradation; that the city officials who inaugurate a "wide-open" policy are to be excused because a portion of the public likes vice; that the men who jeer at philanthropy are to be excused because among philanthropists there are hypocrites, and among unfortunates there are vicious and unworthy people. To pander to depravity inevitably means to increase the depravity. It is a dreadful thing that public sentiment should condone misconduct in a public man; but this is no excuse for the public man, if by his conduct he still further degrades public sentiment. There can be no meddling with the laws of righteousness, of decency, of morality. We are in honor bound to put into practice what we preach; to remember that we are not to be excused if we do not; and that in the last resort no material prosperity, no business acumen, no intellectual development of any kind, can atone in the life of a nation for the lack of the fundamental qualities of courage, honesty, and common sense.

64

THE CITIZEN AS A MEMBER OF
A POLITICAL PARTY

Elihu Root

Elihu Root (1845–1937), prominent New York lawyer and member of the Hague Tribunal (Permanent Court of Arbitration), also served in politics. He was appointed Senator from New York, Secretary of War, and Secretary of State. In 1912, he was chairman of the Republican National Convention, adhering to the Taft faction when the party split. His straightforward advice to the young person who would become an activist seems as much to the point today as when it was written.

*

IT IS quite simple and easy for any intelligent young man to take part in the activities of a political party in the United States. He has only to select the party the ascendancy of which he considers most desirable and let the recognized party officials of his own home know that he is willing to work. He will promptly find himself admitted to membership in whatever may be the simplest form of political organization or association in the locality and will find himself provided with plenty of work to do. He cannot begin by leadership or by dictating party policies, and he probably cannot assume in the beginning any such position of superiority as he may think his education and intelligence entitle him to have. The work in which he will be engaged at first may be simply the details of local organizations, which will perhaps seem of little consequence; or engaging in struggles

Reprinted by permission of the publishers from *Addresses on Government and Citizenship* by Elihu Root, edited by Robert Bacon and James Brown Scott. Cambridge, Mass.: Harvard University Press, Copyright 1916.

between candidates for small offices, in which he does not take very much interest; or canvassing from house to house to ascertain the political affiliations or preference of the residents. It may be very far from that advocacy of principles and influence on the policies and direction of government in which he would like to engage. He may, however, be sure that he will ultimately find the exact level and rise to the full height of opportunity and influence and dignity of employment to which his abilities, character, and devotion to his duties entitle him. If he is able and willing to render effective service, he will gradually find himself moving along until he is at last engaged in the most important duties on the broadest fields of political action. In the meantime, or if he should never rise above mere local activity, let him remember that the first and chief duty of citizenship is to serve in the ranks—not to await some great and glorious occasion to win fame and power. It is the active service of the men in the ranks that makes the difference between popular self-government and popular submission to an absolute monarch. Without the great body of workers who never rise to leadership, popular government would be as impossible as a successful army composed entirely of officers.

In the performance of the simple duties of the political beginner there are certain principles of conduct so indispensable to usefulness that observance of them is a clear duty.

Men influence the conduct of others chiefly through personal association and intercourse. There is such a preponderance of good in human nature that association with men ordinarily begets a liking for them. As men come to know each other, each comes to receive from the others the respect and confidence to which he is entitled; his character and his opinions insensibly acquire their due weight and influence. It is not the stranger who says, "Go there," or "Do that," who is obeyed; but it is the old acquaintance who says, "Come with me," or "Let us do thus and so," who is followed. The knowledge of the tendencies and prejudices of men acquired through personal acquaintance makes the suggestion of a wish from a friend often of greater weight than the most eloquent speech or the most profound essay from a stranger. This power of association is the chief thing which enables political organizations, even when they are going wrong or in bad hands, to resist attacks from without, even from the best and most highly respected citizens, when these occasionally and for the moment are moved to instruct the men actually engaged in political affairs as to what they should and should not do.

There is no monopoly of this power of association. Unselfish and public-spirited men can qualify themselves to exercise it if they take the trouble, just as well as self-seeking men of low aims.

To accomplish very much with other men, one must have a considerable degree of sympathy with their feelings and interests. The man who never cares or thinks about anything but himself cannot expect anybody to think or care about him. If he has no interest in the hopes and ambitions of others, no consideration for their sensibilities, they will be equally indifferent so far as he is concerned. Political bodies, especially primary political bodies, are made up, to a degree unequaled in any other association, of men of widely varying conditions in life, with different opportunities for knowledge and capacity for reflection, with different prejudices and ways of thinking, differing widely in information, in previous reflection, in breadth and scope of thought, in motives, in characters, in tempers, in ambitions. Each one of them is entitled equally with all the others to have his opinions, his wishes, and his ambitions considered; and the feeling that any one gives kindly consideration to them is in itself a great source of influence. The man who has never had anything above a day's wages or a small clerk's salary, or who perhaps has no income but is looking for one, is just as much entitled to aspire to a place in the custom-house, or in a post office, or to be a letter-carrier, as the very successful and able man distinguished in his community is entitled to aspire to be governor or senator; and the small man is just as much entitled as the big man is to have his aspiration considered and treated as an honorable aspiration. The small trader who hopes that the legislation and administration of government will be such as to promote the prosperity of his little business is just as much within his rights as the great banker who hopes for currency legislation or the great manufacturer who hopes for tariff legislation beneficial to his business. Sympathetic recognition of such considerations is a natural and necessary basis for influence and leadership among political associates.

A rightly constituted man brought into association with a great number of others cannot fail to acquire some degree of proper humility. It matters not how well educated or intelligent a man may be, the combined experience, knowledge of life, range of thought, fertility of suggestion, thoroughness of criticism, to be found in any great body of men taken together are so far beyond him that he is bound to gradually take an attitude of receiving and learning, as well as endeavoring to instruct and lead. He will thus escape from the fatal attitude which ruins one's influence with others by giving an impression of assumed superiority in wisdom or virtue. . . .

65

THE DISSENTER'S ROLE IN A
TOTALITARIAN AGE

Norman Thomas

The late President Kennedy observed in his introductory chapter to
Profiles in Courage* *that when he entered the United States Senate he was*
told that "the way to get along is to go along." Legend has it that his
successor, Lyndon B. Johnson, was the source of this sobering advice. Such
has been the emphasis in this book; such is the conventional wisdom of
politics. In most places, at most times, the cooler heads prevail, for better
or for worse. But they also serve who only bellyache about current con-
ditions and demand change. And in America, as Woodrow Wilson once
observed, the kickers are in short supply. After all, we are often re-
minded by the culture, "If you can't boost, don't knock." One who con-
spicuously has ignored all such advice is Norman Thomas (b. 1884).
His own life testifies to the usefulness of dissent, and he sees a special
need for the dissenter as we move ever more securely into the mass
society.

*

DISSENTERS have played more than one role in history. At various times,
at various places, and on issues big and little, they have been responsible
for confusion, division, and discontent; and, for progress. Your true
prophets have always been dissenters. Heretics have often been gravely in
error. Nevertheless, as I am not the first man to observe, the heretic has

From *The New York Times Magazine,* November 20, 1949. Copyright © 1949 by The
New York Times.
* New York: Harper, 1955.

always been the growing point in society. When he is repressed by force, society stagnates. A virile society follows its true prophets and has better ways to deal with error than the club, the noose, or the stake.

Prometheus, according to ancient legend, was punished by the gods for bringing fire as a gift to men. For that punishment I have always suspected that fearful men, slaves to the old ways, not jealous gods, were responsible.

Certainly, in historic times the man with new ideas, not alone in religion and politics, but in what we now call science, has rarely been honored by his own generation. "Your fathers killed the prophets and you have builded their tombs" is a judgment on us which was by no means completely altered either by the coming of Christianity or by the advent of the modern, scientific method. A few famous dissenters have been successful rebels, and when success had led them to power they sometimes tasted the dregs of disillusion within its cup.

When one talks of dissenters, however, one is discussing a far more numerous company than the famous pathfinders and prophets who have proved themselves the leaders of men. The capacity of just plain folks for dissent is important. It is today an expression of the kind of courage on which the very life of democracy depends.

The menacing conflicts of our time are not between the individual prophet in high place or low, and his prejudiced or apathetic neighbors. Increasingly they are between rival groups with different interests and ideologies, all of them inclined to act like mobs rather than fellowships of freemen. Neither the Communist nor the Fascist deserves the honored name of dissenter. He is merely the docile, but often fanatic, slave to his own particular group and its leaders. He wants no true freedom of dissent. In this respect, Communists and Fascists exaggerate a common failing. Most men want the freedom of which they talk for themselves, so that they may advance their particular truth. If and when their group gets power, freedom becomes only a right to agree with them or docilely submit to their sway.

We Americans have visited harsh judgment on Russians and Germans who assented to the practices of demagogues and dictators, even when in their hearts they disapproved of them. We have seen very clearly what tragedy fell on Germany and mankind because there were so few bold dissenters, unknown soldiers of truth, in towns or villages when the Nazis were consolidating their power. Most of our written and spoken comment carries the implication that that sort of thing couldn't happen here in our America. Yet it does happen here whenever and wherever a community condones mob violence, whether in Groveland, Florida, or in Westchester County, New York.

There was a grim and terrible warning in a story which received little notice in the press or radio. Only the other day, at long last, a persistent wife won from an honest judge freedom for her husband who had spent twenty-six years of his life in a state prison for a rape which he did not commit. The man was James Montgomery, a poor Negro worker of good repute. At a time and in a place—Illinois, not Georgia— cursed by the Ku Klux Klan, James Montgomery was accused of rape on the unsupported word of an eccentric woman who later was committed to an insane asylum. The frightening thing, it is now discovered, is that the police played along with the Klan and that the physician who examined the woman knew all along that no rape had been committed, and yet he lacked courage to testify to the truth because he liked "a quiet life," and the Klan was strong. How often, one wonders, he and his fellow citizens in that Illinois community thanked God that they were not as other men, even these Germans?

The guilty silence of the physician, and the overt hostility of the police, in the Montgomery case represented the extreme antithesis to dissent, a conformity to the wishes of the powerful without regard to any values except safety and the poor satisfactions that belong to the members of the herd. Such things threaten any decent democracy.

Philosophers have sometimes argued that the business of living in groups requires that most of our actions shall be traditional and habitual, rather than reflective. The dissenter can be, indeed he often has been, a crackpot or a fanatic. Every great religion is obliged to warn us against false prophets. On this basis, the observer from the windows of his ivory tower (or the lesser security of an editor's office) may comfortably conclude that, on the whole, it is well that men do not change capriciously or follow every Pied Piper who may pipe them a tune; yet, clearly our danger is not from the honest dissenter, but from the passions of the mob and those who manipulate it in the struggle for profit and power.

It may seem that I have been talking in melodramatic terms, and that, for our American, the role of the dissenter is neither so necessary nor so dangerous as some of my illustrations and historical observations would imply. Thank God, it is true that for most of us dissent requires no superhuman courage and that there is even some fun to be derived from it. Americans are kept in line by their own fears of what might happen, far more than by the bitterness of what does happen.

The list of dissenters, even in America, who have been held back in their trade or profession, or black-listed altogether, who have faced hostile audiences or ugly mobs, who have known arrest or imprisonment is long; but it is very short compared with men who have been kept in line simply by fear of being different, or by determination to keep up with the Joneses. I speak against the background of some experience when I say that if dissenters rarely are troubled by the weight of income taxes in the higher brackets, they by no means furnish a chief recruiting ground for relief rolls. If fame and fortune are not the usual rewards of dissent in America, neither is the poorhouse.

Trouble often comes not to the open dissenter but to one who is suspected of hiding the degree of his nonconformity. I have spoken with complete impunity before audiences of considerable size at times and in places where men were denied the right to speak, or whose meetings were badly disturbed, because they were suspected of socialism or some other heresy which they denied.

So I come to my own dissenting experience. The editor who suggested this article hinted that I might. With the natural egotism of every writer thus encouraged, let me record the fact that I have enjoyed my role as dissenter, only regretting my lack of success. More than once, I have said that I would rather be right than be president, but was perfectly willing to be both. (Henry Clay, author of that much quoted sentiment, succeeded in being neither.)

I certainly have not run repeatedly for office out of any masochistic pleasure in recurrent defeat. I never ran merely to make a protest, which at times has value, or to be a "gadfly." (The only notable achievement of a gadfly, in my experience, was to make my horse run away.) A dissenter worth his salt never dissents just for the pleasure of being "agin' the Government." He dissents from the established rule, custom, or theory, because clearly or vaguely, he envisages something better which he positively desires for himself and his fellows. The religious dissenter believes that he has found a better road to heaven; the political dissenter, a better way of life upon earth. If he is to be useful, his capacity for dissent must not be at the price of incapacity for constructive cooperation.

Assuredly, I never coveted the dubious honor of being the most often defeated candidate for high office in American history; neither did I ever run with the expectation of election. I ran because of an honest conviction that by running I could, better than in any other way, further two related causes dear to my heart: the education of the public in democratic socialism, and the realignment of American political parties so that our political divisions would be meaningful and we should have a genuine party responsibility. I was, in other words, a dissenter from the old-line parties not so much because I disliked them, as because I wanted something different.

In respect to promoting a political realignment such as my heart desired, I have been a failure, and failure hurts. In respect to a certain degree of public education and a kind of indirect influence on the old parties, my failure was by no means so complete. I can honestly claim that something had been accomplished. And, it is more than a pious platitude to say that in many respects the struggle is its own reward. In short, I have enjoyed life more as a dissenter than, so far as I can judge, many of my conforming friends and acquaintances—including some of those who have won elections. I have suffered no more than they from current—and damnable—smear techniques.

In my role of aging sage, bestowing advice—unasked—upon the young, I should not dare to promise them as good a life as I have found as a dissenter. I am gratefully and humbly aware of what fortune has done for me. But I would insist that to believe in something enough to stand on your own feet in its behalf, to feel that you are something more than a member of the herd, is a satisfaction transcending inescapable duty. You can find in it a real joy in life, especially if you hang on to a sense of humor. Yet, there's fun in trying to be the Joneses with whom others should seek to keep up.

The editors of *The Daily Worker,* if for purposes of objurgation they read this article at all, will cry to high heaven that I have no right to speak as a dissenter; that I am and have been only a "capitalist lackey"; and that the real dissenters are those recently on trial, and picket duty, in Foley Square. Let me repeat that, today, your Communist is not so much a dissenter as an ultra-orthodox member of an opposing political church, subject in every respect to its discipline.

In the campaign of 1944, more than once Communists called on the government to prevent me from speaking because I was a heretic or dissenter against the government policy, which the Communists then vociferously approved, of winning lasting peace by total vengeance against Germans and by appeasement of Stalin.

The Communists applauded the conviction of Trotskyite heretics under the very law under which their [own] leaders have been convicted. Of all men, they have least use for the individual dissenter. As for their claim that their efforts at secrecy and their use of special party names are necessities because otherwise, in a cruel America, they would face loss of jobs or even imprisonment, that also is not true on the record.

After the conclusion of Mitchell Palmer's "obscene anti-red raids"— the phrase is that of a conservative historian—of which raids the Communists were by no means the chief victims, there was a very high degree of political freedom in America until the "cold war" and Communist subservience to Stalin created an opposition which is often unwise and even hysterical. William Z. Foster lived with complete impunity in America and traveled unnecessarily on false passports for years after he had written the revolutionary book, *Towards a Soviet America,* which he now says is obsolete.

To a very considerable degree, the Communists have created a problem new in American history because they have deliberately flouted the established practice of American radicals from Colonial times on. That practice was not long-continued secret conspiracy, deceit, and concealment, but a flamboyant honesty which, for instance, led the Wobblies of old to fill the jails in towns in which one or more of their comrades had been arrested. Your true dissenter loves the light, and believes in the capacity of the common man to walk in it when it is allowed to shine.

I should like to end this article on something other than a historic or explanatory note. Our democracy is in desperate need of intelligent and constructive dissenters. The particular dissent which haunts me day and night is against the notion that peace for my children and grandchildren can be guaranteed by the present race in arms.

For unnumbered centuries, men have accepted the notion that peace can be had, or at least security, by preparing for war. But today, by every precedent of history and every rule of logic, there can be but one end of this armament race if we continue it: that is, the war of the age of atomic bombs and bacteriological agents of destruction which are already possessed by both groups of potential billigerents.

Our technology has driven us to a new sort of war, and gives a new significance to war. Yet we plod along, simply intensifying the sort of arms race which in the past has led straight to the wars which nominally it was intended to prevent. Lasting peace requires much more than the end of the arms race; but there will be no peace without the end of our frantic competition in weapons of death. So long as our present rivalry continues, our minds will be too preoccupied, our emotions too absorbed, to be capable of the constructive thinking required for the conquest of hunger and a just and equitable rule of law in our one world.

While the arms race continues, it is a mockery to talk of a successful attack upon poverty. Nations feel themselves obliged to spend from 20 to 50 per cent of their current budgets on getting ready for war. The British Labour Government has been denounced for its reckless extravagance in providing for social welfare; but, all its expenditures for social welfare outside of education fall 34,000,000 pounds short of what it is spending in the arms race on its current military commitments.

Already, so tied are we Americans to an arms economy that our fantastic military expenditures are even now hailed as a bulwark against depression. A proclamation of universal peace would mean economic panic, except as we might rapidly substitute planning for life instead of planning for death.

There is no easy answer to this problem of armament in Stalin's world. Our immediate hope lies in the fact that such is the nature of atomic war that it is to everybody's interest, indeed, it has become almost a condition of survival, that conflict between democracy and totalitarianism be transferred from the realm of atomic war and preparation for it. This cannot and will not be done except as we banish war.

And yet, so afraid are we of dissent from habitual reliance on arms and yet more arms, so unable are we to match our boldness in physics with boldness in politics, that neither our government nor people seems willing even to try the effect upon governments and masses of men of a well-thought-out appeal for the universal end of the armament race, under supervision of the United Nations, with international arrangements for security.

The best that Secretary Acheson could do, when addressing the U.N., was to promise that his government would contribute to confidence, and with its attainment would "play its full role in the regulation and reduction under effective safeguards of armaments and armed forces." Here is no mighty and passionate dissent calculated to warm men's minds and hearts that they walk the path to destruction. Here is, instead, a continued failure to make that beginning in sounding out the trumpet call which may yet stir men to the only way of life and safety.

We live in a time when certain dissents against mass folly have become an essential condition of the progress, if not the very life, of mankind. The most necessary of these dissents concerns the method of war; if its articulation is successful, it must drive us to cooperative action for peace.

INDEX

Abraham, Karl, 425, 427
absolutism, ethics of, 54
Acheson, Dean, 485
acting out, 5
actors, role-playing and, 179–180
administrative faults, ethics and, 91–92
administrative organization, domination and, 20
Administrative Procedure Act, 94–95
adolescence, voting behavior and, 381–382
Adorno, T. W., 375
Adventure in Politics (Neuberger), 228 n.
adventures, 176
AFL, 230–231, 415
age, life views and, 59–60
agency, executive functions in, 345
agnosticism, of bureaucrat, 414
Aiken, George D., 85 n., 237
Alexander the Great, 172, 174
Althoff, Friedrich, 28
ambivalence, in politician's social status, 352–363; theory of, 357–360
American Bar Association, 142
American Civil Liberties Union, 310
American Heritage Foundation, 3 n.
American Legion, 233
American Politician, The (Salter), 201 n.
American Revolution, 57
anal personality, 426–427
Anderson, Clinton P., 237
Anderson, Jack, 147–154
Anderson, W. A., 383 n.
anticommunism, 10
Antigone (Sophocles), 218–220
anti-intellectualism, 10, 408
Antioch Review, The, 255 n.
apoliticals, versus politicals, 364–378
appointees, backgrounds of, 345
Arduna, 57

aristocracy, 20; nobility and, 30
Aristotle, 62–68, 76
arms race, 485
arrondissements, 164
artistic rationalization, 73
Ashly, Henry, 288
association, leadership and, 478–479; advocates', 100
Astor, Nancy Langhorne, Lady, 406
atomic war, 485
Augustine, Saint, 169–171, 406
authoritarianism, 366, 374–376
Authoritarian Personality, The (Christie & Jahoda), 391
authoritarian state, 17, 58
autonomy, individual, 73

Babel, August, 47 n.
Bacon, Robert, 477 n.
Baker, John W., 281
Baltzell, E. Digby, 2 n.
bank deposits, salary and, 106–107
Bar Association, New York City, 437–442
Bar Association, New York State, 463
Barkley, Alben W., 135, 138
Barnett, Ray, 286
Barton, Allen H., 381 n.
Bashford, R. M., 293
Beach, Albert, 285
Beach, Marjorie M., 285–290
Beasley, Clara D., 421
Bentivogli, Giovanni, 278
Benton, William L., 6 n., 234–240
Berelson, Bernard, 383 n.
Bergson, Henri, 77, 410 n.
Berle, Milton, 263
Bermondsey Story (Brockway), 405 n., 406 n.
Bernstein, Eduard, 412 n.
Bernstein, Marver H., 342–351

best evidence, rule of, 149–151, 153
Betz, Henry, 293
Bevan, Aneurin, 409 n., 410
Bhagavad-Gita, 57
Bhuddist priests, 29
Bingham, Barry, 139
Bismarck, Otto von, 15, 173
blackmail, 267
Blakeman, Robert A., 462
Blumenthal, Albert H., 463
Blythe, Joseph Lee, 116
body politic, end of, 73
Bolingbroke, Henry St. John, Viscount, 155–156
Bolshevism, 35, 52, 55
Bonaparte, Napoleon, 174–176, 428
bond issues, 285–286
Boorstin, Daniel J., 8 n.
Boss Cermak of Chicago (Gottfried), 416 n.
bosses and bossism, 38, 44, 166, 203, 267–275, 285, 359 n., 373, 416–428, 467
Bowles, Chester, 260
Brahmins, 29, 56
bribery, 90, 130, 159, 294–300
Brill, A. A., 425
British Labour party, 403, 404 n., 485
Brockway, Archibald Fenner, 404 n., 405 n., 406 n., 410 n.
Brome, Vincent, 410
Bronx County, N.Y., 269–275
Brookings Institution, 342
Brooks, Phillips, 474
brotherhood, in race relations, 82
Brown, John Young, 134, 139
Brownlow Committee, 202 n.
Bryan, William Jennings, 167
Buchanan, William, 379–394
budget, political executive and, 348–349
Budget Bureau, U.S., 343
Bullitt, Stimson, 6–7, 241–251
Bundesrat, 48
Bunn, Romanzo, 296
Burckhardt, Jacob, 172–177
bureaucracy, authority and, 141; channels in, 409 n.; growth of, 25, 180; as stabilizing force, 181
bureaucrat, agnosticism of, 414; defined, 403; enthusiast and, 402–415; motivation of, 407–408; politician as, 366
Burke, Edmund, 236
Burleson, Omar, 147, 149
Busch, Francis X., 420 n.
businessman, in government post, 86; *see also* political executive
Byrne, Brendan, 3 n.
Byrnes, John W., 110

cabinet, role of, 26
Caesar, Julius, 173
cahiers, 31
Calhoun, John C., 43
California, poverty plan for, 198
Calvinism, 58
campaign contributions, 434–435; from candidates, 203
campaign costs, President's Commission on, 431–436
campaigning, financial presure of, 88–89, 431–436; methods used in, 92–93; political interest and, 389; *see also* presidential campaign
Campbell, Angus, 383 n.
Campbell, Donald, 463
candidates, political contributions of, 203
Cann, Norman, 116–118
carpetbagger, 163
Carroll, John A., 140
Carthage, 63
Cary, Joyce 226–227
Case, Clifford P., 8, 140, 454–456
Case, Francis, 237
caste, 56
Catholic Center party, Germany, 25, 46
"cause," as motivation, 404, 411
Cermak, Anton, Jr., 335, 416–428; anal characteristics of, 426–427; as business-man, 422; chronic illness of, 435–436; colitis attacks of, 426; czar-like personality of, 423; energy reserve of, 421; gastro-intestinal illness of, 417; power drive of, 421; pugnaciousness of, 420; troubled youth of, 419
Cermak, Anton, Sr., 417
Cermak, Katherine, 417
Chamberlain, Joseph, 40, 147
Chandler, Albert B., 134–139
Chandragupta, 57
change, structured and unstructured, 181
channels, bureaucracy and, 409 n.
charisma, 17
charismatic leadership, 17–19
Charlemagne, 173, 176
Charles V, 26
Chelf, Frank, 131
Chelf Committee, 131
Chicago, gangs of, 419; Hoosier Republicans in, 395–401; precinct captain in, 339; precinct workers in, 334; ward committeemen in, 335
childhood, leadership and, 180, 416; and political interest, 382
Childs, Dave, 286, 288–289
chiliasm, 55
Chinese mandarin, 29
Christ, mercy of, 84; *see also* Jesus

Christianity, ethical problem of, 83; impact of, 73; politics and, 80–84
Christie, Richard, 391 n.
Churchill, Winston S., 249, 404
CIO, 230, 407 n.
citizen, as party member, 477–479; as politician, 467 ff.
citizens' organization for better government, 95
City of God, The (St. Augustine), 169
civic courage, 215 ff.
civilization, politics and, 73
Civilization in the United States (Stearns), 163 n.
Civil Rights Bill (1957), 236
civil service, 343; executives and, 345; *see also* government employees
Civil Service Reform, 25, 45
Civil War, 215–217, 224, 447, 475
Clapp, Charles L., 6 n.
Clark, Charles B., 294
class struggle, 58, 406 n.
Claudius, 250
Clausewitz, Karl von, 237–238
Clay, Henry, 483
Clemens, Samuel (Mark Twain), 224–225
clergy, prince and, 29
Cleveland, Grover, 389
Cleveland, Harlan, 5
Clovis, 173
clubs, political, 37; precinct, 336
Cobden, Richard, 42
Cogwheels of Democracy (Forthal), 325
Colbert, Richard J., 139
cold war, 484
Cole, G. D. H., 404 n., 406 n., 411 n.
colitis, 417, 423, 426
collectivism, 409
Collings, Ben H., 136–137
Commission on Ethics in Government, 93
communes, free, 22
Communist, label of, 310, 312–313
Communists and communism, 310–311. 404 n., 481, 484
compromise, willingness for, 370–371
Comte, Auguste, 97
condottiere, 18, 24
Confessions (St. Augustine), 169
Confessions of a Congressman (Voorhis), 193 n.
conflict of interest, 262–265, 437–442; Kennedy's message on, 443–453; reform of statutes in, 445–449
Congress, U.S., 43, 148; adjournment of, 282; confidence in integrity of, 454–456; as legislative body, 255–257; political executive and, 349; sessions of, 281

Congressional Quarterly, 143
Congressional recess, 281
Congressional Record, 140, 149, 455
Congressmen, "commuting," 319–321; conscience of, 234–240; ethical problems of, 88–89; expulsion of, 148; felonious acts, by, 147–154; financial pressure on, 88–89; meeting with constituents, 282–284; motives of, 193–200; newspaper influence on, 202; from New York City, 319–321; patronage and, 168; political involvement of, 90; pressure groups and, 201–202; "right" and "wrong" votes of, 235; salary of, 321; voting principles of, 202
Connelly, Matthew J., 135–136
Conrad III, 175
Conrad IV, 175
Conrad, Joseph, 250
conscience, of statesman, 69–71; strong versus tender, 69; votes and, 234–240
Constantine I (the Great), 173
constituency, nature and location of, 164
constitution, forms of, 62, 67
Constitution, U.S., 148, 165; truth about, 310
contracts, public official and, 440–442
conventions, national, *see* national conventions
Conway, John, 4 n.
Coolidge, Calvin, 197
Cooperative League of the United States of America, 193
Cooper Institute, New York, 8, 221
corporations, organized power of, 302
corruption, 11, 130, 157, 159, 226–227; in English politics, 69; power of, 74
Corrupt Practices Act, 96, 116–117, 123, 203
Coughlin, Charles E., 309
courage, moral, 224–225
court reform, 202 n.
Craig, Agnes M., 270
Crete, 63
criminal law, proposed changes in, 95
Cripps, Stafford, 404 n., 406 n., 410 n.
Cromwell, Oliver, 415
culture, civilization and, 73
Curia, 22
Curley, James M., 359
Curtin, Willard S., 147
cynicism, 250, 474

Daily Worker, The, 484
Darkness at Noon (Koestler), 413 n.
David, 173
Davis, Harry, 80 n.
Davis, John W., 197
decency, reform and, 471

decision-making, model of, 179; religious element in, 82
Defense Department, U.S., 351
Delagi, Michael N., 270–271
Delano, Ray, 288
demagoguery, 39, 307, 312–313, 409, 481
democracy, moral rationalization in, 76; plebescite, 38; politician's fear in, 201–202; technocracy and, 77
Democracy (Adams), 258
democratic associations, 41
Democratic National Committee, 110, 112, 121–122, 125, 129, 131, 269
Democratic party, 115, 117, 120, 186, 190–192, 197, 199, 230, 269–275, 289, 293, 305, 309, 369, 373 n., 398
Demosthenes, 307
Denning, Lord, 266
dependency wishes, 424
Derge, David R., 395–401
despotism, 20; slavery and, 64
Dewey, Thomas E., 272, 457
Dharma, 56
dictatorship, 200, 481
Dienhart, John, 426
diletante, political, 50
Dirksen, Everett M., 140–146
Disraeli, Benjamin, 155
dissenter, role of in totalitarian age, 480–486
Division of Labor in Society, The (Durkheim), 97
doctor, ethical duty of, 97
domination, desire for, 169; legitimations of, 17; organized, 19
Donatists, 406
Donnelly, Ignatius, 158–159
"don't care" policy, 221–223
"Dooley, Mr.," 315–318
Dos Passos, John, 311
Dostoevski, Fyodor, 55
Douglas, Paul H., 85–96, 130, 260, 443–445
Douglas, Stephen A., 222
Dunne, Finley Peter, 315–318
du Pont de Nemours Company, E. I., 136
Durkheim, Émile, 97–100

Eaton, Charles, 420 n.
Eddy, William A., 4 n.
education, ministries of, 28
educational achievement, political activity and, 2–3, 355, 387
efficiency, morality and, 468–469
ego, commonweal and, 172–177
Eisenhower, Dwight D., 5, 230, 236, 249, 251, 432–433
elected officials, 86–90; *see also* public officials

election, personality in, 39
election agent, 40
Election Finance, Registry of, 435
elite, analyses of, 380; management by, 263
embezzlement, 131
Emerson, Ralph Waldo, 9, 474
emotional life, elemental tendencies in, 424
Encyclopaedia Britannica, 234
end-justifies-means principle, 55–56, 72–74
England, gentry in, 30; Parliament in, 27, 42; party organization in, 40
entertainment, of government officials, 87–88; as party boss, 38–39, 44; role of, 23
enthusiast, bureaucrat and, 402–415; faith of, 409–410
enthusiast-politician, 366
EPIC (End Poverty in California) plan, 198–199
Epstein, Leon D., 411
Escape from Freedom (Fromm), 406 n.
espionage, 267
ethic, Christian, 83
ethical standards, administration of, 452
ethics, of elected officials, 86–90; exploitation of, 52; lawbreaking and, 124; New York legislature report on, 457–460; paradoxes of, 59; politics and, 52, 85–96; professional, 97–100; religious, 56; state commission on, 460; truthfulness and, 54; and two aims of human life, 77; two branches of, 77
Ethics in Government (Douglas), 85
Eugene (Oreg.) *Register-Guard,* 232
Eulau, Heinz, 379–394
evil, versus good, 56, 74; power of, 74
executive, political, *see* political executive
executive appointments, politics and, 91
executive branch, confidence in, 454–456
extremists, reform and, 470
Eysenck, H. J., 366, 372–373

factions, 406–407
Fainsod, Merle, 413 n.
Fair Employment Practices Act, 82
faith, need for, 84; politics and, 81
family, close-knit, 418
family income, of "politicals," 367
family members, politics and, 384
family services, of precinct worker, 328–329
Farley, James A., 183–194
Farley, Thomas A., 106
Farragut, David G., 471
Farris, Charles D., 376 n.
fascism, 313, 481

Faubus, Orville E., 235, 236 n.
Federal Communications Act, 435
Federal Elections Act, 455
Federalist, The, 352
Federal Lobbying Act, 455
Federal Power Commission, 447
Federal Trade Commission, 143
Fenichel, Otto, 427 n.
Ferdinand and Isabella, 174
Ferguson, Leroy, 379–394
Fichte, Johann Gottlieb, 54, 59
financial interest, disclosure of, 459
financial pressure, on Congressmen, 88–89
Flanders, Ralph E., 235
Flynn, Edward J., 269–275
Foley, Samuel J., 269, 271
force, domination by, 19; legitimate use of, 17
Force and Freedom: An Interpretation of History (Burckhardt), 172 n.
Fordham, Jefferson B., 445
Forrestal, James V., 350
Förster, F. W., 56–57
Forthal, Sonya, 325–341
fortune, politics and, 276–278
Foster, Matt, 286, 288
Foster, William Z., 484
Fourteenth Amendment, 237
France, party organization in, 37; prefects in, 27
Francis, St., 53
Frederick I, 175
Frederick the Great, 176
French, T, M., 424 n.
French Labor Movement, The (Lorwin), 407 n.
French Revolution, 31
Freud, Sigmund, 416, 425
friendship, in politics, 248
Fromm, Erich, 406
From Max Weber: Essays in Sociology (Gerth & Mills), 405 n.
F-scale, 374
Fulbright, J. William, 131

Gandhi, Mohandas K., 240
gastrointestinal disorders, 423–426
Gaudet, Hazel, 383 n.
Gay, Peter, 412 n.
gentry, English, 30
George I, 155
George Lansbury (Postgate), 404 n.
Germany, Catholic Center party in, 46; declaration of war on, 291; parliament in, 45–46; party organizations in, 37; political management in, 45; political patronage in, 24; Reichstag of, 42; Social Democratic party in, 39, 46, 412 n., 415

Gerth, H. H., 15 n., 405 n., 415 n.
gifts, to public officials, 87–88, 439, 450, 459, 462
gift tax, 126
Gill, Hiram, 251
Giraud, Émile, 76
Gladstone, William Ewart, 41, 48
Glinski, Frank, 462
glory, desire for, 169
God, history and, 83; true worship of, 171
Golden Rule, 469
Goldstein, Jonah, 272
Goldwater, Barry, 397
good, common, 73; versus evil, 56, 74
Good, Robert C., 80 n.
Goodman, Walter, 11 n.
good will, 187
good works, 405
Gorkin, Jess, 151
gospel, ethic of, 53; inspiration of, 77
Gottfried, Alex, 416–428
government, best form of, 62–63; despotic, 66–67; ethics in, 86–96; federal, 90, 443–453; versus governed, 66; versus statesmanship, 64
government agencies, work done by, 141–146
government employees, and conflict of interests, 262–265, 437–459; gifts and entertainment for, 87–88, 439, 450, 459, 462; prior and subsequent employment of, 86–88; suggested regulations for, 437–442; venality of, 90, 130, 155, 444
government reform, citizen's organization for, 95–96
graft, 90, 293; honest and dishonest, 103–105; *see also* corruption; gifts; venality
Grand Vizier, 26
Grant, Ulysses S., 471
Great Depression, 389–390
great man, quest for, 174–177
greatness, vocation of, 172
Gresham's law, 344
Guelfs and Ghibellines, 35
Guenther, Richard, 293
guilt, 424, 461
Guises, 174
Gurin, Gerald, 383 n.

Hacker, Andrew, 3 n.
Hague Tribunal, 477
Hamilton, Alexander, 207–211
happiness, of state versus individual, 62
Harding, Warren G., 165
Harper, Sam, 294, 298, 301, 303
Harriman, W. Averell, 359

Harrison, Benjamin, 303
Harshaw, Henry B., 293–294, 298
Hatch, Carl A., 136
Hatch, Robert, Jr., 462
Hatch Act, 117, 121, 123–124, 126
Hays, Brooks, 235, 236 n.
Heard, Alexander, 431
Heflin, Tom, 204
Henderson, Arthur, 404 n., 406 n.
Henderson, David B., 303–304
Henderson, J. Howard, 138
Hennessy, Bernard C., 364–378
Henry IV, 175
Henry VI, 175
hero worship, 58
Hilton-Young, W., 413 n.
Hinduism, 56–57
History of Florence (Machiavelli), 59
Hoard, William Dempster, 294, 304
Hobbes, Thomas, 179–180
Hoffer, Eric, 409 n., 412
Hoffman, Paul G., 230
Hoover, Herbert C., 197
Hoover Commission, 342 n., 343
Horse's Mouth, The (Cary), 226
House of Representatives, U.S., 43, 148,
238, 257; Administration Committee,
149–150; Committee on Appropria-
tions, 145; Judiciary Committee, 445;
Office Building of, 148; *see also* Con-
gress; Congressmen
Houston, Sam, 311
Hughes, Charles Evans, 131, 389
Hughes, Emrys, 408
Hughes, John, 463
Hughes, Thomas L., 260–261
humanist schools, 29
humanity, biological hope of, 76
Humphrey, Hubert H., 85 n., 260, 276
Huxley, Aldous, 73
Hyman, Herbert, 380 n.
Hyman, Sidney, 361

idealism, 276, 360, 412, 468, 474
ideology, and political interest, 392–393
illness, psychosomatic approach to, 417
Impellitteri, Vincent R., 269
imperatives, absolute, 57
income, mandatory disclosure of, 95
Independent Labour party, 404 n., 406 n.,
410 n.
India, politics in, 29–30
Indiana delegation, in 1960 Republican
Convention, 395–401
indignation, political, 371
individual, versus state, 62
Indra, 57
information, sale of, 439
Ingram, Verner M., 462

"in's," versus "out's," 10
*Inside Politics: The National Conven-
tions 1960* (Tillett), 395 n.
Inside the Left (Brockway), 405 n.,
410 n., 411 n.
interest, conflict of, 262–265, 437–454
Internal Revenue Bureau, 110, 128
international peace, 84, 485–486
Interstate Commerce Commission, 142,
292
Irish Catholic vote, 272
irrationality, of world, 56
Islam, 30
issues, choosing sides on, 246–247
Italian Left, The (Hilton-Young), 413 n.
Italian vote, 272
Ivanov, Capt. Eugene, 267

Jackson, Andrew, 42, 108–109
Jackson Subcommittee on Conflict of In-
terest, 452
Jahoda, Marie, 391 n.
James, William, 215–217
Janowitz, Morris, 380 n.
Jaudon, Ben, 289
Jefferson, Thomas, 232, 257
Jenner, William, 396
Jensen, Vernon, 407 n.
Jesus, 53, 84, 409 n.
Jewish bloc, 272
Jirka, Frank, 417, 426
job finding, precinct worker and, 329
Johnson, Louis, 121
Johnson, Lyndon B., 237–238, 262, 480
Johnson, Samuel, 470
Jones, Ernest, 425, 428
Jones, Harry W., 5 n.
Joseph, Lazarus, 269, 272
journalist, political, 33–35
Jouvenel, Bertrand de, 178
Julius II, Pope, 278
justice, ends of, 74; residual capacity for,
83
Justice Department, U.S., 131

Kansas City, Mo., boss rule in, 285–290
Kant, Immanuel, 59
karma, 56
Kautaliya Arthasastra, 57
Kean, Robert W., 110–129
Keeler, Christine, 266–268
Kefauver, Estes, 130
Kelly, Daniel, 463
Kelly, Edward J., 419, 425
Kennedy, John F., 238, 359, 431, 433,
443–453, 480
Kennedy, Joseph, 263
Kennedy, Robert F., 163
Kent, Frank, 5

Key, V. O., Jr., 432
kickback, 148
Kimball, Dan A., 432
king, *see* monarch
King, Cecil, 131
King Lear (Shakespeare), 9
Kinsley, Philip, 420 n.
Knox, Ronald, 403 n., 409 n., 414 n.
Koestler, Arthur, 409, 413 n.
Korean War, 344
Krishna, 57
Kuehn, Ferdinand, 293
Ku Klux Klan, 482

Labor Department, U.S., 448
Lacedaemonian constitution, 63, 67
La Follette, Robert M., 143, 197, 291–306
Langstrom, Julian P., 147, 405 n., 406 n.
Laporte, Cloyd, 457, 461
Laporte Committee, 459–463
Lasdon, William S., 110–129
Lasswell, Harold D., 5, 169 n., 391 n., 426
Last Hurrah, The (O'Connor), 359 n.
law, "fixing" of by precinct worker, 332–333; humanizing of, 331; politics and, 30
Lawson, George, 288
lawyer, as legislator, 263; as political executive, 348–349
Lazarsfeld, Paul F., 381 n., 383 n.
leader and leadership, charismatic, 17, 48; independent, 16; personal association and, 478; plebiscitarian, 48; plutocratic, 23; political versus charismatic, 18; psychosomatic analysis and, 416–428; ruthless, 173; types of, 18
League of Nations, 76
League of Women Voters, 369
legal aid, from precinct worker, 329
legality, dominance through, 18–19
legislative employees, code of ethics for, 457–460
Legislative Reorganization Act, 143
legislator, "big dilemma" of, 234–240; conflict of interests in, 263–265; conscience of, 234–240; economic and political involvement of, 87–91; socialization of, 379–394
legislature, organization and functions of, 166, 255–257
legitimation, need for, 51; three types of, 18
Levitt, Arthur, 457
Lewin, Bertram D., 427 n.
liberalism, politics and, 376–377
life, conscience and, 70; political, 28,

280 ff.; two ends of, 77; two parts of, 67; understanding of, 82
life spheres, laws of, 56
Li Hung Chang, 29
Lincoln, Abraham, 8, 48, 221–223, 239, 243, 251, 433, 471–472, 475
Lincoln-Douglas debates, 314
Lindsay, John V., 320
Lindzey, Gardner, 381 n.
Linz, Juan, 381 n.
Lippmann, Walter, 181
Lipset, Seymour, 381 n.
Little Rock (Ark.) segregation situation, 235–238
living faith, of enthusiast, 409–411
Livingston, Louise, 195
lobbying, 143, 455
Lodge, Henry Cabot, Jr., 397
loneliness, 249
Long, Huey, 309
Long, Norton E., 178–182, 276
lord, as director of administration, 20
Lord Denning's Report, 266 n.
Loreto, Charles A., 270–271
Lorwin, Val R., 407 n.
Louis XIV, 175
Louisville Courier-Journal, 134–135, 137–138
love, versus violence, 55
Lovett, Robert, 350
loyalty, to machine, 275; norms of, 181; of public officials, 88
loyalty oath, for teachers, 228–233
luck, factor of, 276–278
Ludendorff, Gen. Erich, 15
Lutheranism, government power and, 81–82
Lyman, William, 270–271
Lyons, James J., 269, 271

Macaulay, Thomas Babington, 472–473
McCarran Bill, 230
McCarthy, Joseph R., 10, 229, 234–235, 238, 248
McConaughy, John, 366
MacDonald, Ramsay, 404 n., 405 n., 406 n., 410 n.
Macedonia, 63
McFettridge, Edward C., 293
McGrath, Christopher C., 270–271
Machiavelli, Niccolò, 26, 59, 74, 276–278
Machiavellianism, 57, 407, 413; immediate success of, 74–75; Lutheran politics and, 81; strength of, 74; weakness and doom of, 76
machine, 272–273, 473; bossism and, 269–275; floaters and repeaters in, 339–340; loyalty to, 275; power and,

machine (*cont'd*)
166; precinct worker and, 325–341;
voting and, 473
McKinley, William, 304, 389
McLean, Joseph E., 344 n.
McPhee, William N., 383 n.
Madison, James, 352
Magnuson, Warren, 140–146
Magruder, Calvert, 445
Mahoney, Walter J., 463
Man for Himself (Fromm), 407 n.
Mannheim, Karl, 7–8
Manning, Bayless, 445
Maritain, Jacques, 72–79
Mark Twain in Eruption (De Voto),
224 n.
Markus, Louis, 111, 113, 120
Marshall, George C., 350
master–slave relationships, 64, 68
Mau Mau, 179
Maverick, Maury, 307–314
Maverick American, A (Maverick), 307 n.
Maximilian I, Emperor, 26
Maylock, Wilburn S., 110–129
Mayor's Wife, The (Beach), 285 n.
means, hierarchy of, 78; problem of, 72–
79
Medici, Catherine de', 174
Member of the House (Baker), 281 n.
Memories and Studies (James), 215 n.
Mencken, H. L., 163–168
Mendès-France, Pierre, 244
Men Who Ruled India, The (Woodruff),
403
Merriam, Charles E., 379, 422
Messianism, 412
Meyer, Karl E., 11 n.
Michels, Robert, 405 n., 412 n.
Middle Ages, 23, 31
Military Affairs Committee, 138
Miller, Clem, 281–284
Miller, Warren E., 383 n.
Mills, C. Wright, 15 n., 405 n., 415 n.
Milwaukee Sentinel, 300
Mimamsa School, India, 30
Mitchell, Steve, 131
Mitchell, William C., 352–363
monarch, versus parliament, 26–27; pa-
tronage of, 36
monarchomachists, 31
Monroney, A. S. Mike, 143
Montgomery, James, 482
Moose, Malcolm C., 432
moral courage, 224–225
moral discipline, authority and, 100
moralizing type, 371
moral particularism, 98
moral principles, strategy and, 82
moral rationalization, 75–77

morals and morality, forms of, 97; funda-
mental, 468; human nature and, 173;
professional ethics and, 98–99; public
opinion and, 99
Morrissey, Pat, 185
Morse, Wayne L., 85 n., 231, 236
Morton, Thruston B., 397
Mosca, Gaetano, 405 n.
Moscow Trials, 413 n.
motives, political, 163 ff.
murder, 159; in self-defense, 78
Murphy, Charles F., 190–191, 275
Murphy, Lawrence, 463
Myers, Rodes K., 137

Napoleon Bonaparte, 174, 176, 428
narcissism, 427
Nast, Thomas, 373
National Association of Manufacturers,
143
National Center for Education in Politics,
3, 364
national conventions, 43; delegates to,
401; *see also* Democratic National Com-
mittee; Republican National Conven-
tion
National Defense Education Act, 283
National Defense Program, 135
national honor, 52
National Opinion Research Center, 4,
352, 356, 358
naturalization, precinct worker's help in,
333
Nazi party, 481
Neely, Matthew M., 85 n.
Nepera Chemical Company, 110
Nero, 170
Neuberger, Maurine, 32, 228
Neuberger, Richard L., 228–233
neurosis, 423
New Aspects of Politics (Merriam),
379 n.
Newberry, Truman H., 203
New Deal, 145, 230, 232, 274, 307, 359,
397
Newman, A. W., 297
newspapers, political influence of, 34, 37,
202, 474, 476
New York City Bar Association, 437–
442, 463
New York City Ethics Committee, 461
New York State, policies of, 189–192
New York State Bar Association, 463
New York State Legislature, code of
ethics of, 457–460
New York Times, The, 319–321, 457 n.
461–463
New York Times Magazine, The, 234 n.
Nicaraguan Canal, 302

Nichols, James Hastings, 172 n.
Niebuhr, Reinhold, 80–84, 178
Nietzsche, Friedrich, 409
nirvana, 57
Nixon, Richard M., 10, 193, 395–396, 433
nobility, court, 30
nominalism, 414
norms, multiplicity of, 181
Northcliffe, Alfred Charles Harmsworth, Viscount, 34
Nothingness of the International Policy of Great Democracies, The (Giraud), 76

obedience, to leader, 18
O'Brian, John Lord, 137
occupations, ethical code and, 56; political consciousness and, 387–388; social status and, 354; thirteen highest, 353
Ochrana, 36
O'Connor, Edwin, 359 n.
O'Dwyer, William, 269
officeholder, ethics of, 85–96
oleomargarine bill, 302
O'Mahoney, Joseph C., 237
open mind, quality of, 177
oral-aggressive type, 424
Organisation Armée Secret, 179
organ neuroses, 423
Orient, leadership in, 26
original sin, 56–57
Origins of the Labour Party, The (Pelling), 411 n.
Ortega y Gasset, José, 406
Orwell, George, 414
Ostrogorsky, M., 39 n.
"out's," versus "in's," 10

Palmer, Mitchell, 484
Paolucci, Henry, 169 n.
Parade, magazine, 147–154
paradoxes, ethical, 59
Parkinson, C. Northcote, 69 n.
parliament, in Germany, 45–46; versus monarch or prince, 26–27; parties and, in England, 37; "whip" in, 40
Parsons, Talcott, 382
participation, political interest and, 386–388
parties, citizen as member of, 477–479; parliament and, 37; *see also* British Labour party; Democratic party; Republican party; Socialist party
party boss, 44
party finances, 41
party following, 38–39
party leader, 18
party organization, 38–43; politician and, 241–242

party workers, 333–334; *see also* precinct workers
patriotism, 470
patronage, 24, 43, 274; Congressmen and, 168
Pausanias, King, 68
Payne, Henry B., 292, 304
peace, international, 84; versus war, 485–486
Pearson, Drew, 150
Pelling, Henry, 411 n.
Pendergast, Tom, 289
Penrose, Boies, 2, 203, 258–259
People's Choice, The (Lazarsfeld *et al.*), 383 n.
Pepper, George Wharton, 203–204
perjury, 124
Perry, J. W., 289
Persia, 63
personality, disorders of, 416; dynamic concept of, 416; of politician, 363; power-seeking, 426
Pfister, Charles F., 293
Pfister, Guido, 293
Philadelphia Chamber of Commerce, 117
Philadelphia Lawyer (Pepper), 203 n.
philistinism, 58
Phillips, Wendell, 471
philosopher, versus statesman, 63
Pilgrim's Progress (Bunyan), 405 n.
Pinney, S. U., 293
Plato, 9
Plunkitt, George W., 103–105
Plunkitt of Tammany Hall (Riordan), 103 n.
political act, as act of will, 178–182
political activist, 3
political amoralism, 77
political behavior, associative, 3
political executive, 342–351; budget and, 348–349; factors influencing behavior of, 347–350; lawyer as, 348–349; typical day of, 346–347
political family, 385
political interest, major sources of, 393–394
political life, 280 ff.; moral rationalization of, 73–77
political motives, 163 ff.
political office, differential status in, 361–362; training for, 361
Political Parties (Michels), 405 n.
political party, *see* parties; party (adj.)
political philosophy, ends and means in, 72–74
political power, status of, 357; *see also* power
politicals (political personalities), 364 ff.; family income of, 367; female, 370–

politicals (political personalities) (*cont'd*) 374; power drive of, 377; pressure-group, 369

political science, versus politics, 18

political socialization, 380; ideology and, 392–393; personal predispositions and, 390–392; primary groups and, 383–385; of state legislatures, 379–394; time of, 381–383

politician, abuse of, 247–248; as actor, 179, 313, 365; ambivalent social status of, 352–363; versus apolitical person, 364–378; archetype of, 258; attacks on, 247; behavior of, 362–363; as businessman, 245–246; citizen as, 467 ff.; as demagogue, 307–313; educational level and, 355; ethical problems of, 85–96; friendships of, 248; "great fear" of, 201–202; honest, 205–206; liabilities of, 241–251; "natural," 5; "occasional," 21; opinions of, 245–246; personality of, 363, 416–426; power drive of, 51 (*see also* power); press and, 33; primary role of, 77; private work of, 243; professional, 21, 29, 37; property-less, 24; public opinion and, 244; "qualifications" for, 258–259; recruitment of, 362; remuneration for, 23; variety in, 50; wealthy, 360; wife of, 316–318

politics, anti-intellectualism in, 10; as art, 9; Christianity and, 73, 80–84; corruption and, 11, 69, 74, 130, 157, 159, 226–227; devotion to, 50; drudgery of, 242; educational achievement in, 2–3, 355, 387; ethics and, *see* ethics; family members in, 384; fortune or luck in, 276–278; as income source, 22; as independent leadership, 16; insidiousness of, 284–290; liabilities in, 241–251; loneliness in, 249; Mr. Dooley on, 315–318; morality of, 97–99, 173, 468; versus officeholding, 203; pay in, 242; people engaged in, 2; power from, 49 (*see also* power); reasons for becoming interested in, 380–381; relatives in, 384; as role-playing, 179, 313, 365; rules for success in, 7; social science view of, 325 ff.; speech in, 245–246; as sport, 316; state legislator and, 380–381; violence and, 55; as vocation, 15–61; Weber's concept of, 16

Politics (Aristotle), 62–68

polls, politicians and, 360

polymorphism, moral, 99

polytheism, Hellenic, 56

Pool, Ithiel, 375, 377

popular fronts, 407

Porter, Paul A., 432

Postgate, Raymond, 404 n., 405 n., 406 n., 411 n., 412

Post Office Department, U.S., 436

power, as goal of politician, 51; legitimacy of, 18; maintenance of, 63; military, 63; orientation of, 365; personality and, 416–417; politics and, 49; self-interest and, 81; social status of, 357–358; values system and, 358; violence and, 52; voting and, 35

Power and Glory: The Life of Boies Penrose (Davenport), 258 n.

power drive, of politicals, 377

power-holder, domination of, 19

Power in Men (Cary), 226

power scale, of politicals, 367–368

precinct captain, 326, 335

precinct club, 336

precinct workers, 325–341; canvassing by, 337–338; election technique of, 339; family services of, 328; good deeds of, 330–331; legal aid from, 329–330; local government and, 333; and party organization, 333–334; social activities of, 336; stock in trade of, 327; tax fixing by, 331; traffic fixes by, 332–333; types of, 325; votes controlled by, 338

predestination, 56

predispositions, personal, 390–392

President, U. S., patronage of, 43

presidential campaigns, financing of, 433–434; machine and, 166–167; political interest and, 389

President's Commission on Campaign Costs, 431–436

press, freedom of, 153; politician and, 33

pressure groups, 201–202; politicals in, 369; women in, 374–375

prestige, occupational, 353

price-fixing, 444

priest, ethical duty of, 97

primaries, U.S., 43

primary groups, influence of, 383–385

prince, clergy and, 29; versus parliament, 27; nobility and, 30; politics of, 21

Prince, The (Machiavelli), 57, 74, 276–278

"principal men," iniquity of, 155–157

problem-solving, 365

Professional Ethics and Civic Morals (Durkheim), 97

Profiles in Courage (Kennedy), 238–239, 480

Profumo, John D., 266

progress, belief in, 51

Progressive party, 203

Prometheus, 481

Protestantism, 57–58

protocol, legislative, 256

Prussia, 28
psychosomatic analysis, leadership and, 416–428
Psychosomatic Medicine (Alexander), 424 n.
public conduct, standards of, 101–159
public events, political interest and, 388–390
public issues, interest in, 388–390
public officials, appointed by President, 451; bank deposits and salary of, 106; code of ethics for, 457–460; conflict of interest and, 262–265, 437–453; conscience of, 234–240; contracting for services by, 440–441; differential status among, 360–361; dilemma of, 234–240; dishonest, 130; duty to community, 106; ethics of, 86–96; *ex parte* communication by, 449–450; gifts and entertainment for, 87–88, 439; loyalty of, 88; pension and group security plans for, 438; rotation of, 108–109; routine performance of, 92; sale of information and speculation by, 439–440; seduction of, 88; suggested regulations for, 437–442; venality of, 90, 130, 155–158, 444; *see also* civil service; government employees; political executive
public opinion, 99, 244
public relations, 461
public service, commitment and, 392
Puritans, 415
Puttkamer, Robert von, 28

Quakers, 57
Quarles, Joseph V., 293, 299

race relations, 82
Räte von Haus, 22
rationalization, artistic, 73–74; of political life, 73–76; technical, 73–75
rational principle, 66
realism, Christian, 83
Reconstruction Finance Corporation, 197
Redfield, Robert, 239
Reed, James A., 204
reference, in federal government, 90–91
Reform Bill of 1832, 36
reformer, practical, 467–476; socialist as, 471
reform movements, 45
religious awakening, 193
Renaissance, 58
rentiers, 23–24, 30, 36
Reporter, The, 260 n.
Republican National Convention, 395–401
Republican party, 117, 135, 185–186, 198, 230, 272, 300–306, 369, 373 n., 389, 395–401
Republican State Central Committee, Wisconsin, 304–305
responsibility, Christianity and, 81–82; ethic of, 54–60
Revolt of the Masses, The (Ortega y Gasset), 406 n.
revolution, romantic nature of, 49
revolutionary socialism, 55
Reynolds, Mrs. Maria, 207–208
Richard III, 173
Richards, Peter G., 6 n.
Rideout, Walter B., 158 n.
Riesman, David, 371, 406
Riordan, William L., 103–105
risk, willingness for, 372
Robinson, Joseph T., 204
Roche, John P., 402–415
Rockefeller, Nelson A., 359
Rogow, Arnold A., 169 n.
role-playing, 179, 313, 365
Roman Empire, domination urge in, 170
Roman law, 30
Roosevelt, Franklin D., 106–107, 175, 183, 198, 202 n., 247, 269, 274, 335, 356, 359, 416–417
Roosevelt, Theodore, 5, 167, 467–476
Root, Elihu, 477–479
Rosenthal, Benjamin S., 319–321
Rosenzweig, Robert, 359, 362 n.
Ross, D. W., 62 n.
rotation in office, 108–109
ruler–subject relationship, 65–66
Ruling Class, The (Mosca), 405 n.
Russia, bolshevism in, 36
ruthlessness, in leader, 173

Sachs, Stephen, 402–415
St. Bartholmew's Day Massacre, 174
Salem (Oreg.) *Statesman,* 232
Salinger, Pierre, 163
Sallust (Gaius Sallustius Crispus), 169
Salter, John T., 201–202
Salvation Army, 42
Savage, Marjorie, 147
Sawyer, Philetus, 292–305
scales, for politicals and apoliticals, 368–374
school studies, political consciousness and, 387; *see also* educational achievement
scientist, ethical duty of, 97
Scott, James Brown, 477 n.
Scylax of Caryandra, 66 n.
Scythia, 63
Seabury, Samuel, 106
Secret Life of Walter Mitty, The (Thurber), 5
secret police, 36

self-defense, murder and, 78
self-government, 30, 472
self-interest, 81, 84
self-righteousness, 58
self-seeking, competitive, 82
Senate, U.S., as "club," 10; Committee for Labor and Public Welfare, 445; Education Committee, 230; Judiciary Committee, 237; Military Affairs Committee, 231
Senator, ethical problems of, 88–89
Sereno, Renzo, 1
Serge, Victor, 413 n.
Sermon on the Mount, 53, 57
service club luncheons, 282–283
service contracts, 441
Seward, William H., 471
Shakespeare, William, 60
Shaw, Robert Gould, 215
Sherman Anti-Trust Law, 292
Siebecker, Robert G., 293–295, 297, 299
Simmel, Georg, 49
Sinclair, Upton, 198–199
slavery, 64, 239, 471; Lincoln's view of, 221–222
Smith, Alfred E., 189–192
Smith, T. V., 235, 255–257
Snowden, Philip, 406 n.
Snyder, John W., 118–119
Social Democratic party, 39, 46, 412 n., 415
socialism, versus capitalism, 406 n.; revolutionary, 55
Socialism over Sixty Years (Brockway), 404 n., 406 n., 410 n.
socialist, as reformer, 471
Socialist League, 404 n.
Socialist party, 412 n., 413 n., 415
socialization, political, *see* political socialization
socializing, by political executive, 350
social movements, history of, 415
social reform, 424; *see also* reformer; reform movements
social science, politics and, 325 ff.
Social Security Act, 309
social status, hierarchy of, 357; occupational types and, 354
Social System, The (Parsons), 383 n.
social welfare, 485
society, value system and, 357–358
Solicitor General, U.S., 116
Solomon, William, 111, 113, 118
Sophocles, 218–220
soul, two parts of, 66
Spain, elections and revolutions in, 25
Sparta, 55, 67
special interests, 133; *see also* pressure groups

speculation, by public official, 439–440
spoils system, 19, 43
Spooner, John Coit, 304
sport, politics as, 316
Sprague, Charles, 232
Staebler, Neil O., 432
Stalin, Joseph, 484–485
state, authoritarian, 58; defined, 16; versus individual, 62; violence and, 17; Weber's concept of, 20–21; *see also* state legislatures
State Ethics Commission, 460
state legislators, political socialization by, 379–394
state legislatures, 166, 255–257
statesman, conscience of, 69–71; "qualifications" for, 258–259
Statesman, The (Taylor), 69
statesmanship, versus government, 64
status quo, 254 ff.
Stearns, Harold E., 163 n.
Steffler, Paul, 308
Stevenson, Adlai E., 130–133
Stone, Donald C., 343, 344 n.
strategy, and moral principles, 82
Student Friendship Fund, YMCA, 194
Sturmthal, Adolf, 413 n., 414 n.
success, morality and, 468–469
Suicide (Durkheim), 97
Sultan, power of, 26
Supreme Court, U. S., 203
Swift, Jonathan, 4
swimming pool, as campaign issue, 134–139
Switzerland, patronage in, 25
sycophancy, 5
symbols, manipulation of, 180
Symington, Stuart, 131
syndicalism, 54

Tacitus, 250
Taft-Hartley Act, 246
Talmadge, Herman, 140–146
Tammany Hall, 38, 45, 103, 190–191, 275, 373 n., 428
Tammany Hall (Werner), 205 n.
tax fixing, by precinct worker, 331–332
tax laws, 440
Taylor, Henry, 69–71
teachers, in politics, 243
teacher's oath bill, 228–233
Teacher's Union, 230, 232
technocracy, democracy and, 77
tendermindedness, 366, 373
Terrenova, Ciro, 271
T-factor, 372–373, 377
Thayer, Walter N., 432
theodicity, 56
Thom, H. C., 304

Thomas, Norman, 197, 480–486
Thoron, Gray, 457
Thrace, 63
Thurber, James, 276
timorousness, 5
To Be a Politician (Bullitt), 241 n.
Tobin, John E., 110–129
toilet training, 427
Tolstoy, Leo, 59, 470
Tories, English, 40, 155
totalitarian age, dissenter's role in, 480–486
toughmindedness, 366, 372–373
Towards a Soviet America (Foster), 484
town meetings, 283
Townsend, Francis E., 309
trade unionism, 47, 406–409, 413 n.
traffic fixes, by precinct worker, 332–333
Tragedy of European Labor, The (Sturmthal), 413 n.
Traylor, Melvin A., 422
treason, 158
Treasury Department, 128
trickery, political, 226
Trotsky, Leon, 16 n.
True Believer, The (Hoffer), 410 n.
Truman, Harry S., 4–5, 135, 230, 243, 359 n.
Truman Committee, 135–138
truth, duty and, 54; good and, 405
Tugman, William M., 232
TVA (Tennessee Valley Authority), 309
Twain, Mark, 224–225
Tweed Ring, 205–206

Union League Club, 303
United Nations, 485
United States, Budget Bureau, 343; civil service reform in, 25; Congress, 43, 148; Defense Department, 351; Internal Revenue Bureau, 110, 128; Labor Department, 448; party organization in, 42–43; political boss in, 44–45; Post Office Department, 436; Solicitor General, 116; spoils system in, 43–44; Supreme Court, 203
Unruh, Jesse M., 262–265

Valhalla, 57
value system, social status and, 357–358
Vanderbilt, Arthur T., 3
Van Hise, Charles, 301
vanity, in politician, 50
venality, in public officials, 90, 130, 155–158, 444
Veterans Administration, 231
Vilas, Col. William, 293
violence, immediate success of, 75; politics and, 55; power and, 52; as sign of weakness, 75; state and, 17
Virgil, 170
virtue, practice and pursuit of, 62–68
visionaries, 177
Voorhis, Jerry, 193–200
Voorhis School for Boys, 196, 200
Vortragender Rat, 28
Vorys, John M., 236, 432
Voter Decides, The (Campbell *et al.*), 383 n.
voting, compulsory, 35; versus conscience, 234–240; "floaters" or "repeaters" in, 339; machine and, 473; precinct worker and, 326–328; psychology of, 381–382
Voting (Berelson *et al.*), 383 n.

Wagner, Karl, 233
Wahlke, John C., 379–394
Walker, James J., 106
Wallas, Graham, 9
Wall Street, 105, 411 n.
Walsh, Thomas J., 204
war, abolition of, 485; horror of, 52; versus peace, 485–486; virtue of, 63
War and Peace (Tolstoy), 59
war contracts, graft and, 134–139
ward club, 336
ward committeeman, 326, 335
War Production Board, 137
Warren, Earl, 230
Washington, George, 5, 42, 475
weakness, violence as sign of, 75
Weber, Max, 15–61, 403 n., 405 n., 412, 415 n.
Webster, Daniel, 43, 238
Welch, Joseph, 248
Weltanschauung, 46, 51, 60
Werner, M. R., 205–206
Whigs, English, 40
whip, Parliamentary, 40–41
White, Leonard D., 422
White House Conference on Campaign Finances, 436
Whitelaw, Robert, 218 n.
Wilde, Oscar, 69
will, political act as, 178–182
William II, Kaiser, 61
Williams, G. Mennen, 359
Williams, Philip, 412 n.
Willkie, Wendell, 246, 357
Wilson, H. H., 10 n., 134–139
Wilson, Woodrow, 16, 165, 167
Wisconsin, graft in, 293
Wisconsin Republican State Central Committee, 304
Wisconsin treasury cases, 293

witch-hunting, 230
women, authoritarianism in, 374–375; political and apolitical, 369–370; tough-mindedness in, 372–373
women's clubs, 285–286
Woodruff, Philip, 403
worker, role of, 23
world, irrationality of, 56
World War I, 412 n., 422

World War II, 344
Worthy, James C., 432

YMCA, 194
Younglove, Joseph C., 462
Young Men's Republican Union, 221
You're the Boss (Flynn), 269 n.

Zaretzki, Joseph, 463
Zilboorg, Gregory, 427 n.